Measurement for Leisure Services and Leisure Studies

Mounir G. Ragheb, PhD
Florida State University

Idyll Arbor, Inc.

39129 264th Ave SE, Enumclaw, WA 98022 (360) 825-7797

Idyll Arbor, Inc. Editor: Thomas M. Blaschko

Printed in the United States of America.

ISBN 9781882883424

Library of Congress Cataloging-in-Publication Data

Ragheb, Mounir G.
  Measurement for leisure services and leisure studies / Mounir G. Ragheb.
    p. cm.
  Includes bibliographical references and index.
  ISBN 978-1-882883-42-4
  1. Leisure industry. 2. Leisure--Psychological aspects. 3. Leisure--Study and teaching. I. Title.
  GV188.R34 2012
  790.06'9--dc23
                                                                    2011049140

To my daughter, Dena,
and my two sons, Nader and Sharif,
whose existence inspired me in my work

Contents

Preface

In the absence of a guide to the content's formation, the book design evolved following a logical scheme and sequence from whole to part to whole again. The grand idea behind this development was stated first, searching for more details to follow, and then crystallizing the total direction again. This process kept repeating to fill identified gaps in the main design, while navigating in uncharted waters and literature to formulate the main trusts of this book. That process was uncharted since it is the first book in recreation and leisure to address the three parts that are covered within.

These three parts grew and changed positions occasionally during organizational design and I modified contents accordingly. In the final design I realized that the best method was to outline and analyze existing instruments first, which can help the major scheme and flow of the intended design, to be followed by the methodology, and then the theoretical foundations.

To put my efforts into clear perspective, the incentive behind this book is to compile as many measurements of leisure and recreation as possible for practical and scientific uses. Then to further employ this compilation to present the methods and strategies of their development to contribute to future scale construction, evolving to a demonstration of the background concepts of those measurements.

Moreover, this book is an attempt to enhance the development and utilization of leisure and recreation measurements. Improvement in the development and use will be attained through the availability of existing leisure measurements for field and research applications. As a result, practical utilization will be facilitated, serving numerous fields of services that can benefit. Examples of those fields are therapeutic recreation, rehabilitation, programming, management, academic training, park involvement, and leisure services in general. Also, practical utilization will stimulate scientific studies that explore behavioral leisure and recreation phenomena and enhance future development of leisure measurements.

Recreation field practitioners, established researchers in leisure and other studies, educators, policy makers, and graduate and undergraduate students will find the three parts of the book useful and applicable. Part I will make leisure measurements accessible and handy for users, based on a logical classification of existing scales. Part II outlines the art and science of measurement developments in leisure and how to use scales, crunching their numbers, and help in providing substantiated interpretations as basis for field actions.

Lastly, Part III looks at the behavioral and social-psychological bases of leisure and helps measurement developers delineate the boundaries of some basic behavioral, social, and cultural concepts relevant to recreation and leisure. As a result, indicators and their items can be identified, extracted, and formulated to be incorporated into future scales based on ideas and views presented here. This part will elaborate on each domain's theoretical concepts, which will allow application of the outlined steps in the art and science of measurement construction as presented in Part II. The interaction between theory and steps of measurement validation can enhance the final product of the attempted measurement — in turn, helping to advance the understanding of the theory itself through a measurement's findings.

The theoretical part is based on four basic behavioral and social sciences: Social Psychology, Positive Psychology, Sociology, and Culture Anthropology.

Acknowledgments

My first thanks goes to Dr. Allen V. Sapora, one of the eminent founders of academic preparation of recreation and leisure professionals. Many educators, practitioners, and scientists — nationally and internationally — are in debt to Professor Allen V. Sapora for his sincere efforts and good care. I was lucky to be one of his graduate students at the University of Illinois, Urbana-Champaign (1970-1975). Dr. Sapora was the initiator and supporter of the utilization of the scientific method to reveal and understand the social and behavioral impacts of recreation and leisure on the individual and society.

Special recognition goes to Drs. Francis C. Cannon and Jean C. Mundy, both Professors Emeritus; and Drs. Cheryl S. Beeler and Julia K. Dunn, College of Education of the Florida State University (FSU), who witnessed and encouraged the many phases of the development of the instruments that I participated in constructing, besides supporting the unfolding of the content of this book.

My especial gratitude goes to Dr. Jacob G. Beard, Professor Emeritus of Tests and Measurements, Educational Research, College of Education at FSU, who collaborated with me from 1979 to 1991 in developing four standardized measurements. Those instruments are assessing leisure satisfaction, leisure motivation, leisure attitude, and leisure interests. Through our encounters for 12 years, I was thrilled and thankful to learn and sharpen my knowledge and skills pertinent to measurement development from Dr. Beard. Without Professor Beard this book and the eight scales, which evolved and improved over my career, would not have seen the light.

My thanks go to all the scientists that developed measurements that are included in this book. Without their achievements and cooperation, Part I of this book would not be attainable; for their scales are the core and focus of that first part. My special gratitude goes to those who approved including their actual scales after the abstracts that summarize the content of their technical reports of their measurements. These inclusions of scales and abstracts will help the needed dissemination of measurements, making instruments accessible for this book's users.

I would like also to extend my sincere appreciation to my students who helped me to grow in the initiation and application of the measurements that I collaborated in developing. In all honesty, students' presence in my classes: Philosophy of Recreation and Leisure, Social Psychology of Leisure and Recreation, and Positive Psychology of Leisure and Recreation — for more than 30 years — enabled me to pierce through and to gain insights into many leisure concepts and how they relate to other life domains. Examples of such concepts are free time, technology, work, leisure, and recreation in their relevancies to wellness, vitality, stress, life satisfaction, happiness, and the quality of life of the American society compared to other cultures. Graduate and undergraduate students in their listening, discussing, challenging, and investigating relevant phenomena, crystallized my understanding of ideas and views that were the foundations of the eight standardized scales and the structure of this book.

A word of recognition goes to my Finnish friend Professor Seppo E. Iso-Ahola for the early discussions and scholarly stimulation, which both of us engaged in while we were in the doctoral program under Professors Sapora, Michele J. Ellis, and Rainer Martens, and serving as research assistants in the Leisure Behavior Research Lab. Those discussions of our field's issues, problems, and aspirations have helped to give birth to the concepts and books of social psychology of leisure and recreation, and their measurements.

Special appreciation goes to Mr. James (Jim) I. Austin, one of the early graduate and undergraduate students in my career (1976-1979) for his esteem of the scientific method and its value. Jim reported that his knowledge and skills of the methods of problem solving based on the scientific method saved his life in practical applications as a USAF pilot. Based on Jim's knowledge of problem/hypothesis relationships and uses, besides deduction and induction as bases of science; Jim survived the height, speed, and complexity of the settings in space; maneuvering a number of high performance aircraft. Moreover, Jim's following-up and attention to my research over the years inspired me a great deal, showing me the relevancy of what I teach, as well as the value of what I investigate.

Finally, I would like to extend my thanks to the College of Education at the Florida State University, Tallahassee, for the support and encouragement while I was serving as a faculty and especially after retirement in doing my scholar work. The college's help enabled me to complete this book and two other books in the Arabic language, as follows:

1. Olympic Performance: Policies and Institutions (2010)

الأداء الأولمبي: سياساته ومؤسساته

2. *The Pathway to Sport Excellence* (at press)

الطريق للتفوق الرياضي

It is important to note that without Ms. Betty L. Willard's extensive word processing: typing, organizing, editing, and reediting, the content of this book would not be completed.

MGR   November 2011

Chapter 1

Introduction to Measurement

Focus of Chapter

This chapter introduces the three pillars of measurement for leisure services and leisure studies: 1. existing leisure and recreation measurements, 2. methods used to construct standardized and non-standardized measurements, and 3. basic techniques to develop constructs from concepts.

Key Terms

- assessment
- behavior
- evaluation
- measurement
- performance
- scale

Objectives

- Explain the related concepts: assessment, evaluation, and measurement.
- Be able to classify a leisure and recreation assessment.
- Realize the rationale behind creating assessment tools.

This book is about measuring various areas of interest in leisure, recreation, and parks. The book provides the basic information and existing instruments that may be used to measure aspects of recreation and leisure in an accurate, meaningful, and practical manner. This book presents the fundamental requirements to measurement. Therefore, it is geared towards the needs of professionals and students who work or plan to work in the many different areas associated with leisure, recreation, and park services. We hope that this information will help improve the quality of leisure experiences and increase the effectiveness of leisure, recreation, and parks' systems and research.

There are many terms that relate to measurement. Some of these terms are interchangeable, while others have subtle differences. Key terms that are often used are measurement, evaluation, and assessment. While these three terms have a lot in common, they have important but subtle differences.

Measurement is the process of documenting observed actions, observed behaviors, or reported attitude (burlingame, 2001). It is the recording of raw data. With measurement, when a value is assigned to represent the observed actions, observed behaviors, or reported attitudes, the intention is that no opinion of the inherent degree of "right" or "wrong" is being determined during the process of data collection. Measurement tends to be one of three different types of activity: 1. Measuring a process, 2. Measuring a product, or 3. Measuring a behavior.

Assessment tends to have a slightly broader and less uniformly accepted definition. Some publications use the terms measurement and assessment interchangeably to refer to the process of gathering data. Other publications, especially related to health care, education, and psychology, tend to use a broader definition of assessment as a process of gathering data and then assigning some kind of value judgment to the data obtained. This second, broader definition will be the one used throughout this book.

Evaluation is the process of reviewing the data collected and placing a value judgment on the whole of the data as a means to arrive at a judgment. While not a hard and fast rule, the term evaluation is typically used when one is determining how successful a curriculum was, how well a procedure worked, or how well a program achieved its stated goals or objectives. The determination of the degree of success or failure is the core of evaluation. Assessment is typically used when one is referring to values made about an individual's performance or behavior.

There are two other terms that are important in the understanding of measurement and evaluation: test and scale. The term *test* typically refers to the actual instrument used to obtain the data. A test may be a set of questions on a piece of paper (for example, a quiz given by your professor to see how much of the information from this chapter you remembered), a protocol of activity to see how well you can perform a specific task (for example, the demonstration of how to right yourself in an upside-down kayak), or a mechanical device that helps measure a quantity (for example, a blood pressure cuff that helps measure blood pressure). Other terms frequently used interchangeably with the term test are *instrument* or *assessment tool*.

A *scale* is a method of determining "where" or "how much" by using commonly recognized increments. One example is a Likert scale where the person selects how much s/he agrees with a statement by selecting a number between one and five. Another example is the Faces Pain Scale — Revised (Bieri et al., 1990) where the client identifies the level of pain s/he is feeling by picking a face that has an expression that matches how s/he feels. A more complex scale may be composed of many questions that are combined to come up with a number that represents a value of what is being measured. One example is the Life Satisfaction Scale (Neugarten, Havighurst, and Tobin, 1961), which sums up 22 questions to determine how satisfied a person is with life. A test may be composed of several scales or several questions using the same scale.

Measurement and evaluation is the process that identifies 1. The scope of issues and actions to be evaluated, 2. The criteria that will be used to determine what specific elements are to be measured, and 3. The types of data that will be collected to help answer the question(s) to be answered through the process (burlingame, 2001). The rest of this book will take you on the journey to understand and feel comfortable with the process and the professional

standards and ethics that that are an intrinsic part of it.

Measurements, Methodology, and Behavioral Concepts

There are three distinct parts to this book, functioning as structural pillars to the development and use of measurement:

I.   Existing leisure and recreation measurements.
II. Methods used to construct standardized and non-standardized measurements.
III. Basic techniques to develop constructs from concepts.

The rationale for using this three-pronged approach to exploring measurement is simple:

Firstly, the main goal of this book is to make leisure measurements accessible. Available assessment tools are scattered in journals and books. Compiling them under their most relevant classification will enhance their utility and application. Moreover, by the virtue of their compilation, scales can be improved by revising them and, most importantly, identifying gaps and shortages in what needs to be measured. When instruments are available, they can contribute to many groups. The tests and scales in this book are now easily available for many practical and scientific uses.

Secondly, the methodology part discusses the guidelines for developing measurements, spelling out criteria and outlining procedures to be employed. When we talk about methods of test development we are answering the questions: Why do we need to have standardized tools? When are these tools used? What might happen if we don't use well-thought-out tools? What steps do we need to take to construct a good tool? How can we use them? This second part will help the reader understand how and when assessment tools are used. It will also discuss the process and mechanics involved in developing a quality tool.

Thirdly, one of the basic requirements is to build a measure on the basis of available information including theories, philosophies, scientific research results, academic work, and common sense. Therefore, part three presents leisure concepts such as interests, involvement, and satisfaction. Scales, as constructs, must be anchored and rely on sound theoretical backgrounds for their development. Making sure that those who wish to develop useful testing tools have an understanding of the concepts required is the reason for the third pillar.

In sum, sequential procedures start with an identification of leisure measurements that already exist. This is followed by a discussion of the methodology used to develop a scale. Last is the discussion of the conceptualization of domains (practical ideas, philosophies, and theories) used in building constructs. Model 1 illustrates how those three pillars interact and overlap.

Pillar 1: Classification of Leisure and Recreation measurements

The focus of the first pillar is to compile all existing measurements pertinent to fields and subfields of leisure and recreation. The availability of these instruments, in the years to come, can have positive effects not only for practice but also for research. Altogether, close to 100 scales are reported, covering a very broad array of areas: leisure, recreation, free time, exercise, fitness, recreational sports, outdoor recreation, travel and tourism, play, humor, management, and supervision in leisure delivery systems are all included in the available scales and measurements.

The report on each available measurement was abstracted in a short summary format, designed to be readable by all. Abstracts are concise and informative. Abstracts are not intended to replace full articles about the measurement. Rather, they give a summary of the background of the scale and identify its source. Every reported measurement is presented simply; following a standardized format: name of the scale, developer(s), references, goals or purpose for the results, background literature, methodology employed, findings (scale's factor analysis, reliability, and validity), and investigator(s) comments. In many cases the complete scale or measurement is included in this book. This approach is designed to be user-friendly and helpful for the instruments' dissemination and use. We expect readers of this book to respect professional standards and copyright law, which means they will ask the author(s) of each scale for permission to use the scale and/or purchase commercially available scales as required for use.

Being able to see the scales in their entirety can be extremely useful not only for educators and their students but also for practitioners and researchers. Items on the scales were requested from their developers and in many cases the developers agreed to have their scales in this book. However, not all developers responded positively to the requests. Therefore, scales included in this book are either permitted by their developers or published in scientific journals or books. The ultimate intention is to facilitate the maximum utility of available tools. This can stimulate interest to construct what is lacking, to fill existing gaps; and to test relations that incorporate variables measured by the scales reported here. Future editions of the book will include more

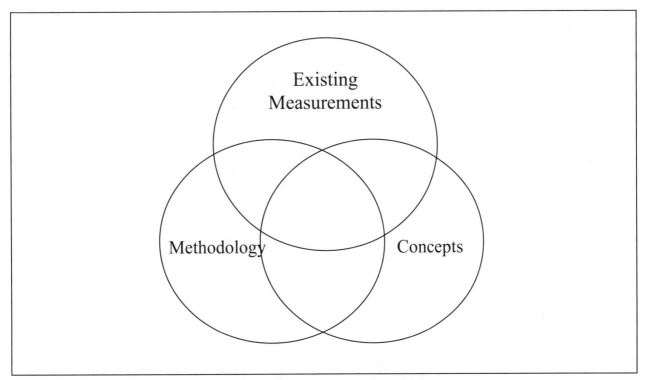

Model 1: Mutual overlap, interaction, and interdependence among three major entities: existing measurements, methodology, and measurement concepts

scales as they become available.

The measurements are grouped under their most pertinent concepts, facilitating their retrieval, comparison, evaluation, and use. The measurements are divided into categories as described in Chapter 2. These categories are

- Leisure Involvement
- Leisure Attitude
- Leisure Motivation
- Free Time Boredom
- Leisure Interests
- Leisure Satisfaction
- Playfulness and Humor
- Leisure Administration and Supervision Functions

It is important to note that the first seven of these domains are fully conceptualized in the third part of this book. The eighth domain (on administration and supervision) is reported in Chapters 11 and 12, in Part II of the book, within the methodology procedures.

Pillar 2: Methods Used to Construct Measurements

A quality measurement cannot be constructed (formally or informally) without the rigorous steps presented in Part II of this book. Chapter 11 presents the rationale for the assessment and measurement process. It discusses the importance of having measurements and the impact of their absence. Examples from facilities, users, programs, personnel, and policies and administrative procedures show how the methodology presented guarantees the relevancy of assessment to practice. Chapter 12 discusses the contributions of assessment to performance, efficiency, and effectiveness. In conducting assessment, qualitative and quantitative methods are usually employed, relying on observation, interviews, and/or paper and pencil instruments. Chapter 13 elaborates on the necessity to be equipped with all data collection methods, as tools to achieve the task. These three chapters are designed to enable the reader to be oriented with what lies ahead in the book, as well as to stimulate interest in the book's relevance to practice.

Moving to the most technical procedures in measurement development, Chapter 14 demonstrates criteria of quality assessment tools: reliability, validity, and usefulness. Different reliability and validity tests are introduced, showing how they are used to measure the quality of leisure scales. Due to the technicality of the steps used to construct a measure, an informal example is used in Chapter 15

to illustrate the sequence. All procedures are introduced in down-to-earth examples, which humans confront frequently in life. The nine steps representing the methodology of scale construction are elaborated on in Chapter 16. These steps are similar in their logic to steps in scientific research.

Since the field of leisure services is based on application, uses of measurements in practice is emphasized in Chapter 17. An instrument is either selected from a pool of quality instruments or constructed — informally or formally — according to the guidelines in earlier chapters. How to select scales, collect data, analyze (crunch) the data, interpret, and report the results are demonstrated through actual use of scales. This will help to reinforce practical application of the content of all prior chapters and give the reader practice using the skills required to determine solutions based on assessment. The fundamental principal behind Chapter 17 is this: "Learning the theory or knowledge about how to swim without being in a pool, getting wet, and performing routines does not make the person a swimmer."

Finally, in concluding Part II, Chapters 18 and 19 show the impact of social change on leisure assessment. Chapter 18 presents the use of technology and computers to assess individuals and community needs, interests, functioning, and constraints. The skills required to develop programs, set policies, and give guidance and awareness are described. Chapter 19 is on assessment and the future: Which subfields of leisure will demand more assessment? How can assessment competencies be developed?

Part II of the book is primarily for undergraduate and graduate students; however, the content will be beneficial to many practitioners, educators, and scientists who did not receive detailed information about these topics in their earlier studies.

Pillar 3: Techniques to Develop Constructs

No quality scale is built without sound basis. The stronger the foundations of a measurement, the higher its quality. In turn, a scale constructed on the good foundations is known for its quality. A scale that meets the criteria of sound background lasts longer, gains trust, and serves practice and research effectively (see Cohen and Swerdlik, 2002; and APA, 1996, for criteria of outdated scales that need revisions). The foundation of such endeavor, for scale's longevity, lies in the reliance on sound and pertinent literature as foundations for concepts, views, ideas, theories, and philosophies.

One of the seven conditions reported by Cohen and Swerdlik (2002; 217) that compel a revision of existing measurements coincides with the development of Part III of this book. That condition says, "The theory on which the test was originally based has been improved significantly, and the changes should be reflected in the design and content of the test." Therefore, as conceptual knowledge advances, the leisure instruments need to catch up with concept's progress. These are the central concerns of the second part of this book. An excellent example is the theory of motivation by Deci and Ryan (1985) living past its usefulness and being overhauled extensively by Ryan and Deci (2000).

The third part of the book is somewhat advanced. It can serve not only upper level undergraduate students, but also graduate students and professionals. Model 2, as a behavioral model, was developed as a theorization to postulate interrelationships among relevant domains of leisure and recreation functioning. The model can assist in putting concepts into perspective, organizing interrelationships among domains, and stimulating investigation and measurement development. Therefore, chapters are developed and positioned following the flow of this model.

The central core of the model is leisure involvement and participation. All antecedent domains and consequences are drawn to the model to explain, predict, and advance leisure involvement. Chapter 20 focuses on demonstrating the background of the notion of ego involvement, initially originating as a social psychological idea, followed by applied areas such as marketing. The study of leisure involvement had a birth defect, evolving from marketing concepts more so than its originator: social psychology.

Manifestations of birth defects will be recognized as gaps, essential experiential and aesthetic ideas of leisure that are missing, as reflected in components such as flow, intensity, and intrinsically motivated choices. Finally, leisure involvement scales are listed. These measurements are characterized as being related to specific leisure activities such as camping and fitness, demonstrating a severe shortage in assessing leisure and recreation in their totalities.

In explaining leisure involvement, a logical sequence in the flow of the model is leisure motivations and needs (see Chapter 21). Five major theoretical structures are identified that can be of good service to the leisure field, with emphasis on the last of them: psychoanalytic, behavioral, cognitive, humanistic or developmental, and positive psychological theories. An attempt is made to map leisure motivation boundaries to understand it as a construct, contributing to the structure of its construct. Fortunately, these sorts of scales have gained the highest

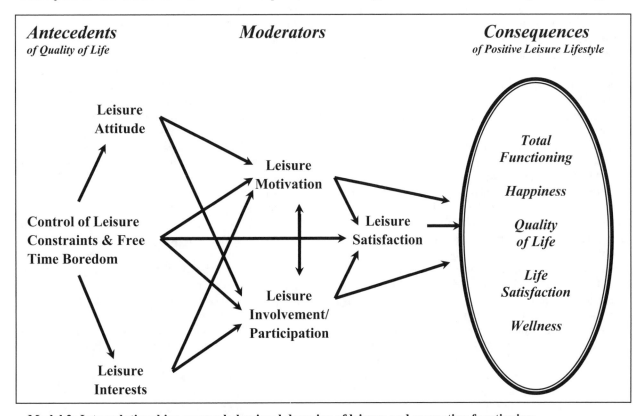

Model 2: Interrelationships among behavioral domains of leisure and recreation functioning

attention with more than 20 scales available. Many social and behavioral phenomena can be tested and understood by using these leisure motivation scales.

Leisure interests as presented in Chapter 22 are equivalent to leisure involvement. Without interests, individuals would not seek leisure participation. This chapter illustrates how interests motivate a person to engage or not engage in activities. The study of interests has a long history of investigation that originated the 1920s. All of the assessments presented here helped pave the road to better understanding of leisure interests. Most of the knowledge about interests gained from these assessments is relevant to "interests in activities." "Psychological dispositions" that lead to interest has not been a major topic for the development of assessments. Factor analysis was employed to reveal diversified interests in leisure as they were assessed.

Chapter 23 explores leisure attitude as an important antecedent to leisure involvement and participation. Some major unintended omissions of critical moderators for each phenomenon were ignored in the 1970s and 1980s. This led to inconsistent findings about attitude-behavior associations. Therefore, gaps were recognized, guarding against repeating the same mistakes, restoring confidence in the methodology employed and its results. Neglected moderators were identified as the causes of inconsistencies in the results. The concept of attitude and its components was traced in the literature. Mainly, three components were extracted and outlined: cognitive, affective, and behavioral. In an applied sense, those interested in leisure attitude aim to help participants change negative impressions, feelings, or practices to more desirable and beneficial ones. That is an approach called attitude change, which is elaborated in the chapter. Contemporary attention to leisure attitude constructs has been lacking development and momentum.

More frequently than expected, constraints and barriers prevent individuals from fulfilling their motivations, and restrict their healthy and normal leisure involvement. Some of these constraints were identified as free time pathologies. Modern advancements, inventions, and technologies have worsened the existence and impact of those pathologies.

Chapters 24 and 25 provide elaborate details on free time boredom (FTB) as a pathology that has diverse impacts on substance abuse, gambling, depression, and suicide attempts. FTB is developed instrumentally in Chapter 24 to help in its diagnosis, prevention, and treatment, drawing attention to the needs for excitement and stimulation in leisure choices, programs, and environments. To put FTB into the proper perspectives, the major three life domains (work, family, and free time) were put into a

context, demonstrating the existence and spillover of boredom from one to the other. Finally, this chapter ends with a broad demonstration of boredom's impact on behavioral disorders including alcoholism, drug abuse, gambling, depression, and suicide.

Chapter 25 is designed to demonstrate the conditions that help diffuse boredom. Medically, to treat an illness, doctors should understand the nature of the illness. Therefore, 15 kinds of boredom were extracted from very broad literature. A synthesis of these 15 kinds integrated them into three main categories: environmental, acquired habits, and genetic. A discussion of the prevalence of these categories, pertinent practical considerations, and serious implications are provided. Bases for diagnosis of boredom, its prevention, and treatment strategies are presented, showing how measuring boredom can assist those strategies. An important consideration is that boredom is devastating our culture not only nationally, but also internationally, evolving from its original form to a new strength called *ennui*: more cyclical, chronic, and severe. Therefore, to help in gaining insights in handling boredom, 13 implications of how research findings are relevant to leisure professionals are presented. Knowledge of these two chapters can be of help to diverse practices.

One of the important consequences of leisure involvement is leisure satisfaction as a final outcome. The next two chapters present this domain. Chapter 26 identifies the specific satisfactions that individuals experience in leisure pursuits and the roots of their concepts.

Measurements developed on the basis of knowledge available are presented, demonstrating the low attention they gained, despite their importance. To serve the formal development, Chapter 27 looks at the diversification of satisfaction concepts in many domains of life (e.g., health, family, and financial). Characteristics of life satisfaction are presented, such as positive affect and intensity. A cross-cultural comparison between life satisfaction in the East (China and Japan) and the West (France and USA) is presented, showing the pertinence of leisure. Different satisfactions will be put into a context in terms of individuals' values. Finally, theories of life satisfaction will be presented that can be used as bases for measurement development. A formula is suggested to compute personal satisfaction.

Finally, Chapter 28 focuses on playfulness and humor. Why people behave playfully and humorously is elaborated on, showing biological and psychological benefits. Usually, maximum manifestations of playfulness and humor are exhibited during individuals' free time. Therefore, instruments are identified and presented to help in their assessment.

Questions and Exercises

1. Name and explain the main parts of this book.
2. How are leisure and recreation instruments classified?
3. Name the major areas of the classification utilized.
4. Explain the methods employed to construct measurements.
5. What are the bases to be used as foundations to develop instruments?

Part I

Classification of Leisure and Recreation Scales

Chapter 2

Classification and Categorizations of Available Leisure Measurements

Focus of Chapter

The goal of this chapter is to be used as a map. It will help readers navigate their way through the more than 100 measurements presented in this book. To map existing scales, a classification categorizing existing instruments is suggested. This is based on logic and content. A social psychological model is developed to identify a flow from antecedents to consequences with a middle critical moderator — leisure involvement and participation. The moderator, as it pertains to the use of measurements, is one of the central issues in this book.

A set of criteria to fit domains in this classification is described. The criteria allow us to list the benefits of such classification, followed by a list of its categorized components. How the proposed classification can serve research and practice is presented, followed by a list of all identified measurements. Comments about utility and revision of scales are included. Finally, illustrations of potential usability of the classification are reported.

Key Terms

- benefits to practice
- benefits to research
- categorization
- classification
- scale revision
- scale usability
- social psychology
- taxonomy

Key Names

- Gaylene M. Carpenter
- Ronald Jay Cohen
- Christine Z. Howe
- Norma Stumbo
- Mark Swerdlik
- Steven R. Thompson

Objectives

- Identify the purposes for categorizing leisure measurement.
- Explain suggested classification of leisure measurements.
- List criteria for formation of leisure domains.
- List benefits of classification of leisure scales.
- Cite reported conditions that require revision of an instrument.

The purpose of the categorization of leisure measurements is to organize and catalog existing scales under their most logical domains. This can enhance the work of three groups: field professionals, researchers, and leisure students. The benefits of this categorization include:

1. Providing an inventory for leisure measurements in existence. Accessibility of instruments can help their familiarity and utilization. Utility of the classification, as an outcome, will be beneficial for all users.
2. Generally, the categorization suggested could demonstrate gaps within certain leisure and recreation domains, requiring more attention to what are missing and neglected.
3. Specifically, within each domain, shortage or lack of necessary scales will be self-evident, stimulating scientific endeavors to develop the needed concept and its tools.
4. More scientific explorations of leisure phenomena and their categorizations can be explored as a result of being oriented with what is classified.
5. The classification can help in training new professionals by orienting them to instruments that can be utilized and enhancing provision whether practical or scientific.

Professionally, there are compelling needs to arrange leisure instruments in a manner that can facilitate their uses and applications. Assessment tools were constructed starting in the 1920s, and the 1960s saw a rapid growth of development for practical and research uses. At times, the variety of assessments can cause confusion; at worst, prevent availability and use. Therefore, arranging measurements according to certain classifications and categorizations can enhance usability. It is important to note that the nature of classifications of objects is never science; it is always art and philosophy. Scientific explanations evolved on the basis of philosophical sorting and classifications of, for instance, rocks, leaves, liquids, animals, fish, and physical features of different races, then, later, behavior and social processes. These types of sorting established sciences like physics, chemistry, and psychology.

The strategy for this classification of leisure instruments is to follow an integrated procedure assigning scales to their most relevant concepts. (Concepts as basis for the development of instruments will be presented in the third part of the book.) Logic and reasoning will be the main approaches to assign scales to their most pertinent classification. The sorting uses identified criteria (content, relevance, deduction, and analysis), to describe the measurements' taxonomy. Taxonomy is defined as the orderly classification of *objects* according to their presumed natural relationships. Each category will incorporate concepts, constructs, and measurements that demonstrate logical relevance and content.

At best, the category would be supported by existing empirical evidence. Accordingly, there will be greater accessibility to both concepts and measurements. In case there is a lack of instrumentation in any given area, it will be clearly manifested and identified. The interest stimulated by the realization that there are gaps should lead to research to fill in the gaps in knowledge about certain concepts and/or relevant instruments. As a result of the availability of each classification, both practice and theory can advance.

Suggested Classification of Leisure Measurements

In the mid 1980s, two classifications were formulated, as chapters in books: one by Carpenter and Howe (1985) and the other by Stumbo and Thompson (1986). The former included 21 scales, while the later incorporated 24. Instruments reported in the two developments were clustered under almost the same domains: leisure attitudes, leisure values, leisure states, leisure behavior, leisure satisfaction, and leisure interests. A similar approach is followed in this book.

To map existing measurements, a social psychological model as presented in Model 2 was developed to guide the process of assigning instruments to categories. This model is utilized here to help arrange and sort most available assessment tools in leisure (general and specific), categorizing them into a meaningful and appealing order. More than 100 measurements are presented below. According to this model, leisure involvement (LI) is viewed as the focus or central domain, around which other leisure concepts revolve. This is done in an attempt to understand and predict LI's antecedents and consequences. Developmentally, these attempts can function as prerequisites for hypotheses testing, theorization, and field application.

Ultimately, the model evolves to achieve a humanistic outcome: maintenance and improvement of wellness, vitality, empowerment, quality of life, and total functioning. These can be regarded as consequences of leisure's social psychological impact. To do so, constructs and measurements are presented, demonstrating their relevance to two major stages and levels: involvement's antecedents and involvement's consequences.

In the model, the identified antecedents to involvement are leisure attitude, controlling constraints (such as free time boredom), interests, and motivation. The consequences manifest in leisure satisfaction, vitality, life satisfaction, quality of life, and total functioning, to put them in what seems to be a logical sequence. Within this model, domains in the middle switch their operating positions, acting as antecedents in some cases and consequences in others, depending on what is predicted and how it is treated. In this manner, if they are between two domains, they are considered moderators.

Criteria for Domain Formation

Specific criteria will be followed to construct and present each domain's concepts and scales, as identified in the classification suggested by the model. Measurements do not exist into a vacuum; they must represent or reflect a specific, agreed-upon domain (e.g., leisure motivation, leisure satisfaction). This is why a concept's familiarity is indispensable, not only just to know its background and content, but also for evaluating the measurement's utility. Accordingly, criteria will be employed to delineate each classification, as follows:

1. What is the body of literature or background representing the domain?
2. Are there sufficient philosophical and theoretical knowledge and explanations to support and represent the domain?
3. How would the current domain relate to other phenomena or domains?
4. Are there sufficient instruments assessing the domain's identified grounds?
5. What are the instruments that represent or serve this domain?
6. How valid, reliable, accessible, and usable are available measurements?
7. Within a domain and among domains, are there gaps in concepts and/or assessment tools?
8. If yes, what are they?

Following the above model, measurements will be grouped, categorically, under their most appropriate and logical domains. Other classifications, following reasonable logic, can be desirable not only to promote identification of scales, but also future theorization and hypotheses testing. Such procedure will enable users of measurements to locate, review, evaluate, and employ available instruments. Moreover, developments of future scales can find a point of reference and origination, both for their concepts and for examples of the relevant tools.

It is important to note that one area of interest to the leisure delivery systems is unclassifiable within the proposed social and behavioral model. However, this area, Leisure Administration and Supervision, has concepts that are very meritorious to practice and has been the focus of significant assessment development. This area will be presented at the end.

For scale users, it is an advantage to know the concept that they are interest in measuring (e.g., leisure involvement, attitude, or interest). This helps in selecting quality scales, and also puts their findings into a logical context, which leads to a sound perspective and realistically interpreted results. Consequently, instrument users can give accurate and well-founded guidance, provide more effective counsel to participants, or plan quality programs and services. For example, to work with someone who has been complaining about free time boredom (FTB), a professional provides a quality service when s/he is equipped with the following:

- The prevalence of causes and effects of boredom in society.
- The behavioral disorders that can manifest themselves as a result of boredom.
- Specific information on the magnitude of boredom in this person's life.
- The person's specific ratings on FTB components: lack of physical involvement, lack of metal involvement, lack of meaningful involvement, and speed of time.
- The components that need the most/least attention?

Most practically, professional services will be more effective because of having specific scores on a person's FTB and how s/he rated boredom's components. Data will pinpoint areas of free time suffering, helping to make understanding clearer, diagnosis more accurate, and treatment more effective.

Based on Model 2 and the unclassified area of leisure provision, the sequence of units will be as follows:

1. Leisure Involvement
2. Leisure Motivation
3. Free Time Boredom
4. Leisure Interests
5. Leisure Attitudes
6. Leisure Satisfaction
7. Playfulness and Humor
8. Leisure Administration and Supervision Measurements

Both the design and objectives of the above categorizations are to help not only instrument development, but also their practical and scientific uses for practitioners, researchers, and students.

Contributions of the Classification to Diverse Services

Due to categorization's comprehensive coverage, contents, and their pedagogical pertinence, the classification can serve several identified fields, research investigations, educational goals, and functions as follows:

First, in many field settings, practitioners are required to strengthen their assessment competencies. Therefore, in-service training and workshops can be planned to expose professionals to the latest assessment instruments and approaches. Also, training can incorporate two fundamental skills: how to treat or use data and how to construct homemade scales. Availability of scales presented here can make assessment more feasible, attainable, and user-friendly. Sometimes the lack of assessment procedures is attributed to the lack of available instruments or a lack of knowledge of how to construct them.

Second, for research purposes, knowledge of assessment tools is crucial to the success of scientific studies. Most leisure scientists use measurements to assess their variables. Therefore, that research will gain a great deal by knowledge of the categorization presented here.

Last, the categorization provides a framework for undergraduate students. By focusing on subjects related to social and behavioral issues and trends of leisure, such as motivation, interests, FTB, and satisfaction, new students will be better able to understand not only why people engage in leisure, but also potential problems. Moreover, mapping and categorizing available leisure scales can enable students to easily locate existing instruments, serving training purposes and future field applications. Future professionals can be better prepared, being oriented to the scales in existence.

For graduate students, content relevant to the domains presented can be utilized on two different levels.

- Existing content can supplement classes relevant to behavioral issues of leisure, such as positive psychology and social psychology of leisure. Moreover, content can be used as foundations for the development of measurements, to assist students to advance methodologically from concepts to measurements.
- Content lays the groundwork for a higher level of abstraction, which would help to delineate concepts further and to advance knowledge while constructing sound, usable tools.

Clearly, then, this graduate level of use tends to represent both a sophisticated and a challenging endeavor for doctorate students in leisure. That is a needed level of application of "Concepts and Measurements."

In other words, the above classification can assist and be employed with a number of academic, scientific, and applied levels — depending on the scope of utility, level of experience, intended goals, and on how concepts are related and implemented in a professional's field of services.

Comments about Utility, Future Challenges, and Needs for Revision

Close to 100 scales represent most of the leisure and recreation assessment tools in existence. Their utility depends on the users' needs, competencies, problems, and professional orientations. However, users need to be cautious about the usefulness of existing measures. For some, they may be outdated. How can users and developers of scales judge the survivability level of an instrument? How can we determine a scale's need for revision? Cohen and Swerdlik (2002: 217) posted seven conditions. If any of them are present, the instrument needs to be revised:

1. The stimulus materials look dated and current test takers simply cannot relate to them.
2. The verbal content of the test, including the administration instructions and the test items, contains dated vocabulary that is not readily understood by current test takers.
3. As popular culture changes and words take on new meanings, certain words or expressions in the test items or directions may be perceived as inappropriate or even offensive to a particular group and must therefore be changed.
4. The test norms are no longer adequate as a result of group membership changes in the population of potential test takers.
5. The test norms are no longer adequate as a result of age-related shifts in the abilities measured over time, and an age extension to the norms (upward, downward, or in both directions) is necessary.
6. The reliability or the validity of the test, as well as the effectiveness of individual test items, can be significantly improved by a revision.
7. The theory on which the test was originally based has been improved significantly, and the changes should be reflected in the design and content of the test.

Cohen and Swerdlik observed that some scales age faster than others. They cite APA (1996, Standard 3.18) offering a general ruling that an existing measure be used for the duration of staying "useful" and it would be revised "when significant changes in the domain represented, or new conditions of test use and interpretation make the test inappropriate for its intended use." In applying the above rulings and criteria, how would the leisure instruments measure up? This evaluation of the merit of the existing leisure measurements presents a challenge: Which instruments need to be discarded? Which measurements need to be revised and modified? Which scales are absent and needed?

Illustrations of Possible Usability of the Classification

A small sample of questions can demonstrate some possible uses for the domains in advancing field applications and scientific explorations:

1. How would leisure attitude, interest, motivation, and control of free time boredom determine leisure involvement?
2. Are there relationships between leisure attitude, interest, motivation, involvement, and leisure satisfaction?
3. How much does each of the social psychological domains of leisure contribute to an individual's total functioning?
4. Which of the social psychological domains contribute the most to an individual's wellness and vitality?
5. Which ones contribute to life satisfaction?
6. What is the level of free time boredom that results in behavioral disorders, such as the following?

   a. Depression
   b. Suicide attempts or actual suicide
   c. Drug abuse
   d. Alcoholism
   e. Gambling
   f. Crime/juvenile delinquency
   g. Excessive work absenteeism, lack of productivity
   h. Divorce
   i. Lack of active leisure interests
   j. Low grade-point average

7. How would the reported social psychological domains contribute to involvement in specific activities such as camping, traveling, picnicking, physical recreation, exercise and fitness, arts, cultural activities, and social activities?

Such answers and findings can enhance not only theorization and hypotheses testing, but also field practice, leisure counseling, leisure education, services, and classroom instruction in preparing new generations for leisure and recreation pursuits.

Classification of Measurements

Table 1 shows the classification of each of the assessment tools presented in this book.

Table 1: Classification of Measurements under Their Most Relevant Categories

Category	Tool
Leisure Involvement	Leisure Activities Blank (LAB) (McKechnie, 1974)
	Measuring Commitment to Running (MCR) (Cormack and Martens, 1979)
	Enduring Involvement in Camping (EIC) (McIntyre, 1989)
	Processes of Change Questionnaire (PCQ) (Marcus, Rossi, Selby, Niaura, and Abrams, 1992)
	Exercise's Stages-of-Change (ESoC) (Marcus, Selby, Niaura, and Rossi, 1992)
	Self-Efficacy for Exercise Behavior Scale (SEEBS) (Marcus et al., 1992)
	Commitment in Recreational Tennis (CRT) (Siegenthaler and Lam, 1992)
	Ego Involvement in Recreational Tennis (EIRT) (Siegenthaler and Lam, 1992)
	Married Couples' Involvement with Family Vacation (MCIFV) (Madrigal et al., 1992)
	Adventure Recreation Involvement (ARI) (Schuett, 1993)
	Adolescent Ethical Behavior in Leisure Scale (AEBLS) (Widmer et al., 1996)
	Assessment of Leisure and Recreation Involvement (LRI) (Ragheb, 1996)
	Leisure Deficit Scale (LDS) (Beach, 1997) [Insufficient information to present]
	Exercise Imagery Questionnaire — Aerobic Version (EIQ-AV) (Hausenblas et al., 1999)
Leisure Attitude — General	Leisure Orientation Scale (LOS) (Burdge, 1961) [Insufficient information to present]
	Measurement of Leisure Attitude (MLA) (Neulinger and Breit, 1971)
	Leisure Ethic Scale (LES) (Bryan and Alsikafi, 1975) [Insufficient information to present]
	Leisure Ethic Subscale (LES) (Buchholz, 1978) [Insufficient information to present]
	Leisure Attitude Scale (LAS) (Crandall and Slivken, 1980)
	Leisure Attitude Measurement (LAM) (Ragheb and Beard, 1982)
	Leisure Coping Belief Scale (LCBS) (Iwasaki and Mannell, 2000)

Table 2: Classification of Measurements under Their Most Relevant Categories (continued)

Category	Tool
Leisure Attitude — Specific	Attitudes Toward Jogging Questionnaire (ATJQ) (Riddle, 1980) [Insufficient information to present]
	Children's Attitude toward Physical Activity Inventory (CATPAI) (Schutz et al., 1985)
	Attitudinal Beliefs Regarding Exercise Questionnaire (ABREQ) (Godin et al., 1986) [Insufficient information to present]
	Attitudes Toward Exercise Questionnaire (ATEQ) (Anshel, 1991) [Insufficient information to present]
Leisure Motivation — General	Measurement of Leisure Needs (MLN) (Iso-Ahola and Allen, 1982)
	Leisure Motivation Scale (LMS) (Beard and Ragheb, 1983/1989)
	Self-as-Entertainment Scale (SAES) (Mannell, 1984)
	Measurement of Perceived Freedom in Leisure (MPFL) (Ellis and Witt, 1984)
	Intrinsic Leisure Motivation (ILM) (Weissinger, 1986)
	Leisure Experience Battery for Adolescents (LEBA) (Caldwell, Smith, and Weissinger, 1992)
	Measurement of Perceived Freedom in Leisure and Satisfaction (MPFLS) (Ellis and Witt, 1994) [Insufficient information to present]
	The Motivation for Leisure Scale (MLS) (Pelletier et al., 1994) [Insufficient information to present]
	Intrinsic Motivation in Leisure (IML) (Weissinger and Bandalos, 1995) [Insufficient information to present]
	Recreation Experience Preference (REP) (Manfredo and Driver, 1996)
	Measuring the Search for Meaning in Leisure and Recreation (MSMLR) (Ragheb, 1997)
	Free Time Motivation Scale for Adolescents (FTMS-A) (Baldwin and Caldwell, 2003)
Leisure Motivation — Specific	Fitness Locus of Control Scale (FITLOC) (Whitehead and Corbin, 1988)
	Racquet Sports Competence Scale (RSCS) (Aguilar and Petrakis, 1989)
	Exercise Decisional Balance Measure (EDBM) (Marcus, Rakowski, and Rossi, 1992)
	Exercise Identity Scale (EIS) (Anderson and Cychosz, 1994)
	The Flow State Scale (FSS) (Jackson and Marsh, 1996)
	The Exercise Motivation Inventory-2 (EMI-2) (Markland and Ingledew, 1997)
	Behavioral Regulation in Exercise Questionnaire (BREQ) (Mullan, Markland, and Ingledew, 1997)
	Exercise Motivation Scale (EMS) (Li, 1999)
	Motivations for Participation in Recreational Running Scale (MPRRS) (Clough, Shepherd, and Maugham, 1999)
	International Leisure Travel Motivation (ILTM) (Toh and Yeung, 2000)
Boredom in Leisure and Free Time Measurements	Measuring Susceptibility to Monotony (MSM), (Thompson, 1929) [Insufficient information to present]
	Curiosity Scale (CS) (Maw and Maw, 1965) [Insufficient information to present]
	Stimulus-Variation Seeking Scale (SVSS) (Penney and Reinehr, 1966) [Insufficient information to present]
	Sensation Seeking Scale (SSS) (Zuckerman et al., 1970) [Insufficient information to present]
	Arousal Seeking Tendency Scale (ASTS) (Mehrabian and Russell, 1973) [Insufficient information to present]
	Intrinsic Enjoyment and Boredom Coping (IEBC) (Hamilton, Haier, and Buchsbaum, 1984) [Insufficient information to present]
	Boredom Proneness Scale (BPS) (Farmer and Sundberg, 1986) [Insufficient information to present]
	Adopted Curiosity Scale (ACS) (Padhee and Das, 1987) [Insufficient information to present]
	Leisure Boredom Scale (LBS) (Iso-Ahola and Weissinger, 1990)
	Telic Paratelic Scale (TPS) (Cook et al., 1993) [Insufficient information to present]
	Free Time Boredom (FTB) (Ragheb and Merydith, 2001)

Table 3: Classification of Measurements under Their Most Relevant Categories (continued)

Category	Tool
Leisure Interest Measurements	Inventory of Leisure Interest (ILI) (Hubert, 1969) [Insufficient information to present]
	Mirenda Leisure Interest Finder (MLIF) (Mirenda, 1973) [Insufficient information to present]
	Avocational Counseling Manual (ACM) (Overs, 1977) [Insufficient information to present]
	Measure of Leisure Interest (MLI) (Frisbie, 1984) [Insufficient information to present]
	Life Interests Inventory (LII) (Leisure/Work) (Williams, 1987) [Insufficient information to present]
	Leisure Interests Checklist (LIC) (Rosenthal et al., 1989) [Insufficient information to present]
	Recreation Interest Inventory (RII) (Kirkcaldy, 1990) [Insufficient information to present]
	State Technical Institute's Leisure Assessment Process (STILAP) (Navar, 1990)
	The Leisure Interest Inventory (LII) (Stangl, 1991) [Insufficient information to present]
	Leisure Interest Measure (LIM) (Ragheb and Beard, 1992)
	Adolescence Leisure Interest Profile (ALIP) (Henry, 1998) [Insufficient information to present]
	Leisure Assessment Inventory (LAI) (Hawkins, Ardovino, and Hsieh, 1998)
	Leisurescope Plus and Teen Leisurescope Plus (Schenk, 1998)
Leisure Satisfaction Measurements	Milwaukee Avocational Satisfaction Questionnaire (Overs, Taylor, and Adkins, 1977) [Insufficient information to present]
	Leisure Satisfaction Inventory (LSI) (Rimmer, 1979) [Insufficient information to present]
	Leisure Satisfaction Measure (LSM) (Beard and Ragheb, 1980/1991)
	Racquet Sports Satisfaction Scale (RSSS) (Aguilar and Petrakis, 1989)
	Physical Activity Enjoyment Scale (PAES) (Kendzierski and DeCarlo, 1991)
	Global Leisure Satisfaction Scale (GLSS) (Ellis and Witt, 1994)
	Leisure Coping Strategy Scale (LCSS) (Iwasaki and Mannell, 2000)
	Leisure Time Satisfaction (LTS) (Stevens, Coon, Wisniewski, Vance et al. 2004)
	Vitality Through Leisure (VTL) (Ragheb, 2005)
Playfulness and Humor Measurements	Lieberman's Playfulness Instrument (LPI) (Lieberman, 1965, 1966) [Insufficient information to present]
	Coping Humor Scale (CHS); (Martin and Leftcourt, 1983) [Insufficient information to present]
	Situational Humor Response Questionnaire (SHRQ) (Martin and Leftcourt, 1984) [Insufficient information to present]
	Children's Playfulness Scale (CPS) (Barnett, 1991)
	Adult Playfulness Scale (APS) (Glynn and Webster, 1992, 1993) [Insufficient information to present]
	Sense of Humor Scale (SHS) (Thorson and Powell, 1993) [Insufficient information to present]
	State-Trait Cheerfulness Inventory (STCI) (Ruch, Koehler, and Ban Thriel, 1996) [Insufficient information to present]
	Playfulness Scale (PS) (Schaefer and Greenberg, 1997) [Insufficient information to present]
	Test of Playfulness (ToP) (Okimoto et al., 2000) [Insufficient information to present]
	Humor Styles Questionnaire (HSQ) (Martin, Puhlik-Doris, Larsen, Gray, and Weir, 2003) [Insufficient information to present]
Leisure Administration and Supervision Measurements	Quality of Recreation Services (QRS) (MacKay and Compton, 1990)
	Recreation Service Quality Assessment (RSQA) (Wright, Duray, and Goodale, 1992)
	Motivation Assessment and Performance Scale (MAPS) (Williams and Neal, 1993)
	Center for Environmental and Recreation Management — Customer Service Quality (CERM CSQ) (Howat, Absher, Crilley, and Milne, 1996)
	Volunteer Functions Inventory (VFI) (Clary et al, 1998)*
	Special Event Volunteer Motivation Scale (SEVMS) (Farrell, Johnston, and Twynam, 1998)*

* Although motivations for volunteering belong to leisure choices, as a motivation for services, these scales were evaluated to relate also to the classification of Leisure Administration and Supervision Measurements.

Questions and Exercises

1. Report on the classification's scope of services.
2. Locate the most useful measurements with the needed category that serve intended functions. (Five users can attempt to locate given scales for identified functions. Evaluation, through inter-rater agreement can test the fulfillment of this objective.)
3. Report on the usability of the classification.

Chapter 3

Measurements of Leisure Involvement

Focus of Chapter

This chapter lists the measurements of leisure involvement currently available for use in recreation and leisure and earlier measurements that can be drawn upon in creating new, more modern measurements.

Key Terms

• leisure involvement

Objectives

• Describe the content and functions of available measurements of leisure involvement.

Measurements presented in this chapter represent a wide range of involvement in leisure activities. Scales can range from involvement in exercise, running, and vacationing to camping and tennis. Few scales were developed to assess global leisure involvement and participation. To assess involvement in other activities that lack instrumentations, measurements can be adapted from what they were developed to serve. To do so, caution needs to be exercised and permissions to adapt scales should be requested from copyright holders first.

Assessment tools in this chapter are as follows.

1. Leisure Activities Blank (LAB) (McKechnie, 1974)
2. Measuring Commitment to Running (MCR) (Carmack and Martens, 1979)
3. Enduring Involvement in Camping (EIC) (McIntyre, 1989)
4. Processes of Change Questionnaire (PCQ) (Marcus, Rossi, Selby, Niaura, and Abrams, 1992)
5. Exercise's Stages-of-Change (ESoC) (Marcus et al., 1992)
6. Self-Efficacy for Exercise Behavior Scale (SEEBS) (Marcus et al., 1992)
7. Commitment in Recreational Tennis (CRT) (Siegenthaler and Lam, 1992)
8. Ego Involvement in Recreational Tennis (EIRT) (Siegenthaler and Lam, 1992)
9. Married Couples' Involvement with Family Vacation (MCIFV) (Madrigal et al., 1992)
10. Adventure Recreation Involvement (ARI) (Schuett, 1993)
11. Adolescent Ethical Behavior in Leisure Scale (AEBLS) (Widmer et al., 1996)
12. Assessment of Leisure and Recreation Involvement (LRI) (Ragheb, 1996)
13. Exercise Imagery Questionnaire — Aerobic Version (EIQ-AV) (Hausenblas, Hall, Rogers, and Munroe (1999)

One other assessment was found in the literature, but there was not enough information to do an evaluation of it.

1. Leisure Deficit Scale (LDS) (Beach, 1997)

Questions and Exercises

1. Describe the content of leisure involvement measurements.
2. Explain the functions of leisure involvement measurements.
3. Is there a need for measurements to assess involvement in specific leisure activities and other measurements to assess general leisure involvement? Elaborate.
4. Name and explain possible components of specific and general leisure involvement.

Involvement 1

LEISURE ACTIVITIES BLANK
(LAB)
George E. McKechnie

Reference: McKechnie, G. E. (1974). The psychological structure of leisure: Past behavior. *Journal of Leisure Research, 6*, 27-45.

Goal of the Measurement: To tap past and future rates of participation in a list of 121 leisure and recreation activities, identifying predominant patterns of leisure.

Background Literature: Expanding free time is claimed to be leading to possible crises. This is due to potential inability to cope with free time, converting it to meaningful experiences to enhance human development and satisfaction. Studies of participation in specific activities (e.g., camping, group activities, swimming) were cited. Studies indicated that meager attention was offered "to explore the boundaries of the domain or attempt to uncover the factor or typological structure of leisure activities" (p. 28). Available studies identified a variety of factors underlying recreation and leisure participation, such as Passive-Free Play, Active-Expressive, Outdoor-Nature, and Aesthetic-Sophisticate. The author's reason for this study was that the small range of activities limits the identification of the psychological dimensions of leisure and recreation participation.

Methodology Employed: The measurement's developer generated a list of the most frequently used leisure activities, then evaluated by colleagues (content validity), resulting in a revised set of 121 activities, designated as LAB. Respondents were asked one time about their past participation and another time about their future intentions for each of the 121 activities. A door-to-door, stratified, random sample (288) of community residents was employed. Factor analysis and Varimax rotation were utilized, followed by alpha and split-half reliability estimates.

Findings: Six interpretable factors were found for past participation: Mechanics, Crafts, Intellectual, Slow Living, Sports, and Glamour Sports. As for the future, eight factors were found: Adventure, Mechanics, Crafts, Easy Living, Intellectual, Ego Recognition, Slow Living, and Clean Living. Activities clustering together under each factor were tested for reliabilities. Alpha reliability coefficients ranged between .89 and .81, while split-half reliabilities ranged between .93 and .81. No reliability tests were reported for the total LAB Scale. The measurement's validity is based on the extensive literature (conceptual and empirical findings) employed to identify possible components, followed by peer reviews of content validity.

Investigator's Comments: It is recommended that this study be replicated, using the same list of activities in other counties and states as well as with individuals of different socioeconomic levels. Many directions for future application and uses of the LAB instrument were suggested including studies of the most common recreation patterns nationally and regionally, personality characteristics of specific activity users, an individual's changes in LAB score profile over time, and societal shifts in recreation preferences.

Involvement 2

MEASURING COMMITMENT TO RUNNING
(MCR)

Mary A. Carmack and Rainer Martens

Reference: Carmack, M. A., and Martens, R. (1979). Measuring commitment to running: A survey of runners' attitudes and mental states. *Journal of Sport Psychology, 1,* 25-42.

Goal of the Measurement: To be able to measure commitment to running (CR).

Background Literature: Due to the contribution of running to wellness, health, and mood, many empirical investigations were conducted. However, there is no clear information about two main behavioral variables: 1. the reasons why people run (motivation) and 2. outcomes that runners derive from running (satisfaction, rewards). Speculative ideas have been tested to verify the notion that running can be utilized to treat depression. Also, it has been suggested that running has addictive qualities as well as beneficial psychological effects when it is used "meditatively." More importantly, the literature yielded a conceptual notion that runners become "positively addicted" to running because the psychological effects "feel so good." Positive addiction was defined by Glasser (1976) as an activity that increases mental strength and, when missed, results in some kind of pain, misery, or upset. Glasser suggested the idea that "spinning free" generates pleasurable and euphoric mental effects. An assumption was made that this causes the brain to grow and become stronger. All of the above were used as bases for the development of a commitment to a running scale.

Methodology Employed: Scanning the popular literature and interviewing runners helped to develop scale items. For content validity, 10 runners and 5 experts reviewed items. An initial list of 30 items was drafted and administered to 180 persons; then analysis helped to reduce the list to 12 usable items. These items were stated to describe feelings about running, using a five-point scale, from "Strongly Disagree" (marked as "1") to "Strongly Agree" (marked as "5"). The commitment to running scale was administered to a sample of 315 runners. Finally, alpha reliability was administered.

Findings: The Commitment to Running Scale (12 items) demonstrated a reliability coefficient of .93 and the Kuder-Richardson formula 20 resulted in another reliability coefficient of .97. Moreover, concurrent validity of the above scale was provided through consistent patterns with Glasser's Positive Addiction Scale and two other constructs.

Investigator's Comments: Although the amount of explained variance is not great, the results are noteworthy. Findings on the classification of over- and under-40 minute runners stimulate a variety of research problems.

Notes: To improve this scale, more conceptual work needs to be done, more concepts must be identified, further items should be drafted, and factor analysis should be employed first, before reliability tests. Engaging in running other than for sports or athletic functions is by all means a physical recreation. For those who choose active leisure lifestyles, running is one of their pursuits.

Contact Information:
Dr. Rainer Martens, President
Human Kinetics, Inc.
P. O. Box 5076
Champaign, IL 61820-5076

Phone: 800-747-4457
Email: humank@hkusa.com

MEASURING COMMITMENT TO RUNNING (MCR)

Carmack, M. A.; and Martens, R.

Feelings about Running

DIRECTIONS: The following statements may or may not describe your feelings about running. Read each statement and then circle the appropriate number to indicate how well the statement describes *your feelings most of the time*. If you **"Strongly Disagree"** with the item, circle "1"; if you **"Strongly Agree,"** circle "5." Otherwise, circle a number between 1 and 5. There are no right or wrong answers. Do not spend too much time on any one item, but give the answers that seem to describe how you *generally feel* about running.

	Strongly Disagree	Disagree	Uncertain	Agree	Strongly Agree
	1	2	3	4	5
1.	I look forward to running.				
	1	2	3	4	5
2.	I wish there were a more enjoyable way to stay fit.				
	1	2	3	4	5
3.	Running is drudgery.				
	1	2	3	4	5
4.	I do not enjoy running.				
	1	2	3	4	5
5.	Running is vitally important to me.				
	1	2	3	4	5
6.	Life is so much richer as a result of running.				
	1	2	3	4	5
7.	Running is pleasant.				
	1	2	3	4	5
8.	I dread the thought of running.				
	1	2	3	4	5
9.	I would arrange or change my schedule to meet the need to run.				
	1	2	3	4	5
10.	I have to force myself to run.				
	1	2	3	4	5
11.	To miss a day's run is sheer relief.				
	1	2	3	4	5
12.	Running is the highest point of my day.				
	1	2	3	4	5

SAMPLE
Do Not Copy

Items 2, 3, 4, 8, 10, and 11 are scored in reverse; for item reversal, see Chapter 17.

Involvement 3

ENDURING INVOLVEMENT IN CAMPING
(EIC)
Norman McIntyre

Reference: McIntyre, N. (1989). The personal meaning of participation: Enduring involvement. *Journal of Leisure Research, 21*, 167-179.

Goal of the Measurement: To assess enduring involvement (levels of participation) in activities. While this version (the original version) specifically measures enduring involvement in camping, the author allows users of this tool to replace the word "camping" with other types of activities.

Background Literature: The main concern of this instrument's development is the personal meaning of recreation participation. The author believes that personal meaning is equivalent to terms found in a variety of other studies including commitment, centrality, affective attachment, and involvement. The literature demonstrates that, although commitment or involvement may lack sufficient operationalization, it is perceived as an important component of recreation specialization. Another critical concept is enduring involvement, with empirical evidence showing that it has four components: importance, enjoyment, self-expression, and centrality.

Methodology Employed: Mainly, items were adopted from Laurent and Kapferer (1985) measuring consumer involvement. Item wordings were altered to fit the camping context for 12 items previously utilized in consumer behavior and recreation. A five-point, Likert-type scale was utilized. A pilot study on 52 persons was conducted; two items were eliminated from the centrality domain. Data was gathered from 347 campers at three localities at a national park in Australia. The principle components' factor analysis with Varimax rotation and Cronbach's alpha reliability were performed to test the construct of enduring involvement.

Findings: The reported findings were completed on the original version of the testing tool as reported in the 1989 article in the *Journal of Leisure Research*. A second version (1990) was used in Dr. McIntyre's Ph.D. dissertation. The second version lacks that psychometric work and is not recommended for use in research. The version presented in this book is the 1989 version that has reported psychometric properties. In the 1989 version the use of factor analysis resulted in three factors explaining 54 percent of the variance: Attraction (enjoyment and importance of camping), Self-Expression, and Centrality. Factors demonstrated trait and discriminant validity. Alpha reliability ranged between .82 and .64 for the three subscales, and .86 for the total *Enduring Involvement Scale*.

Investigator's Comments: Recognizing that there are the three major dimensions within the overall enduring involvement concept should help its operationalization. Findings can be more applicable and generalizable to a broader camping clientele.

Usage: The author, Dr. McIntyre, gives others permission to use this testing tool at no charge for both programs and research. He does not require that the professional using the tool contact him first. The author does allow others to replace the word "camping" for use with other activities (e.g., replacing the word "camping" with "rock climbing"). It is recommended that the tool remain single subject, such as camping, instead of mixing activity types (e.g., mountain biking, road biking). He also allows professionals to pull out the questions from specific subscales. Please acknowledge the author's work in any publication in which part or all of this testing tool is used.

Note to Researchers: Idyll Arbor would appreciate researchers and practitioners who use this tool to report their findings (e.g., send a copy of the write up) to Idyll Arbor for inclusion in its research library. This will add to the research findings library that Idyll Arbor is building to advance the knowledge in the fields of leisure, recreation, and parks.

ENDURING INVOLVEMENT IN CAMPING
(EIC)

N. McIntyre

DIRECTIONS: We want to find out how you feel about camping. Please indicate your level of agreement with each of the following statements by writing in the number that matches your level of agreement.

1	**2**	**3**	**4**	**5**
Strongly Disagree	**Disagree**	**Neither Agree or Disagree**	**Agree**	**Strongly Agree**

_____ 1. Camping offers me relaxation when life's pressures build up.

_____ 2. I find that a lot of my life is organized around camping.

_____ 3. When I am camping others see me the way I want them to see me.

_____ 4. Camping is one of the most satisfying things I do.

_____ 5. Most of my friends are in some way connected with camping.

_____ 6. When I am camping I can really be myself.

_____ 7. I enjoy discussing camping with my friends.

_____ 8. You can tell a lot about a person when you see them camping.

_____ 9. I have little or no interest in camping.

_____ 10. Camping is one of the most enjoyable things I do.

_____ 11. Camping says a lot about who I am.

_____ 12. Camping is very important to me.

SAMPLE
Do Not Copy

Item # 9 is to be reversed; see Chapter 17 for item reversal.

Involvement 4

PROCESSES OF CHANGE QUESTIONNAIRE (PCQ)

Bess H. Marcus, Joseph S. Rossi, Vanessa C. Selby, Raymond S. Niaura, and David B. Abrams

Reference: Marcus, B. H., Rossi, J. S., Selby, V. C., Niaura, R. S., and Abrams, D. B. (1992). The stages and processes of exercise adoption and maintenance in a work site sample. *Health Psychology, 11,* 386-395.

Goal of the Measurement: To assess stages and processes of exercise adoption and maintenance to involve individuals and to maintain such behavior when it takes place.

Background Literature: Evidence is accumulated to support the contention that regular exercise prevents and treats many ills and health problems. Knowing that exercise promoted better health presented professionals with the challenge of involving the uninvolved and maintaining the involvement of those already exercising. Processes of intervention are not identified; just knowledge regarding the rate of dropping out or relapsing — about 50% of those who exercise will drop out during the first three to six months. Five stages and processes of change were identified: Pre-contemplation, Contemplation, Preparation, Action, and Maintenance. These can be very useful in other recreation and leisure pursuits but further research is needed. The intent of this methodological study was to respond to the challenges of getting more people to adopt activity and getting adopters to maintain their activities.

A cross-sectional comment, presenting leisure orientation on the matter, is referred to under "Leisure Interests," in a note following Anderson and Cychosz's (1994) Exercise Identity Scale.

Methodology Employed: Scale construction followed the sequential method of scale development, identifying 110 definitions reflecting the model of stages and processes of change. Items were adapted and revised for exercise and three experts evaluated the scale for content validity, accepting 10 change processes, yielding 65 items. A five-point, Likert scale was used, ranging from "Never" (1) to "Repeatedly" (5). A sample of 1,172 persons rated the items. Data collected was statistically treated by LISREL, factor analysis, and alpha reliability coefficient.

Findings: LISREL VI structured modeling was employed to analyze the data, which helped to reduce the content to 39 usable items. Four items belonged to each of the 10 change processes, except for one process that was represented by only three items. The 10 identified change processes were confirmed, representing experiential processes and behavioral processes, as follows:

A. Experiential Processes: 1. Consciousness Raising; 2. Dramatic Relief; 3. Environmental Re-evaluation; 4. Social Re-evaluation; and 5. Social Liberation.

B. Behavioral Processes: 6. Counter Conditioning; 7. Helping Relationships; 8. Reinforcement Management; 9. Self-Liberation; and 10. Stimulus Control.

Items' factor loadings ranged between .89 and .43, and alpha coefficients for the 10 process subscales ranged between .89 and .62.

Investigator's Comments: The 10 change processes were used by individuals during the acquisition and maintenance of both exercise adoption and cessation of exercise. Knowledge gained here may assist in designing and testing intervention strategies to help individuals move more quickly from one stage of exercise adoption to another. Such procedures can increase the level of physical activity and help to attain the national fitness objectives. This will improve physical health, mental health, vitality, and the quality of life of the population.

Contact Information:
Dr. Bess H. Marcus, Director

Division of Behavioral Medicine
The Miriam Hospital
Brown University
RISE Building
164 Summit Ave.
Providence, RI 02906

Phone: 401-793-8003
Fax: 401-793-8560
Email: Bmarcus@lifespan.org

PROCESSES OF CHANGE QUESTIONNAIRE
(PCQ)

Marcus, B. H.; Rossi, J. S.; Selby, V. C.; Niaura, R. S.; and Abrams, D. B.

DIRECTIONS: Please respond to the following questions, using the scale below.

Never	Seldom	Occasionally	Often	Repeatedly
1	2	3	4	5

_____ 1. Instead of remaining inactive, I engage in some physical activity.

_____ 2. I tell myself I am able to keep exercising if I want to.

_____ 3. I put things around my home to remind me of exercising.

_____ 4. I tell myself that if I try hard enough I can keep exercising.

_____ 5. I recall information people have personally given me on the benefits of exercise.

_____ 6. I make commitments to exercise.

_____ 7. I reward myself when I exercise.

_____ 8. I think about information from articles and advertisements on how to make exercise a regular part of my life.

_____ 9. I keep things around my place of work that remind me to exercise.

_____ 10. I find society changing in ways to make it easier for the exerciser.

_____ 11. Warnings about health hazards of inactivity affect me emotionally.

_____ 12. Dramatic portrayals of the evils of inactivity affect me emotionally.

_____ 13. I react emotionally to warnings about an inactive lifestyle.

_____ 14. I worry that inactivity can be harmful to my body.

_____ 15. I am considering the idea that regular exercise would make me a healthier, happier person to be around.

_____ 16. I have someone on whom I can depend when I am having problems with exercising.

_____ 17. I read articles about exercise in an attempt to learn more about it.

_____ 18. I try to set realistic goals for myself rather than setting myself up for failure by expecting too much.

_____ 19. I have a healthy friend that encourages me to exercise when I don't feel up to it.

_____ 20. When I exercise, I tell myself that I am being good to myself by taking care of my body.

_____ 21. Exercise is my special time to relax and recover from the day's worries, not a task to get out of the way.

_____ 22. I am aware of more and more people encouraging me to exercise these days.

_____ 23. I do something nice for myself for making efforts to exercise more.

_____ 24. I have someone who points out my rationalizations for not exercising.

_____ 25. I have someone who provides feedback about my exercising.

_____ 26. I remove things that contribute to my inactivity.

_____ 27. I am the only one responsible for my health, and only I can decide whether or not I will exercise.

_____ 28. I look for information related to exercise.

_____ 29. I avoid spending long periods of time in environments that promote inactivity.

_____ 30. I feel that I would be a better role model for others if I exercised regularly.

_____ 31. I think about the type of person I will be if I keep exercising.

_____ 32. I notice that more businesses are encouraging their employees to exercise by offering fitness courses and time off to work out.

_____ 33. I wonder how my inactivity affects those people who are close to me.

_____ 34. I realize that I might be able to influence others to be healthier if I would exercise more.

_____ 35. I get frustrated with myself when I don't exercise.

_____ 36. I am aware that many health clubs now provide free babysitting services to their members.

_____ 37. Some of my close friends might exercise more if I would.

_____ 38. I consider the fact that I would feel more confident in myself if I exercised regularly.

_____ 39. When I feel tired I make myself exercise anyway because I know I will feel better afterward.

_____ 40. When I'm feeling tense, I find exercise a great way to relieve my worries.

Involvement 5

EXERCISE'S STAGES-OF-CHANGE
(ESoC)
&

Involvement 6

SELF-EFFICACY FOR EXERCISE BEHAVIOR SCALE
(SEEBS)

Bess H. Marcus, Vanessa C. Selby, Raymond S. Niaura, and Joseph S. Rossi

Reference: Marcus, B. H., Selby, V. C., Niaura, R. S., and Rossi, J. S. (1992). Self-efficacy and the stages of exercise behavior change. *Research Quarterly for Exercise and Sport, 63*, 60-66.

Goal of the Measurement: To assess stages of change for exercise behavior and to test the ability of a self-efficacy scale to differentiate among individuals according to stage of readiness to change.

Background Literature: Evidence was provided that a large percentage of individuals do not exercise regularly and half of the participants drop out within the first six months. This coincides with an accelerated relapse curve in tobacco, heroin, and alcohol addiction. Two theoretical structures were employed as foundations for the two measurements:

(I) The stages-of-change model was utilized as a framework to describe the phases in the acquisition and maintenance of a behavior. People move forward or backward or "get stuck" with four stages of change: 1. Pre-contemplation, 2. Contemplation, 3. Action, and 4. Maintenance. Identifying an individual's stage can assist treatment or enable progress, as demonstrated through success with health behavior, such as smoking, weight control, and mammography.

(II) Self-efficacy theorization formed the basis for the second measurement. The theory postulates that confidence in one's ability to perform a given behavior is strongly related to one's actual ability to perform that behavior. Self-efficacy beliefs have been consistent with performance of exercise, smoking cessation, and weight loss.

Methodology Employed: Two instruments were developed for validation. The "Stages of Change" measure was adapted from a measure initially assessing smoking cessation, by Prochaska and DiClemente (1983). This scale incorporated the conceptualized four stages of change: Pre-contemplation, Contemplation, Action, and Maintenance. After the first trial, a fifth stage was added before Action — Preparation. A five-point, Likert-type scale was employed, marking "1" if "Strongly Disagree" to "5" if "Strongly Agree." The second is the self-efficacy instrument (five items), assessing confidence in one's ability to persist with exercising in different situations. A seven-point scale was used: "1" if "Not At All Confident" to "7" if "Very Confident." Frequency counts, factor analysis, test-retest reliability, and coefficient alpha were utilized to analyze data.

Findings: Reliability of the Stages for Change was tested, employing the Kappa index over a two-week period, yielding .78. The internal consistency of the self-efficacy scale was .82; test-retest over a two-week period was .90. The six Stages for Change are Pre-contemplation, Contemplation, Preparation, Action, Maintenance, and Relapse.

Investigator's Comments: An individual's stage in exercise determines her/his self-efficacy. Intervention should be designed to match stages to enhance efficacy expectations. In other words, provide information and increase motivation of a person in early stages: Pre-contemplation and Contemplation.

Note: Leisure and recreation practitioners providing exercise and fitness as free time pursuits must be able to handle behaviors and changes on an individual basis instead of designing a fitness program "for all." According to knowledge gained from current development, this requires understanding social-psychological dynamics, changes, value clarification, and counseling approaches.

Contact Information:
Dr. Bess H. Marcus, Director
Division of Behavioral Medicine
The Miriam Hospital
Brown University
RISE Building
164 Summit Ave.
Providence, RI 02906

Phone: 401-793-8003
Fax: 401-793-8560
Email: Bmarcus@lifespan.org

EXERCISE'S STAGES-OF-CHANGE
(ESoC)

Marcus, B. H.; Selby, V. C.; Niaura, R. S.; and Rossi, J. S.

DIRECTIONS: Please rate the following items. Marking "1" indicates that you **"Strongly Disagree"** with the item. Marking "5" indicates that you **"Strongly Agree"** with the item.

Strongly Disagree	Disagree	Uncertain	Agree	Strongly Agree
1	2	3	4	5

_____ 1. I currently do not exercise, and I do not intend to start exercising in the next 6 months.

_____ 2. I currently do not exercise, but I am thinking about starting to exercise in the next 6 months.

_____ 3. I currently do exercise some, but not regularly. *

_____ 4. I currently exercise regularly, but I have only begun doing so within the last 6 months.

_____ 5. I currently exercise regularly, and have done so for longer than 6 months.

_____ 6. I have exercised regularly in the past, but I am not doing so currently.

*Regular exercise = 3 or more times per week for 20 min or more at each time.

The above six items represent six stages of exercise in the following order:
1. Pre-contemplation.
2. Contemplation.
3. Preparation.
4. Action.
5. Maintenance.
6. Relapse.

SELF-EFFICACY FOR EXERCISE BEHAVIOR SCALE (SEEBS)

Marcus, B. H.; Selby, V. C.; Niaura, R. S.; and Rossi, J. S.

DIRECTIONS: Please use the following scale to score the items below. Marking "1" indicates that you are "Not At All Confident." Marking "11" indicates that you are "Very Confident." If the item "Does Not Apply At All" mark "0."

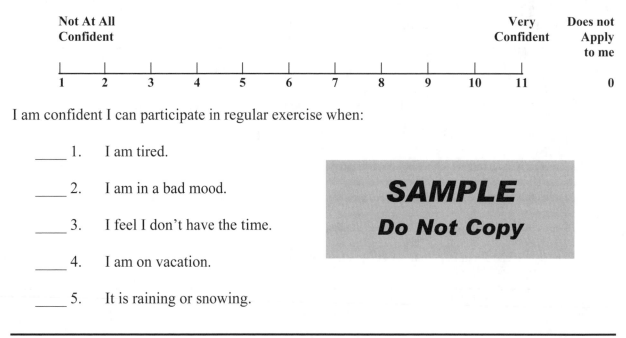

I am confident I can participate in regular exercise when:

_____ 1.   I am tired.

_____ 2.   I am in a bad mood.

_____ 3.   I feel I don't have the time.

_____ 4.   I am on vacation.

_____ 5.   It is raining or snowing.

Involvement 7

COMMITMENT IN RECREATIONAL TENNIS (CRT)

K. L. Siegenthaler and T. C. M. Lam

Reference: Siegenthaler, K. L., and Lam, T. C. (1992). Commitment and ego involvement in recreational tennis. *Leisure Sciences, 14*, 303-315.

Goal of the Measurement: To assess commitment to engage in recreational tennis.

Background Literature: What motivates some people to continue participating in leisure activities, such as tennis, while others do not? This is a question raised by Backman and Compton (1990), chosen here as the focus of construct development (commitment in recreational tennis). Some research studies were conducted, testing relationships between commitment and other variables in the leisure pursuits of running, fishing, and camping. Because tennis offers lifetime opportunity and accessibility in many environments, understanding what motivates people to continue to play tennis can help recreation professionals understand how to provide successful leisure experience. Becker (1960) is cited as defining commitment as consistent behavior that persists over time and that, in part, is characterized by the rejection of comparable alternative activities. The literature yields a sufficient number of components that are utilized as bases for the measurement's development: continuance; sacrifice; dedication; consistency; loyalty; satisfying continuous activity; willingness to invest money, time, and energy; willingness to undertake a disciplined mental and physical effort in learning and mastering an activity.

Methodology Employed: A sample of 331 persons was drawn from 1,047 members in a Tennis Association/Volvo Tennis League. Items were adapted or selected from previous assessment tools of commitment in other recreational activities. Two of the criteria for adapting items were 1. their contents and 2. their applicability to continuance, sacrifice, and dedication reflecting commitment to tennis. For content and face validities, 15 tennis players, 12 students in a tennis class, and five graduate students reviewed items for wording, clarity, and readability. After evaluations, revisions, and changes were made, a scale of 18 items for tennis commitment was ready for final testing. A six-point, Likert-type scale was employed, ranging from "Very Strongly Agree" (6) to "Very Strongly Disagree" (1). The higher the score, the greater the commitment. A mail questionnaire was used to collect data. Factor analysis and reliability tests were employed to test the construct of the *Commitment to Recreational Tennis*.

Findings: Employing point-biserial correlation and factor analysis helped to reduce the scale to 13 substantiated items. Further principal-axis factor analysis yielded two factors (37.4% variance): Dedication and Continuance. Internal consistency reliability for the total scale was .82; .81 for Dedication subscale and .69 for Continuance.

Usage: This testing tool has been released to the public domain. Please follow professional standards of practice and ethics in the use of this testing tool.

Investigator's Comments: Further investigations are recommended to examine the stability of the *Commitment to Recreational Tennis Scale*.

Note: Two scales were developed simultaneously: *Commitment to Recreational Tennis* and *Ego Involvement in Tennis* (reported in another abstract). In a final analysis, the scores of the two measures were correlated (r = .69).

COMMITMENT IN RECREATIONAL TENNIS
(CRT)

Siegenthaler, K. L. and Lam, T. C.

DIRECTIONS: We want to find out how you feel about tennis. Please indicate your level of agreement with each of the following statements by writing in the number that matches your level of agreement.

Very Strongly Disagree	Strongly Disagree	Disagree	Agree	Strongly Agree	Very Strongly Agree
1	2	3	4	5	6

_____ 1. I watch tennis on TV whenever possible.

_____ 2. I miss work in order to play in tennis tournaments.

_____ 3. I make important decisions based on how they will affect opportunities to play tennis.

_____ 4. I rearrange my schedule to play tennis.

_____ 5. I think about tennis while I am at work.

_____ 6. I get up early on weekends to play tennis.

_____ 7. I would change jobs if it would allow me more time to play tennis.

_____ 8. I work on drills to improve my performance.

_____ 9. I continue to play tennis regardless of my performance.

_____ 10. I play tennis only when the temperature is comfortable.

_____ 11. I don't expect to play tennis next year.

_____ 12. I would rather play tennis than any other sport.

_____ 13. Tennis is in my life to stay.

Developed (1992) by Siegenthaler, K. L., and Lam, T. Authors have released this tool to the public domain.

Scoring: Items #10 and #11 are reversed. There are two subscales in this testing tool:
Dedication   = Items 1 to 8
Continuance   = Items 9 to 13

Involvement 8

EGO INVOLVEMENT IN RECREATIONAL TENNIS (EIRT)

K. L. Siegenthaler and T. C. M. Lam

Reference: Siegenthaler, K. L., and Lam, T. C. M. (1992). Commitment and ego-involvement in recreational tennis. *Leisure Sciences, 14*, 303-315.

Goal of the Measurement: To measure ego involvement in recreational tennis.

Background Literature: Identification with an object seems to be a central core for ego involvement. Involvement with an activity or a person can reach the point of altering behavior. A person who reports being a participant in a given activity manifest attributes such as being proud, animated, showing excitement for affiliation with that activity, organizing other activities around the activity, sacrificing other things, having a positive self-image, interest, enjoyment, centrality (focus of attention), and importance. These attributes can be used conceptually, either as components to be enlarged or as indicators to be utilized for item development. Ego involvement was defined as the identification of self with an activity.

Methodology Employed: As reported under the same heading in constructing *Commitment in Recreational Tennis*, a sample of 331 individuals was drawn from a large pool of tennis players. Consumer research provided scales assessing ego involvement and only one measure on ego involvement in leisure. Watkins (1986) was employed with one modification: replacing "activity" with "tennis." Similar to Watkins' intent, the constructed scale here attempted to measure self-expression, interest, and a combination of enjoyment, interest, centrality, and importance. A 6-point Likert-type scale was employed, ranging from "Very Strongly Disagree" (1) to "Very Strongly Agree" (6). Questionnaires were mailed to collect data. Factor analysis and alpha reliability coefficients were utilized to test the scale.

Findings: The principle axis factor analysis revealed two factors, accounting for a total variance of 45.7%. Factors were labeled as Self-Image (identity) and Interest (attention devoted). The alpha reliability coefficient for the total scale was .88; for Self-Image it was .86 and for Interest it was .79.

Investigator's Comments: As recommended previously, further exploration is needed to substantiate the stability of EIRT.

Usage: This testing tool is one of the standardized revisions to Norm McIntyre's *Enduring Involvement in Camping*.

Note: Two scales were developed simultaneously: *Commitment to Recreational Tennis* (reported before this abstract) and *Ego Involvement in Tennis*. In a final analysis, the scores of the two measures were correlated (r = .69).

EGO INVOLVEMENT IN RECREATIONAL TENNIS
(EIRT)

Siegenthaler, K. L. and Lam T. C. M.

DIRECTIONS: We want to find out how you feel about tennis. Please indicate your level of agreement with each of the following statements by writing in the number that matches your level of agreement. Write "1" if you "Very Strongly Disagree." Write "6" if you "Very Strongly Agree." If your response is between 1 and 6, write the number that corresponds to your response.

Very Strongly Disagree	Strongly Disagree	Disagree	Agree	Strongly Agree	Very Strongly Agree
1	2	3	4	5	6

_____   1.   Tennis says a lot about who I am.

_____   2.   You can tell a lot about a person by seeing him/her play tennis.

_____   3.   Tennis is me.

_____   4.   When I play tennis, others see me the way I want them to see me.

_____   5.   Because of my lifestyle, I feel tennis should be important to me.

_____   6.   Tennis helps me maintain the type of life I strive for.

_____   7.   When I am with a friend, we often talk about tennis.

_____   8.   Tennis offers me relaxation and fun when life's pressures build up.

_____   9.   I have little or no interest in tennis.

_____   10.   I get bored when other people talk to me about tennis.

_____   11.   I could talk about tennis for a long time.

_____   12.   Tennis is interesting.

Developed (1992) by Siegenthaler, K. L., and Lam, T. C. M. Based on N. McIntyre's (1989) *Enduring Involvement in Camping.* **Authors have released this tool to the public domain.**

Reverse the scoring for Items 9 and 10.

There are two subscales in this testing tool:
Self-Image Component   = Items 1 to 7
Interest Component   = Items 8 to 12

Involvement 9

MARRIED COUPLES' INVOLVEMENT WITH FAMILY VACATION (MCIFV)

Robert Madrigal, Mark E. Havitz, and Dennis R. Howard

Reference: Madrigal, R., Havitz, M. E., and Howard, D. R. (1992). Married couples' involvement with family vacation. *Leisure Sciences, 14*, 287-301.

Goal of the Measurement: To assess married couples' involvement with family vacation, realizing the underlying dimensions.

Background Literature: Knowledge is available on involvement and consumer behavior in leisure products and services. However, historically the relevance of the role of involvement toward tourism has gained meager attention. Involvement construct development reported here relied on the social judgment theory and the notion of ego involvement by Sherif and Cantril (1947) and others in the 1960s and 1970s. Social judgment theory postulates that involvement is an attitude formed or learned during interaction with the social environment. Literature available helped the authors to arrive at an underlying assertion: Family vacations represent a high-involvement decision, so they should have the five dimensions of involvement Laurent and Kapferer (1985) identified as associated with a product purchase — importance, pleasure or hedonic value, sign or symbolic value, risk probability, and risk consequences.

Methodology Employed: In the development and validation of the instrument assessing MCIFV, 15 items from Laurent and Kapferer's (1985) *Involvement Profile Scale* (IPS) were adopted, using the same wording, except for one item. A five-point, Likert scale was employed, ranging from "Strongly Disagree" (1) to "Strongly Agree" (5). Factor analysis with Varimax rotation was employed to identify the components, and alpha reliability tested the internal consistency of the items. A sample of 70 married couples was a part of the study. To avoid a spouse's influence on responses, spouses were separated from their partners at the testing site.

Findings: Factor analysis with Varimax rotation yielded two factors: one combining Pleasure and Importance and another as Sign Value. Alpha reliability coefficient for the first component was .83 and .69 for the second.

Investigator's Comments: Factors reported in this study are consistent with what was found in another investigation. IPS, by Laurent et al., obtained mixed results when applied to MCIFV. A conceptual reason for the mixed findings is that "items did not apply in the context of family vacations."

Note: Items that do not apply in a context can be a major content validity concern; other components might be highly relevant to the domain of involvement in family vacationing.

MARRIED COUPLES' INVOLVEMENT WITH FAMILY VACATION (MCIFV)

Madrigal, R.; Havitz, M.; and Howard, D.

DIRECTIONS: The following items pertain to your feelings about family vacations. If you "**Strongly Disagree**" with the statement mark "**1**", if you "**Strongly Agree**" mark "**5**"; otherwise mark the appropriate number from the scale below. There is no right or wrong answers. [Directions added by Ragheb.]

Strongly Disagree	Disagree	Uncertain	Agree	Strongly Agree
1	2	3	4	5

_____ 1.   I attach great importance to family vacations.

_____ 2.   Family vacations leave me totally indifferent.

_____ 3.   I have a lot of interest in family vacations.

_____ 4.   I get pleasure from going on family vacations.

_____ 5.   For me, family vacations are a pleasure.

_____ 6.   You can tell a lot about a family by whether or not they go on vacation.

_____ 7.   Where we go on vacation gives people an indication of the type of family we have.

_____ 8.   Where you go on a family vacation says something about your family.

Reverse the scoring for Item 2.

There are two subscales in this testing tool:

Pleasure and Importance	= Items 1-5
Sign Value	= Items 6-8

> **Involvement 10**

ADVENTURE RECREATION INVOLVEMENT (ARI)

Michael A. Schuett

Reference: Schuett, M. A. (1993). Refining measures of adventure recreation involvement. *Leisure Sciences, 15,* 205-216.

Goal of the Measurement: To develop a more comprehensive method of measuring engagement in adventure recreation.

Background Literature: Past studies have been limited in the explanation of adventure recreation because of methodological drawbacks such as sample design, lack of theoretical foundations, and limited field-testing. No scale or index was created to adequately measure an individual's engagement in adventure recreation. The enduring involvement construct was utilized to advance the measure of engagement used by Ewert and Hollenhorst (1989). McIntyre (1992) tested the motives of rock climbers in studying enduring involvement. Involvement was defined by Laurent and Kapferer (1985) as a perception that a product is related to centrally held values. Enduring involvement implies permanent attachment or a trait rather than a situational feeling or a state.

Methodology Employed: Thirteen domains were chosen from the Recreation Experience Preference scales (Driver, 1977). A total of 42 items were chosen for the designated domains. Data was collected from 301 persons, 72% males. Internal consistency, reliability, and factor analysis were employed for statistical treatment.

Findings: Alpha reliability for the enduring involvement scale was .87. Factor analysis yielded four subscales of enduring involvement: enjoyment, centrality, self-expression, and importance.

Investigator's Comments: Theoretical foundations of this adventure recreation construct justify its continued use in attempting to learn more about its nature. The complex nature of this construct opens up an area for further investigation into "personally meaningful involvement" (McIntyre, 1992). More representative samples and other risk recreation activities should used in future research of adventure recreation involvement. Continued investigation in adventure recreation is needed to widen the scope of knowledge and to contribute to the development of leisure theory.

Contact Information:
Dr. Michael A. Schuett
Department of Recreation, Park, and Tourism
Texas A & M University
College Station, TX 77843-2261

Phone: 979-845-0872
Fax: 979-845-0446
Email: maschuett@ag.tamu.edu

Involvement 11

ADOLESCENT ETHICAL BEHAVIOR IN LEISURE SCALE (AEBLS)

Mark A. Widmer, Gary D. Ellis, and Wayne W. Munson

References: Widmer, M. A., Ellis, G. D., and Munson, W. W. (2003). Development of the Aristotelian ethical behavior in leisure scale short form. *Therapeutic Recreation Journal, 37*, 256-274.

Widmer, M. A., Ellis, G. D. (1998). The Aristotelian good life model: Integration of values into therapeutic recreation service delivery. *Therapeutic Recreation Journal, 33,* 290-302.

Widmer, M. A., Ellis, G. D., and Trunnell, E. P. (1996). Measurement of ethical behavior in leisure among high- and low-risk adolescents. *Adolescence, 31,* 397-408.

Goal of the Measurement: To discriminate between the ethical behaviors and attitudes of high- and low-risk adolescents regarding their recreation and leisure.

Background Literature: There are strong indications that adolescents are designated as "high risk" because of an epidemic of alcohol-related incidents. Leisure is seldom used in the treatment and prevention of such at-risk youth. In assessing individual differences in ethical behavior relating to leisure and recreation, a scale would be needed.

The conceptual bases of the Adolescent Ethical Behavior in Leisure Scale (AEBLS) are philosophically guided. The AEBLS is founded on Aristotle's assumption that individuals should act in ways that will bring them happiness, focusing on character, and the habit of making right choices and actions (virtue), based on reflection, moderation, prudence, wisdom, justice, and friendship (meaningful relationships). Moreover, in Aristotle's view, leisure was the peak of ethical life, engaging in speculative thought, contemplation, being able to learn and grow in a state of mind free from obligations, acquiring intellectual virtues. Deductively, the AEBLS is a reflection and an abstraction of the Aristotelian ethical leisure behavior theory. Components within the philosophical boundaries of the concept include intellectual activity, creative activity, meaningful relationships, and moral behavior.

Methodology Employed: For the original scale, 62 items were drafted, tapping the identified four components (intellectual, creative, meaningful relationships, and moral behavior) as components of AEBLS. Two experts in Aristotelian philosophy and three test-construction experts reviewed items for face and content validity. Data was collected from 346 high-school adolescents in an effort to gather information regarding the reliability and validity of inferences of the AEBLS. Cronbach's alpha was calculated to estimate internal consistency. For further psychometric refinements, two measures were employed to test criterion validity: School Bonding (Durrant, 1986) and Leisure Boredom Scale (Iso-Ahola and Weissinger, 1990).

A second study focused on the creation of a shorter form for clinical and research applications. The original 62 items were analyzed to identify the best items for inclusion in the shorter version of the AEBLS. Twenty-six items representing four components of Aristotelian ethical behavior in leisure were selected through item analysis. Participants in this study included 2,502 adolescents from California, Ohio, and Utah who represented a variety of agencies (e.g. high schools, correctional institutions, and psychiatric centers). Data were collected regarding educational performance, substance abuse, legal involvement, leisure boredom, social desirability (CSD), and demographic variables. Internal structure analysis of the short form produced internal consistency estimates ranging from .87 to .90 across the 15 agencies. Analyses providing insight into criterion-related evidence of validity revealed significant relationships between AEBLS-S and educational performance, substance abuse, and leisure boredom. Non-significant correlations resulted between the AEBLS-S and CSD providing additional criterion-related evidence of validity. These findings provide support for validity of inferences that may be made about adolescent's ethical behavior in leisure from scores produced by AEBLS-S.

Findings: The AEBLS alpha reliability coefficient was .90. Regarding the criterion-related evidence of validity, AEBLS correlated with School Bonding (r = .60) and Leisure Boredom Scale (r = .45). No factor analysis on the AEBLS was performed. In another study on 2,502 persons, factor analyses showed two consolidated domains: Intellectual/Creative Activity and Moral Behavior/Friendships.

In the second study, internal structure analysis of the short form produced internal consistency estimates ranging from .87 to .90 across the 15 agencies. Analyses providing insight into criterion-related evidence of validity revealed significant relationships between AEBLS-S and educational performance, substance abuse, and leisure boredom. Non-significant correlations resulted between the AEBLS-S and CSD providing additional criterion-related evidence of validity. These findings provide support for validity of inferences that may be made about adolescent's ethical behavior in leisure from scores produced by AEBLS-S.

Investigator's Comments: The evidence supporting the validity of inferences of the AEBLS suggests that the Aristotelian ethical construct represents a meaningful factor in the lives and development of adolescents. Data from the 2500 subjects in the second study provide normative data from which inferences may be made with respect to the different populations included in the sample. With further development and research, the scale can be utilized as a screening device to identify high-risk youth engaging in delinquent behaviors. The AEBLS should be further examined to assess its latent structures, through factor analysis as well as arriving at a short scale for AEBLS.

Contact Information:
Dr. Mark A. Widmer, Professor
Department of Recreation Management and Youth Leadership
Brigham Young University
273 Richards Building
Provo, UT 84601

Phone: 801-422-3381
Email: Widmer@byu.edu

ADOLESCENT ETHICAL BEHAVIOR IN LEISURE SCALE (AEBLS) Short Form

Widmer, M. A.; Ellis, G. D.; and Trunnell, E. P

Instructions: The following questions deal with what you do in your leisure or free time. This is time when you are not in school, working, doing homework, or household chores. This is time when you can choose to do what you enjoy. Please read each question carefully and fill in the bubble on the answer sheet that best represents how you spend your leisure time. Please use the scale below to respond to each statement.

Never= 1   Seldom= 2   Sometimes= 3   Often= 4   Always= 5

1.	I think about world problems in my free time.	1	2	3	4	5
2.	I spend my free time doing things that build meaningful relationships.	1	2	3	4	5
3.	I study literature in my free time.	1	2	3	4	5
4.	I help those in need during my free time.	1	2	3	4	5
5.	I try to make new friends during my free time.	1	2	3	4	5
6.	I do creative writing in my free time (poetry, stories, etc.).	1	2	3	4	5
7.	I do things to increase my practical knowledge in my free time (for example: read *Popular Mechanics*, *Home and Garden*, or learn to fix things).	1	2	3	4	5
8.	I like to spend my holidays with people who are important to me.	1	2	3	4	5
9.	I think about difficult (philosophical) questions during my free time. (For example: What is good, right or wrong, why do natural disasters occur, why there are wars, etc.)	1	2	3	4	5
10.	I learn new crafts in my free time (for example: sewing, bullet reloading, leather work, quilting, woodworking, etc.).	1	2	3	4	5
11.	In my free time I do or make things for people who are important to me.	1	2	3	4	5
12.	I think about human rights in my free time.	1	2	3	4	5
13.	During my free time I do dangerous activities (for example: drive fast, take drugs, fight, etc.).	1	2	3	4	5
14.	I find new and interesting things to do in my free time.	1	2	3	4	5
15.	I like to be with my family during my free time.	1	2	3	4	5
16.	I solve practical problems in my free time (for example: make my bike work better, find new ways to sew, etc.).	1	2	3	4	5
17.	I am fair when I play games.	1	2	3	4	5
18.	I spend my free time reading classical books (for example: Shakespeare, *Moby Dick*, *Walden*, etc.).	1	2	3	4	5
19.	I use my free time to learn new skills.	1	2	3	4	5
20.	I participate in service organizations in my free time (for example: Key Club, Boy or Girl Scouts, homeless shelters, environmental groups).	1	2	3	4	5
21.	I use my free time to be creative.	1	2	3	4	5
22.	I watch TV news/information programs.	1	2	3	4	5
23.	I use my free time to become a better person.	1	2	3	4	5
24.	I develop new and different ways of doing things in my free time.	1	2	3	4	5
25.	I volunteer for service in my free time.	1	2	3	4	5
26.	I prefer to do things alone during my free time	1	2	3	4	5

Item 13 is reversed.

Involvement 12

ASSESSMENT OF LEISURE AND RECREATION INVOLVEMENT (LRI)

Mounir G. Ragheb

References:

Ragheb, M. G. (1996). Measuring leisure and recreation involvement. Symposium on Leisure Research, National Recreation and Park Association. Kansas City, MO.

burlingame, j. and Blaschko, T. (2010). *Assessment Tools for Recreational Therapy and Related Fields, 4ᵗʰ Edition.* Enumclaw, WA: Idyll Arbor, Inc.

Goal of the Measurement: To assess the totality of involvement (importance, centrality, and interest) in leisure and recreation in general.

Background Literature: Involvement, the degree of interest in, and commitment to an object are concepts first described by psychologists about 50 years ago. Later on, the concept found a strong application in marketing for attempting to predict consumer behavior (interest in and importance of a product). With further conceptual development, fields such as education, marriage, and work found new applications for involvement concepts — recreation and leisure were included. Attention to involvement in recreation has been with specific activities such as fishing, traveling, vacationing, camping, tennis, athletics, adornments, and canoeing. Involvement in global leisure and recreation has been neglected.

To understand specific recreation/leisure involvement, heavy relevance was given to and gained from consumer and marketing literature. In identifying the possible boundaries of recreation involvement in specific activities, the literature from psychology, marketing, and leisure yielded several components. Nine of these components were of interest to this investigation: importance, pleasure, commitment, ego involvement, sign-value, centrality, intensity/absorption, meaning, and interest. Incorporating these components, a conceptual definition — an early step in measurement development — was comprised and tested.

Methodology Employed: Sixty-three items were generated, reflected in 90 identified indicators representing the nine hypothetical components. A five-point, Likert-type scale was employed, ranging from "Strongly Disagree" to "Strongly Agree." In pre-testing, the initial pool of over 90 items was exposed to careful revisions by the investigator and three faculty members, then by eight graduate and undergraduate students in recreation and leisure studies. Then, the first pilot study (n = 123) helped to reduce the items to 57. It was followed by the second pilot study (N = 176) which yielded 52 items to be verified in a final field test (n = 218 employees and students). Statistical treatments in all testing employed factor analysis (Varimax rotation), inter-item correlations, item-total correlations, and Cronbach alpha reliability coefficients. To test concurrent validity, Laurent and Kapferer's (1985) Involvement Profile Scale (IPS) was utilized after being adapted for leisure.

Findings: Factor analysis yielded six interpretable factors, accounting for 57.5% of the Varimax in item responses. Suggested in prior studies, the six factors were Importance, Pleasure, Interest, Intensity/Absorption, Centrality, and Meaning. Alpha reliability coefficients (alpha) for the total scale (37 items) was .95, suggesting that a global leisure and recreation involvement score would discriminate among persons. For the six subscales, alpha ranged between .90 and .78. Inter-factor correlations among the six LRI subscales ranged from .70 to .52, with a median of .61. To test concurrent validity, correlation between the Laurent and Kapferer's (1985) Involvement Profile Scale was performed, obtaining r = .54, while reliability of the Involvement Profile Scale was .58.

Investigator's Comments: Reflecting the involvement literature, the obtained six factors of LRI seem to be well documented and substantiated. On the multidimensionality of LRI, the current findings demonstrate further evidence. The factor importance-pleasure that has been consistently reported in a number of studies was split into two distinct ones, composing a global recreation involvement scale. Due to the low reliability of the IPS by Laurent et al., it is suggested that the concurrent validity of the LRI scale be retested.

Contact Information:
Idyll Arbor, Inc.,
39129 264th Ave SE
Enumclaw, WA 98022

Phone: 360-825-7797
Fax: 360-825-5670
Email: sales@idyllarbor.com

ASSESSMENT OF LEISURE AND RECREATION INVOLVEMENT (LRI)

Ragheb, M. G.

DIRECTIONS: The following statements refer to your leisure, recreation, and tourist activities. By "leisure and recreation," we mean non-obligatory pursuits chosen freely during your free time. Using the scale below, if you **STRONGLY DISAGREE** with the statement, score "1" on the answer sheet; if you **STRONGLY AGREE**, score "5." If your response is in between, blacken the number that corresponds to your answer. There are no right or wrong answers.

Strongly Disagree	Disagree	In Between	Agree	Strongly Agree
1	2	3	4	5

Leisure activities mean leisure, recreation, and tourist activities.

_____ 1. I reserve sufficient time to engage in my favorite leisure activities.
_____ 2. My favorite leisure activities give me pleasure.
_____ 3. I usually want to know more details about the leisure activities that interest me.
_____ 4. The leisure activities I do occupy my feelings.
_____ 5. I feel that I am responsible about choices made to participate in leisure activities.
_____ 6. Without engaging in my favorite leisure activities, life has no flavor.
_____ 7. I continue to do the leisure activities of my choice, even when I am busy.
_____ 8. After completing my leisure activities, I usually feel satisfied and full.
_____ 9. Engaging in my favorite leisure activities expresses my wishes.
_____ 10. My favorite leisure activities help me to discover many things about myself.
_____ 11. I am willing to devote mental and/or physical effort to master my preferred leisure activities.
_____ 12. I express myself best when I am doing my favorite leisure activities.
_____ 13. There is a focus for my leisure choices.
_____ 14. I identify with the leisure activities I favor.
_____ 15. Engagement in my favorite leisure activities is worthwhile.
_____ 16. My choices of leisure activities give a sense of inner freedom for me to do what I desire.
_____ 17. I like to do my leisure activities well, even when they require a great deal of time and effort.
_____ 18. My leisure activities give me a sense of value in my life.
_____ 19. My leisure activities are parts of my lifestyle.
_____ 20. I take pride in the leisure activities in which I engage
_____ 21. I practice the skills required to improve my leisure performances, if needed.
_____ 22. I expect something good to come out of my participation in my favorite leisure activities.
_____ 23. For my preferred leisure activities, I am willing to invest my money, time, and energy.
_____ 24. I do not know what to do without my leisure activities.

Add up all 24 items for a total score for the whole instrument. Add the items to find a total a score for each component, as follows:

Importance	=	Items 1, 7, 13, and 19.
Pleasure	=	Items 2, 8, 14, and 20.
Interest	=	Items 3, 9, 15, and 21.
Intensity	=	Items 4, 10, 16, and 22.
Centrality	=	Items 5, 11, 17, and 23.
Meaning	=	Items 6, 12, 18, and 24

Dividing the total scores by the number of components (24 for the whole instrument or 4 for each subsection) will yield a set of scores for Leisure and Recreation Involvement.

Involvement 13

EXERCISE IMAGERY QUESTIONNAIRE — AEROBIC VERSION (EIQ-AV)

Heather A. Hausenblas, Craig R. Hall, Wendy M. Rogers, and Krista J. Munroe

Reference: Hausenblas, H. A., Hall, C. R., Rogers, W. M., and Munroe, K. J. (1999). Exercise imagery: Its nature and measurement. *Journal of Applied Sport Psychology, 11,* 171-180.

Goal of the Measurement: To assess exercise imagery as a mental process.

Background Literature: Knowledge has steadily accrued regarding the use of mental imagery as an enhancing technique to sport and athletic performance. Mental imagery has been utilized not only for motivational and cognitive functions but also for improvement and learning skills, as well as in mental training programs. The authors speculate that imagery may be used in other forms of physical activity — exercise in particular. The literature proposes that imagery may be as powerful a motivator in exercise as it is in sport. However, some claim that there is a lack of empirical evidence in exercise imagery; what is available is merely a spillover of findings on imagery from investigators on athletics and sports.

Methodology Employed: Three systematic phases were used to develop the exercise imagery scale. Phase One attempted to reveal the nature of imagery used with exercising through answering three questions: 1. When do exercisers use imagery? 2. Why do exercisers use imagery? and 3. What do exercisers imagine? A sample of 144 aerobic exercisers responded to open-ended questions relevant to the above three questions. (Previously, they had read a sufficiently developed definition, which began by stating, "Imagery involves mentally seeing yourself exercising...") It was found that imagery use is relatively high during numerous daily encounters. Response components were classified as Body Image, Techniques/Strategies, Feeling Good about Oneself, Motivation, General Exercise, Fitness/Health, Music, Goals, and Maintaining Focus. Phase Two concentrated on instrument construction. Twenty-three items were developed on the basis of what was identified in the prior phase and administered to a sample of 307 exercisers. A nine-point scale was employed, ranging from "Never Engaging in this Type of Imagery" marking "1" to "Always Engaging in This Type of Imagery" marking "9." Content validity was performed through six judges. As a result of Phase Two, factor analysis (Varimax rotation) yielded three factors: Energy, Appearance (becoming healthier), and Technique. Alpha reliability was very adequate and concurrent validity was established. The above procedures paved the way to the final field verification of the instrument called Exercise Imagery Questionnaire — Aerobic Version (EIQ-AV) in Phase Three.

Findings: A confirmatory factor analysis was performed, yielding the three domains resulting from Phase Two: Appearance, Energy, and Technique. Cronbach's alpha reliability ranged from .85 to .71, and test-retest reliability of the total items was .88.

Investigator's Comments: Based on the finding that frequent exercisers use more imagery than less frequent exercisers, it is suggested that use of imagery may be related to exercise participation. (This notion needs to be tested and verified on other leisure and recreation activities to see if it has applied value.) Moreover, it is suggested that other exercise activities be assessed (such as jogging and weightlifting) to test the status of imagery and to increase the generalizability of the developed scale. Imagery training programs can be utilized for intervention by changing participants' image content. (This can also be validated on the total picture of the leisure lifestyle.)

Note: Due to the status of physical movement, exercise, and fitness as physical recreation and as a critical choice of active leisure lifestyles, imagery tends to serve motivation and maintenance of exercising. If imagery actually exists in exercising, there could be a wide use for its measurement: perhaps by using counseling and guidance for those who score low on EIQ-AV and attempting to improve expectations, motivations, and attitudes. Moreover, the assessment can be explored for possible use in other areas of leisure education and leisure involvement, such as outdoor recreation, the arts, hobbies, cultural activities, and social recreation.

EXERCISE IMAGERY QUESTIONNAIRE — AEROBIC VERSION (EIQ-AV)

Hausenblas, H. A.; Hall, C. R.; Rogers, W. M.; and Munroe, K. J.

These are sample items from the scale. Developers of the scale should be contacted for the complete scale, including directions.

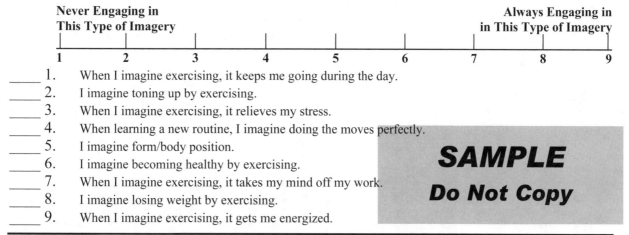

Never Engaging in This Type of Imagery ... **Always Engaging in in This Type of Imagery**

1   2   3   4   5   6   7   8   9

_____ 1. When I imagine exercising, it keeps me going during the day.

_____ 2. I imagine toning up by exercising.

_____ 3. When I imagine exercising, it relieves my stress.

_____ 4. When learning a new routine, I imagine doing the moves perfectly.

_____ 5. I imagine form/body position.

_____ 6. I imagine becoming healthy by exercising.

_____ 7. When I imagine exercising, it takes my mind off my work.

_____ 8. I imagine losing weight by exercising.

_____ 9. When I imagine exercising, it gets me energized.

Energy Component   = Items 1, 3, and 7
Appearance (becoming Healthier) Component   = Items 2, 6, and 8
Technique Component   = Items 4, 5, and 9

Chapter 4

Measurements of Leisure Attitude

Focus of Chapter

This chapter lists the measurements of leisure attitude currently available for use in recreation and leisure and earlier measurements that can be drawn upon in creating new, more modern measurements.

Key Terms

- general attitude
- leisure attitude
- specific attitude

Objectives

- Describe the available measurements of leisure attitude.

Measurements in this chapter are divided in two major sections: one for general leisure attitude scales and the other for specific leisure attitude scales. The general scales assess leisure orientation, ethics, and coping belief. Specific scales assess attitudes toward jogging, children's play, exercise, and physical activity.

General Leisure Attitude

1. Measurement of Leisure Attitude (MLA) (Neulinger and Breit, 1971)
2. Leisure Attitude Scale (LAS) (Crandall and Slivken, 1980)
3. Leisure Attitude Measurement (LAM) (Ragheb and Beard, 1982)
4. Leisure Coping Belief Scale (LCBS) (Iwasaki and Mannell, 2000)

Specific Leisure Attitude

5. Children's Attitude toward Physical Activity Inventory (CATPAI) (Schutz et al., 1985)

Other **general** assessments found in the literature without enough information to evaluate them include.

1. Leisure Orientation Scale (LOS) (Burdge, 1961)
2. Leisure Ethic Scale (LES) (Bryan and Alsikafi, 1975)
3. Leisure Ethic Subscale (LES) (Buchholz, 1978)

Other **specific** assessments found in the literature without enough information to evaluate them include.

4. Attitudes Toward Jogging Questionnaire (ATJQ) (Riddle, 1980)
5. Attitudinal Beliefs Regarding Exercise Questionnaire (ABREQ) (Godin et al., 1986)
6. Attitudes Toward Exercise Questionnaire (ATEQ) (Anshel, 1991)

Questions and Exercises

1. What do leisure attitude scales measure?
2. What is the difference between general and specific leisure attitude measures?
3. Name and explain possible components of leisure attitude?

Attitude 1

MEASUREMENT OF LEISURE ATTITUDE (MLA)

John Neulinger and Miranda Breit

Reference: Neulinger, J., and Breit, M. (1971). Attitude dimensions of leisure. *Journal of Leisure Research, 2*, 108-115.

Goal of the Measurement: To assess leisure attitude and to identify its dimensions.

Background Literature: Concepts are developed in response to scholars' and economists' perceptions that leisure may become a serious problem in the near future. It was assumed that an excess of free time may have great psychological and social implications. It was felt that more information is needed to help evaluate leisure in all of its aspects. The issue of work and its relation to leisure was dominant in this conceptualization process. One of the intents of the scale is to deal meaningfully and quantitatively with various aspects of leisure, as identified in Neulinger's past work. Seven factors were considered as bases for conceptualization: 1. Amount of work or vacation desired; 2. Society's role in leisure planning; 3. Self-definition through work or leisure; 4. Amount of perceived leisure; 5. Autonomous versus passive leisure pursuits; 6. Affinity of leisure; and 7. Importance of public approval.

Methodology Employed: The following closed-form item was asked: "If you did not have to earn your living, would you work anyway?" If the answer to the question was "yes," respondents were further asked to state the reasons why. The majority (88%) said that they would work anyway. The reasons given were of two types: one for intellectual stimulation and satisfaction or, conversely, the need to escape boredom. Qualitative, open-ended items supplied extensive statements and indicators as reasons to work anyway (e.g., to keep my mind active; to get a feeling of being useful; it is good for your body, mind, and soul). Indicators within statements were used to draft 150 items. A number of studies were employed to arrive at a scale to be included in the final phase. To explore differences in meaning of leisure and work, a semantic, differential-type section was included. A sample of 335 working adults responded to 32 attitudinal items. Most items were tested before this replication.

Findings: The factor analysis of the 32-item scale resulted in five factors, accounting for 38% of the variance. These factors were Affinity for Leisure, Society's Role in Leisure Planning, Self-Definition through Leisure or Work, Amount of Perceived Leisure, and Amount of Work or Vacation Desired. No reliability tests were reported.

Investigator's Comments: There is a surprising similarity of factors in this and a previous study by Neulinger. The authors claim that the factors identified represent some real dimensions in the leisure domain.

Note: Copyright permission to include the scale was not obtained; however, all items are listed in Neulinger's (1974) book.

Attitude 2

LEISURE ATTITUDE SCALE (LAS)

Rick P. Crandall and Karla Slivken

Reference: Crandall, R., and Slivken, K. (1980). Leisure attitudes and their measurement. In Iso-Ahola, S. (Ed.). *Social psychological perspectives on leisure and recreation.* Springfield, IL: Charles C. Thomas, Pub.

Goal of the Measurement: To assess a person's general view of and mental state toward leisure.

Conceptual Background: The Leisure Attitude Scale (LAS) is designed to estimate individuals' mental reactions to leisure. Types of leisure attitudes were conceptualized as beliefs, cognitions, stereotypes, evaluations, expectations, satisfactions, behavioral intentions, and general affect. As reported, the investigators' intention was focused on leisure perception and views (cognitive), with less or no emphasis on affective and behavioral domains of leisure. A master's thesis by Slivken (1976) was the basis of this scale.

Methodology Employed: The investigators constructed the LAS on the basis of previous scales in the field of leisure. A pool of 158 items was selected from Burdge (1961), Bryan and Alsikafi (1975), and Neulinger and Breit (1971). A 4-point scale was employed, ranging from "Completely Disagree," marking "1" to "Completely Agree," marking "4." The LAS was administered to over 1,000 persons. Statistics employed were factor analysis; test-retest reliability one to five weeks apart; and correlation coefficients between LAS and three other measures.

Findings: The reported factor structure for the final scale (10 items) yielded three components, with some overlapping — Liking Leisure, Desire for Leisure, and Positive Spontaneity. The test-retest reliabilities were .82, .59, .87, and .85. As evidence of concurrent validity, LAS correlated around the .50s, with the Burdge scale, a leisure satisfaction item, and Neulinger's leisure affinity factor.

Investigator's Comments: Conceptually, attitudes are causal attributions, or cognitive judgments about events or experiences. These judgments determine future interests and choices. Professionally, leisure attitude scales can contribute to a better understanding of leisure theory and help guide practitioners providing services. Moreover, investigators claim that the LAS can be used as a barometer of social attitudes toward leisure, detecting changes in work and leisure ethics and determining differences in leisure attitudes between active and passive participants. It can also compare leisure attitudes to an individual's state of health (wellness, stress, or depression).

Contact Information:
Dr. Rick P. Crandall
Business Owner and Editor
San Francisco Bay Area

web: www.rickcrandall.com

LEISURE ATTITUDE SCALE
(LAS)

Crandall, R. and Slivken, K.

DIRECTIONS: This scale measures your attitudes toward leisure. By this we mean how you feel about your leisure, your recreation, or the things you do in your free time. Please answer as quickly and accurately as possible by indicating whether you agree or disagree with each of the following statements.

Completely Disagree	Moderately Disagree	Moderately Agree	Completely Agree
1	2	3	4

_____ 1.   My leisure is my most enjoyable time.

_____ 2.   I admire a person who knows how to relax.

_____ 3.   I like to do things on the spur of the moment.

_____ 4.   I would like to lead a life of complete leisure.

_____ 5.   Most people spend too much time enjoying themselves today.*

_____ 6.   I don't feel guilty about enjoying myself.

_____ 7.   People should seek as much leisure as possible in their leisure.

_____ 8.   I'd like to have at least two months vacation a year.

_____ 9.   Leisure is great.

_____ 10. It is good for adults to be playful.

*Item 5 is to be reversed; for item reversal see Chapter 17.

$$\boxed{\textbf{Attitude 3}}$$

LEISURE ATTITUDE MEASUREMENT
(LAM)

Mounir G. Ragheb and Jacob G. Beard

Reference: Ragheb, M. G., and Beard, J. G. (1982). Measuring leisure attitude. *Journal of Leisure Research, 14*, 155-167.

Goal of the Measurement: To assess persons' leisure attitudes identified as beliefs and knowledge (cognitive), feelings and evaluation (affective), and intentions (behavioral) toward leisure.

Background Literature: Attitude, a social-psychological construct, has been anchored in three different domains. One of these domains was dominant through the middle of the 1900s at the expense of the other two; that is, the affective — feelings and liking (see Thurstone, 1946; and Fishbein, 1965). Many investigators add two potentially critical domains: cognitive and behavioral. The leisure literature demonstrated that, in measuring and using leisure attitude, there was no differentiation among the three components, although some have included items that might relate to scales in all three. Conceptualizations and definitions of the three domains were theory-driven from the science of social psychology. Moreover, all past leisure attitude scales were reviewed to classify and draw indicators under their relevant domains.

Methodology Employed: A pool of more than 100 indicators was identified, which were based on the knowledge from social-psychological theories and available leisure measurements (Burdge, 1961; Neulinger and Breit, 1971; and Crandall and Slivken, 1980). Items were developed, centered on the identified indicators. Using a process of critical analysis (by the investigators), the set of items was reduced to 61. This new set of items was exposed to external evaluations by 35 faculty and students and was then reduced to 55 revised items. Following that, two pilot studies, on 155 and 254 students, were conducted to verify the scale, yielding 36 items. Fifteen faculty members from academic leisure programs evaluated the final field test further. Then the scale was administered to 1,042 subjects, with half employees and half students. For concurrent validity, two other leisure attitude scales were employed: one by Burdge (1961) and another by Crandall and Slivken (1980). Basically, statistical analyses utilized were factor analysis (Varimax solutions), alpha reliability coefficients, and correlations.

Findings: The factor structure confirmed the differentiation of the three component domains. Each item correlated more highly with the intended factor than either of the other two factors. Alpha reliabilities were sufficiently high for the three components and their total: .91 for the cognitive; .93 for the affective; .89 for the behavioral; and .94 for the total scale of 36 items. Regarding the validity of LAM, two tests were performed. First, content and face validity was established through the evaluation of 15 leisure/recreation educators — demonstrating a positive reaction. Second, concurrent validity, correlating LAM with Burdge's scale yielded r = .50, and .54 with Crandall and Slivken.

Investigator's Comments: The results of the study support a widely held view that attitudes are composed of the cognitive, affective, and behavioral domains. The confirmed three subscales are short (12 items each), easily administered, and having acceptable internal consistency and reliability.

Contact Information:
Idyll Arbor, Inc.
39129 264th Ave SE
Enumclaw, WA 98022

Phone: 360-825-7797
Fax: 360-825-5670
Email: sales@idyllarbor.com

LEISURE ATTITUDE MEASUREMENT
(LAM)

Ragheb, M. G. and Beard, J. G.

DIRECTIONS: We would like to know some of your views and beliefs on leisure. "Leisure activities are nonobligatory and non-work activities." If you **Strongly Disagree**, write 1; if you **Strongly Agree**, write 5; if you are in between, circle the number which describes your degree of agreement. There are no right or wrong answers.

Strongly Disagree	Disagree	In Between	Agree	Strongly Agree
1	2	3	4	5

Cognitive Component of Attitude

_____ 1. Engaging in leisure activities is a wise use of time.
_____ 2. Leisure activities are beneficial to individuals and society.
_____ 3. People often develop friendships in their leisure.
_____ 4. Leisure activities contribute to one's health.
_____ 5. Leisure activities increase one's happiness.
_____ 6. Leisure increases one's work productivity.
_____ 7. Leisure activities help to renew one's energy.
_____ 8. Leisure activities can be means for self-improvement.
_____ 9. Leisure activities help individuals to relax.
_____ 10. People need leisure activities.
_____ 11. Leisure activities are good opportunities.
_____ 12. Leisure activities are important.

Affective Component of Attitude

_____ 13. When I am engaged in leisure activities, the time flies.
_____ 14. My leisure activities give pleasure.
_____ 15. I value my leisure activities.
_____ 16. I can be myself during my leisure.
_____ 17. My leisure activities provide me with delightful experiences.
_____ 18. I feel that leisure is good for me.
_____ 19. I like to take my time while I am engaged in leisure activities.
_____ 20. My leisure activities are refreshing.
_____ 21. I consider it appropriate to engage in leisure activities frequently.
_____ 22. I feel that the time I spent on leisure is not wasted.
_____ 23. I like my leisure activities.
_____ 24. My leisure activities absorb or get my full attention.

Behavioral Component of Attitude

_____ 25. I do leisure activities frequently.
_____ 26. Given a choice, I would increase the amount of time I spend in leisure activities.
_____ 27. I buy goods and equipment to use in my leisure activities as my income allows.
_____ 28. I would do more new leisure activities if I could afford the time and money.
_____ 29. I spend considerable time and effort to be more competent in my leisure activities.
_____ 30. Given a choice, I would live in an environment or city which provides for leisure.
_____ 31. I do some leisure activities even when they have not been planned.
_____ 32. I would attend a seminar or a class to be able to do leisure activities better.
_____ 33. I support the idea of increasing my free time to engage in leisure activities.
_____ 34. I engage in leisure activities even when I am busy.
_____ 35. I would spend time in education and preparation for leisure activities.
_____ 36. I give my leisure high priority among other activities.

Twelve (12) items constitute each component, as follows:

Cognitive Component = **Items 1 to 12.**
Affective Component = **Items 13 to 24.**
Behavioral Component = **Items 25 to 36.**

Add each set of 12 responses to obtain a total for its subscale, divide by 12 to obtain a mean. The same should be done with all the 36 items to obtain a mean for the person's total leisure attitude.

Attitude 4

LEISURE COPING BELIEF SCALE
(LCBS)

Yoshitaka Iwasaki and Roger C. Mannell

References: Iwasaki, Y., and Mannell, R. C. (2000). Hierarchical dimensions of leisure stress coping. *Leisure Sciences, 22*, 163-181. (This article yielded another scale assessing Leisure Coping Strategy, listed under the classification of Leisure Satisfaction.)

Iwasaki, Y., Mannell, R. C., Smale, B. J. A., and Butcher, J. (2002). A short-term longitudinal analysis of leisure coping used by employees of police and emergency response service workers. *Journal of Leisure Research, 34*, 311-339.

Goal of the Measurement: To assess individuals' beliefs about the role of leisure in coping with stress.

Background Literature: People are confronted frequently with stressful events or circumstances in many aspects of their lives. Stress is becoming a major contributor to serious health problems such as cancer and heart disease. Both stress and how people cope with it can impact health both physically and psychologically. The theory of adaptation and health acknowledges coping as a central concept. For example, survival and functioning are assumed to be determined by coping skills. Leisure has the potential to help people cope with stress and improve health. Attention has been given to the buffering role of leisure, for instance, in controlling the negative aspects of stress. Leisure coping beliefs refer to people's generalized beliefs that their leisure helps them cope with stress. These beliefs develop over time, constituting relatively stable psychological dispositions. It is assumed that there are two major types of beliefs: leisure autonomy and leisure friendship. Leisure autonomy is composed of two subdimensions: *self-determination* and *empowerment*. Friendship is formed of four subdimensions: *emotional support, esteem support, tangible aid,* and *informational support*. These six subdimensions were the conceptual bases of the LCBS.

Methodology Employed: A list of 70 initial items was given to a panel of judges (i.e., four leisure scientists) to evaluate the content and face validity. Irrelevant items were removed and redundant items were rewritten, yielding a total of 48 items. A sample of 247 students was recruited from two Canadian universities to test validity and reliability of the scales. A 7-point Likert-type scale was utilized, ranging from 1 (very strongly disagree) to 7 (very strongly agree). Statistical treatments employed alpha reliability coefficients, inter-total correlations, and confirmatory factor analysis.

Findings: Reliability coefficients of the total LCBS was high (.91), while for the subscales they were .71 for Self-Determination; .82 for Empowerment; .70 for Emotional Support; .85 for Esteem Support; .85 for Tangible Aid; and .76 for Informational Support. Next, confirmatory factor analysis was performed documenting the existence of the above components with loadings between .99 and .29.

Investigators Conclusions: The construct validity of the scale was supported. This scale was originally tested with a sample of college students, while subsequent studies have used this scale with police and emergency response personnel (Iwasaki, Mannell, Smale, and Butcher, 2002), and with a general representative sample as suggested in the current report. However, other populations need to be examined for the generalizability of the scale. Authors suggest investigating the influence of different types of leisure activity on actual coping with stress.

Contact Information:
Yoshitaka Iwasaki, Professor
College of Health Professions and Social Work
Temple University
1700 N. Broad Street, Suite 301C
Philadelphia, PA 19121

Phone: 215-204-0011
Fax: 215-204-1386
Email: yiwasaki@temple.edu

LEISURE COPING BELIEF SCALE
(LCBS)

Yoshitaka Iwasaki and Roger C. Mannell

Instructions: This questionnaire is designed to assess your beliefs about leisure. By leisure we mean the things you do in your free time and the recreational activities you engage in. Please read the following statements and indicate the extent to which you agree with each statement by writing in the number which best corresponds to your answer. In the statements, *leisure companions* refers to those individuals with whom you often engage in leisure.

Very Strongly Disagree	Strongly Disagree	Disagree	Neutral	Agree	Strongly Agree	Very Strongly Agree
1	2	3	4	5	6	7

_____ 1. My leisure companions help me feel good about myself.
_____ 2. Leisure provides opportunities to regain a sense of freedom.
_____ 3. My leisure companions assist me in deciding what to do.
_____ 4. My leisure involvements strengthen my ability to manage problems in life.
_____ 5. I gain feelings of personal control in leisure.
_____ 6. Leisure is a self-determined activity for me.
_____ 7. My leisure companions listen to my private feelings.
_____ 8. For me, leisure is a means of developing friendships.
_____ 9. My leisure pursuits are freely chosen.
_____ 10. My leisure companions hold me in high esteem.
_____ 11. What I do in my leisure allows me to feel good about myself.
_____ 12. When I need to borrow something, my leisure companions will lend it to me.
_____ 13. Leisure contributes little to giving me energy to handle problems.
_____ 14. If I need extra hands for doing tasks, I can turn to my leisure companions.
_____ 15. I am able to openly express who I am in my leisure time.
_____ 16. My leisure companions would lend me money if necessary.
_____ 17. I have difficulty in deciding what to do in leisure.
_____ 18. My leisure companions give me advice when I am in trouble.
_____ 19. The things I do in my leisure help me gain confidence.
_____ 20. My leisure companions often provide me with useful information.
_____ 21. I'm respected by my leisure companions.
_____ 22. I feel constrained in leisure.
_____ 23. I can talk to my leisure companions when I am not sure what to do.
_____ 24. I feel that I'm valued by my leisure companions.
_____ 25. Most of my leisure companions are happy to take care of my house (apartment), children, or pets when I am away.
_____ 26. My leisure participation enhances my self-concept.
_____ 27. I decide what to do in my leisure time by myself.
_____ 28. I feel emotionally supported by my leisure companions.
_____ 29. I lack emotional support from my leisure companions.
_____ 30. Opportunities to express myself in leisure enhance my self-concept.

Dimensions:
Leisure-generated self-determination—Items 2, 5, 6, 9, 17 (reverse item), 22 (reverse item), 27
Leisure empowerment—Items 4, 11, 13 (reverse item), 15, 19, 26, 30
Leisure friendship—Items 1, 3, 7, 8, 10, 12, 14, 16, 18, 20, 21, 23, 24, 25, 28, 29 (reverse item)
The leisure friendship dimension consists of four subdimensions:
Emotional support—Items 7, 8, 28, 29 (reverse item)
Esteem support—Items 1, 10, 21, 24
Tangible aid—Items 12, 14, 16, 25
Informational support—Items 3, 18, 20, 23

Attitude 5

CHILDREN'S ATTITUDE TOWARD PHYSICAL ACTIVITY INVENTORY (CATPAI)

Robert W. Schutz, Frank L. Smoll, F. Alex Carre, and Richard E. Mosher

Reference: Schutz, R. W., Smoll, F. L., Carre, F. A., and Mosher, R. E. (1985). Inventories and norms for children's attitudes toward physical activity. *Research Quarterly for Exercise and Sport, 56*, 256-265.

Goal of the Measurement: To assess children's attitudes toward physical activity.

Background Literature: A similar scale — developed and used for young adults (Kenyon, 1968) — was related to many other domains. It was known that attitudes toward physical activities form during middle childhood. Later, this critical attitude gained attention and research was done to study its importance to formal classes, improve attitude-behavior models, and test its relationships to other critical factors.

Methodology Employed: Kenyon's (1968) pioneering model and scale were used as bases for item generation. Other items for children (grades 4-6) came from Simon and Smoll (1974) Kenyon's multidimensional model identified six components: Social Experience, Health and Fitness, Pursuit of Vertigo, Aesthetic Experience, Catharsis, and Ascetic Experience. In a pilot study, the adopted items from Simon and Smoll went through item analysis of eight bipolar adjectives of the semantic differential scales. Basically, internal consistency and factor analysis were employed. The analysis of one factor — Health and Fitness — showed the need to split it into two factors. In the final field test, data was collected as part of a Physical Education Assessment project, from 1,015 grade seven students and 864 grade 11 students.

Findings: Investigators reported that the factor structure of CATPAI was provided by Kenyon (1968) and in a revised form by Schutz, Smoll, and Wood (1981). Because each subdomain is represented by one item, further tests of factor structure were not possible. Secondary evidence of the scale's validity (construct, concurrent, predictive, and convergent) was mentioned. Alpha reliability of CATPAI ranged between .90 and .80, and test-retest reliability (6 weeks) was .60.

Investigator's Comments: Users are cautioned that attitude measures are not recommended for assessing individual change. In using this scale, careful attention needs to be exercised, guarding against the impact of contamination by social desirability on responses. Finally, CATPAI demonstrates high internal consistency, reasonably strong convergent validity, and acceptable face validity.

CHILDREN'S ATTITUDE TOWARD PHYSICAL ACTIVITY INVENTORY (CATPAI)

Schutz, R. W.; Smoll, F. L.; Carre, F. A.; and Mosher, R. E.

This is a sample page provided in the report by Schutz, R. W.; Smoll, F. L.; Carre, F. A.; and Mosher, R. E. (1985). Developers of the scale should be contacted for more details, including information on their subdomains listed below:

DIRECTIONS: Read the idea in the box. Then mark a spot between the pairs of feelings that shows how the idea makes you feel.

How do you feel about the idea in the box?

PHYSICAL ACTIVITY FOR SOCIAL GROWTH
Taking part in physical activities which
give you a chance to meet new people.

Always think about the Idea in the Box.
If you do not understand this idea, mark this box ☐ and go on to the next page.

1.	good	_____ . _____ . _____ . _____ . _____	bad
2.	of no use	_____ . _____ . _____ . _____ . _____	useful
3.	not pleasant	_____ . _____ . _____ . _____ . _____	pleasant
4.	nice	_____ . _____ . _____ . _____ . _____	awful
5.	happy	_____ . _____ . _____ . _____ . _____	sad

CATPAI Inventory: Subdomain Descriptions

1. **Physical Activity for Social Growth (Social Growth)**
   Taking part in physical activities which give you a chance to meet new people.

2. **Physical Activity to Continue Social Relations (Social Continuation)**
   Taking part in physical activities which give you a chance to be with your friends.

3. **Physical Activity for Health and Fitness (Health and Fitness)**
   Taking part in physical activities to make your health better and to get your body in better condition.

4. **Physical Activity as a Thrill But Involving Some Risk (Vertigo)**
   Taking part in physical activities that could be dangerous because you move very fast and must change direction quickly.

5. **Physical Activity as the Beauty in Movement (Aesthetic)**
   Taking part in physical activities which have beautiful and graceful movements.

6. **Physical Activity for the Release of Tension (Catharsis)**
   Taking part in physical activities to reduce stress or to get away from problems you might have.

7. **Physical Activity as Long and Hard Training (Ascetic)**
   Taking part in physical activities that have long and hard practices. To spend time in practice you need to give up other things you like to do.

Chapter 5

Measurements of Leisure Motivation

Focus of Chapter
This chapter lists the measurements of leisure motivation currently available for use in recreation and leisure and earlier measurements that can be drawn upon in creating new, more modern measurements.

Key Terms
- general leisure motivation
- leisure motivation
- specific leisure motivation

Objectives
- To be able to report on the available measurements of leisure motivation.

Measurements included in this chapter assess motivation from different dimensions. Instruments are divided between general and specific leisure motivation. For the general scales, while one of them measures leisure needs, others assess self-as-entertainment, perceived freedom in leisure, intrinsic motives, experience preference, and meaning. On the other hand, specific motivations assess fitness locus of control, racquet sports competence, exercise identity, flow in sport and physical activity, exercise regulation, running, coping strategy, and travel. By far, leisure motivation gained the most attention in scale development.

General Leisure Motivation

1. Measurement of Leisure Needs (MLN) (Iso-Ahola and Allen, 1982)
2. Leisure Motivation Scale (LMS) (Beard and Ragheb, 1983/1989)
3. Self-as-Entertainment Scale (Mannell, 1984)
4. Measurement of Perceived Freedom in Leisure (MPFL) (Ellis and Witt, 1984)
5. Intrinsic Leisure Motivation (ILM) (Weissinger, 1986)
6. Leisure Experience Battery for Adolescents (LEBA) (Caldwell, Smith, and Weissinger, 1992)
7. Recreation Experience Preference (REP) (Manfredo and Driver, 1996)
8. Measuring the Search for Meaning in Leisure and Recreation (MSMLR) (Ragheb, 1997)
9. Free Time Motivation Scale for Adolescents (FTMS-A) (Baldwin and Caldwell, 2003)

Specific Leisure Motivation

10. Fitness Locus of Control Scale (FITLOC) (Whitehead and Corbin, 1988)

11. Racquet Sports Competence Scale (RCSC) (Aguilar and Petrakis, 1989)[*]
12. Motivations for Participation in Recreational Running Scale (MPRRS) (Clough, Shepherd, and Maugham, 1990)
13. Exercise Decisional Balance Measure (EDBM) (Marcus, Rakowski, and Rossi, 1992)
14. Exercise Identity Scale (EIS) (Anderson and Cychosz, 1994)
15. The Flow State Scale (FSS) (Jackson and Marsh, 1996)
16. Exercise Motivation Inventory-2 (EMI-2) (Markland and Ingledew, 1997)
17. Behavioral Regulation in Exercise Questionnaire (BREQ) (Mullan, Markland, and Ingledew, 1997)
18. Exercise Motivation Scale (EMS) (Li, 1999)
19. International Leisure Travel Motivation (ILTM) (Toh and Yeung, 2000)

General assessments found in the literature without enough information to evaluate them include.

1. Measurement of Perceived Freedom in Leisure and Satisfaction (MPFLS) (Ellis and Witt, 1994)
2. The Motivation for Leisure Scale (MLS) (Pelletier et al., 1996)
3. Intrinsic Motivation in Leisure (ILM) (Weissinger and Bandalos, 1995)

Questions and Exercises

1. Explain the nature of leisure motivation measurements.
2. What are the differences and similarities between general and specific leisure measurements?
3. Compare the magnitude of attention given to leisure motivation and the prior domain.
4. Why has leisure motivation gained the highest attention in measurement development?

---

[*] This study has another scale that can be classified as, and incorporated, under Leisure Satisfaction Measurements.

| Motivation 1 |

MEASUREMENT OF LEISURE NEEDS
(MLN)

Seppo E. Iso-Ahola and Jon R. Allen

Reference: Iso-Ahola, S. E., and Allen, J. R. (1982). The dynamics of leisure motivation: The effects of outcome on leisure needs. *Research Quarterly for Exercise and Sport, 53,* 141-149.

Goal of the Measurement: To examine the psychological foundations of leisure needs referred to as perceived reasons for participation in recreation and leisure activities.

Background Literature: Due to the importance of leisure needs, numerous studies were cited to investigate the concept. The assumption of need stability was reported by past studies, ignoring a similarly important aspect: changeability as a function of the nature of leisure experience. Past studies were founded on the assumption that leisure needs are stable and unchangeable motivators to participate in leisure. Nevertheless, leisure needs were perceived as both static and dynamic. One of the principles of this study is that leisure needs change as a result of participation. A social psychological consideration was accounted for, that is, "The perceived outcome is one of the most powerful determinants of human feelings and cognitions" (p. 142). Two major questions were raised: 1. Do the expressed leisure needs vary from before to after participation? 2. Does the outcome of leisure experience influence leisure needs?

Methodology Employed: Previous scholars, such as Crandall (1979), London et al. (1977), and Tinsley et al., (1977) identified many need-satisfying attributes. Investigators have since added further items. In selecting items, two criteria were utilized: items' perceived relationship to intramural basketball and items' ability to cover most needs underlying subjects' participation. A five-point scale was used, from "Never True," marking "1" to "Always True," marking "5." Team captains were telephoned one day in advance of their games. Questionnaires were filled out before and after the game. Responses were exposed to factor analysis and Cronbach's alpha reliability coefficient.

Findings: Factor analysis demonstrated an interpretable six-factor structure and a seventh minor factor for the 40-item scale: Interpersonal Diversion and Control, Personal Competence, Escape from Daily Routine, Positive Interpersonal Development, Diversionary Relaxation, Interpersonal Competence, and Meeting the Opposite Sex. Eigenvalues were higher than 1.0 for all factors, cumulative variance was 58%. Moreover, it was reported that Cronbach's alphas were, on the average .94, with no details on subscales reliabilities.

Investigator's Comments: The seven factors can be integrated in three main structures: Three of them dealt with interpersonal relationships, while two were related to competence, and two others were pertinent to escape or diversion. On the basis of current findings, it seems that leisure needs are quite stable and invariant across various populations.

Contact Information:
Dr. Seppo E. Iso-Ahola, Professor
Kinesiology
College of Maryland
HHP Building, Room 2142
College Park, MD 20742-2611

Phone: 301-405-2505
Email: isoahol@umd.edu

MEASUREMENT OF LEISURE NEEDS
(MLN)

Iso-Ahola, S. E. and Allen, J. R.

Directions: How important was each of the following items or reasons for your participation in the program? If the item is "Never True," write in the number 1; if it is "Always True," write in the number 5, as follows:

1	2	3	4	5
Never True	**Seldom True**	**Sometime True**	**Often True**	**Always True**

_____	1.	Relax physically	_____ 21.	Do things with companions
_____	2.	Competition	_____ 22.	Meet people of opposite sex
_____	3.	Effort and exercise	_____ 23.	Ability to play basketball
_____	4.	Avoid boredom	_____ 24.	Contribute to team performance
_____	5.	Opportunity to make decisions	_____ 25.	Excitement
_____	6.	Creativity	_____ 26.	Enjoy scoring and performing well
_____	7.	Use personal skills/talents	_____ 27.	Be away from friends and family
_____	8.	Nature of game	_____ 28.	Think of personal values
_____	9.	Bring friends/family together	_____ 29.	Get away from other people
_____	10.	Pressure to do well	_____ 30.	Coincidental participation
_____	11.	Talk to new and varied people	_____ 31.	Keep busy
_____	12.	Develop personal skills/abilities	_____ 32.	Be with people of the opposite sex
_____	13.	Get away from civilization	_____ 33.	Help others
_____	14.	Have control over others	_____ 34.	Keep in shape
_____	15.	Ask to play	_____ 35.	Show others I could do it
_____	16.	Learn personal capabilities	_____ 36.	Be in a position of authority
_____	17.	See results of personal efforts	_____ 37.	Risks involved
_____	18.	Slow down mind	_____ 38.	Build friendships with new people
_____	19.	Others think highly of me	_____ 39.	Use mind
_____	20.	Change daily routine	_____ 40.	Get away from responsibilities of everyday life

The above 40-items represent the following components*:
- Interpersonal Diversion and Control
- Personal Competence
- Escape from Daily Routine
- Positive Interpersonal Development
- Diversionary Relaxation
- Interpersonal Competence
- Meeting the Opposite Sex

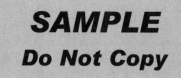

*Identification of items that belong to the above components should be requested from Dr. Seppo E. Iso-Ahola.

Motivation 2

LEISURE MOTIVATION SCALE
(LMS)

Jacob G. Beard and Mounir G. Ragheb

Reference: Beard, J. G., and Ragheb, M. G. (1983). Measuring leisure motivation. *Journal of Leisure Research, 15,* 219-228.

Goal of the Measurement: To assess the psychological and sociological reasons for participation in leisure activities.

Conceptual Background: The latent structure of need-satisfying attributes has been explored from the late 1970s. Studies identified several need-satisfying properties (motivations), such as companionship, diversions, exercise, and intellectual aestheticism. In conceptualizing and measuring leisure motivation, more than 10 theories of leisure, recreation, and play were considered and examined as bases for a theory-driven scale. Some of the identified theories were very useful in explaining leisure motivation. One of the major theoretical structures utilized here was stimulus seeking and stimulus avoidance (Ellis, 1973); that is, the need for optimal arousal. Another overlapping theory was relaxation (Patrick, 1919). A third theory employed was competence-affectance (White, 1959), which claims that humans have an urge for competence in and mastery of the environment through exploration and experimentation. Altogether, these theories assume that persons — in their waking hours — swing between maximum excitement (what they can optimally afford) to full withdrawal from excitement, which seems appropriate for the moment (avoidance and relaxation). To achieve that swing, individuals sense the need for and seek physical competence, mental competence, and social competence. These form the ebb and flow of daily choices. Otherwise, mental and physical starvation can result, leading to maladaptive behavior resulting from understimulation — known popularly as boredom. This extensive theoretical background was used to extract a smaller number of factors in order to build more general subscales.

Methodology Employed: A systematic procedure was employed to find the major dimensions of leisure motivation, which were based on existing literature. First, a pool of more than 150 indicators was identified, catalogued, and classified; then relevant items were constructed to assess about 12 tentative categories of leisure motives. Secondly, in refining items, some steps were taken: investigators' critical analyses of the items' appropriateness; followed by a similar evaluation through 28 faculty members and students; yielding a reduced list of 106 items. Thirdly, the modified list was pretested twice on samples of 65 and 174 students. Finally, after more refinements were made, 48 items were administered to a sample of 1,205 employees, retirees, and students. Statistically, in the two pretests and the final field test, conventional item and test analysis was used, as well as factor analysis, reliability, and correlation.

Findings: As demonstrated in the two pretests, the factor structure, in its final field verification, confirmed the differentiation of four subscales out of the identified 12 categories: Intellectual, Social, Competence-Mastery, and Stimulus Avoidance. The first three components represent Stimulus Seeking. The alpha reliability coefficient for these subscales ranged from .92 to .90 for the four long subscales (12 items each). A shorter version of the measure was also studied by using 32 questions. The short subscales on that version (eight items each) ranged from .90 to .89.

Investigator's Comments: The four recognized factors assess clearly differentiated leisure motives. The criteria of parsimony, utility, and communication were dominant in arriving at this particular subscale structure, constituting acceptable psychometric properties. Practically, leisure motivation can help in predicting leisure demand, as well as leisure counseling, and compatible programming, as suggested by Crandall and Slivken (1980). The short scale is especially recommended for use in practice and research settings where time for administration is a major consideration.

Contact Information:
Idyll Arbor, Inc.
39129 264th Ave SE
Enumclaw, WA 98022

Phone: 360-825-7797
Fax: 360-825-5670
Email: sales@idyllarbor.com

LEISURE MOTIVATION SCALE
(LMS)

Beard, J. G. and Ragheb, M. G.

DIRECTIONS: The following statements are on the reasons which lead an individual to engage in leisure activities, the nonobligatory and non-work activities, active or inactive. Read each statement and then write in your answer. If the statement is **NEVER TRUE**, write **"1"**; if the statement is **ALWAYS TRUE**, write **"5"**; and if you are in between, write the number that describes how true the statement is for you. There are no right or wrong answers.

1	2	3	4	5
Never True	**Seldom True**	**Sometime True**	**Often True**	**Always True**

ONE OF MY REASONS FOR ENGAGING IN LEISURE ACTIVITIES IS …

_____ 1. to learn about things around me.

_____ 2. to satisfy my curiosity.

_____ 3. to explore new ideas.

_____ 4. to learn about myself.

_____ 5. to expand my knowledge.

_____ 6. to discover new things.

_____ 7. to be creative.

_____ 8. to use my imagination.

_____ 9. to build friendships with others.

_____ 10. to interact with others.

_____ 11. to develop close friendships.

_____ 12. to meet new and different people.

_____ 13. to reveal my thoughts, feelings, or physical skills to others.

_____ 14. to be socially competent and skillful.

_____ 15. to gain a feeling of belonging.

_____ 16. to gain others' respect.

_____ 17. to challenge my abilities.

_____ 18. to be good in doing them.

_____ 19. to improve my skill and ability in doing them.

_____ 20. to be active.

_____ 21. to develop physical skills and abilities.

_____ 22. to keep in shape physically.

_____ 23. to use my physical abilities.

_____ 24. to develop physical fitness.

_____ 25. to slow down.

_____ 26. because I sometimes like to be alone.

_____ 27. to relax physically.

_____ 28. to relax mentally.

_____ 29. to avoid hustle and bustle of daily activities.

_____ 30. to rest.

_____ 31. to relieve stress and tension.

_____ 32. to unstructure my time.

Each set of 8 items constitutes a component, as follows:

Intellectual Motivation	=	Items 1 to 8.
Social Motivation	=	Items 9 to 16.
Competence-Mastery Motivation	=	Items 17 to 24.
(*Total Stimulus Seeking Motivation*)	=	Items 1 to 24.
Stimulus Avoidance Motivation	=	Items 25 to 32.

SAMPLE
Do Not Copy

Motivation 3

SELF-AS-ENTERTAINMENT SCALE
(SAES)
Roger C. Mannell

Reference: Mannell, R. C. (1984). Personality in leisure theory: The self-as-entertainment construct. *Society and Leisure, 7,* 229-242.

Goal of the Measurement: To assess individuals' capacity or ability to occupy their free time with satisfying and meaningful activities.

Background Literature: It is assumed that both personality traits and situational factors are the roots and sources of behavior and experience. The scale was originally developed because the interaction of personality differences and situational factors, as they impact on leisure behavior, had been ignored due to lack of appropriate leisure-specific personality measures. The Self-as-Entertainment (SAE) concept was seen as a good fit with the interactionism approach. Individuals' ability to occupy their free time with meaningful activities is viewed as a function of both inherited and learned personality traits. The SAE concept is based on the assumption that people entertain themselves based on three sources or modalities: going to new places, meeting new people, and using one's capacity for mental play. Poor self-entertainers will suffer most often from boredom.

Methodology Employed: SAES was revised from a 40-item scale to 28 items. Four studies on samples between 253 and 400 persons were conducted for the scale's refinement and verification. Factor analysis and alpha reliability coefficients were performed.

Findings: Factor analysis confirmed the existence of three subscales: Mind-Play, referring to the ability to use one's imagination and cognitive resources; Environmental, which is an individual's ability to entertain herself/himself with the use of social and physical environmental resources; and Self, which refers to a reliance on inner personal resources, abilities, and talents. Cronbach's alpha reliability for the total scale (28 items) ranged between .85 and .87 in all studies. Predictive validity was reported for SAES and life satisfaction.

Investigator's Comments: The findings showed the SAES to be reliable with a variety of populations, and to be related in predictable ways to other relevant constructs.

Contact Information:
Dr. Roger C. Mannell, Professor and Dean
Faculty of Applied Health Sciences
University of Waterloo
Waterloo, Ontario, Canada N2L 3G1

Phone: 519-888-4567, Ext. 5404
Fax: 519-746-6776
Email: mannell@healthy.uwaterloo.ca

SELF-AS-ENTERTAINMENT SCALE
(SAES)

Mannell, R. C.

DIRECTIONS: Most people have periods of free time, ranging from a few moments during the course of their daily activities to large amounts of vacation time. The following statements reflect how different people feel about their free time and how they use it. Please respond as quickly and accurately as possible by indicating the extent to which each of the statements describes you.

Doesn't Sound Like Me		Sounds a Little Like Me		Sounds a Lot Like Me
1	2	3	4	5

_____ 1. I have an active imagination.

_____ 2. I like to go places where there is lots to do.

_____ 3. I can make almost anything fun for myself.

_____ 4. I find at this stage of my life that there is not enough to occupy my time.*

_____ 5. When I have to wait for something, I usually get so engrossed in my thoughts that I fail to notice the time.

_____ 6. My most enjoyable vacations are those where I go someplace new.

_____ 7. Filling my free time is a problem for me.*

_____ 8. If something I have planned is cancelled, I have difficulty finding an enjoyable substitute.*

_____ 9. I am good at entertaining myself.

_____ 10. I like to go out a great deal.

_____ 11. I enjoy relaxing and letting my mind wander.

_____ 12. If I have a day free, I prefer to go somewhere away from home.

_____ 13. When I have time on my hands, I usually find someone to spend it with.

_____ 14. I am a person who likes to go to new places.

_____ 15. I am never at a loss for something to do.

_____ 16. I am good at thinking of things to do with my free time.

_____ 17. I often have a difficult time deciding what to do with my free time.*

_____ 18. I am good at thinking of fun things to do.

_____ 19. I remember my good times by the places I've been.

_____ 20. My life would be dull without my daydreams.

_____ 21. I often use my imagination to entertain myself.

_____ 22. I have too much time on my hands.*

_____ 23. I am good at making up games.

_____ 24. My favorite activities require me to use my knowledge and skills.

_____ 25. When I am bored, I go some place where there are things happening.

_____ 26. I like teaching myself to do new activities.

_____ 27. I often feel there is nothing to do.*

_____ 28. It doesn't matter where I am, I enjoy myself.

**SAMPLE
Do Not Copy**

* Items to be reversed; for item reversal see Chapter 17.

Components and their items were as follows:

Self Mode   = Items: 3, 4, 7, 8, 9, 15, 16, 17, 18, 22, 23, 24, 26, 27, and 28

Environmental Mode   = Items: 2, 6, 10, 12, 13, 14, 19, and 25

Mind-Play Mode   = Items: 1, 5, 11, 20, and 21

| Motivation 4 |

MEASUREMENT OF PERCEIVED FREEDOM IN LEISURE (MPFL)

Gary D. Ellis and Peter A. Witt

Reference: Ellis, G., and Witt, P. A. (1984). The measurement of perceived freedom in leisure. *Journal of Leisure Research, 16,* 110-123.

Goal of the Measurement: To assess perceived freedom in leisure based on the "state of mind" view.

Conceptual Background: This scale is a theory-driven assessment tool: attribution theory, arousal-seeking theory, and the concepts of flow. Moreover, freedom was conceptualized philosophically, educationally, and psychologically, demonstrating relevance of these concepts to leisure experiences. For an experience to be considered as leisure or non-leisure, it was assumed that the level of perceived freedom is a determining aspect. Based on extensive literature, this assessment tool was centered on the notion that perceived freedom in leisure is composed of four major elements: perceived competence, perceived control, intrinsic motivation, and playfulness.

Methodology Employed: The literature provided domains representing the assumed four components. Outside reviewers (30), knowledgeable in leisure concepts, evaluated the content of the domains as bases for item development. To refine the scale, several pilot studies were conducted. A three-point scale was used. Statistically, factor analysis (Varimax rotation) and reliability tests were employed.

Findings: The four subscales were confirmed, identifying the degree of homogeneity of items incorporated under each scale. Alpha reliabilities for the four scales ranged between .90 and .88. The alpha for the total scale, labeled "Perceived Freedom," was .96. Test-retest stabilities for the subscales ranged from .82 to .75, and for the total was .89. Two measures were utilized to test concurrent validity: Barriers to Leisure Involvement (BLI) and Knowledge of Leisure Opportunities (KLO). The BLI produced substantial evidence, with correlations ranging between -.62 and .37. The KLO scale had no correlation with the Perceived Freedom Scale and its four subscales.

Investigator's Comments: The four scales and their total received acceptable scores for their reliability and validity. This scale can be utilized in many practical settings where assessment is required, as well as testing relationships in other social and behavioral domains. Fundamentally, the scale can be used to explore the nature of leisure itself.

Contact Information:
Dr. Gary D. Ellis, Head
Department of Recreation, Park, and Tourism
106 Francis Hall
Texas A & M University
College Station, TX 77843-226

Phone: 979-845-7324
Fax: 979-845-0446
Email: gellis@tamu.edu

Motivation 5

INTRINSIC LEISURE MOTIVATION
(ILM)

Ellen M. Weissinger and Deborah L. Bandalos

Reference: Weissinger, E., and Bandalos, D. L. (1995). Development, reliability, and validity of a scale to measure intrinsic motivation in leisure. *Journal of Leisure Research, 27,* 379-400.

Goal of the Measurement: To assess individual differences in the disposition toward intrinsic motivation — to seek intrinsic rewards — in leisure behavior.

Conceptual Background: ILM is a theory-based instrument, constructed on the basis of Deci and Ryan's (1985) Cognitive Evaluation Theory of Intrinsic Motivation. The theory assumes that individuals differ in the degree to which they desire intrinsic rewards, impacting on behavioral choices, needs, motives; and whatever energizes goal selection. Competence and self-determination are two other key concepts used as bases for intrinsic motivation that applies to leisure.

Methodology Employed: The initial pool of 44 items was drafted. Eleven items represented each of the four theorized components: Self-determination, Competence, Commitment, and Challenge. A seven-point scale was utilized, ranging from 1=Very Strongly Disagree to 7=Very Strongly Agree. A sample of 55 college undergraduates responded to the scale. Confirmatory factor analysis and Cronbach's alpha reliability coefficients were employed. Moreover, this study reported a comparison among the findings of nine studies using ILM, and how this scale demonstrated consistency.

Findings: Alpha reliabilities for the four subscales ranged from .83 to .64. Few items were shown that, if deleted, alpha would increase. Moreover, a test-retest, eight weeks apart, received a correlation of .63. A convergent/discriminant validity of the ILM scale was reported, correlating it with 15 theoretically related constructs. The nine studies showed stabilities for the usage of ILM across settings, age groups, and other backgrounds.

Investigator's Comments: The ILM scale proved through the nine studies that it possesses sufficient internal consistency, as well as validity, measuring the intended underlying construct. However, the investigators recommend additional cross-validation of the scale before any modifications of the items that did not cluster well with their subscales are carried out. On the scale's usability, they noted that the ILM scale is not a diagnostic tool. Ultimately, this scale applies to scientific studies that test models or relationships among theoretical variables or concepts. More work is needed before it is used clinically or in other applied areas.

Contact Information:
Dr. Ellen M. Weissinger, Executive Associate Dean of Graduate Studies
Professor of Educational Psychology
University of Nebraska
1100 Seaton Hall
Lincoln, NE 68588-0619

Phone: 402-472-2875
Fax: 402-472-0589
Email: eweissinger@unl.edu

INTRINSIC LEISURE MOTIVATION
(ILM)

Weissinger, E. and Bandalos, D.

DIRECTIONS: This survey is intended to find out how you feel about the things you do in your leisure time. By "leisure time" we mean the non-work hours of your day, or your "free time." Please respond by circling the number that represents your agreement or disagreement with each statement as it applies to your leisure time. Please use the following scale:

Very Strongly Disagree 1	Strongly Disagree 2	Disagree 3	Neutral 4	Agree 5	Strongly Agree 6	Very Strongly Agree 7

1.   I feel in control of my life during my leisure time.
     1   2   3   4   5   6   7
2.   I am as dedicated to leisure as I am to other parts of my life.
     1   2   3   4   5   6   7
3.   I know what I want from my leisure time activities.
     1   2   3   4   5   6   7
4.   I strive to be effective in my leisure pursuits.
     1   2   3   4   5   6   7
5.   I like leisure time activities that are a little beyond my ability.
     1   2   3   4   5   6   7
6.   I feel like I don't get to do what I want with my leisure.*
     1   2   3   4   5   6   7
7.   I am aware that I feel good about my ability to use my leisure time.
     1   2   3   4   5   6   7
8.   My leisure time activities absorb all my attention.
     1   2   3   4   5   6   7
9.   My friends think that I am skilled at leisure time activities.
     1   2   3   4   5   6   7
10. I like a challenge in my leisure time.
     1   2   3   4   5   6   7
11. My leisure time activities are a central part of my life.
     1   2   3   4   5   6   7
12. Leisure time is important in my life.
     1   2   3   4   5   6   7
13. Leisure is OK, but other things are more important in my life.*
     1   2   3   4   5   6   7
14. I am willing to try the unknown in my leisure time.
     1   2   3   4   5   6   7
15. I feel good when my leisure time activities challenge my skills.
     1   2   3   4   5   6   7
16. My participation in leisure time activities makes me feel competent.
     1   2   3   4   5   6   7
17. The thing I like best about my leisure time is that I make free choices.
     1   2   3   4   5   6   7

Seventeen of the 44 items on the INTRINSIC LEISURE MOTIVATION scale.

* Items to be reversed, 6 and 13; for item reversal see Chapter 17.

Motivation 6

LEISURE EXPERIENCE BATTERY FOR ADOLESCENTS (LEBA)

Linda L. Caldwell, Edward A. Smith, and Ellen Weissinger

Reference: Caldwell, L. L., Smith, E. A., and Weissinger, E. (1992). Development of a leisure experience battery for adolescents: Parsimony, stability, and validity. *Journal of Leisure Research, 24*, 361-376.

Goal of the Measurement: To assess what adolescents do with their free time, why they do what they do, and how they feel about what they do.

Description: Based on the fact that free time activities occupy about half of an adolescent's life, understanding how they experience it and what they feel about it would be important in explaining other behaviors (e.g., adjustment, deviation, risk, and challenge). An adolescent's free time needs to provide personal development, challenge, stimulus (optimal arousal), psychological rewards, and meaning. Otherwise, individuals may seek deviant behavior and delinquent acts, overindulge in drugs, alcoholism, cigarette use, and a host of other problematic processes. Four leisure dimensions are proposed to explain adolescent behavior: boredom in leisure (free time), leisure awareness, leisure challenge, and leisure (free time) anxiety.

Methodology Employed: For the first three of the above dimensions, the initial pool of items was adapted from other scales. Leisure anxiety was developed for the purpose of this measurement. Two data sets, over 1,700 students, were utilized (grades 6, 7, 8, 10, and 11). Factor analysis, reliability tests, and correlational analysis were utilized to test the structure of the battery.

Findings: Factor analysis revealed that the clustering of four structural features accounted for over 54% of the total variance. Some items needed to be excluded, which made subscales shorter. Alpha reliability coefficients were performed for the four subscales, ranging from .70 to .55. The low alphas were attributed to the low number of items (3 to 4) in subscales. Test-retest reliabilities were provided, demonstrating some stability over time. Theoretically related measures were correlated with the four subscales, providing further evidence of construct validity.

Investigator's Comments: The LEBA needs more research and further refinement. Reliability dimension scores are low to weak and warrant caution in their uses, especially for diagnostic purposes. Meantime, this battery can be used evaluatively, to test the effects of leisure education on boredom coping skills, leisure preparedness, and anxiety coping skills. Also, LEBA can assess changes in leisure (free time) boredom, anxiety, awareness, and challenge, as well as testing relationships among such changes and other program goals (e.g., drug use, teenage pregnancy, delinquency, cigarette smoking, and alcohol abuse).

Contact Information:
Dr. Linda L. Caldwell
Department of Recreation, Park, and Tourism Management
The Pennsylvania State University
201 Mateer Building
University Park, PA 16802-1307

Phone: 814-863-8983
Fax: 814-863-4257
Email: lindac@psu.edu

LEISURE EXPERIENCE BATTERY FOR ADOLESCENTS
(LEBA)

Caldwell, L. L.; Smith, E. A.; and Weissinger, E.

Directions: Free time refers to the time outside of scheduled school and/or work and required home activities. The following questions are about how you feel about your free time. Read each statement and think about it. Write in the one number that best describes how you usually feel, using the scale given below:

Strongly Disagree	Disagree	Neutral	Agree	Strongly Agree
1	2	3	4	5

_____ 1.   In the community where I live I am aware of exciting things to do in my free time.

_____ 2.   I know of places where there are lots of things to do.

_____ 3.   My community lacks things for people my age to do.

_____ 4.   I've never really given much thought to whether free time could be good for me.

_____ 5.   For me, free time just drags on and on.

_____ 6.   Free time is boring.

_____ 7.   I usually don't like what I am doing in my free time, but I don't know what else to do.

_____ 8.   I almost always have something to do in my free time.

_____ 9.   I like activities that are a little beyond my ability.

_____ 10. I like a challenge in my free time.

_____ 11. I am willing to try the unknown in my free time.

_____ 12. I feel good when my free time activities challenge my skills.

_____ 13. The worst feeling I know is when I have free time and don't have anything planned.

_____ 14. I get uptight when I have a whole weekend with nothing to do.

_____ 15. I feel relaxed about free time when I don't have any plans.

The following items are reversed 3, 4, 5, 6, 7, 13, 14; for item reversal see Chapter 17.

The above items represent the following components:

Leisure Awareness   = Items 1 to 4.

Boredom in Leisure*   = Items 5 to 8.

Leisure Challenge   = Items 9 to 12.

Leisure* Anxiety*   = Items 13 to 15.

* Could also be referred to as "free time"

SAMPLE
Do Not Copy

Motivation 7

RECREATION EXPERIENCE PREFERENCE (REP)

Michael J. Manfredo and B. L. Driver

Reference: Manfredo, M. J., and Driver, B. L. (1996). Measuring leisure motivation: A meta-analysis of the recreation experience preference scales. *Journal of Leisure Research, 28*, 188-213.

Goal of the Measurement: To assess the desired goal states that are attained through participation in leisure.

Conceptual Background: A central focus for the development of this scale is to consider recreation and leisure as a psycho-physiological experience, which is self-rewarding. One of the underlying assumptions in the context of the motivational theory utilized here is that recreation activities are instrumental in attaining certain psychological and physiological goals. Hence, recreation experience was defined, from a psychological perspective, as the "package" or "bundle" of psychological outcomes desired from recreational involvement.

Methodology Employed: Two phases were administered to develop the scale: 1. To identify reliable and valid scales that measure desired goal states in leisure; and 2. To establish scale reliability and validity of the identified scales. Data utilized were accumulated from 36 studies that applied the Recreation Experience Preference (REP) scales. These studies met another sets of criteria (e.g., using similar methods, employing a large number of REP items). Meta-analysis, factor analysis, LISREL, and correlation were utilized in treating the data.

Findings: The 36 studies yielded four response scales: Satisfaction, Importance, Valence (how would the outcome add to satisfaction), and Experience. Analyses revealed the existence of 11 domains or scales, demonstrating reliability and, to some extent, construct validity.

The confirmed 11 domains are as follows: Achievement/Stimulation, Autonomy/Leadership, Similar People, New People, Learning, Enjoy Nature, Introspection, Escape Personal-Social Pressure, Escape Physical Pressure, Teaching-Leading Others, and Risk Reduction.

Investigator's Comments: Since the analyses were based on studies conducted between 1975 and 1979, it is possible that changes would affect the generalizability over time. The scales, being trip-specific and activity-specific motivations, warrant further verifications to determine the extent to which leisure generally achieves goal states in life. The scales are claimed to be appropriate for measuring satisfaction obtained from participation. There are concerns regarding content validity — whether all important experience preferences are measured or not. This requires a pretest every time scales are utilized. Finally, validation of scales should continue as an unending process.

Motivation 8

MEASURING THE SEARCH FOR MEANING IN LEISURE AND RECREATION
(MSMLR)

Mounir G. Ragheb

Reference: Ragheb, M. G. (1997). Development and validation of a multidimensional scale: Measuring the search for meaning in leisure and recreation. Symposium on Research, National Recreation and Park Association. Salt Lake City, UT.

Goal of the Measurement: To assess the existence and magnitude of the search for meaning or sense of purpose in leisure and recreation pursuits.

Background Literature: The concept of the "search for meaning," initiated by Frankl (1962, 1992), has been utilized extensively in many areas to understand human motivations and strivings. Despite the concept's wide use, meager attention was given to its application in recreation and leisure. Recently, work has been described as mechanized, routine, and less satisfying, lacking the meaning it once had. Measuring the search for meaning in leisure and recreation is a theory-driven assessment tool. Fortunately, three theoretical structures were available to guide this development. (The theories are anchored in the philosophy of existentialism, which is concerned with an individual's existence: the nature of humanity, fearing the loss of individuality in mass society, and the loss of meaning in life.) The three psychological theories that lend themselves to the search for meaning in leisure and recreation are Rotter's (1954) Locus of Control, Maslow's (1954) Human Motivation, and Frankl's (1962) Man's Search for Meaning. Seven components were extracted from these theories: 1. Physical, 2. Mental (psychological or cognitive), 3. Social, 4. Spiritual (Frankl), 5. Esteem, 6. Self-actualization (Maslow), and 7. Locus of control or self-determination/self-responsibility (Rotter). Apparently, the three theories overlap a great deal in relating to these seven components.

Methodology Employed: Based on the available seven components and their large numbers of identified indicators, items were generated. Items were critically analyzed by the investigator, which was followed by critiques by nine judges for face and content validity. A five-point, Likert-type scale was used. Two pretests were conducted on samples of 127 and 133 subjects, yielding a scale ready for a final field test. To check concurrent validity, two theoretically relevant constructs to meaning were included: the *State Hope Scale* (Snyder et al., 1996) and *Psychological Well-Being* (Ryff, 1989). Statistically, factor analysis (Varimax rotation), alpha reliability coefficients, and correlations were used to analyze the data.

Findings: By utilizing the Scree test and Varimax rotation, six factors emerged, accounting for 58.8% of the variance. These factors and their loadings were Physical Fulfillment (.84 to .79), Self-Determination/Locus of Control (.78 to .43), Mental Realization (.76 to .44), Spiritual Reminiscence/Spiritual Exultation (.72 to .42), Social Meaning/Love and Belongingness (.64 to .45), and Esteem/Positive Image (.73 to .46). Alpha reliability coefficients (alpha) were performed for each subscale and their total. Alpha for Physical Fulfillment was .93, .84 for Self-Determination, .80 for Mental Relaxation, .84 for Spiritual Reminiscence, .84 for Social Meaning, and .69 for Self-Esteem. For the total scale (36 items), reliability was .94. Interfactor correlations among the six components ranged between .69 to .31, with a correlation coefficient square of 31.6% of the common variance. As to the concurrent validity, the *Search for Meaning in Leisure and Recreation* scale correlated .57 with the *State Hope Scale* and .62 with the *Psychological Well-Being Scale*. These two correlations are further evidence of the validity of *Search for Meaning in Leisure and Recreation* scale.

Investigator's Comments: Evidence provided supports the notion that multidimensionality of meaning is sought in leisure and recreation pursuits. Self-actualization, a hypothesized domain that was not confirmed, was distributed among other components. This is not a negative endorsement of self-actualization from respondents but rather a positive indication. In reality, self-actualization might achieve its meaning through a variety of domains (such as physical, social, and mental), an issue that warrants further study. Characterizations of Meaning in Leisure were identified in this study, making it a unique, concept-based look at the structure of its components. The psychometric qualities of the subscales and their total is from high to moderate besides achieving concurrent, content, and face validities. Validating the construct of the *Search for Meaning in Leisure and Recreation* is needed to ascertain its theoretical background, which might reveal variables that explain individual differences. Further investigations are suggested, as well as applications in field settings.

Scoring: This scale produces both a total score and subscale scores. While the theory behind the tool was proven to be strong, the actual meaning of the scores will need to be determined through further study. To obtain a score for the whole test, add up all the scores for the 36 items and divide the outcome by 36. For individual factors, add up the items in the factor (as shown on the assessment) and divide by the number of items.

Contact Information:
Dr. Mounir G. Ragheb
Recreation and Leisure Services Administration
Sport Management Recreation Management, and Physical Education
123 Tully Gym
Florida State University
Tallahassee, FL 32306-4280

Phone: 850-345-9682
Fax: 850-644-0975
Email: mragheb@fsu.edu

MEASURING THE SEARCH FOR MEANING IN LEISURE AND RECREATION
(MSMLR)

Ragheb, M.

Directions: The following statements refer to your leisure, recreation, and tourist activities. By "leisure and recreation," we mean nonobligatory pursuits chosen freely during your free time. Using the scale below, if you STRONGLY DISAGREE with the statement, write "1" on the answer sheet; if you STRONGLY AGREE, write "5." If your response is in between, write the number that corresponds to your answer. There are no right or wrong answers.

Strongly Disagree	Disagree	In Between	Agree	Strongly Agree
1	2	3	4	5

"Leisure activities" mean leisure, recreation, and tourist activities.

_____ 1.   Most of the time, I test my physical abilities through my leisure activities.

_____ 2.   Most of the time, my leisure activities are usually my personal responsibility.

_____ 3.   My leisure pursuits help me to discover new social meanings.

_____ 4.   I look back fondly and with admiration to what I used to do as leisure activities.

_____ 5.   It is interesting to do leisure activities with others.

_____ 6.   Most of the leisure activities I do help me to gain reasonable attention.

_____ 7.   Through leisure pursuits, I improve my physical abilities.

_____ 8.   Most of the time, I determine my own leisure choices.

_____ 9.   In evaluating my lifestyle, my engagement in leisure activities brings me closer to the reality of life.

_____ 10. Every now and then, I remember things about my past leisure experiences.

_____ 11. Most of the leisure activities I do help me to "hang in there."

_____ 12. Leisure activities give me a chance to be different.

_____ 13. Compared to other things in life, physical activities are important aspects in my leisure pursuits.

_____ 14. I usually have an enjoyable leisure activity to do.

_____ 15. In a variety of ways, my leisure pursuits help me to discover what I can do mentally.

_____ 16. No one can take from me the leisure experiences and memories I had.

_____ 17. Friends and family members are an enjoyable part of my leisure pursuits.

_____ 18. My social encounters through leisure make sense.

_____ 19. For me, most leisure pursuits help me to discover what I can do physically.

_____ 20. I often have some leisure choices that are worth my effort.

_____ 21. I always have future goals regarding what I am going to do as leisure activities.

_____ 22. It means a lot to me to remember how I did my past leisure activities, with whom, and where I did them.

_____ 23. I would not trade for anything what I get socially through leisure pursuits.

_____ 24. During my leisure engagements, I have a strong sense of humor.

_____ 25. I find it thrilling and exciting to be involved physically in my recreation activities.

_____ 26. Most of the time, I experience freedom in the choices of my leisure activities.

_____ 27. My leisure activities ignite and spark my life.

_____ 28. During my daily chores, ideas and images about my leisure activities come to my mind.

_____ 29. In many ways, leisure pursuits help me to get into significant relationships with others.

_____ 30. I am proud of developing physical fitness through my leisure activities.

_____ 31. Most of the time, leisure endeavors provide me with opportunities to express myself.

_____ 32. My leisure activities provide me with opportunities to learn.

_____ 33. Usually, memories of simple leisure experiences move me.

_____ 34. I see nature's beauty and aesthetics in the leisure activities I engage in.

_____ 35. For me, leisure activities have a lot of meaning and significance.

_____ 36. My emotions are usually centered on what I do as leisure choices.

To obtain subscale scores, add up all the scores for each subscale and divide by the number of items. Items constituting each of the six components are

Physical Fulfillment	Items 1, 7, 13, 19, 25, and 30
Self-Determination	Items 2, 8, 14, 20, 26, and 31
Mental Realization	Items 3, 9, 15, 21, 27, 32, and 34
Spiritual Reminiscence	Items 4, 10, 16, 22, 28, 33, 35, and 36
Social Meaning	Items 5, 11, 17, 23, and 29
Esteem/Positive Image	Items 6, 12, 18, and 24

Motivation 9

FREE TIME MOTIVATION SCALE FOR ADOLESCENTS (FTMS-A)

Cheryl K. Baldwin and Linda L. Caldwell

Reference: Baldwin, C. K. and Caldwell, L. L. (2003). Development of the free time motivation scale for adolescents. *Journal of Leisure Research, 35*, 129-152.

Goals of the Measurement: To assess the free time motivation of adolescents.

Background Literature: Teenagers' leisure motivation is complex. This scale is theory-based, employing Ryan and Deci's (2000) theory of self-determination. This theory accounts for intrinsic and extrinsic motivation. The intended measure of free time motivation is uniquely different from other existing scales. The developmental demands of adolescence make autonomy critical for individuality during one's free time. The conceptual framework of the self-determination theory lies in the innate needs of competence, relatedness, and autonomy. Optimal human functioning relies on the fulfillment of these needs. Two other theories were employed to explain intrinsic and extrinsic motivations: cognitive evaluation and organismic integration. Based on Deci and Ryan's theory, between intrinsic and extrinsic motivation there are four extrinsically motivated behaviors. They are external, introjected, identified, and integrated motivation. Non-intentional and non-regulated behavior —as a lower level motivation— is labeled amotivation.

Methodology Employed: FTMS-A was developed as a part of a leisure education program (The Wise: Learning Lifelong Leisure Skills) to prevent substance abuse among middle school students. A questionnaire was constructed, FTMS-A, based on five components: amotivation, external, introjected, identified, and intrinsic motivation. Pelletier et al. (1991) scale of high school, as well as other existing scales, was adapted to generate an item pool. Items were rated on a 5-point Likert scale. In a pilot study eight persons were interviewed after they completed the questionnaire for scale refinement. Respondents for the final field test were 634 grade seven students, 315 (49.7%) females. Statistical treatments started with internal reliability, then correlational and confirmatory factor analysis.

Findings: Five factors were confirmed: Amotivation (alpha reliability = .70), External (.79), Introjected (.69), Identified (.67), and Intrinsic (.68). Total scale reliability was .72.

Investigators' Comments: Subscales displayed acceptable measurement properties. Deletion of two items improved scale's validity. Further analysis is recommended to document reliability and validity. It is suggested that an item be developed to better capture the competence-based nature of introjected motivation.

Contact Information:
Dr. Cheryl K. Baldwin
Aurora University
Aurora, IL 60506

Phone: 630-892-6431
Email: cbaldwin@aurora.edu

FREE TIME MOTIVATION SCALE-FOR ADOLESCENTS (FTMS-A)

Baldwin, C. K. and Caldwell, L. L.

In this survey, we are asking you to think about your free time. Free time means things that you do outside of school. These can include after-school activities like sports or clubs, and activities like 4H, music, spending time with friends, reading, and watching TV.

Directions: Circle the answer that best reflects WHY you do what you do in your free time.

I DO WHAT I DO IN MY FREE TIME BECAUSE…

AMOTIVATION (AMT)
1. I don't know why I do my free time activities, and I don't really care.
2. I don't know, nothing much interests me.
3. I don't know, I have never really thought about it.
4. I don't know but it doesn't matter because I don't do much of anything.

EXTERNAL MOTIVATION (EXT)
1. I would get in trouble if I don't.
2. I am supposed to.
3. That is the rule in my house.
4. So others won't get mad at me.
5. My parents expect me to.

**SAMPLE
Do Not Copy**

INTROJECTED MOTIVATION (IJ)
1. I want people to think I am good at what I do.
2. I will feel badly about myself if I don't.
3. I want to impress my friends.
4. I want people to like me.
5. I want to earn rewards, medals, trophies, or certificates.

IDENTIFIED MOTIVATION (ID)
1. I want to understand how things work.
2. What I do is important to me.
3. I develop skills that I can use later in life.
4. The activities help me develop into the person I want to become.

INTRINSIC MOTIVATION (INT)
1. I want to have fun.
2. I enjoy what I do.
3. I like what I do.
4. I want to.

Motivation 10

FITNESS LOCUS OF CONTROL SCALE
(FITLOC)
James R. Whitehead and Charles B. Corbin

Reference: Whitehead, J. R., and Corbin, C. B. (1988). Multidimensional scales for the measurement of locus of control of reinforcements for physical fitness behavior. *Research Quarterly for Exercise and Sport, 59,* 108-117.

Goal of the Measurement: To assess locus of control of reinforcement beliefs for physical fitness behaviors that usually take place during individuals' free time.

Background Literature: The main foundation for the development of the FITLOC is Rotter's (1954) theory of internal versus external locus of control of reinforcement. The theory proposed that the locus of control was unidimensional, with an individual's beliefs falling somewhere along a continuum ranging from internal perceived control to external perceived control. However, Levenson (1973, 1974, 1975) demonstrated the advantages of separating the external pole of the locus of control construct into two dimensions: chance (C) and powerful others (PO). The pioneering modification advanced the view of simple unidimensionality to a more realistic multidimensional reality. Literature boiled down to three identified domains as bases for FITLOC: Internal (I), Powerful Others (PO), and Chance (C). Fitness pursuits presented here are not exclusive for athletes and sport performances, but also include those done leisurely as a recreational choice.

Methodology Employed: Generated items were evaluated regarding their merit by four experts (content validity), suggesting possible modifications based on this definition of physical fitness behavior: any behaviors that would be likely to result in a change in a subject's organic physical fitness status. These processes yielded an 18-item instrument to be empirically verified. A 6-point Likert-type scale was used: "1" for "Strongly Disagree" and "6" for "Strongly Agree." Two pretest trials were conducted to ensure the factor structure and the reliability of the scale (115 and 111 student responses were utilized). For the final phase, a sample comprised of 133 persons (67 male) responded to the scale. Two other measures were included for testing concurrent validity. A principal component analysis with Varimax rotation, alpha reliability coefficient, and an item discrimination analysis were performed.

Findings: The three conceptual components were confirmed as factors demonstrating the construct of FITLOC. Item loadings were in the .70s and .80s, except one (.44). Test-retest reliability of subscales ranged between .75 and .59, and the alpha reliability coefficients ranged between .84 and .62. Concurrent validity with the two other scales was demonstrated.

Investigator's Comments: The instrument has a theoretically sound foundation. However, generalizability is limited due to having a sample that included only students.

FITNESS LOCUS OF CONTROL SCALE (FITLOC)

Whitehead, J. and Corbin, C.

This is a sample with 11 of the 18 items on the scale. Developers of the scale should be contacted for the complete scale, including exact wording of the directions.

DIRECTIONS: Select a number between 1 (Strongly Disagree) and 6 (Strongly Agree) to show how much you agree with each statement.

Strongly Agree   **Strongly Disagree**

1   2   3   4   5   6

_____ 1. By carefully planning my behavior I can maintain my physical fitness at the level I choose.

_____ 2. I have the power to change my physical fitness status through self-planned, self-directed behaviors.

_____ 3. Carefully self-planned, self-directed behaviors enable me to control my physical fitness as I like.

_____ 4. My physical fitness is determined by those of my behaviors which are a result of the expectations of others.

_____ 5. Somebody who is powerful or important to me controls the personal behaviors that affect my physical fitness.

_____ 6. People who have a considerable influence on me determine whether I behave in ways that affect my physical fitness status.

_____ 7. Friends, parents, or group leaders determine my physical fitness because of their influence or control over my behaviors.

_____ 8. The personal behaviors that affect my physical fitness status are determined by luck, chance, fate, or daily circumstances.

_____ 9. It is just a matter of chance if I behave in a way that will change my physical fitness status.

_____ 10. My physical fitness status is mostly the result of behaviors determined by luck or circumstances.

_____ 11. Chance determines the personal behaviors that affect my physical fitness status.

Components of the scale are as follows:

Internal Locus of Control	= Items 1-3
Powerful Others Locus of Control	= Items 4-7
Chance Locus of Control	= Items 8-11

Motivation 11

RACQUET SPORTS COMPETENCE SCALE (RSCS)

part of the

PERCEIVED COMPETENCE AND SATISFACTION MEASURES FOR RACQUET SPORTS

Teresita E. Aguilar and Elizabeth Petrakis

Reference: Aguilar, T. E. and Petrakis, E. (1989). Development and initial validation of perceived competence and satisfaction measures for racquet sports. *Journal of Leisure Research, 21*, 77-91.

Goal of the Measurement: To assess perceived skills (competence) and rewards gained (satisfaction) from participation in racquet sports: tennis, badminton, and racquetball.

Conceptual Background: This investigation answered the following question: What tends to influence an individual's selection and frequent participation in a physical activity? One of the assumptions was that skill level and/or positive experience (intrinsic pleasure) can influence selection and participation in activities. Harter's model was utilized, illustrating that there are interrelationships among motivation, mastery attempts, perceived competence or lack of it, resulting in either intrinsic pleasure (enjoyment) or anxiety. Consequently, pleasure and enjoyment feedback were assumed to motivate positively, while anxiety was assumed to impact negatively.

Methodology Employed: Item development was based on informal interviews with racquet sport players and observation. A total of 20 items were drafted, employing a five-point, Likert scale, from 1=Almost Never to 5=Almost Always. A pilot study was conducted on 36 students; a second pilot study was performed on 26 students. A further revision was done, making items generic to all racquet sports instead of just tennis or racquetball. The revised 20-item scale was utilized to collect data in two consecutive field tests: 1. a sample of 163 students; 2. another sample of 208 students. Factor analysis and Cronbach alpha reliability were performed to statistically test the structure of the scale.

Findings: Factor analysis, oblique rotation, yielded three factors: Competence (ability), Satisfaction, and Sport Enjoyment. The last two factors (satisfaction and sport enjoyment) were considered as satisfaction obtained. Alpha reliability coefficient was .90 for the 10-item competence subscale, and .74 for satisfaction, including sport enjoyment. Content and face validity were achieved through the evaluation of the review panel. Two other validations were reported: criterion-referenced and construct.

Investigator's Comments: Since the satisfaction scale was reduced to a six-item scale, its validity should be addressed in future studies. Moreover, the scale needs to be validated on backgrounds other than students to represent different ages (childhood, teens, adults, and older persons) and other types of populations. Finally, the issue of concurrent validity should be addressed further.

Contact Information:
Dr. Teresita E. Aguilar, Dean
School of Professional Studies
Our Lady of the Lake University
411 S.W. 24th St.
San Antonio, TX 78207
Phone: 210-431-4140
Fax: 210-431-3962
Email: teaguilar@ollusa.edu

RACQUET SPORTS COMPETENCE SCALE
(RSCS)
Aguilar, T. E. and Petrakis, E.

DIRECTIONS: Developers of the scale should be contacted for the directions.

Never	Almost Never	Sometimes	Almost Always	Always
1	2	3	4	5

_____ 1. I can use a variety of good shots.
_____ 2. I can give anyone a good match.
_____ 3. I can use good strategy.
_____ 4. I am good enough to play in a tournament.
_____ 5. I can make my opponent run.
_____ 6. I can play well in the forecourt.
_____ 7. I have the ability to beat players who have stronger skills than I have.
_____ 8. I can change the pace of the game.
_____ 9. I can beat players who have weaker skills than I have.
_____ 10. I can use a variety of serves.
_____ 11. I am satisfied with my skills in this sport.
_____ 12. I enjoy playing only when I win.

SAMPLE
Do Not Copy

| Motivation 12 |

MOTIVATIONS FOR PARTICIPATION IN RECREATIONAL RUNNING SCALE (MPRRS)

Peter Clough, John Shepherd, and Ronald Maughan

Reference: Clough, P., Shepherd, J., and Maughan, R. (1990). Motives for participation in recreational running. *Journal of Leisure Research, 21*, 297-309.

Goal of the Measurement: To assess individuals' motives (reasons) for participating in recreational running.

Conceptual Background: Due to public demand for recreational physical activities and exercise, it would be useful to know the main reasons behind that popularity. Instead of mainly relying on a theory to construct the instrument, the investigators used mostly personal interviews and extracted reasons recognized in the literature that explain why individuals engage in leisure and other relevant choices, such as sports.

Methodology Employed: Based on personal interviews, categories and indicators were identified to draft items. Two main sources of indicators were used. The first was the literature on leisure, exercise, and running. The second was through a series of face-to-face interviews with 100 volunteers (runners and physically active persons). These two sources yielded 105 items. A pilot study employing 25 runners was conducted. A debriefing session was used to revise, modify, and reduce the scale to 81 items. A five-point scale was used, ranging from "No Influence" scored as "1"; to "Very Strong Influence" scored as "5." The questionnaire was mailed to 250; 173, mostly males, replied. Factor analysis resulted in six factors, and items were reduced to 70 for the final verification on 357 subjects.

Findings: Through factor analysis, the six pretested components were confirmed, accounting for 51% of the variance. Factors for running motivation were named as Well Being, Social, Challenge, Status, Addiction, and Fitness/Health. Only face and content validity were reported.

Investigator's Comments: The motivational categories identified in this study appear to support and extend the findings of prior research into running motivation. Moreover, the results indicate that running shares many of the motivations that underlie leisure-time activities in general.

MOTIVATIONS FOR PARTICIPATION IN RECREATIONAL RUNNING SCALE (MPRRS)

Clough, P.; Shepherd, J.; and Maughan, R.

DIRECTIONS: Please endorse each item as to its influence on your desire to be actively involved in running. If what the item represents has "No Influence," mark 1; if it has "Very Strong Influence," mark 5; and if you are between the above two, choose the number that represents your response.

No Influence	Slight Influence	Some Influence	Strong Influence	Very Strong Influence
1	2	3	4	5

MOTIVATION ITEMS:

(I) Well Being
_____ 1. It brings me peace of mind.
_____ 2. It helps me to understand myself better.
_____ 3. It enlivens my mind.
_____ 4. It gives me a chance to control my life.
_____ 5. It improves my general mood.
_____ 6. It gives me feelings of independence.
_____ 7. It helps me feel less anxious.
_____ 8. I enjoy the state of mind experienced whilst doing it.
_____ 9. It gives me an opportunity to be totally absorbed.
_____ 10. It increases my discipline.
_____ 11. It helps me to relax.
_____ 12. It makes me feel more confident.

SAMPLE
Do Not Copy

(II) Social
_____ 13. It allows me to meet new people.
_____ 14. It allows me to share ideas and feelings with someone.
_____ 15. It allows me to share skills and knowledge with someone.
_____ 16. It allows me to maintain old friendships.
_____ 17. It provides me with interesting experiences which I can tell my friends about.
_____ 18. It improves my close personal relationships.
_____ 19. It enables me to benefit the community.
_____ 20. It provides me with a feeling of belonging.
_____ 21. I receive encouragement and support from other people.
_____ 22. It allows me some sort of artistic expression.

(III) Challenge
_____ 23. It gives me a sense of achievement.
_____ 24. It brings me a chance to compete with others.
_____ 25. It is an activity in which you see the results of your efforts.
_____ 26. It gives me a chance to learn what I am capable of.
_____ 27. It provides me with a physical challenge.
_____ 28. It allows me to compete against myself.
_____ 29. I feel that I'm getting better at it.

No Influence	Slight Influence	Some Influence	Strong Influence	Very Strong Influence
1	2	3	4	5

(IV) Status

_____ 30. It makes me feel superior.

_____ 31. It makes me feel special or important.

_____ 32. It brings me recognition from others.

_____ 33. It allows me some influence over other people.

(V) Addiction

_____ 34. I feel anxious, irritable, or depressed if I stop.

_____ 35. I feel guilty if I stop.

_____ 36. I feel bloated if I stop.

_____ 37. I feel physically unwell if I stop.

_____ 38. I feel I should do it.

_____ 39. It has become a habit.

(VI) Fitness/Health

_____ 40. It keeps me healthy.

_____ 41. It helps keep me fit.

_____ 42. It helps me prolong my life.

_____ 43. It improves my physical appearance.

_____ 44. It helps ward off the effects of old age.

_____ 45. It gives me more energy in my other activities.

SAMPLE
Do Not Copy

Motivation 13

EXERCISE DECISIONAL BALANCE MEASURE (EDBM)

Bess H. Marcus, William Rakowski, and Joseph S. Rossi

Reference: Marcus, B. H., Rakowski, W., and Rossi, J. S. (1992). Assessing motivational readiness and decision making for exercise. *Health Psychology, 11,* 257-261.

Goal of the Measurement: To assess the decisional balance aspect of the transtheoretical model to be applied to exercise adoption.

Background Literature: Exercising influences diseases and conditions affecting both physical and mental health. Two concerns are of interest: 1. How to get people to initiate exercise behavior and 2. When they are active, how to maintain their exercise behavior. This study attempted to extend the transtheoretical model (Prochaska and DiClemente, 1983) to other health-related behaviors, such as exercise-changing behavior, from pre-contemplation, contemplation, preparation, action, to maintenance. The model identifies a set of outcomes that includes decisional balance — the pros and cons of behavior change. The pros and cons are the bases for the instrument developed.

Methodology Employed: A pool of about 75 items was generated, covering the positives (pros) and negatives (cons) of exercise. Items went through critical review and analysis by the investigators, arriving at a final pool of 40 items, of which 20 represented the pros of exercising. A 5-point Likert scale was utilized: "Not At All Important" at 1 to "Extremely Important" at 5. Analysis was based on a sample of 778 subjects (54% female, with an average age of 41.5 years, and 70% married). Employees received a letter from their chief executive officers inviting them to participate in the study, achieving a response rate of 66%.

Findings: A principle component analysis with a Varimax rotation was employed, demonstrating two interpretable factors (explaining 60.4% of the total variance). Six items clustered together, representing what can be unfavorable perceptions (cons) of exercise and reasons not to exercise. Ten other items represented a positive perception (pros) of exercise. Alpha reliability coefficient of the cons subscale was .79 and for the pros was .95.

Investigator's Comments: The scale comprised of 16 items provided indices with adequate empirical properties and conceptual fit to the transtheoretical model of behavior change. It is suggested that other versions be developed, to test reliability and validity of other scales of the same nature, on the bases of the above model.

Note: As an essential part of active leisure lifestyles, fitness and exercise are increasing in value and use as free time pursuits. Therefore, it is necessary for recreation and leisure practitioners to comprehend the concepts of fitness and exercise, assess them, and use strategies to maximize rewards gained from exercise.

Contact Information:
Dr. Bess H. Marcus, Director
Division of Behavioral Medicine
The Miriam Hospital
Brown University
RISE Building
164 Summit Ave.
Providence, RI 02906

Phone: 401-793-8003
Fax: 401-793-8560
Email: Bmarcus@lifespan.org

EXERCISE DECISIONAL BALANCE MEASURE
(EDBM)

Marcus, B. H.; Rakowski, W.; and Rossi, J. S.

<u>DIRECTIONS</u>: How important are each of the following statements, regarding your decision to exercise or not? Mark "1" if it is **Not At All Important**, mark "5" if it is **Extremely Important**, and choose the corresponding number if you are between 1 and 5, as illustrated by the following scale.

Not at All Important				Extremely Important
1	2	3	4	5

<u>Pros</u>
_____ 1. I would have more energy for my family and friends if I exercised regularly.
_____ 2. Regular exercise would help me relieve tension.
_____ 3. I would feel more confident if I exercised regularly.
_____ 4. I would sleep more soundly if I exercised regularly.
_____ 5. I would feel good about myself if I kept my commitment to exercise regularly.
_____ 6. I would like my body better if I exercised regularly.
_____ 7. It would be easier for me to perform routine physical tasks if I exercised regularly.
_____ 8. I would feel less stressed if I exercised regularly.
_____ 9. I would feel more comfortable with my body if I exercised regularly.
_____ 10. Regular exercise would help me have a more positive outlook on life.

<u>Cons</u>
_____ 11. I think I would be too tired to do my daily work after exercising.
_____ 12. I would find it difficult to find an exercise activity that I enjoy that is not affected by bad weather.
_____ 13. I feel uncomfortable when I exercise because I get out of breath and my heart beats very fast.
_____ 14. Regular exercise would take too much of my time.
_____ 15. I would have less time for my family and friends if I exercised regularly.
_____ 16. At the end of the day, I am too exhausted to exercise.

* Directions are summarized from the technical report in *Health Psychology, 11*, 257-261.

Motivation 14

EXERCISE IDENTITY SCALE
(EIS)

Dean. F. Anderson and Charles M. Cychosz

Reference: Anderson, D. F. and Cychosz, C. M. (1994). Development of an Exercise Identity Scale. *Perceptual and Motor Skills*, *78*, 747-751.

Goal of the Measurement: To assess the salience or strength of the role of exerciser or exercise behavior as an integral part of one's concept of self. This scale can be used in the exercise and health promotion areas to differentiate individuals that are likely to drop out of programs from individuals that are more likely to adhere to exercise behavior.

Background Literature: Health care costs in the United States have topped $1 trillion and physical inactivity is a major contributor to these increasing costs. Low participation and persistence in physical activity programs has led researchers to explore a number of theoretical models including social cognitive theory, personal investment theory, the health belief model, and theory of planned behavior as a basis for explaining the process of adopting exercise as part of one's lifestyle. To date, this research has met with only limited success (Dishman, 1990).

Methodology Employed: A primary tenet of identity theory is that an individual's concept of self is comprised of multiple role-identities that give meaning to one's past behavior and provide direction for future behavior (Ervin and Stryker, 2001). The Exercise Identity Scale (EIS) was developed to measure the salience or importance of exercise behavior related to one's concept of self. Items aimed at exploring the place exercise behavior has in the hierarchy of multiple role-identities were developed. Items and scale are listed below. Initially data were collected from 51 college students. Exploratory factor analysis and Cronbach's alpha were utilized to assess internal consistency. Self-reported measures of exercise behavior were used to examine validity.

Findings: Exploratory factor analysis yielded a single factor model with loadings between .91 and .62. Cronbach's alpha was .94. One-week test-retest reliability was .93. Assessment of the relationship between exercise identity scores and self-reported indicators of exercise behavior documented evidence for validity.

Investigator Comments: Additional research utilizing 441 law enforcement employees (Anderson, Cychosz, and Franke, 1998), 1253 employees at a large financial services corporation (Anderson, Cychosz, and Franke, 2001), and 505 community residents (Anderson, Cychosz, and Franke, 2000) supports the findings for college students. The EIS is a valid measure across a wide variety of populations, making it a valuable addition to the exercise adherence instruments available.

Note: The literature on long-term adoption and maintenance of exercise seems to be controversial and intriguing. Scientists suggest that practitioners devise a variety of strategies to attract individuals to exercise and to pay attention to their fitness. The reasons include physical and mental health benefits, attempting to increase the percentage of participation to more than 25%, which was one of the goals of this series of studies.

This issue will remain controversial until we address some realistic points: What is the national goal for exercise and fitness? Is it satisfactory to reach 80% or 90% participation levels? Perhaps just 25% to 40% is logical and reasonable for two reasons. 1. It is a military boot-camp lifestyle to have 80% or more participation rate, ignoring individuals' freedom of choice, changing needs, and life cycles. 2. Due to the nature of life, which we have not realized fully, individuals follow a pattern of behavior in engaging in leisure lifestyles. In assessing motivational readiness and decision making for exercise, Marcus et al. (1992) identified, based on the transtheoretical model, five stages of exercise-changing behavior: Pre-contemplation, Contemplation, Preparation, Action, and Maintenance. Accordingly and realistically, in any given period of time, individuals will be distributed on those five stages, swinging back and forth.

Moreover, it seems that the literature on leisure behavior accumulated some interesting answers. Available explanations can give practical insights in strategizing attempts to increase fitness and exercise participation, as well as attracting individuals to be involved in other leisure pursuits.

More than thirty years ago, Kelly (1974, 1977) presented evidence that participation in leisure activities were evenly divided among those begun as children and those begun in adult years. In other words, individuals maintain 50% of what they were exposed to in earlier stages of life, while introducing 50% of new activities. This notion is explained as the need for novelty and stimulus seeking (Ellis, 1973). Also, Wyman (1982) introduced the concept of interchangeability as the basis for new choices: People can find similar satisfaction when they substitute activities in one area for experiences in another. Later on, Iso-Ahola (1986), in a theory of substitutability of leisure behavior, postulated the following: Substitution means that the originally intended or desired behavior is no longer possible and must be replaced if leisure involvement is to continue.

In sum, for practitioners offering physical recreation, leisure and exercise lifestyles should be realized carefully, to establish realistic goals for percentages of individuals who engage in active pursuits. Further, individuals must be enabled when going through stages of Pre-contemplation, Contemplation, or Preparation to actualize these stages and remove potential constraints. This will maximize the benefits (satisfaction) of exercise and fitness as important pursuits in leisure lifestyles.

Contact Information:
Dr. Dean F. Anderson
Department of Health and Human Performance
Iowa State University
Ames, IA 50011

Phone: 515-294-3427
Fax: 515-294-8740
Email: deanf@iastate.edu

EXERCISE IDENTITY SCALE
(EIS)
Anderson, D. F. and Cychosz, C. M.

DIRECTIONS: Please indicate in the space provided the response that best describes yourself and how you feel. For each item indicate on a scale from (1) disagree to (7) agree, how you feel.

	Disagree					Agree	
	1	2	3	4	5	6	7
1. I consider myself an exerciser.	1	2	3	4	5	6	7
2. When I describe myself to other people, I usually include my involvement in physical activity.	1	2	3	4	5	6	7
3. I have numerous goals related to exercising.	1	2	3	4	5	6	7
4. Physical exercise is a central factor to my self-concept.	1	2	3	4	5	6	7
5. I need to exercise to feel good about myself.	1	2	3	4	5	6	7
6. Other people see me as someone who exercises regularly.	1	2	3	4	5	6	7
7. For me, being an exerciser means more than just exercising	1	2	3	4	5	6	7
8. I would feel a loss if I were forced to give up exercising.	1	2	3	4	5	6	7
9. Exercise is something I think about often.	1	2	3	4	5	6	7

| Motivation 15 |

THE FLOW STATE SCALE
(FSS)

Susan A. Jackson and Herbert W. Marsh

Reference: Jackson, S. A., and Marsh, H. W. (1996). Development and validation of a scale to measure optimal experience: The Flow State Scale. *Journal of Sport and Exercise Psychology, 18,* 17-35.

Goal of the Measurement: To assess the flow state in sport and physical activity settings.

Background Literature: Flow as an optimal psychological state has been used in a variety of life activities. Theorizing on the characteristics of positive flow, Csikszentmihalyi (1976) helped to produce nine dimensions relevant to physical activity and sports. These nine dimensions resulted from a study on elite athletes using qualitative content analysis, to be tested and verified on participants of physical activity and any level of sport engagement.

Methodology Employed: Items were developed to reflect the nine dimensions that were referred to: Challenge-Skill Balance, Action-Awareness Merging, Clear Goals, Unambiguous Feedback, Concentration on Task at Hand, Sense of Control, Loss of Self-Consciousness, Transformation of Time, and Autotelic Experience. Definitions of the nine domains, concepts of flow, and results of interviews were pooled to create an initial scale (54 items) to measure flow with six items per dimension. For content validity, seven referees evaluated the scale for relevance of items to their dimensions. A pilot study (n = 252) was conducted on active participants in either recreational physical activities at club level or in regional, state, and national representations. The final verification utilized a sample of 394 persons, 244 from the United States and 150 from Australia. A five-point, Likert-type scale was employed, ranging from "Strongly Disagree" "1" to "Strongly Agree" "5." Confirmatory factor analysis and coefficient alpha estimates were utilized to test the construct of FSS.

Findings: The confirmatory factor analysis provided a reasonable fit of responses to the 36-item scale, better than the total 54 items. Coefficient alpha estimates for the nine subscales ranged between .86 and .80, with a reported mean of .83, and "Total" including all items together.

Investigator's Comments: Founders of the scale addressed the classical issue of global score versus specific scores on components. They pointed to the importance of a single global measure similar to that reported when assessing intelligence, yet no knowledge on the properties of the global structure, scores, or measure was reported. Scale developers identified a limitation citing Csikszentmihalyi, cautioning against putting too much weight on any empirical measures of flow, lest the experience of flow be lost in the process. More work needs to be conducted that goes beyond FSS, comparing data of different methods, such as observation, diaries, interviews, and current standardized tests.

Because "Neither Agree nor Disagree" may mean "No Response" or "Irrelevant," it is suggested using "In Between" when choosing a mid-point between "Disagree" and "Agree."

Note: A standardized procedure must be followed whenever it is appropriate, especially regarding analysis and information on global measures and their components as parts of the measurement construction. Uses, applications, and logical reviews can determine the scope of reliance on global measures and/or components.

Contact Information:
Dr. Susan A. Jackson
School of Human Movement Studies
Queensland University of Technology
Victoria Park Road
Kelvin, OLD, Australia 4059

Phone: 61-7-3864-3508
Fax: 61-7-3864-3980
Email: sjackson@hms.uq.edu.au

THE FLOW STATE SCALE
(FSS)

Jackson, S. A. and Marsh, H. W.

DIRECTIONS: Please answer the following questions in relation to your experience in the event you have just completed. These questions relate to the thoughts and feelings you may have experienced during the event. There are no right or wrong answers. Think about how you felt during the event and answer the questions using the rating scale below. Circle the number that best matches your experience from the options below each question.

Strongly Disagree	Disagree	Neither Disagree Nor Agree	Agree	Strongly Agree
1	2	3	4	5

1. I was challenged, but I believed my skills would allow me to meet the challenge.
    1   2   3   4   5
2. I made the correct movements without thinking about trying to do so.
    1   2   3   4   5
3. I knew clearly what I wanted to do.
    1   2   3   4   5
4. It was really clear to me that I was doing well.
    1   2   3   4   5
5. My attention was focused entirely on what I was doing.
    1   2   3   4   5
6. I felt in total control of what I was doing.
    1   2   3   4   5
7. I was not concerned with what others may have been thinking of me.
    1   2   3   4   5
8. Time seemed to alter (either slowed down or speeded up).
    1   2   3   4   5
9. I really enjoyed the experience.
    1   2   3   4   5
10. My abilities matched the high challenge of the situation.
    1   2   3   4   5
11. Things just seemed to be happening automatically.
    1   2   3   4   5
12. I had a strong sense of what I wanted to do.
    1   2   3   4   5
13. I was aware of how well I was performing.
    1   2   3   4   5
14. It was no effort to keep my mind on what was happening.
    1   2   3   4   5
15. I felt like I could control what I was doing.
    1   2   3   4   5
16. I was not worried about my performance during the event.
    1   2   3   4   5
17. The way time passed seemed to be different from normal.
    1   2   3   4   5
18. I loved the feeling of that performance and want to capture it again.
    1   2   3   4   5
19. I felt I was competent enough to meet the high demands of the situation.
    1   2   3   4   5
20. I performed automatically.
    1   2   3   4   5

Strongly Disagree	Disagree	Neither Disagree Nor Agree		Strongly Agree
1	2	3	4	5

21. I knew what I wanted to achieve.
    1   2   3   4   5
22. I had a good idea while I was performing about how well I was doing.
    1   2   3   4   5
23. I had total concentration.
    1   2   3   4   5
24. I had a feeling of total control.
    1   2   3   4   5
25. I was not concerned with how I was presenting myself.
    1   2   3   4   5
26. It felt like time stopped while I was performing.
    1   2   3   4   5
27. The experience left me feeling great.
    1   2   3   4   5
28. The challenge and my skills were at an equally high level.
    1   2   3   4   5
29. I did things spontaneously and automatically without having to think.
    1   2   3   4   5
30. My goals were clearly defined.
    1   2   3   4   5
31. I could tell by the way I was performing how well I was doing.
    1   2   3   4   5
32. I was completely focused on the task at hand.
    1   2   3   4   5
33. I felt in total control of my body.
    1   2   3   4   5
34. I was not worried about what others may have been thinking of me.
    1   2   3   4   5
35. At times, it almost seemed like things were happening in slow motion.
    1   2   3   4   5
36. I found the experience extremely rewarding.
    1   2   3   4   5

SAMPLE
Do Not Copy

| Motivation 16 |

THE EXERCISE MOTIVATION INVENTORY-2 (EMI-2)

David Markland and David K. Ingledew

Reference: Markland, D., and Ingledew, D. K. (1997). The measurement of exercise motives: Factorial validity and variance across gender of a revised Exercise Motivations Inventory. *British Journal of Health Psychology, 2*, 361-376.

Goal of the Measurement: To assess exercise motivation.

Background Literature: Concerning the motives for adherence to exercise, research evidence has been accumulated documenting physical and psychological benefits. Based on Deci and Ryan (1985, 1990), self-determination theory, intrinsic, and extrinsic motives of exercise adherence were discussed. A wide range of methodological strategies were presented, demonstrating the identification and reliance on multivariate structures to assess exercise motivations. Identified structures ranged from 12 to three components: Enjoyment, Competence, and Body-Related motives (Frederick and Ryan, 1993). Markland and Hardy (1993) constructed the Exercise Motivations Inventory (EMI) to fill gaps in prior scales. Despite the fact that EMI demonstrated promise in relation to many other important variables, some structural weaknesses were identified and elaborately presented. Therefore, it was appropriate for one of its initial developers and a colleague to revise EMI. The revised scale accommodated for exercisers and non-exercisers alike to motivate initial involvement or re-involvement.

Methodology Employed: Three phases were utilized to improve and refine the original EMI. Many indicators were identified to be developed as a part of the new pool of items. Fitness and health pressures as a factor required additional indicators (items) to broaden it. Many new parts were added, recognizing their indicators sufficiently. Moreover, the items were modified to accommodate for non-exercisers. As a part of a larger study, data was collected from 425 respondents to verify the EMI's original 44 items and the added 25 new items. Fourteen factors were hypothesized as the exercise motivational structure. Statistics employed to test the scale's structure were factorial validity through LISREL alpha reliability coefficients, inter-item correlations, and subscales correlation.

Findings: The hypothesized factor structure of Exercise Motivation Inventory-2 (EMI-2) was confirmed, yielding these 14 components: Stress Management, Revitalization, Enjoyment, Challenge, Social Recognition, Affiliation, Competition, Health Pressures, Ill-Health Avoidance, Positive Health, Weight Management, Appearance, Strength, and Nimbleness. All components obtained very adequate reliability coefficients, ranging between .95 and .83, with one exception — Health Pressures — a bit lower at .69.

Investigator's Comments: Following the deletion of irrelevant statements, items clustered under their factors. Evidence here and elsewhere suggests that it is difficult to categorize some motives as exclusively intrinsic or extrinsic. A current study found that there were sufficient correlations between an extrinsic factor (Social Recognition) and four other intrinsic factors (e.g., Challenge). Moreover, many factors do not seem to belong to either orientation. Investigators suggested following Deci and Ryan's (1985, 1990) theorization of behavioral regulation, ranging from Completely Non-Self-Determined to Completely Self-Determined. Current subscales attempted to account — validly and reliably — for this diversity of motives.

Contact Information:
Dr. David A. Markland, Director of Research Studies
School of Sport, Health and Exercise Sciences, George Building
University of Wales
Bangor, Gwynedd LL57 2PX, Wales, UK.

Phone (from the USA):   011-44-1248-382756.

Fax (from USA):   011-44-1248-371053.
Email: d.a.markland@bangor.ac.uk
Web: www.bangor.ac.uk/~pes004/emi_info.htm

THE EXERCISE MOTIVATION INVENTORY-2
(EMI-2)

Markland, D. and Ingledew, D. K.

DIRECTIONS: On the following pages are a number of statements concerning the reasons people often give when asked why they exercise. *Whether you currently exercise regularly or not,* please read each statement carefully and indicate, by circling the appropriate number, whether or not each statement *is true* for you personally, *or would be true* for you personally if you did exercise. If you do not consider a statement to be true for you at all, circle the "0." If you think that a statement is very true for you indeed, circle the "5." If you think that a statement is partly true for you, then circle the "1," "2," "3," or "4," according to how strongly you feel that it reflects why you exercise or might exercise.

Remember, we want to know why *you personally* choose to exercise or might choose to exercise, not whether you think the statements are good reasons for *anybody* to exercise.

Not at all true for me					Very true for me
0	1	2	3	4	5

Personally, I exercise (or might exercise)…

_____ 1. To stay slim
_____ 2. To avoid ill-health
_____ 3. Because it makes me feel good
_____ 4. To help me look younger
_____ 5. To show my worth to others
_____ 6. To give me a space to think
_____ 7. To have a healthy body
_____ 8. To build up my strength
_____ 9. Because I enjoy the feeling of exerting myself
_____ 10. To spend time with friends
_____ 11. Because my doctor advised me to exercise
_____ 12. Because I like trying to win in physical activities
_____ 13. To stay/become more agile
_____ 14. To give me goals to work towards
_____ 15. To lose weight
_____ 16. To prevent health problems
_____ 17. Because I find exercise invigorating
_____ 18. To have a good body
_____ 19. To compare my abilities with others peoples'
_____ 20. Because it helps to reduce tension
_____ 21. Because I want to maintain good health
_____ 22. To increase my endurance
_____ 23. Because I find exercising satisfying in and of itself
_____ 24. To enjoy the social aspects of exercising
_____ 25. To help prevent an illness that runs in my family
_____ 26. Because I enjoy competing
_____ 27. To maintain flexibility
_____ 28. To give me personal challenges to face
_____ 29. To help control my weight
_____ 30. To avoid heart disease
_____ 31. To recharge my batteries
_____ 32. To improve my appearance

Not at all true for me					Very true for me
0	1	2	3	4	5

Personally, I exercise (or might exercise)…

_____ 33. To gain recognition for my accomplishments
_____ 34. To help manage stress
_____ 35. To feel more healthy
_____ 36. To get stronger
_____ 37. For enjoyment of the experience of exercising
_____ 38. To have fun being active with other people
_____ 39. To help recover from an illness/injury
_____ 40. Because I enjoy physical competition
_____ 41. To stay/become flexible
_____ 42. To develop personal skills
_____ 43. Because exercise helps me to burn calories
_____ 44. To look more attractive
_____ 45. To accomplish things that others are incapable of
_____ 46. To release tension
_____ 47. To develop my muscles
_____ 48. Because I feel at my best when exercising
_____ 49. To make new friends
_____ 50. Because I find physical activities fun, especially when competition is involved
_____ 51. To measure myself against personal standards

SAMPLE Do Not Copy

Motivation 17

BEHAVIORAL REGULATION IN EXERCISE QUESTIONNAIRE (BREQ)

Elaine Mullan, David Markland, and David K. Ingledew

Reference: Mullan, E., Markland, D., and Ingledew, D. K. (1997). A graded conceptualization of self-determination in the regulation of exercise behaviour: Development of a measure using confirmatory factor analytic procedures. *Personality and Individual Differences, 23*, 745-752.

Goal of the Measurement: To assess behavioral regulation in exercise.

Background Literature: For the widespread appreciation of exercise, many attempts were made to explain its motivation on the basis of self-determination theory. Reliance solely on the concept of intrinsic motivation began to wane with the incorporation of the influence of extrinsic motivation. A new theoretical structure was born out of Deci et al.'s self-determination concept called Organismic Integration Theory (OIT) that proposes a variety of motivations. OIT outlines forms of behavioral regulation such as external, introjected, identified, and integrated. When placed on a continuum, they range from non-self-determined at one extreme, to being completely self-determined motivation at the other extreme.

Methodology Employed: An initial modified pool of 30 items was derived from the Academic Motivation Scale by Vallerand et al. (1992) and Self-Regulation Questionnaire for academic settings by Ryan et al. (1989). Items were scored on a five-point, Likert-type scale, ranging from *not true for me* (0) to *very true for me* (4). A sample of 298 (mostly employees and students) was drawn from attendees at a local sports center. Confirmatory factor analysis, internal consistency, and discriminant validity were utilized to test the psychometric values of the scale.

Findings: In the first of the two studies, the subscale amotivational regulation was eliminated from further consideration, just because items were irrelevant to the sample. Four other factors (15 items) were endorsed: external regulation, introjected regulation, identified regulation, and intrinsic regulation, with Cronbach's alpha reliability coefficient ranging from .90 to .76. Discriminant validity was found with reference to subscale inter-correlations. Similar results were obtained by utilizing a sample of 310 white- and blue-collar workers and retirees.

Investigator's Comments: The Behavioral Regulation Exercise Questionnaire may allow finer analysis of the motivational forces of exercising: adoption and maintenance. The scale seems to be valid for both genders. The scale focuses on underlying source level motives for exercise, as represented by behavioral regulation continuum rather than surface-level motives (e.g., weight control, socialization, and fitness), and may increase the interpretive value of perceived self-determination. Employing a developmental continuum would enable investigating possibilities of what can be initially non-intrinsically interesting behaviors, allowing for testing motivational change as a part of exercise adoption.

The removal of the amotivational motivation seems to be acceptable in this setting but it would be worth investigating whether it is relevant in other settings.

BEHAVIORAL REGULATION IN EXERCISE QUESTIONNAIRE (BREQ)

Mullan, E.; Markland, D.; and Ingledew, D. K.

DIRECTIONS: Why do you engage in exercise? Using the scale below, please indicate to what extent each of the following items is true for you.

Not True for Me		Sometimes True for Me		Very True for Me
0	1	2	3	4

_____ 1.   I exercise because other people say I should.
_____ 2.   I feel guilty when I don't exercise.
_____ 3.   I value the benefits of exercise.
_____ 4.   I exercise because it's fun.
_____ 5.   I take part in exercise because my friends/family/partner say I should.
_____ 6.   I feel ashamed when I miss an exercise session.
_____ 7.   It's important for me to exercise regularly.
_____ 8.   I enjoy my exercise sessions.
_____ 9.   I exercise because others will not be pleased with me if I don't.
_____ 10. I feel like a failure when I haven't exercised in a while.
_____ 11. I think it is important to make the effort to exercise regularly.
_____ 12. I find exercise a pleasurable activity.
_____ 13. I feel under pressure from my friends/family to exercise.
_____ 14. I get restless if I don't exercise regularly.
_____ 15. I get pleasure and satisfaction from participating in exercise.

Scale's components and their items:

External Regulation	= Items 1, 5, 9, 13
Introjected Regulation	= Items 2, 6, 10
Identified Regulation	= Items 3, 7, 11, 14
Intrinsic Regulation	= Items 4, 8, 12, 15

| Motivation 18 |

EXERCISE MOTIVATION SCALE
(EMS)

Fuzhong Li

Reference: Li, F. (1999). The exercise motivation scale: Its multifaceted structure and construct validity. *Journal of Applied Sport Psychology, 11,* 97-115.

Goal of the Measurement: To assess motivational tendencies in the exercise context.

Background Literature: There has been a growing interest in what motivates individuals to exercise, and to engage in physical activity. On the basis of the self-determination theory (Deci and Ryan, 1985, 1990), three components were proposed: Amotivation, Extrinsic Motivation, and Intrinsic Motivation. Further elaboration on the components yielded a six-point continuum from external to internal perceived locus of control of causality: Amotivation, External Regulation, Introjected Regulation, Identified Regulation, Integrated Regulation, and Intrinsic Motivation. On the basis of other existing sport motivation measures, relevance of self-determination theory to exercise behavior warranted its inclusion in the current scale. Availability of such a measure can create much practical and scientific impact. Prior to this development, exercise motivation scales focused on intrinsic aspects only, not accounting for the multidimensionality of concepts, including extrinsically motivating reasons for exercising. Therefore, three studies were conducted to create the EMS scale and to test its structural foundations.

Methodology Employed: The three studies were used to develop the EMS. Within the first study, three phases were designed: conceptual formulation, identification of indicators or reasons, and uses of open-ended questions to generate answers to why people exercise, employing a Delphi method to identify categories of exercising. As a result, 32 items were agreed upon, representing eight subscales. Study Two utilized a sample of 371 college students — engaging in different types of exercises — to verify the psychometric structure of the EMS. A six-point, Likert-type scale was used ranging from "Strongly Disagree," marking "1" to "Strongly Agree," marking "6". The structural equation modeling methodology (LISREL) was used. Study Three investigated the validity of the EMS's factor structure, using a sample of 598 college students. Five other measures were included to establish EMS validity: *Perceived Exercise Competence, Perceived Exercise Autonomy, Perceived Social Relatedness, Exercise Interest,* and *Exercise Effort.* The LISREL program was used to analyze the data.

Findings: Elaborate results were presented, providing sufficient evidence supporting the eight subscales identified in Study One, Phase Three (see scale). Item loadings ranged between .84 and .50. The internal consistency reliability of the subscales was .90 to .75 and test-retest reliability ranged from .88 to .78. The five scales utilized to test EMS validity provided a reasonable fit of the data.

Investigator's Comments: In applying the theory of self-determined motivation, conceptual and empirical procedures helped to realize the existence of the dimension of integrated regulation. Examples of items that represent this domain are "Because it is consistent with what I value" and "Because exercising is an important aspect of how I perceive myself." EMS can serve many functions, some of which may establish a baseline to monitor change while investigating exercise adherence in intervention settings. Program execution might require assessing exercise motivation in different phases for diagnostic or treatment needs. The generalizability of EMS needs to be established on different populations, such as participants in recreation-based exercise programs, community, and other groups.

Contact Information:
Dr. Fuzhong Li, Senior Research Scientist
Oregon Research Institute
1715 Franklin Blvd.
Eugene, OR 97403

Phone: 541-484-2133
Fax: 541-484-1108
Email: Fuzhong@ori.org

EXERCISE MOTIVATION SCALE
(EMS)
Li, F.

DIRECTIONS: Please read each of the statements listed below and indicate how strongly you agree or disagree with each statement by circling the appropriate response to the right of the statement. Use the following response categories.

Strongly Disagree (SD) 1	Disagree (D) 2	Moderately Disagree (MD) 3	Moderately Agree (MA) 4	Agree (A) 5	Strongly Agree (SA) 6

WHY ARE YOU CURRENTLY PARTICIPATING IN THIS ACTIVITY?

	SD	D	MD	MA	A	SA
1. For the pleasure it gives me to experience positive sensations from the activity	1	2	3	4	5	6
2. For the satisfaction it gives me to increase my knowledge about this activity.	1	2	3	4	5	6
3. Because other people believe that it's a good idea for me to exercise.	1	2	3	4	5	6
4. Because I must exercise to feel good about myself.	1	2	3	4	5	6
5. Because I believe that regular exercise is a good way to enhance my overall development.	1	2	3	4	5	6
6. Because it is consistent with what I value.	1	2	3	4	5	6
7. I can't understand why I'm doing this.	1	2	3	4	5	6
8. Because I feel pressure from others to participate.	1	2	3	4	5	6
9. Because I think that exercise allows me to feel better about myself.	1	2	3	4	5	6
10. For the pleasure I experience while learning about this activity.	1	2	3	4	5	6
11. For the satisfaction I feel when I get into the flow of this activity.	1	2	3	4	5	6
12. Because I feel I have to do it.	1	2	3	4	5	6
13. To satisfy people who want me to exercise.	1	2	3	4	5	6
14. Because exercising is an important aspect of how I perceive myself.	1	2	3	4	5	6
15. For the pleasure of understanding this activity.	1	2	3	4	5	6
16. I have no idea.	1	2	3	4	5	6

Strongly Disagree (SD)	Disagree (D)	Moderately Disagree (MD)	Moderately Agree (MA)	Agree (A)	Strongly Agree (SA)
1	2	3	4	5	6

WHY ARE YOU CURRENTLY PARTICIPATING IN THIS ACTIVITY?

	SD	D	MD	MA	A	SA
17. For the pleasure of mastering this activity.	1	2	3	4	5	6
18. Because I think it is a good thing for my personal growth.	1	2	3	4	5	6
19. For the pleasure I experience when I feel completely absorbed in the activity.	1	2	3	4	5	6
20. For the satisfaction I feel while I try to achieve my personal goals during the course of this activity.	1	2	3	4	5	6
21. Because I would feel guilty if I did not take the time to do it.	1	2	3	4	5	6
22. Because I value the way exercise allows me to make changes in my life.	1	2	3	4	5	6
23. It is not clear to me anymore.	1	2	3	4	5	6
24. Because I think exercise contributes to my health.	1	2	3	4	5	6
25. To comply with expectations of others (e.g., friends).	1	2	3	4	5	6
26. For the enjoyment that comes from how good it feels to do the activity.	1	2	3	4	5	6
27. Because I enjoy the feelings of discovering more about this activity.	1	2	3	4	5	6
28. Because I enjoy the feelings of improving through participating in this activity.	1	2	3	4	5	6
29. Because I feel that changes that are taking place through exercise are becoming part of me.	1	2	3	4	5	6
30. For the pleasure I experience while trying to become the person I want to be.	1	2	3	4	5	6
31. Because I would feel ashamed if I was not doing anything to improve my current situation.	1	2	3	4	5	6

Motivation 19

INTERNATIONAL LEISURE TRAVEL MOTIVATION
(ILTM)

Kain L. Toh and Suk Y. Yeung

Reference: Toh, K. L., and Yeung, S. Y. (2000). International leisure travel motivations among students in Hong Kong. *International Council for Health, Physical Education, Recreation, Sport, and Dance, 36*, 56-58.

Goal of the Measurement: To assess international leisure travel motivations (ILTM).

Conceptual Background: This instrument was developed as part of a larger project to test certain hypotheses. Investigators utilized motivations reported in a study on sightseeing tourists' motivation (Dunn-Ross and Iso-Ahola, 1991). Also, ILTM was based on a pool of items generated from two studies: one by Fisher and Price (1991) on international pleasure travel motivations and the other study by Lang and O'Leary (1997) on motivation, participation, and preference. These empirical bases were utilized to conceptualize international leisure travel motivation, to identify components and their relevant indicators. This pool of items was the focus of verification in this study.

Methodology Employed: An initial 36-item scale was reduced to 26 involving leisure travel motivations. A five-point, Likert scale was used, ranging from "Strongly Disagree" marking 1, to "Strongly Agree" marking 5. For pilot testing, the 36 items were given to a random sample of 100 students. Factor loadings of less than .30 helped to delete 10 items. The final test was administered to a random sample of 343 college students. Statistical treatments employed were the principal components of factor analysis with Varimax rotation and Cronbach alpha coefficients.

Findings: Factor analysis yielded six components with eigenvalues more than one. These six factors explained a total of 89.7% of the total variance: Challenge, Stress Reduction, Entertainment, Education and Culture, Kinship, and Meeting New People. Reliabilities for the subscales were very reasonable, ranging from .99 to .81, with .91 for the total scale.

Investigator's Comments: The International Leisure Travel Motivation Scale needs to be further verified regarding tourists in general, to gain a better understanding of their travel motivations and preferences.

INTERNATIONAL LEISURE TRAVEL MOTIVATION
(ILTM)

Toh, K. L. and Yeung, S. Y.

Contact the authors for direction.

Strongly Disagree	Disagree	Neither Disagree Nor Agree	Agree	Strongly Agree
1	2	3	4	5

Challenge

_____ 1. I travel in order to see things few travelers are likely to see.

_____ 2. I travel in order to challenge myself.

_____ 3. I travel in order to understand myself better.

_____ 4. I travel in order to build up my sense of independence.

_____ 5. I travel in order to make myself feel more confident.

Stress Reduction

_____ 6. I travel in order to participate in sports or recreation activities.

_____ 7. I travel to the places my friends have not been for a sense of satisfaction.

_____ 8. I travel in order to release stress from home.

_____ 9. I travel in order to release stress from schoolwork.

_____ 10. I travel in order to talk about the trip after I return.

Entertainment

_____ 11. I travel in order to attend my favorite concerts or performances.

_____ 12. I travel in order to find excitement and thrills.

_____ 13. I travel in order to shop.

_____ 14. I travel in order to have fun.

SAMPLE Do Not Copy

Education and Culture

_____ 15. I travel in order to experience as many customs about a country as possible.

_____ 16. I travel in order to experience as many cultures about a country as possible

_____ 17. I travel in order to increase my knowledge about different places.

_____ 18. I travel in order to see a lot of cultural heritage.

_____ 19. I travel in order to see the famous sites.

Kinship

_____ 20. I travel in order to have as much time with my friends or family as possible.

_____ 21. I travel in order to enjoy activities with my whole family.

_____ 22. I travel in order to help strengthen ties with my family or friends.

Meeting New People

_____ 23. I travel in order to learn or practice foreign languages with new friends.

_____ 24. I travel in order to meet with different people of the country I traveled to.

_____ 25. I travel in order to have the opportunity to interact with new friends.

_____ 26. I travel in order to make new friends.

Chapter 6

Measurements of Leisure and Free Time Boredom

Focus of Chapter

This chapter lists the measurements of leisure and free time boredom currently available for use in recreation and leisure and earlier measurements that can be drawn upon in creating new, more modern measurements.

Key Terms
- free time boredom
- leisure boredom

Objectives
- Explain the content, functions, and concerns of available measurements of leisure and free time boredom.

Scales listed in this chapter date back to the 1920s, but attention to boredom slowly increased from the 1960s, Most of the scales were obtained from the literature with insufficient information to abstract them and present their items. The two scales presented below assess boredom in two settings: one in leisure and the other in free time.

These scales measure construct related to boredom.

1. Leisure Boredom Scale (LBS) (Iso-Ahola and Weissinger, 1990)
2. Free Time Boredom (FTB) (Ragheb and Merydith, 2001)

Other assessments discussed in the literature, which to not have enough information to evaluate, include:

1. Measuring Susceptibility to Monotony (MSM) (Thompson, 1929)
2. Curiosity Scale (CS) (Maw and Maw, 1965)
3. Stimulus-Variation Seeking Scale (SVSS) (Penney and Reinehr, 1966)
4. Sensation Seeking Scale (SSS) (Zuckerman et al., 1971)
5. Arousal Seeking Tendency Scale (ASTS) (Mehrabian and Russell, 1973)
6. Intrinsic Enjoyment and Boredom Coping (IEBC) (Hamilton, Haier, and Buchsbaum, 1984)
7. Boredom Proneness Scale (BPS) (Farmer and Sundberg, 1986)
8. Adopted Curiosity Scale (ACS) (Padhee and Das, 1987)
9. Telic Paratelic Scale (TPS) (Cook et al., 1993)

Questions and Exercises

1. What are some of the differences between leisure boredom and free time boredom?
2. Is there a need for measurements to assess boredom in informal activities and times?
3. Elaborate on the history of developing measurements assessing boredom in informal activities and times.

Boredom 1

LEISURE BOREDOM SCALE
(LBS)
Seppo E. Iso-Ahola and Ellen Weissinger

<u>Reference</u>: Iso-Ahola, S., and Weissinger, E. (1990). Perceptions of boredom in leisure: Conceptualization, reliability, and validity of the Leisure Boredom Scale. *Journal of Leisure Research, 22*, 1-17.

<u>Goal of the Measurement</u>: To assess the mismatch between desired arousal-producing characteristics of leisure experiences, perception, and actual availability of such leisure experiences. This mismatch is treated as resulting in boredom.

<u>Background Literature</u>: Leisure should be optimally arousing if it is to be psychologically rewarding. Leisure boredom may result from too much time available and too little to do. Another conceptual aspect that can lead to boredom is the lack of a match between available skills and available challenges. Moreover, a balance of novelty and familiarity occurring between and within leisure experiences is also critical to perceptions of leisure as optimally arousing. Therefore, leisure boredom was defined as a negative mood or state of mind that reflects a mismatch between optimal experience and the experiences that the individual believes are available.

<u>Methodology Employed</u>: One of the main bases for item development was Patrick's (1982) qualitative study, using open-ended questions for over 100 persons seeking treatment in a boredom clinic run by recreational therapists. Patrick's study yielded six components (e.g., dissatisfaction, disinclination to action, passive expectant attitude). An initial pool of 28 items was developed; 35 faculty members and graduate students reviewed the items for content and face validity, yielding positive reactions and acceptance of the scale's content. Also, a pretest on 55 students was conducted suggesting all items to be retained for final testing. A scale from one to five was used, ranging from "Strongly Disagree" marking 1, to "Strongly Agree" marking 5. Higher scores indicated higher levels of boredom. Factor analysis and reliability tests were performed on data collected from three independent studies with varying samples: 175, 174, and 344. Using some other theoretically relevant scales, construct validity tests were performed.

<u>Findings</u>: Employing principal axis factor analysis clustered all items except one under a single factor. Cronbach's alpha coefficients of the total scale in the three studies were .85, .88, and .86. Construct validity tests against relevant theoretical constructs produced a series of significant relations with the Leisure Boredom Scale (LBS). The exception was one construct (social desirability) that did not correlate with LBS.

<u>Investigator's Comments</u>: The scale may be used in clinical and practical situations involving leisure dysfunction. However, the use of the scale as a diagnostic device is uncertain until it is validated in those settings. The scale may also be used in the area of basic research in testing relationships to other constructs, to develop a theory. Investigators suggest further psychometric verifications of the scale, validating its ability to predict problematic behaviors (e.g., drug and alcohol abuse, vandalism, lethargy), and to verify the scale on non-student populations.

Contact Information:
Dr. Seppo E. Iso-Ahola, Professor
Kinesiology
College of Maryland
HHP Building, Room 2142
College Park, MD 20742-2611

Phone: 301-405-2505
Email: isoahol@umd.edu

LEISURE BOREDOM SCALE
(LBS)
Iso-Ahola, S. and Weissinger, E.

Instructions: The statements listed below are intended to find out how you feel about your leisure time. Just respond to each item as it applies to *your* leisure time. By "leisure time" we mean the *non-work* hours in your day.

Please respond to each of the 16 statements. You do this by writing, on the line next to each item, the number that shows how much you agree or disagree with the statement. For example, by writing in a "5" on the line to the left of a statement, you are showing that you "**Strongly Agree**" with the statement as it applies to your leisure time. Please use the scale below to respond to each statement.

Strongly Disagree	Disagree	Neutral	Agree	Strongly Agree
1	2	3	4	5

_____ 1. For me, leisure time just drags on.

_____ 2. During my leisure time, I become highly involved in what I do.

_____ 3. Leisure time is boring.

_____ 4. If I could retire now with a comfortable income, I would have plenty of exciting things to do for the rest of my life.

_____ 5. During my leisure time, I feel like I'm just "spinning my wheels."

_____ 6. In my leisure time, I usually don't like what I'm doing, but I don't know what else to do.

_____ 7. Leisure time gets me aroused and going.

_____ 8. Leisure experiences are an important part of my quality of life.

_____ 9. I am excited about leisure time.

_____ 10. In my leisure time, I want to do something, but I don't know what I want to do.

_____ 11. I waste too much of my leisure time sleeping.

_____ 12. I like to try new leisure activities that I have never tried before.

_____ 13. I am very active during my leisure time.

_____ 14. Leisure time activities do not excite me.

_____ 15. I do not have many leisure skills.

_____ 16. During my leisure time, I almost always have something to do.

Items to be reversed are # 2, 4, 7, 8, 9, 12, 13, and 16.

Boredom 2

FREE TIME BOREDOM
(FTB)

Mounir G. Ragheb and Scott P. Merydith

Reference: Ragheb, M. G. and Merydith, S. P. (2001). Development and validation of a multidimensional scale measuring free time boredom. *Leisure Studies, 20,* 41-59.

Goal of the Measurement: To assess the magnitude of boredom in individuals' free time — time remaining after daily obligations have been met.

Background Literature: Due to increasing free time in post-modern societies, individuals are faced with greater opportunities to select from a wide range of choices. Despite this fact, there is a strong likelihood for maladaptive behaviors to manifest themselves, such as drinking, drug use, and boredom. What is the concept of boredom? The root of this concept is anchored in the notion of individuals' needs for optimal arousal, a need for excitement, to stay alert, focused, and awake. Boredom was investigated in a number of settings but not in free time. The Leisure Boredom Scale was the exception (Iso-Ahola and Weissinger, 1990). Settings that gained attention in their relevance to boredom were industry, school, and marriage. Accumulated observations reached certain conclusions about common characteristics leading to boredom: tasks lack sufficient optimal arousal by being repetitive, of no interest, causing apathy, or destroying initiative. How relevant is boredom to a person's free time? No direct attempt had heretofore been made to fully comprehend and develop this concept. The closest effort was the research initiated by Iso-Ahola (1984) on measuring leisure boredom. Conceptually, boredom can occur in free time as a leisure constraint, but not in leisure itself as an experience.

Boredom in free time seems to be multidimensional. The literature revealed some possible components, as a theoretical rationale for the measurement of free time boredom (FTB): physical, mental stimulation, social isolation, affective, and environmental. Knowledge about the theoretical rationale of these components provided the basis to verify and test, as a validation procedure, its measurement and construct. "The body in flow" by Csikszentmihalyi (1990) is an example to substantiate the physical dimension. Physical pursuits must rely upon rhythmic activities or harmonious movements in order to generate optimal performance. Other evidence by Csikszentmihalyi suggests that boredom has a cognitive component (lack of mental stimulation). The absence of others, especially intimate ones, proved to be relevant to boredom. Extensive literature was used to outline the boundaries of the FTB construct.

Methodology Employed: Items tapping the five identified domains were drafted. They went through the process of critical analysis by the investigators, then by colleagues. A five-point, Likert-type scale was employed, ranging from "Strongly Disagree" to "Strongly Agree." Two preliminary trials (67 and 50 items) helped to reduce the number of items to 37 for final field verification on a sample of 347 (47% employees). Farmer and Sundberg's (1986) Boredom Proneness Scale (BPS) and Burisch's (1984) two items on boredom were correlated with FTB for concurrent validity. Conventional items and test analysis (factor analysis), alpha reliability coefficients, and correlation were utilized to analyze the data in all stages.

Findings: Although five domains were extracted from the literature and developed, only four factors were confirmed, accounting for 45% of the variance in the item responses. The four extracted factors that compose the FTB scale are Lack of Meaningful Involvement, Lack of Mental Involvement, Slowness of Time, and Lack of Physical Involvement. The alpha reliability coefficients for the subscales ranged from .91 to .78, and .92 for the total FTB scale. Regarding the concurrent validation tests, FTB correlated with BPS (r = .34) and with the combined two items by Burisch (r = .69).

Investigator's Comments: Empirical tests, demonstrated in this study, further document the literature, suggesting the multivariate nature of FTB. The scale exhibited psychometric qualities in terms of validity and reliability. Relevant to a large number of subpopulations, more verification of the characteristics of the FTB scale is needed. Prominent subpopulations that have excessive free time are teens, the elderly, the unemployed, homemakers, patients, and prisoners. One of the limitations of the FTB scale is the need to validate it on groups different from employees and students. For comparison and validation reasons, it is sometimes necessary to employ other methods of data collection (observation and interviews) to detect the real existence of FTB. Lastly, FTB stability over time requires further investigation. Cautious interpretations of the above findings need to be exercised until these limitations have been tested.

Contact Information:
Idyll Arbor, Inc.
39129 264th Ave SE
Enumclaw, WA 98022

Phone: 360-825-7797
Fax: 360-825-5670
Email: sales@idyllarbor.com

FREE TIME BOREDOM
(FTB)

Ragheb, M. G. and Merydith, S. P.

Directions: The following statements refer to your free time. **By "free time," we mean time left to you after daily obligations are met, such as sleep, work, or school.** Please read each statement, and then write the appropriate number on the line in front of the question. If you **STRONGLY DISAGREE** with the statement, write "1," if you **STRONGLY AGREE** with the statement, write "5." Possible choices in between are described on the following scales. There are no right or wrong answers.*

Strongly Disagree	Disagree	In Between	Agree	Strongly Agree
1	2	3	4	5

During My Free Time, …

_____ 1. I do not use a lot of my physical skills.
_____ 2. I feel excited.
_____ 3. I feel that my surroundings are dull and "blah."
_____ 4. It feels that time stands still.
_____ 5. I am physically energetic.
_____ 6. I am provided with many experiences.
_____ 7. I feel empty.
_____ 8. I feel that too much of it is on my hands.
_____ 9. I do things below my physical ability level.
_____ 10. New ideas are stimulated.
_____ 11. I tend to be busy with meaningless things.
_____ 12. I want it to last longer.
_____ 13. I enjoy getting my body toned up.
_____ 14. I have a variety of places to go to.
_____ 15. I am without focus.
_____ 16. The time flies.
_____ 17. My physical abilities are challenged.
_____ 18. I usually have something interesting to do.
_____ 19. It seems like I am wasting my time.
_____ 20. I wish I had more of it.

SAMPLE
Do Not Copy

Reverse items 2, 5, 6, 10, 12, 13, 14, 16, 17, 18, and 20 so the higher scores indicate higher Free Time Boredom.

Five items constitute each component, as follows:

Lack of Physical Involvement	=	Items 1, 5, 9, 13, and 17.
Lack of Mental Involvement	=	Items 2, 6, 10, 14, and 18.
Lack of Meaningful Involvement	=	Items 3, 7, 11, 15, and 19.
Slowness of Time	=	Items 4, 8, 12, 16, and 20.

To get a total Free Time Boredom score add up all the 20 item scores and divide by 20. To get a component score add up the item scores in the component and divide by five.

Chapter 7

Measurements of Leisure Interests

Focus of Chapter

This chapter lists the measurements of leisure interests currently available for use in recreation and leisure and earlier measurements that can be drawn upon in creating new, more modern measurements.

Key Terms

• leisure interests

Objectives

• Describe the available measurements of leisure interests.

Leisure interests can be divided between two major domains: interest in specific activities such as camping, tennis, or travel and interest as a psychological inclination that drives the individual to a large area of activities such as outdoor interest that can be satisfied by a large number of outdoor pursuits.

These scales measure constructs related to leisure interests.

1. State Technical Institute's Leisure Assessment Process (STILAP) (Navar, 1990)
2. Leisure Interest Measure (LIM) (Ragheb and Beard, 1992)
3. Leisure Assessment Inventory (LAI) (Hawkins, Ardovino, and Hsieh, 1998)
4. Leisurescope Plus and Teen Leisurescope Plus (Schenk, 1998)

Other assessments discussed in the literature, which do not have enough information to evaluate, include:

1. Inventory of Leisure Interest (ILI) (Hubert, 1969)
2. Mirenda Leisure Interest Finder (MLIF) (Mirenda, 1973)
3. Avocational Counseling Manual (ACM) (Overs, 1977)
4. Measure of Leisure Interest (MLI) (Frisbie, 1984)
5. Life Interests Inventory (LII) (Leisure/Work) (Williams, 1987)
6. Leisure Interests Checklist (LIC) (Rosenthal et al., 1989)
7. Recreation Interest Inventory (RII) (Kirkcaldy, 1990)
8. The Leisure Interest Inventory (LII) (Stangl, 1991)
9. Adolescence Leisure Interest Profile (ALIP) (Henry, 1998)

Questions and Exercises

1. What are the differences between specific leisure interest measurements and general leisure interest measurements?

2. Elaborate on leisure interests as psychological inclinations that move the individual to engage in activities such as outdoor, mechanical, or artistic.

| Interest 1 |

STATE TECHNICAL INSTITUTE'S LEISURE ASSESSMENT PROCESS (STILAP)

Nancy Navar

Reference: Navar, N. (1990). State Technical Institute's Leisure Assessment Process (STILAP). Idyll Arbor, Inc., Ravensdale WA.

Goal of the Measurement: To help clients achieve a balanced lifestyle through leisure interests in different activities, assessing leisure skill participation patterns, yielding leisure competence areas, and providing guidelines for leisure decision making that enhances involvement.

Background Literature: The scale is a theory-driven measurement, based on the assumption that an individual needs to engage freely in leisure activities of one's own choices. Activities should be varied in their competency areas and domains to provide healthy leisure lifestyles. This development is based on the work done by Navar and Clancy (1979) and Navar (1980), where fourteen competencies have been listed as the main thrust and pillar of the this scale. The fourteen competencies are extracted from Peterson and Gunn's (1984) leisure education concepts. A competency as utilized in this assessment was defined as "One of the fourteen skill areas that assist adults in responsible uses of their leisure."

Methodology Employed: The literature cited above under Background Literature is considered the basis for the establishment of two validities: face and content. The checklist by Navar (1974) was field tested on several hundred persons with disabilities. The 1990 version, which required some modifications to the score sheet, was updated by the developer and burlingame. However, the formal validation of the 1974 and 1990 scales have not been established.

Findings: A confirmation of the fourteen competencies of leisure skills.

Investigator's Comments: The STILAP scale's results should not be utilized as the sole assessment tool. Depending on the services offered by the therapeutic recreation department, the therapist will need to select and rely on other assessment tools to measure areas that are not accounted for by the STILAP.

Contact Information:
Dr. Nancy Navar
Idyll Arbor, Inc.
39129 264th Ave. SE
Enumclaw, WA 98022

Phone: 360-825-7797
Fax: 360-825-5670
Email: sales@idyllarbor.com

STILAP (1990)
State Technical Institute's Leisure Assessment Process
Navar, N.

Purpose: The purpose of the *STILAP* is to help the client/patient achieve a balanced leisure lifestyle.

DIRECTIONS: Below is a list of various leisure activities.
Circle "M" (much) for those activities you participate in regularly (daily, every other day, when in season, etc.)
Circle "S" (sometimes) for those activities you have done but not on a regular basis
Circle "I" (interested) for those activities you would like to learn (you may or may not have done these before, but you are still interested in learning more about the activity)

M	S	I	1. Pool, Billiards, Snooker	M	S	I	31. Tobogganing
M	S	I	2. Dieting, Nutrition	M	S	I	32. Snow Skiing (downhill)
M	S	I	3. Bowling	M	S	I	33. Snow Shoeing
M	S	I	4. Roller Skating	M	S	I	34. Fishing
M	S	I	5. Archery	M	S	I	35. Ice Fishing
M	S	I	6. Riflery	M	S	I	36. Hiking
M	S	I	7. Shuffleboard	M	S	I	37. Bird Watching
M	S	I	8. Pin Ball Playing	M	S	I	38. Football
M	S	I	9. Ice Skating	M	S	I	39. Softball/Baseball
M	S	I	10. Auto Mechanics	M	S	I	40. Frisbee
M	S	I	11. Jogging, Running	M	S	I	41. Judo, Self-Defense
M	S	I	12. Physical Fitness (exercises)	M	S	I	42. Table Tennis (Ping Pong)
M	S	I	13. Yoga	M	S	I	43. Paddleball, Racquetball
M	S	I	14. Relaxation Techniques, Isometrics	M	S	I	44. Handball
M	S	I	15. Darts	M	S	I	45. Squash
M	S	I	16. Horse Shoes	M	S	I	46. Tennis
M	S	I	17. Horseback Riding	M	S	I	47. Badminton
M	S	I	18. Miniature Golf	M	S	I	48. Deck Tennis
M	S	I	19. Golf	M	S	I	49. Volleyball
M	S	I	20. Hunting	M	S	I	50. Basketball
M	S	I	21. Biking	M	S	I	51. Ice Hockey, Hockey
M	S	I	22. Motorcycling	M	S	I	52. Meditation
M	S	I	23. Sailing	M	S	I	53. Jigsaw Puzzles
M	S	I	24. Canoeing	M	S	I	54. Crossword Puzzles
M	S	I	25. Boating	M	S	I	55. Reading
M	S	I	26. Trailer Camping	M	S	I	56. Watching Football
M	S	I	27. Tent Camping	M	S	I	57. Watching Baseball
M	S	I	28. Backpacking	M	S	I	58. Watching Basketball
M	S	I	29. Orienteering (map & compass)	M	S	I	59. Watching Other Sports
M	S	I	30. Cross Country Skiing	M	S	I	60. Watching TV

Client's Name	Physician	Admit #	Room/Bed

DIRECTIONS: Below is a list of various leisure activities.
Circle "M" (much) for those activities you participate in regularly (daily, every other day, when in season, etc.)
Circle "S" (sometimes) for those activities you have done but not on a regular basis
Circle "I" (interested) for those activities you would like to learn (you may or may not have done these before, but you are still interested in learning more about the activity)

M	S	I	61. Touring	M	S	I	96. Batik (wax fabric dyeing)
M	S	I	62. Traveling	M	S	I	97. Lapidary (rock polishing)
M	S	I	63. Listening to Music	M	S	I	98. Copper Enameling
M	S	I	64. Art Appreciation	M	S	I	99. String Art
M	S	I	65. Theater (movies or plays)	M	S	I	100. Sewing, Needle Point, Crewel, etc.
M	S	I	66. Party Going	M	S	I	101. Knitting, Crocheting
M	S	I	67. Backgammon	M	S	I	102. Other Crafts
M	S	I	68. Checkers	M	S	I	103. Baking, Cooking
M	S	I	69. Dominos	M	S	I	104. Canning
M	S	I	70. Other Table Gaines	M	S	I	105. House Plants
M	S	I	71. Cribbage	M	S	I	106. Gardening
M	S	I	72. Bridge	M	S	I	107. Wood Refinishing
M	S	I	73. Chess	M	S	I	108. Wood Working
M	S	I	74. Euchre	M	S	I	109. Pets
M	S	I	75. Hearts	M	S	I	110. Sweepstakes, Lottery
M	S	I	76. Poker	M	S	I	111. Basketball Officiating
M	S	I	77. Other Card Gaines	M	S	I	112. Softball Officiating
M	S	I	78. "Ham" Radio Operating ("CB")	M	S	I	113. Volleyball Officiating
M	S	I	79. Writing	M	S	I	114. First Aid Certification
M	S	I	80. Leather Crafts	M	S	I	115. Life Saving Certification
M	S	I	81. Jewelry Making	M	S	I	116. Member of a Church
M	S	I	82. Pottery/Ceramics	M	S	I	117. Member of a School Club
M	S	I	83. Ceramics (molds)	M	S	I	118. Member of a Community Organization, Politics
M	S	I	84. Horn Playing				
M	S	I	85. Guitar Playing	M	S	I	119. Signing Group, Deaf Sign Language
				M	S	I	120. Volunteer Work
M	S	I	86. Other Musical Instruments				
M	S	I	87. Ballroom Dancing	M	S	I	121. Swimming
M	S	I	88. Social Dancing	M	S	I	122. Water Skiing
M	S	I	89. Square Dancing	M	S	I	123. Skin Diving, Scuba Diving
M	S	I	90. Drawing, Painting	M	S	I	124.
				M	S	I	125.
M	S	I	91. Collecting Items (coins, stamps, etc.)				
M	S	I	92. Singing	M	S	I	126.
M	S	I	93. Participation in Drama Production	M	S	I	127.
M	S	I	94. Macramé	M	S	I	128.
M	S	I	95. Photography	M	S	I	129.
				M	S	I	130.

STILAP (1990) Profile Score Sheet

SAMPLE
Do Not Copy

Client's Name	Physician	Admit #	Room/Bed

STILAP (1990) COMPETENCY SUMMARY

Enter color codes here:	M	S	Interest Areas	Prescription Choice
A. Physical Skill That Can Be Done Alone				
B. Physical Skill That S/he Can Participate with Others, Regardless of Skill Level				
C. Physical Skill That Requires the Participation of One or More Others				
D. Activity Dependent on Some Aspect of the Outdoor Environment				
E. Physical Skill Not Considered Seasonal				
F. Physical Skill With Carryover Opportunity for Later Years				
G. Physical Skill With Carryover Opportunity and Vigorous Enough for Cardiovascular Fitness				
H. Mental Skill Participated in Alone				
I. Mental Skill Requiring One or More Others				
J. Appreciation Skill or Interest Area That Allows for Emotional or Mental Stimulation Through Observation or Passive Response				
K. Skill Which Enables Creative Construction or Self-expression Through Object Manipulation, Sound, or Visual Media				
L. Skill Which Enables Enjoyment/Improvement of the Home Environment				
M. Physical or Mental Skill Which Enables Participation in a Predominantly Social Situation				
N. Leadership and/or Interpersonal Skill Which Enables Community Service				
O. Other				

SAMPLE
Do Not Copy

ASSESSMENT SUMMARY STATEMENT:

RECOMMENDATIONS:

Client's Name	Physician	Admit #	Room/Bed

Interest 2

LEISURE INTEREST MEASURE (LIM)

Mounir G. Ragheb and Jacob G. Beard

Reference: Ragheb, M. G., and Beard, J. G. (1992). Measuring leisure interests. *Journal of Park and Recreation Administration, 10*, 1-13.

Goal of the Measurement: To assess leisure preferences and interests based on persons' psychological and social tendencies, collectively and individually.

Background Literature: What would make a person interested in camping, fishing, gardening, boating, and/or mountain climbing? Is there a core interest to seek these activities? Meanwhile, if activities fail to be interesting, would an individual substitute them within the same area of interest or the same core? What is the logical name for such a core of interests? There is a general agreement to call that core "outdoor recreation." Besides outdoor interests, are there other identifiable core interests — cultural, physical, or social — that might behave and cluster in similar ways? Core interests rather than activities were the target of this development, which tests whether the leisure interest categories exist or not, and to what extent.

In attempting to understand leisure interests, the literature yielded at least four conceptual reports (e.g., Butler, 1959; Kaplan, 1960) and eight empirical (theoretical) studies using factor analysis (e.g., Proctor, 1962; Bishop, 1970; Witt, 1971; Allen, 1982). Each report or study identified four to nine categories (subscores) of leisure interests, with a total of 27. Identified categories overlapped with each other. Examples of leisure interest categories are artistic, nature-outdoors, mechanics, physiological (sports), and social. Interests were defined as "preferences for leisure activities." All past measurements of leisure interests utilized checklists or inventories of activities, to study individual leisure preferences. The literature lacked identification of individuals' psychological and social characteristics and tendencies for leisure and recreation. There was no direct measure to assess a person's leisure inclinations as traits, described as avocational interests, similar to vocational interests by Holland (1978). Without regard to interest in activities, are the person's tendencies artistic, mechanical, cultural, or nature/outdoor? Most likely, individuals would show diversified interests, depending on identifiable aspects, such as age, gender, marital status, and income. How would individuals rate themselves on categories of recreation and leisure interests? Lacking was knowledge about the boundaries and content of these leisure interests, or the psychological core.

Methodology Employed: Several stages were employed to arrive at a smaller, more parsimonious set of leisure interest categories. The list compiled from the review of literature yielding 27 categories (areas) of leisure interests was exposed to a cluster analysis. In the initial methodological strategy, categories were described on separate cards, as defined in their original study, and then sorted by 21 leisure experts, by pair similarities. Detecting natural grouping in data, a similarity matrix was formed statistically, yielding 10 clusters. In the second stage, the 10 clusters and their definitions were arranged in a list of all 45 possible pairs. Twenty leisure judges compared each cluster to every other one and rated them according to their similarity on a nine-point scale. After redefining several categories and adding a new one (service), items were prepared (five to eight items for each category) to assess interest in their identified cluster. Based on responses and critiques of 51 persons, a scale of 50 items was ready for the final testing (252 persons). Data was statistically treated, employing factor analysis, alpha reliability coefficients, and simple correlations.

Findings: The final stage failed to confirm clearly three categories as unique leisure interests: intellectual, achievement, and relaxation. It seems conceptually logical that there are no interests that can be called achievement, relaxation, and intellectual. This was realized as a clarification based on the available empirical evidence (shuttling among steps, from conceptualization, to data collection and analysis, back to conceptualization again). Items relevant to the above categories were potentially loading on other categories, such as mechanical or artistic interests, instead of achievement; reading instead of intellectual; outdoor and cultural interests instead of relaxational. After several analyses and deliberations, a 29-item scale was composed, constituting the final Leisure Interest Scale. The 29-item scale represented eight components, explaining 77% of the variance: Artistic (creativity), Cultural,

Mechanical, Outdoor (natural), Physical (sports), Reading, Service, and Social. The alpha reliability coefficient for the scale was .87, and ranged from .93 to 75 for the subscales.

Investigator's Comments: Similar to occupational interests, the investigation focus has gone from specific activities to constructs, representing families of activities having common characteristics. The leisure interest scale can help respondents in many respects: on community or county levels; information gained from use of the scale could be used in scheduling, resulting in cost-effective offerings and programs, comparing options available within the program, and conducting feasibility studies on areas that interest the population. Moreover, on a personal level, the scale can assist in developing leisure awareness of individual interest, exploring leisure options available, and for leisure counselors to recommend opportunities for particular areas of leisure interests (mechanical, social, or service) in which the person prefers to excel.

Contact Information:
Idyll Arbor, Inc.
39129 264th Ave SE
Enumclaw, WA 98022

Phone: 360-825-7797
Fax: 360-825-5670
Email: sales@idyllarbor.com

LEISURE INTEREST MEASURE
(LIM)

Ragheb, M. G. and Beard, J. G.

DIRECTIONS: The following statements refer to your interests or preferences in leisure activities. It does not matter whether you participate in the activities or not; we need to know about what you prefer or are inclined to do. Please read each statement and then mark the appropriate circle on the answer sheet. If you "**STRONGLY DISAGREE**" with the statement, mark "1"; if you "**STRONGLY AGREE**" with the statement, mark "5"; if you are in between, mark the number which describes your response. There are no right or wrong answers.

Strongly Disagree	Disagree	In Between	Agree	Strongly Agree
1	2	3	4	5

_____ 1. I like to read in my free time.
_____ 2. I prefer being outdoors.
_____ 3. I like to work with materials, such as metal or wood, in my leisure time.
_____ 4. I like to be original in my leisure activities.
_____ 5. I appreciate the cultural arts.
_____ 6. I am committed to serve as a volunteer worker in one or more service organizations or activities.
_____ 7. I prefer competitive physical activities.
_____ 8. I use my leisure as a chance to meet new and different people.
_____ 9. I like the fresh air of outdoor settings.
_____ 10. I often use tools in my leisure activities.
_____ 11. I like to create artistic designs in my leisure time.
_____ 12. I prefer to engage in leisure activities such as going to plays, lectures, or visiting museums.
_____ 13. I often participate in service activities in my leisure time.
_____ 14. I prefer leisure activities that require a high degree of physical activity.
_____ 15. I use my leisure to develop close relationships with others.
_____ 16. I prefer leisure activities that help me to learn about nature.
_____ 17. I like repairing or building things in my leisure activities.
_____ 18. I prefer leisure activities that require creativity.
_____ 19. I like to observe local and national cultural events.
_____ 20. I regularly contribute time to service organizations or activities.
_____ 21. I prefer physically oriented activities such as sports.
_____ 22. I prefer to engage in leisure activities which require social interaction.
_____ 23. I prefer to be involved in leisure activities that take place in outdoor environments.
_____ 24. I like to work with mechanical devices in my leisure activities.
_____ 25. I like leisure activities that help me to explore new ideas.
_____ 26. I have a strong attraction to the cultural arts.
_____ 27. I prefer to be of service to others in my leisure time.
_____ 28. I like leisure activities that require physical challenge.
_____ 29. I prefer leisure activities that help to develop friendships.

Four items constitute each component, with the exception of item #1 for reading, as follows:

Reading	= Item 1.	Cultural Interests	= Items 5, 12, 19, and 26.
Outdoor Interest	= Items 2, 9, 16, and 23.	Service Interests	= Items 6, 13, 20, and 27.
Mechanical Interests	= Items 3, 10, 17, and 24.	Physical Interests	= Items 7, 14, 21, and 28.
Artistic Interests	= Items 4, 11, 18, and 25.	Social Interests	= Items 8, 15, 22, and 29.

To obtain scores, add all the items in a component (or the whole test) and divide by the number of items.

Interest 3

LEISURE ASSESSMENT INVENTORY
(LAI)

Barbara Hawkins, Patricia Ardovino, and C. Hsieh

Reference: Hawkins, B., Ardovino, P., Rogers, N., Foose, A., and Ohlsen, N. (2002). *Leisure Assessment Inventory* (LAI). Idyll Arbor, Inc., Enumclaw, WA.

Goal of the Measurement: To measure the leisure behavior of adults.

Background Literature: The conceptual basis of this instrument relies on several perspectives. A fundamental one is anchored in psychology and was presented by Neulinger (1981). He postulated that perceived freedom and motivation are basic characteristics that distinguish leisure from non-leisure. Another perspective is presented by Kelly (1972) as a sociological interpretation. He categorized experiences as unconditional leisure, recuperative and compensatory leisure, relational leisure, and role-determined leisure. Other perspectives by Hawkins (1994) viewed leisure as a major domain of life activity that is found across all socioeconomic levels. As a social psychological perspective, leisure incorporates a person's beliefs, values, knowledge, attitudes, and motivations that are exemplified by freedom of choice that generates rewards and satisfactions. Finally, there was a theological and cultural view presented by Pieper (1963), which stated that leisure pursuits are a condition of the soul.

Methodology Employed: Four indexes were extracted from the literature as pillars of the *Leisure Assessment Inventory* (LAI): The Leisure Activity Participation Index, the Leisure Preference Index, the Leisure Interest Index, and the Leisure Constraints Index. A panel of five experts reviewed these indexes and interviews were conducted to evaluate indexes' contents in terms of appropriateness, clarity, and accuracy. Two experts were practitioners, two were academicians, and one was a measurement expert; all showed sufficient agreement about the quality of the contents of the four subscales. Based on the literature available, an instrument to assess "leisure activity involvement" was drafted. To test scale's validity and reliability, a longitudinal study was conducted. Subjects employed were recruited from 31 community-based agencies, serving individuals with disabilities. To help standardized the LAI and for reproduction of the scale, some changes were made to create the commercial product. A guide interview was developed.

Findings: Inter-correlations among LAI indexes was performed to determine scales validity, which ranged between $r = -.08$ to $r = .47$, with only two significant relationships. Convergent and discriminant validities were determined by examining correlations with other relevant variables (i.e., life satisfaction and adaptive behavior). Three of the four LAI subscales correlated significantly with life satisfaction. As to the power of discrimination between high and low performances, utilizing U-test converted to z scores provided significant evidence. As to the reliability of the scale, data proved that the LAI is moderately consistent and stable measure of the four subscales.

Investigator's Comments: Scale's users should be familiar with all aspects of the LAI prior to its implementation. LAI should be administered in a quiet area and a comfortable room. This process takes about 45 minutes. It is to be hoped that the LAI will be used by professionals who design leisure programs and to evaluate the effectiveness of leisure education interventions.

Contact Information:
Dr. Barbara Hawkins
Idyll Arbor, Inc.
39129 264th Ave. SE
Enumclaw, WA 98022

Phone: 360-825-7797
Fax: 360-825-5670
Email: sales@idyllarbor.com

LEISURE ASSESSMENT INVENTORY
(LAI)

Hawkins, B.; Ardovino, P.; and Hsieh, C.

See the assessment manual for instructions on how to give the assessment.

Sample Score Sheet for Leisure Interests (Showing Scoring for 18 of the 53 Items)

√		Card	1 Yes	2 If "Yes" then ask: Less	Same	More	3 No	4 If "No" Past? Yes	No	5 Like to Try? Yes	No	Comments
1	√	Telephone	√	√								My phone bill is too high.
2	√	Relaxing	√			√						I would like to learn some new ways to relax to feel better.
3	√	Reading	√		√							
4	√	Table Games					√	√				When the kids were younger we played every Saturday night.
5	√	Visiting	√		√							
6	√	Movies					√	√				
7	√	Television	√	√								I waste too much time watching TV.
8	√	Radio/CD	√		√							
9	√	Cooking	√	√								
10	√	Sewing					√		√	√		
11	√	Gardening					√	√				
12	√	Pets					√	√				Pets are a bother.
13	√	Instrument					√		√	√		
14	√	Singing	√		√							
15	√	Painting					√	√				
16	√	Crafts	√			√						I want to learn how to make necklaces.
17	√	Museum					√	√				
18	√	Concert					√	√				I used to go to concerts with my friends. Now we seem to all be busy.
Leisure			Sum = LAP Score			Sum = L-PREF Score				Sum = L-INT Score		**Total Scores:** LAP Score ___9___ L-PREF Score ___2___ L-INT Score ___1___

The interviewer should check the appropriate space for the response to each picture. The steps are outlined in the *Flow Chart for Administering the Leisure Assessment Inventory*. Points to remember while filling out the *LAI* Part 1 Score Sheet:

- Place a check in the column next to the number if the client gives a reasonably close description of the activity.
- Each row will have *at least* two check marks in columns 1 to 5.
- If Column 1 has a check, then there *must* be a second check placed in Column 2.
- If Column 1 has a check, there will be *no* checks in Columns 3, 4, or 5.
- If there is no check in Column 1, then there *must* be a check in Column 3.
- If there is a check in Column 3, then there must be a check in Column 4.
- Column 5 will have a check for a "no" answer in column 4.
- If Column 3 has a check, there will be *no* checks in Columns 1 or 2.

Interest 4

LEISURESCOPE PLUS AND TEEN LEISURESCOPE PLUS

Connie Nall Schenk

Reference: Schenk, C. (1998). *Leisurescope Plus* and *Teen Leisurescope Plus*. Idyll Arbor Inc., Ravensdale, WA.

Goal of the Measurement: *Leisurescope Plus* and *Teen Leisurescope Plus* assess areas of high leisure interest, emotional motivation for participation in leisure choices, and identify individuals who need higher arousal experiences.

Background Literature: The instrument is based on early field experiences of the developer as a recreation therapist, combined with developer's hobby of photography and her training in neurolinguistic programming. Research results supported developer's intuition that visual images helped individuals to process information more quickly and soundly. The literature yielded ten (10) categories of leisure pursuits such as Games, Nature, Crafts, and Adventure, with the last category being added in the latest version due to Zuckerman's (1979) work on "sensation seeking."

Methodology Employed: As stated above, the scale was initiated based on intuitive impressions and academic training in sociology and leisure studies. Therefore, there are face and content validations for the proposed categories. Simple correlations were utilized to test relations among components, employing samples of 144 and 231 persons.

Findings: It was reported that Sensation Seeking correlated positively with the Adventure category ($r = .4$, $p < .001$), and with the subscale of Thrill and Adventure Seeking, correlation was ($r = .68$, $p. < 001$). Validity and reliability tests were performed on the instrument. Using a sample of 144 persons, test-retest validation was performed on the ten categories. Results yielded correlations between $r = .69$ and $r = .84$, which is quite adequate. Utilizing a panel of five professional judges, construct validity was established. There were perfect agreements among all panel members on all of the ten categories. In another study on a sample size of 231 individuals, correlations were provided among Holland's (1973) six personality types and the ten categories of *Leisurescope Plus*, showing few relations.

Investigator's Comments: Individuals involved in changing their behavioral lifestyles find the scales' information helpful, as it creates renewed awareness that can positively serve to establish new behaviors and interests. Professionals like the two scales because they provide instant information about participants' interest areas and emotional motivation, allowing professionals to be more effective.

Notes: The Manual of the *Leisurescope Plus* describes a Leisure Activities Filing System; includes instructions for its administration; how to interpret assessment results; measuring progress; changes in configurations from one administration to another; interpreting and customizing the feelings charts; modifications for individuals with significant impairments; using the assessment in different settings, such as occupational retraining, eating disorders, wellness, substance abusers, geriatric, marriage, and education; and making statements based on assessment results.

Contact Information:
Idyll Arbor, Inc.
39129 264th Ave SE
Enumclaw, WA 98022

Phone: 360-825-7797
Fax: 360-825-5670
Email: sales@idyllarbor.com

LEISURESCOPE PLUS AND TEEN LEISURESCOPE PLUS

Schenk, C.

Teen Leisurescope Plus   *leisure interest assessment*

Instructions: You will be shown 10 groups of pictures which show leisure activities. You will be comparing each group to another. Begin by comparing photo group #1 with #2. Decide quickly which one you like best. Then decide how much better you like your favorite using the example below. Once you decide which phrase (see example) best describes how much better you like your favorite, shade in the appropriate number of squares in the row number that matches your favorite. Always begin shading in the first square on the left and shade from left to right. If you choose the same group another time, you will just continue to add shaded squares in that row. This creates a bar graph which represents your preference by shading

squares, look at the words to the right of the example in the Feelings Chart and pick **one word only** which describes the feeling you associate with the photo group you have just selected. Place a tally mark (|) in the box underneath that word in the same row as your favorite photo group. For example, if you scored #2 as having high interest, you would shade in three squares in row #2 and, if you said that the word that describes your feeling for that group is "Fun", you would make a tally mark on row #2 underneath the word "Fun". After you have recorded your responses for 1 vs. 2, place a check mark next to this comparison in the Comparison Tracker at the bottom of the page. Then continue on to the next comparison, 1 vs. 3. Continue in this fashion for all of the comparisons.

Step 1: Leisure Activities Graph

EXAMPLE

- Low interest
- Medium interest
- High interest

Step 2: Feelings Chart (You may cross out any of the words provided below and write in a word of your choice.)

	Accomplishment	Excitement	Friendship	Relaxation	Contentment Pleasure	Release	Health Fitness	Happiness	Escape	Fun
1											
2																	
3										
4										
5												
6												
7												
8												
9										
10																
	Total 7	Total 7	Total 7	Total 2	Total 0	Total 3	Total 6	Total 4	Total 4	Total 5

Step 3: Comparison Tracker Place a check mark next to each comparison after you have recorded your response above.

1 vs 2 | 2 vs 3 | 2 vs 4 | 3 vs 7 | 4 vs 6 | 5 vs 6 | 6 vs 7 | 7 vs 9
1 vs 3 | 2 vs 4 | 2 vs 5 | 3 vs 8 | 4 vs 7 | 5 vs 7 | 6 vs 8 | 7 vs 10
1 vs 4 | 2 vs 5 | 2 vs 6 | 3 vs 9 | 4 vs 8 | 5 vs 8 | 6 vs 9 | 8 vs 9
1 vs 5 | 2 vs 6 | 2 vs 7 | 3 vs 10 | 4 vs 9 | 5 vs 9 | 6 vs 10 | 8 vs 10
1 vs 6 | 2 vs 7 | 2 vs 8 | 4 vs 5 | 4 vs 10 | 5 vs 10 | 6 vs 8 | 9 vs 10

Idyll Arbor, Inc., PO Box 720, Ravensdale, WA 98051 425-432-3231

Teen Leisurescope Plus Interpretation

Step 1

For each of the 10 Leisure Categories (See Step 1, other side), notice whether each shaded line ends in the low (L), medium (M) or high (H) range. Circle the appropriate letter in the chart below for each category.

Leisure Category	Low	Medium	High
1 Games	(L)	M	H
2 Sports	L	M	(H)
3 Nature	L	M	(H)
4 Collection	(L)	M	H
5 Crafts	(L)	M	H
6 Art & Music	L	(M)	H
7 Entertainment	L	(M)	H
8 Volunteerism	(L)	M	H
9 Social Affiliation	(L)	M	H
10 Adventure	L	M	(H)

Step 2

List the categories in order by looking at your longest line of shaded squares (step 1, other side). Write the category name here as your 1st choice and highest interest. Look at the next longest line and write that category name as your second choice. Continue until all 10 categories have been listed. Write the word "tie" in the margin where appropriate. The line with the fewest (or no) shaded squares will be you 10th and lowest interest.

1st   Adventure
2nd   Sports
3rd   Nature
4th   Entertainment
5th   Art & Music
6th   Crafts
7th   Games
8th   Volunteerism
9th   Social Affiliation
10th   Collection

Step 3

Write in the name of the Feeling that received the highest number of tally marks and place an X beneath the leisure categories associated with that feeling. Do the same thing for your second and third highest totals.

	Games	Sports	Nature	Collection	Crafts	Art & Music	Entertainment	Volunteerism	Social Affiliation	Adventure
Feeling word with the highest total: Accomplishment		X			X			X		X
Feeling word with the second highest total: Excitement	X	X X			X	X X				X
Feeling word with the third highest total: Friendship	X				X			X X	X X	X X

It is important to notice which feelings are the most important ones for you to achieve and to notice which activities provide those desired feelings. Once you become more aware of what you want to feel and the activities that you can participate in to provide those feelings, you will be more apt to use your time in ways that satisfy your needs. Self-awareness is the first step in changing behaviors and attitudes.

Idyll Arbor, Inc., PO Box 720, Ravensdale, WA 98051 425-432-3231

Things to think about: Spend some time thinking about how often you participate in activities that leave you feeling joyful and satisfied. If you determine that your life isn't as you wish it to be, make a list of steps to take toward making some positive changes.

Chapter 8

Measurements of Leisure Satisfaction

Focus of Chapter

This chapter lists the measurements of leisure satisfaction currently available for use in recreation and leisure and earlier measurements that can be drawn upon in creating new, more modern measurements.

Key Terms

* leisure satisfaction

Objectives

* To be able to explain the available measurements of leisure satisfaction.

These scales measure constructs related to leisure satisfaction.

1. Leisure Satisfaction Measure (LSM) (Beard and Ragheb, 1980/1991)
2. Racquet Sports Satisfaction Scale (RSSS) (Aguilar and Petrakis, 1989)
3. Physical Activity Enjoyment Scale (PAES) (Kendzierski and DeCarlo, 1991)
4. Global Leisure Satisfaction Scale (GLSS) (Ellis and Witt, 1994)
5. Leisure Coping Strategy Scale (LCSS) (Iwasaki and Mannell, 2000)
6. Leisure Time Satisfaction (LTS) (Stevens, Coon, Wisniewski, Vance et al. 2004)
7. Vitality Through Leisure (VTL) (Ragheb, 2005)

Other assessments discussed in the literature, which do not have enough information to evaluate, include:

1. Milwaukee Avocational Satisfaction Questionnaire (Overs, Taylor, and Adkins, 1977)
2. Leisure Satisfaction Inventory (LSI) (Rimmer, 1979)

Questions and Exercises

1. Describe the nature of leisure satisfaction measurements.
2. Is there a need for specific and general leisure satisfaction measurements?

Satisfaction 1

LEISURE SATISFACTION MEASURE
(LSM)
Jacob G. Beard and Mounir G. Ragheb

<u>Reference</u>: Beard, J. G., and Ragheb, M. G. (1980). Measuring leisure satisfaction. *Journal of Leisure Research, 12,* 20-33.

<u>Goal of the Measurement</u>: To assess the extent to which individuals perceive that certain personal needs are met or satisfied through leisure activities.

<u>Background Literature</u>: The novelty of the application of satisfaction, which was borrowed from marketing products, to the field of recreation and leisure contributed to its limited attention and conceptual development. A main orientation with leisure and play satisfaction is achieved through realizations of recreation, parks, and leisure goals in the process of need gratification. It was realized that one of the major goals of leisure and park services is their contribution to individuals' pursuit of happiness manifested through perceived satisfaction. For the purpose of measurement development, leisure satisfaction was defined as the positive perceptions or feelings that an individual forms, elicits, or gains as a result of engaging in leisure activities and choices.

Conceptually, the literature revealed that leisure is motivated intrinsically by the search for freedom, self-actualization, challenge, realizing abilities, accomplishment, and self-expression. (These indicators and others formed the Psychological component.) Another cluster of indicators reflected individuals' needs for intellectual stimulation in leisure, learning, seeking new experiences, satisfying curiosities, and trying new things (categorized as Educational, Learning, or Intellectual). Moreover, the Social component was very evident due to its indicators: Developing freely chosen relationships, need for social adjustment, need for communication or social interaction, enjoyment of good fellowship, belonging, identification with others, gaining attention and recognition, and being altruistic. A fourth part was the Relaxational component: A need for restoration, recuperation, resting, and relieving stress and strain from work. A Physiological component was also identified, based on elements such as physical restoration, challenge, development, fitness, muscular and heart strength, prevention of obesity, controlling weight, increasing energy, and enhancing health. Finally, an Aesthetic component was realized, presented through a need for the leisure and park environments to exhibit complementary qualities, such as beauty, quality in design, cleanliness, being interesting, and being pleasing. These were mostly the theoretical rationale for the construct of leisure satisfaction, awaiting empirical testing and validation to confirm or disconfirm their structures.

<u>Methodology Employed</u>: Reviewing the conceptual background of the positive impacts (satisfaction) of leisure and play yielded several parts that were catalogued and abstracted. Five of the following six domains were the assumed components of a hypothesized structure of leisure satisfaction. Originally, an assumed category of recreation was split — in an early analysis of one of the trials — to one of the parts already accounted for and the other was previously unaccounted for. The unaccounted part was developed as the physiological domain.

Indicators were used to develop items, adopting a five-point Likert-scale. Then the instrument was exposed to extensive revisions by the investigators and critiques by external reviewers. When the instrument was judged ready for field verification, several tests were conducted. Content validity was established through experts in leisure and recreation behavior. Then the scale was administered to two samples of 603 and 347 persons after minor revisions had been made. The data was analyzed first using factor analysis, followed by reliability tests and inter-factor correlations.

<u>Findings</u>: Factor analysis (Varimax solutions) on the data from the sample of 603 persons revealed an empirical justification for six interpretable factors. Results were confirmational, for items were deliberately written to measure certain component parts. In this stage, the physiological emerged to replace what was originally conceived as a "recreation" component. After necessary revisions and additions of items were made, the new scale (51 items) was administered, in another final test, to a sample of 347 persons. Based on confirmational factor analysis, six subscales

were tested for reliability. The total scale obtained an alpha reliability coefficient of .96, and the six subscales ranged from .92 to .85. The long scale (51 items) was shortened (24 items, four for each subscale) and obtained an alpha reliability coefficient of .93.

Investigator's Comments: Beyond face and content validity, the scale is awaiting further validation through its application in studies testing relationships between LSM and other theoretically relevant variables. Investigators recommended that the utility of the scale remains to be demonstrated. Research is needed to test stability and predictable changes in leisure satisfaction based on life spans (stages). However, LSM can be used in counseling, examining the use of individuals' free time. LSM can help in the development and validation of theoretical structures to predict leisure behavior. Many questions still need to be answered before we fully comprehend the concept of leisure satisfaction.

Contact Information:
Idyll Arbor, Inc.
39129 264th Ave SE
Enumclaw, WA 98022

Phone: 360-825-7797
Fax: 360-825-5670
Email: sales@idyllarbor.com

LEISURE SATISFACTION MEASURE

Beard, J. G. and Ragheb, M. G.

DIRECTIONS: Below are some statements on how persons feel about and perceive their leisure activities. Leisure activities are defined as non-work activities in which the individual has a free choice as to whether or not to participate. Please read each statement and then mark the appropriate circle on the enclosed answer sheet.

Strongly Disagree	Disagree	In Between	Agree	Strongly Agree
1	2	3	4	5

____ 1. My leisure activities are interesting to me.

____ 2. My leisure activities give me self-confidence.

____ 3. My leisure activities give me a sense of accomplishment.

____ 4. I use many different skills and abilities in my leisure activities.

____ 5. My leisure activities increase my knowledge about things around me.

____ 6. My leisure activities provide opportunities to try new things.

____ 7. My leisure activities help me to learn about myself.

____ 8. My leisure activities help me to learn about other people.

____ 9. I have social interaction with others through leisure activities.

____ 10. My leisure activities have helped me to develop close relationships with others.

____ 11. The people I meet in my leisure activities are friendly.

____ 12. I associate with people in my free time who enjoy doing leisure activities a great deal

____ 13. My leisure activities help me to relax.

____ 14. My leisure activities help relieve stress.

____ 15. My leisure activities contribute to my emotional well being.

____ 16. I engage in leisure activities simply because I like doing them.

____ 17. My leisure activities are physically challenging.

____ 18. I do leisure activities, which develop my physical fitness.

____ 19. I do leisure activities, which restore me physically.

____ 20. My leisure activities help me to stay healthy.

____ 21. The areas or places where I engage in my leisure activities are fresh and clean.

____ 22. The areas or places where I engage in my leisure activities are interesting.

____ 23. The areas or places where I engage in my leisure activities are beautiful.

____ 24. The areas or places where I engage in my leisure activities are well designed.

Each four items constitute a component in the following order

Psychological	= Items 1-4
Educational/Intellectual	= Items 5-8
Social	= Items 9-12
Relaxation	= Items 13-16
Physiological	= Items 17-20
Aesthetic-Environmental	= Items 21-24

Satisfaction 2

RACQUET SPORTS SATISFACTION SCALE (RSSS)

Teresita E. Aguilar and Elizabeth Petrakis

Reference: Aguilar, T. E., and Petrakis, E. (1989). Development and initial validation of perceived competence and satisfaction measures for racquet sports. *Journal of Leisure Research, 21,* 77-91.

Goal of the Measurement: To assess perceived skills (competence) and rewards gained (satisfaction) from participation in racquet sports: tennis, badminton, and racquetball.

Conceptual Background: This investigation attempted to answer the following question: What tends to influence an individual's selection and frequent participation in a physical activity as a leisure pursuit? One of the main assumptions of the study was that skill level and/or positive experience (intrinsic pleasure) can influence selection and participation in activities. Harter's model was utilized, illustrating that there are interrelationships among motivation, mastery attempts, perceived competence or lack of it, resulting in either intrinsic pleasure (enjoyment) or anxiety. Consequently, pleasure and enjoyment feedback were assumed to motivate positively, while anxiety was assumed to impact negatively.

Methodology Employed: Item development was based on informal interviews with racquet sport players and observation. A total of 20 items were drafted, employing a five-point, Likert scale, from 1=Almost Never to 5=Almost Always. A pilot study was conducted on 36 students; a second pilot study was performed on 26 students. A further revision was done, making items generic to all racquet sports instead of just tennis or racquetball. The revised 20-item scale was utilized to collect data in two consecutive field tests: 1. a sample of 163 students; 2. another sample of 208 students. Factor analysis and Cronbach alpha reliability were performed to test statistically the structure of scale.

Findings: Factor analysis, oblique rotation, yielded three factors: Competence (ability), Satisfaction, and Sport Enjoyment. The last two factors (satisfaction and sport enjoyment) were considered as satisfaction obtained. Alpha reliability coefficient was .90 for the 10-item competence subscale and .74 for satisfaction, including sport enjoyment. Content and face validity were achieved through the evaluation of the review panel. Two other validations were reported: criterion-referenced and construct.

Investigator's Comments: Since the satisfaction scale was reduced to a six-item scale, its validity should be addressed in future studies. Moreover, the scale needs to be validated on backgrounds other than students to represent different ages (childhood, teens, adults, and older persons) and other types of populations. Finally, the issue of concurrent validity should be addressed further.

Contact Information:
Dr. Teresita E. Aguilar, Dean
School of Professional Studies
Our Lady of the Lake University
411 S.W. 24th St.
San Antonio, TX 78207

Phone: 210-431-4140
Fax: 210-431-3962
Email: teaguilar@ollusa.edu

RACQUET SPORTS SATISFACTION SCALE
(RSSS)

Aguilar, T. E. and Petrakis, E.

DIRECTIONS: Developers of the scale should be contacted for the complete scale, including directions.

Never	Almost Never	Sometimes	Almost Always	Always
1	2	3	4	5

_____ 1. When I lose, I feel like quitting the game forever.
_____ 2. I enjoy competition.
_____ 3. I enjoy the game each time I play.
_____ 4. I enjoy the challenges of this sport.
_____ 5. Whether I win or lose, I feel a sense of accomplishment.
_____ 6. I feel a sense of freedom while I am playing.
_____ 7. I derive great satisfaction from playing.

Scores of item 1 should be reversed, see Chapter 17 for item reversal.

PHYSICAL ACTIVITY ENJOYMENT SCALE (PACES)

Deborah Kendzierski and Kenneth J. DeCarlo

Reference: Kendzierski, D., and DeCarlo, K. J. (1991). Physical activity enjoyment scale: Two validation studies. *Journal of Sport and Exercise Psychology, 13*, 15-64.

Goal of the Measurement: To assess the extent to which an individual enjoys doing any given physical activity, regardless of whether the activity is done for exercise or for sport.

Background Literature: Enjoyment obtained from doing physical activities is not recognized nor sufficiently investigated. To assess this type of enjoyment, scientists utilized a single- or two-item approach, both of which have inherent difficulties in meeting basic criteria for quality instruments: validity and reliability. Enjoyment has been established as a primary motivator to engage in physical activities. To develop a reliable and valid set of items, literature conceptualizing exercise adherence and exercise enjoyment was examined.

Methodology Employed: The literature yielded a set of 39 items (some of which were previously used), descriptors of feelings experienced, words or phrases used to express enjoyment with activities, the dictionary, interviews, and brainstorming. A seven-point bipolar scale was employed, ranging from "1" to "7" to rate the items. Items went through content validity examination by three experts, then two raters, reducing the scale to 19 items. Responses from a sample of 30 students were tested for internal consistency (.93), giving indications of high reliability. One item, which did not advance the item-total correlation, was discarded. Another similar pilot study (33 students) obtained consistent results. The final test utilized a sample of 37 students. Two reliability tests were performed: alpha reliability coefficient and test-retest.

Findings: In the final analysis, Cronbach's coefficient alpha reliability was .96. Also, the test-retest for jogging was .93 and .60 for bicycling.

Investigator's Comments: Evidence obtained yielded a valid and reliable instrument assessing PACES. It is suggested that PACES should be validated further with other physical activities, such as sport, leisure activities, and outdoor settings. Also, validating the scale on populations in different ages and occupations, accounting for larger samples of males and females for comparisons, can enhance the scale's application. Since a one-dimensional construct of enjoyment was reported, further investigation is needed to test the factor structure, examining possibilities of its multidimensional nature.

Contact Information:
Dr. Deborah Kendzierski
Tolentine Hall Room 346
Villanova University
800 Lancaster Ave
Villanova, PA 19085

Phone: 610-519-4753
Email: Deborah.kendzierski@villanova.edu

PHYSICAL ACTIVITY ENJOYMENT SCALE
(PACES)

Kendzierski, D. and DeCarlo, K. J.

DIRECTIONS: Please rate how you feel *at the moment* about the physical activity you have been doing.

#	Left	Scale	Right
1.	I enjoy it*	1 2 3 4 5 6 7	I hate it
2.	I feel bored	1 2 3 4 5 6 7	I feel interested
3.	I dislike it	1 2 3 4 5 6 7	I like it
4.	I find it pleasurable*	1 2 3 4 5 6 7	I find it unpleasurable
5.	I am very absorbed in this activity*	1 2 3 4 5 6 7	I am not at all absorbed in this activity
6.	It's no fun at all	1 2 3 4 5 6 7	It's a lot of fun
7.	I find it energizing*	1 2 3 4 5 6 7	I find it tiring
8.	It makes me depressed	1 2 3 4 5 6 7	It makes me happy
9.	It's very pleasant*	1 2 3 4 5 6 7	It's very unpleasant
10.	I feel good physically while doing it*	1 2 3 4 5 6 7	I feel bad physically while doing it
11.	It's very invigorating*	1 2 3 4 5 6 7	It's not at all invigorating
12.	I am very frustrated by it	1 2 3 4 5 6 7	I'm not at all frustrated by it
13.	It's very gratifying*	1 2 3 4 5 6 7	It's not at all gratifying
14.	It's very exhilarating*	1 2 3 4 5 6 7	It's not at all exhilarating
15.	It's not at all stimulating	1 2 3 4 5 6 7	It's very stimulating
16.	It gives me a strong sense of accomplishment*	1 2 3 4 5 6 7	It does not give me any sense of accomplishment at all
17.	It's very refreshing*	1 2 3 4 5 6 7	It's not at all refreshing
18.	I felt as though I would rather be doing something else	1 2 3 4 5 6 7	I felt as though there was nothing else I would rather be doing

* Items to be reversed; for item reversal see Chapter 17.

SAMPLE
Do Not Copy

Satisfaction 4

GLOBAL LEISURE SATISFACTION SCALE (GLSS)

Gary D. Ellis and Peter A. Witt

Reference: Ellis, G. D. and Witt, P. A. (1994). Perceived freedom in leisure and satisfaction: Exploring the factor structure of the perceived freedom components of the *Leisure Diagnostic Battery*. *Leisure Sciences, 16,* 259-270.

Goal of the Measurement: To measure perceived freedom in leisure, arriving at a single (total) score for the components.

Background Literature: Perceived freedom in leisure (PFL) was assumed to assist in operationalizing the continuum model of providing therapeutic recreation. It was also assumed that a high level of PFL would be attributed to greater levels of independence, intrinsic motivation, and satisfaction. To the contrary, lower levels of PFL lead to helplessness in leisure, depression, and dependence on providers. For more usefulness and possible comparisons, users of the Leisure Diagnostic Battery (LDB) (Witt and Ellis, 1989) recommended adding up scores of the five subscales. This is to produce a meaningful and more interpretable measure of perceived freedom in leisure. For further details on the LDB, see Witt and Ellis, 1989.

Methodology Employed: Secondary data were utilized, re-analyzing matrices of correlation among the five subscales from the LDB, Part 1. Three different investigations were combined. Three life stages were represented by these investigations: adolescence (200 persons), young adulthood (513 adults), and mid-life (297 persons). The names of the five subscales of the LDB are Perceived Leisure Competence, Perceived Leisure Control, Leisure Needs, Depth of Involvement in Leisure, and Playfulness. The intent of the current analysis was to discover the latent factors of the concept investigated, perceived freedom in leisure. Factor analysis and correlations were used for further analysis of the data.

Findings: Each of the five scales produced moderate to high loadings on the factor that was extracted. Loadings of factors ranged from .91 to .45, supporting the notion of the unitary perceived freedom concept. Extensive analysis was performed, suggesting that a two-factor model provides a greater fit for the data than the one-factor model. Another analysis yielded a 14-item, more efficient, Global Leisure Satisfaction Scale, with an average alpha reliability coefficient of .87.

Investigator's Comments: As an extension of efforts to develop the LDB, the validation described here enabled the focus and extent of LDB to be sharpened. Investigators suggest further examination of the internal structure of the five subscales. Moreover, the relatively low correlations of the Leisure Needs and the Depth of Involvement subscales with the Perceived Freedom subscale necessitate further verifications. Also suggested is further conceptual work to develop an understanding of the nature of relationships among the five subscales.

Contact Information:
Dr. Gary D. Ellis, Head
Department of Recreation, Park, and Tourism
106 Francis Hall
Texas A&M University
College Station, TX 77843-226

Phone:　979-845-7324
Fax:　　979-845-0446
Email:　gellis@tamu.edu

GLOBAL LEISURE SATISFACTION SCALE
(GLSS)

Ellis, G. D. and Witt, P. A.

Contact the authors for directions and the complete scale.

_____ 1. When I have been working for a long time at something, recreation activities help me to relax.
_____ 2. When I am tired, doing recreation activities helps me to relax.
_____ 3. I do recreation activities to help me feel less restless.
_____ 4. When I'm restless, recreation activities help me calm down.
_____ 5. When I have had a day in which nothing seems to go right, I do a recreation activity to make me feel better.
_____ 6. When I have failed at something I tried to do well, doing recreation activities helps me feel less restless.
_____ 7. When I get mad at someone, doing recreation activities makes me feel better.
_____ 8. When I'm angry, recreation activities help to calm me down.
_____ 9. I often do recreation activities that are new and different to me.
_____ 10. I often do recreation activities in which I have to solve difficult problems.
_____ 11. Sometimes, when I'm involved in a recreation activity, I can forget everything else.
_____ 12. When I'm doing recreation activities I feel good inside.
_____ 13. Sometimes when I'm involved in a recreation activity, I can really let my feelings go.
_____ 14. There are times when I really feel powerful and in control while doing recreation activities.

Components obtained:
Leisure Needs   = Items 1-10
Depth of Involvement Scale   = Items 11-14

Satisfaction 5

LEISURE COPING STRATEGY SCALE
(LCSS)

Yoshi Iwasaki and Roger C. Mannell

References: Iwasaki, Y., and Mannell, R. C. (2000). Hierarchical dimensions of leisure stress coping. *Leisure Sciences, 22,* 163-181. (This article yielded another scale assessing Leisure Coping Strategy, listed under the classification of Leisure Attitude.)

Iwasaki, Y., Mannell, R. C., Smale, B. J. A., and Butcher, J. (2005). A short-term longitudinal analysis of leisure coping used by employees of police and emergency response service workers. *Journal of Leisure Research, 34,* 311-339.

Iwasaki, Y. (2006). Counteracting stress through leisure coping: A prospective health study. *Psychology, Health & Medicine, 11,* 209-220.

Goal of the Measurement: To assess the extent to which leisure helps people cope with stress as a situation-specific strategy.

Background Literature: Besides the details on the content of this report on leisure coping beliefs, information on leisure coping strategies as a satisfying outcome is presented under this measure. These "strategies" are actual leisure involvement behaviors that help to cope with stress in specific situations. These are intentional, leisure-involvement behaviors chosen to obtain coping rewards. Specifically, when people face a stressful event, they may — by design — select a given coping action in response to the event. It is assumed that leisure coping strategies represent a process by which a certain stressful event triggers the use of a specific type of leisure to cope with stress and to maintain good health. Three subdimensions or types of leisure coping strategies were conceptualized: leisure companionship, leisure palliative coping, and leisure mood enhancement. These three subdimensions were the conceptual bases of the LCSS.

Methodology Employed: LCSS and the other measure were verified together employing the same method, as follows: For face and content validity, a list of 70 initial items was exposed to a panel of judges, four leisure scientists, to evaluate the content and face validity of the items. Irrelevant items were removed and redundant items were rewritten, yielding a total of 48 items. A sample of 247 students was recruited from two Canadian universities to test the scale. A 7-point Likert-type scale was utilized, ranging from 1 (*very strongly disagree*) to 7 (*very strongly agree*). Statistical analyses were performed including alpha reliability coefficients, inter-total correlations, and confirmatory factor analysis.

Findings: The reliability coefficient of the total LCSS was high (.93), while for the subscales they were .87 for Companionship; .86 for Palliative Coping; and .85 for Mood Enhancement. Next, confirmatory factor analysis was performed yielding the aforementioned three components with loadings ranged between .89 and .12.

Investigators Comments: The authors provided the same conclusions as stated under the LCBS. They suggested that it is important to explore other ways in which leisure contributes to coping with stress. The construct validity of the scale was supported. This scale was originally tested with a sample of college students, while subsequent studies have used this scale with police and emergency response personnel (Iwasaki, Mannell, Smale, and Butcher, 2005), and with a general representative sample (Iwasaki, 2006).

Contact Information:
Yoshitaka Iwasaki, Professor
College of Health Professions and Social Work
Temple University
1700 N. Broad Street, Suite 301C

Philadelphia, PA 19121

Phone: 215-204-0011
Fax: 215-204-1386
Email: yiwasaki@temple.edu

LEISURE COPING STRATEGY SCALE
(LCSS)

Iwasaki, Y. and Mannell, R. C.

Instructions: The following statements assess to what extent your leisure helps you cope with stress in your life. In some cases, you may intentionally choose your leisure involvements to help you deal with stress. At other times, you may find that what you do in your leisure has helped reduce stress even though you chose to participate for other reasons. By leisure we mean the things you do in your free time and the recreational activities you engage in. Please think back to stressful events you encountered in the past month. Now recall how you coped with these events. Read each of the following statements and circle the number which best corresponds to your answer.

	Very Strongly Disagree	Strongly Disagree	Disagree	Neutral	Agree	Strongly Agree	Very Strongly Agree
1. My leisure helped me feel better.	1	2	3	4	5	6	7
2. My leisure allowed me to be in the company of supportive friends.	1	2	3	4	5	6	7
3. I engaged in a leisure activity to temporarily get away from the problem.	1	2	3	4	5	6	7
4. Escape through leisure was a way of coping with stress.	1	2	3	4	5	6	7
5. Socializing in leisure was a means of managing stress.	1	2	3	4	5	6	7
6. I gained a positive feeling from leisure.	1	2	3	4	5	6	7
7. I dealt with stress through spending leisure time with my friends.	1	2	3	4	5	6	7
8. Engaging in social leisure was a stress-coping strategy for me.	1	2	3	4	5	6	7
9. Leisure was an important means of keeping myself busy.	1	2	3	4	5	6	7
10. I maintained a good mood in leisure.	1	2	3	4	5	6	7
11. Engagement in leisure allowed me to gain a fresh perspective on my problem(s).	1	2	3	4	5	6	7
12. My leisure involvements failed to improve my mood.	1	2	3	4	5	6	7
13. Leisure made me feel miserable.	1	2	3	4	5	6	7
14. By escaping from the problem through leisure, I was able to tackle my problem(s) with renewed energy.	1	2	3	4	5	6	7
15. Lack of companionship in leisure prevented me from coping with stress.	1	2	3	4	5	6	7
16. Leisure helped me manage my negative feeling.	1	2	3	4	5	6	7
17. I took a brief break through leisure to deal with the stress.	1	2	3	4	5	6	7
18. One of my stress-coping strategies was participation in social leisure.	1	2	3	4	5	6	7

Dimensions:

Leisure companionship = Items 2, 5, 7, 8, 15 (reverse item), 18
Leisure palliative coping = Items 3, 4, 9, 11, 14, 17
Leisure mood enhancement = Items 1, 6, 10, 12 (reverse item), 13 (reverse item), 16

| Satisfaction 6 |

LEISURE TIME SATISFACTION
(LTS)

A. B. Stevens, D. Coon, S. Wisniewski, D. Vance, S. Arguelles, S. Belle, A. Mendelsohn, M. Ory, and W. Haley

Reference: Stevens, A., Coon, D., Wisniewski, S., Vance, D., Arguelles, S., Belle, S., Mendelsohn, A., Ory, M., and Haley W. (2004). Measurement of leisure time satisfaction in family caregivers. *Aging and Mental Health, 8*, 450-459.

Goal of the Measurement: To assess the distinct psychological dimension of satisfaction with the amount of time spent in leisure activities, to be used with family caregivers who are taking care of someone with Alzheimer's disease or a related dementia.

Background Literature: Family caregivers provide extensive assistance with self-care activities and manage behavioral problems. Thus, they become highly involved in their care giving, leaving less time for other meaningful and satisfying activities. The impact of care giving on leisure activities has gained meager attention. However, there is growing evidence that leisure involvement contributes positively to physical and psychological well-being. Family caregivers reported constraints on their leisure activities such as vacations and hobbies. Two outcomes were theorized to be very prevalent: stress and depression. Lewinsohn and his group (e.g., 1986) emphasized the need for sufficient pleasant activities to control depressive mood states. Measures available (Pleasant Events Scale — Elderly, Multilevel Assessment Instrument, and Leisure Satisfaction Scale) fail, either in content or length, to meet certain criteria pertinent to care giving.

Methodology Employed: The Leisure Time Satisfaction (LTS) scale was developed by a team experienced in family caregiver research (face validity), to obtain a report on the level of satisfaction caregivers felt regarding the amount of time spent in leisure activities. Items aimed at activities commonly listed on existing leisure measures and were judged to be relevant to this type of care giving. Items and the scale utilized are listed below. Other scales were employed for validity testing. Data was collected from a sample of 1229 caregiver/care-recipient dyads, as a basis for the analysis. Exploratory and confirmatory factor analysis was used, then Cronbach's alpha to assess internal consistency. For convergent and divergent validity, Spearman rank correlation coefficients were calculated among measures.

Findings: Exploratory factor analysis yielded a single factor model with loadings between .90 and .60. Cronbach's alpha was .80. Besides the established face validity, convergent validity was found through association of LTS with two other measures.

Investigators Comments: Recent evidence suggests the importance of investigating leisure within studies of care giving. Items were carefully chosen to capture the various categories of leisure activities and the diverse settings in which leisure occurs. LTS is a valid measure across a number of subgroups identified by gender, race/ethnicity, relationship of the caregiver to the care recipient, and by research site. This makes the scale a valuable addition to the leisure assessment instruments currently available. The LTS focuses on an individual's feelings of satisfaction with leisure time, a construct we believe to be relevant to caregivers who are frequently charged with providing 24-hour service.

Contact Information:
Dr. Alan B. Stevens, Director
Dementia Care Research Program,
Division of Gerontology and Geriatric Medicine
University of Alabama
1530 3rd Avenue South, CH 19, Suite 218
Birmingham, AL 35294-2041

Phone: 205-934-7916
Fax: 205-975-5870
E-mail: AStevens@uab.edu

LEISURE TIME SATISFACTION
(LTS)

**Stevens, A.; Coon, D.; Wisniewski, S.; Vance, D.; Arguelles, S.;
Belle, S.; Mendelsohn, A.; Ory, M.; and Haley W.**

We are interested in how satisfied you are with the amount of time you have been able to spend in various activities that you might enjoy. Over the past month, how satisfied are you with the amount of time you have been able to spend:

		Not at all	A little	A lot
1	In quiet time by yourself?	0	1	2
2.	Attending church or going to other meetings of groups or organizations?	0	1	2
3.	Taking part in hobbies or other interests?	0	1	2
4.	Going out for meals or other social activities?	0	1	2
5.	Doing fun things with other people?	0	1	2
6.	Visiting with family and friends?	0	1	2

Satisfaction 7

VITALITY THROUGH LEISURE (VTL)

Mounir G. Ragheb

Reference: Ragheb, M. G. (2005). Vitality through leisure. Idyll Arbor, Inc.

Goal of the Measurement: To assess a person's vitality level as a result of leisure involvement.

Background Literature: Throughout history vitality has gone through extensive practical uses, conceptual developments, and theorizations. Practically, Athenians knew how to vitalize themselves — as a cultural influence — through involvement in sports, music, physical recreation, dance, the arts, the intellect, contemplation, meditation, and relaxation. Activities were pursued for their vitality contribution such as inward calm, peace, and serenity. All of these are viewed as promoters of Vitality Through Leisure (VTL). Conceptually, more than 250 years ago, Lord Kames, as a philosopher, had the view that play is sought for recreational purposes to refresh a person after labor. Still, 150 years ago, GutsMuths reported on the procreative values of play. All evolved to theoretical explanations for the need for recovery from fatigue of labor after the American Industrial Revolution in 1850. Therefore, Patrick (1921) theorized that activities were needed for relaxation and recuperation to regain vigor and vitality lost in labor. Three other theories lend themselves to the explanation and development of VTL. First, in White's (1959) theory of competence mastery, White observed that people strive beyond their basic necessities, seeking mastery of activities and competency. As a result, they feel alive, up-to-something, and active. Second, Ryan and La Guardia (2000), in their self-determination theory, claim that vitality would diminish when such needs as autonomy, competence, and relatedness are neglected. Last, burnout is caused by demands of certain levels of effort, leading to stress pathologies. Burnout and stress were the basis for Ellis's (1973) subtheory of stimulus avoidance (SA) and the need for relaxation. SA through leisure endeavors is essential in coping, refreshing, and recovering from fatigue to recharge one's vitality.

Methodology Employed: To construct a scale assessing VTL the following steps were followed: First, identifying possible components and indicators of the concept of VTL, nine components were recognized. Second, indicators were checked linguistically for word difficulty and reading level, achieving simplicity. Third, components were defined and external reviewers evaluated the indicators' relatedness to definitions, yielding 100 indicators. Fourth, scale development went through item generation, then item reduction by graduate and undergraduate students. Fifth, a final scale of 69 items was ready for final field settings. Sixth, a sample of 309 students and employees responded to the survey, which included two other questions: one on health satisfaction and another on weight satisfaction. Statistical treatments employed factor analysis, alpha reliability coefficients, item-scale correlations, and subscale inter-correlations.

Findings: The nine assumed components were not confirmed through factor analysis, only five were confirmed: Broaden-and-Build (alpha reliability = .94), Physical Condition (alpha = .92), Relaxation and Stress Control (.89), Optimal Arousal (.81), and Personal Betterment and Restoration (.76). The alpha value for the long scale (49 items) was .96 and for the short scale (28 items) was .93. Health satisfaction correlated more than weight satisfaction with VTL. Moreover, Broaden-and-Build and Relaxation and Stress Control correlated higher than Physical Condition with VTL.

Investigator's Comments: To gain VTL, a person needs to be exposed to a variety of experiences that contribute to broaden-and-build (mental) of personal resources. Relaxation and Stress Control were hypothesized in the literature as two separate components. Empirically, they were consolidated, which makes sense. The psychometric properties of the VTL are reasonable for practical and scientific uses. Uses of the VTL scale can contribute to personal awareness, attitude, development, practice and policymaking, and research. However, the scale is new, requiring further validations on different populations as well as different demographics. Also, VTL scores need to be compared to data collected through other means such as observation and personal interviews.

Contact Information:
Idyll Arbor, Inc.
39129 264th Ave SE
Enumclaw, WA 98022

Phone: 360-825-7797
Fax: 360-825-5670
Email: sales@idyllarbor.com

VITALITY THROUGH LEISURE (VTL)

Ragheb, M. G.

DIRECTIONS: As a result of engaging in your leisure activities, there are some outcomes and impacts on you. We want to know how you rate possible outcomes of your leisure activities. By "Leisure Activities," we mean the activities you do after work, school, and/or other obligations. These include jogging, visiting others, going to the beach, and listening to music. Please use the scale below: If you *STRONGLY DISAGREE*, with the statement select "1," if you *STRONGLY AGREE* select "5"; otherwise, choose a number between "1" and "5". *There are no right or wrong responses.*

Strongly Disagree	Disagree	In Between	Agree	Strongly Agree
1	2	3	4	5

The Leisure Activities I do …

_____ 1. help me to be in touch with my spirit.
_____ 2. maintain or increase my fitness.
_____ 3. help me to recover from the demands of life.
_____ 4. are enjoyable.
_____ 5. improve my relationships with others.
_____ 6. help me to realize that I am a part of a bigger picture.
_____ 7. improve my physical shape.
_____ 8. help me to relax.
_____ 9. are rich sources of delightful experiences.
_____ 10. improve my mood.
_____ 11. help me to be in touch with the supreme power of my choice.
_____ 12. make me feel stronger.
_____ 13. help me to unwind.
_____ 14. provide me with rich experiences.
_____ 15. restore me to a new state.
_____ 16. improve my views or perspectives of life.
_____ 17. contribute to my health.
_____ 18. help me to regenerate from fatigue.
_____ 19. make sense to me.
_____ 20. make me enthusiastic about life.
_____ 21. allow for me to make life changes.
_____ 22. improve my energy level.
_____ 23. soothe me.
_____ 24. give me excitement.
_____ 25. help me to pursue my life dreams.
_____ 26. help me to feel positive about how I look.
_____ 27. take my mind off other things in life.
_____ 28. are self-determined.

Items that constitute each component:

Broaden-and-Build	= Items 1, 6, 11, 16, 21, and 25.
Physical Condition	= Items 2, 7, 12, 17, 22, and 26.
Relaxation and Stress Control	= Items 3, 8, 13, 18, 23, and 27.
Optimal Arousal	= Items 4, 9, 14, 19, 24, and 28.
Personal Betterment and Restoration	= Items 5, 10, 15, and 20.

Add all the 28 items to obtain a score for total "Vitality Through Leisure."

Chapter 9

Measurements of Playfulness and Humor

Focus of Chapter

This chapter lists the measurements of playfulness and humor currently available for use in recreation and leisure and earlier measurements that can be drawn upon in creating new, more modern measurements.

Key Terms

- humor
- playfulness

Objectives

Know the available measurements of playfulness and humor.

These scales measure constructs related to playfulness and humor.

1. Children's Playfulness Scale (CPS) (Barnett, 1991)
2. Sense of Humor Scale (SHS) (Thorson and Powell, 1993)

   Other assessments discussed in the literature, which to not have enough information to evaluate, include:

1. Lieberman's Playfulness Instrument (LPI) (Lieberman, 1965, 1966)
2. Coping Humor Scale (CHS); Martin and Leftcourt, 1983.
3. Situational Humor Response Questionnaire (SHRQ); Martin and Leftcourt, 1984.
4. Adult Playfulness Scale (APS) (Glynn and Webster, 1992, 1993)
5. State-Trait Cheerfulness Inventory (STCI); Ruch, Koehler, and Ban Thriel (1996).
6. Playfulness Scale (PS) (Schaefer and Greenberg, 1997)
7. Test of Playfulness (ToP) (Okimoto et al., 2000)
8. Humor Styles Questionnaire (HSQ) Martin, Puhlik-Doris, Larsen, Gray, and Weir, 2003.

Questions and Exercises

1. Discuss the nature and benefits of assessing playfulness and humor.

| Playfulness 1 |

CHILDREN'S PLAYFULNESS SCALE
(CPS)
Lynn A. Barnett

Reference: Barnett, L. A. (1991). Playfulness: Definition, design, and measurement. *Play and Culture, 3,* 319-336.

Goal of the Measurement: To identify and measure children's playfulness or internal predisposition to be playful.

Background Literature: An attempt was made to demonstrate difficulties facing scholars to define, conceptualize, and theorize about play and its psychological attributes. A turning point has been identified, that is by focusing on play as a characteristic of the individual (as an internal personality predisposition trait), rather than the child's behavior and overt interactions (what the child does). To illustrate this point: a highly playful child will create her/his play world out of even the most sterile environment. Speculatively, scholars have been delineating the boundaries and contents of playfulness components for five decades, such as:

1. Surgency — cheerful, joyous, humorous, witty, and energetic.
2. Siza-affectia — being good-natured, laughs readily, and likes to participate with people.

Insightfully Lieberman (1965, 1966), in her pioneering efforts, identified five components of the playfulness trait: cognitive spontaneity, social spontaneity, physical spontaneity, manifest joy, and sense of humor. Later, Lieberman (1977) added horseplay, enthusiastic participation in a wide range of social activities, hostile wit, and taunting pranks directed at others. Further research added to playfulness being imaginative, humorous and playful attitude, emotional expressiveness, novelty seeking, curiosity, openness, and communicativeness. Evidence demonstrated that children who rated high on playfulness were characterized as having positive affect, being physically active, having a high degree of social and imaginative play, and being more verbal than their less playful preschool counterparts. The above theoretical conceptualization was used as the basis for empirically testing the structural foundations of the playfulness construct.

Methodology Employed: Lieberman's five components identified above were the starting point, with additions from another study, to help construct the current measurement. A five-point, Likert-type scale was employed to rate 25 items from "Sounds Exactly Like the Child" to "Doesn't Sound At All Like the Child." Items were revised and reconstructed following review by colleagues and students. Moreover, two expert panels — 26 in child development and 9 faculty members — evaluated the 25 items for content and face validities, dropping them to 23 revised items. A sample was selected, composed of 388 children (179 boys), ranging from 29 months to 61.5 months. Factor analysis with Varimax rotation and test-retest reliability were performed.

Findings: Factor analysis confirmed the five-factor structure, gaining loads of .55 or greater, accounting for two-thirds of the variance. The five factors were Physical Spontaneity, Social Spontaneity, Cognitive Spontaneity, Manifest Joy, and Sense of Humor. Alpha reliability coefficients ranged between .89 and .84, and test-retest .95 to .84. Scale validity (convergent and discriminant) was also demonstrated.

Investigator's Comments: The CPS is offered as a reliable, valid, and efficient means for measuring the child's intrinsic tendency toward playful encounters with his/her surroundings (people, places, or things).

Contact Information:
Dr. Lynn Barnett-Morris, Professor
Department of Recreation, Sport, and Tourism
The College of Applied Health Sciences
104 Huff Hall
University of Illinois
Champaign, IL 61820

Phone: 217-244-5645
Fax: 217-244-1935
Email: lynnbm@illinois.edu

CHILDREN'S PLAYFULNESS SCALE
(CPS)

Barnett, L. A.

DIRECTIONS: The developer of the scale should be contacted for the exact directions. Generally, the directions say to mark how closely the description matches the child being evaluated on the following scale.

Sounds exactly like the child	Sounds a lot like the child	Sounds somewhat like the child	Sounds a little like the child	Doesn't sound at all like the child
1	2	3	4	5

Physical Spontaneity

_____ 1. The child's movements are generally well coordinated during play activities.

_____ 2. The child is physically active during play.

_____ 3. The child prefers to be active rather than quiet in play.

_____ 4. The child runs (skips, hops, jumps) a lot in play.

Social Spontaneity

_____ 5. The child responds easily to others' approaches during play.

_____ 6. The child initiates play with others.

_____ 7. The child plays cooperatively with other children.

_____ 8. The child is willing to share playthings.

_____ 9. The child assumes a leadership role when playing with others.

Cognitive Spontaneity

_____ 10. The child invents his/her own games to play.

_____ 11. The child uses unconventional objects in play.

_____ 12. The child assumes different character roles in play.

_____ 13. The child stays with one activity rather than changes activities during play.

Manifest Joy

_____ 14. The child expresses enjoyment during play.

_____ 15. The child demonstrates exuberance during play.

_____ 16. The child shows enthusiasm during play.

_____ 17. The child is restrained in expressing emotion during play.

_____ 18. The child sings and talks while playing.

Sense of Humor

_____ 19. The child enjoys joking with other children.

_____ 20. The child gently teases others while at play.

_____ 21. The child tells funny stories.

_____ 22. The child laughs at humorous stories.

_____ 23. The child likes to clown around in play.

SAMPLE
Do Not Copy

Reverse scoring on items 13 and 17.

Playfulness 2

SENSE OF HUMOR SCALE
(SHS)

James A. Thorson and F. C. Powell

Reference: Thorson, J. A., and Powell, F. C. (1993). Development and validation of a multi-dimensional sense of humor scale. *Journal of Clinical Psychology, 49*, 13-23.

Goal of the Measurement: To assess the sense of humor as a situational reaction.

Background Literature: Humor has been identified as a mechanism to cope with life's difficulties. Evidence was cited that humor helped with successful aging. Many studies on death, anxiety, or fear of death were restricted from investigating critical relations due to the lack of a reliable and valid multidimensional scale that assessed the sense of humor. Humor can serve many functions: self-protection, getting along, showing kindness, easing tension, or gaining someone's confidence. Six elements were identified which may make up an individual's humor repertoire, as follows: recognition of oneself as a humorous person; recognition of others' humor; appreciation of humor; laughing; perspective (an individual's outlook, coping vs. getting upset, and being good-natured and tolerant); and coping humor or adaptive humor to ease tension as a social lubricant — the highest form of humor usage.

Methodology Employed: As a result of literature review, six elements of the sense of humor were extracted: 1) humor production and creative ability; 2) playfulness or a sense of whimsy, *joie de vivre*, the ability to have a good time; 3) the ability to use humor to achieve social goals; 4) recognition of humor; 5) appreciation of humor; and 6) use of humor as an adaptive or coping mechanism. Brainstorming to develop items yielded 20 to 21 items for each element, forming a total pool of 124, which was responded to by 264 volunteers, using a 5-point, Likert-scale. Analysis helped to reduce the 124 items to 70, of which 22 were loaded (principal component, Varimax rotation) at .60 or higher. Eight items were added on humor for social purposes. Further analysis settled on 29 items, which were administered to a sample of 234 individuals. Statistical treatments utilized factor analysis and alpha reliability.

Findings: Employing principal component factor analysis and a Varimax rotation identified five items that did not load at .50 or higher. The other 24 items clustered under four factors, as follows: Humor Production and Social Uses of Humor; Coping or Adaptive Behavior; Humor Appreciation; and Attitudes toward Humor. The alpha reliability coefficient for the total scale was .92.

Investigator's Comments: Most existing scales of the senses of humor assess only one element (component), despite the evidence that humor is a multidimensional construct. Some earlier approaches attempted to combine different scales, which resulted in an unclear focus regarding what is measured. The current scale is a multidimensional structure, validated through three trials, and tested for reliability. The current scale may have a variety of research and clinical applications.

SENSE OF HUMOR SCALE
(SHS)

Thorson, J. A. and Powell, F. C.

DIRECTIONS: Please rate the following items on the following scale.

Strongly Disagree				Strongly Agree
1	2	3	4	5

_____ 1. I'm regarded as something of a wit by my friends.
_____ 2. I can say things in such a way as to make people laugh.
_____ 3. My clever sayings amuse others.
_____ 4. People look to me to say amusing things.
_____ 5. I use humor to entertain my friends.
_____ 6. I'm confident that I can make other people laugh.
_____ 7. Other people tell me that I say funny things.
_____ 8. Sometimes I think up jokes or funny stories.
_____ 9. I can often crack people up with the things I say.
_____ 10. I can ease a tense situation by saying something funny.
_____ 11. I can actually have some control over a group by my uses of humor.
_____ 12. Humor helps me cope.
_____ 13. Uses of wit or humor help me master difficult situations.
_____ 14. Coping by using humor is an elegant way of adapting.
_____ 15. Trying to master situations through use of humor is really dumb.
_____ 16. Humor is a lousy coping mechanism.
_____ 17. Uses of humor help put me at ease.
_____ 18. I can use wit to adapt to many situations.
_____ 19. I appreciate those who generate humor.
_____ 20. I like a good joke.
_____ 21. Calling somebody a "comedian" is a real insult.
_____ 22. I dislike comics.
_____ 23. People who tell jokes are a pain in the neck.
_____ 24. I'm uncomfortable when everyone is cracking jokes.

When scoring, reverse items 15, 16, 21, 22, 23, and 24.

Complete directions were not provided.

Chapter 10

Leisure Administration and Supervision Measurements

Focus of Chapter

This chapter lists the measurements of leisure administration and supervision currently available for use in recreation and leisure and earlier measurements that can be drawn upon in creating new, more modern measurements.

Key Terms
- administration
- supervision

Objectives

Know the available measurements of leisure administration and supervision.

Measurements included in this chapter assess administrative and supervisory functions. The limited assessment tools available here measure quality of recreation services, employees' feelings and how managers react to them, volunteer functions, and special event volunteer motivation. Despite the critical importance of administrative functions in recreation, very meager attention has been given to their assessment.

1. Quality of Recreation Services (QRS) (MacKay and Compton, 1990)
2. Recreation Service Quality Assessment (RSQA) (Wright, Duray, and Goodale, 1992)
3. Motivation Assessment and Performance Scale (MAPS) (Williams and Neal, 1993)
4. Center for Environmental and Recreation Management — Customer Service Quality (CERM CSQ) (Howat, Absher, Crilley, and Milne, 1996)
5. Volunteer Functions Inventory (VFI) (Clary et al, 1998)
6. Special Event Volunteer Motivation Scale (SEVMS) (Farrell, Johnston, and Twynam, 1998)

Questions and Exercises

1. How can assessment procedures improve recreation administration and supervision?
2. Elaborate on the issue of "Quality" as basis for assessment for managers and supervisors.
3. Which areas lack assessments that are needed to enhance leisure management and supervision?

Administration 1

QUALITY OF RECREATION SERVICES
(QRS)

Kelly J. MacKay and John L. Compton

Reference: MacKay, K. J., and Compton, J. L. (1990). Measuring the quality of recreation services. *Journal of Park and Recreation Administration, 8,* 47-56.

Goal of the Measurement: To assess service quality in the context of recreation service delivery. That would be achieved through investigating customers' perceptions of service quality in selected recreation services.

Background Literature: Due to increasing competition from nonprofit organizations and commercial companies, increasing service quality of recreation agencies will be the key to future viability. Most studies find two types of competitive advantage: 1. low price and 2. superior quality of service. For recreation and park departments the trend has been to phase out subsidization, which has made lower prices less of a possibility. Therefore, recreation and park administration gradually favored paying more attention to improving service quality. Defining quality, philosophically and empirically, has been debatable due to its subjectivity. For the purpose of this development, quality was agreed to be the degree to which opportunities satisfy the motivations for which they are designed. This is achieved when recreation opportunities meet the needs of the participants. A baseline needs to be established when assessing users' service expectations to evaluate how positive or negative their perceptions have been. The index to be suggested is as follows: The more positive the expectations, the higher the service quality.

Two concepts were differentiated elaborately: service quality and satisfaction. While service quality is intangible, it can be considered as the summation of past transactions or experiences. In comparison, satisfaction with service is related to the psychological outcome that emerges from experiencing the service. Also, it is the psychological outcome from a specific transaction or experience. There had been a growing conceptualization of service quality in the field of marketing that has been adapted to park and recreation services. Using a quantitative method in the field of marketing, data were gathered from more than 1,000 users. Five dimensions were recognized: tangibles, reliability, responsiveness, assurance, and empathy. This assessment attempted to explore the above marketing dimensions in the field of park and recreation.

Methodology Employed: The instrument focused on the five dimensions of service quality reported in the marketing literature. A seven-point scale was used; one negative, one neutral choice, and five positive choices as follow: disagree, neither agree nor disagree, slightly agree, agree, strongly agree, very strongly agree, extremely strongly agree. Although this approach is unconventional, the investigators' rationale was that respondents rarely disagree with positive features described by the scale items in the "desires" section. Twelve experts generated 128 items, assessing the five dimensions of service quality. That was regarded as the basic structure of the recreation service quality domain. Other experts (15), putting each statement into the dimension in which they perceived it belonged, performed further classification. Consensus on statements was used to choose five items for assessing each of the five domains, yielding a 25-item scale. Twelve out of the 25 items in the scale were raised in the 22 items by marketing investigators. This demonstrates uniqueness of park and recreation services, as well as making this instrument a recreation-specific scale. Relying on global scales developed in non-recreation areas would not be as effective. Coefficient alpha analysis was used to test the reliability of the scale items. A sample of 199 was drawn from the population of municipal recreation program participants. Data were collected on-site through a self-administered questionnaire handed out at the start of four recreation sessions (fitness class, senior trips, painting, and ice hockey).

Findings: Utilizing the reliability test provided Cronbach's alphas, ranging from .86 to .62, suggesting sufficient internal consistency within the scale. Validity was established through two different analyses, one of which was correlating overall quality and the difference (perception-desire) score for each dimension. Results supported the structure of the 25-item scale assessing quality of recreation services.

Investigator's Comments: Comparing desires and perceptions can provide an overall measure of service quality in the form of average score across all dimensions. Moreover, individual responses can provide insights into which particular aspects of a dimension were superior, indicating directions for improvement. On the agency level, assessment can include not only perceptions of its own services, but also for perceptions of the attributes of similar services offered by other service suppliers.

Note: The assessment is given twice using different wordings in the directions and items. The first directions read, "Please show the extent to which you think the program should possess the features described by each of the following statement(s)." The second wording is, "Please show the extent to which you think the program in which you are now participating has the features described by each of the following statement(s)." The items are changed from "should be" to "is." The first wording assesses "Service Quality Desired." The second assesses "Perceived Service Quality."

Contact Information:
Dr. Kelly MacKay, Professor & Associate Dean (Academic)
106 Frank Kennedy Centre
Faculty of Kinesiology and Recreation Management
University of Manitoba
Winnipeg, Manitoba, R3T 2N2

Phone: 204-474-7058
Fax: 204-474-7634
E-mail: mackay@cc.umanitoba.ca

QUALITY OF RECREATION SERVICES

MacKay, K. J. and Compton, J. L.

DIRECTIONS: Please show the extent to which you think the program [should possess | in which you are now participating has] the features described by each of the following statement(s).

Disagree	Neither Agree nor Disagree	Slightly Agree	Agree	Strongly Agree	Very Strongly Agree	Extremely Strongly Agree
1	2	3	4	5	6	7

TANGIBLES
_____ 1. The facility [should be | is] visually aesthetically attractive.
_____ 2. The staff [should be | is] well dressed and appears neat.
_____ 3. The equipment provided by the department [should be | is] up-to-date.
_____ 4. The facility [should be | is] comfortable.
_____ 5. The other participants [should not be | are not] bothersome.

RELIABILITY
_____ 6. The facility/program [should start | starts] on time.
_____ 7. Information provided [should be | is] accurate.
_____ 8. What is promised [should be | is] delivered.
_____ 9. The staff [should perform | perform] duties consistently well.
_____ 10. The department [should be | is] concerned with quality control.

RESPONSIVENESS
_____ 11. The staff [should be | is] willing to go an extra step to help participants.
_____ 12. The staff [should take | takes] time with participants.
_____ 13. The staff [should respond | responds] to requests quickly.
_____ 14. Problems [should be | are] solved quickly.
_____ 15. The department [should act | acts] on participants' suggestions.

ASSURANCE
_____ 16. The staff [should be | is] polite.
_____ 17. The staff [should be | is] trustworthy.
_____ 18. The staff [should be | is] competent.
_____ 19. The staff [should be | is] credible.
_____ 20. The staff [should have | has] enthusiasm.

EMPATHY
_____ 21. The staff [should give | gives] individual attention to you.
_____ 22. The staff [should understand | understands] your needs.
_____ 23. The program/service [should be | are] offered at a convenient time for you.
_____ 24. The program/facility [should be | is] at a convenient location for you.
_____ 25. The staff [should make | makes] you feel as though you belong.

Administration 2

RECREATION SERVICE QUALITY ASSESSMENT (RSQA)

Brett A. Wright, Nick Duray, and Thomas L. Goodale

Reference: Wright, B. A., Duray, N., and Goodale, T. L. (1992). Assessing perceptions of recreation center service quality: An application of recent advancements in service quality research. *Journal of Park and Recreation Administration, 10*, 33-47.

Goal of the Measurement: To assess service quality to be utilized in diagnosing and improving service provisions.

Background Literature: In contemporary times, improving service quality has gained growing attention, mainly initiated by marketing specialists. Evidence showed that products received much higher ratings than services. It was realized that providing superior service produces competitive advantages and substantial cost efficiencies by reducing service-related mistakes. Similar attention to service quality in recreation and park services began in the late 1980s. Hence it was felt that, in order for organizations to improve service quality, they must first assess their customers' perceptions of the existing quality. Surprisingly, it was found that managers are not necessarily reliable predictors of users' opinions.

Qualitative studies conducted by Parasuraman, Zeithamal, and Berry (1985) laid the conceptual framework for developing a service quality scale. The main theoretical assumption utilized in Parasuraman's measurement development was, "Total service quality is perceived by the customer as a comparison between the expected service, which he or she expects to get, and that perceived service, which the customer feels he or she has in fact received" (Gronroos, 1982). Parasuraman and his colleagues realized five criteria. These criteria or dimensions were tangibles, reliability, responsiveness, assurance, and empathy. For future applications, the above dimensions need to be verified every time a park and recreation scale is developed in the above context

Methodology Employed: An item pool from Parasuraman et al. (1985) and MacKay and Crompton. (1990) was adapted to recreation centers. Furthermore, recreation-center-specific items were added, but within the same five marketing dimensions described by Parasuraman. Center-specific items were obtained through focus-group sessions and on-site observations. All in all, 70 initial items were drafted. After a refinement of the 70 items, they were evaluated and reduced by a panel of administrators, managers, and researchers, resulting in 30 items. In the final verification, ratings were obtained on a seven-point scale, ranging from "Not at All Essential for Excellence" = "1" to "Absolutely Essential for Excellence," = "7." A stratified, proportionate sample of 2,063 was drawn, representing eight centers (rate of return = 39%).

Findings: Results were not reported on the instrument's factorial structure nor on its reliability, but only on the service quality in the centers. The instrument initiated above remains in need of further verification, using factor analysis, reliability, and validity tests.

Investigator's Comments: Many recommendations and conclusions were offered, but almost all were irrelevant to scale development. A set of recommendations was provided for applying Parasuraman et al.'s scale.

Note: In the conceptualization of recreation service quality, it is important to keep in mind the uniqueness of recreation and park services being experiential and non-material. Recreation quality might have different characteristics as compared to product quality, yielding somewhat different dimensions. Differences can be due to the nature of the clientele, settings, expectations, or rewards. What actually applies to the dimensions of quality products might not necessarily fit the picture of quality park and recreation services. It is important to test a recreation-specific construct, discovering the proportion of overlap with quality products and, more importantly, what is uniquely experiential or aesthetic in recreation services.

RECREATION SERVICE QUALITY ASSESSMENT
(RSQA)

Wright, B. A.; Duray, N.; and Goodale, T. L.

DIRECTIONS: Please rate the following items as they relate to the quality of services offered by your recreation center. If the content of the statement is "**Not at All Essential for Excellence**" mark 1 on the line in front of the content. If the statement is "**Absolutely Essential for Excellence**" mark 7. If you are in between, choose the number that corresponds to your rating.

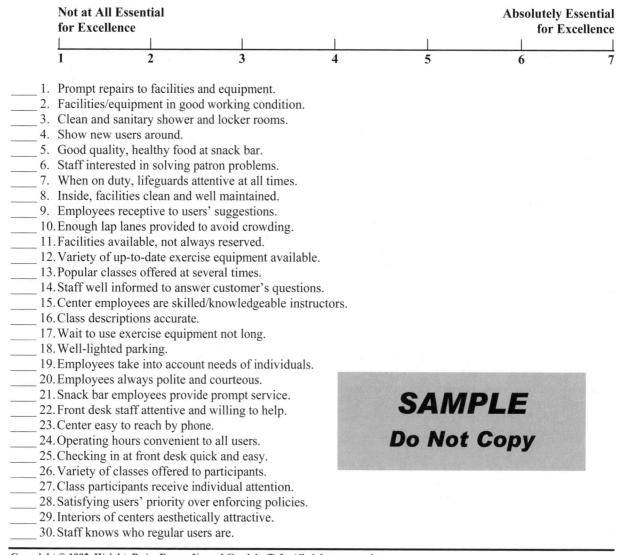

Not at All Essential for Excellence						**Absolutely Essential for Excellence**
1	2	3	4	5	6	7

_____ 1. Prompt repairs to facilities and equipment.

_____ 2. Facilities/equipment in good working condition.

_____ 3. Clean and sanitary shower and locker rooms.

_____ 4. Show new users around.

_____ 5. Good quality, healthy food at snack bar.

_____ 6. Staff interested in solving patron problems.

_____ 7. When on duty, lifeguards attentive at all times.

_____ 8. Inside, facilities clean and well maintained.

_____ 9. Employees receptive to users' suggestions.

_____ 10. Enough lap lanes provided to avoid crowding.

_____ 11. Facilities available, not always reserved.

_____ 12. Variety of up-to-date exercise equipment available.

_____ 13. Popular classes offered at several times.

_____ 14. Staff well informed to answer customer's questions.

_____ 15. Center employees are skilled/knowledgeable instructors.

_____ 16. Class descriptions accurate.

_____ 17. Wait to use exercise equipment not long.

_____ 18. Well-lighted parking.

_____ 19. Employees take into account needs of individuals.

_____ 20. Employees always polite and courteous.

_____ 21. Snack bar employees provide prompt service.

_____ 22. Front desk staff attentive and willing to help.

_____ 23. Center easy to reach by phone.

_____ 24. Operating hours convenient to all users.

_____ 25. Checking in at front desk quick and easy.

_____ 26. Variety of classes offered to participants.

_____ 27. Class participants receive individual attention.

_____ 28. Satisfying users' priority over enforcing policies.

_____ 29. Interiors of centers aesthetically attractive.

_____ 30. Staff knows who regular users are.

Administration 3

MOTIVATION ASSESSMENT AND PERFORMANCE SCALE (MAPS)

Albert E. Williams and Larry L. Neal

Reference: Williams, A. E., and Neal, L. L. (1993). Motivational assessment in organizations: An application of importance — performance analysis. *Journal of Park and Recreation Administration, 11*, 60-71.

Goal of the Measurement: To depict how leisure employees feel and how managers act relative to their motivations and performances.

Background Literature: In contemporary, interconnected environments, employees' motivations in public, private, and nonprofit organizations remain important. A major theoretical base is Herzberg's (1966) motivation/hygiene theory, which was used to develop a marketing tool called Motivation Assessment and Performance Scale (MAPS). Herzberg's theory assumes that certain factors in the work environment can influence motivations and hygiene. The motivations factors were generally intrinsic, related to job content, and linked to growth and personal development. Meanwhile, hygienic factors, extrinsic in nature, were associated with job dissatisfaction.

Herzberg's theory is a derivation of Maslow's (1954) hierarchy of needs. As a marketing tool, it identifies salient, qualitative features and rates importance and performance in the workplace. Moreover, it is a method to evaluate a program, a product, or a concept from the perception of the user. Recently, this method has been used in recreation to evaluate program planning, therapeutic recreation services, communication effectiveness, and citizens' views of government services.

Methodology Employed: Three stages were used to create the importance-performance instrument, MAPS. First, an item pool was identified, using experts, participants, and literature. These items were developed and refined by the authors in another study. Secondly, in developing the actual measurement, separate versions were developed for employees and their managers. A five-point, Likert-type scale was utilized to assess the responses. Lastly, mean values were calculated and used in the analysis of importance and performance items. The resulting scores were then plotted on a two-dimensional, actual grid for importance and performance. A systematic, random sample of 32 agencies out of 60 was drawn to represent park and recreation departments, yielding 26 participating agencies. A total of 635 respondents were identified from the 26 agencies: 158 managers and 477 employees (336 responded = 53%).

Findings: Two main factors emerged: "Concentrate Here" and "Keep up the Good Work." Cronbach's alpha reliability coefficient for the adopted MAPS scale was .87. Moreover, content validity was established through experts' approval and satisfaction with what the scale is measuring.

Investigator's Comments: The MAPS scale has proven to be a "user friendly" method of gathering and interpreting data, as well as a viable method of assessing employees' motivations. MAPS could provide agencies with a means to open the communication process among employees and managers, with respect to their motivations. However, additional refinements of MAPS in terms of establishing statistical significance and placement of the interpretive grids are needed.

Note: Numeric order of the items is based on original work of Neal, Williams, and Beach.

MOTIVATION ASSESSMENT AND PERFORMANCE SCALE (MAPS)

Williams, A. E. and Neal, L. L.

FOR EMPLOYEES

DIRECTIONS: Please rate **"How Important"** each item is for you. As demonstrated on the scale below, if the item was **Not At All Important,** mark 1; if the item was **Very Important,** mark 5; if your response falls between 1 and 5, choose the number that corresponds to your response. Place the rating of your choice on the line to the left of each item.

Not At All Important				**Very Important**
1	2	3	4	5

____ 1. Having a role in the decision making process.
____ 2. Being informed about job performance.
____ 3. Job security and steady work.
____ 4. Being part of the work team.
____ 5. Receiving raises and awards.
____ 6. Help agency attain its goals.
____ 7. Appreciated and recognized by supervisors.
____ 8. Receiving good wages.
____ 9. Safe work conditions.
____ 10. Learning new skills.
____ 11. Opportunity for promotion and advancement.
____ 12. Getting along with others.
____ 13. Achieving personal goals related to work.
____ 14. Increased freedom on job.
____ 15. Doing important, interesting, and quality work.
____ 16. Being leader of a work group.
____ 17. Receiving a good benefit package.

**SAMPLE
Do Not Copy**

Items belong to the following two components:

Motivator	= 1, 7, 10, 13, 15, and 16.
Hygiene	= 2, 3, 4, 5, 6, 8, 9, 11, 12, 14, and 17.

FOR MANAGERS

DIRECTIONS: Please rate **"How Important"** you feel that each item is for your employees. As demonstrated on the scale below, if the item was **Not At All Important,** mark 1; if the item was **Very Important,** mark 5; if your response falls between 1 and 5, choose the number that corresponds to your response.

Not At All Important				**Very Important**
1	**2**	**3**	**4**	**5**

_____ 1. Having a role in the decision making process.
_____ 2. Being informed about job performance.
_____ 3. Job security and steady work.
_____ 4. Being part of the work team.
_____ 5. Receiving raises and awards.
_____ 6. Help agency attain its goals.
_____ 7. Appreciated and recognized by supervisors.
_____ 8. Receiving good wages.
_____ 9. Safe work conditions.
_____ 10. Learning new skills.
_____ 11. Opportunity for promotion and advancement.
_____ 12. Getting along with others.
_____ 13. Achieving personal goals related to work.
_____ 14. Increased freedom on job.
_____ 15. Doing important, interesting, and quality work.
_____ 16. Being leader of a work group.
_____ 17. Receiving a good benefit package.

SAMPLE
Do Not Copy

Items belong to the following two components:
     Motivator   = 1, 7, 10, 13, 15, and 16.
     Hygiene   = 2, 3, 4, 5, 6, 8, 9, 11, 12, 14, and 17.

Administration 4

CENTER FOR ENVIRONMENTAL AND RECREATION MANAGEMENT — CUSTOMER SERVICE QUALITY (CERM-CSQ)

Gary Howat, James Absher, Gary Crilley, and Ian Milne

Reference: Howat, G., Absher, J., Crilley, G., and Milne, I. (1996). Measuring customer service quality in sports and leisure centers. *Managing Leisure, 1*, 77-89.

Goal of the Measurement: To assess customer service quality at a macro level.

Background Literature: Increased accountability demands evaluation and measurement of outcomes and outputs. Goal attainment and effectiveness have been gaining importance in not only Australia and New Zealand, but also the United Kingdom. Two main areas gained attention: 1. the development of efficiency performance indicators and 2. the development of effectiveness indicators based on customer service quality for sports and leisure centers. Both resource utilization and customer satisfaction are considered by managers as criteria for success. Total quality management focuses on results pertinent to customers' expectations. A discrepancy between customers' expectations and their perceptions of performance is a measure of customer service quality. The service provider's knowledge and skill in dealing with customers will significantly influence how customers perceive the quality of the service they receive at a specific "moment of truth." Numerous moments of truth accumulate, creating a cumulative effect, which must be backed by quality in the rest of the organization's activities. Customer expectations are composed of word-of-mouth communication, personal needs, and past experiences.

Methodology Employed: Past work by MacKay and Compton (1988, 1990) and Wright et al. (1992) was reviewed to identify dimensions and attributes. All were reduced to 15 attributes to be tested in this study. Moreover, a focus group of managers participated in four sessions to list service attributes. A total list of 60 attributes was generated, and then exposed to experts. As a result, the list was reduced to 15 core items. The scale was judged through ranking and rating processes. Respondents were asked to rate them in terms of how important each attribute was to them. A five-point scale was used with "Very Unimportant" = 1, "Unimportant" = 2, "Neither Important nor Unimportant" = 3, "Important" = 4, and "Very important" = 5. Two pilot studies were conducted after that to refine the scale. The scale was administered to a sample in 15 centers, yielding 2575 respondents.

Findings: Four factors were obtained: Core Services (loadings from .73 to .55), Staff Quality (.78 to .64), General Facility (.84 to .70), and Secondary Services (.78 to .64).

Investigators Comments: The generic nature of the CERM-CSQ attributes is intended to reduce the potential of respondent fatigue in completing the questionnaire. In turn, analyses of the CERM-CSQ attributes allow managers to focus on individual attributes by developing "ranking" items to determine what aspects of an attribute are problems or strengths. CERM-CSQ dimensions are different from financial services, which is not surprising, due to the unique nature of leisure industry's services. However, the obtained factor structure needs to be replicated in other contexts.

CENTER FOR ENVIRONMENTAL AND RECREATION MANAGEMENT — CUSTOMER SERVICE QUALITY (CERM-CSQ)

Howat, G.; Absher, J.; Crilley, G.; and Milne, I.

Directions: Please rate the following items in terms of how important each of them is to you. If the item is "**Very Unimportant**" mark 1, "**Unimportant**" mark 2, "**Neither Important nor Unimportant**" mark 3, "**Important**" mark 4, and "**Very Important**" mark 5.

Very Unimportant	Unimportant	Neither Important nor Unimportant	Important	Very Important
1	2	3	4	5

_____ 1. Parking area very safe and secure (cars, bikes, etc.).

_____ 2. Facilities always clean and well maintained.

_____ 3. Up-to-date information available on activities, results, events, etc.

_____ 4. Programs always start and finish on time.

_____ 5. Offer a broad range of activities.

_____ 6. Center well organized and well run.

_____ 7. Center physically comfortable and pleasant.

_____ 8. Programs and facilities provide value for money.

_____ 9. Equipment of a high quality and well maintained.

_____ 10. A good canteen or kiosk.

_____ 11. Adequate child minding.

_____ 12. Staff friendly and responsive.

_____ 13. Staff presentable and easily identified.

_____ 14. Staff experienced and knowledgeable.

_____ 15. Officials (umpires, judges, etc.) qualified, experienced and consistent.

SAMPLE Do Not Copy

> **Administration 5**

VOLUNTEER FUNCTIONS INVENTORY (VFI)

E. Gil Clary, Mark Snyder, Robert D. Ridge, John Copeland, Arthur A. Stukas, Julie Haugen, and Peter Miene

Reference: Clary, E. G., Snyder, M., Ridge, R. D., Copeland, J., Stukas, A. A., Haugen, J., and Miene, P. (1998). Understanding and assessing the motivations of volunteers: A functional approach. *Journal of Personality and Social Psychology, 74*, 1516-1530.

Goal of the Measurement: To assess the functions served by volunteers.

Background Literature: More than 89 million individuals invest a great deal of their (free) time and energy in the service of others. Volunteerism, a worldwide phenomenon, is an expression of relieving helplessness: providing companionship, tutoring, counseling, health care, and numerous other useful services. Based on literature, volunteers can be characterized as seekers of opportunities to help others; may deliberate a degree of involvement according to how the activity interests them; and may make a degree of commitment of their resources (time, energy, and opportunity). Investigating volunteers' motivations — the processes that initiate, direct, and sustain action — can be useful and functional, attempting to answer two main concerns: 1. Why do people volunteer? and 2. What sustains voluntary helping? To serve these ends, a strategy called "functional analysis" was devised and defined as an approach that is explicitly concerned with the reasons, purposes, plans, and goals that underlie and generate psychological phenomena, such as the motivation of volunteers. Acts of volunteerism may appear similar to each other, but they may, in reality, come from different motivations. In the end, though, what is important is that the volunteer feels effective. Attitude theories were used to explain motivations, yielding several of them such as bringing a sense of understanding the world and helping people to express deeply held values. Further, more contemporary functional theories were equated with volunteering motivation, extracting six components: values, understanding, social, career, protective, and enhancement.

Methodology Employed: Six studies were conducted to generate items, pretest the scale, formally testing the final inventory, and cross-validating it. Thirty items were composed initially to reflect the psychological and social functions of volunteerism on the bases of the conceptual analysis. Items were administered to currently active volunteers in a variety of settings; that is, with the assumption that their volunteering motives were the reasons for the enjoyment. The six studies employed samples of 321, 534, 65, 39, 61, and 369 persons. A seven-point, Likert-type scale was utilized, ranging from "Not at All Important/Accurate" = 1 to "Extremely Important/Accurate" = 7. Statistics employed were exploratory and confirmatory factor analysis (principal component), LISREL, regression analysis, Cronbach's alpha coefficients, and test-retest reliability.

Findings: The uses of factor analyses provided evidence supporting the six-subscale structure. Cronbach's alpha coefficients for the six confirmed subscales ranged between .89 and .80. Moreover, test-retest reliabilities were .78 to .64. Predictive validity was established in one of the studies.

Investigator's Comments: The validation of VFI contributes to understanding the helping motivations. Organizations that rely on volunteers to provide critical services can employ VFI to pre-measure their potential volunteers and devise a strategy to maximize their output.

Contact Information:
Dr. E. Gil Clary
15200 Kutztown
Kutztown, PA 19530

Phone: 610-680-1315

VOLUNTEER FUNCTIONS INVENTORY
(VFI)

Clary, E. G.; Snyder, M.; Ridge, R. D.; Copeland, J.; Stukas, A.; Haugen, J.; and Miene, P.

<u>DIRECTIONS</u>: Please indicate how important or accurate each of the following reasons for volunteering was for you in doing volunteer work. If the reason is "**Not at All Important/Accurate**," mark 1, if the reason is "**Extremely Important/Accurate**," mark 7.

Not at All Important/Accurate   Extremely Important/Accurate

| 1 | 2 | 3 | 4 | 5 | 6 | 7 |

_____ 1.   No matter how bad I've been feeling, volunteering helps me to forget about it.
_____ 2.   By volunteering I feel less lonely.
_____ 3.   Doing volunteer work relieves me of some of the guilt over being more fortunate than others.
_____ 4.   Volunteering helps me work through my own personal problems.
_____ 5.   Volunteering is a good escape from my own troubles.
_____ 6.   I am concerned about those less fortunate than myself.
_____ 7.   I am genuinely concerned about the particular group I am serving.
_____ 8.   I feel compassion toward people in need.
_____ 9.   I feel it is important to help others.
_____ 10. I can do something for a cause that is important to me.
_____ 11. Volunteering can help me to get my foot in the door at a place where I would like to work.
_____ 12. I can make new contacts that might help my business or career.
_____ 13. Volunteering allows me to explore different career options.
_____ 14. Volunteering will help me to succeed in my chosen profession.
_____ 15. Volunteering experience will look good on my resume.
_____ 16. My friends volunteer.
_____ 17. People I'm close to want me to volunteer.
_____ 18. People I know share an interest in community service.
_____ 19. Others with whom I am close place a high value on community service.
_____ 20. Volunteering is an important activity to the people I know best.
_____ 21. I can learn more about the cause for which I am working.
_____ 22. Volunteering allows me to gain a new perspective on things.
_____ 23. Volunteering lets me learn things through direct, hands-on experience.
_____ 24. I can learn how to deal with a variety of people.
_____ 25. I can explore my own strengths.
_____ 26. Volunteering makes me feel important.
_____ 27. Volunteering increases my self-esteem.
_____ 28. Volunteering makes me feel needed.
_____ 29. Volunteering makes me feel better about myself.
_____ 30. Volunteering is a way to make new friends.

SAMPLE
Do Not Copy

Each set of five items constitute a component, as follows:

Protective	=	Items 1-5
Value	=	Items 6-10
Career	=	Items 11-15
Social	=	Items 16-20
Understanding	=	Items 21-25
Enhancing	=	Items 26-30

Administration 6

SPECIAL EVENT VOLUNTEER MOTIVATION SCALE (SEVMS)

Jocelyn M. Farrell, Margaret E. Johnston, and G. David Twynam

Reference: Farrell, J. M., Johnston, M. E., and Twynam, G. D. (1998). Volunteer motivation, satisfaction, and management of an elite sporting competition. *Journal of Sport Management, 12*, 288-300.

Goal of the Measurement: To assess dimensions of volunteers' motivation and the relative importance of these motivations.

Background Literature: Special events are unique in the way they recruit volunteers. Events are characterized to be one shot, for short duration, and to occur annually or seasonally. Volunteers are a major part of an event's success; therefore, their motivations and satisfaction gained from their work is crucial. Volunteers' motivation can be intrinsic and extrinsic, with evidence demonstrating three categories for those incentives: Purposive, Solidarity (Social), and Material. A notion borrowed from consumer behavior, called "disconfirmation," presents satisfaction as a comparison between the rewards and costs of a purchase experience relative to an anticipated result. Previous satisfaction experiences influence a consumer's decision to purchase a given product or participate in a service. Voluntary behavior follows a process similar to the above.

Methodology Employed: Twenty-two items that constitute Volunteers' Motivation were adopted from an earlier investigation (Cnaan and Goldberg-Glen, 1991), which developed a scale assessing motivation to volunteer in human services. New items, specific to the event, were added as used by Getz (1991). Participants were asked on a five-point, Likert scale to indicate the importance of each item that influenced their decision to volunteer at a tournament. Questionnaires were mailed, and then followed up a month later, yielding 137 sets of responses (45.7% rate of return). Factor analysis with Varimax rotation was performed.

Findings: Factor analysis with the Varimax rotation yielded four components, explaining 49.7% of the variance: Purposive, Solidarity, External Traditions, and Commitments. No reliability tests were performed.

Investigator's Comments: Results on the components and item rank order differ as compared to the instrument developed by Canaan and Goldberg-Glen (1991). The difference suggests that motivation for special event volunteers is different from that for other volunteers. In application, managers should be prepared to address a variety of motivations when seeking volunteers for special events. It is speculated that attachment and involvement in a sport or recreational activity may influence motivation to volunteer for special events. Therefore, testing attachment and involvement, as developed in the recreation involvement construct, can be beneficial for segmenting volunteers.

SPECIAL EVENT VOLUNTEER MOTIVATION SCALE (SEVMS)

Farrell, J. M.; Johnston, M. E.; and Twynam, G. D.

<u>DIRECTIONS</u>: Developers of the scale should be contacted for directions and the complete, five-point scale.

Factor 1: Purposive
_____ 1. I wanted to help make the event a success.
_____ 2. I wanted to put something back in the community.
_____ 3. I wanted to do something worthwhile.
_____ 4. I wanted to feel part of this community.
_____ 5. Volunteering creates a better society.
_____ 6. Volunteering at this tournament makes me feel better about myself.
_____ 7. I wanted to help out in any capacity.
_____ 8. I am involved in curling.
_____ 9. I wanted to vary my regular activities.
_____ 10. It was a chance of a lifetime.
_____ 11. If I did not volunteer, there would be no one to carry out this volunteer work.

Factor 2: Solidarity
_____ 12. I wanted to broaden my horizons.
_____ 13. I wanted to gain some practical experience.
_____ 14. I wanted to work with different people.
_____ 15. I could obtain an educational experience.
_____ 16. I wanted to develop relationships with others.
_____ 17. I wanted to interact with others.

**SAMPLE
Do Not Copy**

Factor 3: External traditions
_____ 18. My family/friends were also volunteering.
_____ 19. A relative or friend is involved in curling.
_____ 20. I wanted to continue a family tradition of volunteering.
_____ 21. I did not have anything else to do with my time.
_____ 22. I wanted an opportunity to meet the players and see the games.
_____ 23. I have more free time than I used to have.

Factor 4: Commitments
_____ 24. My skills were needed.
_____ 25. I am expected to volunteer.
_____ 26. I have past experience providing similar services.
_____ 27. Most people in my community volunteer.
_____ 28. Being a volunteer with this tournament is considered prestigious.

Part II

Methods Used to Construct Measurements

The next nine chapters will focus on the art and science of developing measurements. The art pertains to the activities that delineate the boundaries of the concept, extracting it mainly from existing tested hypotheses, theories, and philosophies. The science is the application of the scientific method to verify what the art has yielded and composed. There should be continuous interaction between the art and the science until the final product in the form of quality instrument is secured. This is through maintaining a balance between the two, between the literature and its findings and theories on one hand and the rigorous validations of the measurement on the other. Ultimately, this produces an assessment tool that manifests good quality: valid, reliable, and usable. Part II looks at the methodology. Part III will present some of the most pertinent concepts and backgrounds that can be used as foundations for measurements in leisure services and leisure studies.

Chapter 11

Importance of Assessment in Recreation and Human Services

Focus of Chapter

The intent of this chapter is to describe the place of assessment and measurement in providing human and social services. Assessment, whether intentionally or unintentionally, formally or informally, has a central role in making good decisions. Reasons for the variations in attention to assessment — from one service to another — will be explored. The position of assessment in the decision-making process of leisure delivery systems will be introduced in relation to four major applications: administrative procedures, performance appraisal, program offerings, and therapeutic recreation. The impact of the absence of assessment in a delivery system will be investigated in relation to some basic processes: judgment, confidence in the outcome, efficiency, and generalizability of the services from one location or agency to another.

Key Terms

- absence of assessment
- decision making
- efficiency
- generalizability
- objectivity

- performance appraisal
- program evaluation
- scales and instruments
- status of assessment

Key Names

- Rabel J. Burdge
- Donald W. Fiske

- Richard Kraus
- John Neulinger

Objectives

- Describe the reasons for the importance of assessment in different fields.
- Identify the reasons for reliance on assessment in providing leisure and services in allied areas.
- Explain the impact of the absence of assessment tools in some critical services.
- Identify major aspects to be considered in using assessment.
- Describe the scope of providing leisure that lends itself to assessment such as administrative actions and performance appraisal.

Assessment, *the process of estimation and appraisal of leisure behavior and actions for decision-making,* is the central focus of this book. As a *process,* it is an ongoing operation that leads to problem solving, resulting in a decision. As *estimation,* it approximates judgment or opinion —

numerically — of the value, significance, or worth of an object (personal, social, or behavioral). As an *appraisal*, it is an advanced evaluation of qualities inherent in or possessed by that object. Finally as *problem solving*, it is utilized in the decision-making procedures (formally or informally) to meet needs, plan actions, or execute provisions. Scales and measurements are utilized to make accurate appraisal and estimation for quality decisions when deciding on leisure actions.

Often these days, neither the status nor the need for assessment in recreation and leisure provision are clearly perceived. Moreover, rigorous orientation and training in assessment approaches and use are not provided. That is due to three deficiencies:

- Lack of understanding the functions that assessment serves.
- Lack of assessment competencies.
- Lack of quality assessment tools.

For relevance of assessment to evaluation and to leisure delivery functions, see Riddick and Russell (1999), Henderson and Bialeschki (2002), Theobald (1979).

To start with, this chapter will demonstrate the status and need for rigorous assessment in leisure provision, showing functions that assessments can fulfill. Most of the leisure tools available in leisure and recreation are shown in Part I. As a foundation, a brief discussion of assessment approaches in fields concerned with life encounters, including leisure and recreation services, will be provided. Comparisons will be performed to see the centrality of assessment whenever there is a demand for information and decision-making.

There are many indications of the critical impact of free time on modern cultures. Nevertheless, there is no parallel match in attention to the assessment of related concepts. Let us imagine the absence of critical instruments in some sensitive fields of services, such as medicine or engineering. (An *instrument* can also refer to a measure, test, scale, inventory, questionnaire, survey, finder, or a tool. All serve the function of data acquisition.)

What would happen in the absence of such tools? How could doctors or engineers achieve their goals? By comparison, how much better would areas such as leisure provision, exercise, fitness, and health be at providing services if they had equally good assessment procedures? A number of answers to these questions will be is provided.

In responding to the above concerns, some basic considerations for the uses of assessment, such as objectivity, confidence, and efficiency, will be presented. Hopefully, by the time you complete reading this chapter, you will have not only a better understanding of the needs for assessment in leisure and allied services, but will also develop a better attitude toward assessment processes. Consequently, you will have better motivation to seek well-rounded orientation to basic assessment concepts and a desire to develop homemade assessment tools, as needed in your area, if standardized scales do not exist. Your assessment understanding, attitude, and motivation can shape your assessment competencies.

Assessment as a Decision-Making Device

All fields that are pressed for information and decisions demand assessment. Illustrating the broad demand for assessment, Cohen and Swerdlik (2002, p. 563) say, "In the area of interface between behavioral assessment and new technology, we foresee research focused on questions related to how a wide range of interventions in inpatient and outpatient settings (*ranging from leisure activities to medicine*) affect behavior." (Italic added) How critical the decision (a life on the line versus no threat at all) decides whether there should be strict or lenient demands for assessment. Decisions are made in war and in peace; therefore, competencies in assessments are needed for both.

What are some of the most critical incidents in human existence that necessitate rigorous assessment? Without exclusivity, some examples of having a life on the line range from surgery and wars to orbiting the earth and flying through our solar system. Therefore, these areas have the most sophisticated technological assessment tools. Medical technology, for instance, can penetrate into human bodies, with both accuracy and precision, collecting data and operating with ease and accuracy. Moreover, the Armed Forces and space agencies can collect excellent details before they encounter an enemy or navigate safely going into orbit within our solar system. The underlying reason for success in all these endeavors is accurate assessment, which enables practitioners to make not only sensitive decisions and strategies, but also successful executions. In comparing uses of assessment in medical technology and space travel to social services, a wide gap exists, as presented below.

The Status of Assessment in Human and Social Services and Sciences

Assessment is widely utilized in society. It serves not only all age groups and specific services across life span, but also goals for organizations. Examples of age groups gaining assessment attention can range from infants, preschoolers, toddlers, adolescents, middleagers, and the elderly (e.g., Findling, Schulz, Kashani, and Harlan, 2001; Smith and Kampfe, 2000). There are numerous examples of specific services that operate across developmental stages. These services require assessment to achieve their goals, as reported in mental health promotion (Findling et al., 2001; Barry et al., 2000), management (Lichtveld, 2005), career counseling (Bronson, 2001), medicine (Wilson and Nutt, 2005) drug abuse prevention (Arthur and Blitz, 2000), rehabilitation counseling (Smith and Kampfe, 2000), providing for the homeless (Acosta and Toro, 2000), psychiatry (Huffman and Kunik, 2000; Lehman et al., 2000), and neuropsychological (Mateer, 2000). In sum, different groups and ages demand accurate assessment for a variety of functions.

Many fields of human services also are required to make sensitive decisions in their delivery systems, although decisions are not as critical as in surgery or in war. In principle, it is logical to assume that the more the service is perceived (by individuals and society) as both important and critical, the greater the demands and reliance on assessment. Examples of social and behavioral services that utilize assessment — without an attempt to rank-order them — are psychiatry, mental and physical health, counseling, rehabilitation, social work, education, management, advertising, criminology, therapeutic recreation, sports performance, physical therapy, physical education, occupational therapy, and recruitment (civil and Armed Forces).

In the search for efficiency in industry, a Harvard professor, Robert Kaplan, and a consultant, David Norton (1996) postulate that you cannot manage what you can't measure, and you can't measure what you can't describe. Warning of over-reliance on measurements in industry, Witzel (2005) wrote an article on, "The danger of mistaking the science of measuring as divine." He observed that, "some aspects of management will always be intuitive. That said, measurement yields knowledge, and no source of knowledge should ever be overlooked. The mistake is to treat measurement as a God… After all, you cannot measure what you cannot manage." (p. 8) Assessment in all fields should not be viewed as one-size-fits-all. Rather, it should be utilized as a tool to gather usable data for managerial decision-making. Moderation in the uses of measurements (as Socrates points out) allows for other realistic perspectives to be present.

Depending on the values of society, attention is demanded regarding what is being assessed. The implication is that there are some political, ethical, moral, and economic differences and considerations regarding the status of assessment and its value in given areas. Moreover, guidelines are suggested that can be considered parameters to identify and weight the level of attention devoted to assessment. Five criteria can be utilized to evaluate that status in any given field:

1. Number of assessment tools developed in a designated area of services.
2. Accessibility of developed measurements for professional and public use.
3. Quality of existing assessment instruments, in terms of usability, validity, and reliability.
4. The number of published textbooks, focusing on assessment in a given field.
5. The ability to use assessment tools or overall assessment competency.

It is assumed that no progress in knowledge and precision in practice can be made until quality assessment procedures are performed. In an era of rapid changes and efficiency in the use of resources, data-based decisions (quantitative or qualitative) are required. Advances in assessment strategies seem to be one of the signs of improvement in recent years.

The Status of Assessment in Leisure and Recreation Provision

In utilizing assessment, how would the fields of recreation, leisure, fitness, and play compare against the above fields or professions? How critical and sensitive are the decisions made in recreation services to individuals and society? In answering, it is sufficient to say that there is *no single general book on assessment* in the field of leisure and recreation services. The only two that exist are on recreational therapy (see burlingame and Blaschko, 2010; Stumbo, 2002). However, there are small chapters in books, articles in journals, and infrequent mention of assessment in different resources (e.g., Carpenter and Howe, 1985; Henderson and Bialeschki, 2002; Riddick and Russell, 1999). Moreover, the number and quality of assessment tools is meager (less than 100 measurements), without the rigorous methodology and attention required to develop formal or standardized assessment tools, as well as informal or homemade assessment devices. Sometimes you cannot locate the assessment instruments or reach their developers. Available tools are a start, but there is a clear need for more rigorous procedures.

Historically, in recreation and leisure, the first standardized tool was constructed to assess "Recreation and Play Interests" by Patrick (1921). That marked the beginning of formal, quantitative assessment devices. A steady momentum of scale development was established later, starting with the pioneering leisure attitude scale by Burdge (1961). In comparison, the history of psychology and educational assessments goes back more than 120 years, when Cattell founded the testing (assessment) laboratory at the University of Pennsylvania in 1888, although a few steps were taken before Cattell's major work (see Walsh and Betz, 1985; Aiken, 1989).

A major component of this book, as well as of classes taught on the subject, is the orientation to available scales in leisure and recreation. Therefore, the first part of this book presented 97 abstracts of technical reports on leisure measures, classified and developed in the following areas: leisure involvement, motivation, attitude, interests, satisfaction, leisure time boredom/free time boredom, playfulness and humor, and administrative functions. Fitness, exercise, recreational sports, and outdoor activities were incorporated where they best fit in the above classifications. Moreover, when they were available, the measures themselves (or portions thereof) were included with the abstracts, enabling reviewers to make appropriate decisions on their selection of instruments.

It is in the best interest of leisure practitioners to become familiar with the scales available. The classification is user friendly and self-explanatory. The author is confident that the content and coverage of that classification will intrigue the reviewer and relate to practice in many respects. All in all, a well-developed practitioner is one who is competent in assessment and its utilization in the decision-making process.

Relative to the sensitivity of decisions about individuals, in a society initially dominated by work and Protestant ethics; non-work pursuits were viewed as less critical, less important, and sometimes even trivial and a waste of time. Adult play (recreation), for instance, was forbidden during weekdays; it was considered a sin like many other taboos, which were perceived to jeopardize work productivity, reputation, and responsibility (see Kraus, 2000).

When informal and non-utilitarian activities are not valued, why would organizations and society need assessment of recreation, exercise, and leisure functions? Fundamentally, individuals and society did not fully perceive the growing role that informal activities could contribute to individuals' lives beyond the notion of fun and games. Cultural developments have since improved the image of recreation because we have realized that recreation can be fun and still contribute to work productivity and other positive outcomes.

Moreover, the trivial — what was viewed as a waste of time and as "just fun and games" — are now gradually demonstrating potentiality and viability.

Major breakthroughs have shown how critical free time, leisure, recreation, and play can be in their influences on individuals and society. The following analogy illustrates the importance of informal pursuits:

> Because of leisure's nature and characteristics (spontaneous, relaxed, freely chosen, with laughter and humor, mastering playful skills, and being self-initiated), it functions as a garnet silk shirt — an existing covering, though, it is not felt.

Due to the earlier misperceptions, recreation and leisure as pursuits and services gained less attention and budget, less value and political concern; consequently, lower attention was paid to their assessment. This is changing. For about 25 years now, many scientific fields of inquiry gradually documented positive impacts of informally chosen activities. Examples include relationships between recreation or leisure and the following life domains: *health* (Coleman and Iso-Ahola, 1993; Stephens, 1988; Taylor, Sallis, and Needle, 1985); *wellness* (Ragheb, 1993; Hettler, 1986; Ketchum and Marion, 1982); *vitality* (Kramer and Willis, 2001; Frank, Vaitl, and Walter, 1990); *stress* (Iwasaki and Mannell, 2000; Hull and Michael, 1995; Ragheb and McKinney, 1993; Zayas, 1990; Kabanoff and O'Brien, 1986); *life satisfaction* (Russell, 1987; Foret, 1985; Keller, 1983); *mood or depression* (Reddon, Pope, Friel, and Sinha, 1996; Elliott and Shewchuk, 1995); *and work morale and productivity* (McGrew, Johnson, and Bruininks, 1994; Edmonson, 1991; Nock and Kingston, 1989; Marino-Schorn, 1985-86). So, contrary to common misperceptions and old beliefs, the informal, the fun and games that humans pursue in their free time, are growing in their importance. Those pursuits have been realized for their possible positive impacts.

There is evidence that one-third of an individual's free time is experienced as leisure (see Neulinger, 1974). Besides, Yankelovich (1978) provides evidence that leisure doubled between 1955 and 1977 in its contribution to the search for meaning, as compared to work and the family. Consequently, leisure and recreation pursuits can touch on the very core of human existence and the search for significance in what is done (see Ragheb, 1996). In social evolution, what seemed less critical and less sensitive for existence, requiring less attention and assessment; turned out to be as essential as any other critical social entity.

Lack of assessment for informal pursuits can leave blind spots in tracing human development and change. For instance, certain phenomena will occur in given times and disappear as society changes. That would be possibly due to rapid advancements and the dynamics of change. Without recording them, without a point of reference as a baseline for future comparisons, they will be missed. Assessment is a process for registering developments and constraints at given times as points of reference in the human struggle, change, growth, and existence.

The Effects of the Absence of Assessment Tools

In current era, leisure provision, like many other services, has been expanding enormously, covering all life's settings. Lacking assessment of individual and community needs can jeopardize the processes of planning or securing sound policies and strategies. The level and quality of assessment will determine the possibility of many future successes.

Like cameras, assessments capture and register events in the moment they occur. Many examples illustrate these dynamics:

1. Free time can increase or decrease due to advancements in technology, economic crises, demographic changes, cultural norms, and trends. These are causing many uniquely unrepeatable responses.
2. Based on what is done as labor, work, soft computer work (pushing buttons), or high rates of unemployment, human energy utilized in leisure pursuits can be accumulated or wasted, contributing to or hurting individuals by that extra or missing energy.
3. Inventions can invade society and individuals' lives without our detecting or realizing their impact, such as television in the 1950s, when only 50% of the people had it, or cars in eras when the majority of people did not own them. Without cars, televisions, computers, and modern communication media how did individuals and communities pursue free time and leisure activities?

The impact of these critical devices and phenomena cannot be understood without accurate assessment.

Specifically, in contemporary times, do we know why many age groups (especially adolescents) seek drugs, alcohol, and tobacco in their free time? Do we know why people are seeking high-risk and excessive challenges in some of their leisure pursuits? How do lack of activity and low levels of exercise relate to health conditions, weight or obesity, and the level of wellness? How would free time and lack of leisure and recreation opportunities relate to violence, deviant behavior, crime, and terrorism? Do we have past records of these activities and other domains to compare with present behaviors?

Medically, when a patient is facing a health problem, doctors usually compare current functioning against the past records. Comparisons are made based on previous assessments and diagnoses to discover the origination of the disease that led to the present state. Past individual and national assessments can be sensitive indicators of present phenomena. Historical records and outcomes can help in explaining, interpreting, and comprehending present leisure, recreation, and play behaviors.

With greater advancements in measurements, both past and present assessments can also help predict future trends, patterns, and phenomena. Quality assessment and information function as the most powerful tools for quality predictions. Their outcomes may be utilized for sound planning and sound policy-making. In addition to that, they also provide information about crucial human and behavioral phenomena in the society at large.

It is critical to note that the absence of assessment devices impacts different fields in different ways. Some fields or trades cannot operate without good assessment devices, while others can deliver services without noticing the need or the impact of their absence. For example, an electrician is trained to use specific devices to help in getting the job done. If connections or repairs are not done properly, precise instruments can point to the malfunctioning device, avoiding the negative results of possible electrocution or fire. Clearly, lack of such devices can cause grave impacts, jeopardizing lives.

Unfortunately, in social and human services, including leisure, sports, and rehabilitation, practitioners are not similarly equipped with sensitive instruments to give information, helping to detect trouble and decide on needed repairs (actions or treatments). Comparatively, if a service did not achieve its goals or correct what was intended, (such as recreation programs with at-risk youth) no clear negative impact like electrocution happens. Subjectivity most likely is what professionals in these fields are left with. Service users would not voice reactions; practitioners are mostly content with their performance and no parties point out needs for service modifications. Administratively, this is the reason for unchanged offerings by service agencies. Without good assessment, practitioners do not know whether they succeeded or failed.

Based on the limited examples reported above, how can we assess relevant recreation, leisure, and free time behaviors? Are there any assessment tools available for those behaviors? More importantly, how are critical and sensitive decisions made and services provided in response to the above issues and demands? In free time and leisure, is there something like a life on the line, as in the war zone or in an operating room? Although the degree of sensitivity of free time and recreation is no match for war and surgery, there are indications that the positive impacts of leisure on health, wellness, vitality, stress control, life satisfaction, and quality of life are crucial to well-being, and they are growing in their importance.

There is a strong argument in favor of the need to assess informal and non-utilitarian behaviors, from childhood to the golden years. Nevertheless, developing and using assessment tools requires knowledge, skills, competencies, and resources. Other chapters in this book will contribute to these and the development and use of assessment tools.

Luckily, as human systems advance, assessment is becoming more important, so now it is often planned deliberately and executed skillfully as a basis for improvement.

The leisure field has accumulated almost 100 measurements, with a momentum to reach 150 scales in future decades. Moreover, evaluation studies cannot be conducted without the use of measurements. Therefore, like almost all other applied fields of services, a class in measurement needs to be incorporated in academic curricula, to teach assessment competencies to future practitioners. Major applied academic areas that teach classes in assessment are like the following: Measurement is Social Work, Measurement in Sport, Measurement in School Psychology, Measurement in Education, Measurement in Criminology, Measurement in Counseling, Measurement in Rehabilitative Services, and Measurement in Gerontology. Suffice it to say that service expansion and need for effectiveness, efficiency, and accountability require similar attention to assessment in leisure, recreation, park use, and fitness.

Basic Considerations for the Use of Assessment

Why there is a need for assessment instruments in recreation and leisure? Nunnally (1978), in his presentation of advantages of standardized measures, raised five points: objectivity, quantification, communication, economy, and scientific generalization. In relation to the leisure delivery systems, his five points show the need for

- objectivity in judgment processes
- confidence in results as the basis for good decisions
- ability to communicate findings to others
- efficiency in assessment use

- generalizability to other settings

Below are how Nunnally's five points relate to the field of leisure and recreation.

Objectivity in Judgment Processes

As demonstrated above, in many practical recreation settings, practitioners need to make decisions. Two approaches are available and exercised in different delivery settings: the subjective basis and the objective one. Subjectivity in assessment and decision-making is the reliance on gut feelings, personal orientations, views, and biases. Fundamentally, reliance on objective assessment demonstrates how critical and sensitive the decision is. Examples of important decisions are administrative: budget allocation, initiating a new service or action (requiring feasibility studies and needs assessment), program initiation or modification, and designing a new facility. Some other decisions are therapeutic: diagnosis, prevention, referral, treatment, or intervention.

The underlying required feature to all decisions is objectivity. An objective practitioner, in making professional judgment, removes his/her own personal preferences, inclinations, feelings, and biases. Therefore, relying on data generated through assessment makes decisions not only fairer and more accurate, but also sounder.

On the other hand, when measurements are utilized in field studies of leisure and recreation — helping practitioners to found their practice on valid assumptions — they remove guesswork from conclusions. Studies presenting viable findings can be replicated to validate results and establish consistency before they are utilized in practice, programming, therapy, or newly emerging services. However, invalid and unreliable assessment tools yield not only conflicting results and disagreements, but also frustrations and lack of confidence in scientific outcomes.

Due to fluctuations in the content and quality (validity and reliability) of assessment tools, for instance, an investigator may find a very strong relationship between recreation involvement and wellness, while another finds no significant relationship. How would practitioners in corporate fitness or therapeutic recreation view and utilize such findings? Which finding do they trust? Is there a chance of confusion and distrust in both results? Objectively stated, standardized instruments tend to minimize these scholarly, practical, and professional hazards and difficulties. Thus, they remove subjectivity or at least minimize its impacts. A quality instrument tends to gather consistent information. (See Chapter 14 on "Basic criteria for quality assessment tools").

Confidence in Results as the Basis for Good Decisions

Well-developed assessment procedures and the use of standardized tests can produce more accurate and trustworthy results. The value of the data collected depends on either personal motivation and efforts invested in a practitioner-made tool or on a standardized test's reliability and validity. Accurate results increase decision makers' trust in their actions.

On the other hand, shaky and inconsistent results lead to weak bases for programs and actions, jeopardizing their usefulness, impact, and trust. Therefore, it is to the best interest of all leisure professionals, administrators, supervisors, leaders, programmers, therapists, and evaluators, to employ trustworthy procedures; thus, maximizing both confidence and goal achievement.

Ability to Communicate Findings

Subjective findings are based strongly on personal biases. When it is necessary to communicate findings to another professional, it can be difficult to convey sufficient information about biased findings. Beyond that, different professionals will have different interpretations of results and may often reach different conclusions.

Standardized assessments eliminate many of the problems because of their objective nature. While it is still possible for professionals to reach different conclusions about what needs to be done, each has an objective basis (the assessment results) for making the decision. Bias in what was observed is eliminated and that leads to clearer communication.

Efficiency in Assessment Use

Quality assessment processes require good investments: time, money, effort, and public convenience. In an age of accountability and competition for resources, especially in public and corporate services, practitioners need to rely on efficient procedures. Developing a good homemade tool or a standardized device, although it requires more investment, yields quality data and results, more so than subjective procedures and personal guesses.

To illustrate the above, in making programmatic decisions in a nursing home based on individuals' leisure motivation, administrators and practitioners can employ a combination of three strategies for the acquisition of data:

1. Observation;
2. Personal interview; or
3. A practitioner-made or standardized test.

Obviously, the first and second approaches take weeks of observation and interviews (costing time, money, and public convenience); also, they require training of observers or interviewers. Whereas in the third strategy, the use of a test can be both efficient and effective. It can yield dependable data for less cost and with reasonable training. In most nursing homes the MDS (an assessment of resident status required for all facilities receiving U.S. Medicare funding) is fulfilling part of this requirement. Depending on the setting and other circumstances, it is recommended that the third option (practitioner-made or standardized devices that you trust) be used to gather more information.

Generalizability to Other Settings

Drawing a generalization to other behaviors or settings is the central focus of assessment and science. It can be done if appraisal procedures are valid and reliable. In a chaotic world, characterized by disorder, appropriate assessment procedures can find consistency and order, enhancing organization. The goal of assessment is to discover the underlying processes, consistent patterns, and order in evolving phenomena.

Surprisingly, accumulated evidence reveals that behaviors and reactions have a great deal of regularity and consistency. That is, under specific circumstances individuals' reactions are very close to each other, with minor variations. For example, people who are stressed show similar manifestations, with potential burnout. Many of them seek similar types of relaxation, solitude, and stimulus avoidance. Individuals who exercise claim a unified set of patterns, report given levels of functioning, health, wellness, and vitality; going through similar stages. This is fundamental for the meritorious status that assessment tools have in terms of generalizability.

Assessment generalizability can be verified and further validated by the use of multiple methods. If and when a self-reporting assessment procedure coincides, agrees, and correlates with other methods (namely observation and interview), assessors can claim that their assessment procedure is powerful and sufficient to achieve their goal(s).

Assessment of program intervention is also generalizable. For example, assume that the Department of Parks and Recreation in Phoenix, Arizona, experimented with the use of recreation and leisure programs for at-risk youth, assessing that the intervention was successful under conditions A and B, but not C. It is probable that replicating this intervention in Tampa, Florida, under the same conditions would achieve similar results. Consistently, if program execution is the same and the assessment tools are within the guidelines (valid and reliable), similar predictable outcomes are likely to occur. This is even more certain if the assessments have been tested for generalization across populations, time, and localities.

Pertinence of Assessment to Leisure and Recreation Services

Assessment can be viewed as a necessary basic step in four major operations or areas within the leisure delivery system. For instance, to appraise personnel, a program, a client, an agency, or total services, a practitioner needs information to rely on. This information should be sufficiently reliable to give an accurate judgment or appraisal.

In the absence of employing accurate assessment procedures, information can be useless or misleading. For data to be useful, collecting it must follow certain procedures. Also it necessitates attaining specific competencies in utilizing assessment steps such as making accurate observations, conducting good interviews, or employing quality instruments. Moreover, experience in data analysis would be needed, as well as objectivity in drawing interpretations. Lacking one or more of the above competencies not only will limit the value of the assessment process, but also can destroy the whole process and its usefulness. Greater attention to these details will be provided in separate chapters.

In order for the leisure delivery system to operate successfully, assessment has to be utilized on a variety of levels. Applications of assessment can be on four main levels: administration, personnel, programs, and therapeutic recreation procedures.

Assessment in Administration

Administrators can use assessments of specific types in one or more phases of service and policy implementation. Successful administrators should seek and rely upon accurate information to make decisions about programs and their sizes, funds, and the future of services — expanding or canceling them. During this Information Age, assessment has been proven to be one of the most efficient and useful procedures for administrators when planning and organizing data, described as "information technology management" (Smissen et al. 1999, p. 361). Therefore, managers in any system cannot operate effectively in the absence of information and its required skills in assessment.

Administratively, assessment is an ongoing process that changes as practitioners progress in their work. For example, before beginning recreation programs or services in a given setting, such as a

corporation, community, campus, or military base, accurate information is needed for good planning. The appropriateness and accuracy of the assessment determines the success of the next steps. This start — as outlined above — incorporates not only the assessments of needs and interests but also feasibility studies considered as a "marketing situation assessment" (see Smissen et al., 1999). While a program or a service is implemented on the basis of what has been assessed, ongoing assessment can help to further define direction, suggesting possible changes or modifications of programs or services.

Finally, both administrators and boards of directors would like to know how successful the program or the service has been or will be. This knowledge can be achieved using the widespread strategy of "satisfaction-based evaluation" (see Rossman and Schlatter, 2000). Moreover, administrators plan to periodically update systems, services, and/or programs. Updating systems is focused on improving offerings, increasing efficiency and effectiveness, increasing user satisfaction, and/or following emerging trends. In all of the services, no serious advancement and updating will occur unless the data is accurately representative, measuring the "pulse" of what is offered and how it is offered, in valid and reliable ways.

Assessment in Performance Appraisal

Performance appraisal, the process of evaluating personnel and the achievement of their duties, is a common concern of all organizations. Performance appraisal processes in leisure services, like all other organizations, face several difficulties, mostly in finding objective measures for the quality of services (see Culkin and Kirsch, 1986). It is viewed from myriad perspectives, depending on the individual's position in the system (e.g., the appraised, appraisers, administrators, or beneficiaries). A lack of quality in appraisal procedures can be misleading and frustrating, making performance appraisal, as a procedure, "in" for a period of time and "out" for another. The pendulum of how appraisals are perceived swings from trust to no trust, then trust again.

In commenting on the history of performance appraisal, Lazer and Wikstrom (1977) view it as shifting from "initial enthusiasm" to "deepening disillusionment," repeatedly followed by "new mechanisms." "That appears to be still underway." (p. 1). It is very possible that this frustration and the level of trust stem from dissatisfaction with the quality of data gathered. In a historical review Fiske (1971, p. 8) admits that, "The measurement of professional competencies is always a hard problem." Apparently, that is due in part to the methodology of appraising performance and what is appraised, which is the main focus of this book.

This issue needs careful attention. For performance appraisal to achieve its ends, it has to be conducted according to guidelines and tested methods. Aspects that need to be considered in assessment were suggested by Fletcher (2000). They include ongoing work performance, giving feedback, trying to increase work motivation, enhancing quality and quantity of output, and developing an individual's potential.

The issue of performance is straightforward, but what to include in an appraisal and the procedures to follow tend to be sources of trouble. Due to the rigorous nature of assessment methodology, both appraisers and their organizations need to be aware of potential difficulties. We assume that most of the dissatisfaction in the data gathered is due to the methodologies employed; these are the procedures and assessment tools utilized to reveal the level of performance.

For the data gathered to be useful, it must be valid and reliable. Therefore, performance appraisal must be viewed as an assessment strategy that follows all the steps and procedures of measurement development as discussed in Chapters 15 and 16. Without following these steps, problems will occur again and again.

To break this cycle, the initial step in measurement must be fulfilled to the letter. That first step is understanding the "concept" or "behavior" that we are attempting to evaluate. The concept of certain performances must be clearly defined and understood. Otherwise, all of the frustrations and the distortions will keep on reoccurring, without apparent explanations and reasons.

Before a quality appraisal process is conducted, some basic questions should be asked, such as: What is performance? Under what conditions is performance to be viewed? What is the expected quality of that performance? Fundamentally, how can we delineate the boundaries and content of what is appraised? The next step is to follow the art of measurement development as outlined in Chapters 15 and 16.

After knowing what is to be appraised, empirical validation of possible contents to be used will be found. Through employing a systematic method for the steps in measurement development, trustworthy outcomes can be assured. Dissatisfaction with the findings of performance appraisal and the cyclical dilemma of difficulties will be reduced and hopefully eliminated by using empirical validation of what we are trying to appraise.

One of the consistent problems is that no serious attention is invested in assessment procedures. There are some forms that have been utilized for years with no confidence in their outcomes. This is due, in part, to the limited utility for each performance appraisal. (In an agency with 20 kinds of jobs, it would require 20 different performance appraisal scales.) Besides this large number of performances that do not overlap, serious difficulties can result from the administrator's lack of training and competence in assessment procedures. That includes knowledge about assessment, its necessary tools, selection or development of quality tools, and data reduction and interpretation.

Are having quality appraisal tools, as suggested above, going to be the answer to the cyclical problems and disappointments of work performance assessment? A simple response is "no." But, at least this part of the process will have the best of available methods. The total picture also has to be continuously reevaluated, improving all other relevant parts of the appraisal process.

Appraisers' competencies are considered major determinants to both improvement and success of what is evaluated. Hence, what are the main competencies that need to be acquired by the appraiser? In order to be successful in performance appraisal, a supervisor needs to acquire specific skills, mastering all of these competencies:

1. Clear view of the duties a performer should achieve.
2. Indicators of desirable performance, to be utilized as the core of a scale.
3. Comprehensive knowledge of appraisal tools available to evaluate each specific performance.
4. Knowledge of what determines the quality of tools and measurements (validity and reliability).
5. Skills in adapting and modifying a generic tool to make it job-specific, followed by a number of verifications or pilot studies.
6. If there are no existing tools, the ability to take a list of duties and responsibilities for a certain job and convert it into an appraisal tool.
7. Ability to pretest a homemade appraisal tool (#6) to validate, change, and improve it.
8. Skills in handling data reduction, analysis, and interpretations as discussed in Chapter 17.

Following such a systematic and rigorous approach will ensure confidence in and reliance on appraisal outcomes.

System and Program Evaluation

Evaluation is recognized as a necessary procedure in program planning and service delivery (Suchman, 1976; Rossman and Schlatter 2000; Henderson and Bialeschki, 2002). Fundamentally, evaluation methodology always identifies assessment as a required step. In that sense, Farrell and Lundegren (1993) stress the importance of assessment to evaluation. Moreover, Edginton, Hanson, Edginton, and Hudson (1998) observe that, as a key concept to evaluation, it requires inquiry, appraisal, and assessment to estimate the efficiency, effectiveness, and output of a service organization.

Central to evaluation is the process of appraisal. The intent of the appraisal process is to make an estimation of the worth of a product, a service, or an outcome. The more accurate (valid and reliable) that estimate, the better the evaluation and its contribution to success. Appraisal, judgment, and estimation of an object are all fulfilled through assessment procedures. Therefore, no system or program evaluation can be conducted appropriately — according to evaluation guidelines — unless a careful assessment is performed.

Treatment Settings

Assessment is considered a fundamental step in the process of providing recreational therapy (see Carter, Van Andel, and Robb, 1995). For recreational therapy personnel to be competent practitioners, they must possess certain qualities. Among these qualities, a practitioner should be aware of the following:

- The goals of assessment
- Available assessment instruments
- What instruments are lacking
- How to administer available assessment tools
- How to interpret assessment results
- The utility of the results produced and interpretations in delivering appropriately selected actions

These competencies can assist critical functions. Delivering quality actions, with the aid of proper assessment, can be related to program planning, service design, and policy-making.

Recreational therapy requires carefully planned assessment before and after delivering what is needed. Therefore, assessment is an indispensable procedure. As a matter of fact, recreational therapy can be considered the most credible frequent user of assessment instruments and procedures in leisure and recreation services. Possible reasons for recreational therapy's inclusion of the assessment process and use of standardized tools is accountability, requirements for specific medical or rehabilitative outcomes, and the nature and strategy of recreational therapy.

Fundamental to a treatment plan in recreational therapy is an accurate assessment of the disability. Assessment, prior to planning a program, secures information about four basic levels that demand attention: an individual's makeup, level of functioning, potential, and needs. These four levels can be explained as followed:

1. Baseline data on a patient's behavior, such as physical, emotional, mental, psychological, spiritual, and social, represent a patient's background. These behavioral characteristics can draw an accurate profile of a patient's makeup. (Behavioral and social sciences can furnish excellent assessment tools to achieve the goals of attaining baseline data. Tools can assess domains such as life satisfaction, life's meaning, adjustment, depression, stress, mental health, and total functioning.)
2. A patient's functioning can be gathered through assessment of critical leisure domains. This can incorporate interests, frequency of use of activities or facilities, free time availability, leisure motivation, perceived freedom in leisure, leisure attitudes, leisure satisfaction, leisure wellness, and perceived constraints. All are based on the specific behavioral and social aspects of leisure, recreation, and play. (A growing number of behavioral leisure and recreation instruments are in existence to satisfy this requirement. Many of them are presented in Part I of this book.) However, most available leisure instruments need to fit their designated therapeutic recreation population. A required competency is to be able to use standardized assessments that fit the skills and needs of the client, based on the client's functional ability.
3. Incorporating a patient's desires can help in assessing and drawing a nearly complete profile of needs, possibilities, and difficulties.
4. Leisure inhibitors or barriers should be realized to account for their removal as a part of service or program planning and executions.

Note that recreational activities can be used therapeutically by all persons for improving mood, controlling stress, changing self-perception, offsetting depression, and improving mental health. Therefore, recreational therapy and non-recreational therapy practitioners are therapists by nature or function, requiring equal levels of assessment competency to be able to provide designated services.

Summary and Conclusion

Is there a place for assessment in leisure and recreation? If yes, what is the magnitude of assessment demand now and in the future? Realistically, assessment as a decision-making device is a relatively new approach in informal services. Making good decisions requires situational and personal assessment of some kind. Moreover, the importance of decisions determines the level of assessment: the higher the sensitivity of decisions, the greater the attention to assessment.

In many cultures, recreation and leisure suffered due to excessive attention to work. But work has been on the decline in providing meaning and rewards. Therefore, leisure choices have been gaining in importance. They have been elevated from their previous place as neglected trivia to be fun and games for pleasure, and lately to be experienced as sources for meaning, success, achievement, and self-actualization. As recreation and leisure pursuits grow in importance and status, demands for precise information through assessment will increase.

Besides assessing individuals' leisure needs, interests, and constraints, assessment procedures and strategies can assist many operations, such as administration, supervision, evaluation, specific therapeutic recreation functions, and in many other settings. In such procedures, assessment can enable not only objectivity in the judgment process but also confidence in efficient and generalizable results as the basis for good decisions. Greater utilizations of assessment will show even more areas in the provision of leisure services that can use measurement and assessment procedures. A wide range of settings will be the focus of the next chapter, demonstrating the contribution of assessment to different leisure functions.

Questions and Exercises

1. Name some of the reasons for the importance of assessment in different fields.
2. Why is it important for the fields of leisure and recreation to conduct assessment studies?
3. Explain possible relations between assessments and decision-making processes.
4. What is the status of assessment in human and social services as compared to surgery and wars?
5. What are some of the impacts of the absence of leisure and recreation measurements?
6. Name the main reasons for the use of leisure and recreation assessment tools.
7. Debate how relevant assessment is to leisure and recreation services.

Chapter 12

Contributions of Assessment to Providing Parks and Recreation Services

Focus of Chapter

This chapter will demonstrate the usability of assessment in diverse areas of recreation and leisure, helping the process of decision-making. Applications of assessment will be shown for program planning, evaluation of services and personnel, administration, and policymaking. The wide uses of assessment will be explained mainly through two models — one by Suchman to assess effort, performance, adequacy of performance, and efficiency. The other model was generated by Henderson and Bialeschki called "5 Ps" for participants, personnel, policies, places, and programs. Assessment is not an end in itself. The purposes of assessment will be discussed as a means towards securing knowledge about relevant operations, improving quality of services, and modifying or changing services as needed.

Key Terms

- adequacy of performance
- efficiency
- effort
- participants
- performance
- personnel
- places
- policies
- programs
- scope of assessment

Key Names

- M. Deborah Bialeschki
- Gaylene M. Carpenter
- Karla A. Henderson
- Christine Z. Howe
- John K. Larsen
- Ananda Mitra
- Robert A. Stothart
- Edward A. Suchman
- Albert A. Tillman

Objectives

- Identify the broad utility of assessment in diverse areas of leisure and recreation.
- Describe the uses of assessment to serve models by Suchman and Henderson and Bialeschki.
- Understand the specific uses in programming versus administration versus personnel.

The utility of assessment tools in providing recreation services can range from policymaking, marketing of services, and administrative procedures to dealing with disabilities and rehabilitation. Tools serve these operations by helping to achieve goals or gain insights into needs and interests of participants, as bases for actions. Ultimately, utilization of tools is centered on serving needs adequately, making reasonably accurate decisions, and meeting professional requirements. (For more on needs assessment, see Mitra, 2011.)

What is assessable in leisure systems? Is the intent here to invite all recreation and park practitioners to measure all parts of what they provide? This is an issue of assessment scope and needs. Despite the fact that assessment processes are used daily, not all situations require formal (planned) assessment. In most situations, practitioners use their assessment knowledge and skills informally. However, at times formal assessment must still be deliberately planned to best benefit participants, programs, and organizations.

By design, assessment can be formative (as the program forms and evolves) or summative (as a service summary at the end). Certain settings require more assessment than others, formal and informal, formative and summative. In some situations, assessment is performed periodically (every one to three years). Assessment protocols are available to practitioners to help in making informed and effective decisions.

The rest of this chapter will respond to the following two aspects: 1. Describe the many recreation areas that can benefit from assessment through three available service models and 2. Explain the numerous functions to which assessment procedures can contribute. The main four levels of leisure (administration, performance appraisal, program evaluation, and therapeutic recreation) presented in chapter 11 will be incorporated under their most relevant areas within the three service models.

Scope of Utility and Usefulness of Assessment in Recreation

In presenting the numerous uses of assessment procedures in recreation, three models will be used to show their relevance and applications: Henderson and Bialeschki's (2002) model, Suchman's (1976) model, and a model by Larsen and Stothart (1986).

Firstly, attempts will be made to demonstrate how the assessment strategies can serve Henderson and Bialeschki's classifications of leisure service organizations, designated as "the Five Ps." These five Ps that compel assessment stand for *Participants, Personnel, Policies/Administration, Places* (Areas and Facilities), and *Programs*.

Secondly, Suchman's model incorporates five categories for evaluation purposes. The first four lend themselves extensively to assessment: *Effort,*

Performance, Adequacy of Performance, Efficiency, and *Process.*

Lastly, the third model to be included, shedding light on assessment applications, was developed by Larsen and Stothart (1986) in a cross-cultural report. Due to the novelty of this third model, a further elaboration is made. Three nations — Australia, New Zealand, and Canada — were compared to each other and to the United States. Comparisons were made on how recreation and park services evolved in those four countries. They looked at history, focus of services, and evolved needs. The three stages of services progressed in the four nations, but with a time difference. A fourth and even fifth stage might have evolved since the time of the report in 1986.

The three stages of development, and more so for contemporary stages, lend themselves precisely to the processes of assessment. In the compared countries, recreation and park stages began in the 1940s with facility structures (parks, playgrounds, and sports fields), moving in the 1950s to programming for games and activities, mostly for children and youth, and finally reaching a people-orientation stage — starting in the 1970s — based on social services and humanism that attended to persons' needs and interests.

Speculatively, due to the enormous changes from the 1970s on, people's orientation should have been followed by a new stage. What is the nature and possible name for this new stage that demands more assessment efforts? Some speculations arrived at the following possible names based on the nature of leisure services in the contemporary era: "Environments for Humans (or for All)," "Community Living for All," "Healthful Living and Wellness." And "The Search for Vitality Though Leisure." Clearly, all the four names necessitate assessment of the environment, community, health, wellness, and vitality.

The above four stages will be incorporated where they fit best into Henderson and Bialeschki, and Suchman's classifications. Since Larsen and Stothart's model blends under the preceding two, no specific section will be presented to relate assessment to their classification. In using the three models, there will be abundant opportunities to show how assessment is practically involved in regular procedures and actions of delivery systems.

Henderson and Bialeschki's Five Ps Model

The five Ps model lists the parts of providing services that need to be assessed. The five Ps are places, participants, programs, personnel, and policies. How each part can be assessed is demonstrated as follows.

Places

Facilities, as physical resources, and their administration can experience more success when using assessments. All phases in handling facilities lend themselves to use of appraisal: ranging from facility preplanning, demand, safety of their environment, and distribution to altering or modifying their functions and uses. Without assessing needs, resources can be wasted. Therefore, facility assessment is indispensable for accountability and quality management.

Recreation facilities, historically thought of as all that was required to recreate (Larsen and Stothart, 1986), have been improved through assessment and evaluation. Facility assessment serves the administration by looking at areas and places and providers:

- Firstly, the areas and places that require appraisal can include facilities such as parks, playgrounds, stadiums, recreation centers, outdoor facilities, open fields, exercise and fitness centers, entertainment places, travel sites, commercial facilities, senior homes, and golf courses. These physical resources, mostly real estate, necessitate considerable financing and maintenance.
- Secondly, providers can be governments, communities, members or users, corporations, taxpayers, organizations, and investors. All stakeholders — participants, practitioners, boards of directors, and legislators — require mechanisms that ensure cost-effectiveness, user satisfaction, and accountability. Both assessment and evaluation can help achieve these goals.

How can recreation areas and facilities benefit from the processes of assessment and evaluation? First and foremost in contributing to facility development, attention should be paid to assessment processes, starting with the *preplanning* phase in facility design. Some preplanning efforts neglect utilizing assessment procedures. Without doubt, facilities are designed for human uses, needs, and enjoyment. Therefore, logically, they must seek potential users' feedback through assessment of their preferences, needs, and expectations.

If organizations do not listen to users, they will have nonfunctional resources, such as traditional American playgrounds designed between the 1960s and 1980s. Billions of dollars have been spent on American playgrounds (real estate and equipment), that are neglected by children after only 15 minutes of use (Wade, 1968). Because playgrounds are fixed — considered to be unidimensional — and their users

were not consulted when they were designed (needs were not assessed); children grow disinterested, then bored, with fixed equipment, attempting to generate challenges through changing their uses.

Another similar experience is in designing a senior home without needs assessment. A residency can end up with an oversupply of single rooms that stay vacant. In the meantime, the demand for two-person rooms is much greater. A long waiting list can result. Feasibility studies, feedback, and reactions must be assessed; data should be collected from users of all facilities. That is, if designers and practitioners care about users' duration of stay, usability, enjoyment, growth and development, and the functions served.

After seeking pre-design feedback, some basic aspects of the facilities require assessment. One of these aspects is the *number of users,* or the use level of an area (frequency), which is easy to assess, for it is based on counting heads. Historically, recreation and park providers have been using this assessment approach since services began.

Another aspect calling for assessment is *demand* for facilities and resources. Due to its nature, demand can be tricky. If, for example, community residents or corporate employees ask for facilities, assessment would not be necessary. If available, the magnitude of the expressed demand can actually be used as an indicator of what facilities are needed.

However, a problem can exist when needs are unidentified or unexpressed because unrealized needs for facilities lead to areas that are lacking. In these cases, utilization of the most creative applications of assessment procedures would be required to measure demands, interests, needs, and wants for facilities and places. Usually, there is an absence of clear criteria for demand, unless certain parks and recreation standards are employed.

In addition to pre-design feedback, level of use, and demand, facility *safety* can require some assessment. Here, safety is used as a broad concept, including the safety of equipment, fitness areas, camping facilities, and security (e.g., crime rate). Assessment of these aspects can be formal or informal (interviews, observation, and rating scales).

Moreover, the distribution of areas and facilities — in a city, county, or state; corporate organizations; or Armed Forces bases — as recommended by Henderson and Bialeschki (2002) also would require assessment. Henderson and Bialeschki suggested, "Master plans done for long-range planning are a form of assessment and evaluation" (p. 22). Similarly important is appraisal of the *carrying capacity.* This is based on assessment of recreation environment and facilities and is critical in providing information pertinent to decision making. This measures the amount of use an area can bear before recreation enjoyment begins to decline.

In sum, assessment and evaluation processes must be implemented for physical assets to maximize their returns. Assessment procedures can be applied in many respects, not only in facility preplanning phases and counting the number of users and demands, but also in safety, distribution of resources, and carrying capacity. As outlined here, the main goal for assessment is to obtain data proving or disproving the effectiveness and efficiency of leisure, recreation, and park facilities. Hence, decisions can be made to expand, improve, modify, and/or cut back services.

Participants

Logically, all services are provided to meet the needs and demands of individuals and communities. The goals may include maximizing enjoyment, improving health and fitness, solving problems, or removing recreation constraints. Therefore, service users are considered the pivot of almost all strategies in recreation, park, and leisure provision.

Usually needed programs, environments, and services start with requests from participants (e.g., needs, wants, interests, and pre-services feedback). As resources, and services are utilized, an impression of what was offered (users' attitudes, satisfaction, functioning, and evaluation) is formulated. The people-orientation (third identified) stage, by Larsen and Stothart, corresponds to this P of Henderson and Bialeschki. As it seems, assessment — utilized either formatively or summatively — would be necessary from the beginning to the end of participants' involvement in leisure, recreation, and park services.

Almost all intervention processes are centered on the beneficiaries of the service. Attention given to users and their needs is in the nature of democratic societies. To ensure democracy, to achieve success of efforts, and to attain cost-effectiveness of provisions, participants' feedback through assessment is needed. Assessment by nature is an expression of democracy, especially if the results of the assessment are taken seriously.

Moreover, assessment of users can provide the prerequisite data for decision-making. The rationale behind all of this is simple: The ultimate goals of all social and human services — leisure, recreation, and parks included — are to contribute to the betterment of individuals' conditions. So, among the goals of recreation are individuals' health, well-being, vitality, quality of life, and total functioning. Logically, therefore, providers of leisure, recreation, parks, exercise, play, and their environments are concerned

with users' impressions and feedback as a tool towards enhancement of satisfaction.

What are the tools available in the field of recreation for user assessment? Actually, most of the instruments presented in this book assess social and behavioral domains of leisure, recreation, and parks users. Some adaptations might be required for instruments with other goals and purposes. Examples of areas of instrumentation that can assess users' functions are attitudes, motivations, involvement, interests, constraints, satisfactions, flow, boredom, and competency in or acquisition of activities. (For more details, see abstracts presented in the first part of this book.)

Besides, since leisure provision is a people-oriented field, most assessment instruments belong to the behavioral domain of recreation participants. Therefore, to help users effectively and to efficiently enable organizations, professionals can benefit a great deal from familiarity with and competencies in the choice and utilization of existing instruments in the leisure field.

Programs

In Larsen and Stothart, evaluation and comparison of programs represented the second stage in recreation development. As pointed out by Henderson and Bialeschki, "For many leisure service providers, the program is the primary concern when evaluations are discussed" (p. 23). In turn, it is our position that an evaluation cannot be conducted without data, without assessment. Assessment is actually a prerequisite to any sort of evaluation.

Data on programs are required at all stages of their development (Tillman, 1973; Carpenter and Howe, 1985; Edginton, Hanson, Edginton, and Hudson, 1998). Examples of program stages that require data include preplanning (determining needs), participation levels, program impressions, user-acquired competencies, user satisfaction, goal attainment, and the effects of programs on users and their communities. Moreover, Rossman and Schlatter (2000) in their book *Leisure Programming,* incorporate assessment of different functions in a chapter entitled: "Obtaining Client Input," and a section on "Assessing the Macro Environment." In sum, examining these programmatic functions, diversified provisions, and operations necessitates a variety of data through the utilization of different types of assessments.

To assess the impact of a program, answers to the following questions can reflect necessary program criteria: Did the program or event achieve its goals? What are the areas of major successes? What are the areas of major difficulties or failures?

Were there any reported constraints on the program? Were users satisfied with the event or program? Do we have evidence to expand, modify, or cut back the program? Answers to all of the above concerns can be achieved employing an assessment of some kind.

Still in this era of rapid technological progress, a program is a central core of the delivery system. But, due to social change, future strategies might seek non-facility and non-program-bound provisions. Online systems may take the place of physical facilities in our push-button culture. Therefore, attention to assessment remains an essential step in maintaining and improving recreation and leisure programs, offerings, and systems (for more details on these relevancies, see Riddick and Russell, 1999; Henderson and Bialeschki, 2002). One of the differences between classical or face-to-face programming and non-program-bound is the way assessment procedures are conducted; instead of face-to-face, it will be through electronics.

Moreover, as the delivery system evolves to offer outreach services and non-facility-bound options, assessment will be even more important to secure success in identifying and meeting needs. This will require more innovative procedures for assessment.

Personnel

In addition to its pertinence to performance appraisal as reported in the last chapter, models presented here incorporate personnel assessment as a basic requirement for quality operations. Suchman (1976, p. 61) stated, "The presence of a sufficient number of specific kinds of qualified personnel could be a measure of the adequacy of local public services." Assessment of personnel performance is a step toward achieving quality programs and services. Within this context, the assessment process is a part of supervision and the administrative procedures governing organizations.

In order for assessment of personnel performance to be valid and useful, scales must be developed to reflect the precise content of every job, as stated before. Also, assessment must be centered on the results of performance as the job progresses. Performance appraisals provide feedback — mainly from service receivers — necessary for enhancing service quality.

Based on an appraisal, actions for improvement of service are suggested: in-service training, reinforcement, relocation, promotion, and financial rewards. Basically, developing and maintaining qualified staff, logically is a part of adequate programs. Therefore, performance appraisal is a necessary procedure.

Policies and Procedures

Not only do organizations devise plans, schedule activities, and provide programs, but they also structure fees, finance services, and provide personnel. All of these endeavors require assessment of some type. The goals behind providing this tangled web of services are to meet needs and solve problems. In some settings, the goals are merely for users to be satisfied or enjoy themselves. In commercial recreation, making a profit is required. Therefore, assessment of procedures is necessary to indicate success or failure. In a delivery system, assessment findings of policies can be very instrumental in providing suggestions on how to improve services. Riddick and Russell (1999) reported on how to move from evaluation (assessment) results to policy and practice of leisure delivery systems (see also Theobald, 1979).

In allocating funds and budgets, organizations attempt to answer a fundamental question: Did the cost justify the effect (performance)? How far did the service go? How much of the total need (adequacy of performance, Suchman, 1976) did the service meet? None of these cost-effective and cost-benefit models can be tested without data generated through assessment.

Clearly, then, Henderson and Bialeschki's five Ps (Participants, Personnel, Policies, Places, and Programs) lend themselves to formative and summative appraisal and assessment. These appraisals can be informal or formal. Orientation and training in assessment use will determine the scope and quality of data gathered. Therefore, professionals — as decision makers — need to be skillful in and knowledgeable about utilizing assessment procedures such as observations, interviews, and/or surveys. That is, they must be able to choose the specific kind and level of appraisal that will fit their needs, and problems.

Applications of Assessment to Suchman's Model

Suchman's (1976) evaluation model showed where assessment could apply to many service fields. The model is based on five categories that lend themselves to leisure, recreation, travel, play, exercise and fitness, and park offerings:

1. Effort
2. Performance
3. Adequacy of Performance
4. Efficiency
5. Process

To show the place of assessment in leisure service, implementations of these five categories are as follows:

Effort

Effort means conscious action and use of energy toward the accomplishment of an identified goal or target. Assessment of effort is the easiest, because it can be sensed. Assessment of effort is considered sensory only, accounting for what can be seen, heard, touched, smelled, and tasted. This makes the assessment processes easy and affordable, without requiring extensive tools or training. In the 1960s and 1970s assessment of effort was a common sense process, which fit that era's demands and available assessment tools.

How would assessment of effort relate to leisure and recreation services? Assessment of effort is based mostly on counting. For years in parks and recreation, counting has been used as the only index of goal achievement. Counting can apply to how many persons entered the park or the recreation center; number of individuals camping out; how many persons participated in drawing, painting, or music classes; how many hours an agency or piece of equipment operated; and the like. In almost all social and human services, counting as an assessment procedure of the organization's health or condition was viewed as the sole indication of success without regard to more essential aspects such as impact and outcome.

All human and social services require *effort* to exist and survive — recreation provision included. Examples are picnics, classes, and meetings— yet the magnitude of efforts alone cannot guarantee effective outcomes. (This notion will be elaborated further within Suchman's context.) In assessment, little or no effort usually results in failure; but effort by itself as stated above may not produce success. Therefore, well-planned assessment of impact is a fundamental approach to reveal success or failure of a program.

Assessment must evaluate where the agency achieved goals and met needs. Equally important is the identification of negative outcomes. Aspects to be improved and corrected can include showing where failure occurred, where difficulties were found, what kinds of problems or constraints were encountered, and where they were faced. Controlling and removing those constraints enable service providers to reach their goals.

Hence, indices other than mere counting must be employed in order for recreation and park provisions to advance by meeting societal needs and confronting some of the challenges of modern times. Advanced assessment procedures; therefore, are needed. This requires a balance between assessment of effort and effect. In sum, effort and its assessment comprise a mechanism for survival, but they only reveal energy use and lack sufficient evidence of the effect of the effort.

Performance

On the importance of assessing performance, Suchman (1976, p. 62) stated: "The ultimate justification of a public service or community action program in seeking public support must rest with the proof of its effectiveness in alleviating the problem being attacked." In the case of leisure, recreation, and park services, responding to a problem represents part of the provision for higher-level life requirements and needs. These upper levels can be developed to improve lifestyle and contribute to individuals' happiness and wellness, quality of existence, individual and community vitality, and total functioning. As it applies to recreation and leisure provision, Suchman's proof of service effectiveness relates here to the attainment of the preceding states.

Assessment of performance should be considered the focal point for almost all services. Performance assessment can serve many functions. There are four major recreation and park functions that performance assessment can serve:

1. Participant's performance (e.g., skill acquisition, treatment, rehabilitation, satisfaction gained, change of behavior or attitude).
2. Personnel's performance (using rating scales for assessing leadership, programmers, supervisors, or administrators).
3. The impact of actions on individuals and communities (such as the results seen from programs, services, facilities, or strategies).
4. Agency or system performance (such as, influence of the organization on a community, impact of recreation on a corporation or an Air Force base).

Performances of users, staff, actions taken, or programs executed, and the whole delivery system lend themselves to assessment as either part of the evaluation process or as a data supplier, providing necessary information for critical decisions to be made.

Employing performance assessment has been constrained by technical limitations or barriers. Examples of aspects preventing wide-scale use of performance assessment in leisure, recreation, and parks are the following:

1. The shortage of sufficient reliable and valid instruments to do the job.

2. Lack of skills in data collection, reduction, and interpretation as a basis for action and decisions.
3. Lack of ideology, strategy, and commitment to program assessment.

This book will attempt to reduce negative impacts of the preceding three limitations, closing gaps between assessment procedures and applications. However, the third constraint reported above requires an attitude change and increased competence in doing assessments for some professionals, showing greater commitment and motivation to seek and apply assessment when needed. In contemporary culture and for the evolving role of parks and recreation performance, assessment should gain more attention for its ability to guide decisions that improve service quality.

Adequacy of Performance

This procedure is a step higher than just assessing performance. In Suchman's expression, "A measure of adequacy tells us how effective a program has been in terms of the denominator of the total need" (p. 63). In this manner assessment is a basic ingredient revealing program effectiveness. "Total Need" has to be determined in advance by management. The number of recipients of a service can represent the total need, which will be used in the final analysis and decisions.

Adequacy of performance is an index that relies on measuring performance as a first step. This is to demonstrate how much of the total need has been met. That index represents impact of a service.

To test the impact of a service, two pieces of information (data) are needed: A simple piece of data is the number of beneficiaries or participants in the service (head count = effort). The second — not as simple, rather technical — is the rate of effectiveness or performance quality. These pieces of data are incorporated in an elegant index of the adequacy of performance, as demonstrated below.

A few examples will be used to illustrate how to arrive at this informative index. Remember, the intention is to answer the following: What was the impact of the service? How effective was the service?

A technical step is needed, requiring assessment and familiarity with measurement development to calculate the rate of effectiveness. To arrive at what you need, you must employ a set of items or interviews, or use observations covering all possible aspects about the service (as a concept) as follows:

- To find out how effective a state park is, a person might ask respondents to rate the park's safety, availability of rangers, maintenance, cleanliness, hospitality of personnel, and peacefulness, etc.

- Assume that there are 10 aspects or items, rated on a 10-point scale (1 to 10). ("1" is the lowest rating and "10" is the highest rating, with eight other points between 1 and 10.) Then, you add the 10 responses of one person: 7, 9, 6, 9, 8, 10, 5, 8, 7, and 8 = 77 ÷ 10 items = 7.7, or 77% effective for that person.

- If we use a *sample* of 400 park users, we add all of their scores as was done with one person, then divide by the number of people surveyed, which is 400. The result is the rate of effectiveness — let us say, 8.3 out of ten, or 83%. (The sample is a portion of the total population.)

- To compose the index, you need the number of users or total *population* for last year (hypothetically, 12,000 park users) multiplied by the rate of effectiveness, divided by 100. The 400 is the sample employed for the study, but the 12,000 persons are the actual users of the park for a year, avoid confusing one with the other. From the sample of 400, we generalize to the total population for last year, which is 12,000 in our example.

- The index and its result would be like this:

$$\text{Impact} = \frac{\text{Number of Users x Rate of Effectiveness}}{100}$$

$$\text{Users} = \frac{12{,}000 \times 83}{100} = 9{,}960$$

In Suchman's language, this is the strength of influence upon individuals exposed to park services. In other words, 9,960 persons felt the impact of the park, although it was used by 12,000 persons. The rate of effectiveness as you recall is one of two factors that determine impact or influence of a service.

So, what can be gained from this index and knowledge about impact or the rate of exposure? Three recreation scenarios can be used as examples to shed more light on some of the benefits of this index and its need for assessment, as follows:

Type of Service *A* (Tournament)
$$= \frac{700 \times 36}{100} = 252$$

Type of Service *B* (Dance or Other Art Classes)
$$= \frac{25 \times 94}{100} = 23.5 \text{ or } 24$$

Type of Service *C* (Youth Intervention)
$$= \frac{450 \times 60}{100} = 270$$

Consequently, the following number of individuals *felt* or were exposed to these three services:

- 252 persons for Service Type A (a tournament),
- 24 persons for Service Type B (a dance or other art class), and
- 270 persons for Service Type C (a youth intervention).

In retrospect, how many individuals needed each of these services? Was the number of persons who felt the influence of the service adequate to the magnitude of total need? Or was it a drop in a bucket — "too little, too late" and, therefore, ineffective?

A variety of questions can be constructively asked to improve service impact and adequacy of performance. Four examples of questions are as follows:

1. What can be done to improve the impact of these services (if needed)?
2. Based on data included in the index, where do we need to improve the rate of effectiveness?
3. Where do we need to market services and promote offerings to increase the number of participants?
4. Is there a need for more staff or staff reduction? Based on assessment data, why reduce or increase staffing? If so, where?

Many decisions can be reached as we compare services based on well-constructed indices, to meet the total demands for all services. Such decisions would be based on available funds, severity of problems and/or demands, politics, philosophy, users' welfare, strategies adopted, and, sometimes, values. As demonstrated above, assessment of adequacy of performance is a cornerstone necessary for arriving at usable indices.

Efficiency

Like performance's adequacy, efficiency is another administrative action and goal that assessment can enhance. Besides assessing how much of the total need has been met, efficiency assesses alternative, less costly ways to provide the same or better quality of service. Alternative actions are related to expenditure (money, time, effort, and public convenience). That is an issue that has been gaining wide attention in almost all settings, services, and situations. Moreover, Mitra (2011) points out the importance of efficiency to face current changes in the face of limited resources.

Suchman suggests using a ratio to measure efficiency — the ratio is between input and output, between effort and performance. For example, how

efficient is an organization's impact on youth in an at-risk youth program versus a recreation and exercise class for teens? Two pieces of data will be necessary:

1. Rate of performance.
2. Cost (in time and/or money, including personnel and equipment).

For examples, in comparing two programs, one for at-risk youth, 215 persons were impacted by the service (based on the index used under adequacy of performance) at a cost of $37,000. For the other program, 300 teens were affected, at a cost of $42,000. Using this current index, dividing input by output, how efficient were these two services?

1. The cost per person for Program A
   = $37,000 / 215 = $172 per person
2. The cost per person for Program B
   = $42,000 / 300 = $140 per person

Comparison of result should be based on certain considerations to produce logical and reasonable scenarios. Generally, it would be a mistake to compare two unrelated services. Compare apples to apples and oranges to oranges to obtain equitable results.

Two main guidelines need to be regarded in making such comparisons:

- First, a valid comparison requires information on the efficiency of similar programs, in the same environment, or in some other localities or situations in similar-sized cities.
- The second consideration is for an organization to compare the financial costs for its programs to help to decide the most beneficial methods of delivery. Familiarize yourself with these scenarios:

  1. For an organization, the costs per person for six programs are as follows: 97, 185, 120, 370, 27, and 148. Which ones do you maintain, increase, or decrease?
  2. Sometimes decisions can be made to increase users for less costly offerings; to seek alternative methods of providing the same quality but with reduced costs.
  3. Other times just maintaining the service as it is or breaking even, due to stabilized and acceptable levels of user satisfaction would be desirable.
  4. However, a service can prove costly, but for social, behavioral, and/or strategic reasons, it is decided to maintain it.

That is where the managerial, technical, and professional skills and ethics are interwoven with assessment procedures and their outcomes.

Process

Assessment on this level requires adding all data and observation gathered to assess the first four categories: effort, performance, adequacy of performance, and efficiency in one perspective. No data is collected for this category. Within this frame, successes and/or failures of service are put together like a jigsaw puzzle, searching for more meaningful answers through careful and skilled interpretation. The assessor has the opportunity to synthesize numbers and facts together, making sense of what is found, to advance the quality of services provided and administrative procedures.

Accordingly, attempts are made to discover the mechanisms of the service and the underlying dynamics of actions taken. Attempts are made to answer the following questions:

- What went wrong?
- What went right?
- Why did things work out?
- Why did things fail?
- Are there things pointing to any directions of change?

This is done by integrating all of the available information, to make sense of the services offered.

Summary and Conclusion

Assessment in recreation and leisure systems can serve many different decision-making functions.

Assessments can be used for everything from program planning and evaluation to policymaking and administrative procedures, covering a very wide spectrum. The usefulness of assessment procedures was shown for Henderson and Bialeschki five Ps (Participants, Personnel, Policies, Places, and Programs) and Suchman's five categories of evaluation (Effort, Performance, Adequacy of Performance, Efficiency, and Process).

A third model by Larsen and Stothart accounting for three developmental stages: facility, program, and people was incorporated into the above two models and their needs for assessment. A fourth speculative stage was suggested in this book, considering contemporary changes: *environments for living* and/or *healthful living*. Larsen and Stothart's model provides further support for the application of assessment cross-culturally.

In essence, assessment is not an end in itself, but a means toward practical ends. Assessment can include:

- Obtaining knowledge about needs, interests, and problems as a basis for planning programs, establishing services, and policymaking.
- Improving the quality of programs and services based on data.
- Modifying, changing, or canceling programs or services provided when evidence points in that direction.

Accordingly, assessment is utilized as an administrative tool, for the benefit of participants, communities, and society.

Questions and Exercises

1. Explain how assessment applies to a wide area of leisure and recreation services.
2. According to Henderson's model, how can assessment contribute to the fulfillment of this model?
3. According to Suchman's model, how can assessment contribute to the fulfillment of his five categories?

Chapter 13

Qualitative and Quantitative Methods

Focus of Chapter

Data is both necessary and important when providing quality services. This chapter presents the wide scope of methods of data collection, discussing the quantitative and qualitative methods to acquire data. Readers will explore the usability of observation, interviews, and self-reporting tools. The quantitative and qualitative contexts of the methods will be described. Readers will be able to describe strengths, weaknesses, and usability of each method, avoiding conflicts over the merit of each procedure.

Key Terms

- data collection
- interview
- methodology
- observation
- psychology
- psychometric
- qualitative procedures
- quantitative procedures
- sociology
- sociometric
- standardized test

Key Names

- Madeleine M. Leininger
- Jum C. Nunnally

Objectives

- Identify the characteristics of quantitative and qualitative procedures.
- Distinguish the differences between quantitative and qualitative methods of data collection.
- Identify the relevance of quantitative and qualitative methods to field settings, problems, and needs.
- Identify problems and constraints on the uses of the two approaches.
- Describe solutions to overcome the identified problems and constraints to utilize the methods of data collection.

Accurate and up-to-date information is required for making good decisions. To secure information, managers utilize many methods of data collection, varying from informal to formal, non-standardized to standardized, homemade devices to pre-developed instruments. Using the information they collect, park and recreation managers make decisions that affect the fate of their organizations and the services offered to their clients. Contemporary managerial approaches rely on accurate data in arriving at their decisions. In many instances, leisure and park managers, as well as practitioners in many applied services, utilize two paradigms in collecting data: quantitative and qualitative procedures.

These two approaches grew apart in their methodologies, goals, and strategies. As a result, differences and preferences manifested themselves in favor of one over the other. In turn, this created confusion and led people to ask, which one is better? This chapter will explain the nature of this problem, offering solutions regarding which paradigm is most appropriate for leisure, recreation, and park managers, or at least for given settings. (Three chapters are written on the above methodologies in Riddick and Russell, 1999; another comparison is made by Henderson and Bialeschki, 2002.)

Quantitative versus Qualitative Procedures

In an era of service quality and accountability, modern societies strive to rely on valid and reliable data. Almost all services, including leisure and park systems, make important decisions that need to be based on information of some kind. (Examples of diversified human and social services that rely on data are education, counseling, rehabilitation, social work, physical education, sports, criminal justice, and health.) Arriving at accurate and usable data requires practitioners to seek methods adapted and developed mostly through their original sources of methodology; that is, cultural, social, and behavioral sciences.

Unfortunately, each applied field and scientific discipline developed different methodologies. This is mainly to suit each service's interest, science's focus, and pertinent phenomena. Methodological procedures of assessment, utilized sometimes in service evaluation, naturally evolved distinct features. Methods grew apart while solving the science or service's unique problems, yielding what is well known as qualitative and quantitative paradigms. (For the development and uses of qualitative methods, see Posavac and Corey, 1997; Potter, 1996; Lawler and Carley, 1996. For the development and uses of quantitative procedures, see Barkham, 1996; Jaeger and Bond, 1996; Thornicroft and Bebbington, 1996.)

As is the case with almost all related concepts, hot controversies and comparisons of the strengths and weaknesses of the two procedures were debated (e.g., Bennett, 1995; McKeganey, 1995; Pearson, 1995; Sechrest and Sidani, 1995). Accordingly, the heated discussion spurred appraisals of both methodologies to answer a central concern (if possible): Which method is most useful? Which of them is the good one?

As this chapter will show, there are advantages and disadvantages to both methods. The solution is to use both, each in the proper situation.

What are some of the differences between these two main methods of data collection? First, although the qualitative and quantitative methods have the same objectives, securing usable data, the paradigms differ sharply in how the data is collected. In presenting advantages of using quantitative procedures, Nunnally (1978) gave the following five reasons:

1. Objectivity: taking guesswork out of scientific observations.
2. Quantification: being able to report results in finer mathematical detail.
3. Communication: the ability to convey results efficiently.
4. Economy: by saving time, money, and effort while securing usable data.
5. Generalizability: by drawing conclusions explaining some underlying order in naturally occurring human and social phenomena, leading to the ability to compose powerful, predictable theories and, at best, leading to laws (the ultimate goal of science).

The above five reasons seem to be claimed also as disadvantages of qualitative methods.

On the other hand, credibility, confirmability, and meaning-in-context were reported by Leininger (1994), among six criteria (considered advantages) of qualitative research, which also included recurrent patterns, transferability, and saturation. The content of the six criteria illustrates advantages of qualitative procedures, as follows:

1. Credibility is the degree of "truthfulness" and "believability" in findings founded on intensive observations, giving results their "realness."
2. Confirmability is established through "repeated affirmations" of what is seen and heard.
3. Meaning in situational contexts, life events, or lived-through experiences are indicators of the reality of relevant frames of references.
4. Recurrent patterning is related to repeated sequences and events, showing the underlying pattern(s) associated with a phenomenon.
5. Saturation is being immersed in a phenomenon as a step toward comprehending and realizing its scope.
6. Transferability is the ability to transmit findings to another qualitative study that results in similar conclusions without generalizability, but in-depth understanding of a phenomenon as unique and different.

Similarly, as pointed out above, these six criteria can represent disadvantages of quantitative paradigms.

So it seems that, as the two approaches centered on practical and scientific concerns relevant to each field, they grew apart in focus, interest, and rationale. (For more details on the merit of quantitative and qualitative procedures in parks, recreation, and leisure services, see Henderson and Bialeschki, 2002.)

As a result of these controversial comparisons between the two procedures, the intent is to respond to three specific issues:

1. Presenting some methodological notions relevant to procedures of data collection, identifying some gaps that might distract parks and recreation practices, and clarifying the nature of the problem.
2. Showing the relevance, usefulness, and usability of different methods.
3. Demonstrating sources of gaps that can be corrected. Methods should depend on the field settings or phenomena and their demands, not on loyalty toward a specific methodology.

Before getting into more detail, it is important to note that while the author's work falls almost exclusively under quantitative procedures, with a great deal of emphasis on the uses of psychometric theory, it is strongly based on information gathered earlier using qualitative methods.

To help in closing the gaps between paradigms, a model will be presented with suggestions for leisure and park professionals to map their positions among methodologies. The ultimate goal is to use the paradigm that best solves the problem(s) confronted without being lost in details and complexities or heated arguments. After all, for a plumber, a wrench can be as important as a hammer, depending on the situation and what is being repaired.

Background of the Disagreement

Academically, educators in human and social sciences generally fall under one or a combination of three disciplines: cultural anthropology, sociology, and/or psychology (see Model 3). Social psychology can be considered as an amalgamation of the three disciplines above (see Ragheb, 1980). Disciplines such as political science, economics, religion, and criminology share or draw their methodology from one or more of these human and social sciences.

Employing quantitative or qualitative strategies would depend on the nature of the problems to be solved in pertinent disciplines, as well as in specific, applied fields of services. Usually, leisure educators and practitioners bring their academic backgrounds — orientations, training, and preferences — when they attempt to assess, evaluate, and predict leisure phenomena. It is necessary to be equipped with all tools — like a plumber — and, depending on what is confronted, practitioners should employ available strategies, appropriate to that setting.

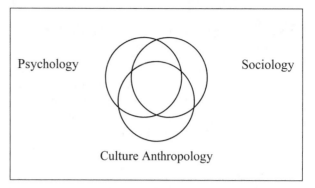

Model 3: Relationship of academic disciplines.

Every discipline looks at specific, defined phenomena. The goal is to explain and solve the scientific problems, based on appropriate strategies by securing needed data. Assessment procedures in psychology and psychiatry can prove to be useless in studying cultural behavior.

Moreover, as depicted in the model, the status of the methods of data collection varies from one discipline to another. Observation, for instance, can be rated the highest (best) in cultural studies. Self-reporting or standardized devices can be rated higher in psychology but they are not as popular in cultural anthropology. Personal interviewing is rated as equally usable in all disciplines. In settings where investigators utilize both procedures as needed (e.g., Levin, Share, and Shatil, 1996), extra verifications across methodologies are employed in establishing knowledge. Finally, technical procedures in collecting data are designated by their most relevant discipline: psychometric (in psychology) and sociometric (in sociology).

The leisure delivery system exhibits a great deal of setting variations, from the very psycho-physiological (therapeutic) to the culturally very broad (recreational). Both extremes encounter difficulties and confusion regarding which approach is best, especially when they attempt to identify a one-size-fits-all procedure. It's even worse when one end of the spectrum tries to say that all implementations, from managers and practitioners to training for future practitioners must use the same (single) procedure.

The nature of these delivery systems demonstrates the reasons for variations, which encompass recreation areas such as outdoor, parks, entertainment, travel and tourism, fitness, playgrounds, community centers, corporate, campus, the Armed Forces, therapeutic, and private recreation activities. The list can be very extensive; each setting tends to be unique. Moreover, the scope of provisions is very broad as well as very complicated, contrary to what it seems on the surface.

For example, comparing two extreme settings (recreational therapy versus a city's annual cultural and recreational special event) demonstrates different needs for using assessment methods (data collection), evaluation, or scientific studies as follows:

- For a therapeutic recreation practitioner, there is an obligation to make decisions to perform some necessary duties to clients: screening, diagnosing, classifying, referring, planning intervention, and evaluating progress of treatment. The focus is on very specific, individualized evaluation. Recreational therapists need to generate quantifiable data (sometimes strict scores) to meet clients' treatment requirements, daily progress, and obligations. They also need to observe a client's actions within a situation qualitatively to determine how newly acquired disabilities are perceived by the client and those around him/her.

- City recreation practitioners, on the other side of the spectrum, are studying vast numbers of people to provide the best opportunities with limited funds. They may need to make some decisions germane to annual cultural events, such as festivals, folklore, circuses, fairs, arts, entertainment, and organized sports and their leagues. They must handle exceptionally large-scale field events and must look for the most relevant devices to assess and evaluate cultural offerings so that they are pleasing to the widest set of participants. In deciding between events, they often employ quantitative methods (assessing experiences and impressions) to determine which event is most pleasing. On the other hand, they will need to use qualitative methods to discover new events that may be added to their lineup.

Practitioners must navigate carefully, identifying the techniques needed to secure specific data. The value of the method used is not inherent within it; but rather is in its adaptability, dependability, and utility. Problems arise when data collection techniques are limited artificially by preconceived notions of what is "proper." The method of data collection needs to be designed to respond to the specific scope and the demands of a given situation, event, or delivery system. Accordingly, selecting the most appropriate procedure is like that of choosing a silk glove to fit a hand, avoiding unfounded uses like trying to wear a garden glove in a delicate situation. In other words, methods should be chosen without an endless and useless heated debate — without being a "wrench-ologist" or a "hammer-ologist" plumber.

Synthesis of Methods

At the heart of the debate is the belief by the quantitative side that you understand what is going on only when you use numbers. The qualitative side believes that non-numeric interviews and observations are the only way to understand the real situation. Thankfully it is becoming clearer that both are right — except the word "only" needs to be replaced with sometimes. *Sometimes* numeric results are the best way to study a problem. *Sometimes* non-numeric results will give you better information. The intent of assessment is to obtain good data (by observations, physiological instruments, electronic devices, interviews, or self-reporting tools). The methods chosen should depend on the situation.

There are times when there is no conceptual basis for the acquisition of data. Newly established services to older persons or at-risk youth, for example, might have no established procedure for assessment and evaluation. Also, a newly occurring phenomenon, caused by the impact of rapidly changing technology, requires new ways of assessing relevant behaviors and reactions. Examples are new types of stress, pain, wellness, vitality, empowerment, and/or boredom (*ennui*). Both evaluators and scientists lack devices to assess the basic orientations in situations similar to the above examples. Hence, users attempting to understand or explain a phenomenon or a concept, or assess a service's quality and functions are actually ignorant of the situation.

It is not insulting to be ignorant of new facts or occurrences. Actually, ignorance is just being uninformed or having a lack of knowledge about a particular thing. It is normal to be unaware or uninformed when new situations or phenomena evolve. If the evaluator doesn't know what to look for, it is very hard to count it quantitatively. In this case, the navigating devices best suited to this new social or behavioral situation are qualitative procedures utilizing observations and/or interviews.

Transitionally, as users (investigators and practitioners) probe into what is happening, knowledge to handle the situation accumulates. Thus, there is a need for a different procedure. Tested hypotheses and theories are developed through qualitative procedures. Users of qualitative methods achieve realism, discover underlying patterns, and grow knowledgeable about given phenomena. In turn, these achievements can be used to create conceptual structures — as prerequisites for the use of more strict and structured quantitative procedures. The quantitative procedures can provide more in-depth testing regarding hypothesis about particular phenomena, but they also spin off insights and knowledge. The new insights guide the search for further understanding, which is usually pursued qualitatively at first.

Methodologically, from the point of view of quantitative paradigms, well-developed theories and hypotheses are considered as the basic ingredients in the composition of a theory-guided instrument for assessment. An example can illustrate where it is a good idea to go beyond qualitative data when making decisions about particular programs:

For a class project to assess and evaluate an "After School Recreation Service," participants utilized open-ended questions. One of the items asked respondents, "What do you like about your After School Programs?" Responses were repeatedly "It is fun," "*FUN*," or they responded by saying, "It is cool" or some similar response. Qualitative responses in this kind of situation are often limited to the most obvious. They can often be included in one capsule, in this case, "I am pleased with it." This is useful information, but it might be more useful to rate "How fun it is." With that kind of quantitative rating users of the service provide a degree of contentment. For example, in one setting an average rating could be 6.5 out of 10; while in another, it might be 9 out of 10. If the goal is to find out reasons that the participants are returning to activities, qualitative results are useful. Quantitative results are useful in this example to improve or change a program or to decide which of two competing programs to keep.

Several decades ago (in the 1940s and 1950s), in an initial attempt to learn about leisure and recreation motivation, an investigator could ask qualitatively, "Why (motive) do you engage in leisure and recreation activities?" "What are some of your reasons (motives) to do recreation activities?" In fact, many open-ended questions could have been asked on any given target area, from motivation and satisfaction to interests and involvement, (see the third part of this book on concept development). As knowledge accumulates, aiding in hypothesis testing, varied theories can be postulated. Many theories during the 1950s and beyond were composed in just that way.

Based on accumulated explanations established qualitatively, quantitative procedures can evolve. Part of the reason for quantifying theories is to verify that they are generalizable across varied populations. A second reason is that quantitative measures can be more useful in making decisions, as shown in the earlier example. The finer mathematical details and more efficient testing procedures can be used more economically to achieve agency or scientific goals. In contemporary times there are many advanced theories available regarding leisure and recreation, which can be used to build quantitative measurements.

For an investigator constructing a measurement in the second decade of the 21st century, to do what was previously done qualitatively would be considered "spinning his or her wheels" or wasting time. In a more advanced stage like ours to measure leisure motivation, a theory such as competence-mastery

motivation (White, 1959) is available. Also, stimulus seeking and stimulus avoidance (Ellis, 1973) is a well-developed theory, as is that of Ryan and Deci (2000).

In conclusion, we should realize the need for a balance among solutions. When we are ignorant of the phenomenon, use qualitative; when knowledgeable, use quantitative. When we want to know why something is happening, qualitative methods are better. When we want to know how much better something is, quantitative measures are required.

It is important to avoid false assumptions undertaken by users of different paradigms, claiming one of the following: 1. Facts and established knowledge, to qualify for recognized existence and/or to be accepted in the body of knowledge, must follow the cultural anthropological paradigm (qualitative). Or, 2. For existing facts to have merit, they must follow the psychological paradigm or the psychometric theory (quantitative). The reality of leisure and recreation is too complicated for either procedure to be used exclusively. Both are required.

In recreation and human services, the more relevant issue is to be knowledgeable and competent in the following: 1. The development and use of reasonably good homemade tools according to guidelines. Or 2. To use of available existing methodologies, disregarding differences between quantitative and qualitative approaches.

As demonstrated here, no absolute truth exists in judging the superiority of either quantitative or qualitative methods. Actually, the two are *simply tools:* They help to solve specific field problems, securing the best kind of data for coming to educated conclusions. In their own way, both tools serve clients' needs or therapies when evaluating community recreational offerings, and testing managerial and scientific hypotheses.

Without ego involvement with one procedure or the other, or entering heated debates for that matter, the two tools are means toward an end, not ends in themselves. Users' training, fields of inquiry, and personal convictions determine users' knowledge and commitment to a given procedure. Users must guard against false assumptions and unnecessary arguments that their procedure is the superior one. As demonstrated above, every one of them serves an indispensable role.

Summary and Conclusion

Data is needed for applied practical and scientific reasons; that is, in order to solve a problem and to make good decisions. In the zeal to secure needed data, different levels of services and scientific phenomena demanded utilization of specific procedures. Although relative methods aim at similar targets, they differ in their means.

As is the case with many practices, users of each paradigm (due to ego involvement and immersion in relative tasks) develop — sometimes irrationally — commitment and loyalty to certain procedures. Thus, conflicts can begin, as differences manifest themselves.

Admittedly, fanatics of each procedure are about half right, and the situation, unlike the debate, requires further integration and reconciliation among procedures, responding to practical and empirical demands. Therefore, recreation and park practitioners, as well as almost all human services personnel, would be more efficient if they were competent in all methods. The heaviest emphasis should be on the procedure that proves to be most useful to their specific requirements, settings, and problems.

Questions and Exercises

1. What are the characteristics of quantitative procedures of data collection?
2. What are the characteristics of qualitative procedures of data collection?
3. What are the main differences between qualitative and quantitative methods?
4. How relevant are both qualitative and quantitative procedures of data collection to leisure and recreation services?
5. What are some of the problems facing use of qualitative and quantitative methods?
6. How can users solve problems that emerge when using qualitative and quantitative procedures?

Chapter 14

Basic Criteria for Quality Assessment Tools: Reliability and Validity

Focus of Chapter

This chapter will explain the criteria of quality assessment tools: reliability and validity. The main concepts and definitions of basic criteria will be introduced. Reliability and validity are considered the most technical requirements for instrument construction. Familiarity with reliability and validity is necessary for all assessment users. For some, extensive familiarity is needed to construct quality scales, while for others, familiarity is needed for careful selection and use of instruments based on differentiations among existing tools. These competencies are indispensable, not only for scale developers, but also for field users. Moreover, the importance of reliability and validity is explained as simply as possible. This is followed by explaining the types of reliability and validity, through describing what to search for in technical reports about a measurement. The purpose is to be able to make good judgments evaluating the quality of existing scales or to construct a new measure with appropriate levels of reliability and validity.

Key Terms
- alpha reliability coefficient
- concurrent validity
- construct validity
- content validity
- criteria validity

- predictive validity
- split-halves reliability
- test-retest reliability
- usability

Key Names
- Ronald Jay Cohen
- Fred N. Kerlinger
- Jum C. Nunnally

- John Salvia
- Mark Swerdlik

Objectives
- Identify fundamental criteria for measurements.
- Explore the importance of reliability and validity for available scales.
- Distinguish and rate the quality of scales.
- Differentiate among types of reliability and validity as criteria for quality instruments.
- Select and screen scales to identify scales that fit users or clients, goals, and agencies or communities.

This chapter is designed so it can be understood by an individual who has no prior exposure to basic criteria for assessment instruments, their requirements, or standards. For readers to be able to evaluate the quality of assessment tools, certain fundamental concepts and guidelines will be presented. This will enable readers to make appropriate selections for meeting minimum standards and an agency's requirements. (For more information on reliability and validity see Chapters 5 and 6 in Cohen and Swerdlik, 2005.)

This chapter will avoid going deep into the complexity of reliability and validity concepts. However, future and current practitioners who employ assessment in their work must understand the two basic criteria of measurements — reliability and validity, as illustrated in Figure 1. While reliability means consistency and accuracy of representation of what is measured, validity is a judgment about concept's merit: sufficiency and truthfulness.

Reliability and validity are considered the highest technical requirements in measurement development. The technical nature of reliability and validity is due to their diversification and their many requirements. For example, reliability has a number of types and meanings, ranging from the need to be consistent and accurate to being predictable and dependable. Also, the types and meanings of validity can range from the simplest (face and content validities) to the most elaborate (concurrent and construct validities). Achieving any of the above necessitates taking certain steps and performing specific procedures during the development process.

Methodologically, precise steps to secure reliability and validity can start with a conceptual definition, and then include delineation of concepts, identifying their indicators and verifications through a number of tests for validity and consistency of items, using certain statistical procedures. Moreover, procedures can incorporate all of the steps known as the art and science of measurement development. When these steps and procedures are performed carefully and precisely, the outcome tends to be a durable, trustworthy, and usable instrument.

While one type of reliability is adequate to establish a quality assessment tool, a single validation (such as content validity) would be inadequate. In other words, an instrument can report only one set of results relevant to alpha reliability coefficient, or split halves, or test-retest and still be considered adequate. For validity, however, that same instrument must also report not only basic validations (face and content) but also one or more of the others (concurrent, predictive, and/or construct validity) as the uses of instrument intensify. This is especially so, after an instrument has been tried for some years, establishing further knowledge.

The Value of Reliability and Validity in Leisure Measurements

The leisure and recreation fields are very promising and viable. Free time is increasing in its importance and impacts individuals and society as a whole. Free time is now found during weekends and holidays, after work, after school, or when unem-

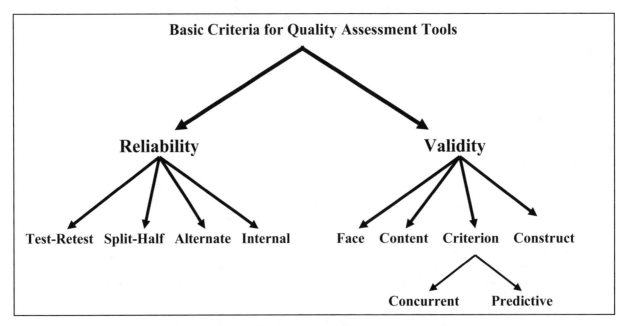

Figure 1: Schematic illustration of basic criteria required for assessment tools

ployed. This extra time and additional activities to be pursued have the potential to shape modern societies and cultures. These impacts can range from the positive to very negative, from the very desirable to the very undesirable.

Within this context, what do we know about phenomena occurring after work or school? What is the actual impact of free time, fitness, and leisure activities on society? How can we measure relevant phenomena of free time and leisure? Sufficiently reliable and valid leisure instruments that measure newly occurring phenomena and the dynamics of change are scarce. Reliability and validity, as defined below, need to be established when developing instruments and before they are utilized in practical or scientific settings if the instruments are to achieve their goals.

As we advance in technology and economics, a great deal of attention must be focused on assessing domains occurring in informal pursuits, such as free time, leisure, travel, exercise and fitness, and recreation. For an assessment instrument to show quality — reliability and validity — extensive procedures must be performed: The required effort currently is lacking in many leisure instruments.

A measurement's set of items cannot be composed and validated in a hurry (not in few days, not even in a month), like writing a short report. To the contrary, it is a painstaking process, taking 12 to 18 months from beginning to end. Carving a valid and reliable concept is neither a "quick fix" nor a simple operation. Like all instruments, a leisure construct must reflect a domain. We must chisel it from a mountain of knowledge and relate it to unique leisure experiences and behaviors, while applying it to specific human functions and needs. After all, the outcome, being valid and reliable, can be a great professional and social investment.

Reliability

In assessing an individual's height, a measuring tape is used to arrive at the true value. In so doing, there is a chance for error to creep in. The measurement procedure strives to be close to the individual's "true" height, attempting to control or, at minimum, reduce error. In physical domains, unlike social and behavioral ones, it is relatively easy to verify their true reality, because they are more reliably assessed. Because true values of behavioral and social domains are unknown (e.g., motivation toward work or family), the reliability of a measure must be achieved through the best possible means available to science. We must work to discover the measurement's accuracy, predictability, consistency, and also its degree of error.

What can cause error in an assessment device? Basically, the reasons are found in unsystematic fluctuation and in response oscillation, due to an item (or items) that is ambiguous, irrelevant, or poorly stated as explained here:

- First, ambiguity and low-quality statements can create unnecessary and unsystematic variability. That is due to the manner in which respondents interpret the content of a given item. For example, in measuring leisure attitude, an item may read: "I value my leisure and my work." Some of those who value leisure but not work might disagree, emphasizing how they value work, while others might agree with the statement emphasizing more how they value leisure. While an unknown number of respondents might be confused as to what to rate, work or leisure. Here, the stimulus, "work and leisure" is unclear and imprecise, yielding hazy or unstable reactions. This type of ambiguity leads to a risky variability. Later, it will be counted in the reliability testing as error. To overcome this problem, a developer simplifies the item by saying "I value my leisure." If needed to account for another item, improving reliability, the developer may have two items: (1) "I value my work." (2) "I value my leisure." Responses will be focused, reducing variability. Item development and its guidelines are never science; they are always part of the art of scale development.

- The second difficulty causing error is irrelevance of an item. For instance, if a scale is composed to assess leisure interests, but somehow an irrelevant item is included, tapping a different domain, such as leisure satisfaction, that item might invite error to creep in. For people who have strong interests in leisure, some might rate highly that satisfaction item while others, who are similarly interested in leisure, might rate the same item on leisure satisfaction low. This is because the item's content does not truly relate to the concept of leisure interests; thus it is irrelevant. For an instrument to be reliable, attempts must be made to reduce, at best eliminate, error or noise. Estimating the score of the unknown true reality is achieved through controlling item ambiguity and increasing relevance.

- The third cause of error is an item that is stated poorly. Quality items demonstrate not only clarity and precision but also brevity and simplicity. For an item to be clear it must be easily understood, free from doubts and other meanings, and not be misunderstood for something else. Item's precision is achieved when the item is sharply and exactly stated, is distinguished from other statements, and summarizes pertinent ideas. Items should be short, 20 words or less. Finally, an item should be simple, being free from complications and having a single meaning.

Failing to meet one or more of the above three guidelines can yield a poorly stated item that can cause error, jeopardizing a measurement's reliability.

In application, generalization of findings is the core reason for being concerned with reliability. Generalizability lets us use a score on a test to predict what will most likely occur in the future or somewhere else. For example, educators generalize from SAT or GRE scores to predict success in academic performance. An instrument's reliability determines its ability to predict outcomes.

Due to the diversity of recreation and leisure systems, it will be helpful to look at some examples that illustrate a measurement's universal outcomes. (Some will relate to you and to your setting, while others might not.)

1. A practitioner serving in corporate recreation or similar settings: Findings would be generalizable if knowledge about employees' job stress (e.g., stress control or reduction) relates to frequency and duration of involvement in recreation activities offered by the corporation. In turn, as a basis for future leisure programs, such findings can be generalized and utilized to contribute to stress control in other corporations, under similar circumstances. This is the power of prediction and consistency from one domain (work stress) to what can be expected to happen (relaxation, productivity, and job satisfaction) through another domain like leisure involvement. This generalization is basically dependent on the reliability of two scales: "Leisure Involvement" and "Stress."

2. For a nursing home, suppose it is found that leisure motivation, attitude, self-determination, and satisfaction contribute to the residents' vitality and wellness; therefore, generalizability from one or more domains can indicate the levels of performance or reaction in other domains. In another setting, leisure professionals can attempt to increase participants' leisure satisfaction, predicting a contribution to wellness, as a generalizable fact or finding. This is based on the use of reliable scales.

3. In a therapeutic recreation setting, when a relationship has been established between the involvement component of the Leisure Diagnostic Battery (Witt and Ellis, 1989) and speed of recovery and adjustment, then to be generalizable, scores on that component must correlate with practitioners' observation of patients' functioning. The observed rate of recovery and adjustment would determine the level of universality for scores of patients' leisure involvement; hence, dependability of a scale is founded. Dependable scales are known to be reliable.

4. In community recreation, assuming that it was established that patrons' satisfaction with recreation services (or service quality) was related to the quality and number of certain programs. Then, what we offer in quality and quantity of services and programs would predict that satisfaction. Practitioners in other similar settings can generalize from that knowledge base to other programming options, through assessing patrons' satisfaction with recreation services. This is based on the utilization of an established reliable instrument.

5. As Alex F. Nunez, a student at Florida State University in 2001, reported in a special communication about at-risk youth: At-risk youth programs have been developed all over the nation with goals of decreasing crime and dropout rates, as well as increasing participation in recreation and education. Nunez adds that the Phoenix, Arizona, Parks, Recreation, and Library Department has recently taken some action in its At-Risk-Youth Program, throwing out the traditional rulebook and becoming a bit more liberal. Relevant to the utilization of assessment to appraise the degree of success reported by Nunez, if a program for at-risk youth is proven successful and effective, a generalization about the impact of recreation on given behaviors from those settings to other cities would be possible.

Such dependable, generalizable, or universal findings of measures — as illustrated above — can be considered the most applicable to field practice and service providers (e.g., activities, programs, interventions, crises, treatments, diagnosis, systems, and policies). Hence, the reliability of what we assess is considered a major concern for its application.

Reliability can incorporate characteristics and types such as accuracy, replicability, dependability, predictability, stability, and consistency. Each characteristic requires precise procedures. Four types of reliability will be presented to demonstrate criteria and guidelines that an instrument needs to follow in its construction. By employing these procedures, a user is better able to evaluate it, whether in applied or research settings. As shown in Figure 1, the four types of reliability are

1. Test-Retest Reliability
2. Split-Half Reliability
3. Alternate Form Reliability
4. Internal Consistency Reliability

Test-Retest Reliability

As implied by the name, test-retest is very easy to understand and perform. It is done by administering the same instrument two or more times to the same subjects. Each test is separated by a time interval sufficient for the subjects to forget prior responses (preferably two or more weeks). The longer the time interval, the less the impact of memory on retest responses.

However, inaccuracy might creep in if the time interval is too long, say six months or more. Individuals' behavior and choices might change as a result of history, seasons, and/or maturity, affecting the stability of the personality aspect under consideration (e.g., satisfaction, mood, or depression). The instrument's findings might reflect lack of stability or lack of consistency between tests, but the changes are actually caused by the passage of time and the individual's experiences, not what the instrument is tapping. Relatively, the more the domain is emotional (e.g., feelings, moods, or sentiments) the greater the impact of the longer time interval on response stability. This is because emotions change faster over time.

Test-retest reliability estimates the degree of stability in the instrument over a period of time. If a test score is stable, a respondent would most likely receive a similar score as s/he repeats his/her responses to the same test in the future. Correlations among repeated administrations are taken altogether as an index, not only of stability, but also of consistency and generalizability. This is called the "Reliability Coefficient." The diagrammatic illustration in Figure 2 should be utilized as a basis for evaluating correlations among repeated administrations, using Mannell's (1984) Self-as-Entertainment Scale, as an example.

In the diagram, r is the correlation between two test administrations. In evaluating the quality of a given test, an index can be established based on the three correlations within the diagram:

- First administration and second administration (r_{12})
- Second administration and third administration (r_{23})
- First administration and third administration (r_{13})

Examples of instruments in the fields of leisure and recreation that employed test-retest reliability include Crandall and Slivken (1980), developing the Leisure Attitude Scale; Ellis and Witt (1984), constructing Perceived Freedom in Leisure; Barnett (1991) in Children's Playful Scale; and Caldwell, Smith, and Weissinger (1992), building the Leisure Experience Battery for Adolescents.

For practical and research uses, if a test-retest reliability coefficient ranges between .60 to .80, it would be considered sufficiently stable and consistent. Test stability greater than .80 would be highly desirable. Scientists and practitioners should attempt repeatedly to improve the stability of scales needed to achieve their ends. Systematically, this can be achieved through two activities: gaining more knowledge of the concept assessed, then modifying

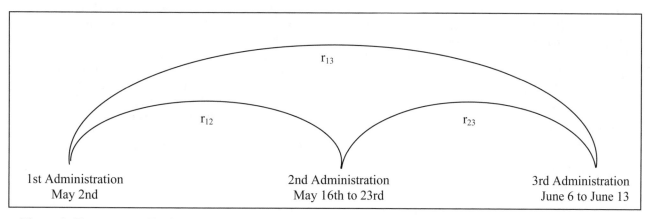

Figure 2: Test-retest reliability procedure and testing for the Self-as-Entertainment Scale

and changing the items of the measurement to reflect a broadly recognized concept.

Split-Half Reliability

Split-half reliability compares one half of a test with the other half to determine whether subsets of the test are reliable in coming up with the same results. In thinking about dividing a scale of 40 items into two halves, the critical question is deciding how you would split the scale. See for yourself as you continue reading, how important it is to divide the questions appropriately.

When trainees are asked about how to split the items of an instrument into two equal parts in order to compare them, they often commit a technical error. They suggest that the 40-item instrument, for instance, be divided into two halves as follows: one-half from items 1 to 20 and the other from items 21 to 40. Three main drawbacks of this method are as follows:

1. Respondents' motives and impressions may be different in their early responses to the first half as compared to the second.
2. Attention may change as they respond to more items.
3. Persons' interests and the effect of time may cause changes in how they view the content of earlier items, as they reach the later ones.
4. The test may be constructed so that different types of items or different subscales are put together in blocks. Splitting the test into the first half and the second half may end up comparing subscales with one another rather than comparing questions that are expected to be similar.

To overcome all potential drawbacks — known and unknown — a split into two parts would be correctly based on having the odd items in one half and the even items in the other half. In other words, we compare the items numbered 1, 3, 5, 7 ... to 39, against 2, 4, 6, 8 ... to 40.

One technique in test construction may require a slightly different approach in dividing the questions. Sometimes subscales are interleaved so that the questions reflect subscales as follows:

1. subscale 1
2. subscale 2
3. subscale 3
4. subscale 4
5. subscale 1
6. subscale 2
7. subscale 3
8. subscale 4 ...

In that case a better division would be to use items 1, 3, 6, 8 ... in one half and items 2, 4, 5, 7 ... in the other half. The goal is to have equal numbers of each subscale in each half of the test while also taking the same number of questions from the first and second half of the test in each sample. The numbers we have chosen give us the first question from subscale 1 (item 1) in the first half and the second question from subscale 1 (item 5) in the second half. Similarly, the second question from subscale 2 (item 6) goes in the first half and the first question from subscale 2 (item 2) goes in the second half. This method of splitting an assessment tool is similar to the alternate forms reliability discussed next.

Comparisons are done initially in terms of means and variances: assuming equality and followed by correlation. The correlation between the two halves demonstrates the measurement's level of reliability, known as "Split-Half Reliability." The higher the correlation, the higher the reliability of the scale. Acceptable levels of split-half reliability are between .75 and .95.

Alternate or Parallel Forms Reliability

To gain confidence in the common attributes that the items represent, if two different forms of the same test are used, they should yield *similar* scores. This similarity of scores demonstrates consistency. The two tests or forms should be equivalent or parallel scales, covering the same domain or concept. For instance, in developing a leisure motivation (needs) scale, if the investigator has 60 items, the developer may create two forms: A and B.

In order for the forms to be parallel and equivalent, pairs of items relevant to each component of the construct would be assigned *randomly* to either form A or B. Hence, the content of the measured domain of each form is assumed to cover similar characteristics of the target domain. Unlike dividing according to odd-even numbering in split-halves, items that have the same content are paired. Then they are randomly assigned to the two forms, making them parallel or equivalent in meaning and content.

After creating two similar forms of 30 items each, the two forms should be administered together to a group of persons. If the scores of Form A correlate adequately with scores of Form B, this can be considered as sufficient evidence of reliability that the two forms are measuring the same domain. Therefore, users can employ either form to assess the intended domain of interest.

Internal Consistency Reliability

Another reliability test is how each item within a test measures the same property as each of the other items. This reliability can be labeled as homogeneity, inter-item association, or internal consistency. The result is demonstrated through a statistical procedure called "alpha reliability coefficient" (ARC), as an index reflecting inter-item correlation. This index ranges from .01 to 1.00. Acceptable ratings will be .60 and higher.

To illustrate with a simple four-item scale, an index is the outcome of all item correlations, as shown below in Figure 3.

Each line is a relation represented by a correlation (r). The correlation between the first and second item, for example, is represented by the correlation r_{12}. The alpha reliability coefficient is calculated on the basis of all of the correlations.

While constructing a scale, through pre-testing, in the process of arriving at or improving the test's ARC, further items belonging to the concept can be added. Also, items gaining lower correlations can be rewritten and further tested, or discarded if proven irrelevant. Then, the ARC will demonstrate the measurement's inter-item correlations.

This is achieved through utilizing an excellent procedure to keep items that show high correlation with the total scale and discard items that show less relevancy — those demonstrating less consistency. For example, items are retained when correlations are in the range of .45 to .60 (or higher) for the item relative to the total scale or subscale. These scores demonstrate homogeneity.

On the other hand, low correlations for an item would be strong empirical evidence to delete it. In turn, ARC can improve if certain low items are deleted in this manner. Some investigators use .30 as a minimum criterion to retain an item, while more stringent investigators use higher correlations, such as .40. Practically, utilizing .30 or .40 would rely on how the items overall correlate with their subscale or total scale.

For evaluation purposes, an ARC of .80 or higher is an appropriate index for field application and research use. To improve a given scale, inter-item correlation can be employed to advance instruments in recreation and leisure to reach an alpha above .90. In the fields of informal activities, internal consistency reliability was employed more than any other reliability procedure. For examples see Leisure Satisfaction Measure, by Beard and Ragheb, 1980; Leisure Boredom Scale, by Iso-Ahola and Weissinger, 1990; Quality of Recreation Services, by MacKay and Compton, 1990; Motivation Assessment and Performance Scale, by Williams and Neal, 1993; and Intrinsic Motivation in Leisure, by Weissinger and Bandalos, 1995; Leisure Coping Belief Scale, by Iwasaki and Mannell, 2000; and Adolescent Ethical Behavior in Leisure Scale, by Widmer, Ellis, and Munson, 2003).

Considerations in Using and Interpreting Reliability

In employing measurements in practice or in research, established reliability must be analyzed and interpreted carefully and skillfully. Understanding major reliability considerations can guard against potential mishaps. Users need to be sensitive to the appropriate applications of an assessment tool based on the explanations of the measurement's reliability. (Validity is important, too, as will be discussed later.) Some major reliability considerations can be raised, such as:

1. The functions of the test must be considered when looking at the scale's reliability. For example, measurements used in therapeutic recreation for treatment functions (diagnosis, referral, or types of therapy) must demonstrate high reliability coefficients, .90 or higher (see Salvia and Ysseldyke, 1991; Nunnally, 1978). A measurement employed in commercial or corporate recreation and the like would be acceptable with reliabilities of .80 or higher. The nature of the setting, relevant to its sensitivity, dictates how high reliability must be.

2. Dependence on reliability should not be absolute. Two competencies need to be acquired and exercised: interpretation and research design. First, a practitioner using an instrument known to be reliable might lack skills in data collection, analysis, and interpretation of findings. The reliability level cannot save the outcome that results from following inappropriate procedures. Second, in testing a relationship, the same high level of reliability cannot compensate for an unsound background of the study, or formulating poorly stated hypotheses, or collecting inadequate data, and/or inappropriately analyzing the data

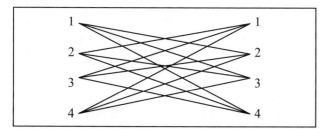

Figure 3: Correlation of items for an alpha reliability test.

collected. In both cases — interpretation and research design — reliability is a prerequisite to field practice and research investigation. Nevertheless, it is viewed as an insufficient requirement by itself, if data is misinterpreted or the study has a poor research design. Some minimum competencies to handle and interpret the data are needed.

3. To improve a measurement, a developer strives to minimize variance error and to maximize the variance of the individual differences. To reach that goal, Kerlinger and Lee (2000) suggests three general procedures:

   - Write items unambiguously (clearly, including only one meaning or aspect).
   - Add more items to an unreliable instrument to reduce the impact of error.
   - Give clear (unambiguous) instructions.

   Measurement improvement is a continuous process through development and revision, for a scale is never perfect.

4. A measurement's user should not expect the reliability coefficient to be the same across all settings and populations. Age, setting, life conditions, and culture dictate preferences in rating items. Sometimes seasons or weather can impact responses. What one group endorses in the form of response might not be suitable for another, causing a reliability coefficient to change, but within a reasonable range.

In conclusion, some basic knowledge of reliability is needed for all users. Locating a reliable scale is insufficient. Like having a gun, without competent use, reliability can be harmful. A measurement's reliability is a fundamental requirement, but it would also be useless without valid content and concept.

Validity

Validity studies attempt to answer several questions, two of which are "What does the test measure?" and "Does it assess correctly what it was designed to measure?" Validity of an assessment tool is not measured but rather judged. Some of the bases for evaluating validity are its representation, relevance, adequacy, comprehensiveness, and, later, its reliability. Other pertinent verifications are the answers to the following:

1. How well does a scale assess what it attempts to measure?
2. What inferences can be made from its test scores?
3. How suitable are the conclusions drawn from the test results?

All of the above must be addressed before we have full confidence in a measurement's attributes.

Validity, unlike reliability, is judged not through one procedure, but through a number of approaches or validations: face, content, criterion, and construct. Analogously, while a car is running reliably, after you turn the ignition key to begin driving it to your target, the car must be correctly directed to specific roads, speeds, signs, and other directions in order to reach its proper destination safely. Reaching a designated destination is an indication of effective, sound, or "valid" process of driving. In sum, while a car is running and moving reliably, it might not achieve any of its true intents —reaching the proper destination (validity) — and it may still violate speed limits or traffic regulations. Therefore, a scale can be reliable but invalid at the same time (see Kruger, 1995).

Four main types of validity are available. These vary in their levels of validations, in their required stages, and in their level of advancement. Figure 1 presented the following means of validation:

- Face Validity
- Content Validity
- Criterion Validity
  - Concurrent Validity
  - Predictive Validity
- Construct Validity

Basic descriptions of the types of validity are as follows.

Face Validity

Technically, face validity of a measurement is the validity judgment given by outside reviewers of the assessment. Effort is invested to determine whether the measure "seems on target" or "looks relevant to its concept" without further technical procedures. The reviewers are asked to determine whether the measure seems to be relevant to what the measure is intended to assess.

The presence of face validity might help in some respects, but its lack can cause much harm. For example, a scale that works well with children may sound funny, unrealistic, off target, or at worst ridiculous when used with other ages like adults or the elderly. Such a scale might have face validity when considered for use with children, but it would not have face validity for use with other groups. Lack of face validity can damage public relations, trust, destroy respondents' ratings of items, or create resistance. It is highly needed, but insufficient in itself.

These efforts, although offered by expert practitioners and scientists, are still superficial in the absence of other evaluations of validity. Users might agree on the use of an instrument due to face validity, but upon using the instrument on the basis of the apparent face validity only, it may later prove short on more important validations. However, an advantage especially applicable to recreation and park provisions is to apply face validity when an area requiring assessment does not have a needed instrument. It is important, when lacking advanced types of technical validation such as content or criterion validities, to apply face validity. This is especially true when it is the only information available in selecting a measurement. Developers need to consider face validity as only *one* of the minimum requirements or as a prerequisite, insufficient in itself alone. However, it cannot be ignored without great damage.

Content Validity

Is the measurement's content representative of its concept? This is the easiest and most realistic manner for defining content validity. Although this validity may be on a lower level, yet it is considered one of the most essential validations. It is related to both the adequacy of the developer's "homework" to secure the concept's relevance and the comprehensiveness of the assessment tool, as a result of the quality of doing the homework. As low in its level of advancement as it is, without valid content you have no quality instrument.

Are the items representative of the universe of behaviors observed? Relevance of items is what makes the content valid. Technically, a measurement's content encompasses and delineates the theoretical universe of a concept. It accounts for an adequate representation of all possible meanings pertinent to an object. Work to secure the concept's relevance must be invested first before any attempts for further validations or reliability tests are performed. Moreover, a measurement's quality cannot exceed the quality of its contents. Quality input — most likely — yields desirable and known outcomes.

The quality of items and what they represent are a critical concern for content validity. This issue has been gaining methodologists' attention (see Lindell, Brandt, and Whitney, 1999; James, Demaree, and Wolf, 1984). A method was developed by Lawshe (1975) to compute interrater agreement in determining the essentiality of each item in a scale. Lawshe used three ratings to determine the importance of a given item:

1. Essential
2. Useful but not essential
3. Not necessary

In Lawshe's criteria, for an item to show content validity, it must be rated "essential" by at least 50% of the raters. More criteria were presented, as well as a content validity ratio to be used to retain an item.

In evaluating given instruments in their totality, a recreation practitioner or researcher looks for two things when studying the content validation of an assessment tool. (They are mainly matters of judgment.)

- First, did the developers of the assessment tool report on their "process of critical analysis of relevant knowledge" or something to this effect?
- Second, was the measure exposed to external referees or judges — persons with expertise in the area assessed? That is to evaluate the content for its relevance to what is measured.

Adequate answers to these two criteria determine the quality of the content. Hence, a professional selecting an assessment tool would need to apply these standards.

Developers' use of both critical analysis and external evaluators secures content validation. A main condition to this internal and external evaluation is familiarity with the body of knowledge (concept) relevant to what the assessment scale is attempting to measure as presented in Part III. All future validating procedures and applications should rely on this step. Analogously, for a train to go west and not some other direction, it must initially be on the right tracks and headed in the right direction.

Implementing the above procedures can be illustrated through the following: The object to be measured might be "rewards obtained from leisure," or leisure satisfaction (see Beard and Ragheb, 1980). Therefore, a main intent to evaluate this assessment tool is to look for evidence based on three criteria:

- Did the instrument's developers identify all possible parts (components) that make the structure that is under consideration?
- Did developers account for all possible rewards obtained/received from leisure?
- Was their delineation of the object, from literature or experience, sufficient?

That part of the body of literature is considered the theoretical universe of what is assessed. Investigators' motivation is a major determinant of success in accounting for the theoretical universe of the concept.

Examples of measures attempting to satisfy these three criteria, establishing content validity in recreation and leisure, are Aguilar and Petrakis' (1989) Racquet Sports Competence Scale, and

Clough et al.'s (1999) Motivations for Participation in Recreational Running Scale.

Criterion Validity

When a measurement developer utilizes an external measure, it is known as criterion validity. An external measure is compared to or correlated with the scores of the newly developed scale. The external measure must demonstrate relevance of its construct to the newly developed one, measuring the same or similar attribute as the scale constructed. Prior validations (content and/or face) can be connected to the current one and other procedures. Two validities are to be considered as criteria for criterion validity: concurrent and predictive validities.

Concurrent Validity

This is established when the developer's measure (called predictor) is administered at the same time as an external, well-established scale related to what is measured (called criterion). In this situation, interest is in the relationship between present performance on the newly developed scale and present performance on the criterion, as a validating mechanism. For example, two scales would be utilized in validating a new scale to measure Vitality Through Leisure (VTL) of older persons; the newly developed scale could be administered simultaneously with another — well-established — scale indicating wellness. Exact findings would determine the validity of the newly developed scale.

The strength of the correlation between the two provides evidence about the newly constructed VTL scale. This is referred to as "Concurrent Validity." The above validation is then demonstrated, fulfilling its objective. In the field of recreation, four measures provide examples of how to use concurrent validity: Leisure Attitude Scale (Crandall and Slivken, 1980), Measurement of Leisure Attitude (Ragheb and Beard, 1982), Measurement of Perceived Freedom in Leisure (Ellis and Witt, 1984), and Leisure Experience Battery for Adolescents (Caldwell, Smith, and Weissinger, 1992).

Predictive Validity

To what extent would a present score foretell future behavior or performance? The predictive criterion is concerned with how accurate a measure is when administered currently, as compared to another criterion measure to be performed in the future. In this application, the prediction is from the developed test to the use of a criterion-related measure after the passage of an interval of time. Future performance or behavior is the one revealed as "Predictive Validity."

Usually, this is employed in the classification of therapeutic recreation patients or selection of personnel in leisure agencies. For example, in the application of predictive validity, selection of recreation managers can be tested through:

1. A decision-making ability scale.
2. Later, by observing successful administration styles and performance.

By correlating the two observations — test score and on-the-job performance — we learn about the predictive validity of the decision-making ability scale. The magnitude of the measurement's correlation with the observed behavior and the success of the tested administrators will determine the predictive validity of the decision-making ability scale.

Broadly stated, predictive validity is not concerned about correlating present reactions to two measurements, but rather with prediction from present scores to future behavior or performance. All of the above procedures also can be applied to attempted forecasts taken from present test scores, as compared to past performance and behavior, illustrated by the following three examples:

1. "How would predictive validity of a scale apply to future choices in leisure and recreation?" When this validation is established, for instance, then prediction of the low frequency of past leisure participation in teenage groups will relate to present or future reporting of, for instance, free time boredom. The correlation between the two is an index of predictive validity. Later, when a relationship is established, tests can be given to assess frequency of leisure participation now, as a predictor of free time boredom in the future.
2. Given that there is evidence showing that employees' wellness or stress reduction associates with leisure awareness or "attitudes." As a prediction, a currently developed measurement of leisure attitudes can foretell future scores of employees' wellness or stress control.
3. In other settings like therapeutic recreation, scoring LOW on a leisure involvement scale, but showing HIGH participation in many leisure activities, calls into question the validity of the leisure involvement scale. Saying it differently, the current scale on leisure involvement does not seem to associate with relevant measures that look at actual leisure participation. Therefore, one of the measures may be an invalid instrument, not useful for field practice.

Certain concerns arise when choosing a criterion: "What criterion can be utilized?" "Whose selection and whose judgment apply?" "How can data be interpreted?" Until further relationships and relevance are established, users need to adopt a conservative strategy and be careful in their application of criterion or predictive correlations.

Construct Validity

As inferred from the name, construct validity is an investigation into the construct's structure — its theoretical background. Therefore, this validation is considered a highly advanced procedure not only in measurement development but also in application. As a higher technical step, it should be performed as an advanced evaluation of the instrument's validation. Basically, construct validation requires an accumulated body of literature relevant to the concept/construct being assessed. Therefore, it is a procedure conducted at a later stage of validation, refining instrumentations.

What factors influence the construct under consideration? Answering this question is a basic attempt to establish construct validity. For example, validating an instrument such as the Leisure Motivation Scale, an investigator wants to know what variables explain its variance. Variables can be demographic (such as age, gender, and income) and/or behavioral (such as need for achievement, need for affiliation, search for meaning, stress control, wellness, leisure interests, and leisure attitude). These are in addition to all other potentially influential variables that form a construct's foundations. In testing relationships between leisure motivation and other demographic and behavioral variables, the theoretical background accounting for its variance is considered "Construct Validity."

The concern with construct validation is not with the measurement itself but rather with how to interpret differences in individuals' responses. In other words, what variables make one individual score high on a leisure motivation scale while another's responses are low? In sum, the effort is not on validating the test itself but its basis — the theorizing behind the test.

Usability: Practical Use

Practical use might seem to be an unimportant and uncritical criterion for available assessment tools. However, it seems to be acute, because a scale can be both reliable and valid enough but not usable in certain settings. Practical use of instruments can be evaluated by responding to questions similar to the following:

- Does the measurement assess something of value to my participants or agency?

- Is the data off-target, so that it seems irrelevant in practice?

- Is the data resulting from the scope of the instrument sufficient, or is it too limited to be useful?

- Is the measurement too long (e.g., 90 items or more) or too short (two to five items), making it impractical and inhibiting its usefulness?

- Would the language and content of the items fit my target population? (For example, children, employees, older persons, varying educational levels, and at-risk youth may all require different language and content to measure the same basic concept.)

Each setting demands that certain considerations be regarded in choosing a tool. Selected scales must be appropriate to setting's nature, goals, problems, and requirements. That will maximize each instrument's usability and outcome.

A Methodological Issue That Needs Attention

Like "the chicken or the egg" dilemma, which comes first: reliability or validity? In other words, must the measurement be consistent and predictable (reliability) before it demonstrates that it is measuring what is to be measured (validity)? Or is it the other way around? In reality, this is a resolvable issue (unlike "the chicken or the egg"), since "reliability or validity" relies on logical sequence.

Contrary to the way almost all textbooks are written, certain validities should be checked first. Reliability chapters are almost always presented first in books, but a set of validity tests should be considered a prerequisite to reliability. The logic and sequence would consider that a certain kind of concept validity (mostly content) must be demonstrated first, followed by the reliability, or accuracy, of the measurement. Finally, another validity, of a different kind and higher level, must be performed.

Initially, validity, not reliability, must gain the attention of developers and users. In application, the review of pertinent literature is the determinant of validity: theories and tested hypotheses, philosophical speculations, and the use of common sense. (See Chapter 15 for more details.) Without clear ideas, the concept that should supply the foundation and structure of a measurement is vague. Performing these systematic procedures represents the art and science of measurement construction.

Diagrammatically, the sequence of intermixing reliability and validity procedures in developing an assessment tool, of a given concept, can be illustrated by Figure 4.

The chain in Figure 4 demonstrates starting with a valid concept; secondly, through one of the reliability tests, items' correlations are demonstrated; followed again by validity tests. When a concept lacks sound delineation and representation, reliability cannot come to the rescue. A valid concept, in terms of its concept, is a prerequisite to a reliable construct. Instrument developers must first be on target, establishing a thorough focus; then accuracy and predictability can be attempted, proven, and improved or sharpened.

Summary and Conclusion

Reliability and validity, as basic criteria for quality assessment tools, are the most technical procedures in measurement development. Meeting reliability and validity criteria ensures a measurement's value, trust, life span, and usability. Measurement developers strive to revisit their measures to advance those qualities, for it is considered a continuous process. A measure is never perfect or complete.

Three frequent users are interested in measurement reliability and validity: instrument developers, scientists testing hypotheses, and field professionals (practitioners). First, measurement developers need competencies in meeting reliability and validity requirements — through courses and training or collaboration with persons who possess such expertise. Second, research scientists using quantitative methods cannot test relations among variables, proving or disproving their hypotheses, unless employing trustworthy measurements. Last, practitioners need quality tools in their practice to perform dependable assessments of clients and evaluation of actions as bases for providing quality services. They need to be competent as good consumers of measurements. That is, performing the following tasks:

- To be able to understand what scientists have done to validate their instruments and why.
- To be able to select measurements that exhibit quality criteria to meet their clients' and organizations' needs.
- To implement measurement criteria and guidelines in their selection, choosing measurements that demonstrate quality.

These three groups would need competencies in assessment in different proportions, depending on the nature of their requirements.

Toward these three ends, this chapter introduced guidelines about measurements useful not only to future developers and research scientists; but also to practitioners, including some basic criteria on how to

---

Content

Content Validity
Valid Concept:
Through common sense,
philosophical speculations,
and scientific explanations

Face Validity
Empirical Evidence:
Evaluated by developers
of the instrument and judges

↓

The Content is Tested for Reliability
Through Predictability,
Homogeneity of Items,
Internal Consistency,
Accuracy,
Repeated use Consistency,
Or
Stability

↓

A Valid Construct

Concurrent Validity
Against other similarly existing constructs

Construct Validity
The sum total of accumulated evidence

Predictive Validity
Against actual behavior

Figure 4: Sequence of systematic procedures: intermixing validity and reliability

seek and review measurement background and methodologies. Four types of reliability tests and four ways of validation were presented, with some main criteria to be considered. Reliabilities are test-retest, split-half, alternate form, and internal consistency. Validity procedures are face, content, criterion, and construct.

Understanding all eight criteria is required to be competent in screening, selection, development, testing relationships, or field implementation of a scale. At least one reliability and one validity criterion (besides face validity, if reported) is required to determine whether a test should be relied on. A measurement lacking evidence of reliability and/or validity should be handled with extreme care and a conservative attitude in terms of interpretation, use, reliance on scale's outcome, and generalizability.

Questions and Exercises

1. Elaborate on the basic criteria that ensure the quality of assessment instruments.
2. What is reliability?
3. What are the kinds of reliability?
4. What is validity
5. What are the kinds of validity?
6. Discuss the issue of usability of measurements.
7. What is the sequence of procedures to secure a quality measurement?

Chapter 15

Prerequisites for the Development of Assessment Tools

Focus of Chapter

This chapter introduces the development of ideas or concepts as the basis for the content of a measurement. It also outlines the strategies (steps) for verifying the relevance of identified details or structures of a designated concept. Developing a concept precedes its abstraction as a construct. Therefore, the differences between concepts and constructs are explored in preparation for identification and development of a measurement. Moreover, sources used for delineating a concept will be presented: suggesting the most important source to be sought, warning against inherent weaknesses in other sources. Those sources — from the most desirable to the least — are theory-guided, philosophical speculations, and common sense. Nevertheless, reducing a concept to a construct is a big leap; going from macro level to micro representation is a process of zooming from reality to artificiality. The outcome is a human-made product. Zooming in on human affairs and minds requires human cameras to assess behaviors, feelings, perceptions, and ways of thinking. This chapter will lay the needed groundwork for a more advanced orientation, leading to "Formal Steps in Construct Development," the focus of next chapter.

Key Terms

- abstract
- concept
- construct
- philosophy
- steps
- theory

Key Names

- Edward L. Deci
- Gary D. Ellis
- Donald W. Fiske
- David A. Markland
- John Neulinger
- Richard M. Ryan
- Robert W. White

Objectives

- Differentiate between concepts and their constructs.
- Identify the boundaries of a concept to be abstracted in a construct.
- Describe the three sources of concept development.
- Report on strengths and weaknesses of common sense, philosophical speculations, and theory-guided explanations as sources of concepts.
- Apply the illustrations and examples provided to other concepts relevant to the reader.
- Recognize the rationale and strategy to seek a concept, in reducing it to a construct.
- Make a smooth transition from the informal orientation to the more formal steps in studying construct development.

Like all intellectual endeavors, assessment requires starting with a clear idea of what is to be achieved. Absence of clarity leads to confusion, causing problems with identifying content, and makes selecting a direction unclear, resulting in inaccurate and/or unknown outcomes.

How clear are novel ideas or concepts? In other words, how clear are newly occurring leisure phenomena? Realistically, most new ideas are not clearly described or fully developed in the literature. Pertinent information on new concepts is scattered or suffers from a lack of agreement in its definition and background. Often this lack of uniformity compels focused efforts to pull together details and elements to arrive at a universally understood meaning. Logically, this is the nature of knowledge. Especially this is the case with novel and unresearched domains. It is common for measurement development to operate as the foundation and driving force behind the increased understanding and universal acceptance of concepts.

A major component of developing a quality assessment tool is thoroughness in reviewing relevant information already developed by others on these novel ideas. By reviewing the research done by others, the individuals developing the novel idea (and the testing tool to measure the novel idea) enhance the measurements ability to exhibit acceptable criteria (validity, reliability, and usability). By clarifying issues related to the novel idea through this process, the researcher helps in identifying the direction and the scope of the assessment tool. A measurement's quality does not exceed the assessor's level of care in delineating clearly what is constructed.

Where can we search for the background of ideas as basis for constructing measurements? The answer to this question is a focal point in measurement development. This main issue will be addressed in this chapter, demonstrating the degree of complexity of different concepts. Part of the strategy is to follow certain steps (methodology) in developing an assessment tool to reduce inherent complexities of concepts. Therefore, in presenting a nearly complete picture of the steps called for, some examples will be raised — to simplify the procedure — demonstrating informally the sequence of these steps. Formally presenting these steps will be the goal of the next chapter, "Formal Steps in Construct Development."

Clarity of Directions and Objectives

Concepts (ideas) — such as satisfaction, quality of life, and vitality — vary in their difficulty and complexity to abstract and outline. For instance, on a continuum, physical and social concepts are less complicated to abstract and measure than moral and spiritual ones, with psychological and mental dimensions falling in between. Examples of physical concepts are height and speed. Social domains can be conformity, friendship, and attraction. Moral domains can be courage and fairness. Psychological and mental domains can be motivation, attitude, aggression, and intelligence. As a rule: the more the object is material, the clearer it is and the easier it is to reach an agreement about its nature. Consequently, it is easier to measure.

In contrast, the closer the concept is to being moral (abstract), the more difficult it is to state it clearly and the harder it is to reach an agreement about it. It is also more difficult to measure. Social concepts can be placed between material and moral (abstract) concepts. Relatively, concreteness of the issue or object makes it easier to understand and to measure. In sum, clarity, concreteness, simplicity, and possibility of measuring an object go hand-in-hand. (More information will be presented later in this chapter on the nature of a given concept and its definition.)

How would play, recreation, and leisure dimensions and provisions lend themselves to conceptualization and assessment? Our belief is that the previous continuum applies here, too. For example, physical dimensions of recreation, exercise, leisure, and park participation are easier to conceptualize and assess (e.g., park attendance, the number of children on a playground, and how many corporate employees attended a recreation event or exercise). Progressively, social dimensions tend to be relatively more difficult to assess than physical dimensions (e.g., the social impact of recreation and leisure activities, kinds of interaction among club or team members, involvement of females versus males in leisure pursuits, with whom people go to parks, or social relationships developed through play or leisure).

Finally, the behavioral and psychological (mental) processes of recreation, fitness, and leisure are lower on clarity and higher on complexity; thus, more difficult to assess. Examples of behavioral domains are the perception of leisure experience, satisfaction, involvement, vitality, awareness of leisure constraints, and why children play. In sum, besides the above-mentioned difficulties, without clear conceptualization and identification of designated domains, abstraction and development of assessment tools are limited. Therefore, a fundamental, early step toward outlining a *concept* is its comprehensive development, to the best of the investigator's ability and the broadest degree of available knowledge.

What Is a Concept?

Since the meaning of the term "concept" is so critical to measurements, we need to understand its nature. A concept is a way of defining an object and intangible idea, drawing the definition from literature, experiences, and observations. To ensure a well thought out concept, the gathered information should examine most of the meanings or related concepts relevant to what is to be abstracted. Often the information gathered will have conflicting ideas, so the development of a concept also includes resolving conflicting information or ideas, sometimes by presenting them. Incomplete conceptualization of ideas logically leads to incomplete assessment tools. It is for this reason that diligence is used in developing a comprehensive concept.

Moreover, a concept is an interconnected collection of unified ideas relative to and known about an object. Unified knowledge about a domain of interest can be established through informal and/or, at best, formal means. Fundamentally, Fiske (1971: 3) postulates a basic criterion saying, "The concept must be spelled out so that we know what we want to measure and have some guidance in developing ways of measuring it." Therefore, in measurement construction, clarity of concepts is essential as a cornerstone criterion; thus, concept development is the point of origination, where all of our work should begin.

Another criterion in constructing measurements is the comprehensiveness of what a concept represents (or the ground it covers). The developer's diligence, perseverance, and motivation are a basic determinant of inclusiveness of concepts. For example, in photographing a huge mountain (concept), your picture will represent that at which you aim — what you can include in the photograph. If you focus on a specific part or limited parts of the mountain, the picture will be less inclusive, reflecting only that part or parts. The further and the wider you aim comprehensively — on all parts — the greater you represent a global view of the mountain, or the concept of what you view. There is a limited picture of an object and there are other, broader ones, possibly with different degrees of quality, all of which are dependent upon the zooming capabilities of a camera (measurement) and the photographer's (measurement's composer) skills. Therefore, if the conceptualization (or composition) is incomplete and/or vague, the end product (scale or picture) will be limited and unrepresentative, reflecting almost exactly that restricted and confined boundary — no more and probably less.

Sources of Concepts

What is the scope of a concept's sources? Or, from where does a concept draw its meaning, content, and ideas? Concepts, as the basis of measurements, can be derived from a number of sources and developed on many different levels: from the down-to-earth notions (daily practice) to the most advanced knowledge (theories). However, the nature of the concept, its available information, and the validity (soundness) of interpretation employed determine the quality of the constructed measurement.

If you are developing or evaluating a measurement for use, you should answer these basic questions:

1. How did the measurement originate?
2. What concepts were behind it?
3. What does it represent?
4. How was it developed? Or, technically what methodology was utilized to construct it?

In this appraisal, a hierarchy exists to determine the quality of the foundations of a concept. This hierarchy includes common sense, philosophy, and theories. On a scale, the lowest quality would be related to concepts derived from common sense and folkways. The highest quality would be for concepts anchored in theories, labeled as a theory-guided or a theory-driven measurement. The latter, when employed in measurement construction, will be strongly predictive and more comprehensive. Between common sense and the use of theories lies philosophical speculation.

To illustrate the nature and importance of the three bases of measurements, further elaboration of these identified sources are presented.

Common Sense and Folkways

Common sense, as a basis for concept development, forms a lower quality in presenting ideas. In this context, common sense means ordinary, widespread, second-hand opinions and knowledge shared by the public ("common knowledge"), characterized by a lack of sophistication and refinement. Developmentally, formation of such concepts was popular in the early years of all intellectual pursuits, fields of service, and disciplines. Historically, folkways and common sense were the roots of different concepts, awaiting further speculative philosophical insights, evolving to clearer views and judgments, followed by theories as sources for testing and assessment. Since then, conceptualization and assessment of many domains improved by their utilization of more advanced approaches.

How much do recreation, park, leisure, and play domains rely on common sense? Of the many early concepts, how many would fit the common-sense description? Suffice it to say that, at its beginning — like all other professional areas — parks and recreation relied heavily on common-sense rationales, explanations, concepts, and ideas. However, two more refined approaches have been gradually replacing folkways and common sense, one of which is philosophy.

Philosophical Speculations

As a foundation for measurement development, philosophy, the central core of all human inquiries, is the oldest organized endeavor of investigation and conceptualization in the pursuit of knowledge and wisdom. In its attempt to answer what is real, philosophy helped — speculatively — classifying and categorizing physical, social, and behavioral aspects. Consequently, philosophy gave birth to all scientific fields, stimulating exploration and experimentation. Therefore, philosophy, as an overall vision, is considered the mother of all sciences from physics and biology to economics and sociology.

Philosophy's method of establishing knowledge is based on truth finding through inquiry and questioning existence and reality. Moreover, philosophy organized knowledge, helping increasingly rigorous explorations to arrive at more precise answers about reality and existence. Behaviorally and socially, for instance, philosophy attempted to explain the nature and reality of aggression, emotions, contentment (happiness), and success. Later on these were investigated and theorized about scientifically.

In the fields of parks, recreation, leisure, and play, how much knowledge is based on philosophy? Historically, again, at the beginning of an organized recreation movement, philosophy was very dominant (replacing common sense) in explaining recreation and play in the absence of science until the 1970s. With heightened social demands for recreation and with increasing free time (Neulinger, 1974; Robinson, 1990), further scientific investigations began sharing in the study of recreation and leisure aspects.

Concepts developed philosophically can be utilized as bases for measurement development. Several concepts can be abstracted and measured, founded on knowledge initiated philosophically through, for instance, idealism, pragmatism, naturalism, realism, and existentialism. For example, a measurement assessing "Perceived Freedom in Leisure" (see Ellis and Witt, 1994) relied partially on assumptions developed in the philosophies of dogmatism and existentialism. Also, park design has much to reap

from the philosophical concepts of aesthetics and harmony (flow), gaining criteria for planning (see Rutledge, 1971) and assessment of those qualities.

Another set of measurements can draw conceptualizations from the philosophical "reservoir" of happiness and contentment; attempting to assess leisure and recreation rewards — enjoyment, pleasure, and satisfaction. Finally, the philosophy of pragmatism can help in understanding the usability of recreation environments, programs designed to meet needs and interests, and in explaining individual functioning — seeking adjustment, success, and adaptive behavior. It is no exaggeration saying that without philosophy, understanding the background of many concepts would have lacked vision and focus. Hence, in the process of measurement construction, philosophical understanding is a fundamental ingredient to be incorporated.

Theory-Guided Explanations

As a cornerstone in scale development, theory is indispensable for many measurements. Theory-driven assessment can be viewed as the most advanced procedure. One of the main reasons for theory-anchored advancement is a better-developed explanation as a basis for measurement development. Knowing contemporary theories and research findings of tested hypotheses would provide strength, based on using more refined views, ideas, and predictions of what can be incorporated in a measurement. Therefore, utilizing a theory-based observation tends to be characterized by being more comprehensive, more accurate, and more logical — arriving at a better quality measurement that is both valid and reliable.

With the emergence of new and better explanations and theories, assessment procedures can improve by accounting for new conceptual grounds, sometimes never before considered. Many assessment tools were founded on the cognitive evaluation theory (CET) by Deci and Ryan (1985), including leisure (see Weissinger, 1985; Ellis and Witt, 1984; Baldwin and Caldwell, 2003). The theory emphasized intrinsic motivation as the predominant reason for certain pursuits. However, Deci and Ryan (1990), the same theorists of CET, realized that the motivational dichotomy pitting external motivation against internal motivation was misleading. They felt that CET outlived its usefulness and introduced the possibility that motivation is more than what is intrinsically motivating; allowing for other reasons such as amotivational and apprehensions components, as well as external motivators (see Li, 1999). As a result, contemporary assessments account for new theoretical assumptions and explanations, validating their relevancies (see also Cokley, 2000; Markland and Ingledew, 1997; Mullan, Markland, and Ingledew, 1997). Thus, theory-guided assessment is a viable pursuit: adaptable, highly refined, and trustworthy.

However, the value of theories is sometimes debated by different users. One group perceives no relationship between theories and practice, assuming that a "theory is just a theory," with limited or no application. Some might consider theories irrelevant to field applications, different from the reality of things. Some might go as far as saying that theorists are in the ivory tower, aloof, and alienated from realities.

On the other hand, another group claims that everything designed is based on a theory (an idea), in order to be successful in achieving its intentions or goals. For example, organizing traffic requires a theory (an idea and/or data). A modern arena or a stadium would be designed on the bases of new concepts, providing a better flow, aesthetics, and/or improved amenities. Also, through theories in physics, chemistry, biology, and engineering (all combined), space travel is achieved with great precision and maximized success.

In this context, for the achievement of goals, a theory is indispensable. As Fred Kerlinger (Kerlinger and Lee, 2000: 10) once said, "There is nothing more practical than a good theory." Familiarity with available theories seems to be critical for measurement construction and for their sound application and explanation. Yet in the empirical test of a measure, some theories can contribute more than others. Each measure is unique, drawing from theories that coincide with the scale's focus and how respondents relate to it.

In attempting to explain recreation, leisure, exercise, and play, it would be very useful to be well versed in pertinent theories. These theories can help in conceptual developments related to social and behavioral aspects of leisure, park, facility designs, recreation programs, and delivery system planning. Theories of leisure and play are categorized as classical theories, recent theories, and contemporary theories (see Ellis, 1973).

Three empirically validated theories were listed under contemporary theories: cognitive dynamics by Piaget (see Flavell, 1963), competence-effectance or mastery (White, 1959), and arousal seeking behavior (Ellis, 1973). These, as well as other theories, provide numerous assumptions and explanations that can help in conceptualizing many recreation, play, exercise, and leisure phenomena. Altogether, these are what make up a great portion of the theoretical bases of recreation and leisure. Furthermore, theories in administration, supervision, marketing, and psychol-ogy are badly needed when scales are developed to serve leisure functions.

Because a theory varies in its levels of explanation, its quality is usually dependent upon its power of prediction of matters and attributes related to its context. Concepts in leisure-specific measurement development should be founded in recreation and leisure theoretical literature. Otherwise, related fields — behavioral, social, economic, or administrative — can provide the needed theoretical framework. In this manner, testing theories from related sciences can be validated for further use to explain leisure behavior and to construct its assessment tools. Foreign and non-leisure scales and theories need to be employed carefully, at least until they are validated and fit leisure settings as a "retailored" silk glove.

A prime example of how concepts can evolve is related to the history of inventions. The beginnings of all types of inventions, if compared after decades to the present state of the art, would illustrate how primitive they were back then. Formerly, inventions were based on certain assumptions; presently, ideas and theories behind inventions have been refined. They are in a state of flux, waiting for more changes and progress. The results are highly advanced inventions (based on imaginative, then tested, ideas). The same progress applies to leisure measurements. Starting with what are available (generic scales) and non-leisure theories, progressively more adaptations can be made, making measurements a leisure-specific product.

By simply applying the above logic, a measurement is founded on current theories or ideas that explain the concept with which we are dealing. The measurement's validity will be determined by its reality, its comprehensiveness of using pertinent ideas, and its underlying theories. That is why we have a range of quality scales, from acceptable to excellent measurements, from a valid scale to a highly valid scale. This notion is relevant to the scope of a given measurement, answering the following: Does the measurement sufficiently comprise or encompass all possible parts of the concept? That is why we strive for better use of existing theories or ideas for the development and revisions of measurements.

In sum, for all sources of concepts, philosophies such as realism, dogmatism, existentialism, and materialism can provide extensive insights into and backgrounds of needed concepts to be constructed in leisure and recreation. Preferably, however, in this contemporary era, there will be increased reliance (in measurement development) on tested assumptions — hypotheses and theories — combined with philosophy. Due to continually advancing knowledge, we need to reduce reliance on common sense, using philosophies to identify perspectives and main sources of ideas. In many occasions, a scholar and/or a practitioner can benefit by shuttling back and forth between theories and philosophies, with an eye toward common sense. However, as knowledge progresses, we should employ scientifically tested notions to their fullest extent — that is, if our target is to construct a high-quality assessment tool.

Like all inventions, measurements should be in a continuous state of change, refinement, and improvement. Moreover, a state of amalgamation should be maintained between all sources of knowledge. But, in practical terms, how can we develop an amalgamated or integrated concept to construct a measurement? A measurement should be a reduced construct of the known concept. Without technical efforts to reduce existing diversified details, a measurement is not feasible.

The Bases for Reduction

By now, we know that concepts are developed through theory, philosophical speculations, and common sense: Utilizing a combination of the three is a better strategy, more comprehensive. But, how can these concepts help in the development of a measurement? An important fundamental is that a concept cannot be measured. For a concept to be built as a construct, it must be reduced. Concepts and constructs share common characteristics; yet, each has its unique and different features, functions, and levels of presentation.

Since we now know how to arrive at concepts, some examples can clarify the nature of and distinctions between concepts and constructs. Also, examples will show how we can successfully arrive at constructs.

As previously described, a concept is a general view or idea about an object, whereas a construct is a specific and human-made structure of that object. Moreover, a concept is the macro (grand) reality of something in existence: an object, a thing, or an idea. While a construct is a concept's micro (limited or small) representation, on a much-limited scale, and alternatives can serve the goal as well. This differentiation can assist efforts to identify, comprehend, communicate, and use concepts and constructs, not only in practice, but also in research and science.

To illustrate the above differences, a person traveling overseas needs a photograph to receive a passport. In this case, the person himself/herself is a concept (the way s/he exhibits the original features on a macro level), known as the reality of the person or the grand entity. The photograph is what we construct to depict these features or realities in a size the passport can accommodate. The person is natural and original, while the photograph is human-made, specific, and reduced (to a micro representation) — in this case, reduced through a camera, to serve selected goals.

Hopefully, with advanced cameras, the human-made effort will depict facial realities with greater accuracy, and will equally represent all dimensions of that face in equal proportions, without distortions: ears, eyes, nose, cheeks, and hair.

Unfortunately, behavioral and social concepts are not as easily reduced as the above example. That is because their macro shape is unknown and without physical existence. Their state compels more extensive work to capture the main features and realities.

In the preceding example, a measurement can be thought of as a camera, a behavioral and social camera. Both measurements and cameras depict, illustrate, represent, and capture a person's features, an object, a mood, or a feeling. While cameras capture physical features, behavioral measurements depict social, psychological, and administrative attributes. Camera technology advanced rapidly (e.g., light control, varied lens use, ability to zoom, focusing, precision, and quality of print). In contrast, the technology and methodology of measuring behavioral attributes lags far behind the physical technology of the camera. Nevertheless, there is a need to depict behavioral and social characteristics and attributes as crude and less advanced as they are (in recreation and other life studies) through the use of psychometric and sociometric theories. Over time, with more progress like all inventions, methodology will improve, capturing realities of feelings and moods.

For practical and research uses, measurements are needed. We still need to make them even though our social and behavioral "cameras" are not as advanced as physical cameras. For some practice and for most scientific studies, a measurement is a cornerstone. Therefore, it is necessary to keep on refining our behavioral lenses and their precision to capture accurate and representative objects (mental states, feelings, perceptions, or behaviors) of individuals, as illustrated through the following informal example about the concept of "love."

From Concept to Construct: An Informal Example about Love

Now to the bottom line, how can developers reduce concepts to constructs or measurements? The following application refers to the concrete example of a person's photograph to understand this process. Switching from an easy physical example of a camera to an emotion can illustrate the degree of difficulty in assessment. Let us take a broad emotional concept like "love." How can we develop a construct (or a camera-like device) to assess the concept of love, *if it is possible at all*? First and foremost, what is the concept of love? How can we define it?

Love, for sure, has been felt and observed by humans since the beginning of life. Moreover, different people in different times have expressed it in numerous ways. For example, in Western cultures the Shakespearean characters of Romeo and Juliet expressed it one way, Josephine and Napoleon showed it another, Abelard and Heloise still another, and, above all, you and I have our own ways, too. On the other hand, ancient Egyptians, Romans, Hebrews, Greeks, Chinese, and other older civilizations had their own distinct and unique ways of expressing love. Although love is both a complex and subjective concept, a definition is inevitable.

Defining Love

One of these definitions — exhibiting some of love's attributes — can be as follows:

> Love between two persons is the intensively loaded positive (rarely negative) feeling, heavily charged with emotions; characterized by attraction, affection, caring, warm attachment, devotion, longing, and admiration. It is a feeling accompanied by some unique physical and mental reactions and manifestations.

This is a very first step that has to be performed before any attempts to assess love are made.

Love is claimed to be a very subjective (emotional) matter; so are all psychological concepts — aggression, motivation, perception, interpersonal relations, and adjustment. However, even with the subjectivity in the concept of love (used here solely for the sake of illustration), we assume that it can be measured. If we can measure attraction, friendship, and interpersonal relationships, we can also measure love!

To do so, after defining it, we look for ideas to explain love (through using, for example, romantic films, love books, songs, authors of novels, poems, etc.). The search would focus upon whatever sources of knowledge are available, as obtained from common sense, philosophy, or theories, as presented before. In essence, we carefully examine all of these sources, exploiting their content, and exploring their possibilities. In this way we add to our own knowledge of the comprehensive concept of love.

Assessing Love

In the second stage of the process, we identify main parts and extract signs that represent lovers' actions and feelings toward the beloved. Emotions to be identified include: having frequent imageries of the beloved one, thinking of no one else, dreaming about the loved one, drawing hearts with initials inside them, being glued looking at the beloved one, drinking poison if the beloved one is found dead. Other feelings can be sharing gifts such as flowers, perfumes, ties, or socks; holding hands; kissing; and many other signs we can identify.

Available tracers (signs) of the concept must be gathered, evaluated, classified, and catalogued, as a further stage in representing the identified domains (parts) of love. All in all, to what degree would a person have these emotions and feelings as a true lover? The answer would be indicative of a person's love, which is the main focus of the following steps we will use to create a construct.

Practically, would all these parts and referents of love that have been suggested prove useful and applicable to contemporary persons of this millennium and this Western culture? This awaits more testing and verification. One further step in the process is developing the construct of love — which is developing statements to which persons are asked to respond. After some elaborate work is done with those statements, actual attempts are made to test both the shape and form of the identified structure. Examples of such statements are centered around manifestations of love based on the above definition and the identified emotions, as illustrated in the preceding lines. They must be expressed clearly. To realistically extract the level of love, identified signs are stated as stimuli. Then we ask the respondent to identify a person in his/her mind that s/he loves and ask him/her to respond to the statements that we think are manifestations of love, such as these:

- It pleases me to present things to the person I love.
- Even while I am so busy, I find myself thinking of the person I love.
- In the presence of the person I love, I am always looking at him/her.
- I cannot survive without being with or around the person I love.
- If my beloved person were found dead, I would not mind drinking poison.

Compiling a large number of statements will not make the instrument; extensive scrutiny will be necessary, as an advanced stage. In other words, the quality and realism of these tracers must be proven through responses and endorsements to given items.

In our case, how can these statements blend together to capture true "love" that respondents agree upon?

The set of statements (a potential "Love Scale") is now ready for field verification, or collecting sufficient reactions to support or deny given emotions within what has been viewed as love. Employing specific statistical procedures, a structure of the parts of love begins to evolve and to merge together. Actually, a clear pattern will start to form as a result of some basic analyses.

This intriguing stage is like looking at a blank wall. But with deeper concentration and closer observation (like focusing a sensitive camera), a drawing on the wall begins to take form and shape, to emerge and evolve. Actually, a mosaic is emerging. Now we can see a new, more meaningful and interesting picture. In most cases, we are familiar with what we see in the mosaic (confirmation), but in a few others, we might see thrilling things we never thought of before (exploration of new possibilities). This intriguing stage, revealing hidden or unknown meanings, adds novel ideas to the reservoir of knowledge. Hence, the original concept will be improving.

Because of what this process and analysis reveal, this activity is one of the most amazing activities in measurement development. It actually can give goose bumps. Latent structures become more vivid; unrecognized domains emerge more clearly.

During this stage, indicators that did not work are screened and discarded from our current constructed picture. With continued analysis, we arrive at a validated list of items. This new set of items would have the power to differentiate (discriminate) between lovers and non-lovers. This is like a classroom test that differentiates between achievers and non-achievers. The list of items is called a scale. Moreover, differentiation between lovers and non-lovers is the main goal behind taking all these elaborate steps to construct a "love" scale.

If the scale predicts and discriminates between lovers and non-lovers in given relationships, this would be a demonstration of the quality of the scale. Hence, the ultimate goal of the designated scale is achieved. Those who score high are suppose to be highly in love. The converse should be also true if the love scale is valid. Later on, scores on the scale can be compared against other observations of the lovers and interviews with those who were rated high, as a necessary validation of the scale.

In sum, all of these steps would represent the "method of measurement development," or the "methodology employed," achieving a giant leap from a concept to a construct. This entails a transition from a general idea to a specific structure, from scattered notions to a focused tool. Formally, more rigorous steps in the psychometric theory need to be studied and applied, as will be illustrated in the next chapter, representing the formal, rigorous steps to be performed in measurement development.

Summary and Conclusion

Knowledge relevant to a topic is considered the foundation of an assessment tool. Lack of basic ideas is a main constraint to instrument development. A concept is recognized as a broad, general view, thought, idea, perception, or feeling of what is conceptualized. Concepts vary in their degrees of clarity and completion, which in turn determine the quality and scope of their representative constructs.

To clarify and compose a complete picture of a concept, a developer seeks integrated knowledge from three sources: common sense and popular knowledge, philosophical explanations, and theoretical formations and tested hypotheses. The last source — theoretical and hypothetical — provides highly advanced information, predictions, and views as bases for measurement development. However, pooling and uniting the outcome of the three resources yields a trustworthy tool, thus gaining wider approval and acceptance by the public, confirmation about speculative assumptions, and scientific conclusions. This is an issue of validity, as a first step, which is a crucial concern in assessment.

Finally, to reduce a concept (the original entity on a macro scale) to a construct (a representational dimension on a micro level) is a big leap, requiring the recruitment of different rigorous scientific procedures. A popular concept "love" was utilized as an example, simply to illustrate informally the sequence of scientific steps in measurement development. The next chapter represents a highly disciplined set of guidelines, acquainting readers with necessary steps to be performed. Also, some users — as consumers of assessment and research — can have three benefits from knowing measurement guidelines: (1) employ these guidelines as criteria for evaluating the merit of an existing assessment tool, (2) make a decision on which ones to utilize, and (3) appraise a scientific study with respect to its reliance on sound measurements.

Questions and Exercises

1. Why there is a need for clarity and objectivity to arrive at a quality assessment tool?

2. What is a concept?
3. What is a construct?
4. Explain the procedures to reduce a concept to a construct.

Chapter 16

Formal Steps in Measurement Construction

Focus of Chapter

Ensuring food is cooked well requires a good recipe; constructing a good measurement to serve important functions also requires logical steps. The content of this chapter explains the "recipe" or the logical steps for measurement development. One scale can employ a single item, while another incorporates more. This is an issue of sufficiency — which will be explained further — uni- versus multi-item constructs. Nine logical, systematic steps that provide the recipe for developing a measurement will be described. These represent a delicate balance between the art and the science of measurement. Examples of the art part are steps like concept definition, review of literature, and item development, while science steps include pre-testing, data collection, and statistical analysis. All possible procedures are employed to ensure the acquisition of a sound and quality scale that exhibits the basic criteria of validity, reliability, and usability.

Key Terms

art and science
components
conceptual background
eigenvalues
indicators
item loading

measurement dissemination
multi-item
pretest
scales
uni-item

Key Names

- Anne Anastasi
- Hubert M. Blalock
- Kenneth A. Bollen

- Andrew L. Comrey
- Richard F. Gorsuch
- Jum C. Nunnally

Objectives

- Describe the issue of uni- versus multi-items in scale selection.
- Identify steps in construct development.
- Define steps in measurement construction.
- Use, skillfully, measurement criteria to judge the merit/quality of given scales.

In developing a stable and thorough assessment tool or in its evaluation, two critical questions are asked. First, on what basis was the instrument constructed? (Or, what does it represent?) Secondly, how was the instrument constructed? While the first question relates to the *conceptualization* process, the second represents the *methodology* employed to validate it.

Among other procedures, the above two concerns will be addressed, demonstrating procedures — for standardized or non-standardized assessment tools — necessary to arrive at a trustworthy scale. Basically, any quality structure must be based on sound foundations, constructed with refined systematic procedures, guidelines, principles, and criteria to obtain a good product. Technically, this is labeled as "Measurement Methodology." For example, leisure educators, Theobald (1979), Henderson and Bialeschki (2002), and Riddick and Russell (1999) reported similar methodology in conducing evaluative research investigations.

For some users, one item can be considered good enough to capture a concept. For instance, to obtain knowledge about an individual's leisure interests, an item can be cast as such: "I am interested in leisure activities." For others, this procedure would have shortcomings. Some can claim that a single item cannot tap a domain's comprehensive structure. That is especially true with phenomena characterized as being behavioral, diverse, complicated, or technically multidimensional. Therefore, early in this chapter, a comparison will be made, showing some of the main reasons to search for the broader concept and depend on or use what the literature yields as foundations in constructing a scale.

Uni-item and Multi-item Testing Considerations

Using one or very few items, as was mentioned above, is known as uni-item or singular-item testing. On the other hand — with different degrees of adequacy — most standardized measures are composed of a larger number of items. These can be described as multi-item constructs. Most likely, they achieve the status of being multi-component constructs as well.

Taking less response time, the uni-item measures are considered more efficient. On the other hand, there are claims that, quite often, they capture neither the essence nor the scope of the concept. This is due to concept's complexity. In other words, usually they do not account for diverse grounds that the concept might actually cover. Comparatively, multi-item scales do not exhibit those weaknesses; yet, they take a longer time to construct and to respond to.

Revealing some of the concept's hidden aspects, multi-item measures can have a further advantage. They can help the process of understanding the concept's structure itself. They require studying a concept's underlying foundations and meanings diligently. A single item lumps all of the details together, without discrimination.

Multi-item tests, on the other hand, constructed according to sound guidelines, are assumed to be better developed, reflecting wider scope, and having improved validity. For example, in an attempt to measure "Leisure Satisfaction," a uni-item assessment procedure can use one of the following: "My leisure gives me a great deal of satisfaction." or "I am satisfied with my leisure activities and experiences." A singular item of this nature fails to cover diverse grounds and benefits gained from leisure. Logically, one item cannot reveal unrealized or hidden positive impacts of an endeavor like leisure or fitness, for instance. Therefore, many other potentially satisfying attributes of leisure or exercising might be missed, unintentionally unrecognized, or ignored.

The person responding to the above uni-item assessing leisure satisfaction, for instance, might focus on just his/her physical gains: Exercising, excelling, controlling weight, increasing energy, and giving vitality. That is because the physical domain is presently occupying that person's mind, dominating current attention and thinking. Other leisure benefits and rewards that are actually experienced might not be considered in that person's frame of mind.

This omission can be due to a lack of awareness of such impacts, or due to memory, or benefits being taken for granted such as being relaxed or controlling stress. Recalling all or at least most leisure rewards requires knowledge on the concept of leisure satisfaction that is not available to a respondent who is a layperson. (A layperson is someone who is not knowledgeable or specialized in a subject matter.) The person might not account, in his or her responses, for the variety of all of the possible rewards from leisure, such as mental gains, social rewards, relaxational impacts, positive psychological outcomes, and the enjoyment of the aesthetics of the leisure environments. According to improved conceptualization, all should be part of the leisure satisfaction concept when it is measured.

Respondents to the uni-item measurement, in most cases, would not validly account for the above diversification, variety, and unrevealed structures of the concept. This requires prior extensive effort on the concept by the measurement's developer. Moreover, respondents to a single-item scale tend to simplify how they respond to it; missing potentially critical details and limiting their reactions to what is currently on their minds.

On the other hand, when employing quantitative procedures utilizing a limited number of items, respondents can be misled. That is due to investigators' failure to provide necessary details and a well-rounded set of items to represent the concept. Analogously, this case resembles the old comment, "the blind leading the blind" or as it fits the above context "the disoriented investigating the disoriented." Therefore, a fundamental question to ask here is "Do we really have a clear idea and broad coverage of the nature of the concept that we are abstracting?" If yes, use it.

If scale developers assume expertise in the subject matter they intend to assess (which should be the case), they must take a leadership position. This is through paving the road to the discovery of concept's salient domains. The developers must be responsible about the development of the concept they are investigating and its construct. Otherwise, assessors do not actually understand what they are assessing; consequently, respondents do not react correctly when they are responding.

Furthermore, in application, if we have a good concept of leisure satisfaction (or any designated concept, for that matter), with knowledge about its attributes, we can practically, clinically, and scientifically identify persons' ratings. They can be used as the bases for programming or treatment, investigating or testing relationships for hypothesis verification. Without a well-developed concept, all of the above efforts are in vain and cannot achieve their goals.

Ultimately, this is how a concept improves practice or provides "building blocks" for further verified knowledge, in some cases arriving at theories.

In sum, it could be postulated that early assessment trials can employ a uni-item approach for a short duration. But sooner rather than later, multi-item and multidimensional considerations must be pursued and attempted, thus refining the initial uni-item construct. Multi-item procedures tend to be less efficient and costly; however, they are trustworthy and worth the investment. (*Nothing good is cheap; nothing worthy comes without investment.*)

Toward the above end, this chapter outlines nine steps in constructing multi-item and multi-dimensional measurements. These steps are the art and science of reducing concepts to manageable, attainable, and adequate constructs. This investment is useful to practice and contributes to the advancement of the body of knowledge. One of the criteria for scale users is this: Evaluate the merit of a given instrument on the basis of the steps outlined here as a guide to learn about the scale's quality.

In executing the following steps properly, a measurement developer must strike a balance between both the art of an instrument's construction and the science of verifying the final product. Hence, a reliable and a valid scale is born, as a "star" in its field. Such scales last for years, serving professionals and researchers effectively and efficiently.

Steps in Constructing a Multi-Item Measurement

Constructing a measure is an elaborate endeavor, requiring time, skill, and concerted effort. One of the reasons for requiring elaborate procedures is that the details for the construct to be built are entangled with other concepts. They are not easily recognized and outlined. Sometimes, relevant ideas are unclear, most often unknown. Thus, to clarify and extract a concept, a considerable effort, length of time, as well as patience are required.

The very nature of the outcome necessitates elaborate procedures: If we plan for a resilient and sturdy product, we must build it on well-established foundations, using appropriately refined methodology and tools. Luckily, a well-established methodology is readily available. In fulfilling all of the above, a measurement not only stands the test of time, but also is useful for field application, able to face challenge, scrutiny, and change. By attaining these qualities, a scale can last a long time serving different functions, groups, agencies, and communities.

Before any scientific procedures are conducted, an investigator's task is to extract the construct and clearly draw its boundaries. This is a major part of the art of a scale's construction. The *art* of developing a measurement should incorporate all steps taken before and after collecting the data and analyzing it. The *science* of measurement development, on the other hand, is composed of data collection, analyses, and validation of the scale. The art and science of construct development must be sufficiently balanced. All in all, a set of logical and flexible steps is summarized below. They should be taken judiciously. They can function as guidelines to ensure a sturdy, trustworthy, long-lasting, quality measurement. (For a similar strategy for test development, see Cohen and Swerdlik, 2005, pages 188-223.)

These steps are presented below in a logical order. (Measurement construction and science are founded on logic: proper sequence and soundness of procedures.) However, investigators can shuttle back and forth, from one step to another, until the requirements of each step are satisfied:

1. Defining the Concept

Looking for "a needle in a haystack" requires a definition of a needle and another definition for hay. This answers the questions: "What are we looking for? What are we constructing?" In presenting procedures for test design and construction Aiken (1991, 35) emphasizes that, "Ideally, however, construction of any test or psychometric instrument begins by defining the variables or constructs to be measured and outlining the proposed content." To emphasize the importance of early definitions remember that definitions determine clarity of direction. As the situation evolves, three definitions will represent stages of growth: conceptual, hypothetical, and empirical.

The literature in the field of parks, recreation, and leisure has been growing at a high rate. Nevertheless, in order for investigators to achieve their assessment goals and to be efficient, they need to identify their direction and goal, focusing on (tentatively) defining what needs to be assessed. That is mainly because, as it stands; knowledge of the concept is not readily available, not waiting in publications on the shelf for quick identification and use. Rather it is scattered, confusing, uncovered, and unrelated. Therefore, to identify the measurement's direction, an early and tentative definition of the concept is indispensable.

Two opposing views exist regarding definitional needs. Howe and Rancourt (1990) take the stand that definitional consensus is a major necessity for researching and developing the body of knowledge. On the other hand, Samdahl (1988: 27) does not endorse the notion of reaching consensual definitions for basic terms, only for terms to be explicit, specifying their nature as the basis for building a theory (*or a measure*).

In this book the belief is that there is nothing wrong with definitional disagreements. As a matter of fact, differences in judgments should be encouraged. This should be considered a healthy practice, for the domains that we deal with — free time, recreation, play, and leisure — are multi-dimensional, changeable, and complex. Moreover, due to recent technology and social change, society is experiencing phenomena that have not been observed and defined before.

These phenomena can include, but are not limited to, uses of computers and electronics, four-day and three-day work weeks, unemployment, economic crisis, work stress, high mobility, communication networks, early retirement, urban expansion, vitality, empowerment, boredom, *ennui*, and high-risk activities in outdoor recreational pursuits. Many of those phenomena will evolve more as a result of new developments in the economic, social, educational, and behavioral sectors. Therefore, definitions can operate as a compass, pointing toward newly evolving directions. Definitions are needed before constructing their pertinent measurements or before including them in scientific explorations.

Conceptual definitions must reflect philosophical understanding and available theoretical evidence; both must be as diversified as possible. Conceptual definition is just a "blueprint," awaiting further

exploration and applications through literature review and scientific studies. We continue to evolve toward the hypothetical definition and on to an empirical definition, scientifically validated. Even though prior conceptual and empirical definitions form a new understanding, they must be tested again as a part of the perpetual process of improving views and knowledge on given phenomena.

In sum, measurement construction can employ three types of definitions, as suggested above: a conceptual definition, a hypothetical definition, and an empirical definition. The conceptual definition, utilized at this stage, is related to the distinction and clarification of the concept. This lets us look for the concept and comprehend it. In effect, it is more of a tentative procedure; followed by a hypothetical assumption for what the literature yields and what we are trying to outline or chart in knowledge.

On the other hand, the empirical definition (usually one of the latest steps in measurement construction) is the product of scientific verification. Considered as the verified or tested version of the conceptual definition, an empirical definition is the end result of construct development. In essence, measurement development begins with a definition, conceptual, ending with another definition, empirical. The latter one is usually utilized in future clinical, research, theorizing, field assessments, and evaluation studies. Fundamentally, without a clear and well articulated, early conceptual definition, efforts to arrive at an empirical one lack a critical step.

2. Reviewing the Conceptual Background of the Idea to be Abstracted

After securing a conceptual definition, the next step is to use it as a "flashlight in the attic of information." The developer must search through all of the sources available to put together everything that can be found regarding the concept at the heart of the measurement being developed. As previously presented, the conceptual background lies in three areas of knowledge: common sense, philosophical speculations, and theory. Eclectically, the more the concept is anchored in the three areas of knowledge, the higher the measurement's representation of reality and the greater its validity. Achieving these criteria can secure both comprehensiveness and a logically deduced concept.

How critical is the careful review of the conceptual background? Formulating and following incomplete and underdeveloped concepts end in having a similar quality measurement. The output in the form of measurement is dependent on the conceptual input. Analogously, for a train to arrive at Champaign-Urbana, Illinois or Cairo, Egypt, the train must be put on the right track. Concept identification is similar to road familiarization.

Moreover, the quality of conceptualization is similar in behavior to the laws of physics: "For every action, there is an equal and opposite reaction." Without exaggeration, this effort (reviewing the background) is not only badly needed; it is most critical for attainment of a good measurement. Professionally, an investigator's motivation to invest in this process is the secret of the instrument's success. Therefore, the most critical stage in measurement development is a careful review of the existing broad conceptual background.

Another basic criterion for a quality measurement is its validity. As is generally known, validity is a prerequisite to reliability; validity comes first. In other words, if a concept is not valid (does not represent the idea), efforts to achieve reliability will not help to save it. Hence, in order to achieve the concept's content validity, reviewing the conceptual background comprehensively must reflect eclectically and adequately the state of the knowledge.

Where can information and knowledge of leisure be found to serve conceptual development? Related background ideas are rather diverse within two main sources:

- First, knowledge is found in the literature describing and exploring free time, leisure, recreation, play, exercise, parks, and their facilities. This can be found in the growing number of books, magazines, and journals.
- Second, it can also be found in numerous areas allied to informal activities and services, such as psychology, sociology, cultural anthropology, criminology, biology, physiology, economics, administration, marketing, regional planning, environmental sciences (such as forestry and botany), geography, history, and philosophy.

This state of the art in knowledge forms a challenge to those who plan to develop measurements, but the challenge can be met.

3. Extracting Components and Indicators

Practically speaking, how would the conceptual background aid the process of measurement development? There are two indispensable levels in processing the background knowledge: encompassing the concept's structure (components) and identification of specific indicators representing these components. Investigators cannot proceed successfully without realizing not only important "*components*" but also their "*indicators*." For example, to develop a theory-driven scale assessing "Perceived Freedom in Leisure" (PFL), its investigators, Ellis and Witt

(1984), relied upon three theoretical structures: attribution, arousal seeking, and flow. Such theories provided possible parts and their indicators. A component is defined as a constituent element, ingredient, and part of the grand composed structure. An indicator, on the other hand, is a sign or a symptom serving as a manifester, tracer, and pointer to an underlying process or substructure.

Investigators are responsible for forming and distinguishing components and indicators by identifying them. Then they codify, classify, and categorize them. Background information provides a hypothetical structure and boundaries, including the various parts, of the concept. Consequently, through precise steps as developed herein, the assumed structure awaits further empirical confirmation or disconfirmation (validation) through data collected. However, the road to a clear picture of the concept is not paved, rather it is full of obstacles.

Goodale and Witt (1991) in their introduction to their book elaborated on "Clarifying Concepts: The Ongoing Struggle for Understanding." The same concern is fundamental to measurement development.

The issues of components and indicators are essential in measurement development; therefore, more details of the two will be provided. The question is which of them comes first? It is important to note that measurement developers shuttle back and forth between components and indicators. The two are interwoven as follows:

1. Component Identification: Almost all social and behavioral concepts have parts. These parts are called "components," and together they form the assumed total concept. In reviewing a concept's background information, an investigator might miss one of the possible components. In the end, it will be unaccounted for in the final construct. That will be missed from the structure of the instrument, absent from the hypothesized and composed construct.

   In identifying the boundaries of a concept, components need to be recognized as suggested by theories, tested hypotheses, and/or philosophies. Components can be labeled as the concept's "dimensions" or "domains" or "factors"; therefore, most quality measurements have multi-dimensional structures. That is why all possible components of the target concept should be in place, to be validated further by investigators. Empirically, analysis to follow (reported as a later step) will reveal which components make it through the testing process as significant parts of the construct.

2. Indicator Extraction: Indicators are very instrumental in measurement development. They can be considered a structural part of the bridge between a given concept and its attempted measure. To elaborate further, an indicator is a descriptor or a pointer to attributes that hint and characterize a domain or its substructures. A medical example of an indicator can illustrate this point: to diagnose that a person has a fever; s/he should show some specific signs. These signs are used as *indicators* of fever. Signs are what a doctor looks for, pointing to a judgment on how feverish or not a patient is and how severe the case is, so that the fever may be effectively treated.

The same applies to measurement development; indicators need to be identified carefully. For example, constructing a scale to assess leisure motivation requires identification of signs that would potentially push a person to engage in leisure activities, constrain the person from engaging, or cause the person to stop engaging in the activities. Each sign is called an "indicator" and is usually a word or a phrase that suggests or points out to a constituent component.

Indicators and components are similar to what they point to; however, they differ in scope or their levels of representation. Accordingly, indicators differ in their importance to the constructed measure.

Examples of leisure motivation signs (indicators) can be "to learn," "to explore," "to interact," "to improve skill," "to relieve stress and strain." A measure can start with over 150 indicators and then reduce them (using critical judgment, then statistics) to a manageable number (say 24 to 36 items) as a final scale. The approximately 150 indicators is a rough sample constituting the universe of signs, waiting for further analysis to test their representation and relevancy.

The final set of indicators/items represents a larger potential pool. Each indicator stands for more unreported signs, but is depicted by what respondents endorse via their choices in the way they respond. (The issue of endorsing items will be discussed under the step "Analysis of Data Collected.") Identifying comprehensive knowledge is crucial, but insufficient in itself. In this step the developer must continue the process by mapping the position of components and their importance as big sections, enabling landmarks, signs, or indicators to be extracted.

Definitions Operating as Hypotheses: Comprehensively covering the conceptual background, mapping components and indicators, should by now have helped in obtaining a much clearer idea of what will be constructed. More details and knowledge are now available on the total concept, its components, and relevant indicators. A logical, repeatable step presents itself; that is, a revised definition of the global concept and its newly identified components. Step 1 speculated a tentative and informal conceptual definition, but by now literature reviewers can speculate an educated, hypothetical, and formal definition to guide scientific steps in measurement development.

Without components, indicators, and items a measurement does not exist. Future success is founded on these three aspects that belong to the art of measurement development.

4. Item Development

Item development, according to specific guidelines, is the next step toward testing the structure of a construct. Items can operate as a bridge between art and science, between concepts and respondents who endorse the appropriate items (indicators) and their components. This process is centered on transforming indicators to items, enabling respondents to understand and respond to them.

Converting indicators into items enables scientists to communicate their intent to the people who are taking the measurement. By virtue of the developed items a scientist is able to test, empirically, how respondents see the relevance of the identified indicators to their construct. This is how a scientist presents his/her formulated concept. Practically, this is used as a further step in knowing about the content and boundaries of a designated concept from the respondent's point of view.

Item development follows all guidelines accumulated over the years on the art of questionnaire design. Mainly, two areas of guidelines must be followed: wording and content. Examples of the basic wording guidelines are to keep the items simple — readable, at a 10-year-old level — and to make statements as short as possible — 20 words or less. Shorter items are not only clearer but also more efficient and they minimize response fluctuation.

On the content of the items, each statement should present a single indicator — no more. For example, in assessing family relationships, an investigator might err by stating: "I love my father and my mother." Apparently, humans do not love parents equally. In correcting this item, two statements are needed: one for the mother and another for the father. Two statements can accurately assess the quality of family relationships without respondent confusion that may, in turn, jeopardize a construct's reliability.

Another aspect to consider is a double-negative statement. Instead of saying, "I do not hate my leisure," say, "I like my leisure." Items stated with double negatives blur a respondent's judgment, which also jeopardizes reliability. (For many more guidelines regarding item drafting see references on questionnaire design.)

5. Item Refinement

At this point all indicators have been transformed into items, assumingly according to guidelines. But before conducting pilot studies (the next step), four procedures are required to refine items. Usually, they are performed in this order:

First, about two weeks after the items are developed, investigators critically review the items. This is to be able to reevaluate content, wording, and their relevance to components and indicators. (Investigators should discard items that do not fit or do not work, using a reasonable period of time that ensures objectivity or nonbiased reaction to the created items.)

Second, administer these items to 10 to 20 respondents. The persons would be instructed to identify items that they do not understand, that are duplicates of other items, or are unclear. This procedure will reveal the need for some specific changes.

Third, interview five to ten persons for extra verification. Interviewees are instructed to read items aloud in the presence of the investigator. Notes on non-verbal reactions are taken. Items that potentially can be misunderstood or are ambiguous will consistently manifest themselves from one interviewee to another. Respondents are asked to evaluate the relevance of each items' contents to the definitions yielded from the literature review. For a given item, changes should be considered if two or three interviewees point, verbally or nonverbally, to a difficulty or weakness.

Certain characteristics of the interviewer can help refine the scale. The interviewer should posses interviewing skills such as good listening, non-defensive attitude, objective reactions, and keen observation — detecting items that work and others that do not work by watching respondents' non-verbal cues. The outcome can help to refine the scale. Modifications and changes can be done on the basis of interviewees' recommendations and reactions.

Last, following all of the above refinements, the measurement is ready for peer or expert evaluation. Peer reviews provide formal "content validity." The intent in employing peer reviews is to validate the relevance of the content of items to its target concept. Drafted hypothetical definitions should be used as the basis for evaluation. Construct developers, peers, and

experts utilize something like the following questions as criteria to evaluate the merit of the scale:

1. Do the items represent the target concept definition?
2. Are there any missing parts from the concept?
3. Do the items fall within the provided definitions?
4. Are the items sufficient in scope, representing all possible grounds?
5. Did the measurement follow the guidelines for item, format, and content development?

If there is a positive consensus among external reviewers, investigators can proceed for now to the next step.

In all of the above four procedures, there certainly will be suggestions. The investigators should integrate them as much as possible. In very few occasions, suggestions can be considered consultative, without necessarily applying the recommendations. Investigators are ultimately responsible for selecting and screening evaluations objectively. Possible reasons are that sometimes suggestions can be in conflict with each other or do not account for all the facts that the investigators, as experts in their subject matter, know.

This step concludes the art of measurement development. The next steps apply the science of measurement construction, which is the bulk of the psychometric theory.

6. Pre-testing the Workability and the Basic Structure of the Measurement

Before navigating into space, it is crucial to ensure that all parts of the space shuttle will function properly. The first step in the science of measurement development is the process of securing its workability, called a "pretest" or a "pilot study." Like the space shuttle, the final test of the measurement is a big investment of resources: time, money, and effort. Accordingly, concerned persons plan to succeed; therefore, conduct pilot trials.

In measurement construction, how many trials or pretests are needed? Basically, two pilot studies are the minimum. Sometimes three are needed before the final field application. The first pretest should utilize a minimum sample of about 100 persons. The second should secure, at least, 150 or more individuals. In principle, the greater the sample size is, the less the potential error when computing means and other scores.

As a follow-up, how can investigators benefit from pre-testing? One of the goals of these pilot studies is to check on the workability of items and their components. This step is a mini-final, on a limited scale. Consequently, investigators modify items and/or expand components. They delete what is unnecessary and/or add what is necessary, missing, or seems to be lacking.

If many changes were needed because of two pilot studies, it would be an indication that components and items are unstable. Then, a third pretest utilizing another sample size of about 150 persons might be required. In all pilot studies, conventional statistical procedures (described later under Step 8) are performed. Results of such pre-testing will suggest when the measurement is ready for its final, full-scale field verification.

7. Collecting Data for the Final Field Testing of the Measurement

After *careful refinements* through the pilot studies, a final field test is the formal evidence of how the instrument works. Based on data (empirical evidence) collected during this step, the measurement will demonstrate how the items and the assumed components actually behave. This is the final exploratory or confirmatory support, providing evidence or denial of the hypothesized structure. Therefore, investigators invest heavily in collecting sufficient and adequate data.

In securing needed data, sample design should account for the number of items in the measurement. The number of subjects required is ten times the number of items or 300 subjects, whichever is greater. Like all scientific studies, as previously reported, the larger the sample size, the less the error and the more confident the researchers can be in the results. Sometimes — depending on the investigators' motivation — sample sizes can exceed 1,000 persons. As a criterion, Comrey (1988) noted that a sample size of 200 is reasonably good for factor analytic work with 40 or fewer items. Comrey adds that more variables require larger samples, and with 400 subjects, few apologies are needed.

There are practical reasons in securing an adequate sample size. For a standardized instrument to survive scrutiny and the test of time, it must be well founded and investigated. Moreover, until better theories are developed to challenge their content, measurements are intended to last for decades. If users have faith in the quality of the content and instrument's functions, this faith should be dependent on consistent reactions from adequate numbers of respondents. In sum, no sound measurement can be well established on inadequate or limited samples.

Simultaneously, with the constructed measure to be verified in its final stage, investigators usually include one or more measurements that possess relative theoretical properties. Testing construct validity of the new measurement is the main reason

for this inclusion. For example, in developing a new leisure attitude scale, other measurements assessing similar concepts — such as life satisfaction, quality of life, or wellness — can be included in the final field test. Preferably, if available, investigators include other existing leisure attitude instruments for the process of concurrent validation.

8. Analyzing the Data Collected

This step is the most intriguing phase in the whole encounter of measurement construction. Now is the time for discoveries to be revealed, the time for explanations to be made. Consequently, new findings and structures are added to our existing body of knowledge. Within this context, data analysis can operate as a transition between speculative assumptions made to start with and the testing of the assumed knowledge, through analysis described here.

In establishing these new results, specific conventional statistical procedures must be performed, as follows:

A. Factor Analysis

This procedure is the very first to be executed in both pilot tests and final phases. With the use of factor analysis (Varimax), a certain number of interpretive domains will be revealed, from two or three up to 14 factors. All factors demonstrate the portion they explain of the assessed construct. That portion is referred to as "variance." Gorsuch (1983) observed that extracted variances of 40% to 50% reflect a factor structure of substantial impact for self-reporting scales.

By employing factor analysis, the following specific considerations in treating items and domains should be regarded:

For an item to be retained within its designated domain, it needs to be loaded sufficiently (.30 to .40 at minimum) on its factor. This loading is the correlation between the item and its obtained factor. The determination that an item belongs to one factor or another is subject to how respondents endorsed the item, how respondents viewed and considered the content of the item. This is manifested by the size of the correlation with designated factor.

Respondents do not do this intentionally or with awareness; but rather their consistency answering a set of items similarly produces these scores. For example, almost all "lovers" think intensely of the beloved one, present gifts (offerings of some kind), and other similar emotions, but do not commit suicide if the beloved one is found dead. Homogeneity of items that belong to one factor is always demonstrated when respondents rate given items similarly. Other items fluctuate randomly not showing relevance to the realized factor, while a third group of items demonstrate complete irrelevancy. This is what factorizes or clusters items together. Unintended or un-thought-of endorsements are the underlying determinants of this elegant procedure; consistency in rating creates a given factor.

Item Endorsement: How do respondents endorse an item or a set of items? For a given component, for instance, seven items gained loadings of .79, .74, .68, .65, .52, .46, and .42. The item that says, "I always think of my beloved person in her/his absence," gained the highest loading of .79. What does it mean? The underlying process here is that, whenever a person rates the seven items favorably, the first item is rated consistently high.

This first item is loading .79 with its interrelated and homogeneous set of items. This item was reported high among lovers across most respondents. While the seventh item that gained the least loading (.42) was within the clustering, it was not as consistently acclaimed across all respondents as the first item. For a shorter scale, when there is a need to reduce the seven items to four or five, the loading scores of .42 and .46 are reasons to remove those items, based on respondents' endorsements.

The loading of each item on its given factor is the criterion of clustering, belonging, selecting, and retaining. Analogously, knowledge of an item's loading can function as a "chisel" for carving structures of relevancy. Within a well-developed factor, when an item is loaded high on its relevant subscale, that indicates that another set of items within this factor associate together in content and meaning with this item. This item's content was felt to tap a common domain, felt but unexpressed. The opposite is also true; for those who rate themselves low on that subscale, they react less favorably to this item and the items that associate with it.

In another scenario, if an item is loaded equally, either moderately or highly on two or more factors (e.g., .48, .41, .34, and .36 out of 1.00), an action or two is required:

It looks like a "muddy" item or "unclean diamond." The item did not gain precise endorsement to a given factor. The way it was written needs to be cleaned. Respondents were confused as to where to place the meaning of this item, or how to respond to it. While for some it meant one thing, for others it meant something else. Hence, in order to make it more relevant to the factor that it was designed to represent, it requires modifications.

The item needs to be refocused by removing any multiple parts. For example, a moderately loaded item can be the result of its content. If it reads, "Engaging in leisure activities *with others* gives me *self-respect*." This can cluster under psychological impacts (self-respect) or social benefits (with others). In rewriting this item, it needs to be more focused on just the social benefits *or* the psychological impacts, as follows: "Engaging in leisure activities give me self-respect." With another item that says, "I enjoy engaging in leisure activities with others." This is how a given item can be purified. Sometimes it is unfeasible to correct an item of this nature; therefore, the second daring action must be taken.

If an item cannot be cleaned or refocused, simply have the courage to throw it out. Delete it from the structure; other cleaner items can represent the factor better, especially if the review of the literature provided sufficient indicators to be incorporated into items.

Scale Modifications: Interestingly, contrary to the hypothesized structure, the investigator may find that a few items that were meant to represent a given component may cluster under another factor. This represents a new empirical finding, found with the use of factor analysis. Therefore, new discoveries must be evaluated very carefully, for they might shed more light upon a hidden, unrealized domain. Such a finding can be either a new discovery or an unintended omission of an important part of the concept as it was developed.

Accounting for what was omitted is a big gain. Definitely this is considered an improvement in the way the concept should be viewed and constructed. Therefore, an objective evaluation of this domain might suggest re-weighing this part by enlarging it — shuttling back to the conceptual background for an understanding of what has been revealed. If a significant number of changes like the above ones are made, another field test might be required.

Factors should be labeled, giving them both logical and realistic names. To do so, review the indicators carefully, and identify the thread that ties them all together. Find the underlying meaning that appears across all of them. Moreover, in naming or giving a label to a factor, the highest loading items (the top two or three) will be useful to point to the possible name, according to the meanings of their indicators. In some cases, it is unfeasible to find a common, shared ground for all indicators under an obtained factor. If so, invent a logical name or a fictitious one. For overlapping domains, names can be such as psychosocial, bio-psycho-culture, or bio-psychosocial, and the like.

It is important to note that, early in the analysis, a decision needs to be made on the number of factors to be included in the analysis. Investigators apply an important technical procedure, called "eigenvalues." For a factor to be retained in the final analysis, it should gain an eigenvalue of 1.0 or higher. This procedure determines the number of factors to work with and analyze.

B. Reliability Tests

After realizing the number of factors — as the first step in the analysis — now it is time for reliability tests. *(Reliability verification cannot be performed before identifying the construct's factors.)* Reliability tests are conducted to check the inter-consistency of items that have been factorized. Performing reliability tests before factor analysis is a grave mistake. Both irrelevant and relevant items, when performing reliability before factor analysis, will distort and destroy the findings. Irrelevant items should be chiseled out first.

As presented earlier, four possible reliability tests are available, at minimum one of them will be sufficient: test-retest, split-halves, the use of alternate forms, and internal consistency (alpha-coefficient). The fourth — utilized to improve the scale's internal relatedness — intends to test the homogeneity of items. That is how items correlate with each other under their designated factors, as well as with their total. Bollen (1989) observed that alpha coefficient is a conservative estimate of internal reliability for most scales. As a criterion, what is the acceptable range of internal reliability? As reported by Nunnally (1978), for research purposes, internal reliabilities in the .70 to .80 ranges are acceptable.

In the application of alpha reliability, when coefficient analysis for an item is inadequately correlating with its subscale, it may be deleted or modified under these two conditions to improve the scale's reliability:

1. If the item-total correlation is much lower than what the rest of the items have received.
2. Sometimes, analysis suggests that removing an item improves reliability. If such an item is deleted, the total reliability will be higher by one or more points. It is important to note that removing unnecessary items adds to the cohesiveness, durability, and longevity of the scale because the retained items have extra relatedness and consistency, generating more confidence in field usage.

Ultimately, each refined and tested item will be like a diamond or a pearl. The nucleus of an item is its originally identified indicator. A number of items will harmoniously form a uniquely composed pattern as a necklace: called here a scale.

Each item in its constituent scale is a diamond with given quality. Some diamonds are cheaply or unskillfully cut, having structural flaws, but they are still considered diamonds. Better ones, represent the state of the art in purity and cut, possess rare quality.

The same evaluation applies to the total number of items. Accordingly, to arrive at a quality scale, a number of diamond-like items are needed to form the structure. Scale developers need competencies in cutting, sorting, and selecting diamonds and pearls-like items, based on clear criteria.

In sum, factor analysis and reliability tests enable the process of clustering, "sifting," and cleaning components and their items. In the final analysis, a proven reliable instrument demonstrates cohesiveness on two fronts: items and factors (components). The end product is an enduring instrument that can withstand the test of time and sometimes the fluctuation of situations giving users confidence in its durability, usefulness, and longevity.

C. Validity Tests

Three main tests are important to validity. Content validity should have been performed earlier. The other two are concurrent and construct validity. As explained before, content validity requires the use of experts evaluating the relevance of the items to the assessed concept. Experts, receiving the instrument and a set of definitions, are asked to rate how much the components represent the designated domain and to what degree the items belong to their components and their total concept. General agreement among experts will suggest a measurement's content validity. This is an indication that items tap the defined domain. Face validity should also have been a part of the early steps.

The second validation is concurrent validity, performed through the use of other pertinent scales. This is administered simultaneously with the newly developed instrument. Sufficient correlations among this set of measurements will be a criterion indicative of present scale's validity.

Construct validity, the third necessary test, demonstrates how the psychometrics of the scale merges with its theoretical background (Blalock, 1979). Or, from the point of view of Anastasi (1988), it is placing measurement scores in a theoretical frame of reference of associations with presumed interrelated domains. In this process, the assessed domain is tested in terms of how it fits into the context of relevant properties to the construct. In other words, construct validity is established when the new construct represented by its scale shows reasonable association with other scales within the same area of study. This evidence (valid construct) gives credence to the newly developed instrument. Usually, construct validity is conducted as more results — relevant to the construct — accumulate. Finally, while a single reliability test is sufficient, eventually all validity checks need to be performed as data accumulates to ensure a sound scale.

9. Redefining Components and Their Total Construct

This step requires that the newfound parts and their total be redefined. Two early definitions were the initial definition in Step One and the hypothetical, which is theoretically founded, in Step Three, This third definition is empirical. Tracing commonalities among the indicators (making up each component) can assist in arriving at their empirical (tested) definitions. Careful review of newly found and substantiated items under each subscale should be utilized to make up the empirical definition of the designated component. Definitional strategies are based on exact research findings.

Review of the meanings of all components that have been confirmed is used to state the construct's total empirical definition. These definitions (components and their total) can be available for future use in field practice (services), as well as hypothesis and research testing. Improving concepts follows a rigorous methodology, aimed toward advancing theories, as a process that adds new and verified knowledge to our intellectual heritage.

In conclusion, this endeavor began with a definition, ended with another. It began with an unsubstantiated concept and ended with a revealed and well defined, proven construct, which may now be incorporated in new theorization and research.

Measurement Dissemination

There are claims that one of the weaknesses of leisure and recreation instruments is their inaccessibility (see Loesch and Wheeler, 1982). If an instrument's developer invests heavily in its construction, what would be its value if it were unavailable? Professionally, it is a part of the investigators' responsibility to report the procedures and findings of their constructed measurements so others can use it. Unfortunately, until an instrument is disseminated on a large scale, it is not going to be fully of adequate service.

To disseminate a scale, there are some possible directions to be sought:

- First and foremost, a technical report needs to be written, describing all of the steps performed in developing the instrument and evidence obtained: items confirmed, components realized, and scale's functions identified.

- Second, attempting to inform potential users can include conference presentations, journal publications, and/or commercial distribution.

- Finally, responding to users' concerns, copyrights, and providing permissions to use measurements, as quickly as possible, will help the process of dissemination. So, accessibility of a measurement is one of the determinants of its usefulness and value.

In sum, writing a measurement report, its presentation, and its publication can all help its wide use and improvement of services.

Summary and Conclusions

In developing a measurement, there are strong rationales to employ systematic and refined steps. This can be labeled as methodology. The methods utilized are considered an amalgamation of art and science, to secure a quality (multi-item and multidimensional) product in the form of a scale. Besides, following a well-advanced methodology can help in gaining more knowledge about the developed construct and its concept. Those systematic and refined procedures can assist in composing an assessment tool that endures the test of time, scrutiny, and challenge.

Nine steps were presented, incorporating the required delicate balance between the art and science of measurement development. Steps begin with the artistic steps of these undertakings. That is the need to define the concept and its components, and then to use definitions to search for relevant knowledge to build the assessment tool. Progressively, that evolves using more steps to expose attained information to empirically test the structure that makes the developed construct or tool.

On the other hand, empirical testing requires the use of scientific guidelines. Steps are taken, exposing the identified construct to other experts and respondents, collecting data, and employing statistical treatments. Following measurement methodology seems to be time consuming, expensive, and inefficient; however, in the long run, these steps are actually the most efficient means to arrive at a sound and usable structure. Moreover, generated knowledge can be a part of future theorizations and tested information.

Arriving at a worthwhile, usable instrument is the ultimate outcome of following these meticulous procedures. For some, arriving at a measurement is just a simple effort, putting a number of items together. As a matter of fact, if each step is followed correctly, the measurement construction process can take a long time. It is no exaggeration to state that it can take about 18 months to construct and report on a scale.

There are very good reasons for a standardized measurement to take that long. For example, it is clear by now that outlining a concept requires concentrated effort to comprehend it reasonably and then extract indicators and components from its philosophical and theoretical background. Consequently, it is a painstaking effort to carve a concept from the literature.

A well-designed structure must be systematically built to achieve dependability and accuracy. No more effort will be required to revisit — unless needed — the structure to correct things. This is what it means to be efficient. Also, outcomes will be trustworthy, valid, and reliable. Steps taken can be achieved through specific procedures: internal and external reviews, modifications, pre-testing, data collection, testing, analyzing, redefining, and reporting findings. Through verification, every step must be ensured of success. Ultimately, the measure must be assumed to assess the concept that was to be measured, as a validity check.

These requirements might seem inhibiting; however, nothing of quality and value can be done in haste. Step by step, backed up with high motivation, knowledge of the concept, and acquisition of basic skills, all can enable the creation of badly needed, concept-refining measurements in their given areas.

Questions and Exercises

1. Compare uni-item and multi-item tests of variables.
2. What are the steps employed to construct a multi-item instrument?
3. What is the art and what is the science in the steps to develop measurements?
4. Name the steps that belong to the art of measurement development.
5. Name the steps that belong to the science of measurement development.
6. What are the procedures used in analyzing the data collected to arrive at a standardized scale?

Chapter 17

Application of Recreation Assessment Tools in Field Settings: A Practical Example

Focus of Chapter

Learning about assessment, its tools, and required criteria without the ability to use a scale is like teaching swimming without getting in the water. This chapter shows you how to actually practice assessment. All practical details on how to use assessment tools will be systematically presented to expose you to step-by-step data reduction "crunching." Data collected is massive, usually useless in its original form; therefore, reducing it allows patterns to evolve and trends to emerge. Data reduction is like melting raw gold ore to extract the best out of it. This is not difficult; it just needs discipline and practice, like swimming and tennis.

Key Terms

action and treatment
analysis
application
assessment competencies
compute

crunching
data reduction
interpretation
item reversal
mean

Key Names

- Patricia Farrell
- Karla A. Henderson
- Richard Kraus

- Herberta M. Lundegren
- Roger C. Mannell

Objectives

- Administer and score assessments accurately.
- Use means comparatively to interpret phenomena based on numbers and scores.
- Use judgment objectively.
- Prescribe action, treatment, strategy, and policy, based on facts and numbers.

As part of this practical example, some basic information presented before will be reemphasized to reinforce its application in real-world settings.

It is human nature to assess the world around us. We constantly make appraisals of and decisions about emerging conditions. We do this in our relationships, our work, our play, and all of the other actions, procedures, and processes of life. We assess the world to gather information about and gain knowledge of events and people in our lives. It is safe to say that assessment and advancement are intertwined in their relationship.

Sometimes, assessment is done intentionally; most of the time it is done unintentionally. Whenever the task is critical, assessment is not only intentional but also following a design: planned and deliberate. So, assessment (judgment) seems to be a habit, second nature, for human functioning and survival.

In providing parks and recreation services, assessment tools are needed for improvements in many stages of delivery systems. Recreation scholars identified assessment and evaluation to serve comprehensive functions (see Kraus and Allen, 1987; Lundegren and Farrell, 1985; Henderson and Bialeschki, 2002). The latest categorization, by Henderson et al., requiring assessment of some kind, includes five areas (or "Ps"): participants, personnel, policies/administration, places (areas and facilities), and programs, as presented earlier. These operations encompass almost all aspects within any given subsystem of leisure. Delivering a service well requires evaluation. To achieve the evaluation's intentions, data needs to be secured through assessment procedures.

How necessary is it for leisure and park personnel to be trained in assessment protocols? Which service areas would benefit from assessment competencies? What will happen if leisure practitioners lack basic assessment competencies? Finally, is there a relationship between assessment and evaluation of services? We know that all researchers (scientists) and some practitioners require formal training in assessment. Yet, even those who do not need formal training in assessment will still benefit both indirectly to a great extent and directly to a lesser extent by having a better understanding of the assessment process. The benefits obtained by leisure and park practitioners are from familiarity with the processes of assessment, instruments available, and knowledge about potential uses.

In most cases, the constraint on utilizing assessment procedures results from either a lack of understanding the nature of assessment or absence of skills in assessment. In many instances both are lacking. It is safe, therefore, to assume that all practitioners and investigators use assessment processes for decision-making and evaluation, but in different degrees. Moreover, no evaluative study is conducted successfully without assessment of some kind. Therefore, assessment is considered a prerequisite to both evaluation and making decisions. That is because we need data to arrive at accurate appraisals of services and programs or to test relationships.

Due to its nature, assessment is broader and more generic than evaluation. Evaluation, by nature, compels the use of assessment. However, not every assessment ends up with either an evaluative investigation (e.g., diagnosis and treatment or policy-

making and management), or in scientific testing of a relationship between variables.

In the process of assessment and evaluation, data is collected. Handling data requires competencies not only in its reduction, but also in its interpretation and how it is used to suggest actions (e.g., treatment, programming, administration, or policy making*). To be skillful in handling data, avoiding possible pitfalls and biases, requires certain protocols (practice and training) in treating assessment data.* Examples will be presented below, demonstrating how both knowledge and skill attained through practice are necessary to acquire competencies.

Knowledge and Skills Needed to "Crunch" Data

Instruments available, that practitioners need to be familiar with, are classified here in two types: general scales and scales specific to park, leisure, and recreation. The general scales are in fields such as marketing, administration, or psychology. As much as you can, use recreation-specific measurements. Otherwise, adapt general scales to the needs of the organization and your patrons; be extra careful in your interpretations of data collected through general scales. For a scale to qualify as being recreation- and park-specific, it must be validated in these settings. This is the process of adaptation of a scale. As a recreation specialist, you should strive to familiarize yourself with existing assessment tools — specific and general — applicable to your area of emphasis.

In this text, many recreation-specific instruments are presented. Applying instruments in some recreation and leisure settings might require consultation with existing tools to assess one of your functions, as presented by Henderson et al. Basically, quality assessment protocol depends on the practitioners' familiarity with recreation-specific measurements and skills in using them: knowing what measurements assess, their quality (validity and reliability), how to use them, and how to derive explanations and connotations from data.

Procedures and Functions of Data Reduction

Utilizing an assessment tool can produce massive data. In response to a 30-item instrument, using a five-point scale, one person can mark items numerically, such as 3, 1, 4, 3, 2, 5, 5, 2, etc. (making 30 choices). How can a recreation and park practitioner make sense of the reported numbers? Moreover, if 40 recreation participants (50% females) responded to the above 30-item instrument, how would the assessor handle a comparison based on gender? The "flood" of numbers might seem not only chaotic, but also actually uninterpretable. However, with further work, the numbers can evolve into meaningful patterns and shapes. For example, for item number 1 on creative leisure pursuits (interests), females' responses were 4, 3, 5, 4, 4, 5, 4, 4, etc.; while males' responses were 2, 3, 1, 2, 1, 1, 2, 2, etc. Scoring "1" would represent "Very Low" interest in participation or motivation, while scoring "5" would represent the "Very High" level.

The above two scenarios require data crunching and reduction, centered on the use of means and standard deviations followed by appropriate statistical treatments. Before any advanced statistics can be utilized, reduction of data needs to be performed correctly, which is considered a relatively easy task. Many small mistakes can happen, which can cause grave errors, but with good training mistakes can be eliminated.

In reducing data, underlying patterns start to evolve and emerge, with different degrees of clarity. Emerging trends — evident from data reduced — can help in making logical deductions, leading to insightful conclusions. Accordingly, more accurate decisions are made. These well-founded decisions — based on patterns and trends — can serve many purposes, such as treatment, programming, policy-making, facility design, marketing strategy, or modifying an agency's goals and objectives.

Reducing Data to Meaningful Patterns: An Exercise

To do a service for your participants, you should practice acquiring and mastering skills and competencies needed. Then you will be able to use these tests and measurements for the benefit of your organization. Hopefully, by now, we offered you a strong rationale for the importance of data reduction and some possible uses.

For the sake of this exercise, one of the antecedents of leisure and recreation involvement will be chosen to illustrate how to apply assessments to field settings. The exercise will be on the assessment shown below: Free Time Boredom (FTB).

First of all, before adding any scores and in order to make it a boredom scale, the user must be very careful in converting positively stated items (showing no boredom) to negative expressions (showing boredom). For instance, let us take item 16 from the scale to illustrate the need for reversing an item. A five-point scale was utilized, ranging from: "Strongly Disagree" scored as "1" to "Strongly Agree" scored as "5."

Item 16 reads like this: "During my free time, the time flies." Logically, if you "Strongly Agree" with this item and score "5," your response will indicate that you are not showing a sign of boredom in your free time. Therefore, every statement reporting "NO boredom" or expressed in a *positive* manner should be reversed. To proceed with the reversal, transform

Free Time Boredom   *Sample*
Do Not Copy

Directions: The following statements refer to your free time. By "free time" we mean time left to you after daily obligations are met, such as sleep, work, or school. Please read each statement. To the left of each statement is a line for you to indicate how much you agree (or disagree) with the statement. Use the following responses:

1	**2**	**3**	**4**	**5**
Strongly Disagree	Disagree	In-between	Agree	Strongly Agree

During My Free Time, ...

_____ 1. I do not use a lot of my physical skills.
_____ 2. I feel excited.
_____ 3. I feel that my surroundings are dull and "blah."
_____ 4. It feels that time stands still.
_____ 5. I am physically energetic.
_____ 6. I am provided with many experiences.
_____ 7. I feel empty.
_____ 8. I feel that too much of it is on my hands.
_____ 9. I do things below my physical ability level.
_____ 10. New ideas are stimulated.

During My Free Time, ...

_____ 11. I tend to be busy with meaningless things.
_____ 12. I want it to last longer.
_____ 13. I enjoy getting my body toned up.
_____ 14. I have a variety of places to go to.
_____ 15. I am without focus.
_____ 16. The time flies.
_____ 17. My physical abilities are challenged.
_____ 18. I usually have something interesting to do.
_____ 19. It seems like I am wasting my time.
_____ 20. I wish I had more of it.

responses according to the scale from 1 for "Strongly Disagree" to 5 for "Strongly Agree." In this manner, you need to change the scores as follows: 1 to 5, 2 to 4, 3 to 3, 4 to 2, and 5 to 1. All future reversals must be treated as illustrated here.

On the other hand, a "Strongly Disagree" response with a positively stated item such as "I feel excited," indicates partial boredom — "partial," because possibly some people may feel unexcited in their free time, but still not be bored. Thus, a respondent must rate a series of items indicative of boredom to be considered bored. This point on the issue of reversal will be clearer when you go through the example in the box below.

Procedures to reverse scores are done as instructed by the test designer. To do the reversal in the FTB scale, convert responses of the following numbers: 2, 5, 6, 10, 12, 13, 14, 16, 17, 18, and 20. Respond to the scale yourself to experience the reason for the reversal of items.

After the reversals, data is now ready for computation. The step after the reversal process is to calculate means related to the components of FTB.

Let us take one component to illustrate this step. The component chosen is "Lack of Physical Involvement." On the Free Time Boredom this component is made up of items 1, 5, 9, 13, and 18. Items 5, 13, and 18 need to be reversed. Any number of persons can be included in the analysis, such as 50, 500, or much less (such as 4 to 10, in some settings). In this example we will use five persons to illustrate required procedures. Items representing this component obtained the scores presented under *Subjects' Original Responses* for our five respondents, as shown in the table on the next page.

First, perform the reversal procedure in the column entitled: *Scores after Reversal.* Then, add the scores as posted in the column designated as: *Scores after Reversal.* It looks like this = 23, 20, 21, 20, and 19 = 103). Since we have used 25 scores to obtain the average, divide the total by 25: 103 divided by 25 = 4.12. This average (between 1 and 5) is the mean of this group for the lack of physical involvement component. Where does this group stand on the utilized scale? Is it a physically involved group in its free time?

As shown on the next page under "Location of the Average Score," the mean of the five items for lack of physical involvement is placed on the scale where the X is, between 4 and 5. (Remember, it is a boredom scale, meaning the higher the point on the scale the more the boredom.) The closer the mean is to "5," the more the severity of what the component presents; whereas, a mean closer to "1" illustrates a strong lack of boredom relevant to the specific component. For future interpretation, the lower the

Table 4: An Example of Item Reversal

Quality of Family Relationships

By Professor Florida S. Universe, Ph. D.

Directions: The following items ask you to rate the quality of family relationships. Circle the responses of your choice: Mark "1," if you "Strongly Disagree" with the statement; mark "5," if you "Strongly Agree." There are three more choices in between, as the scale below demonstrates.

Strongly Disagree	Disagree	In Between	Agree	Strongly Agree
1	2	3	4	5

1 2 3 4 5   1. I have positive relationships with my parents and siblings.
1 2 3 4 5   2. I care about my family members.
1 2 3 4 5   3. My family means a lot to me.
1 2 3 4 5   4. I try very hard to spend Thanksgiving and other holidays away from my family.
1 2 3 4 5   5. I share deep secrets with my family members.

Add the scores of the five items, and then divide by 5 to obtain your average score to represent the strength of your family relations.

You might be puzzled by now; asking, how can I add the score of item #4 on the holidays? That procedure, adding, will not be representative of my true score. By saying so, you are right. In this manner you see the value of reversing your score on item #4.

After you reverse this item, add the five scores and divide by 5, arriving at a mean (now you are on the correct path). See how close the new mean is to your general impression and feeling.

Lack of Physical Involvement of the *FTB*

Item in Scale	Text of Item **During my free time,…**	Subjects' Original Responses 1 | 2 | 3 | 4 | 5	Scores after Reversal By Subject 1 | 2 | 3 | 4 | 5	Group Means
1.	I do not use a lot of my physical skills.	4 | 3 | 5 | 4 | 3	4 | 3 | 5 | 4 | 3 (NC)	19/5 = 3.8
5.*	I am physically energetic.	1 | 2 | 1 | 3 | 1	5 | 4 | 5 | 3 | 5	22/5 = 4.4
9.	I do things below my physical ability level.	5 | 4 | 3 | 4 | 4	5 | 4 | 3 | 4 | 4 (NC)	20/5 = 4.0
13.*	I enjoy getting my body toned up.	2 | 1 | 1 | 2 | 3	4 | 5 | 5 | 4 | 3	21/5 = 4.2
18.*	My physical abilities are challenged.	1 | 2 | 3 | 1 | 2	5 | 4 | 3 | 5 | 4	21/5 = 4.2
Totals	Person's Total Scores	Not to be computed	23 | 20 | 21 | 20 | 19	
	Person's Averages	Not to be computed	4.6 | 4.0 | 4.2 | 4.0 | 3.8	103/25 = 4.12

Items requiring reversal. NC = No change, because there is no reversal.

Location of Average Score

Strongly Disagree 1	**Disagree** 2	**In Between** 3	**Agree** 4	**Strongly Agree** 5
			X	

mean score is, the lower the boredom for physical reasons.

The same calculation should be repeated with the other three components. Table 5 fictitiously demonstrates the means of all four components for the five persons.

Table 5: Scores on the FTB

Person	Physical	Mental	Meaning	Speed	Mean
1	4.6	4.2	4.6	4.2	4.40
2	4.0	3.6	4.4	4.4	4.10
3	4.2	4.0	4.2	4.6	4.25
4	4.0	4.4	3.8	4.2	4.10
5	3.8	4.6	4.8	3.8	4.25
Mean	4.12	4.16	4.36	4.24	4.22

Three basic calculations, based on the means of the components, are still required to reduce chaos or, at best, to control and regulate the flood of data. Accordingly, data reduction can lead to order and organization. First, what is the reported level of FTB for each person? (In following the next steps, use the table to be able to understand the logic behind the procedures needed to answer the question.) By adding horizontally the four means for each person's components, and dividing by 4, we obtain the mean for the person's FTB. This can be used in future comparisons, analyses, and interpretations.

The second essential calculation responds to two questions:

1. How did the five persons score on the four components?
2. Which area(s) demonstrated higher scores or higher free time boredom?

To answer, you need to add the five individuals' means for each component. For the lack of mental involvement, for instance, add 4.2 + 3.6 + 4.0 + 4.4 + 4.6 = 20.6; and then divide by 5 = 4.16. This procedure needs to be performed for all subscales. The averages of the five persons are used for comparisons and to perform the final calculation.

Lastly, as a summary of the total data and a focus of the whole endeavor: "What is the reported level of FTB of this group of five persons?" Two possible ways — both are correct — can be used to obtain this grand mean for this group: You can add either of the two sets of means that belong to "Total Free Time Boredom." One is horizontal; the other is vertical. The two calculations should be identical; in this case, as you see, the result is 4.22. Hopefully, by now you have realized how elaborate this process of "data reduction" is, the need for the above treatments, and potential usability of such data as will be presented below.

For further analysis, means in the table can be used for insights into individuals' behaviors. Sometimes information can be used for diagnosis, referral, or treatment. Also, means can have many practical uses: comparisons among participants or groups, bases for consultations; and detection of patterns and trends in a group, an agency, or a community. Moreover, when means are rank-ordered, they can be used as the basis for further interventions, comparisons, prescriptions, treatment strategies, or goal modification. In essence, the initial high chaos in numbers can be regulated and transferred to meaningful order, demonstrating patterns and pointing to evolving trends.

Similarly, previously presented computations apply not only to service delivery or scientific studies examining relationships between variables, but also to evaluate services and programs, as well when testing an agency's goal attainment and performance. Based on available literature, for example, investigators can test how the components and their total FTB associate with variables of interest to their studies.

Needless to say, the process reported in this chapter applies to all constructs that are proven to be comprised of identified components. In an article on one of the leisure concepts, Mannell (1989) claimed that investigators did not utilize the identified components of the measurement they used, only the total scale. This example of not using components is a very practical example of why we need orientation and competencies in employing existing components. Analysis based on components can provide "down-to-earth" understanding, ensuring more practical explanations while interpreting data.

Item Reversal

In developing and applying a measurement, some items can be stated in opposite ways or meanings. This called item reversal. For example, if the intent of a scale is to assess positive domains such as empowerment or happiness, some items can represent reversed moods to tap sentiments such as sadness, grievance, and misery. This gives the instrument power to extract or pull realistic emotions, which enhances scale's validity.

If the intent is to assess negative domains such as depression, anxiety, and boredom, reversed items ought to represent positive feelings. This would include being active, hopeful, or alive, all of which reflect non-depressed states. For example, items in the leisure literature that tap boredom reversibly include:

1. Leisure time gets me aroused and going (Iso-Ahola and Weissinger, 1990).
2. I get a kick out of most things I do (Farmer and Sundberg, 1986).
3. During my free time, I want it to last longer (Ragheb and Merydith, 2001).

Scoring high on these items shows no boredom. Therefore, positive items in a depression scale must have their scores reversed to reflect the intended sentiment. Otherwise, grave errors will be reflected in computing final scores, in field interpretations; and in hypotheses tested.

There are reasons for an item's content to be reversed. Besides achieving extractive power and realism as mentioned, items should tap authentic meanings, reflect truthfulness, create variations in responses, and reach a high degree of believability.

In some cases reversed contents do not achieve what is intended. The examples from Ragheb and Beard (1982) and Carlson et al. (2011) can show this point.

When Ragheb and Beard (1982) assessed leisure attitude, they employed in their pilot studies, items such as:

1. I feel that I am wasting my time when I am engaging in leisure activities.
2. I regret the time I put into my leisure activities.
3. I feel guilty for engaging in leisure activities.

In the item analysis reliability was jeopardized because of these statements, yielding low point-biserial correlations between the item and its total subscale score. The reasons for the items to behave this way are unknown.

In another study on reversal items, Carlson et al. (2011) showed that among older adults' respondents, reverse-scored items were associated with measurement difficulties. (This can lower face validity for this age group.) In cases such as these, item reversal is not desirable and should be avoided at all costs.

In conclusion, despite logical rationale to use and rely on opposite or reversed contents in scale developments, in some cases this does not work. Caution and substantiations need to be performed, demonstrating that there is no harm found during the analysis that jeopardizes reliability and/or validity of the scale.

Using Data to Contribute to Participants and Their Organizations

Organizations (practitioners) can use the data to improve performance in several areas. These can range from executive strategies, policy making, planning, and marketing to treatment, diagnosis, and referral. Also, results can be used to the benefits of participants (intervention, consultation, or programming), as shown below.

Knowing the nature of the concept that respondents are reacting to is critical in offering interpretations of findings. The model shown in Figure 5 — presented in more detail in Chapter 25 — can help in gaining insights into interpretations as well actions taken.

To complete the exercise, as a way to illustrate utility of data, we will assume that the five respondents to the FTB are residents in a senior home. Their scores will be utilized to answer the following questions. Your answers should be objective, based on exact numbers and statistical means. It is important to emphasize removing practitioners' biases in treating data. That is, remove personal tendencies to interpret data based on feelings of liking or disliking, personal emotions, or defensiveness. Biased reactions are referred to as subjective interpretations.

Based on data in the tables presented in this chapter, what are your best answers to the following concerns?

1. Is this group of older persons in your senior residence bored or not in its free time? Why?
2. Who is (are) the most (least) bored person(s) in this group? What is your evidence? Rank order the five persons from high to low, or the reverse. How can you use the rank order to devise a strategy? Is the rank order consistent with your observations, relatives' judgments, and/or reports from others? Based on available records, you might know why.
3. What is the rank order of the four components of FTB and their total in terms of their reported severity of boredom, experienced in free time, by this group?
4. What strategy can be used to reduce or control the reported severity of FTB (if any)?
5. Do you sense any potential suicidal inclinations? Why? (Knowing that severe boredom leads to depression and depression leads to suicide attempts.) Do the obtained results on the potential suicide coincide with any other practitioners' reports or observations? (Careful attention needs to be paid, avoiding overgeneralizations and misinterpretations of data, demanding extra verifications through available means such as peers, relatives, and caretakers.)
6. Who would have the potential to be depressed? (Others' observations and consultations are necessary to make accurate and trustworthy decisions.)
7. In terms of actions to be taken, to whom, of the five persons in Table 5, do you prescribe to or work with to achieve the following:
   a. Increasing involvement in physical activities.
   b. Increasing involvement in mental activities.
   c. Increasing the meaningfulness of what is encountered.
   d. Developing strategies, programs, plans, and activities to increase the speed of free time.
   e. Increasing overall excitement, interest, and enjoyment that eliminate or at least control FTB.
8. You might plan actions to control and reduce boredom, and then assess FTB again — let us say three months from the time you start. What is the average score for each component and the total FTB that you would set for your goal? (The value of available valid and reliable scales is that they can help in assessing and reassessing domains with confidence for action.)

As a stage in the assessment process, the above answers provide a strong rationale for the importance of developing both experience and competencies in

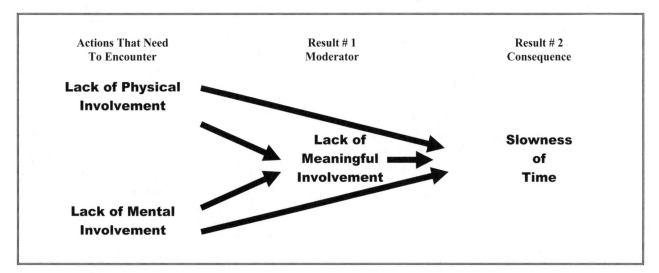

Figure 5: Interrelationships among Free Time Boredom components requiring actions to speed time and remove boredom

"crunching" data. Obtaining and using available data is important in assessment, interpretation of situations, and treatment.

Field Actions and Policymaking Based on Data

As demonstrated above, after reducing the data and interpreting it, certain decisions will be self-evident. Decisions can be made by a single practitioner: a manager, a supervisor, a therapist. But for accuracy and credibility, decisions are preferably made collectively, involving all concerned parties, including relatives. That is because data can lend itself to many interpretations — never science, but rather art. For moving from data and results to policy and practice, see Riddick and Russell (1999).

Moreover, collaborative decisions can motivate employees, relatives, and patients to be a part of the solution, and help in gaining their support. Although some trends demonstrate prevalence, mobilization of staff as a team is a main ingredient in the successful implementation of findings. To put assessment in its context, self-evident patterns alone in assessment findings are insufficient without the positive involvement and commitment of sufficient human resources. In some odd settings, data and observation point one way, but staff and patients act and respond another way. Staff involvement in assessment is a critical ingredient in commitment, action, and success.

Obtained results based on data can impact organizations on many levels. For example, data can serve to initiate new actions, modify current provisions, or sometimes stop nonfunctional offerings. In principle, actions and provisions based on reliable tools and trustworthy findings would ensure more desirable and successful outcomes than relying on trial and error, personal preferences, or just common sense. Objectively made decisions can impact organizations, not only to make them more effective, but also to make changes more positively and strongly.

The aspects that can profit from both data and quality decisions derived from data can contribute to numerous areas in field settings: for instance, the most realistic programs are the ones designed on the basis of assessed needs, which are then accounted for in planning what is offered. Also, community recreation activities, where high vandalism has been reported, can gain from data to be able to respond to crises, to meet needs for certain localities, or to program for certain age groups.

Intervention programs, too, can achieve greater success, depending on the quality of data collected. Treatment is one of the critical areas that rely extensively on data. Treatment in recreation settings can be at correctional institutions, senior housing, therapeutic recreation settings, at risk-youth programs, rehabilitation centers, and the like. Other areas to which data can contribute strongly include facility design, resource allocation, policymaking (fees, operating times, and scheduling), marketing targets, and agency strategy.

In sum, almost all leisure and park provisions require competencies in the acquisition of data and its interpretations to arrive at good decisions. Moreover, in order to meet the challenges of competition for funds and accountability in our rapidly changing society, securing data through assessment protocols can be proven not only to be an efficient means, but also the most effective procedure.

Summary and Conclusions

All humans perform assessment for survival, many times every day. That is, when we make judgments, estimates, or appraisals of our various situations and confrontations. Assessment can be applied informally or formally, depending upon each situation and tools available. Recreation and leisure services provide numerous settings that can make use of assessment. Besides informal leisure assessment, data can be collected formally for practical reasons that necessitate making sense of information gathered. The above development followed systematic and logical procedures in using data to gain knowledge as the basis for improving performance.

Contemporary leisure and recreation practitioners must be competent in using assessment tools. Therefore, the above information is used to develop skills in utilizing data in terms of reduction: to make understandable findings, followed by how to interpret results, then how those findings can contribute to services, users, participants, and agencies. A fictitious example, employing a standardized instrument, was utilized to orient the reader to the steps and procedures to handle data. Practitioners who wish to master relevant skills need to practice three to five fictitious examples with different leisure instruments such as leisure motivation, fitness and exercise, vitality through leisure, and leisure interests to attain most of the competencies required.

Questions and Exercises

1. What are the specific knowledge and skills required to "crunch" data?
2. How can you use data gathered to contribute to the quality of services and the welfare of the participants?

3. How can assessment and the data contribute to policymaking and field actions?
4. For three to five assessment tools, do the following:

- Collect data.
- Reverse items that require reversal.
- Compute necessary scores such as means.
- Cluster component scores, leading to total average.
- Use means comparatively to interpret phenomena based on numbers and scores.
- Use judgment objectively.
- Prescribe action, treatment, strategy, and policy, based on facts and numbers.

Chapter 18

Technology and Computer-Managed Assessment

Focus of Chapter

The intent of this chapter is to demonstrate the applicability of computer-managed assessment (CMA). We will look at how CMA applies in recreation, leisure, parks, and travel and tourism to study pursuits taking place in an individual's free time. Also, we will look at how the assessment strategy can enhance leisure delivery systems. CMA requires user-friendly software, an issue that will be addressed, inviting concerned entities to take charge of the financial support of software. Phases for processing CMA will be identified. Examples of phases to be presented include selections of assessment tools suiting each situation and function, administration of the appropriate instruments, and interpretations of results to help participants or patients make personalized leisure choices, judgments, and decisions.

Uses of CMA can be numerous. Therefore, examples will illustrate some possible applications, which can lend themselves to a multitude of settings. Use of any technology in any given setting is accompanied by serious problems. Hence, possible advantages and disadvantages of this extremely powerful, high-speed, and rapidly changing technology in leisure assessment will be discussed. In a later stage of development, when the proper software for assessment is available, how can we employ it to the benefit of society, all groups, and individuals? This issue of accessibility to all potential users, to enhance their self-knowledge and self-change, will be presented.

Key Terms

- applications
- computer-managed assessment (CMA)
- leisure delivery systems
- phases of the computer assessment process

Key Names

- James N. Butcher
- Ronald Jay Cohen
- Howard N. Garb
- James Sampson
- Douglas K. Snyder

Objectives

- Identify current reasons for the use of computers in leisure assessment.
- Recognize future trends and their reasons for further CMA uses.
- Use CMA and latest technologies to reach leisure users in their environments.
- Recognize potential contributors to the process of CMA and its software.
- Utilize the Internet in selecting assessments.
- Orient users with CMA.
- Administer CMA successfully to remote users.
- Score users' responses.
- Interpret users' data and results carefully.

- Identify strategies to make CMA accessible.

Assessing leisure behavior and functions has been on the rise since 1980. Generally, a variety of instruments have been constructed since that time. However, the value of instruments resides in their uses and contributions to both individuals and society. A similar concern was expressed by Garb (2000: 3), who insightfully observed:

> To improve psychological assessment (that is, to bring psychological assessment into a new age), it is necessary to do more than construct new tests and structured interviews. We also need to improve the way that assessment information is used to make judgments and decisions.

In parks and leisure fields, more instruments need to be developed. Equally important is their accessibility to users — a phenomenon that the Age of Information will need increasingly as society progresses and free time increases.

Reasons for the Use of Computers in Leisure Assessment

Computers and modern technologies, with their characteristics of high speed and efficiency, can impact tremendously on leisure services through possibilities of assessment. Computer managed assessment (CMA) can contribute to the fulfillment of the ultimate goals of leisure, recreation, parks, and travel and tourism. Some noted benefits could be to experience quality leisure and goal attainment, as a basic ingredient to an individual's quality of life and high-level wellness leading to vitality.

Good and realistic CMA of leisure needs, interests, and functioning can lead to better uses of available resources. Examples of resources to be used by contemporary individuals are free time, personal energy, existing facilities, and activity. All can be employed to help persons enjoy what they do, achieving satisfaction as a growing portion of modern quality of life.

Specifically, technology and the use of computers are becoming more dominant and inescapable. They can provide numerous benefits to human and social services (see Psychological Assessment Resources, Inc., 1999). Computerized assessment has been in operation for over 50 years, contributing to human functioning (see Butcher, Perry, and Atlis, 2000; Snyder, 2000). Today, leisure services are expanding rapidly and are considered one of the most expansive fields (see Edginton, Jordan, DeGraaf, and Edginton, 2002).

By comparison, the leisure system lags far behind its counterparts in the use of computers to deliver its services. Examples of more advanced areas are medicine, pharmaceuticals, distance learning and other new forms of education, sports, counseling, psychological assessment, and marketing. Logically, in utilizing computers and modern technologies, an available leisure service/program requires that it be matched with those who need it or have interest in it. This is a simple job that can easily be performed through computers and CMA strategies.

Far beyond using computer matchmaking in providing leisure, CMA can contribute effectively to the process of making wholesome choices. This is through individuals' leisure insights, health promotion, and self-learning. By using CMA, an individual can gain insights into several personal domains and functions. To achieve these two goals considerations need to be accounted for, as follows:

- First, knowing about dormant or unused abilities, talents, interests, and motivations.
- Second, possibilities exist to discover resources that are available but unknown to the user (such as programs, services, and facilities).
- Third, being able to control or minimize self-imposed restraints. Attempts can be made to remove many constraints, such as negative attitudes, social alienation, fears, lack of skills or confidence, misconceptions, lack of motivation or interest, free time boredom, and lack of knowledge of leisure provisions.

CMA can help individuals realize what influences their leisure lifestyles and enable them to exercise self-empowerment through leisure self-determination, self-change, and self-development. Leisure self-empowerment can be considered the essence of leisure functioning and adjustment.

Future strategies in leisure services will incorporate the application of CMA, as societal needs, demands, and changes open new avenues for technological uses. Not only experiencing increasing discretionary time and longevity but also abundance of human energy and vitality characterize demands and needs of contemporary society. This is due to enhanced technology use and massively produced goods. (A large portion of these products is utilized for the enjoyment of leisure, recreation, fitness, and travel and tourism.)

CMA can operate as one of the bridges to supply options and services for these newly created demands and functions. This is besides meeting such societal goals as personal leisure, recreation, and fitness needs. However, computer usage in assessment has disadvantages as well. For a presentation of pros and cons of computers and modern technologies, see Cohen and Swerdlik (2005).

Computer Managed Assessment and Technologies Enhancing Assessment

What technologies are available that can help assessment? With the aid of computers, e-mails, phone apps, social media, faxes, and other technologies, assessment procedures in recreation, leisure, fitness, and travel and tourism can be more accessible. This can remedy the persistent problem of the lack of accessibility of leisure and recreation instruments that has been hindering their usability.

Data, then, can be collected and compared to understand participants' leisure needs, problems, constraints, frequency of use or lack of use of free time services. Consequently, collected data can be employed for programming, services, and funds allocation; as well as bases for personal guidance, counseling, health protection, and health promotion.

CMA application can be very broad. Generally, people in diverse settings can be interested in gaining knowledge about the nature of their leisure lifestyles. Individuals like to be oriented with options available, what can interest them, and possible difficulties acting as constraints that might prevent them from meeting their leisure needs. People in many settings — such as employees, military and police personnel, senior citizens, prisoners, at-risk youth, college students — can be interested in learning about their leisure needs (motivations), free time boredom (if it exists), attitudes, and what kinds of satisfaction they are getting from their current recreation and leisure activities.

Moreover, leisure users might like to explore possibilities new to them, such as new places to travel to, original art to experience, novel hobbies to pursue, or fresh outdoor recreational activities to do. Responding to a number of CMA tools can draw a personal profile, helping not only to meet newly realized needs but also to impact upon and change that person's lifestyle.

The use of the Internet — through appropriate phases to be elaborated on later — can help to change and shape leisure lifestyles. Perhaps, too, the Internet can help overcome problems and perceived constraints that prevent a person's full enjoyment of recreation and leisure. Moreover, recreation and leisure can contribute to the promotion of mental and physical health, as a step toward further high-level wellness and vitality.

Initiatives that Support the Development of Software

Who would support CMA software? Financial supporters of such systems should possess common characteristics — being concerned about the well-being of individuals, their functioning, and society's quality of life. Moreover, supporters should not be concerned about limited use or profitability rather than caring about national responsibility, facilitating leisure lifestyles as postulated in the *Charter of Leisure,* "Leisure is the Right of All."

The intent of such development is to make it available and usable by all groups. Individuals who can benefit from such services range from employed to unemployed persons, able to disabled, indigent to affluent, females and males, from younger to older ages. This is without regard to position in life, ethnicity, levels of education, marital status, or socioeconomic status.

Three main contributors can help in developing leisure CMA software — nonprofit organizations, philanthropic agencies, and concerned corporations. Examples of nonprofit organizations can start with the most concerned and specialized one — the National Recreation and Park Association. Some other concerned organizations are the American Alliance of Health, Physical Education, Recreation, and Dance; American Camping Association; National Intramural Recreational Sports Association; Young Men's and Young Women's Hebrew Association; the YMCA; and the YWCA.

The second main contributor comprises endowments by philanthropic agencies, such as the Fulbright, Rockefeller, and Ford organizations. The third entity, which employs a very high percentage of the total population, is corporations, starting with their main organization, the National Employee Services and Recreation Association. The following corporations and similar businesses would be interested in developing such software: General Motors, IBM, Dell, America on Line, Yahoo, Coca-Cola, Microsoft, AT&T, Philip Morris, and Proctor and Gamble. In return, benefits to the corporations sponsoring software can be advertisement, free use of the developed software by their employees, contributing to community functioning, public relations, and enhancing their public image.

Goals of the computer-managed assessment in leisure cannot be attained unless pioneering agencies or organizations can see CMA's benefits and sponsor its implementation.

Phases of Computer-Managed Assessment

In a broad utility of CMA, Garb (2000: 31) pointed to certain purposes for computerized psychological assessment: collecting data, scoring protocols, and making judgments and decisions. Based on standards proposed by the American Educational Research Association (1985) and a Joint Committee on Testing Practices (1988), Sampson (1998) presents five phases for common elements of the assessment process to be computer-managed:

- Selection of assessment tools
- Orientation
- Administration
- Scoring
- Interpretation

Using the Internet to enhance their utility, these five phases can apply to almost all delivery systems, including parks and recreation. These five phases can apply to leisure provision, as illustrated below.

1. Using the Internet in the Selection Process

Logically, availability of software and tools on the Internet are prerequisites to the selection process. Practitioners should be familiar with instruments available on the Internet, the nature of these tools, their qualities (reliability and validity), what they measure, and how the results can be interpreted. Diagnosis and careful understanding of user settings and needs are of extreme importance in the selection process. Hence, experience and training in the nature and utility of assessment tools in field practice (as a basis for selection) determines the level of success in meeting needs and community or personal goal attainment.

In the selection process, software should be developed and identified through two basic sources: leisure-specific and non-leisure assessment tools. As mentioned before, "specific" refers to instruments being leisure-related; that is, related to needs, interests, and functioning in recreation, leisure, play, park activities, and travel and tourism. All measurements abstracted and presented in Part I of this book are leisure-specific.

Non-leisure measurements, on the other hand, are tools that are indirectly related to leisure services but can be of help to leisure users. These non-leisure measurements can originate in psychology, sociology, gerontology, economics, marketing, administration, physical education and sports, health, counseling, and rehabilitation. Comparatively, leisure-specific instruments, unlike non-leisure measurements, are very limited in number and are probably less accessible. In adapting a non-leisure instrument, extreme care needs to be exercised. Moreover, before adaptations are made, sufficient knowledge must be obtained about the nature of those assessment tools.

In the future, extensive in-service training will be required to make accurate instrument selections. This training should be aimed at practitioner competencies in the basic features of instrumentations. Features can include, but are not limited to: the reading level of instruments, their language, established norms, evaluation of their quality, time required to respond, cost, how to reduce data, and how to interpret results for field uses as discussed in Chapter 17.

2. Computer-Managed Assessment Orientation

The orientation is a kind of mini-self-training, walking through procedures step-by-step, to ensure a thorough understanding of the instrument. Orientation should include basic familiarity with an instrument's purpose, nature, utility, administration, and possible interpretative scenarios. In designing software, a skillfully developed orientation is fundamental to achieve success, just as availability of a map and sufficient directions allows us to find our way in a city.

Included in well-designed software, there should be a comprehensive orientation through some basic features. An instrument's orientation should help a practitioner or participant to make accurate selections and use the instrument with a clear goal to contribute to an intended outcome. The outcome of CMA can be both decision-making and behavior change. Ultimately, in designing an orientation to produce valuable results, a participant or a patient can make decisions on leisure or recreation choices, places to visit, or facilities and resources to use. Moreover, s/he can use assessment findings to learn about himself/herself through value clarification (in part), how his/her recreation motivations are rated, what kind of attitude s/he possesses, and how this self-knowledge can help in self-changing behavior.

3. Administration of Computer-Managed Self-Assessment

This phase is straightforward and self-explanatory. Its success depends upon the prior phases, instrument selection and orientation. Self-assessment administration through the Internet overcomes many problems and barriers that may prevent assessment. Potential problems that may prohibit assessment can include lack of time, the nature of a disability, distance, and availability of transportation. Moreover, performing assessment from a remote site removes completely the need to coordinate the presence of a practitioner/clinician and a participant/patient.

If results and interpretations of self-assessment are not self-explanatory, further help needed from a trained specialist could be performed later. This would be done through accessing data and results, thus offering insights, value clarification, interpretations, and guidance to users. Nevertheless, in administering self-assessment procedures, there are many potential confounding factors and problems that need to be realized, studied carefully, and solved through a continuous evaluative mechanism of software and administrative procedures that help to reveal any potential difficulties or confusing factors.

4. Scoring Mechanisms and How to Use Them

Measurement scoring is the most mechanical phase, with computer software performing all tasks. Data "crunching" is completed automatically, computing means, standard deviations, and comparisons to norms and to relevant individuals or groups. An individual's means can be compared against three scores.

- Means obtained by members of the same group (e.g., participants in a recreation center, employees in a corporation, prisoners in a specific facility, similar at-risk youth, or patients in a rehabilitation center).

- Means relevant to a norm group (e.g., persons of the same age, such as a teenager or a senior adult; persons from the same gender; persons with similar deficiencies; or persons with corresponding circumstances).

- The absolute mean of the scale regardless of what is described under the prior two comparisons (compare against the midpoint of the scale, e.g., 3 on a five-point scale or 4 on a seven-point scale).

As a result, an individual is more self-knowledgeable, which can change attitudes and generate motivations for actions.

5. Interpretations of Data and Results

All of the prior four steps are means toward an end — to help respondents. The end product is reduced to this question: "How would my scores, help me in my leisure enjoyment, skills, lifestyle, wellness, vitality, and functioning?" All prior procedures are narrowed down to the power of the "flashlight," in the form of interpretations and possible suggestions. These can focus an individual's attention on self-change and self-development. To interpret data and results is to make sense of massive, chaotic numbers called responses. Interpretation

helps a respondent to see matters that are, sometimes, taken for granted.

In this process, results point to certain leisure or recreation realities. These realities can be problems, deficiencies, lack of skills, lack of behavioral readiness; or a state of inertia, or adjustment, successful functioning, or attainment of desired quality of life and wellness. For example, when individuals respond to certain assessment tools, they can be more aware of their realities. Some may be constrained from leisure participation or enjoyment due to a sense of guilt toward being in a state of leisure (Neulinger, 1974). In another case, a negative attitude toward playfulness might be realized; or lack of motivation may restrict leisure enjoyment and benefits. A "flashlight" with clarification power can help persons gain self-understanding so they can make good leisure decisions and/or change perspectives toward their leisure lifestyles, fulfilling the essence of self-determination.

Practitioners providing interpretations of results must receive professional training. They should be competent in assessment, basic statistics, leisure services, guidance and counseling, and social and behavioral aspects of leisure. As lay-users, a careful and complete orientation must be a part of the software, as well as accessibility to lists of trained personnel and/or agencies that are concerned about specific users or outcomes (e.g., corporations, therapeutic recreation, community recreation, special events, armed forces, seniors, prisoners, or at-risk youth).

The purpose of all of the above effort is to maximize user benefits and minimize potential problems or restrictions as illustrated below through some scenarios. Otherwise, misusing the power of interpretations and clarifications will be like giving a real gun as a toy to a four-year-old child.

Computer-Managed Assessment in Leisure Services

How can professionals and users of leisure delivery systems benefit from CMA? Initially, practitioners and users should be oriented with the nature and function of leisure and recreation computerized scales. Then, based on an individual's situation, users can identify the assessment tools that respond best to their current situation. These situations can vary a great deal. The following scenarios can be generalized to other settings, three of which are presented:

1. To Increase Leisure Participation

An individual who wants to know what s/he can do for leisure choices would select a leisure interest assessment tool. By virtue of his/her responses and with the aid of the computer to crunch data provided by the user, results can be available as bases for insights about the user's tendencies and inclinations. The results of this leisure interests inventory can show the individual how much s/he is inclined to seek some of the following: creative (artistic) pursuits, mechanical, physical (sports and fitness), cultural, social, outdoor activities, reading, or service (volunteering). With the help of computers, a user profile can be drawn and suggestions offered regarding appropriate choices that match reported personal interests.

Moreover, any combination of these interests can reflect an individual's real preferences. In the same self-assessment session, the computer might suggest leisure and recreation options and alternatives. For instance, if a person scored highly on artistic and creative pursuits, a list of options would be made available, as well as where to go to receive these services. On the other hand, and even more importantly, individuals who scored low on physical or cultural interests may need to receive guidance and/or counseling. An exploration with such users can furnish them with possible real or imagined constraints (environmental or personal) that might have prevented them from approaching their chosen pursuits. Suggestions would be proposed regarding where to go, what to do, and how to learn further about potential interests. (Non-physically active children and teens can benefit a great deal to control the growing negative impacts of obesity.)

2. To Control Free Time Boredom

A second situation that can benefit from CMA is the issue of boredom after school or work. Teens, college students, and corporate employees can respond to a measurement identifying their levels of boredom, or lack thereof, after work or school. By comparing users' scores against norm groups similar to them, findings would be communicated. These findings can enable users to gain self-awareness and knowledge of what is actually happening to them after school or work and what can be done.

Practically, self-assessment can result in insightfully knowing the three negative "H's" about boredom: the Hidden, the Habitual, and the Hurtful; as well as the three positive "H's" about after work or school: the Healthy, the Healer, and the Helpful. Assuming that data is both valid and reliable, as a logical sequence, this step can be followed by suggestions of areas of recreation and leisure choices to emphasize, avoid, seek, or develop certain lifestyles. Unlike treatment, this preventive strategy can assist individuals to focus on their recreation and leisure choices, attitudes, awareness, competencies, and potential constraints that need to be removed.

Acquired insights and self-awareness can use approaches like self-prescription or self-motivation. For example, if I actually do A, B, and C, this can lead to boredom after school or work. To the contrary, if I engage in K, L, or M, with certain attitude or goal orientation, most likely I will not complain about boredom after work/school. Users also need to be cautioned that, if facing difficulties in the interpretations of assessment, or if they do not notice changes in their complaints of boredom, they need to consult with their leisure professional, who should be skillful in assessment and counseling. Further assessments might be required to diagnose the causes of after-school or after-work complaints. A personal interview can be insightful. Following such a strategy can highlight possible trouble and point to potential solutions or strategies.

3. To Remove Barriers to Leisure

A final CMA scenario can relate to leisure constraints or barriers, which might restrict obtaining rewards from recreation and leisure. What are some of the possible constraints to be incorporated in a measurement? Constraints can be very personal and subjective, not only relevant to what an individual lacks (such as time, money, skills, and companions with whom to do activities or enjoy experiences), but also safety, transportation, physical disabilities, or health conditions. Through assessments of severity of constraints, combined with background information (e.g., age, gender, financial and marital situations), portfolios can be drawn; directions can be suggested.

Constraints confronted by CMA can be applied to almost all settings and populations: older persons, or at-risk youth, the able and disabled, work force, armed forces, prisoners, urban or rural dwellers, college students, or homemakers. Most individual constraints are imaginary or traps, sometimes self-imposed. Hence, self-guided assessment can encourage users to escape those difficulties and prescribe a course of feasible actions to be self-empowered.

When users prefer exclusive self-guided assessments for confidentiality or other reasons, computer-generated solutions can be offered. Confidentiality can be related to names of agencies providing services, programs, facilities, cost (fees), locations, telephone and fax numbers, and e-mail addresses.

Summary of Scenarios

Generally, each individual's situation is uniquely different. Therefore, persons must use assessment tools and technology in diversified ways. Based on what is illustrated above, scenarios may be limited; however, applications can be limitless. The above scenarios intend to demonstrate how the availability of leisure opportunities, through CMA, can facilitate

— despite possible limitations — their positive impacts on all individuals and society.

Evaluation of Computer-Managed Assessment

CMA includes all of the advantages of computer operations. It is extremely efficient, highly adaptable to individual differences in important characteristics (e.g., age, gender, education, work or school load, and income). Computers have numerous capabilities, providing on-the-spot data crunching, and offering usable interpretations of assessment findings. Butcher, at al. (2000: 6) observed that the benefits to the field from computers continue to expand as technology becomes more advanced, allowing for more sophisticated operations.

It is expected that with the current rate of development, before the year 2020, computers will perform jobs and activities never thought of before. Thus, users will be allowed more insightful realizations of their leisure interests, what is available for them, what can satisfy them, and what is possibly restraining them from involvement.

On the other hand, some disadvantages are potentially present, such as the high cost of the operation, the inadequacy of software (especially in newly expanding service areas like leisure and parks), lagging far behind the state-of-the-art in hardware. Moreover, in terms of applicability, there might be a lack of availability of assessment norms to compare against. Results can be misinterpreted because they are sometimes communicated mechanically, due to the nature of computers. Effort should be made to control or, at minimum, to reduce the impact of those disadvantages, posting possible limitations. Then CMA will be useful in enhancing users' leisure lifestyles.

Accessibility of Computer-Managed Assessment

How can CMA reach users (individuals and communities) to contribute to their leisure and recreation lifestyles? Basically, software must be both creatively and skillfully developed. Through funding by service agencies or grants, software must incorporate all possible recreation and leisure assessment tools, with clear instructions about how to respond to this self-administered assessment. Consulting with assessment developers, users will learn about how to "crunch" data relevant to their instruments, in addition to how to interpret that data, providing scenarios that best fit and help.

Upon accessibility of that advanced software, leisure delivery systems and entities concerned about leisure can acquire such advancements. Examples of systems that can purchase such software has a huge range: those who are serving community recreation, campus recreation, armed forces recreation, correctional recreation, corporate recreation, parks, senior homes, travel and tourism, rehabilitation and counseling, and therapeutic recreation settings, as the biggest users. Self-managed assessment can then serve participants or clients through three strategies:

1. Fully free of charge, paid by the agency or the system.
2. Services subsidized by agencies with users paying a small fee, to create accessibility for all.
3. All costs incurred by users.

All copyright laws and procedures should apply to these uses.

Summary and Conclusions

The highest form of a leisure-oriented society is the ability of individuals to take charge of their leisure choices, in other words, to be leisure-competent. Utilization of computers and modern technologies in recreation, health, and leisure can operate as an excellent mechanism to achieve self-responsibility and competency (referred to in psychology as "locus of control"). For this ultimate goal to be achieved and for CMA to fulfill its role, four basic levels of services must be considered:

1. Availability of sufficient quality of leisure-specific and pertinent non-leisure assessment tools.
2. Skillfully created, "user-friendly" software.
3. Preparation of well-trained practitioners, competent in assessment selection, administration, and interpretation.
4. Participants and patients with advanced awareness and education for the impact of leisure in their lives, in order to be self-sufficient.

People can have all the free time that organizations can afford; society can have all the leisure facilities and programs that systems can design and provide; nevertheless, the values and benefits of free time and its resources reside in the way they are used.

Truly, therefore, CMA can connect receivers with providers, beneficiaries with suppliers. Ultimately, CMA can be facilitating for needs to be met, for resources to be available, for obstacles to be removed, and for skills to be acquired. In an era of communication, CMA should and actually can connect.

Leisure services, resources, and facilities are expanding enormously. Hence, CMA can enable users to benefit from these systems by matching their needs and interests with what is available. One of the outcomes can be facilitating both self-care and self- advancement, thus helping to achieve participant satisfaction, well-being, vitality, and quality of life.

Questions and Exercises

1. Discuss the reasons for the uses of computers in leisure assessment.
2. What are the future trends for further computer-managed assessment?
3. Name and discuss the phases of computer-managed assessment.
4. Give examples of computer-managed assessment in leisure and recreation services.

Chapter 19

The Future of Assessment in Recreation and Leisure

Focus of Chapter

The purpose of this chapter is to discuss future directions in the uses of assessment. Future scales will improve in quantity and quality. In terms of quantity, more instruments will be developed to respond to some neglected, evolving areas and newly occurring phenomena. In terms of quality, future scales will employ more psychometric theory, with stringent procedures to satisfy validity and reliability requirements. Moreover, dissemination of developed scales will improve, reaching many concerned users. The next generation of instruments to be developed will focus on leisure-related or specific scales more than relying on non-leisure instruments generated in other areas. Due to demands for assessment competencies, workshops and in-service training will be utilized to orient professionals to data reduction, interpretation, and actions based on results. More technologies will be adapted to assessment implementations. These changes will impact subareas of the leisure delivery systems in different ways. Service areas receiving attention will range from commercial recreation, intervention with at-risk youth, and public recreation, to event management, therapeutic recreation, and facility design.

Key Terms

- assessment
- assessment improvements
- competencies
- dissemination

- in-service training
- leisure-specific scales
- modern technologies

Key Names

- Jum C. Nunnally

Objectives

- Identify societal trends and issues that will require recreation assessment procedures.
- Describe current circumstances that will lead to employment of leisure assessment.
- Foresee conditions that will require improvements in recreation assessments.
- Identify future needs for dissemination of leisure instruments.
- Describe the reasons for growing interest in leisure-specific instruments.
- Identify reasons for providing workshops and in-service training to teach recreation assessment competencies.
- Describe the use of modern technologies to enhance leisure assessment procedures.

Changes and social events that affect personal and societal life occur whether we can measure them or not. The same applies to the rapidly occurring leisure and recreation phenomena and their impact. To capture and understand what is occurring calls for assessment of some type. In the future, instruments will change on many fronts to reflect what is happening to individuals and society. Broadly expressed, many areas will lend themselves to progress in measuring recreation and leisure.

Recreation Areas Affected

On many different fronts, recreation and park assessment tools are expected to go through changes and developments. Areas that will witness changes include a number of leisure subfields such as commercial recreation, youth intervention, event management, marketing leisure services, and facility design. Other fronts that are expected to witness more assessment include improvement in service quality and investigating behavioral aspects (e.g., constraints, awareness, and impacts of free time; fitness, vitality, and positive psychological phenomenon of leisure). Regarding the diversity of these subfields, there will be a better balance — in orientation and use — between qualitative and quantitative methods of data collection.

Besides increasing the quantity of recreation assessment tools and reliance on different approaches, improving the quality of recreation instruments will be another critical front. Developers will be expected to follow strict guidelines for validation. There will be more advanced utilization of science as the basis for instruments (e.g., administration, economics, marketing, psychology, and sociology).

Another major front to be improved is related to users. Measurements will be more accessible; computers and other devices will be available to obtain, store, manage, analyze, and interpret data. Future professionals will be highly trained in the use of assessment. Organizations and participants will have better accessibility to data; contributing to planning, treatment, changes, marketing, and managerial decisions.

In short, with more attention, the use of recreation assessments will serve many fronts, augmenting their progress in an ever-changing age of communication and accountability.

Methods of Data Collection

The future of assessment will be expected to incorporate the use of all available methods of data collection. A balance in training and use will be reached among interviews, observations, physiological devices, and paper-and-pencil scales. Depending on the nature of subfields, methods of data collection will be enhanced and practitioners will develop necessary competencies in them.

Conceptualization and Validation

To improve the quality and usefulness of recreation and park measurements, a portion of the existing ones will need further enhancement by giving more attention to concepts, scale reliabilities, validations, and disseminations. For instance, if certain instruments lack sound conceptualizations, then philosophical bases, theoretical structures, and research findings may be employed more thoroughly to strengthen the concept's foundations, followed by new attempts at validation.

Moreover, scales that lack reliability and validity could be improved through re-evaluation, employing contemporary theoretical backgrounds and well-developed methodologies. These improvements will be achieved by following highly advanced guidelines of both validity and reliability: criteria and strategies in a measurement's research design. Specifically, certain criteria will be emphasized, refining the items by using basic statistics required for measurement development — factor analysis and internal reliability coefficients — to discard weak, irrelevant, and unnecessary items. Thus, the psychometric theory will be utilized more extensively in scale construction.

Dissemination of Recreation Measurements

Usefulness of measurements is achieved when they serve participants, organizations, and communities. This is a notion of a measurement's pertinence to one's life, an agency's objectives, and a community's problems. Future measurements are anticipated to account further for relevant settings and users. Two other criteria will be related to usefulness: their effectiveness (accuracy, dependability, and predictability or reliability; and their efficiency, time to respond, brevity in number of items utilized). Future measurements will demonstrate not only more usefulness, serving broader goals, but also demonstrate greater effectiveness and efficiency.

Moreover, usefulness of instruments can be achieved if they are widely available to all users. A logical question can be asked, "What is the value of a measurement if it is not readily available for those who need it?" This is an issue of dissemination of existing measurements. To serve both dissemination strategies and usability, measurements would be much more accessible if published, either in journals or commercially. Many organizations would benefit from commercially available instruments, such as corporations, the Armed Forces, cities, counties, hospitals, rehabilitation centers, schools, parks, forestry sites, outdoor recreation, leisure counseling, commercial enterprises, and non-profit organizations. In other words, usefulness and dissemination of recreation measurements can be fulfilled through availability in journals and/or commercial publications. Deliberate efforts are expected to make instruments in recreation, park, and leisure available to all potential users.

Coverage and Scope of Recreation Measurements

The content of this book attempted to cover global assessment tools and strategies in all recreation, parks, leisure, fitness, travel, and play to account for all recreation specializations and concepts. In the future, it might be proven that such a global approach is not as useful as expected, or at minimum, limiting, and unrealistic. These constraints are due to the breadth and diversity among recreation and leisure subfields and the difficulty in responding to the complexity of such provisions.

In this context, it is anticipated — meeting accountability challenges and societal demands — that the number of published instruments will more than double, serving specific provisions by the end of the next two decades. Future demands, needs, specializations, and evidence will point to the appropriate path(s) to take in developing and adapting recreation-specific and related assessment procedures. It is possible that assessment will be specialized further in areas such as therapeutic recreation, at-risk youth, event management, physical recreation, commercial recreation, the arts, outdoor recreation and parks, travel and tourism, and leisure behavior.

Future Needs and Demands for Recreation-Specific Instruments.

Evidence might point to persisting needs for more specialized assessment tools. For instance, there can be assessments designed uniquely to parks, activities in natural surroundings, and outdoor recreation, while other tools are designed to assess provision of services, motivations, professional appraisal, management procedures, service quality, marketing strategies, cost-effectiveness, and customer involvement. Other therapeutic recreation subfields that might require specialized attention include assessing clients' abilities, health, well being, and vitality to enable them to function not only in leisure but also in life in general.

Moreover, due to leisure needs and the amount of spending involved, demands for data will be greater in commercial recreation for marketing strategies. Assessment will be required for a variety of goals such as feasibility studies, facility design, carrying capacity, and profitability. Also, three more subareas (worth mentioning for their cross-relevance) that might need assessment specialization are

1. Free time phenomena, changes, and problems.
2. The unique leisure style of children, adolescents, adults, employees, and older persons.
3. Gender and racial differences in free time and leisure with emphasis on women and minorities to secure inclusion of all groups.

These are examples of potential areas that will need further assessment. Social change will reveal more phenomena that will require assessment.

The need for specialized assessment tools in different subfields will depend on demands, advancements, and awakening to the usefulness and application of assessment procedures in decision-making. Practitioners' orientation — training, familiarization, and ability to use assessment — will determine the magnitude of reliance on available, standardized instruments or adapting them to specific needs.

Assessment Workshops for Better Usability

A prerequisite for focused efforts on the uses of measurements in the future, fulfilling their ends, is better orientation and improvement of practitioners' competencies in handling existing instruments. Both better orientation and competency improvement require workshops and applications relevant to each recreation subfield. The goal is to enhance academic preparation and training of assessment competencies.

Extensive exposure to assessment procedures and their criteria will be required for students of leisure and recreation (undergraduate and graduate). Further emphasis on measurement design and construction will be required from graduate students and post-graduates. Courses with titles like, "Measurements in Leisure and Recreation Systems" or "Assessment in Leisure and Recreation Services" will be expected in academic leisure programs. That is similar to almost all applied academic specializations that seek higher professional status.

On the other hand, greater emphasis on comprehending, evaluating, and using measurements should be basic skills acquired at the undergraduate level. Due to its relevance in this context, it is worth repeating Nunnally's impression of the value of measurements and their availability. Nunnally (1978) states that, "The science of psychology will progress neither slower nor faster than it becomes possible to measure important variables" (p. 6). This can apply to three leisure, park, and recreation concerns: service evaluation, applied assessment, and scientific investigations. It is expected for these three areas to expand with widespread provision of leisure and recreation.

Technology and Recreation Assessment

Modern technology — especially computers and electronic devices — will contribute more in the future to the use of instruments. With a high degree of accessibility, tests and measurements will be computerized, making them readily available to users. Moreover, respondents and practitioners will be able to obtain instant results and these responses will be stored electronically.

These results can be utilized for diagnosis, treatment, prevention, and comparisons against norms or any other groups. Self-administered assessment can be employed due to its availability, assisting respondents in their own privacy, gaining an idea about their behavior, knowing what they lack and what prevents them from doing activities, choices to be pursued, and places to go to enjoy their free time.

Through the use of computers, a participant's portfolio of results from recreation instruments can be established and made available. This portfolio can be useful not only for practitioners who make decisions regarding program planning, intervention, and treatment; but also for participants to gain insight into their leisure functioning. This can create further awareness and skill development, which in turn allows for desirable changes. Recreation and leisure measurements can be constantly adapted to use modern technology. This is a part of technology's contribution to individual and societal quality of life and functioning.

Improving the Body of Knowledge

As a result of increasing quality of recreation and leisure measurements, the body of knowledge in the leisure field will evolve further. How would current and future measurements improve the body of knowledge? Basically, besides experience, concepts form a great part of the body of information, if not the majority of it.

More interestingly, it is claimed too that measurements advance concepts as much as concepts advance measurements. There should be a continuous process of feedback between concepts and measurements, which make a cornerstone of the body of knowledge.

It is true that a measurement is founded on its relevant concept (philosophical, hypothetical, and theoretical). However, a concept is advanced more by discoveries of its constructs. This process is known as "mutual interaction" (Fiske, 1971) between concepts and measurements. The above feedback should be an ongoing exploration and discovery, which is in a state of continuous motion and interaction. Therefore, it is expected that research efforts will be more focused on areas that lack empirically validated measurements in order for those measurements to advance the substantiation of ideas.

A research agenda will be composed to fill in the gaps for instruments and assessment procedures. The process in action is referred to as theory-measurement-theory. This is evolving new concepts that lead again to a yet better measurement. Ultimately, the body of knowledge will be in continuous state of motion and refinement to serve individuals and society.

Summary and Conclusions

Future development of leisure measurements will witness elaborate technical efforts, improving their quality and quantity. Some of the technical areas that will gain attention will be relevant concepts with their reliability and validity and also better dissemination and availability. Instrument specialization will move from reliance on non-recreation measurements to recreation-specific instruments serving professional needs.

Further attention will also be paid to advanced training and orientation of practitioners, as well as employing modern technology to improve recreation service quality. Finally, the future will witness better collaboration and feedback among theories and measurements to increase the body of information for improving recreation, parks, leisure, services, and play.

In conclusion, a renaissance of recreation measurements will be upon us when quality and quantity of instruments are achieved. This will require paying more attention to the quality of measurements and their concepts as we utilize further the psychometric and sociometric theories. However, it should be noted that measurement quality (validity and reliability) of concepts covered and availability are among the basic criteria that determine the credibility and value of recreation instruments.

Training of practitioners on the usability of measurements and utility of modern technology are basic requirements. Most importantly, the strength and development of the body of knowledge as a result of mutual interaction between themes and measurements are among the basic criteria that determine the status and value of the movement of recreation, parks, leisure, and play. These are some of the approaches that will, when fulfilled, lead to a renaissance of basic leisure and recreation concepts and knowledge.

Questions and Exercises

1. What are the main issues and social trends pertinent to leisure that will require assessment?
2. Explain contemporary circumstances that will lead to use of leisure assessment.
3. Elaborate on future recreation needs for dissemination of instruments.
4. What are some of the reasons for interest in area-specific leisure scales?

Part III
Conceptualization of Constructs

Chapter 20

Leisure Involvement: From Concepts to Measurements

Focus of Chapter

Due to the importance of involvement, it is introduced first among the social-psychological domains of leisure. History of involvement will be presented, originating in psychology, applied to marketing, then considered in leisure and recreation. In conceptualizing leisure involvement, many components were realized ranging from importance, pleasure, and commitment to interest, identity, and centrality. Types of involvement (felt, enduring, and situational) will be discussed. However, due to leisure involvement's heavy reliance on marketing concepts, some domains were emphasized (perceived risk, sign value, self-image, and risk probability), while some other ones, more relevant to leisure, were underrepresented (e.g., intensity, absorption, flow, and meaning). Evidence of the status of the domains will be presented. Comparatively, with the exception of one general leisure involvement scale, all identified measures assess involvement in specific leisure activities. On another front, when are the following concepts more helpful for leisure practitioners and researchers, frequency of leisure participation or leisure involvement? Answers will be presented demonstrating under which conditions each concept operates best. At the end, scales assessing different leisure involvement will be reported.

Key Terms

- absorption
- centrality
- commitment
- importance
- intensity

- interest
- involvement (ego)
- involvement (felt, enduring, and situational)
- participation
- pleasure

Key Names

- Mark E. Havitz
- Jean-Noel Kapferer
- Gilles Laurent

- Norman McIntyre
- Muzafer Sherif

Objectives

- Identify the most/least relevant components of leisure involvement.
- Describe types of involvement.
- Identify the conceptual development stages of leisure involvement.
- Cite reasons for missing potentially important components of leisure involvement such as intensity, flow, and absorption.
- Distinguish settings that require the use of either frequency of leisure participation or leisure involvement.
- Evaluate theories that can explain leisure involvement.
- Explain functions of scales assessing leisure involvement.

Almost 100 years ago, Calkins (1916) introduced the concept of ego involvement in the psychology literature. About 30 years afterward, the concept began to be shaped and formed by Sherif and Cantril

(1947). Sherif and Cantril presented a psychology of attitudes, using it as a basis for the interpretation of ego involvement. In their discussion, they reported results of experiments on how variables, such as social status and social class identification, could shape and affect ego involvement. Consequently, due to social developments in the past five decades, ego involvement found applications in many fields of service. Marketing and consumer services witnessed the broadest application for the concept of ego involvement, assessing clients' reactions, utilizing scales such as Personal Involvement Inventory (Zaichkowsky, 1985), Consumer Involvement Profile (Laurent and Kapferer, 1985), and Revised Personal Involvement Inventory (McQuarrie and Munson, 1987).

Moreover, examples of diversified fields applying ego involvement included health (Rosenheck, 2000), civic or political involvement (Niemi et al., 2000), and student or academic involvement (House, 2000). The leisure and recreation field was no exception in using involvement to interpret relevant phenomena (see Wiley, Shaw, and Havitz, 2000). Assessment of leisure involvement began with outdoor recreation, evolving from the late 1970s and 1980s (e.g., Bryan, 1977; Wellman, Roggenbuck, and Smith, 1982; McIntyre, 1989). Therefore, it seems that a utilitarian and pragmatic motive is behind the attention given to involvement concepts in all fields; they want to improve their services.

Recreation and leisure assessment instruments focused on measuring involvement in specific activities, such as camping and vacationing, ignoring or being unaware of individuals' recreation or leisure involvement, as a whole. Examples of measurements assessing involvement in specific recreational activities are Enduring Involvement in Camping (McIntyre, 1989), Measuring Commitment to Running (Carmack and Martens, 1979), Married Couples' Involvement with Family Vacation (Madrigal, Havitz, and Howard, 1992), and Ego Involvement in Recreational Tennis (Siegenthaler and Lam, 1992).

Definitions and Conceptualization of Leisure Involvement

An initial generic and conceptual definition can be stated and followed later by a more elaborate one.

Leisure involvement is viewed here as a state of being a part of what is engaged in, characterized by attachment, excitement, sacrifice, sensing oneness or "weness" with the activity, and the sense of time and place disappears while engaging in such activities.

This initial definition will be followed by further details after mapping and drawing boundaries of leisure involvement.

Definitions of involvement in activities, unlike the above conceptual definition, can be presented on the basis of empirical findings (which are more applied and sophisticated), based on what has been investigated in the way of components. This tends to be more comprehensive and closer to reality. Therefore, it would be more appropriate first to comprehend the parts that make up the whole of leisure involvement. Then, by incorporating and integrating these parts, we can obtain a more rounded concept and definition.

Probably due to the long history of involvement study, complexity, and leisure's centrality in life, leisure investigators have been identifying a large number of the components (parts) of activity-specific involvement. Havitz and Dimanche (1997) very elaborately reviewed investigations conducted in the prior 10 years. They identified all reported hypotheses, research questions, and objectives. Moreover, they reported the factor structures (components) observed in 41 investigations of involvement instruments. (The reader is referred to the above reference for more details on the possible components of leisure involvement.)

Components realized range from Importance (Mittal and Lee, 1988) and Pleasure (Selin and Howard, 1988) to Commitment (Buchanan, 1985) and Ego Involvement (Siegenthaler and Lam, 1992), from Sign Value (Madrigal et al., 1992) and Centrality (Selin and Howard, 1988) to Interest (Kauffman, 1984), and Risk Probability (Dimanche, Havitz, and Howard, 1991).

However, Havitz and Dimanche (1997) claim that measuring leisure and recreation involvement in its totality or generically "may be of little use in most managerial and academic contexts" (pp. 265-266). Fundamentally, then, there is no doubt that activity-specific involvement has practical, academic, and scientific benefits; therefore, measures of that involvement need to be improved in quality and quantity. Nonetheless, it is advocated here that knowledge about and assessment of involvement in leisure lifestyle, as a whole, is as important.

Many applied, academic, and scientific areas can benefit from such generic knowledge of leisure involvement in its totality. Valid conclusions about leisure involvement can contribute significantly to the areas of leisure education, leisure counseling, maintenance of physical and mental health, wellness, vitality, life satisfaction, quality of life, and total functioning. For example, leisure involvement was utilized in a study by Hood (2003) on "Women in recovery from alcoholism: The place of leisure." She found interesting functions. Leisure involvement was reported to be critical in moving beyond just "not drinking" toward true recovery. Respondents found that leisure involvement allowed them to learn about themselves, learn how to accept and appreciate their various attributes and limitations, and take risks as another means of developing self-awareness. How can such relationships be tested in the absence of a global leisure involvement scale?

Other useful applications can include academic preparation, philosophies taught, diagnostic procedures of those uninvolved in leisure, and programming strategies. Finally, to arrive at a sound theory, incorporating total leisure involvement, predicting it, assessment of leisure involvement in its totality is indispensable. This can be a very useful guide to practitioners and scientists. Kerlinger and Lee (2000: 10) once said, "There is nothing as practical as a good theory." While Nunnally (1978: 6) added that "The science of psychology will progress neither slower nor faster than it becomes possible to measure important variables." Therefore, in the absence of generic leisure involvement concepts and a leisure involvement scale, how can relationships be tested between leisure involvement and other total domains such as stress, work satisfaction, health, empowerment, vitality, depression, marital adjustment, and the like? To be incorporated into empirical models, many hypotheses cannot be examined without the availability of an assessment tool for global involvement in leisure.

Fortunately, many components that underlie involvement in specific activities are identified on empirical bases; but, unfortunately, no test has yet been published to discover which of these components make up general/global recreation and leisure involvement. Havitz and Dimanche (1990: 180) once attested to this state, noting that "... the involvement construct has not been extensively studied in our field." This implies the need for the development of one or more leisure involvement scales, realizing their underlying factors. Another interesting point is that other concepts such as leisure attitude, leisure interests, and leisure motivation gained attention in concepts and measurements in their totalities, as well as their specific manifestations (see scales presented in the first part of this book).

After comprehending the diversity of leisure involvement's concepts and components, a second but operational definition must be considered, as stated by Ragheb (1996):

> *Leisure involvement is the state of commitment to, centrality of, and interest in an individual's favorite leisure pursuits. This state is demonstrated through the reported degree of importance of choices made, meanings desired, intensity of engagement, ego attachment, self-expression, and how valuable leisure is to one's life.*

Further verification of the leisure involvement construct, testing its definitional structure and the logic behind it, is needed in order for provision of leisure services to advance through research on the subject and improvements in practice.

Types of Involvement

The literature recognizes certain important types of involvement that help in its comprehension: felt involvement (Celsi and Olson, 1988), enduring involvement (McIntyre, 1989), and situational involvement (Richins, Bloch, and McQuarrie, 1992).

1. *Felt involvement* is like "felt needs," described by Edginton et al. (1998) — it is realized but not acted upon.
2. *Enduring involvement* expresses a high level of intensity and duration of current engagement in an activity or endeavor.
3. *Situational involvement* is a short-lived encounter or interest, or a momentary attention span, mostly material or social (such as buying clothes or cars), or going to a park with others on the spur of the moment.

Havitz and Mannell (2005) performed an interesting study to test associations between enduring involvement, situational involvement, and flow. They found that after three months respondents in leisure and non-leisure activities who had higher levels of enduring involvement were more likely to experience higher levels of flow even though situational involvement mediated these associations.

Evaluation of the State of Knowledge of the Parts of Leisure Involvement

Before integrating all available parts in a conceptual frame, some issues should be evaluated and addressed. These issues are relevant to potential gaps and problems with the state of knowledge of leisure involvement. Some components of leisure involvement seem to be missing in their pertinence and development: intensity of involvement, flow, absorption, and meaning behind involvement. In this section we will elaborate on these missing components.

First, what is intensity? In a psychosocial study, Wild, Kuiken, and Schopflocher (1995) illustrate some interesting characteristics of intensity; that is, when "we are 'immersed' in activities, 'captured' by feelings, 'absorbed' in imagery and dreams, 'riveted' by interactions with others, and so on" (p. 569). Knowledge of intensity, in this context, can be very useful to leisure professionals and researchers if they are going to be able to facilitate for it or assess it whenever it occurs. Similarly, Tinsley and Tinsley (1986) and Baldwin and Tinsley (1988) observed important aspects in order for a person to experience leisure — which fit neatly the above-mentioned characteristics: "intensity of emotion" and "absorption of the task."

Absorption — as a central characteristic of intensity — can be illustrated using a fanciful comparison. Absorption in activities is an earthly black hole, which powerfully draws individuals toward the focus of their chosen activities in the same way that black holes in space draw in all surrounding matter and light. Such a "black hole" can forcefully draw a person deep within what is being done, bringing a quick and full unification with the task or experience. This "black hole" involvement can be characterized mainly as being loaded emotionally, mentally, and spiritually. Realistically, not many individuals are fortunate, prepared, or synthesized enough to experience this hypothetical state of "black hole absorption" in their leisure pursuits. However, individuals experience different levels of absorption in their leisure endeavors from very weak to very strong. Achieving strength in absorption contributes to the flow of events and how fast time passes. Sometimes unknown conditions are required to achieve this state.

All earthly matters — marriage and the family, work or school, and free time activities — possess the potential to attain this "black hole" experience. Yet, the nature and characteristics of leisure, in particular, inherently provide numerous opportunities to be powered toward such "black hole" intensity. Ultimately to be drawn toward and unified with a sense of absorption is considered the highest enjoyable state of involvement. This issue can be investigated scientifically, simply by asking people to rate their interest in what they engage in, their absorption, and the intensity they experienced in different life activities: work, family, and leisure (see Yankelovich, 1978). For meanings derived from life domains we can use a tool like Tellegen's (1982) Absorption Scale. Moreover, with further development of leisure absorption and intensity instrumentations, depth of absorption in family, work, and leisure can be investigated; compared, differentiated, and facilitated.

Integrating all of intensity's characteristics (indicators) in a true leisure experience, as noted above, would put the individual in a state of being extremely attentive. Usually, s/he withdraws from daily entanglements, focusing, contemplating, and concentrating on what is pursued, without regard to time, place, and sometimes companions! This state — in its purest sense — can be observed in children's play in their early years (one to five years of age) characterized by being uninterrupted. The identified degree of pertinence of intensity to leisure involvement endorses its position of importance and need for further psychometric development.

Two valuable factors were recognized for their connectedness to leisure intensity: flow and intrinsic motivation. Csikszentmihalyi (1990) illustrates how intensity and flow seem to be interwoven together, describing it as the optimal state of inner feeling. This was labeled further as "psychic energy" or "attention." When skills match opportunities, focusing increases. On the other hand, when there is a lack of flow, certain insightful reactions can take place. This makes us (practitioners and scientists) more informed and appreciative of the above-described *"state of flow."* On the anti-flow relevance to lack of intensity, Vodanovich and Watt (1999) observed that time structure (interrupting flow) seemed to be associated with boredom proneness scores. Furthermore, in a methodological study, it was found that "Slowness of Time" and "Lack of Mental Involvement" were two of four components that compose free time boredom structure (Ragheb and Merydith, 2000). Therefore, it seems that flow and intensity of involvement have negative relationships to boredom.

Moreover, intrinsically motivated leisure feelings associate with intensity of involvement equally well, as does the optimal state of flow. There are social and psychological claims that intrinsic motivation functions as an underlying factor, determining the level of involvement. Activities are perceived as interesting and pleasurable when they are ends in themselves — intrinsically motivated (see Wild et al., 1995; Weissinger and Bandalos, 1995). This view of how intensity and motivation are interwoven illustrates further the uniqueness of leisure involvement as stated before.

In conclusion, there is sufficient knowledge supporting the notion of intensity as an important domain in the concept of leisure involvement. Knowing about the nature of involvement, its definition, and its assessment can have practical and scientific implications. It can be defined as:

Intensity of involvement is an exceptionally high degree of immersion in a self-determined leisure experience that can be characterized as having optimal flow, intrinsic motivation, concentration, and reaching a peak in energizing and contributing to individuals' leisure expectations.

Many benefits can be reaped from familiarity with such concepts: practitioners can provide services that facilitate for intensity, offer guidance and counseling to achieve it, devise strategies for intensity needs, and design facilities conducive to the achievement of this state of involvement. On the other hand, scientists can investigate its relationship to other variables. Ultimately, leisure involvement would be positioned in its deserving place in new theoretical structures. In turn, this would contribute to future psychometric development of leisure involvement in specific activities and general pursuits.

Another potentially useful component to the understanding of leisure involvement is the notion of the *search for meaning*. For mental health maintenance, individuals seek the realization of meaningful experiences in whatever they do, including play, fitness, recreation, and leisure. Most likely, when meaning or purpose ceases, irrelevance and un-involvement follow, with boredom operating as a potential moderator. In many cases, individuals are unaware of this reoccurring process, leading to feelings of emptiness, vacuum, or loss, as follows:

> *Lack of Meaning*
> → *Boredom*
> → *Un-involvement*
> → *Emptiness*

Regarding the missing component of meaning, leisure choices do not exist haphazardly. They exist for a reason or a goal. Frankl (1962 and 1992) observed that the most human motivation is "the will to meaning." He added that meaning is not invented but discovered through actions, attitudes, and achievements. Due to the nature of informal activities (leisure, recreation, fitness, and travel), they seem to be rich providers of actions and achievements, which supply an abundance of meanings. It depends on how a person recognizes it, discovers it, and views it. Meaning can be found in and supplied by many actions and choices: including the arts, outdoor recreation, physical activities, exercise, tourism, hobbies, volunteering, cultural activities, social activities, skill acquisition, reading, meditation, music, and intellectual choices. Individuals maintain involvement in activities like the above as long as they derive meaning and purpose from doing them, quitting them when this sense ceases or deteriorates.

Practically, there seems to be a relationship between lack of meaningful involvement and boredom (see Barbalet, 1999). In another investigation, Lack of Meaningful Involvement (LMI) was the highest contributor to the variance in "Measuring Free Time Boredom," explaining 27.5% out of 45% of the variance (Ragheb and Merydith, 2000). LMI was defined empirically; based on scientific confirmation, as follows: "Individuals regard their free time as boring if it lacks focus, feels empty, consists of meaningless pursuits, occurs in dull surroundings, associates with irritability, and makes it seem as though participants are dragging their feet." In sum, boredom must be removed or at best controlled as a potential constraint before individuals are free to search for meanings and purposes in their leisure involvement. Or, it could be the other way around, when an individual draws meanings from free time involvement, there is no room for boredom to creep into a person's experience.

Possible Reasons for Missing Potentially Important Components

If the relevance of domains such as the search for meaning, absorption, and intensity are critical to leisure involvement — as illustrated — why were they missed or unrecognized in conceptualizations and measurement construction? This issue is fundamentally a content validity concern. Any lack of inclusion of certain components as parts of a concept ultimately will be reflected in its final analysis. The components won't be accounted for in its construct (see the nature of content validity, the first part of this book). This is a validity notion of comprehensiveness of a concept. Also, it is *possible* that the activities investigated (e.g., camping, vacationing, or canoeing) did not exhibit factors that demonstrated intensity or meaning, because intensity and meaning are not parts of the structure of the activities investigated, but are *potentially* parts of other constructs.

Historically, scientists investigating involvement in leisure activities have relied most heavily on ideas and measurements developed to serve marketing and the understanding of consumer behavior (e.g., Dimanche et al., 1991; Twynam, 1993; Havitz and Dimanche, 1997). Naturally, marketing concepts and tools to assess them are different from leisure, recreation, and exercise. The extent of difference is unknown.

Marketing concepts and their tools were forced into the interpretation of informal choices. In that regard, concepts and tools demonstrated the overlap between involvement in informal activities (e.g., leisure) and consumer involvement. They pointed to parts such as risk probability or consequence, self-image, sign value, and perceived risk. All of these might be the primary influence in buying merchandise, but they may be of secondary importance or irrelevant to informal choices. Hence, this can cause ignoring what are possibly primary components to leisure involvement. Primary components of leisure involvement, not the secondary ones, should be tapped and verified.

The concern of advertising and marketing would be more in tune with increasing sales, profits, and maintaining customers, being utilitarian. But much less attention is paid to involving individuals for outcomes of leisure experience, such as aesthetic values, flow, peak experience, intrinsic enjoyment, having a sense of freedom and control, experiencing intensity in engagement, and finding meaning in chosen pursuits. There is no denying that components overlap between marketing and recreation activities; but, as demonstrated previously, leisure involvement must be uniquely characterized and recognized based on its nature. Considering what is known and what is missing about leisure involvement creates a complicated, confusing situation. Therefore, further deliberate effort is needed to discover the real structure of each construct for the following rationale, however complicated the task may be.

All behavioral and social domains seem to be unclear, lacking detailed knowledge. They are highly detailed and tangled. For example, domains such as depression, motivation, interests, vitality, and emotions are as complicated as involvement in activities, if not more so. Despite this complexity, researchers — equipped with scientific tools — attempt to uncover the latent and underlying structures of concepts, such as depression.

Attempts are made, despite the fact that individuals vary in their subjective sadness or depressed reactions to life, because there are common and unique characteristics shared by those who are struck with that mood. For instance, as knowledge of depression and its assessment advance, scholars continue to find that there are certain components in depression, such as hopelessness and helplessness. Beck (1987) realized that there is a cognitive triad that triggers depression — a negative view of self, a tendency to interpret experience in a negative manner, and having a gloomy vision about the future. Leisure involvement is no different in its nature and complexity. Underlying components can be revealed with a high degree of consistency among different populations.

Theories That Can Help Leisure Involvement Scales, Science, and Practice

Some humanistic and growth theories can help explain the nature of leisure involvement. These theories can be used as bases for the development of involvement instruments. Examples of those useful explanations are Self-Determination Theory (Rotter,

1954), Attribution Theory (Heider, 1958), Human Motivation Theory "Peak Experience" (Maslow, 1962), Man's Search for Meaning (Frankl, 1962), and Cognitive Evaluation (Self-Determination) Theory (Deci and Ryan, 1985). In scale development, one of those theories can be used as a foundation of a given scale, assessing certain leisure involvement or functions. At best, a group of these theories are pooled to identify possible structure and components to be tested and verified.

Scientists, after devising a measurement of involvement, can test its relationships to leisure and life satisfaction, quality of life, boredom control, stress control, empowerment, wellness, vitality, total functioning, and even longevity. Moreover, intensity of leisure involvement — like commitment, sign-value, and importance — deserves an exclusive measure to assess it. All conditions to develop the intensity of involvement scale are available: knowledge, components, and indicators. They are waiting for a methodological exploration.

This type of measure can be useful in program planning, leisure education, leisure counseling and guidance, and for the improvement of mental health and stress control. Finally, a large number of measurements assessing leisure involvement, specific and general, were constructed in the last quarter of the 20th century, as presented below. Unlike leisure attitude, where all scales assess general attributes, involvement scales almost exclusively assess involvement in specific leisure activities, such as outdoor activities or physical recreation.

Frequency of Leisure Participation and Leisure Involvement

Based on the above knowledge on leisure involvement, a critical issue needs to be addressed, assessing the magnitude of engagement in leisure. Of the two concepts relevant to the domain, leisure participation or leisure involvement, which is more valid? Which one reflects reality? Also, which one is more useful? In measuring leisure participation, scientists ask, "How frequently do you participate in the following leisure activities?" Then they provide a list of activities to be rated (from 10 or so to more than 200 activities; see the chapter on Leisure Interests). Activities assessed can cover categories such as outdoor activities, physical recreation activities, hobbies, cultural activities, the mass media, and social activities. Accordingly, people are rated as high or low participants (see McKechnie, 1974; Ragheb, 1980; for illustrations of leisure categories).

Utilizing the frequency of leisure participation versus leisure involvement is a major validity concern. Which of the above concepts must be relied on? In response, frequency of participation in leisure activities has been accounted for, testing its relationship to other essential life domains (e.g., Ragheb and Griffith, 1982; Ragheb and McKinney, 1993; Hsieh, 1999). However, assessing leisure involvement seems to be more accurate in representing engagement (or the status of leisure in individuals' lives) than simple Frequency of Leisure Participation (FOLP), for reasons advocated here:

First, involvement seems to possess some unique features. Involvement, more than sheer participation in a number of activities, can reflect interest in what is done without regard to quantity, represented by the term "frequency" and number of activities done.

Second, involvement can tap the importance of, commitment to the activities engaged in, and the magnitude of intensity while doing them. The emphasis in involvement is focused upon the quality of such engagements — on personal regards and subjective meaning, rather than just performing the activities or being there while the activity is performed.

Third, involvement can be considered the spirit of participation, or its life. For example, a given person may show interest in a small number of activities as assessed by FOLP; but, on the other hand, s/he does these activities with high motivation and commitment, showing substantial attraction, attention, concentration, and intensity. The person is more than being there while the activity is being performed. All of these are good qualities that FOLP alone does not reveal. Another person might be rated high on FOLP but with much less focus, less interest, and less attention to the activities.

According to contemporary empirical evidence, this might characterize persons who rate themselves "high" on sensation seeking in their search for the mirage (the illusion) of more frequent participation and high-risk activities (see Spence, 1998; Gordon and Caltabiano, 1996; Iso-Ahola and Crowley, 1991; Rowland et al., 1986). More evidence revealed that sensation seeking associates with leisure boredom (Iso-Ahola and Weissinger, 1990).

Hence, the number of activities alone can produce the illusionary effect of high participation in activities but without density or substance. Leisure's social-psychological impact on behavioral phenomena (mental health, satisfaction, functioning, and stress) is not in the number of activities performed; rather, it seems that it is in the substance or density of outcomes (output) through the manifestations of experiential rewards, self-expression, achievement of a sense of purpose, and positive self-concept. Outputs and outcomes are all expressions of the levels of involvement and their quality, being a part of and unified with leisure actions.

Overall, assessment of FOLP would not be representative of individuals' *true* leisure situation or position. In some cases, a person shows high participation (reporting doing many activities), while s/he is truly uninvolved. In other cases, low participation is shown while the person is immersed and absorbed in just one or a few leisure activities: oil painting, exercising, and/or playing piano, for example. Therefore, it seems that the value of leisure in an individual's life should not be a matter of quantity (FOLP) but rather of quality (Involvement).

The merit and the reliance on scales assessing FOLP needs to be reevaluated, by comparing them to leisure involvement. It is suggested here to employ leisure involvement measurements. This is in order to truly capture individuals' leisure status, positions, and the true "reality" (Kerlinger and Lee, 2000), unless an important need exists to measure FOLP for its merit and relevancy.

In some unique cases, FOLP rather than involvement is indispensable. For example, FOLP should be utilized when a scientist attempts to investigate leisure participation *patterns* as they relate to other domains (Stodolska, 2000; Goldstein, 1998); or relating the level of structured versus unstructured activities to certain functions (Mahoney and Stattin, 2000); or when frequency of participation is employed as an indicator of the level of doing a specific activity, such as whitewater kayaking (see Schuett, 1993). Also FOLP would be needed when programming for activities, requiring frequencies of doing activities. There are times when FOLP is the most appropriate — sometimes the only — tool that fulfills the goals of a certain study, situation, or evaluation. Otherwise, careful considerations need to be applied, utilizing leisure involvement scales as they best fit.

The Network of Relationships of Leisure Involvement to Other Determinants and Consequences

The degree of involvement is determined by a number of aspects that contribute to the level of certain outcomes. Aspects that can determine involvement can be a person's leisure attitudes, leisure motivation, and leisure interests, among other factors. On the other hand, some outcomes can be that person's leisure satisfaction, vitality, wellness, and quality of life. These determinants and outcomes will be demonstrated in the behavior model discussed in the following chapters, as shown in Model 2.

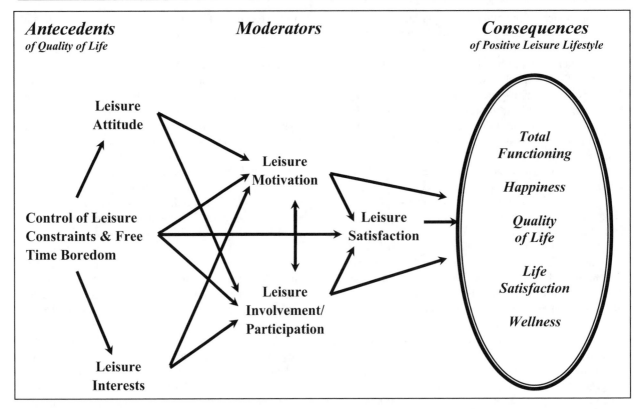

Model 2: Interrelationships among behavioral domains of leisure and recreation functioning (repeated from page 5)

Summary and Conclusions

Involvement has been the concern of many fields. Ego involvement attracted the attention of psychologists in its earliest conceptualization. This was then applied to marketing, consumer behavior, health, sports, politics, students, and (lately) to leisure. The study of involvement in recreation and leisure initially focused on relating it mainly to outdoor activities, travel, and recreational sports. The literature has identified many components to involvement in activities, such as importance, sign value, centrality, and risk probability. Three types of involvement can be recognized: 1. Felt involvement, 2. Enduring involvement, and 3. Situational involvement.

In the zeal to study and explain leisure involvement, five areas were ignored, requiring additional attention because of their potential value and impact. These missing areas are absorption in activities, flow of experiences, intensity in what is done, intrinsic motivation, and meaning in involvement. Accumu-

lated knowledge on intensity of involvement warrants a separate scale to assess it independently. Many psychological theories can help assessing involvement in leisure, recreation, fitness, play, and travel. Finally, it would be unfair to the reader and the field of leisure to pass this opportunity without comparing some of the uses and validities between leisure involvement and frequency of leisure participation. Despite the fact that I engaged in a number of studies relying upon the frequency of leisure participation, it is suggested that leisure involvement is more meritorious for qualities that are inherent in the context of the concept. Some rare and clear exceptions that would demand otherwise were presented.

Many measurements exist (reported below), attempting to abstract their content for practical and research uses. Moreover, these identified scales can stimulate necessary measurements that are lacking and relate the existing ones to other pertinent domains.

Existing Measures Assessing Leisure: Involvement-Specific and Involvement-General

1. Leisure Activities Blank (LAB) (McKechnie, 1974) (Participation)
2. Measuring Commitment to Running (MCR) (Carmack and Martens, 1979)
3. Enduring Involvement in Camping (EIC) (McIntyre, 1989)
4. Processes of Change Questionnaire (PCQ) (Marcus, Rossi, Selby, Niaura, and Abrams, 1992)
5. Exercise's Stages-of-Change (ESoC) (Marcus, Selby, Niaura, and Rossi, 1992)
6. Self-Efficacy for Exercise Behavior Scale (SEEBS) (Marcus et al., 1992)
7. Commitment in Recreational Tennis (CRT) (Siegenthaler and Lam, 1992)
8. Ego Involvement in Recreational Tennis (EIRT) (Siegenthaler and Lam, 1992)
9. Married Couples' Involvement with Family Vacation (MCIFV) (Madrigal et al., 1992)
10. Adolescent Ethical Behavior in Leisure Scale (AEBLS) (Widmer et al., 1996)
11. Assessment of Leisure and Recreation Involvement (LRI) (Ragheb, 1996)
12. Exercise Imagery Questionnaire — Aerobic Version (EIQ) (Hausenblas et al., 1999)

The Assessment of Leisure and Recreation Involvement is shown on the following pages. Looking at the description of how the assessment was developed will help in understanding the concepts described in Part II of this book. The overview of the assessment was presented on page 278. Questions and exercises follow the scale.

Assessment of Leisure and Recreation Involvement

Assessment of Leisure and Recreation Involvement by Mounir G. Ragheb
Manual for the *Assessment of Leisure and Recreation Involvement* by Mounir G. Ragheb and joan burlingame

The *Assessment of Leisure and Recreation Involvement* (*LRI*) measures a participant's perception of his/her involvement in leisure and recreation. There is a difference between participation and involvement in activities. Participation tends to be a linear concept that measures the quality and quantity of effort made by a participant during an activity. Being involved in leisure and recreation means that an individual has specific (usually positive) feelings about the activity, believes that the activity adds a positive value to his/her life, and is committed to engage in the activity. Involvement is feelings, values, and commitment. Leisure involvement, therefore, is a multifaceted cognitive and emotional state. Involvement has six cognitive/emotional elements that influence actual participation in an activity:

- Importance of the activity
- Pleasure derived from the activity
- Interest in the activity
- Intensity of, or absorption in, the activity
- Centrality of the activity to the individual's perception of self
- Meaning of the activity

This involvement is measured by the participant's rating of importance of leisure choices made, meanings derived, and pleasures obtained from his/her own leisure. The development of a valid and reliable testing tool to measure the various components of involvement — a state based on an individual's environment, knowledge, and current situation and which cannot be accurately measured by observation — historically has proven to be a challenge. Following standards for the scientific development of testing tools, the *Assessment of Leisure and Recreation Involvement* was created to measure what is labeled as the cognitive and emotional involvement in leisure and recreation, through a self-report form using a Likert scale.

At first pass the definition of involvement and the concept behind it seem deceivingly simple. However, leisure involvement is not a simple concept due to the diversity and complexity of what compels an individual to become and stay involved. Some individuals can participate in certain leisure and recreation activities without feeling involved — showing no commitment, interest, or importance — while others can be rated high on all accounts. Individual orientation is the determining factor that the *Assessment of Leisure and Recreation Involvement* attempts to measure and record.

When we measure leisure involvement, we are measuring the degree of commitment to, the perceived value (centrality) of, and the interest in leisure that the individual holds. But how can we do that? Because trying to accurately interpret an individual's thoughts and beliefs by observation alone is not possible, we must use other methods. There have been numerous attempts in the past to measure degree of involvement in leisure. One of the greatest challenges has been in defining "commitment," "value/centrality," and "interest." Some of the suggestions have included measuring the reported level (number) of leisure choices made, meanings derived, pleasures obtained, perceived compatibilities with an individual's mental thought process, belief systems (ego attachment), opportunities for self-expression, and perceived values derived.

Using the *Assessment of Leisure and Recreation Involvement* we are now able to define and describe involvement in leisure and recreation. *Table 1: Components of Concepts in Leisure and Recreation Involvement as a Research Finding* provides the six subscales that have been found to make up the construct of involvement and describes the characteristics of high and low involvement. This manual takes the reader through the process used to arrive at these six subscales: the reliability and validity of the *Assessment of Leisure and Recreation Involvement*, instructions for administering the tool, and possible implications of scores.

Why Develop a Tool to Measure Involvement?

How can we use and benefit from involvement in the leisure and recreation domain without knowing two basic aspects about it: concept and measurement? A domain's concept needs to be defined — realizing its details, attributes, and characteristics, leading to the ability to assess it, look for it, and find it, without confusion with other domains — in a complicated network of life dimensions. This required following systematic methods. To this end, leisure is an emerging domain, in terms of importance, that requires more conceptualization and assessment.

Moreover, there is evidence that informal activities (such as leisure) are growing in their positive impacts on individuals and society (Dubin, 1956; Dumazedier, 1967; Inglehart, 1990; Kelly and Kelly, 1994; Newsletter, 1996) and need to be balanced with formal activities (work and family). For instance, in a

Table 1: Components of Leisure and Recreation Involvement as a Research Finding

Concept	Examples
Importance	*High score:* would reserve time for leisure endeavors, rearranges schedule to allow time for these pursuits, has a focus on activities, considers activities as part of lifestyle, gives them special attention.
	Low score: does not allocate time for recreation activities, with no aim or focus toward leisure choices, does not recognize these activities, and does not give them attention as part of daily pursuits.
Pleasure	*High score:* claims enjoyment, speedy time passage, feels full after engaging in recreation activities, identifies with activities, able to entertain self, and proud of chosen activities.
	Low score: finds little or no enjoyment in leisure, claims that time is a drag when engaged in recreation activities, reports dissatisfaction with leisure choices, lacks self-entertainment through recreation, has no pride in leisure and recreation pursuits.
Interest	*High score:* wants to know details about leisure activities that express wishes, considers leisure choices worthwhile, serving certain goals or aims, practices skills needed to improve performance of the activities.
	Low score: feels that leisure activities are trivial, has no desire to learn details about leisure pursuits, does not practice leisure skills, mostly aimless during free time without goal or orientation.
Intensity	*High score:* feels that leisure activities occupy feelings, uses activities to help in discovering things about self, not easily distracted while pursuing favorite leisure activities, claims that leisure pursuits give a sense of inner freedom, expects positive outcome from leisure endeavors.
	Low score: considers leisure activities peripheral, is easily distracted while doing a leisure activity, claims no discoveries or realization through leisure choices, lacks a sense of inner freedom and intrinsic relatedness, with negative or no expectations from leisure and recreation pursuits.
Centrality	*High score:* has a sense of self-responsibility toward choices made to participate in leisure activities, ready to devote effort to master activities, strives to achieve and do well, willing to invest money, time, and energy in leisure pursuits.
	Low score: does not intend to put effort into skill acquisition and activity mastery, does not invest to achieve or succeed in recreation pursuits, lacks self-responsibility about leisure outcome.
Meaning	*High score:* claims that leisure choices give life meaning and flavor, feels that leisure activities help in expressing self, possesses knowledge of chosen leisure activities greater than the average person, gains a sense of value in life through leisure, feels lost without leisure activities.
	Low score: has no self-expression through leisure and recreation activities, shows that these activities do not contribute to the search for meaning in general, has minimum or no knowledge about what is done as leisure choices, lacks sense of value in life derived from leisure.

study of 11 nations (the United States is one of them), Inglehart (1990) observed a shift away from material aspects, toward more attention to quality of life and self-expression. Back in the 1950s, at the root of this shifting phenomenon, Dubin (1956) found that 75 percent of the sample considered the family, leisure, and their well-being to be more important than work, in contrast to 24 percent reporting "work orientation" as more central to their lives. The development of balance among family, leisure, and work — with this order of importance — was confirmed by Kelly and Kelly (1994).

Therefore, with increasing free time (Robbinson, 1990) and time devoted to leisure (Neulinger, 1974), understanding and assessing involvement tends to be critical for engagement in leisure pursuits. This is critical for the following reasons: 1. Knowing and assessing leisure involvement can help to diagnose lack of involvement, which can be used as the basis for leisure education and leisure counseling, thus creating awareness and positive orientation with leisure, maximizing leisure benefits. 2. The availability of such a measurement can help in testing leisure's relationship to other important social and behavioral phenomena (such as health, adjustment, hope, purpose in life, stress, life satisfaction, work productivity, and quality of life). Hence, incorporating the concept of leisure involvement in future studies would help test and establish more realistic models and theories for a growing domain. In sum, to achieve the above practical and scientific goals, a major prerequisite step needs to be satisfied: the development of a psychometrically validated instrument to assess leisure and recreation involvement.

Background in Construct Development of Involvement

Historically, how have researchers defined what it means to be involved in an activity or an action? Involvement concepts went through a long evolution from interpreting observed behavior (empirical studies) to more formal scientific review. These studies were an attempt at explaining why, most of the time, humans keep on doing or choosing certain products or activities. About 50 years ago, psychologists initiated the study of involvement. Since then, many applied fields utilized this concept to understand involvement in their specific practices or products (see Bryant and Wang, 1990; Holbrook and Hirschman, 1982; Rean, 1984; and Sherif and Cantril, 1947; Sherif, Sherif, and Nebergall, 1965). Then, starting with the early seventies, involvement concepts were applied in marketing to help predict consumer behavior (e.g., Good, 1990; Hupfer and Gardner, 1971; Mittal and Lee, 1989; Ram and Jung, 1994; Tybjee, 1979). From the end of the seventies, efforts were made to measure consumers' involvement (Laurent and Kapferer, 1985; Peter, 1979; Zaichkowsky, 1985). Fields such as education, marriage, work, and several other areas began to try to measure involvement.

The fields of leisure and recreation found it relevant to look at basic involvement concepts. Numerous authors worked to define, understand, and comprehend the concept of involvement and its implications for leisure and recreation participation (e.g., Bloch, 1993; Bryan, 1977; Havitz and Dimanche, 1990; McIntyre, 1989; Siegenthaler and Lam, 1992; Wellman, Roggenbuck, and Smith, 1982). Consequently, involvements in specific leisure and recreation pursuits, such as fishing and travel, have been the focus of abstraction and construct development, as a second step. Measurements were constructed, for example, to assess involvement in vacationing, camping, fishing, tennis, athletics, adornments, whitewater kayaking, and canoeing (Bloch, 1993; Bryan, 1977; Dimanche, Havitz, and Howard, 1991; Madrigal, Havitz, and Howard, 1992; McIntyre, 1989; Siegenthaler and Lam, 1992; Wellman, Roggenbuck, and Smith, 1982). In spite of all these efforts and all the data collected, there was a lack of research geared toward discovering the more global construct of involvement.

The original work on defining the concept (ideas about) and construct (elements of) leisure and recreation involvement focused on choices people made engaging in specific activities such as baseball or skiing and on the variables that impacted these decisions. Much of this work relied on research in social psychology. This influence from research in social psychology slowly shifted to influences from research in consumer and marketing behaviors. (For more details, see Bloch, 1993 and Dimanche, Havitz and Howard, 1991.)

For us to better understand the global concept of what influences people to be involved in leisure and recreation activities, we need to look at three different areas: 1. conceptualizations of ideas in an attempt to formally describe involvement in leisure and recreation (e.g., Mannell, 1980; Havitz and Dimanche, 1990; Selin and Howard, 1988), 2. construct development to define how different elements of the concept fit together, and 3. empirical examinations of the relationship between involvement in leisure and recreation activities and other factors (e.g., Ap, Dimanche, and Havitz, 1994; Lee, 1990; Madrigal, Havitz, and Howard, 1992). To arrive at a concept of what *being involved* means, and to understand the subcomponents of involvement (construct) we will need to draw from research that has used standard forms of scientific study to verify the concept and its constructs. We also need to compare our research findings with evaluations of real life experiences (empirical studies) to validate our definition of, and manner of evaluating, involvement in leisure and recreation.

Because so much of our early understanding of involvement came from looking at involvement in other activities, such as marriage (social psychology), shopping (marketing and consumer studies), there is still a lack of conceptualization and available instruments to measure involvement in leisure and recreation in general. The purpose of this work was to employ a scientifically sound strategy to develop a scale assessing leisure and recreation involvement in its totality, and to be able to understand its concept more accurately. This required three steps. The first step was to develop an initial operational definition to guide future studies. The second step was the abstraction of leisure and recreation involvement concepts: identifying its components, connotations, indicators, and items. The third step was to give the newly developed test to different groups to allow us to conduct empirical validations. This required specific phases of test development: 1. evaluating how successful we were in accurately grouping the components or subscales, 2. drawing upon different groups of subjects to fill out their answers on the testing tool, and 3. applying a variety of statistical procedures to calculate how close the concept, construct, and testing tool itself came to defining involvement in leisure and recreation. Finally, steps were taken to gain an understanding of the concept, structure, and meaning of leisure involvement, as well as to assess it.

Conceptualization

Wild, Kuiken, and Schopflocher (1995) used the phrase "experiential involvement" to refer to when an individual is "immersed" in activities, "captured" by feelings, "absorbed" in imagery and dreams, and "riveted" by interactions. Moreover, they proposed that aesthetic experience, flow (Csikszentmihalyi, 1975), intrinsic motivation, and peak experience (Maslow, 1967) also are all instances of experiential involvement. Privette (1983) felt that peak experience and flow are characterized by absorption and involvement. These specific ingredients and characteristics are basic to understanding involvement and its development. The concept of leisure involvement originates from these different works.

A growing body of literature suggested multiple classifications to the concept of leisure involvement. More than ten factors of leisure involvement were documented by scientific evidence. For example, importance-pleasure was found as a factor underlying specific leisure involvement (Dimanche, Havitz, and Howard, 1991; Madrigal, Havitz, and Howard, 1992; Unger and Kernan, 1983; Watkins, 1986). The magnitude of the findings of the importance-pleasure factor endorses the fact that this factor will be excellent in the conceptualization of overall or global leisure involvement. Commitment to the activity or dedication and continuance was a dimension observed in some other studies (Buchanan, 1985; Schreyer and Beaulieu, 1986; Siegenthaler and Lam, 1992). Sign value, defined as belonging to an activity to differentiate oneself from others, was recognized in some of the above studies, as an attribute of involvement (Dimanche, Havitz, and Howard, 1991; Madrigal, Havitz, and Howard, 1992). One component of involvement identified by numerous authors is centrality of the activity, or how important the activity is to the participant (McIntyre, 1989; Wellman, Roggenbuck, and Smith, 1982). Also, intensity was reported as a component underlying involvement (Shields, Franks, Harp, McDaniel, and Campbell, 1992; Stamm and Dube, 1994). Finally, the realization of "meaning" or "meaningful involvement" was reported in other studies (Brook, and Brook, 1989, McIntyre, 1989; Roelofs, 1992; Shaw, 1985). Minor factors were found to be relevant to involvement in different leisure activities, such as risk probability, level of experience, attractiveness, direction, skill, and self-expression (Bloch, 1993; Bryan, 1977; Kauffman, 1984; McIntyre, 1989). Therefore, involvement in specific leisure activities seems well-researched, and is a well-documented phenomenon today. Leisure involvement (in specific leisure activities and global leisure experience) will be needed as societies advance (see Rojek, 1995, for leisure and modernity).

Construct Development

There was no shortage of possible components underlying involvement in specific leisure activities. But the literature was still missing scientifically arrived at knowledge to help us bridge the gap between understanding how the things that make an individual want to be involved in a single type of activity relate to wanting to be involved in leisure and recreation in general. The professional literature in other fields or literature relating to specific activities in the fields of leisure and recreation failed to provide us with guidance as to which elements were really important. In other words, are commitment, sign value, and self-expression the best factors to predict leisure involvement? Or, do importance-pleasure, ego involvement, centrality, and interest explain leisure involvement better? Which combination, empirically, underlies the structure of the construct "leisure involvement?" As Havitz and Dimanche (1990, p. 180) noted, "Despite considerable conceptual discussion suggesting that involvement is a central part of the leisure experience, the involvement construct has not been extensively studied in our field. Several authors have considered involvement in their research without explicitly studying the construct." Therefore, investigating the construct of leisure and recreation involvement required the development of a testing tool to be able to allow us to test both our concept and construct.

Involvement in specific recreation activities has many elements or constructs. To define leisure involvement operationally each of the subcomponents were defined. The definitions assigned to each of the subcomponents are based on theoretical and conceptual definitions found in the literature cited above.

1. *Importance* is the magnitude to which a person equates a situation or stimulus to either salient-enduring or situation-specific goals (Bloch and Richins, 1983).
2. *Pleasure* is the expectation and realization of express rewards (Selin and Howard, 1988).
3. *Commitment* is the pledging or binding of an individual to behavioral acts that result in some degree of affective attachment to the behavior (Buchanan, 1985).
4. *Ego Involvement* is the identification of self with an activity (Siegenthaler and Lam, 1992).
5. *Sign Value* is an individual's association with or belonging to a group of superior

status (Baudrillard, 1970).

6. *Centrality* is the role assigned to a leisure activity relative to other life interests (Selin and Howard, 1988).

7. *Intensity/Absorption* is the depth of engagement in a leisure activity or experience, characterized by a mood of high concentration, and reflected in the level of immersion or absorption in the designated choice (Ragheb, 1999).

8. *Meaning* in leisure is the individual's striving and search for mental, physical, social, and spiritual realization while fulfilling the individual's potential. (Frankl, 1962)

9. *Interest* is preferences for leisure activities (Ragheb and Beard, 1992).

A scale assessing involvement in leisure and recreation was constructed. The literature identified at least nine major components and some minor ones underlying involvement in specific recreation activities. These were used to begin the process of verifying that a viable tool, which would have reasonable validity and reliability, could be developed.

Once this first draft of a tool to measure involvement was developed, it was administered to two different groups. One group had 123 people and the second group had 176 people. Using basic statistical procedures to analyze the way the subjects responded to the questions, the first draft of the testing tool was re-written by refining the items and the number of components included. The final field test (218 subjects) yielded six factors, importance, pleasure, interest, intensity/absorption, centrality, and meaning. All factors were well suggested by the literature. As a result, alpha reliability coefficient of the *Assessment of Leisure and Recreation Involvement* was sufficiently high (.95); the components ranged from .78 to .90, and interfactor correlations ranged from .52 to .70. Laurent and Kapferer's (1985) *Involvement Profile Scale* was adapted to leisure and employed to test the concurrent validity of the *LRI* (r = .54). Moreover, the association between the draft *Assessment of Leisure and Recreation Involvement* and participation in six leisure categories was tested, resulting in some exploratory, interesting findings. Following the above methodology, the *Assessment of Leisure and Recreation Involvement*, a theoretically driven testing tool, was developed demonstrating sufficient psychometric attributes: reliability, validity, and practical usefulness. Details of the development are shown below.

Method

The methodology employed in this investigation started with extracting items relevant to the identified nine major a priori components of involvement in leisure and recreation. Items were developed to incorporate the tapped indicators, then administered in two trials, before final testing. Factor analyses, reliability, and validity tests were conducted to determine the worth of items and subscales.

Item Development

Sixty-three items for leisure and recreation involvement were generated and accepted, incorporating over 90 extracted indicators, tapping the identified nine components yielded from the above literature, in order to be verified in two pilot studies. Components included were 1. importance, 2. pleasure, 3. intensity, 4. interest, 5. commitment, 6. ego involvement, 7. sign value, 8. centrality, and 9. meaning. Items were designed to be easy to read, short, and simple. To develop respondents' frame of reference, each individual was asked — in an open-ended format — to list his or her favorite recreation, leisure, and tourist activities, in which he or she might participate. Illustrations were provided stating that "Examples of such activities are traveling, camping, tennis, oil painting, playing chess, fishing, playing a guitar, gardening, being with others, reading, and personal hobbies." To measure leisure and recreation involvement, a structured set of 63 items was presented. Respondents were asked to indicate the extent of their agreement with each item. A five-point scale was utilized, going from (1) for "Strongly Disagree" to (5) for "Strongly Agree."

Leisure and recreation activities were defined as non-work or non-school activities, taking place in free time, in which an individual has a free choice, with less obligation to participate. Attention was drawn to the activities listed by the respondent in the above open-ended item, to guide an individual's ratings and extent of agreement with items.

Pretests

In the first pretest, the initial pool of over 90 items was exposed to a careful revision by the investigator and three faculty members, then by eight graduate and undergraduate students who had past background in fundamental concepts of leisure. Items were checked for the following: 1. relevance to the domain of leisure and recreation involvement, 2. clarity and simplicity of content, and 3. possible duplications among items. These steps were utilized to modify, delete, add, or maintain items in the pool. As a result, 63 items were retained for verification in the first pilot study. Then, the verified instrument was tested in a second pilot study, containing 57 revised items. Lastly, after some modifications were made, a version of 52 items was ready to be validated in a final field testing.

Samples and Administration

The initial version of the *Assessment of Leisure and Recreation Involvement* (*LRI*) (63 items) was administered in five classes, chosen by random sampling from a southeastern university, representing colleges or schools of business administration, education, human sciences, engineering, and history. Students had the option not to be a part of this study, which yielded a usable sample size of 123 participants. The second pretest employed a sample of 176 from similar classes.

Statistical Analyses

Statistical analyses reported here were utilized in the two pilot studies and the final field test. Data were analyzed using the Statistical Package for the Social Sciences (SPSS) (Release 4.0). To test the factor structure, principle component factor analysis (Varimax rotation) and item and test analyses were employed. Confirmatory factor analysis was most suited to the situation of *LRI*, since there had been extensive relevant findings on the status of those domains. The item and test analyses were based on these treatments: inter-item correlations, item-total correlations, and Cronbach alpha reliability coefficients, for each component and the total scale. An alpha level of .05 was utilized for all statistical treatments. The intention was to form long and shorter versions of the same scale, for there is a need for shorter, more economical, and more efficient scales.

Final Field Test

The purpose of this final stage was to further inspect the stability of the factors, their reliabilities, and test their validity. To test concurrent validity of the *LRI* (52 items), Laurent and Kapferer's (1985) involvement profile scale was adapted for leisure. Examples of adapted items are, "Where I go for leisure choices says something about me" and "I attach great importance to my leisure activities." Moreover, frequency of leisure participation was included to test its relationship to *LRI*. Thirty-nine areas of activities under six categories: mass media, outdoor activities, sports activities, social activities, cultural activities, and hobbies were used. Examples of items assessing participation in outdoor activities are fishing, hunting, traveling, boating, nature study, camping, and sunbathing. The scales were administered to a sample of 218 employees and students. The sample is described in *Table 2: Description of the Final Sample*. Data of this final field test was analyzed, employing the same statistical procedures previously reported.

Results

Factor Structure and Analysis

Testing the confirmatory conceptual structure, factor analysis (Varimax rotation) was performed. Biserial correlation between items and their *LRI* subscales' scores was considered first. To decide on how many factors to use, the Scree test (Cattell, 1966) was conducted and eigenvalues were evaluated carefully. Using the eigenvalue of one criterion, as extracted from the principal components' analysis, 11 factors emerged, showing a variance of 69.3%. By studying the results of the Scree test, it demonstrated a sharp drop in the eigenvalues between the sixth and seventh factors. This finding suggested a clear six-factor solution. Their eigenvalues were 18.6, 3.6, 2.6, 1.9, 1.7,

Table 2: Description of the Final Sample

Sex	n	%	Marital Status	n	%
Female	118	54	Single	114	52
Male	98	45	Married	79	36
Omitted	2	1	Divorced	13	6
			Separated	5	2
Income	**n**	**%**	Widowed	2	1
Less than 10,000	95	43	Omitted	5	2
10,001-25,000	67	31			
25,001-40,000	21	10	**Education**	**n**	**%**
40,001-55,000	13	6	High School	97	45
55,001 or over	17	8	College	89	41
Omitted	5	2	Graduate School	29	13
			Omitted	3	1
Age	**n**	**%**			
Under 23 years	82	38	**Employment Status**	**n**	**%**
24-33 years	33	15	Full-time	106	49
34-43 years	37	17	Part-time	47	21
44-53 years	42	19	Unemployed	24	11
54 or older	18	8	None of the above	17	8
Omitted	6	3	Omitted	24	11

and 1.6, which accounted for 57.5% of the variance in item responses. *Table 3: Factor Structure for Multidimensional Leisure and Recreation Involvement Scale and Item-Subscale Correlations* represents items that were endorsed by respondents in the final field test.

The computer was instructed to drop out items from the subscales if they had low item-total correlations (r < .40); also if an item was loaded equally well above .40 on two or more factors, it was discarded by the investigator. These were the grounds to eliminate an item from the scale and to discard it from future analysis. Hence, the *Assessment of Leisure and Recreation Involvement* yielded 37 endorsed and usable items from the final version of 52 items. Analysis of a number of probable solutions — between ten and five factors — showed that the six-factor structure was the most workable and explainable factorial manifestation. All the resulting factors were suggested in prior studies.

Table 3: Factor Structure for Multidimensional Leisure and Recreation Involvement Scale and Item-Subscale Correlations

#	Statement	Factor 1	Factor 2	Factor 3	Factor 4	Factor 5	Factor 6	r bis
1. Importance								
*18.	I reserve sufficient time to engage in my favorite leisure activities.	.80						.58
* 9.	I continue to do the leisure activities of my choice, even when I am busy.	.80						.56
11.	I rearrange my schedule to allow time to do my leisure activities.	.77						.50
*45.	There is a focus for my leisure choices.	.65						.68
*35.	My leisure activities are parts of my lifestyle.	.61						.70
25.	I can describe myself as a strong participant in certain leisure activities.	.59						.66
46.	Usually, I have an aim toward leisure choices.	.56						.66
17.	I give special attention to a number of leisure activities.	.55						.60
26.	My favorite leisure activities say a lot about who I am.	.43						.78
2. Pleasure								
29.	I enjoy the leisure activities in which I engage.		.70					.46
*15.	My favorite leisure activities give me pleasure.		.68					.59
31.	Time passes rapidly when I am engaged in my favorite leisure activities.		.65					.41
*12.	After completing my leisure activities, I usually feel satisfied and full.		.62					.43
*16.	I identify with the leisure activities I favor.		.61					.68
6.	I can entertain myself through my favorite leisure activities.		.60					.53
1.	Leisure activities are always good for me.		.60					.49
8.	I find it easy to be interested in some leisure activities.		.60					.57
*20.	I take pride in the leisure activities in which I engage.		.48					.68
3. Interest								
*38.	I usually want to know more details about the leisure activities that interest me.			.74				.41
*39.	Engaging in my favorite leisure activities expresses my wishes.			.62				.56
*51.	Engagement in my favorite leisure activities is worthwhile.			.57				.49
23.	My leisure pursuits serve certain goals or aims in my life.			.54				.59
*32.	I practice the skills required to improve my leisure performances, if needed.			.50				.61

Table 3: Factor Structure for Multidimensional Leisure and Recreation Involvement Scale and Item-Subscale Correlations (continued)

#	Statement	Factor 1	Factor 2	Factor 3	Factor 4	Factor 5	Factor 6	r bis
4. Intensity								
*48.	The leisure activities I do occupy my feelings.				.70			.44
*50.	My favorite leisure activities help me to discover many things about myself.				.57			.66
41.	Few things distract me while I am participating in my favorite leisure activities.				.52			.55
*27.	My choices of leisure activities give a sense of inner freedom for me to do what I desire.				.52			.72
*49.	I expect something good to come out of my participation in my favorite leisure activities.				.51			.57
5. Centrality								
*33.	I feel that I am responsible about choices made to participate in leisure activities.					.66		.41
*24.	I am willing to devote mental and/or physical effort to master my preferred leisure activities.					.50		.66
*42.	I like to do my leisure activities well, even when they require a great deal of time and effort.					.46		.61
*19.	For my preferred leisure activities, I am willing to invest my money, time, and energy.					.45		.63
6. Meaning								
*21.	Without engaging in my favorite leisure activities, life has no flavor.						.70	.54
*22.	I express myself best when I am doing my favorite leisure activities.						.68	.54
40.	I have a greater than average knowledge of my favorite leisure activity.						.56	.52
*30.	My leisure activities give me a sense of value in my life.						.50	.68
*36.	I do not know what to do without my leisure activities.						.49	.56
Eigenvalues:		18.60	3.61	2.63	1.88	1.65	1.58	
Variance Explained:		35.7	6.9	5.1	3.6	3.2	3.0	

n = 218   * Short Form

Data presented (Table 3) demonstrated that the final factor structure differentiated among the following six parts of the *LRI* measure named as: "Importance" (loadings of .80 to .43, r bis = .78 to .50), "Pleasure" (loadings of .70 to .48, r bis = .68 to .41), "Interest" (loadings of .74 to .50, r bis = .61 to .41), "Intensity/Absorption" (loadings of .70 to .51, r bis = .72 to .44), "Centrality" (loadings of .66 to .45, r bis = .66 to .41), and "Meaning" (loadings of .70 to .49, r bis = .68 to .52). Gorsuch (1983) noted that variances or loadings between .50 and .40 indicate a structure factor of adequate size for self-reporting scales. The *Assessment of Leisure and Recreation Involvement* and its parts are much higher than the benchmark. Definitions of the above parts were developed reflecting the empirically obtained endorsements of the respondents.

Reliability Tests

Alpha reliability coefficients (Alpha) were performed for the six subscales and their total, ranging from .95 to .78 (see Table 4: Internal Consistency Reliabilities for the Long and Short Scales and Total *Assessment of Leisure and Recreation Involvement*). Alpha for the total *LRI* (37 items) was .95, suggesting that a global leisure and recreation involvement score would discriminate among persons, demonstrating individual differences; this indicates the level of involvement in leisure and recreation pursuits. For the subscales, alpha was .90 for Importance, .88 for Pleasure, .79 for Interest, .82 for Intensity, .78 for Centrality, and .80 for Meaning. Nunnally (1978) reported that alpha reliability coefficients between .80 and .70 are acceptable for research purposes. The

Table 4: Internal Consistency Reliabilities for the Long and Short Scales and Total *Assessment of Leisure and Recreation Involvement*

Subscale		Long				Short			
		# of Items	Alpha*	M**	SD	# of Items	Alpha*	M**	SD
1	Importance	9	.90	3.53	1.23	4	.84	3.51	1.23
2	Pleasure	9	.88	4.10	1.10	4	.82	4.02	1.09
3	Interest	5	.79	3.73	1.12	4	.74	3.76	1.12
4	Intensity	5	.82	3.71	1.11	4	.81	3.75	1.11
5	Centrality	4	.78	3.83	1.03	4	.78	3.84	1.03
6	Meaning	5	.80	3.43	1.33	4	.78	3.34	1.33
	Total	37	.95	3.52	1.23	24	.93	3.70	1.48

n = 218
*Alpha = Alpha Reliability Coefficients.
**Five-point response scale for all the items.

alpha reliabilities for each subscale and their total scale were sufficiently high. The Importance subscale was most reliable and Centrality was least reliable.

The Laurent and Kapferer's (1985) adapted involvement profile scale obtained an alpha reliability coefficient of .58. Analysis showed that deletion of two items would improve the scale's reliability to .69. Those two items seem to have wording and conceptual difficulties: "Leisure activities leave me totally indifferent" and "It is not a big deal if you make a mistake while choosing a leisure activity."

Intercorrelations among the Subscale Scores

The interfactor correlations among the six *LRI* subscales were moderate to slightly higher (see Table 5), ranging from .70 to .52, with a median correlation of .61. Interpreting the correlation coefficient square (.37) as the proportion of common variance and the

reliability coefficient as the proportion of true variance, these results showed that only approximately one-third of the true variance of the subscales was common among them. It is inferred here that the six parts of the *LRI* assess different dimensions of its construct. The strongest correlations were between Centrality and Pleasure and Intensity and Pleasure, while the lowest correlations were between Centrality and Meaning and Pleasure and Meaning.

Concurrent Validity

Examining the correlations between the *LRI* scale and its subscales tested the concurrent validity of the *LRI* and Laurent and Kapferer's (1985) adapted *Involvement Profile Scale* (*IPS*). As demonstrated in *Table 5: Interfactor Correlations among Leisure and Recreation Involvement Subscales and an Adapted Criterion Variable Testing Concurrent Validity,* the long scale of the *LRI* correlated .54 with

Table 5: Interfactor Correlations among Leisure and Recreation Involvement Subscales and an Adapted Criterion Variable Testing Concurrent Validity

Subscale			LONG							
			1	2	3	4	5	6	7	8
1	Importance			.57	.59	.61	.61	.65	.83	.46
2	Pleasure	S	.50		.58	.69	.70	.53	.81	.53
3	Interest	H	.43	.58		.62	.62	.60	.81	.47
4	Intensity	O	.51	.65	.60		.63	.58	.83	.41
5	Centrality	R	.54	.68	.60	.59		.52	.82	.55
6	Meaning	T	.55	.49	.53	.54	.47		.80	.28
7	Total LRI		.76	.81	.78	.81	.81	.78		.54
8	Laurent and Kapferer Involvement (adapted to leisure)		.44	.50	.44	.41	.55	.23	.53	

n = 218
Note: Above the main diagonal represents the long *Assessment of Leisure and Recreation Involvement*.
Below the main diagonal represents the short *Assessment of Leisure and Recreation Involvement*.

IPS. Moreover, *IPS* correlated with all the six *LRI* subscales on the long form, ranging from .55 to .28, with a median correlation of .46. The Pleasure and Centrality subscales of *LRI* associated highly with the *IPS* criterion measure, but Meaning correlated modestly with *IPS.* That modest association indicates that the Meaning subscale assesses different grounds, as compared to what the criterion taps.

Relationships among Leisure Participation and Leisure and Recreation Involvement

Table 6 presents a further test for relationships among leisure participation categories and leisure and recreation involvement. Since that test was exploratory, no hypotheses were proposed, yet interesting findings prevailed. Mass Media activities (watching TV, reading, and going to movies) did not correlate with Centrality or Meaning. It correlated only with Intensity, Pleasure, and Importance (r = .18, .17, and .11, respectively). Outdoor recreation activities (e.g., fishing, traveling, and camping) associated positively with all *LRI* subscales, except Centrality. Two categories — sports (e.g., fitness and team or individual sports) and Social Activities (parties, visiting, or entertaining friends) — correlated the highest and most consistently with the six *LRI* subscale and their totals, ranging from (r = .45 to .22). Cultural activities (e.g., attendance at concerts, opera performances, theater, and playing music) correlated positively with all *LRI* subscales. Finally hobbies (e.g., painting, woodwork, photography, and working on electronics) related to

only Intensity (r = .11) of all the *LRI* subscales. Meanwhile, total leisure and recreation participation correlated significantly and positively with all the *LRI* subscales and the total scale, with Importance (r = .38) the strongest to Centrality (r = .21) the lowest. Based on correlations ranging from "none" to modest obtained and reported in Table 6, it seemed that involvement for this sample required much more than participation and is perhaps determined by other factors. Equally, the reverse also could be true. These relationships need further testing and verification before drawing conclusions.

Short Form

The final version of the short form of the *Assessment of Leisure and Recreation Involvement* has the order of the statements rearranged to group the statements from each subscale together. This allows for easier tabulation of the subsection scores.

Discussion

The six factors seem to be well documented in the empirical and conceptual knowledge of leisure and recreation involvement. The findings of the final field test demonstrate evidence supporting the multidimensional nature of the *LRI.* The six factors are consistent with previous research findings on involvement in specific recreation activities (e.g., Bryan, 1977; Buchanan, 1985; Dimanche, Havitz, and Howard, 1991; McIntyre, 1989; Shaw, 1985;

Table 6: Intercorrelations among Leisure and Recreation Involvement Subscales and Leisure Participation Categories

		Leisure and Recreation Involvement							
Activity Type		*Subscale*							
Leisure Participation Categories		Importance	Pleasure	Interest	Intensity	Centrality	Meaning	Total Leisure & Recreation Involvement	*Adapted Leisure Involvement* by Laurent & Kapferer
1	Mass Media	.11	.17	.10	.18	.07	.00	.12	.08
2	Outdoor Recreation	.25	.11	.15	.13	.10	.19	.20	.02
3	Sports Activities	.45	.31	.34	.39	.22	.42	.44	.05
4	Social Activities	.35	.31	.23	.37	.24	.34	.38	.05
5	Cultural Activities	.22	.13	.26	.16	.13	.20	.23	.11
6	Hobbies	.00	-.02	.08	.11	.01	.05	.00	-.10
7	Total Leisure & Recreation Participation	.38	.27	.32	.30	.21	.34	.37	.04

n = 218
where r = .11 and higher, it is significant at .05.

Siegenthaler and Lam, 1992). The confirmed factors in this study evidently discriminate among levels of leisure and recreation involvement. The six subscales are efficient in size for practical use, differentiate reasonably, and are clear in content.

Interestingly, the Importance-Pleasure component was reported and ranked highly in other studies of involvement (see Madrigal, Havitz, and Howard, 1992; Unger and Kernan, 1983; Watkins, 1986). But it is recognized and endorsed by the respondents in this study as two separate factors: one as Importance and another as Pleasure. The Interest subscale of the *LRI* is supported by past observations (Laurent and Kapferer, 1985; Kauffman, 1984; Selin and Howard, 1988; Siegenthaler and Law, 1992; Watkins, 1986). The Intensity factor is consistent with findings by Stamm and Dube (1994), and Shields et al. (1992). Critical analysis of the content of the Intensity factor revealed similarities with the conceptualization of "absorption," "total attention," devoted to "experiential involvement" (see Tellegen, 1982; also Privette, 1983; Wild, Kuiken, and Schopflocher, 1995). Moreover, the Centrality subscale of the *LRI* scale is consistent with findings by McIntyre (1989) and Wellman, Roggenbuck, and Smith (1982). Finally, the Meaning component is supported by results obtained by Roelofs (1992), McIntyre (1989), and Shaw (1985).

Some factors that were found to relate to specific involvement in leisure and recreation activities did not seem to show up in the *LRI*, such as sign value, commitment, risk probability, and self-expression. A possible explanation is that involvement in general and global leisure and recreation experiences can require different reactions and manifestations (or factors), when compared to involvement in specific activities such as hunting, arts, tennis, reading, or ballet. This requires further investigation to reveal the underlying causes influencing global involvement, and the basis for making specific activities differ in their expression.

In summary, how would the findings of this study fill in the gap in knowledge about the concept of involvement in leisure and recreation? Evidence presented here provides a preliminary delineation of the content of the concept of involvement in leisure and recreation. Specifically, we obtained six factors from the construct of the *LRI*: Importance, Pleasure, Interest, Intensity/Absorption, Centrality, and Meaning. Results on the six factors have denotations that they belong to and outline one thing in common: involvement in leisure. Evidence here should be utilized to further our understanding of involvement in leisure and recreation; consequently, an operational definition incorporating these findings can be restated.

Leisure involvement is the degree of interest in, and centrality of, an individual's leisure and recreation encounters. This state is demonstrated through the reported rating of importance of leisure choices made, meanings derived, and pleasures obtained from one's own leisure.

This definition completes the achievement of the main goals of this investigation, summarized as follows: a. increasing our knowledge of leisure and recreation involvement; b. being able to assess leisure and recreation involvement; and c. having a workable, operational definition to be used in future studies and for further verification.

Some limitations of this investigation, however, are recognized as requiring future research attention. First, due to the fact that the respondents were employees and college students, validation of the *LRI* necessitates testing it with other groups, such as participants of various ages, participants from various cultural backgrounds, or participants with specific disorders and diseases. Second, the instrument's stability over the long and short term needs to be tested. Third, for further validation, it is necessary to apply multi-method studies, employing non-self-report leisure and recreation involvement assessments and ratings (e.g., recreation leaders, family members, peers, and teachers). Finally, to test the practical usefulness of the hypothetical structure of involvement in leisure and recreation, further work on the construct is needed, as well as testing relationships between involvement in leisure and recreation and other variables such as leisure motivation, free time boredom, leisure constraints, wellness, and stress. Pending such verifications, users should be careful in their inferences of the findings reported here, as well as users' results, when employing the *Assessment of Leisure and Recreation Involvement*.

Conclusions

The psychometric characteristics of the *LRI* seem to be acceptable. Factors obtained are interpretable, possessing high internal consistency for the six subscales and their total scale. Moreover, *LRI* is theoretically founded, reliable, short, and seems to demonstrate construct validity. The six subscales are efficient in size for practical use, differentiate reasonably, and are clear. Moreover, the short subscales (four items each) are less time-consuming. For the short scale (24 items), the total reliability is .93, as compared to .95 for the long scale (37 items). Items on the short form are marked with an asterisk (*) in Table 2.

Administering the *LRI*

The *Assessment of Leisure and Recreation Involvement* score sheet should be given to each participant. These score sheets are copyrighted material and a facility, school, or other type of setting must have either purchased sets of the *LRI* from Idyll Arbor or have obtained a license from Idyll Arbor to make copies. In no other situation may copies of the blank forms be made.

Verbal Instructions

It is important that the professional giving the participant the score sheets provides each participant with the same instructions for completing the assessment. The instructions should be the same whether the participant is self-administering the assessment or the professional is reading the assessment to the participant.

The professional should first explain to the participant the purpose of the assessment and how the results could benefit the participant. This explanation should not take more than four or five brief sentences.

The professional should also inform the participant that there are no "right" or "wrong" answers.

Next, the professional should read the directions right from the score sheet and then ask the participant if s/he understands the instructions. If the professional is going to be reading the statements for the participant, the professional should place an example of the 1-5 bar graph with the corresponding words (e.g., "1 Strongly Disagree") in front of the participant to help cue him/her.

Environment

The professional should obtain better results if the assessment is administered in a stimulus-reduced environment. A comfortable room with adequate light and limited visual and auditory distractions should be the professional's goal.

Participant Self-Administration vs. Professional Read

Up to 20% of the population of the United States are nonfunctional readers (*World Book Encyclopedia*, 1989). In addition, numerous participants have visual disabilities making it difficult for them to self-administer this assessment. The professional should always err on the conservative side. If s/he feels that the participant's reading level or visual acuity may affect the participant's score, the statements should be read out loud.

Implications of Scores and Changes in a Client's Leisure Lifestyle

The mean score for the short form is 89 with a standard deviation of 28 for the final sample. That means that about two thirds of the sample fell into the range from 61 to 116. At this point we do not have the research to draw upon to clearly state that a certain score, or scoring pattern, indicates a serious problem. However, drawing upon recognized patterns discussed in the literature of recreation, leisure, and recreational therapy/therapeutic recreation we can draw some conclusions.

Extremely High Scores

An extremely high score would be any total score of 116 or above (one standard deviation above the mean). It would be assumed, based on recognized patterns of behaviors, that if an individual circles all or almost all, fives (strongly agree) throughout the entire test the most likely conclusions would be that either 1. the participant was not able to (or chose not to) read the statements or 2. the participant was over-enthusiastic at the least and possibly manic.

There might be a variety of reasons that the participant would circle almost all fives without paying attention to the content of the statements. First, the participant may not be able to read the statements. This may be due to an inability to read English statements or an inability to read 11-point Times New Roman font. See Table 7: Readability Statistics of the *Assessment of Leisure and Recreation Involvement*. Another reason may be that the participant perceives a benefit to circling almost all fives including the perception that s/he will look "better" with a higher score.

The participant may also circle fives predominantly because over exuberance that may border on

Table 7: Readability Statistics	
Ave. Words Per Sentence	11.9
Ave. Characters Per Word	4.7
Passive Sentences	0%
Flesch Reading Ease	51.2
Flesch-Kincaid Grade Level	9.0
Font Size	11 pt
Font Style	Times New Roman

the pathological. Disorders such as Bipolar Disorders that affect between 0.4% and 1.6% of the population have symptoms that include periods of abnormally elevated or expansive moods that could include inflated self-esteem, grandiose thinking, and increased goal-directed activity, especially toward pleasurable activities. Further studies need to be done to compare norms between participants with manic behaviors and participants who report experiencing a healthy, elevated satisfaction with their leisure and recreation activities.

While a subsection score of 18 or better in many subsections does not necessarily indicate a cause of concern, further inquiry may be necessary if the sub-scale scores all fall between 18 and 20. Check especially questions 2, 9, 21, and 24. Scores of 5 on these questions may be indicative of leisure that is too important (unbalancing) relative to other parts of the participant's life.

High Scores

High scores are total scores between 100 and 115. This would indicate that the individual has achieved a score above 16 in many subsections with most of the answers given falling fairly evenly between fours (Agree) and fives (Strongly Agree). These scores may represent an individual who is fairly independent in his/her leisure lifestyle and finds meaning and satisfaction through leisure and recreation.

Moderate Scores

Moderate scores would be scores that range between 76 and 99. Participants who score in the moderate range usually have other priorities and demands in their life that make it hard for them to justify placing their own leisure and recreation desires in front of the other priorities. Family (especially ones with young children), cycles at work that require a lot of overtime, or a commitment to finish up a degree may all take precedence over leisure and recreation activities. This is not inherently bad; in fact, it is very realistic and healthy as long as the individual maintains some connection to leisure and recreation for physical and mental health. If participants are distressed about scoring in the moderate range, options to help prioritize and/or make time for leisure and recreation activities may be indicated.

Low Scores

Low scores would be scores that range between 55 and 75. Participants who score in the low range may have some barriers to their leisure and recreation involvement. The professional may want to work with participants who score in the low range to see if lack of time or money, health concerns, and other constraints that can be overcome are causing the low score. It is more likely that increasing involvement will require modifications to attitudes, motives, behavior patterns, or knowledge base.

Extremely Low Scores

Extremely low scores would be scores that range between 24 and 54. It would be assumed, based on recognized patterns of behaviors, that if an individual circles all or almost all, ones and twos throughout the entire test the most likely conclusions are that either 1. the participant was not able to (or chose not to) read the statements or 2. the participant was significantly depressed or bored.

As with extremely high scores, the professional should be sure that the participant is able to read the statements.

The participant may also circle ones and twos predominantly because of depression, significant barriers to leisure, guilt, fear, or shame. The reasons for the low scores should be explored in depth with the participants. In addition to low overall scores, a score of 8 or lower in any subsection (12 or below in Pleasure) probably indicates a cause of concern that requires further inquiry.

It is possible that participants who score in the extremely low range only need assistance to identify barriers and develop a plan to increase the participant's involvement in leisure and recreation activities. We feel that it is more likely that the problem is more significant than that, potentially requiring observation and interviews with family members, other professionals, caretakers, and friends.

Leisure and Recreation Involvement

Research has identified six different elements that describe your involvement in leisure and recreational activities. The purpose of the *Assessment of Leisure and Recreation Involvement* is to help identify how important (or not important) each of these six elements is to you. By answering these statements you can better grasp why you might want to engage in leisure and recreation activities. There is no "correct" score. This scale tells you about how you feel about your free time and leisure. Read each statement then circle the number to the right of the statement that best describes you.

		1 Strongly Disagree	2 Disagree	3 In-Between	4 Agree	5 Strongly Agree
1.	I reserve sufficient time to engage in my favorite leisure activities.	1	2	3	4	5
2.	I continue to do the leisure activities of my choice, even when I am busy.	1	2	3	4	5
3.	There is a focus for my leisure choices.	1	2	3	4	5
4.	My leisure activities are parts of my lifestyle.	1	2	3	4	5
5.	My favorite leisure activities give me pleasure.	1	2	3	4	5
6.	After completing my leisure activities, I usually feel satisfied and full.	1	2	3	4	5
7.	I identify with the leisure activities I favor.	1	2	3	4	5
8.	I take pride in the leisure activities in which I engage.	1	2	3	4	5
9.	I usually want to know more details about the leisure activities that interest me.	1	2			5
10.	Engaging in my favorite leisure activities expresses my wishes.	1				5
11.	Engagement in my favorite leisure activities is worthwhile.	1	2	3	4	5
12.	I practice the skills required to improve my leisure performances, if needed.	1	2	3	4	5
13.	The leisure activities I do occupy my feelings.	1	2	3	4	5
14.	My favorite leisure activities help me to discover many things about myself.	1	2	3	4	5
15.	My choices of leisure activities give a sense of inner freedom for me to do what I desire.	1	2	3	4	5
16.	I expect something good to come out of my participation in my favorite leisure activities.	1	2	3	4	5
17.	I feel that I am responsible about choices made to participate in leisure activities.	1	2	3	4	5
18.	I am willing to devote mental and/or physical effort to master my preferred leisure activities.	1	2	3	4	5
19.	I like to do my leisure activities well, even when they require a great deal of time and effort.	1	2	3	4	5
20.	For my preferred leisure activities, I am willing to invest my money, time, and energy.	1	2	3	4	5
21.	Without engaging in my favorite leisure activities, life has no flavor.	1	2	3	4	5
22.	I express myself best when I am doing my favorite leisure activities.	1	2	3	4	5
23.	My leisure activities give me a sense of value in my life.	1	2	3	4	5
24.	I do not know what to do without my leisure activities.	1	2	3	4	5

Scoring the *Assessment of Leisure and Recreation Involvement*

There is no "right" or "wrong" score for the *Assessment of Leisure and Recreation Involvement*. However, the scores indicate the prominence of leisure and recreation activities in your life. Some people find that their work, their families, or education are as important, or more important, than their involvement in free time activities. They generally have low scores. Low scores may also mean that you currently have little that you feel is important in your life. A high score means that leisure and free time are important to you. A *high score* is a score of 16 or above in any one subsection and a *low score* is a score of 12 or below in any one subsection.

Importance of Leisure and Recreation to You
Add all of the scores for Questions 1 – 4.   **Importance Score:** _____
- *High score:* would reserve time for leisure endeavors, rearranges schedule to allow time for these pursuits, has a focus on activities, considers activities as part of lifestyle, gives them special attention.
- *Low score:* does not allocate time for recreation activities, with no aim or focus toward leisure choices, does not recognize these activities, and does not give them attention as part of daily pursuits.

Pleasure You Derive from Your Leisure and Recreation Activities
Add all of the scores for Questions 5 – 8.   **Pleasure Score:** _____
- *High score:* claims enjoyment, speedy time passage, feels full after engaging in recreation activities, identifies with activities, able to entertain self, and proud of chosen activities.
- *Low score:* finds little or no enjoyment in leisure, claims that time is a drag when engaged in recreation activities, reports dissatisfaction with leisure choices, lacks self-entertainment through recreation, has no pride in leisure and recreation pursuits.

Interest that You Have in Your Leisure and Recreation Activities
Add all of the scores for Questions 9 – 12.   **Interest Score:** _____
- *High score:* wants to know details about leisure activities that express wishes, considers leisure choices worthwhile, serving certain goals or aims, practices skills needed to improve activities' performance.
- *Low score:* feels that leisure activities are trivial, has no desire to learn details about leisure pursuits, does not practice leisure skills, mostly aimless during free time without goal or orientation.

Intensity that You Feel when You Engage in Leisure and Recreation Activities
Add all of the scores for Questions 13 – 16.   **Intensity:** _____
- *High score:* feels that leisure activities occupy feelings, uses activities to help in discovering things about self, not easily distracted while pursuing favorite leisure activities, claims that leisure pursuits give a sense of inner freedom, expects positive outcome from leisure endeavors.
- *Low score:* considers leisure activities peripheral, is easily distracted while doing a leisure activity, claims no discoveries or realization through leisure choices, lacks a sense of inner freedom and intrinsic relatedness, with negative or no expectations from leisure and recreation pursuits.

Centrality, or How Central Your Leisure and Recreation Activities are to Your Life
Add all of the scores for Questions 17 – 20.   **Centrality:** _____
- *High score:* has a sense of self-responsibility toward choices made to participate in leisure activities, ready to devote effort to master activities, strives to achieve and do well, willing to invest money, time, and energy in leisure pursuits.
- *Low score:* does not intend to put effort into skill acquisition and activity mastery, does not invest to achieve or succeed in recreation pursuits, lacks self-responsibility about leisure outcome.

Meaning to You of Your Leisure and Recreation Activities
Add all of the scores for Questions 21 – 24.   **Meaning:** _____
- *High score:* claims that leisure choices give life meaning and flavor, feels that leisure activities help in expressing self, possesses knowledge of chosen leisure activities greater than the average person, gains a sense of value in life through leisure, feels lost without leisure activities.
- *Low score:* has no self-expression through leisure and recreation activities, shows that these activities do not contribute to the search for meaning in general, has minimum or no knowledge about what is done as leisure choices, lacks sense of value in life derived from leisure.

Name _____   **Date:** _____   **Total Score:** _____

Questions and Exercises

1. Define leisure involvement, discussing attention given to the concept of involvement in different fields.
2. What are the types of involvement?
3. Evaluate the state of knowledge of the parts of leisure involvement.
4. What are the main reasons for missing potentially important components of leisure involvement?
5. What are the theories that can help understanding of leisure involvement?
6. Compare the merit and validity of utilizing leisure involvement versus leisure participation.

Chapter 21

Leisure Motivation: From Concepts to Measurements

Focus of Chapter

Motivation, to seek leisure pursuits or not, tends to be a major part of the social and behavioral foundations of leisure. Five grand theoretical explanations will be presented, showing their pertinence to leisure needs and phenomenon: psychoanalytic theories will be introduced as the oldest, followed by behavioral and cognitive theories, maturing to humanistic theories, ending with theories of positive psychology. In developing a theory-guided leisure motivation scale, specific applications will be performed to map the boundaries of the concept. A critical issue in mapping leisure motivation domains is the need to account for the concept's multivariate nature, possibly ranging from intrinsic to extrinsic motives, from amotivation to apprehension. Available general and specific scales for leisure motivation will be reported.

Key Terms

- amotivation
- apprehension
- behavioral motivation
- cognitive motivation
- environment
- extrinsic motivation

- extrinsic regulations
- hereditary
- humanistic motivation
- intrinsic motivation
- positive psychological motivation
- psychoanalytic motivation

Key Names

- Gordon Allport
- Gary D. Ellis
- Viktor Frankl
- Seppo Iso-Ahola
- Carl Jung
- Abraham Maslow
- Jay B. Nash

- Jean Piaget
- Carl Rogers
- Julian B. Rotter
- B. F. Skinner
- Edward Thorndike
- John B. Watson
- Ellen Weissinger

Objectives

- Recognize reasons to study leisure motivation.
- Distinguish among the five theoretical structures in explaining behavior.
- Describe how the theories of motivation apply to the development of a motivation construct.
- Identify controversies in applying the growing theories to explain leisure motivation.
- Explain the desperately needed balance among intrinsic and extrinsic motivation, as well as amotivation and apprehension.

- Identify existing leisure motivation scales, explaining what they assess.

Leisure motivation (LM), defined as needs and drives to pursue leisure activities, is a pivotal domain with many other concepts revolving around it. Assessing this status, Iso-Ahola and Allen (1982: 141) emphasize, "Leisure needs (*motivation*) is perhaps the most important concept in the field of leisure studies." (Italics added.)

In a study on leisure motivation in relation to psychosocial adjustment, Munchua-DeLisle and Reddon (2005) found a moderately strong correlation with depression and psychiatric symptomatology. Motivation for sports of adolescent athletes was investigated as a consequence of parents influence by Gutiérrez, et al (2011). Also, in a study by Beggs and Elkins (2010) all subscales of leisure motivation correlated with leisure satisfaction. Another application of the leisure motivation scale to understand sports' tourism was conducted by Yusof and Shah (2008).

Examples of aspects revolving around leisure motivation are leisure attitude, satisfaction, empowerment, interest, vitality, involvement, and meaning, among other domains.

Moreover, in case of lack of leisure motivation or unfulfilled expectations, the phenomenon of boredom could creep into a person's free time due to the dearth of stimulation. Consequently, a host of behavioral problems can be created. Examples of problems are disrupting flow and quality of life, tainting other domains, forming negative attitudes, lacking involvement, and experiencing dissatisfying pursuits. Therefore, developing measurements to assess motivation for leisure is a needed step to help some critical areas ranging from practical application and academic preparation to scientific investigation and philosophical conceptualization.

Motivation Theories

To comprehensively comprehend motivation, numerous theories and some philosophies (e.g., existentialism) lend themselves as bases for conceptual models and the construction of assessment tools of LM. In providing an understanding and an explanation of LM, theories in social psychology and positive psychology can be classified in five groups, as presented below:

1. Psychoanalytic theories
2. Behavioral theories
3. Cognitive theories
4. Humanistic theories
5. Positive psychological theories

Comprehending the basic assumptions of these grand theoretical structures allows sound explanation and utilization of leisure motivation.

Since all sorts of motivations exist in leisure activities and experiences, social-psychological theories can help us understand the complexity of participants' leisure needs. People seem to have a great variety of reasons to engage in or to avoid doing leisure pursuits. Therefore, theories can help us find valid explanations for individuals' leisure motivations in this culture. Better realization of the concept will stimulate instrument construction and development of theory and models for more sound applications.

Psychoanalytic Theories

As it is very well known, the founder of psychoanalysis is the eminent scholar Sigmund Freud, a medical doctor, then a psychiatrist. Freud's work stimulated the discipline of modern psychology, arriving at different theoretical explanations. His conceptualization of the person is not only a model of personality development, but also a philosophy of human nature. Freud focused on the psychodynamic processes, which presented reasons or compulsions for a person's behavior. Many other scholars were members of this family of psychoanalysis: Carl Jung, Alfred Adler, Harry Stack Sullivan, Eric Bern, Erik Erickson, and Karen Horney.

Psychoanalytic theories postulate that an individual's unconscious is the source of motivation. These theories assume that an individual's biologically rooted instincts drive behavior and thought; if they reach a state of deprivation, they energize human actions. Moreover, humans have basic tendencies to gratify primitive instincts, minimizing the demands of society. Two examples of the theories that belong to this classification are the psychoanalytic theory (Freud) and the psychosocial theory (Erikson). However, due to the nature of the unconscious — being unseen and unheard — psychoanalytic theories recognized here have limitations and cannot be employed as bases for the development of a construct nor a measurement in leisure and recreation.

Behavioral Theories

John Watson (1913) founded behaviorism, suggesting that psychology should not focus on the unconscious and subjective experiences. Rather it should focus on behavior that can be seen and heard (things that are observable). Historically, the roots of behaviorism stem from the work of Pavlov and Thorndike in a concept called "classical conditioning," resulting from Pavlov's pioneering experiments on dogs' salivation, stimuli, and conditioning. Thorndike (see Kimble, 1961: 10) later demonstrated that behavior is controlled by its consequences (a notion that applies very much to leisure/recreation/play expectations, anticipations, rewards, gains, and satisfaction). A basic principle stated by Thorndike is that positive rewards function to reinforce certain behaviors, while negative results tend to diminish the repetition of behavior. This principle can be viewed as a core reason for individuals to repeat or strive to avoid certain free time activities pursued as leisure, fitness, recreation, and play. Also, this explains why people repeat rewarding activities and avoid other choices that they experienced as unpleasurable, difficult, or, at worst, as a defeat.

Behaviorism gained both esteem and influence in the 1960s, attempting to generate behavioral changes based on learning theories. New concepts, terminologies, and principles were developed by behavioral theorists: operant conditioning, positive and negative reinforcement (shaping, chaining, and modeling), and behavior modification. Other authorities associated with these themes are B. F. Skinner, Arnold Allan Lazarus, Joseph Wolpe, and Hans Eysenck.

Cognitive Theories

Focusing on the mental structures, cognitive theories are centered on processes of perception and learning. As organizers of beliefs, expectations, and interpretations of the cues perceived in the environment, these theories attempt to explain the functions of the brain and the nervous system. One of the main assumptions of cognitive theories is that the individual is a thinking organism — *Homo sapiens* (McDavid and Harari, 1968).

There are many cognitive theories that apply to informal and avocational choices. Both forming and changing leisure attitudes can employ the theory of cognitive dissonance (Festinger, 1957). Working with children and planning for their play can benefit from the theory of cognitive dynamics (Piaget, 1948). Understanding and interpreting why humans repeat activities can be based on the theory of play as learned behavior described by Thorndike (Kimble, 1961: 10). Another theory that applies to the informal choices of adults is the attribution theory (Heider, 1958), which also has a wide application in leisure studies. The attribution theory attempts to explain individuals' causal reasons for the outcomes of their choices and behavior.

In a practical sense, cognitive explanations (theories) can help greatly in understanding and assessing individuals' awareness, rationales, and knowledge about how leisure and exercise relate to health, wellness, vitality, and quality of life. These theories attempt to explain the underlying mental reasons behind a person's decisions to choose or not choose to engage in activities of their own interests. Moreover, professionals equipped with knowledge of cognitive theories can explain a great deal of leisure and recreation involvement. One of the many reasons for that utility is that many leisure choices, perceptions, expectations, impressions, and outcomes are cognitively anchored. In sum, cognitive explanations both exert and will continue to exert a great influence on leisure assessment and programming, activities, and services. This is simply because humans have brains and demand to engage them in what they do (for relevancy to motivation see Beard and Ragheb, 1983; for pertinence to interests see Ragheb and Beard, 1992).

Humanistic Growth Theories

This name came about after Schultz (1977) published his book, *Growth Psychology: Models of the Healthy Personality*. Theorists that paved the road for humanistic or growth psychology include, but are not limited to Gordon Allport, Carl Rogers, Abraham Maslow, Charlotte Buhler, Viktor Frankl, Julian Rotter, Robert White, and Fritz Perls. This group does not emphasize the negative or the deterministic circumstances of individual's behavior. Instead it focuses on growth theories that show the humanistic, developmental, and creative abilities and talents of the person as reasons to pursue choices.

Growth theorizations deal with the majority of individuals and groups, sometimes called "normal." Consequently, they facilitate healthful functions, stressing the initiation and maintenance of mental health, wellness, and the attainment of quality of life. Major assumptions of humanistic (growth) postulates can be recognized as follows:

1. Individuals have the will and capacity to fulfill their potential for maturity through self-driven searches.
2. Healthy individuals take control of their lives, which in turn, maximizes enjoyment by creating feelings of mastery, being responsible for one's free choices, and self-initiative.
3. Individuals have the emotional and intellectual capabilities to be aware of their existence and to determine their destiny.
4. Most individuals' ultimate aim is gratification, pleasure, satisfaction, or happiness. They also seek and search for meaning, purpose, and a

place in life. This is fulfilled, not through the gratifying moments of existence, but mostly through reversed feelings: pain and suffering, accepted as an individual's destiny.

5. Individuals have the mental capacity to be self-directed, enabling them to attempt success in what they encounter. They can repeat tasks, sometimes seriously challenging, however long it takes to be skillful. They strive to be competent and search for achievement and to master their environments, thereby maximizing control.

Fulfilling potential, taking control, determining destiny, searching for satisfaction and meaning, and performing activities for competency and mastery are all served and fulfilled through leisure pursuits.

Examples of the humanistic theories are as follows:

1. Human Motivation (Maslow, 1962)
2. Self-Determination (Rotter, 1954; Deci and Ryan, 1985)
3. Person-Centered (Rogers, 1956)
4. Competence-Effectance and Mastery (White, 1959)
5. Man's Search for Meaning (Frankl, 1962)

Ultimately, human growth explanations lead us to trust existentially that most individuals possess humanistic characteristics, seeking to flourish and to be fully developed. Examples of such characteristics are the desire for independence and self-determination, to freely choose and make responsible decisions. Consequently, this enables the self not only to master chosen goals and to be competent, but also to maximize potential while searching for the upper limits of being, seeking positive functioning, searching for meanings behind existence and beyond, and attempting to reach an individual's utmost realization.

Obviously, humanistic theories should possess higher status in their contributions to not only the development of leisure assessment tools but also to field practice and settings. More attention should be given to understanding, testing, and implementing these theories within leisure, recreation, travel, and fitness provisions and environments.

Positive Psychological Theories

Instead of being concerned with treatment of pathologies for healing purposes, positive psychology focuses on the unlimited resources of humans. Instead of being victimized and expected to react passively, individuals are perceived to react actively and creatively. Seligman (1998: 1), the founder of positive psychology, discusses features of positive psychology that tend to overlap greatly with leisure

and recreation outcomes. He postulates, "Individuals are now being seen as decision-makers, with choices, preferences, and the possibility of becoming masterful, efficacious, or, in malignant circumstances, helpless and hopeless." In a person's free time such malignant circumstances can be anxiety, boredom, and depression. Persons who are educated for leisure, leisure pursuits, exercise, and travel can face such malignant circumstances and turn them into strength, efficacy, and mastery or competence.

The foundations of positive psychology make it especially relevant to informal activities. It started with a team of psychologists (Danner, Snowdon, and Friesen, 2001) analyzing handwritten autobiographies for 180 Catholic nuns, composed upon their entry to the monastery when they were around 22 years of age. Emotional contents of the autobiographies were related to survival during ages 75 to 95. A strong inverse correlation was observed between positive emotional content in pertinent writing and risk of mortality in late life. One example is that the nuns who reported the most positive emotions lived up to ten years longer than those who reported the fewest.

Similar findings and concepts that go back to the 1950s alerted psychologists about the effects of positive feelings and strength on health and longevity. Those findings triggered this new science of positive psychology. (Strength is viewed broadly to incorporate maturity, fulfillment, optimism, thriving, optimal excitement, and altruism.) Great numbers of applications and implications can be found in positive psychology that can contribute to practical situations and services. In application, recreation, leisure, and park services can reap a great deal of benefits from such knowledge.

Leisure and recreation are about meeting the deepest preferences or interests (Ragheb and Beard, 1992), about motivations to be skillful, the longing to seek effectance, competence, and mastery (White, 1959), and leisure satisfaction. Positive qualities are embedded and deeply rooted in free time activities such as exercise, outdoor recreation, and travel. A person involved in leisure would be on top of matters: experiencing flow, intensity, absorption, and a state of elation. True leisure involvement — when someone achieves it — can be the peak of positive psychological experiences. This can fulfill the state of "meta-satisfaction" (see Maslow, 1969).

The science of positive psychology was defined in a number of ways, demonstrating its characteristics as follows:

- Positive psychology attempts to understand how and why individuals not only invigorate and grow, but also thrive and flourish.

- Positive psychology focuses on humanity's strengths and fulfillments for the betterment of existence, further adjustment, and successful functioning.

- Positive psychology focuses on desirable qualities: initiation, self-control, intrinsic pursuits, maturity, empowerment, expertise, advancement, optimism, hope, resilience, stimulation or excitement, flow, self-leadership, coexistence, and meaning while enjoying the journey of life.

- While negative emotions have downward spiral effects, leading to depression and other pathologies, positive emotions have upward spiral manifestations, leading to happiness and a state of elation. Hence, positive emotions can be considered the working tools of positive psychology.

- Positive psychology is a science that demonstrates how to inject positive qualities into one's life, formulating learned happiness through personal success, vitality, fulfillment, pleasure, flow, joy, satisfaction, and ultimately reaching bliss.

Lazarus (2003) argues that positive psychology is the power of positive thinking and feeling as sources of health and well-being. Meanwhile, Cowen and Kilmer (2002) suggests five pathways to wellness.

Fredrickson (2003), in her Broaden-and-Build Theory of growth and development, claims that positive feelings prepare for future hard times. (It is important to note that this developmental theory applies very much to leisure and recreation endeavors.) Experiencing positive emotions can lead to states of mind and modes of behavior that indirectly prepare a person for later, harder encounters. A person's mindset is broadened momentarily when it is composed of a positive emotion. These accumulations, synthesizing interactive processes, form and crystallize as a result, producing desirable outcomes.

The nature of leisure and recreation endeavors lends itself to the fulfillment of the deepest expectations of Fredrickson's Broaden-and-Build Theory. Synthesizing the interactive processes of leisure endeavors, being freely chosen, self-determined, intrinsically motivated, with flow, intensity, and enjoyment make them prime candidates to supply "broadening feelings and thinking" and "building positive traits and beliefs"; enabling humans to face life's ups and downs, successfully.

In sum, psychoanalysis claims that individuals are driven biologically and unconsciously, through innate instincts to be gratified. Behaviorism focuses on the influence of environmental conditioning, seeking pleasure and avoiding pain. Cognitive theories focusing on the central processes of perception: the brain and the nervous system as regulators of what is confronted. In contrast, growth theories and philosophies — when they apply — tap the wholesome aspects of human beings: their fullness, flourishing, and richness of life, focusing on their recognized and unrecognized reservoir of capacities, abilities and talents, interests, and energies, as viable resources to be maximized to the level each person chooses. Finally, humanistic theories evolved to be positive psychology. More attention is given to human possibilities for strength, flourishing, and thriving. Positive emotions gained from daily encounters and limited experiences contain the power to generate an upward spiral. As a result, an individual is more resilient and better functioning, experiencing meta-satisfaction and learning to be happy.

Application of Motivational Theories and Philosophies to Assessing Leisure

In guiding leisure assessment, how applicable are these five grand theoretical structures? For the psychoanalytic theories, due to their heavy emphasis on the unconsciousness, biological gratification, and instincts as sources of motivation, they cannot be used as bases for recreation and leisure measurements. These theories do not lend themselves to construct formation nor to empirical validation.

Regarding behavioral theories, although environmental determinism explanations are losing some ground, their content holds reasonable merit — lending themselves to empirical validation — as underlying assumptions for some measurements in leisure, recreation, fitness, and play. Corey (2001) looked at behaviorists' merit to therapy by citing Glass and Arnkoff's (1992) relationship between behaviorist explanations and needed attention to health. They suggest that, "With the rising costs of health care, the emergence of national health programs, and the increasing involvement of psychologists in health issues, there will be a need for greater integration of behavioral self-help, coping-skills training, relaxation training, and self-management programs into health care."

In an era of accountability, Glass and Arnkoff's (1992) observation has very sound and practical implications for the contemporary behavioral role of leisure delivery systems. This requires extensive exploration in leisure services of how to implement such concepts of self-management, self-help, and relaxation training. Because leisure, recreation, fitness, and play behaviors can be observed and utilized (developmentally, preventatively, and therapeutically), their verbal or written assessment is not only feasible, but also possibly crucial, depending on the theory and the philosophy employed.

Comparatively, cognitive theories are more useful than behavioral theories as bases for assessment of many leisure processes, functions, and needs for strategies. For example, play and playfulness behaviors operate as mental processes as children develop. Therefore, their assessment can reveal their underlying causes. Knowing the processes can help professionals to facilitate these processes for children. Also, leisure and exercise pursuits can be assessed, employing such explanations as the attribution theory, self-determination, cognitive dynamics, stimulus seeking, and stimulus avoidance. Researchers can explain and predict wants, needs, and interests for informal choices. Apparently, cognitive theories will always exert reasonable influence on conceptualization and assessment of leisure, travel, and recreational sports.

On the other hand, by far the best motivational philosophies and theorizations that lend themselves to explain the nature of leisure and its assessment are those concerned with growth. It is expected that most future assessments of leisure motivations, functions, and outcomes or benefits will rely heavily on the underlying assumptions and explanations of humanistic theories and positive emotions. It is crucial to note that emphasis on the wholesomeness explanation does not cancel the environmental, cognitive, or biological determinants of behavior; to the contrary, their great influence is highly recognized here.

Attention is urgently needed to focus on the fact that humans seek what is beyond their physical, mental, and environmental domains. They exercise their self-initiative and creative talents for healthful living and actualizing themselves, going farther than basic requirements for existence that contribute to human functioning and existence. Biological and environmental domains do exist — this is where humans are locked in and housed. Nevertheless, individuals have the will, freedom, power, choice, determination, and responsibility to act freely. This is beyond potential and perceived constraints (or what they are locked into). Sometimes the body and/or surroundings impose these constraints, but some persons go beyond them. (For more details on leisure constraints, see the special issue of the *Journal of Leisure Research*, 1991, Vol. 23, # 4; all articles are dedicated to the topic of leisure constraints.)

Humanistic and positive psychological theories and philosophies ultimately come in the middle of the heart and focus of the inherent nature of leisure, recreation, exercise, travel and tourism, and play. Leisure benefits have been recognized by users and scholars. In a wave beyond information, possibly a "Push Button" evolution characterized by high-speed encounters, fast delivery, and unlimited possibilities, contemporary humans are different.

The modern concepts of leisure and fitness are fulfilling higher developments: health restoration, healing, curing to a balanced sound state, excelling, tapping inner personal resources, maturing through needs satisfaction, generating new, unheard of vitalities (Murphy, 2008), empowerment, and enhancing self. People are trying to achieve a level of self-chosen wholesomeness and total functioning. Leisure and active lifestyles have the potential to deliver such qualities, with people expecting all these healthful and growth promises. These are a few of the reasons that make such theorizations very close to the spirit of leisure options.

Generally, in terms of assessment, due to the importance of the concepts of motivation in the psychology of informal times, it is no wonder that leisure, recreation, and exercise motivation gained the greatest attention. This is in contrast to other classifications, as demonstrated in Part I (e.g., leisure attitude, leisure interests, and leisure satisfaction). The number of instruments available, as demonstrated in Part I, is strong evidence of attention.

Controversies in Applying Theories to Explain Leisure Motivation

In the zeal to interpret, explain, and predict free time and leisure motivations, many scientists have relied on a variety of theories. As a result, instruments were developed, relationships were tested, and models were constructed. The past 40 years have witnessed many orientations and commitments, growing up with clear distinctions. Intrinsic leisure motivation is one of these orientations and explanations. However, the concept of intrinsic leisure motivation was not adequately debated. All along the way, there have been reasons to believe that both intrinsic and extrinsic motives (as well as other types of motivation) most likely operate on individuals' leisure choices (see Cokley, 2000; Li, 1999; Markland and Ingledew, 1997). But for many years the notion of intrinsic motivation dominated the conceptualization and development of measurements.

The Desperately Needed Balance between Intrinsic and Extrinsic Leisure Motivation

The nature of a given quality concept is a critical, "content validity" issue, attracting the utmost attention of scholars. Here, scholars are attempting to answer a simple question: What are we studying? Without clear answers to this question, incomplete or fragmented concepts can be formed, leading to incorrect directions. Based on logic and evidence, it is assumed that for an average person there is a reasonable mix of intrinsically motivated reasons to engage in leisure blended with extrinsic reasons, but with more emphasis on the intrinsic ones. Moreover, the not as positive reasons can influence leisure choices or lack of choices. This cry for balancing and completing the concept's views, not tipping it solely toward the intrinsic explanation, is the focus of the next discussion.

This issue requires careful consideration. As stated previously, the study of motivation differentiates between extrinsically and intrinsically pursued actions. This is an issue that always surfaces in all areas, including leisure, exercising, and the arts (see Iso-Ahola, 1980, for relevance of motivation to leisure; and Csikszentmihalyi, 1975, for relevance to flow). It is easy to idealize and purify leisure, viewing it as being exclusively intrinsically motivated, as reflected in scale development. Examples are a scale constructed by Weissinger (1986) and a replica by Weissinger and Bandalos (1995). Moreover, extensive research findings have been providing evidence of the influence of intrinsically motivated leisure on other phenomena (e.g., Guinn, 1999; Juniu et al., 1996; Kay, 1993).

In terms of content validity, we need to remember that motivation in general life endeavors is extrinsic as well as intrinsic. In making a choice, it is crucial to note that the influence of others and external factors are always present or perceptually there in different degrees. Social psychology, by definition, is the study of the influence of others on behavior (see Allport, 1994; Asch, 1987) as the study of economics is centered mainly on goods (materialism) and services.

A simple review of social psychological topics can demonstrate the importance of the impact of others: interpersonal relationships, group dynamics, leadership, norms and habits, social identity, socialization, social motivation, and social interaction. (Alfred Adler's individual psychology, presented by Dreikurs, 1953, elaborated on concepts such as "Social Interest," "Community Feeling," and "Social Feeling" as motivators.) This is combined with the nature of leisure, as viewed by Kelly (1996: 7): "Leisure is freely chosen because the activity or the companions (*extrinsic*) or some combination of the two promises personal satisfaction." (Italics added.) So it seems that the social and extrinsic motivators in all life activities, including leisure, are a pillar of human and community existence.

Valid assessment requires having the content of concepts as complete as possible. Therefore, intrinsic motivation appears to realistically represent only a part of the total picture. Both content conceptualization and its validity are urgent. They require an accurate delineation before we embark on the simplest attempts to measure concepts, not yet relating its variable to other variables or incorporating it in constructed theorizations and models.

Naturally, the different domains of motivation, mainly intrinsic and extrinsic, exist and impact differently on many other phenomena such as health, wellness, vitality, longevity, interpersonal relations, life satisfaction, stress, involvement, and work performance. (For further evidence, see Vallerand and O'Connor, 1991.) Therefore, assessors should account for all possible types of motivation, waiting for respondents' endorsements of different life pursuits (including leisure) to acclaim whether their choices are more intrinsic or more extrinsic.

We can compare this to the nature of similar constructs. For instance, we use three components (cognitive, affective, and behavioral) to measure Leisure Attitude. Although respondents in different settings would endorse the three differently, the basic structure (content) of leisure attitude should be presented in all settings, to all respondents in its entirety, without bias or unintended omission. We know that certain groups will rate different domains differently, depending on their settings and other situational aspects. This is the essence of research.

Ignoring Important Aspects of a Construct

If leisure motivation is assessed accounting for intrinsic and extrinsic reasons to engage in activities, a common error has a chance to creep in. Some investigators would claim that leisure is intrinsically motivated if the difference between the means of the two factors is statistically different. This, in itself, is a methodological trap. Unintentionally, this trap can lead to various misinterpretations and future misuses.

A fictitious example can demonstrate this point. Assume that you are utilizing a scale to assess intrinsic and extrinsic motivations (in this case it is limited to just two parts), which yield two means for the identified components. On a five-point scale, the mean for an extrinsically motivated subscale is 3.1 versus 4.7 for the intrinsically motivated subscale. Would this difference make leisure *just* intrinsically motivated? There is certainly a large arithmetic difference of 1.6 on the five-point scale (4.7 - 3.1 = 1.6), and it seems to make a handsomely significant statistical difference as well. Assume this illustration: If glass A is filled to 4.7 out of its size and glass B that is filled to 3.1, this in itself does not make glass B empty or nonexistent!

Results here may create a neat trap that leads some to interpret leisure as intrinsically motivated only, ignoring the scores obtained on extrinsic motivation (i.e., 3.1). For example, they may report that evidence was obtained demonstrating that the intrinsically motivated leisure domain is significantly greater than the extrinsic domain. Therefore, leisure motivation is intrinsically driven.

To elaborate further, the statistical difference, whatever it is, does not make leisure purely intrinsically motivated. How can we ignore the power of a reasonable score such as 3.1 on a scale of five points? Actually, it is higher than the middle point of the scale, which is 3.0. In this case, we must consider both our content validity value and ethical responsibility to inform readers that leisure is extrinsically as well as intrinsically motivated in different degrees, but with the latter being greater and significantly higher (and that is all: *significantly higher*). Then, in subsequent studies, these two types of motivations might be utilized, but will function differently in their associations with different cultures, phenomena, localities, populations, and various ages.

In the above fictitious example, the "poison" is actually hidden within the statistics or the type of statistics utilized! The results seem to be potentially deceptive, are misrepresented, or are unintentionally misrepresented. Some hard-core conceptualizations and logic must be employed to re-evaluate the direction that has been taken when using only intrinsic leisure motivation.

Accounting for the two motivations (intrinsic and extrinsic plus others that have been recognized), in relation to the investigated phenomenon is crucial to determine the magnitude of their contribution to given variables (see Li, 1999; Graef, Csikszentmihalyi, and Gianinno, 1983; Vallerand and O'Connor, 1991). For instance, Larson (2000) provided evidence that the "development of initiative" appears to come from structured (extrinsic) voluntary activities, such as sports, arts, and participation with organizations in which youth experience the rare combination of intrinsic motivation with deep attention *(intensity and flow)*. Moreover, it was found that "freely chosen" extrinsically motivated activities produced the highest levels of intrinsically rewarding flow (Mannell, Zuzanek, and Larson, 1988). Admittedly, intrinsic motivation is an underlying factor when skills, competencies, achievement, and performance are parts of leisure pursuits (largely in the arts, sports, and hobbies). But there are so many other leisure choices that do not require competencies or performance — the average relaxing endeavors, sometimes in the presence of others or for the pleasure of others.

More recently, Li (1999), in a very sound methodological investigation, provided strong evidence that eight factors compose the exercise motivation construct. The eight factors exhibit a fair balance in their content between extrinsically and intrinsically motivated exercise and non-motivated, such as: external regulation, introjected regulation, identified regulation, integrated regulation, intrinsic motivation to learn, intrinsic motivation to accomplish tasks, intrinsic motivation to experience sensations, and amotivation. (Regrouping Li's eight factors, it seems that there are two reasonably large structures: intrinsic and extrinsic; and a minor manifestation, three items of "amotivation.") Therefore, a leisure motivation scale should include an explicit, balanced set of items assessing the two types of motivation: intrinsic and extrinsic (and their possible variations, if proven to exist, as in Li's study). The final analysis in a given study will demonstrate how all types of motivation behave with different characteristics that might be of interest to investigated phenomena.

The logical conclusion is that leisure, with its diversity and complexity, cannot be limited to one set of motivations in any context. People's leisure motivations manifest themselves while they are going through various circumstances, cultures, geographical locations; being influenced by certain developmental stages, incomes, educational levels, states of health, and work demands. Realistically, all sorts of motivations underlie involvement in leisure pursuits — intrinsic, extrinsic, a combination of the two, and others can be experienced in leisure.

A Speculative Explanation of the Nature of Motivation

A notion that might be worth thinking of and debating is that extrinsic versus intrinsic motivation tendencies might stem from personal traits or as personality dispositions. Personality traits such as proneness to boredom, interests, inherited abilities, and intelligence might help in looking at the genetic roots of motivation. These traits (heredity) can manifest themselves in combination with the environment — mostly social environment. Both traits and environment seem to interact together as a bio-psychosocial domain mixed in different proportions and priorities to produce what is labeled as motivation. (For more details on the bio-psychosocial combinations and their influence, see Chapter 22 on Leisure Interests.)

Complexity of the Nature of Leisure Motivation

It is suggested here that limiting motivational interpretations of leisure choices to notions such as "flow" and "peak experiences" as the only reasons to engage in activities is unrealistic. Examples of choices that may require specific skills and performance were reported above. But not all leisure options exhibit characteristics as the above activities. Therefore, searching for a valid concept, we might require an evaluation of potential motivations for other possible and realistic grounds and options.

Perhaps an illustration of diversified leisure settings in post-technological and affluent societies can show the other extreme: the potentially less bright realities of recreation and leisure. J. B. Nash (1953), a U.S. pioneer philosopher of the leisure movement, presented a paradigm showing six levels of leisure participation. Of that paradigm, the lower two dealt with harmful participation. The lowest one is injuries to society through delinquency and criminal acts, while the second lowest level is injury to self through excessive indulgence, such as drinking or smoking. The next higher level has to do with killing time, amusement, and entertainment from without.

Unfortunately, in the years since Nash's paradigm was presented, the situation has steadily worsened. Demonstrating "The shady side of leisure: Morally marginal play," Kraus (2000) courageously admits, "What is not generally acknowledged in scholarly studies of leisure and its effects is that many of the most widely engaged in forms of play in American society have potentially negative outcomes" (p. 306). Kraus goes on to present details on "addictive behaviors" as short-term, immediate gratification, such as "gambling as a leisure pursuit," "substance abuse and leisure," "commercialized sex," pornography as a $7 to $10 billion a year industry, nude shows, and prostitution. What motivations are behind these indulgencies? Therefore, other designations, such as amotivation, fears, anxieties, insecurities, and sensation seeking are needed to describe motives of the above marginal leisure, other than being pure extrinsic or pure intrinsic.

With the wide expansion and dominance of morally marginal leisure, one wonders how many intrinsically motivated individuals are driven to seek these pursuits. Are they experiencing control or being controlled, absorbed by the activity or suffering from peripherality and unrelatedness, achieving high levels of vitality or unwholesomeness, being "alive or merely existing" (Chase, 1966)? All of these negative characteristics can lead to disorientation, irrelevancy of activities, and boredom, all of which can act as leisure constraints. Accordingly, these people can claim (correctly) that they have free time, but there are doubts that they experience positive results (as described, for example, by Nash, 1953) from their leisure. Realistically, instead of limiting explanations to just the intrinsically motivated choices, what we need to conceptualize and validly assess is how much

of people's leisure, recreation, and play is driven by all sorts of motivations, including amotivational reasons as well.

Leisure Motivation Measures

Extensive conceptual efforts by many scholars have laid groundwork for the construction of leisure motivation scales. Broadly, Ellis (1973) in his book, *Why People Play*, presents 15 theories that can be considered exclusively motivational explanations that drive individuals to leisure, recreate, travel, exercise, and play. The efforts by London, Crandall, and Fitzgibbons (1977); Tinsley, Barrett, and Kass (1977); and Iso-Ahola (1980) speculated on the psychological structure of leisure and its need-satisfying properties.

The evolution of knowledge to understand leisure motivation led to holding a conference at the University of Illinois, inviting scholars to join forces in order to comprehend the reasons for leisure motivation. Conclusions were reported by Crandall and Slivken (1980), paving more precise roads to explain leisure motivators. Later, reported conclusions were utilized as the bases for measurement development, as demonstrated thereafter.

In an investigation of the leisure needs before and after engagement in intramural college basketball games, Iso-Ahola and Allen (1982) developed a 40-item scale. Six interpretable factors (and one minor factor, "Meeting the Opposite Sex") were extracted and named: Interpersonal Diversion and Control, Personal Competence, Escape from Daily Routine, Positive Interpersonal Involvement, Diversionary Relaxation, and Interpersonal Competence. Pooling and integrating all of the above conceptualizations, another scale was developed measuring leisure motivation (Beard and Ragheb, 1983). Four main factors were obtained and named: Intellectual (mental), Social, Competence/Mastery (physical), and Stimulus Avoidance. Based on the literature, the first three factors were consolidated, making the construct of Stimulus Seeking.

Ellis and Witt (1984) constructed another theory-driven measurement of perceived freedom in leisure. Four factors were confirmed, representing Perceived Competence, Perceived Control, Intrinsic Motivation, and Playfulness. The first exclusive scale — assessing theory-driven intrinsic motivation in leisure — was constructed as a dissertation subject (Weissinger, 1986). Ten years after their 1984 Perceived Freedom in Leisure Scale, Ellis and Witt (1994) explored the factor structure of the perceived freedom components of the Leisure Diagnostic Battery. Factor analysis yielded five components: Perceived Leisure Competence, Perceived Leisure Control, Leisure Needs,

Depth of Involvement in Leisure, and Playfulness. Based on comparisons among results obtained from nine studies, Weissinger and Bandalos (1995) reported on the demonstrated consistencies of Weissinger's Intrinsic Motivation in Leisure scale. Four components were identified: Self-Determination, Competency, Commitment, and Challenge.

Employing meta-analysis to measure Leisure Motivation, Manfredo and Driver (1996) provided evidence of the desired goal states that are achieved through participation in leisure. They had an underlying assumption that recreation activities are instrumental in attaining psychological and physio-logical goals. Manfredo and Driver's analysis of 36 studies confirmed four subscales: Satisfaction, Importance, Valence (how the outcome would add to satisfaction), and Experience.

Also, the search for meaning in leisure pursuits was recognized as a motivational construct (Ragheb, 1997). Primarily based on Frankl's (1962) theory, a scale was developed and tested, yielding six components: Physical Fulfillment, Self-Determination, Mental Realization, Spiritual Reminiscence, Social Meaning, and Esteem/Positive Image. Finally, Baldwin and Caldwell (2003) developed a Free Time Motivation Scale for Adolescents. Five components were realized in their study: Amotivation, External, Introjected, Identified, and Intrinsic.

Ten motivation-specific leisure activities scales were identified, covering a span of history from 1988 to 2000. These ten scales assess physical recreational motivations, such as running, exercising, fitness, racquet sports, and recreational sports as listed below. Moreover, it is important to note that procedures employed to validate the Exercise Motivation Scale by Li (1999) are very advanced and elaborate, and recommended to be reviewed and used as a model in measurement construction.

Potential Uses of Leisure Motivation Instruments

The leisure motivation scales reported (general and specific) can have a variety of uses. Data obtained can enable users to function better and gain satisfaction, and for practitioners to employ these scales in deciding what they provide. Assessing participants' needs and desires can be used for designing services and prescribing choices through leisure counseling.

Moreover, researchers can identify areas that lack instrumentations, such as motivations in therapeutic recreation settings, measuring motivation in outdoor recreation, measuring travel motivation, or

measuring arts motivation. For example, the Leisure Motivation Scale (Beard and Ragheb, 1983) was investigated in its application to two areas: Ryan and Glendon (1998) applied to tourism in Australia while Yusof and Shah (2007) applied it to sport tourism. Consequently, the need for scales to be developed and verified to fill recognized voids would be clearly realized. Furthermore, with the availability of measures reported here or to be constructed, a variety of relationships can be tested to assist practice, theory development, and model construction.

Leisure Motivation Scales

Existing leisure motivation scales are divided into general and specific leisure motivation groups, as presented below[1]:

A. Measurements of General or Global-Leisure Motivation:

1. Measurement of Leisure Needs (MLN) (Iso-Ahola and Allen, 1982)
2. Leisure Motivation Scale (LMS) (Beard and Ragheb, 1983)
3. Self-as-Entertainment Scale (Mannell, 1984)
4. Measurement of Perceived Freedom in Leisure (MPFL) (Ellis and Witt, 1984)
5. Leisure Experience Battery for Adolescents (LEBA) (Caldwell, Smith, and Weissinger, 1992)
6. Measurement of Perceived Freedom in Leisure and Satisfaction (MPFLS) (Ellis and Witt, 1994)
7. The Motivation for Leisure Scale (MLS) (Pelletier et al., 1994)
8. Intrinsic Motivation in Leisure (IML) (Weissinger and Bandalos, 1995)
9. Recreation Experience Preference (REP) (Manfredo and Driver, 1996)
10. Measuring the Search for Meaning in Leisure and Recreation (MSMLR) (Ragheb, 1997)
11. Free Time Motivation Scale for Adolescents (FTMS) (Baldwin and Caldwell, 2003).

B. Measurements of Motivation-Specific Leisure Activities:

1. Fitness Locus of Control Scale (FITLOC) (Whitehead and Corbin, 1988)
2. Racquet Sports Competence Scale (RSCS) (Aguilar and Petrakis, 1989). (This study has

---

[1] Although motivations for volunteering belong to leisure choices, as a motivation for services, the following two scales were evaluated to relate best to the classification of Assessment for Leisure Administration Functions: 1. Special Event Volunteer Motivation Scale (Farrell, Johnston, and Twynam, 1998) and 2. Volunteer Functions Inventory (Clary et al., 1998).

another scale that can be classified as, and incorporated under, "Leisure Satisfaction: From Concepts to Measurements," Chapter 27.)

3. Exercise Decisional Balance Measure (EDBM) (Marcus, Rakowski, and Rossi, 1992)
4. Exercise Identity Scale (EIS) (Anderson and Cychosz, 1994)
5. The Flow State Scale (FSS) (Jackson and Marsh, 1996)
6. Exercise Motivation Inventory-2 (EMI) (Markland and Ingledew, 1997)
7. Behavioral Regulation in Exercise Questionnaire (BREQ) (Mullan, Markland, and Ingledew, 1997)
8. Exercise Motivation Scale (EMS) (Li, 1999)
9. Motivations for Participation in Recreational Running Scale (MPRRS) (Clough, Shepherd, and Maugham, 1999)
10. International Leisure Travel Motivation (ILTM) (Toh and Yeung, 2000)

Summary and Conclusions

The knowledge of motivation in all life activities seems to be attractive and worth the invested attention. By comparison to work motivation, motivators to engage in leisure, recreation, travel, play, and exercise are, perhaps, more intriguing, for their non-utilitarian reasons. A great body of social psychological theorization enables the process of explaining motivations for informal pursuits. Theories can range from the less usable psychoanalytic explanations to behavioral ones, pointing both to anticipations and expectations from leisure as well as rewards and satisfaction sought. These behavioral experiences determine re-engaging or avoiding doing activities as individuals are conditioned positively or negatively.

Both psychoanalysis and behaviorism explanations can contribute to the study and interpretation of amotivated and apprehended leisure. Moving from psychoanalytic explanations to behavioral ones leads to the realization of the importance of cognition to answer many problems. Being on a higher level of the motivation continuum, cognitive theorizations can assist in understanding how leisure choices are regulated, and provide bases for kinds and feelings about extrinsic motivation. Cognitive theories are applicable mental reasons to pursue leisure, to leisure attitude (ideas and beliefs) and attitude change, perception and awareness of leisure, and children's mental processes and development through play.

On the other hand, instead of following biological (psychoanalysis) or environmental (behaviorist) deterministic causes as reasons to engage in leisure, or to be locked in mental processes, a more viable set of theories can be utilized, labeled as humanistic or developmental and positive psychological. Both theorizations emphasize qualities close to leisure experience: peak experience, flow, self-determination, aesthetic experience, competency and mastery, strength, flourishing, searching for meaning, and maximizing potential to reach one's utmost good. Providing insights into intrinsically motivated choices, humanistic and positive psychological theories with all their qualities and pertinent domains can provide great insights regarding leisure explanations and interpretations.

Finally, a critical issue needs to be considered carefully; that is, striking a balance in studying and assessing intrinsic and extrinsic motivators (and any combination of the two) of leisure, recreation, travel, play, and exercising. This is besides other motives such as amotivation and apprehension. A detailed rationale for that inclusion was offered. Applications of instruments available, 20 of them reported above, need to be explored further, and then implemented.

Questions and Exercises

1. What are the main theoretical structures that can help understanding of leisure motivation?
2. What are the applications of motivational theories and philosophies in developing a leisure motivation measurement?
3. Discuss the controversies in applying theories to explain leisure motivation.
4. How much is leisure motivation considered intrinsically versus extrinsically initiated? Explain.
5. Elaborate on the existing leisure measurements: magnitude, focus, and what they lack.

Chapter 22

Leisure Interests: From Concepts to Measurements

Focus of Chapter

Two levels of interests will be presented: interest-specific and interest-general. The former will be demonstrated as interest in activities, usually in the present moment, while the latter are structural, long-lasting, and durable interests. Most vocational and avocational interests are recognized as interests in careers or in informal activities. However, all interests seem to stem from a genetic basic structure, a bio-psychosocial interaction with the physical environment.

Key Terms

- activity choices
- avocational inclinations
- components of leisure interest
- environment
- genetics
- inner personal core
- vocational inclinations

Key Names

- Doyle W. Bishop
- H. D. Carter
- John L. Holland
- Frederic Kuder
- Stephanie Lehman
- G. T. Patrick
- E. K. Strong
- Donald E. Super
- Peter Witt
- Paul A. Witty

Objectives

- Explain the nature of human interests.
- Distinguish differences and similarities between vocational and avocational interests.
- State stages of studying interests in careers, schools, and leisure.
- Distinguish between interests in activities, genetics-based, and bio-psychosocial mix.
- Describe the relationship between interests and the environment.
- Sort interest scales according to functions served: activities versus core personal structure.

Interests, defined simply as tendencies and desires in life pursuits, have been easy to observe. People can be classified on the basis of what they show or say that they are interested in. Whenever there are possible options and choices, people have naturally expressed preferences, inclinations, and readiness either for or against what is presented. Therefore, attempts to comprehend and assess both vocational and avocational interests began many decades ago. Surprisingly, studies of play and recreational interests (e.g., Patrick, 1921; Lehman and Witty, 1927, and Additon, 1930) were initiated a few years earlier than career and school interests. Now vocational interests receive more emphasis than avocational interests, as progress has been made economically, socially, and educationally.

The Place of Human Interests in Explaining Motivated Choices

Concepts and theories of interest apply equally well to the explanation of interests in many fields: vocational interests (school and career), avocational interests (recreation, leisure, arts, sports, and exercising), and marital or family interests. A major reason for this wide application is the existence of predetermined personality and environmental characteristics that motivationally drive individuals to seek to actualize their interests.

Due to some environmental dominating factors, such as economics, work values, and religion, play and leisure were considered sinful and trivial (Kraus, 2000). That helped vocational interests gain most of the conceptual and assessment work, due to efforts to survive and compete economically and educationally. Nevertheless, as we move toward being a leisure-oriented society (Seassoms, 1974), a renaissance is in the making; the process is moving toward a balanced state. Lately avocational interests have become a larger part of conceptual and assessment development. This is due to social change, technological breakthroughs, and increasing free time.

Evolution and Strategies for Investigating Vocational Interests

The conceptualization and measurement of interests have an extensive history, going back to the early years of the 20th century. Strong (1927) developed a pioneering inventory, Strong Vocational Interest Blank. That was based upon his conceptualization that interests were on a liking-to-disliking continuum. This inventory held sway for a long time. Even after 50 years had passed, this inventory was reported as the fourth most frequently researched assessment tool (Buros, 1978).

Contemporary evidence supported a three-dimensional structure of Stone's Interest Inventory: Data/Ideas, People, and Things (Einarsdottir and Rounds, 2000). On the importance of people or interest in others, Alfred Adler presented elaborate ideas. In Adler's individual psychology in the early 1930s, "Social Interest" was a fundamental pillar to human life. Social interest, in Adler's view, incorporates concepts such as "Community Feeling" and "Social Feeling" (see Dreikurs, 1953). Adler presented ideas centered on the importance of human

community, where people have a natural tendency to show interest in each other through work, friendship, and love.

Kuder (1934) performed the second pioneering effort arriving at The "Kuder Performance Record," assessing individuals' preferences for activities, many of which were recreational. In 1966, he developed the "Kuder Occupational Interest Scale." In 2000, Diamond and Zytowski presented information on the uses and interpretations of Kuder's Occupational Interest Scale. They demonstrated strong evidence concerning both the quality and level of health (content) of Kuder's scale.

Another perspective by Carter (1940) took into account the social dynamics that influence teens in actualizing their interests from choosing a vocation to finding personal fulfillment. In 1956 a theory of vocational choices was proposed by Roe — that an individual would have interests toward others or not toward others; that is, toward things.

On the other hand, Holland (1959) theorized that behaviors comprise the outcome of three factors: Interests, Personality, and Social Environment. Progressively, Holland (1973) suggested that interests are expressions of one's personality, demonstrating one or more of these six types: Realistic, Investigative, Artistic, Social, Enterprising, and Conventional. Use of these types is still employed in scientific studies (see Carless, 1999). Although Holland's hexagonal model was criticized for lack of validity (Tinsley, 2000), Prediger (2000) provided evidence that the model is alive and well.

The Nature of Interests and Their Definitions

A definition based on a sound comprehension of interests in general is a critical key to methodological (i.e., measurement development) and empirical testing of relationships that can be used later in applied settings. There are dedicated efforts to understand and define the concept of interest, as well as to differentiate it from other ideas. Carter (1940) identified interests with self-concept; Forer (1948) equated interests with activities; Darley and Hagenah (1955) conceived interests as expressions of deeply seated needs; and, in a similar vain, Super (1970) recognized needs as prerequisites for interests.

We can speculate about questions such as: How stable are interests in activities? Can interests be created? Can interests be modified, changed, substituted, or manipulated? Tentatively, it seems that interests in activities are flexible and adaptable, but a deeper root (or core) of interests is much more stable, structural, long-lasting, and consistent. Interests seem to be anchored in personality.

A dominant, underlying force that is interwoven in the above concepts and used to explain interests is the "Trait" structure as an ingrained personal characteristic. Moreover, from Carter's (1940) era, considerations were given to the social forces (parents, peers, and leaders) that form interests. Traits (genetics) and the environment (physical, social, and cultural elements) would draw an individual spontaneously "to like or prefer" (Super, 1949; Walsh and Betz, 1985) certain choices, as "goal-oriented activities" (Aiken, 1989).

Considering all of the above, a definition of interest has been composed, as follows:

> *An interest exhibits a stable and consistent preference toward a set of activities. Interests operate as a force stemming from traits and self, interacting with social and physical environments, with potential to be latent or active, dormant or expressed. They can be characterized as a generic core that materializes choice of a specific manifestation.*

This definition demonstrates itself in all life endeavors: vocational, avocational, and familial. It would be interesting to identify how play and leisure interests are a stable and consistent trait, influenced by physical and social environments.

Approaches to the Study of Avocational Interests

Leisure and recreational interests were conceptualized, measured, and tested in relation to other domains. They seem to be founded more on common sense than on theoretical structures. Early efforts in the study of avocational interests focused on understanding and assessment of "recreational and play interests" (e.g., Patrick, 1921; Lehman and Witty, 1927; Trow, 1927; Additon, 1930; Nelson, 1934; Dale, 1935; Toogood, 1939; White, 1939; and Houston, 1940). Patrick's scale preceded Strong's Vocational Interest Blank by six years.

Interestingly, Lehman et al. — as early as the 1920s — accounted for an extensive list of play activities, utilizing Lehman's Play Quiz. Moreover, Nelson in 1934 was one of the earliest investigators to use a title including Leisure-Time Interests and Activities. Dale used similar terminology. Moreover, Houston suggested that teachers must help students to relate each subject of instruction to vocation, leisure time, and other needs and interests. Insightfully, Houston's (1940) vision of relating instructional subjects to leisure can be considered a fundamental

root for leisure education, leisure awareness, leisure counseling, and guidance that is based on leisure interests and needs.

In the assessment of leisure interests, 1940 appears to have witnessed the first transition toward employing avocational and vocational interest inventories. This was seen with the use of the Strong Vocational Interest Blank (Super, 1940) in avocational settings. It seems that for the first time in history, Super applied an empirical or theoretical rationale in assessing leisure interests. Super's rationale for such inclusion was that avocational items gained evidence of discriminative weight in vocational interest inventories, suggesting the presence of avocational interest patterns as well.

Later, leisure interests were tested in their relationships to other variables, such as age and intelligence (Reeves and Slater, 1947). Progressively and internationally, leisure interests began to be accounted for in global life interests. In France Rennes (1952) employed psychometric theory (factor analysis and reliability tests).

All of these developments have led to a new era started with more advanced uses of theoretical and empirical conceptualization of leisure interests (Peel, 1959). For the first time Holland's (1966) theory was employed, testing stability of avocational (leisure) interests (Varca and Shaffer, 1982). A construction of guides pairing occupational and leisure interests based on factor analysis followed (Killcross and Bates, 1968). Conceptually, scholars in the fields of outdoor recreation and leisure gave extensive attention to preferences and interests in activities (see Kaplan, 1960; Procter, 1962; de Grazia, 1962; Sapora, 1966; Reid, 1966; Hopkins, 1966; and Driver, 1976).

So far, the evolution of developing concepts and measurements of leisure interests is very intriguing and encouraging. It began with using common sense focusing on play and recreation and moved to better uses of theoretical bases, empirical findings, and psychometric theory. The concepts were broadened to incorporate leisure and the outdoors.

Revealing Dynamics of Leisure Interest through Factor Analysis

Scholars such as Kaplan (1960) and de Grazia (1962) laid down some speculative groundwork of leisure interests. Kaplan speculated five categories: Games and Sports, Social, Art, Movement, and Immobility, while de Grazia advocated a four-item, bipolar factor explanation: Active-Passive, Participant-Spectator, Indoor-Outdoor, and Solitary-Social. Many studies were conducted thereafter, which helped to uncover the possible empirical factor structures of leisure interests.

A variety of factors began to be demonstrated scientifically around the 1970s. For example, four factors of outdoor interests, such as Passive Choices and Water Sports were reported by Proctor (1962). Bishop (1970) observed three-factor structures of leisure interests (Active-Diversionary, Potency, and Status), while Witt (1971) found other factors (e.g., Aesthetical/Sophisticate). More investigations were conducted, yielding overlapping factors (see McKechnie, 1974, seven factors; Ritchie, 1975, four bipolar clusters; Howard, 1976, four categories; Allen, 1982, nine categories; and Frisbie, 1984, 17 factors of "Leisure and Occupational Interests").

Apparently, there was no scarcity in the dimensions of identified leisure interests. To the contrary, the overlaps among factors were found to be a source of frustration and confusion. They tended to create difficulties such as the inability to understand the real leisure interests, how to measure them, and how to use them in practice and to test their relationships to other phenomena.

Interests in Activities versus a Combination of Personal Inner Core to Interact with the Environment in Shaping Interest

It is important to note that most authorities attempted to explain interests in "activities" historically, which was the way interests actually led to activities. That was *always* considered on target; however, there seemed to be a deeper and more generic structure. This structure allows for interests in activities radiating from an underlying longing. Interest in a given activity can imply a deeper trait. That generic radiant structure can be characterized as being focal, core, very stable, and more consistent than activities. That core operates as a stem, putting the individual in a state of readiness for a broad menu of choices or activities.

Most likely, this is a reciprocal mixture of genetics, environment, and motivation interacting all together (see Cote and Levine, 2000, in an article "Attitude Versus Aptitude"). What we see (overtly) is a person inclined or not inclined to do an activity (relevant to work, family, or leisure), making a choice or not, that can be considered an expression of a deeper nagging, hidden force. For instance, a person's hidden structure — whether artistic or mechanical, seeking physical choice or mental abstraction — can vaguely express inner core or psychological inclinations (interests).

The structure is persistent, but not directly tied to specific activities. The elements of the structure can manifest themselves through a broad range of preferences with potential substitutability for activities, options, or choices. It is also possible that a person does not know his/her core interests (see Iso-Ahola, 1986). Being fairly knowledgeable about what s/he momentarily wants to do (activities that interest him/her) or being able to choose from a menu of activities does not mean that the person understands his/her core structure.

Moreover, one interest can be latent while another is active. The former is actually dormant, waiting for appropriate environmental and behavioral conditions, while the latter is expressed, being in a state of actualization. During an individual's lifetime, some interests are actualized while some others are constrained, mostly due to a combination of lack of financial resources, energy, companions to do activities with, time, climate, or opportunity for skill acquisition.

The number of unfulfilled or enacted-upon interests varies from one person to another, due to potentially unexplored reasons. In some cases, individuals do not fully realize what they are capable of pursuing, while having many latent or dormant interests. Sometimes this is due to a feeling of learned helplessness (see Seligman, 1972) or hopelessness. In the most practical sense, this is the role of four entities:

- Leisure professionals, practitioners, educators, and scientists
- The leisure delivery system
- The family
- The school and the community at-large.

To facilitate fulfillment of leisure and recreation interests and needs the leisure system, parents, and the school should consciously try to control identified constraints (behavioral and environmental) that reinforce learned helplessness. They should work toward increasing hope, competence, mastery, and functioning within the environment.

When elaborating upon the reciprocal interaction between genetics and the physical environment, these can be viewed as the bio-psychosocial amalgamation of elements necessary for the interests to flourish. The reciprocal process crystallizes a person's ways of facing life by seeking acclimatization, yielding choices based on what we label as "interests." In other words, a manifested interest is the product of interactive, reciprocal processes among bio-psycho-social structures with the physical environment (agriculture, desert, mountains, islands, urban, or technical). Consequently, a delicately balanced outcome is manifested, which we call "interests."

With continued advancement in assessment, the delicately balanced outcome can be predicted with a good degree of accuracy.

Moreover, the bio-psychosocial structure, in its interaction with its environment, can operate uniquely and strangely in different proportions. This is due to cultural resources: the media, family background, and financial capabilities. For example, some teenagers might have interests in activities characterized as being thrill and adventure seeking (see Zuckerman, 1977; Wang et al., 2000) while others desire activities characterized as social or mechanical.

Activities desired can be athletics, music, singing, or dancing (psychosocial). But, seekers do not have the basic requirements or talents (bio- or genetics or aptitudes) in the form of abilities to become athletes, musicians, or singers. However, it was reported that motivation (psychological), not intelligence (bio- or genetic/aptitude) was the cause for skill acquisition and academic achievement (Cote and Levine, 2000). Mysteriously sometimes, outcomes can be against expectations and logical odds.

On the other hand, some other teens can have the bio-psychosocial structure (all of what is needed) but reside in remote areas such as islands, the plains, deserts, inner cities, or remote mountains, which might prevent the development of avocational and/or vocational skills. This is how interests remain dormant or latent, sometimes for the person's whole life, without the person even knowing. There is a dire need for the availability of some basic environmental support for interests to express themselves. Therefore, the "delicate balance" should be available in any given situation, as a requirement for interests to be actualized, without feelings of deprivation or frustration or inaccessibility.

Further elaboration on and application of the above concepts will be reported in the next section, regarding their contributions to instrument development in leisure and recreation. In sum, this reciprocal interactive balance among bio-psychosocial structures, as influenced by physical environmental circumstances, represents our theoretical position in comprehending interests in general and leisure interests in particular. A measurement responding to this position would have the power to reveal and predict latent (hidden) and acted on leisure interests.

Another Direction for Conceptualizing and Assessing Leisure Interests

Further concerns were observed with the conceptualization and methodology employed to assess leisure interests when trying to identify the greatly diversified factors listed above. Ragheb and Beard (1992: 3), in a methodological investigation, constructed a scale assessing leisure interests to discover a potential structure. They argue that:

> There are at least two obvious problems in the checklist approach to leisure interest measurement *based on activities*. First, the interests that can be expressed are limited by the activities included in the checklist. Second, when the checklists elicit responses about actual participation in specific leisure activities, the results are biased by restricted opportunities to participate. Some activities might be of interest, but the respondent cannot act upon them. (italics added)

To remedy such concerns, Ragheb and Beard pooled all possible identified factors, including Holland's hexagonal model, in a measurement construction following the psychometric theory. The goal was to hypothetically conceptualize a background of a scale to assess the social-psychological structure of human interests in leisure pursuits in an attempt to reveal their core.

A 29-item scale was constructed, assessing latent leisure interests. As a result of their empirical test, they found eight factors that can underlie an individual's leisure interests in activities, explaining 77.33% of its variance. The realized factors were Service, Physical, Mechanical, Cultural, Social, Outdoor, Reading, and Artistic. The scale can be utilized in practice for program planning, designing facilities, and providing leisure counseling and guidance to participants. Scientifically, many relationships can be investigated, testing how different life domains associate with leisure interests, including stress, boredom, empowerment, health, wellness, vitality, depression, adjustment, and longevity.

How could these eight leisure interest areas be expressed? It is assumed that leisure interest components are to be found in different degrees among individuals. When an individual rates himself/herself high on mechanical leisure interests, for instance, s/he is inclined to seek certain activities, including working with tools, studying mechanical structures, relatively quickly comprehending the theory behind mechanical devices, reading about mechanics, feeling that mechanics attract her/his attention and energy, and repairing or inventing mechanical objects.

The activity here is not the concern; actually, many choices can satisfy this interest. The core, predisposing the person to seek or not to seek, is the problem. This core is the important foundation behind the recognized and nagging interest. It is also assumed that if an activity does not satisfy this interest, other activities that are considered mechanical may be available.

Another example is an individual who rates herself/himself low on interests of outdoor recreation. This person would avoid being in outdoor places, would not read about them, would not watch "Discovery Channel" on the television, does not particularly seek friends who pursue outdoor choices, and does not buy outdoor gadgets. All of this is due to lack of outdoor inclinations. The above examples apply also to artistic interests as well as interests in service, physical, reading, cultural, and social preferences and endeavors. In essence, a core attraction operates to draw the individual to any of unlimited number of choices that can satisfy what is internally nagging.

Existing Measurements Assessing Leisure Interests

Stages of development resulted in a number of instruments assessing leisure interests, as follows:

1. Inventory of Leisure Interests (ILI) (Hubert, 1969)
2. Mirenda Leisure Interest Finder (MLIF) (Mirenda, 1973)
3. Avocational Counseling Manual (ACM) (Overs, 1977)
4. Measure of Leisure Interest (MLI) (Frisbie, 1984)
5. Life Interests Inventory (LII) Leisure/Work (Williams, 1987)
6. Leisure Interests Checklist (LIC) (Rosenthal et al., 1989)
7. Recreation Interest Inventory (RII) (Kirkcaldy, 1990)
8. Leisure Interest Inventory (LII) (Stangl, 1991)
9. Leisure Interest Measure (LIM) (Ragheb and Beard, 1992)
10. Leisurescope Plus (Schenk, 1993)
11. Adolescence Leisure Interest Profile (ALIP) (Henry, 1998)

12. Leisure Assessment Inventory (LAI) (Hawkins, Ardovino, and Hsieh, 1998)

Extra effort needs to focus on assessment of global or general leisure interests, balancing core interests with the many existing interest-specific scales.

Summary and Conclusions

For more than 90 years, scholars have been investigating the nature of the concept of interest. Attempts have been made to assess it for applied reasons, vocational and/or avocational. Concepts related to interests evolved from what people "like or dislike," such as ideas, people, and things, to "preferences for activities," "interests toward others or not toward others (things)," and "needs as prerequisites for interests" accounting for the social and environmental impacts on interests.

Considerations were given to the interactive processes between traits (genetics), self, and the environment (social and physical). Expression and actualization of interests are determined accordingly. Developmental approaches to the conceptualization and assessment of avocational interests were parallel to vocational ones (if not earlier!). But, due to the higher value and importance of careers, personal income, work, economics, and productivity (going through two world wars), more attention was focused on vocational interests, at least in terms of quantity and quality of assessment tools. However, there are over 10 instruments assessing leisure interests. Scales vary in what they measure — from activity finders, inventories, and checklists to core psychological and social traits or structures that can apply to all humans, everywhere. Further work is needed on five fronts, to advance leisure practice and study:

1. Conceptualizing leisure interests.
2. Discovering approaches and ways to implement leisure interest inventories in leisure settings.
3. Improving the quality, validity, and reliability of leisure interest assessment tools.
4. Testing relationships between leisure interests and other important life domains (e.g., health, vitality, stress, depression, and life satisfaction).
5. Utilizing instruments and conceptual developments to enable leisure practitioners to perform quality services, program design, and facility design; responding to participants' needs and interests.

Questions and Exercises

1. How would human interests relate to motivation?
2. What was the evolution of investigating vocational interests?

3. What is the nature of human interests?
4. Define interests.
5. Discuss the approaches to the study of interests.
6. How do leisure interests evolve and how are they revealed?
7. Compare the differences between interests in specific leisure activities and the psychological core of interests.
8. Discuss possible new directions for conceptualization and assessment of leisure interests.

Chapter 23

Leisure Attitudes: From Concepts to Measurements

Focus of Chapter

Attitudes (ideas and feelings toward objects) seem to determine behavior. Therefore, the study of attitude in psychology and many applied fields has been dominant from the 1930s. But due to some methodological omissions, critical moderating variables were not accounted for and considered. That created inconsistencies in findings of the relationship between attitude and behavior. Contemporary advancements in the usage of methodology restored confidence in outcomes when moderators were realized and considered. Moreover, attitude structure faced some controversies: for some it is only how individuals feel toward an object, but for the majority it is what you know (cognitive), how you feel (affective), and what you intend to do toward that object (behavioral intentions) that incorporates feelings and realistically goes beyond just one domain. Attitude change from negative to positive, for its practical benefits, gained momentum in the 1970s and 1980s, with no progress afterwards, especially in measurement construction. Attitude formation and change will be related to the pursuit of leisure choices, demonstrating assessment tools available.

Key Terms

- attitude
- attitude change
- attitude components
- awareness

- behavior
- moderating factors
- opinions
- values

Key Names

- Gordon Allport
- Rabel J. Burdge
- Rick Crandall

- Martin Fishbein
- John Neulinger
- Harry C. Triandis

Objectives

- Describe the importance of and challenges to the study of attitudes.
- Define attitude and its components.
- Identify the boundaries of attitude components.
- Explain the reasons for attitude components to fluctuate from one investigation to another.
- Describe under which conditions attitude fluctuates in its relationships to other domains.
- Identify assessment tools of leisure attitudes.
- Explain how to change an attitude.

When I buy a car — if I am a rational (thinking) person — there must be good reasons for my choice. First, some of the possible dominant reasons can be based on my views about that car (e.g., mechanical quality, price, speed, and size). Second, another set of reasons, as strong as the first, emanate from my feelings about a specific car (comfort, pleasure, importance of its make, how my peers evaluate it, and whether or not it makes me look good). Lastly, some other strong reasons can relate to aims or intentions (e.g., Do I drive a car like this? Do my friends have a car like this? Am I going to exceed the quality and impressions of the cars my friends have? Can I afford it?) In one statement: my ideas, feelings, and aims will work together in mysterious ways, rational or irrational — sometimes unknown to me — to help in finding the car I will buy. The same type of impressions can help me to choose a spouse or business partner or other things. In this we see the arguments of Sanbonmatsu, Prince, Vanous, and Posavac (2005): attitudes guide choice.

A rational person should have good reasons for making appropriate decisions. That is why people seek knowledge about certain things that are called here objects. Why do they like or dislike an object? Then they develop intentions (acceptance or rejection) toward the object. People do not operate haphazardly; they form impressions, which can be called "gut feeling" or attitudes. Therefore, it is logical to assume that we are driven by what we know, how we feel, and what we set out to do, mostly rational but sometimes irrational.

This process is the central issue of the scientific study of attitude and attitude change. It sounds easy and attainable, but actually it is not so easy. The early stages of study (1940s to the 1980s) revealed the nature of attitudes, measured them, and related attitudes to other factors. Yet, this process was confusing and conflicting. Mixed signals and mixed results created confusion and frustration. Difficulties and challenges in the study of attitude lasted for many years. The concerns were so serious that some lost confidence in the results of the attempts to discover how individuals' attitudes related to other aspects of life. Some researchers ceased to rely on the ability of attitudes to predict behaviors.

Persistently, this issue received close attention from social psychology and applied fields, including leisure and recreation. Lately, with the help of advancements in scientific methods and employed statistics, many intervening aspects that created difficulties in obtaining consistencies are in the process of being discovered and controlled. Confidence, accordingly, is in the process of being restored. For example, Sanbonmatsu et al. (2005) developed a framework based on knowledge gained from the attitude-behavior relationship.

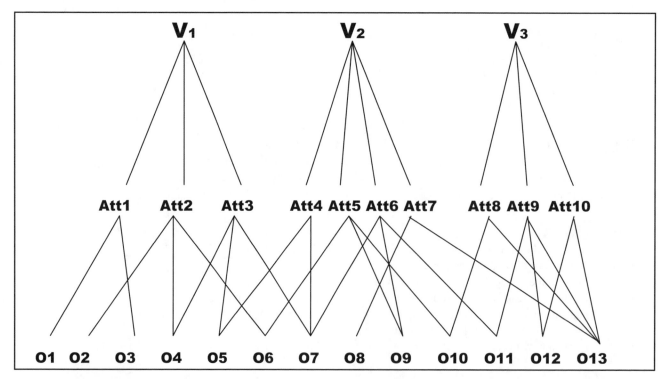

Model 4: Interconnections among values and opinions via attitudes (V = Value, Att = Attitude O = Opinion.)

Conceptualization of Attitudes

What is an attitude? In pioneering efforts, Allport (1935: 805) viewed attitude as: "A mental and neural state of readiness, organized through experience, exerting a directive or dynamic influence upon an individual's response to all objects and situations with which it is related." (Also see Allport, 1994.) Similar orientations were maintained in subsequent conceptualizations, such as McDavid and Harari (1968: 129): "An attitude may be defined as a relatively stable system of organization of the behavior displayed by a person toward a particular object or set of objects." What Allport refers to as a "mental state of readiness" and for McDavid and Harari is a "System," was put into excellent perspective by Hollander (1971), in this manner: An attitude is a chain that links two very distinct and important manifestations that humans confront every day. These are opinions and values. Model 4 illustrates Hollander's explanation and can aid in the understanding of leisure and recreation attitudes.

According to the model, attitudes are influenced by one's values and what is held important. Moreover, attitudes are not seen nor heard, but inferred from one's opinions. While values and attitudes are covert, opinions are overt, with the former limited in number but the latter expressed in many ways. (The number of manifestations increases as we move down in the model.) Finally, in terms of ability to change, a value is the most difficult. An attitude would be possible to change through presentation of ideas, information, or positive and/or negative impressions. Finally, opinions are much easier to change, based on convincing reasons and logic. This issue of attitude change will be related to leisure and elaborated upon later.

Background Perspectives of Attitude Assessment, with Emphasis on Leisure

The study of attitude was used in almost all life concerns and activities. Attitude and its assessment gained extensive initial attention in social psychology. Many other service areas, as spin-offs, found a demand for it, such as education, rehabilitation, sports, work, criminology, the homeless way of life, marketing, management, health, counseling, and social work. All of these rely on knowledge gained from social psychology. (For attitude assessment in education, see Lumpe et al., 2000; in fitness, see Kerner and Grossman, 1998; for consumers, see Bang et al., 2000; for the homeless, see Lester and Pattison, 2000; in criminology, see Samra-Grewal

and Roesch, 2000; in health, see Fleming et al., 2000; and for work, see Fisher, 2000.)

Leisure and recreation fields were no different. They found uses for attitude concepts in understanding what people know and believe about leisure; how they feel; and what they plan to do (see Burdge, 1961; Neulinger, 1974; Iso-Ahola, 1980; Crandall and Slivken, 1980; Mannell and Kleiber, 1997). Leisure scholars emphasized the value of studying individual attitudes toward leisure, to be able to enhance involvement, contributing to personal outcomes (positive emotions, enjoyment, satisfaction, wellness, and vitality) and development.

Importance of and Challenges to the Study of Attitudes

Understanding the nature of attitudes is crucial to all fields. To explain choices and to make changes, different fields required the use of attitudes. At times, the relationship between attitude and behavior was inconsistent, as mentioned above, creating doubts and mistrust in the value of understanding and working on attitudes. But efforts persisted in distinguishing the causes behind inconsistencies between attitude and behavior, such as the work by Kashima and Lewis, 2000; Smith and Mackie, 2000; and Tarrant and Green, 1999. Therefore, interest in studying attitudes has been gradually renewed.

Going back to the very basics of knowledge about attitudes can provide practical insights. For instance, most individuals who go to college value education; those who exercise value health, fitness, and/or appearance; and those who travel value experiencing new places and/or cultures. Two issues arise from these relationships: first, it is true that the above statements do not apply to all users. Second, the relationship, for instance, between exercising (behavior) and having a positive impression and feeling of fitness (attitude) might not be there or applicable in all cases. The following statements contain paradoxes, which at times tend to puzzle listeners, readers, or interpreters: "Leisure is good, but I do not do many activities." "Health is important, but I smoke or I do not exercise." "Television is a waste of time, but I watch it for hours every day." For decades, science has been attempting to explain the causes for such inconsistencies.

The paradoxes in these responses are due to intervening or moderating factors. This will be explained further in the form of constraints or barriers. Those constraints may be norms or habits, traditions or social contexts, lack of skill, lack of companions to do activities with, money, or time. Moderating and modifiable aspects are currently identified and carefully investigated in the study of attitudes (e.g., Fleming et al., 2000; Maio et al., 2000; Crano and Prislin, 1995). To better understand the impact of modifiers, intervening factors must be controlled and careful tests of relationships should be designed and performed to arrive at valid findings. Otherwise, the early confusing and conflicting results will reoccur repeatedly and make observers doubtful of relationships that actually exist: in this case, with attitudes, behaviors, and many other variables.

Components of Leisure Attitudes

Definitions and measurements of attitudes relied most heavily on scientists' conceptual orientations of the nature and structure of attitude. If "attitude" is understood as simply liking or disliking, a definition and measurement of the affective component would be most emphasized (Thurstone, 1946; Fishbein, 1965; and Crandall and Slivken, 1980). On the other hand, when other investigators view it as composed of three components — cognitive, affective, and behavioral — definitions and assessments consequently follow (see Triandis, 1971; Martens, 1975; Ragheb and Beard, 1982). Hence, as a fundamental procedure, careful review of the literature and judgments would be required in this stage. Fundamentally, this is what determines the validity of what can be identified and accepted as content.

Founded on a social-psychological conceptualization of attitude, Ragheb and Beard (1982) obtained evidence for three components in leisure attitude, as defined empirically:

1. *The Cognitive Component* is the beliefs and general knowledge of leisure, its association with domains such as productivity, health, self-improvement, and renewal of one's energy. This component incorporates leisure characteristics, virtues, and how they relate to an individual's quality of life.
2. *The Affective Component* is an individual's evaluation or feelings toward leisure experiences and activities — liking or disliking them.
3. *The Behavioral Component* comprises the behavioral intentions and actions of an individual toward leisure choices, reporting on current and past engagements.

In the final analysis, these three components correlated moderately with each other, ranging between r = .63 to r = .47. This is a highly desirable overlap among any existing parts as evidence of discriminant validity. More recently, Van de Ven et al. (1996), in Australia, employed factor analysis to show that tripartite (cognitive-affective-behavioral) measure-

ment strategy of attitudes was still an appropriate decision.

Fluctuation of Attitude Components between Settings

There is no absolute or clear direction as to how attitude and its components associate with behavior. Interesting conditions will impose directions. These include the nature of the setting, the kind of issue, situational sensitivity, and the presence of others. Two examples will be used as scenarios, demonstrating how misleading research outcomes may constrain the value of the study of attitude in many areas, including leisure and recreation. This happens as a result of confusion, resulting — as stated before — in frustration and loss of trust in the existence of relationships. The influence of some moderating aspects may prevent relationships from appearing.

Most interestingly, one study observed how attitude components shift in their impact on given phenomena. In supporting the validity of a one-component strategy of attitude, Verplanken, Hofstee, and Janssen (1998), in the Netherlands, found that the "affective-based evaluations" are more accessible in memory than "cognitive-based evaluation." Furthermore, Lavine et al. (1998), in a study of attitudes toward presidential candidates, obtained evidence that the affective component exerted a stronger influence than the cognitive one on attitudes toward candidates and voting behavior.

A third documentation, while attempting to solve conflict in developing models to predict consumers' attitudes, Bodur et al. (2000) reported evidence supporting the contention that "affect" does influence attitudes directly and independently of the mediation of the cognitive structure (belief).

Relative to our phenomena of leisure and recreation — if the above results by Verplanken et al., Lavine et al., and Bodur et al., are consistent here and used as scenarios — what may count is not what you know or believe about leisure (cognition) but rather how you feel about it, whether you like or dislike it (affective).

On the other hand, in investigating attitudes toward condom use, de Wit et al. (1997) observed that students reported a negative affect associated with condom use, while overall cognitions were far more favorable. In a second scenario relative to leisure — if this finding is consistent — what may count is what you know and what is in your mind, not how you feel about leisure.

The bottom line here is that, in the most logical and practical sense, the three components of attitudes will behave differently. The exact behavior depends upon the phenomena, situations, issues, circumstances, respondents' ages, and many other moderating factors. Just as components fluctuate in their presence and impact in political situations and the uses of condoms, they will also fluctuate with other domains such as leisure, marriage, divorce, diet, health, or work. Therefore, careful considerations in the control of variables should be given to uses of leisure attitude components.

Moderating Factors Impacting Attitude-Behavior Relationships

It is in vain to invest the most technical efforts and resources in developing sound psychometric procedures to assess attitudes without knowing and controlling moderating effects. How can we benefit from having the most valid and reliable attitude measurement to detect beliefs, feelings, and intentions if components and relations with behavior and/or other pertinent factors (e.g., longevity, health, stress, and satisfaction) fluctuate? The results will seem inconsistent.

Moderating factors tend to sneak in, like foxes that raid chicken coops, concealing existing influences by twisting and distorting results. Therefore, to advance uses of leisure or non-leisure attitude measurements, aspects that modify, intervene, and moderate outcomes should be identified, included, and tested for their possible impacts and relationships to what is investigated (for an example, see Tarrant and Green, 1999).

To further clarify the problems of moderating domains, we need to study how modifiers can change leisure, fitness, and recreation outcomes. Conceptually, Triandis (1971) insightfully identifies social norms, habits, and expected consequences that shape or cause attitude formation. More recently, Terry et al. (2000) observed support for one of Triandis' contention. They found that attitude-behavior consistency is strengthened if a person's attitudes are supported by a congruent, in-group norm that acted as a potential influence to moderate the relationships between attitudes and other behaviors.

Empirically, age and developmental level were modifiers of attitudes in a health promotions intervention with urban, African-American, school-age children (Fleming et al., 2000). Moreover, in a study on attitudes toward women managers, Brown (1995), employing canonical correlation, observed the influence of education, occupational level, and age as moderators of attitudes. Furthermore, Crano and Prislin (1995) found that hedonistic or vested interest is a major aspect fostering attitude-behavior consistency.

Moderators of leisure lifestyles might have neglected the impact of some key aspects on leisure attitude-behavior. The leisure literature identified many constraints and barriers (see Henderson, 1991; Jackson, 1988, 1990), which are potentially operating as moderators, intervening to block positively oriented leisure attitudes and, more importantly, leisure involvement. For example, two persons with the same gender, age, amount of free time available to them, and with similar scores on a leisure attitude scale may seem the same, but their actual behavior (involvement or participation in leisure) proves to be very different. What could be the intervening moderators that can close the doors of the leisure wonderland on one but not the other? Definitely, a whole host of factors can influence the person who is least involved in leisure and recreation. Scholars have identified many of these factors as leisure constraints. Such as I have free time, I like to exercise; but I do not. Why? Someone might ask. The answer is because after my work/school I am drained, lacking energy for exercise.

Of the numerous possible moderators that have potential to influence leisure attitude outcomes are the following: work schedules, school loads, amount of free time, families, stress levels, mood, vitality for leisure, personal energy levels, personality types, skills and competencies, income, locations, ages, health condition, religious beliefs, and many more aspects unique to every setting and each person. In this respect, leisure practitioners have an important professional, social, and moral responsibility to strive for accuracy to deliver their services effectively to those who need them.

Leisure practitioners must be competent in their knowledge of the impacts of attitudes. They must understand the basic concepts of attitude, how to assess it and use the results, how to interpret findings, how attitude-behavior functions, and how to help participants change attitudes, if needed or desirable. Leisure professionals are no longer just providers of activities, programs, services, and environments. Technically, they should be implementing social and behavioral sciences as assessors and agents of social change, enabling constituents to maximize their leisure rewards (see Ragheb, 1980).

Assessing Leisure Attitudes

Assessment of leisure attitude was one of the very first concepts to be studied in leisure appraisal in the modern era. As assessment of attitude was the earliest developed instrument in recent times to be constructed in the field of leisure, setting up a contemporary momentum for measurement construction. One of the points of demarcation for the history of formal, standardized assessment in recreation and leisure was the birth of the pioneering work on assessment of attitude by Burdge (1961). This was followed by the extensive efforts of Neulinger and Breit (1971), reporting on a scale called "A Study of Leisure." (Neulinger devoted extensive attention to understanding leisure attitude concepts and relating it to some other factors. (See his book *Psychology of Leisure*, 1976, which is centered on leisure attitude.)

Next was a Leisure Ethic Scale, developed by Bryan and Alsikafi (1975), utilizing 20 items and yielding three factors: Protestant Work Ethic, Leisure Ethic, and Work-Leisure Fulfillment. Within a scale assessing the cognitive component of work, Buchholz (1978) obtained four factors, one of which was relevant to leisure attitudes (eight items). In 1980, Crandall and Slivken, published their Leisure Attitude Scale emphasizing the affective aspects. Two years after, Ragheb and Beard (1982) constructed a scale measuring leisure attitude, demonstrating a three-factor structure: Cognitive, Affective, and Behavioral.

Specifically, the leisure attitude scales introduced above have unique characteristics. Being aware of these characteristics would be of benefit for professionals and researchers. First, Burdge's pioneering Leisure Orientation Scale asks respondents to rate leisure in comparison to work, such as: "My leisure activities are just as important to me as work activities." and "The only way I can justify my leisure time is to work for it." Relevant to the first item, someone can circle no, because leisure activities are more important; therefore, mistakenly, s/he will be rated low on this item. Crandall and Slivken and Ragheb and Beard identified other problems. In another report, Yoesting and Burdge (1976) concluded that, due to fluctuation in its implementation, the Leisure Orientation Scale "had deteriorated considerably over time," therefore suggesting its abandonment. Similarly, Buchholz's eight items of leisure had the same comparison, contrasting work to leisure.

Neulinger and Breit's scale included 150 items that yielded five factors: Society's Role in Leisure Planning, Self-Definition through Leisure or Work, the Amount of Perceived Leisure, Affinity of Leisure, and Amount of Work or Vacation Desired. Crandall and Slivken recognize the pioneering stimulation of Neulinger and Breit's scale. However, they demonstrated some weaknesses, such as the extreme length of the scale and the lack of psychometric evidence about the measurement's construct. Early measures lacked basic qualities. For example, Bryan et al.'s (1975) Leisure Ethic Scale and Buchholz's (1978) scale have a similar concern to Neulinger's scale

(1971): that is, a lack of psychometric documentation.

Regarding Crandall and Slivken's (1980) Leisure Attitude Scale, psychometric procedures were utilized, producing a 20-item scale, reduced to a short scale of 10 items. Factor analysis yielded three factors: Liking Leisure, Desire for Leisure Time, and Positive Spontaneity. Test-retests were reasonably good, ranging from .85 to .59. Yet, the scale seems to have two main difficulties: one is conceptual and the other is empirical:

First, while the conceptual intent of the scale was to develop an affective scale based on liking and disliking, three of the ten items (short scale), were evaluated as belonging to the cognitive component: knowledge, information, and beliefs (verbs or indicators that determine relevance to components are in italic): "5. Most people *spend* too much time enjoying themselves today." "9. Leisure *is* great." and "10. It *is* good for adults to be playful." The other three that were judged to belong to the behavioral component (intentions and past or current actions) are as follows: "2. I *admire* a person who knows how to relax." "4. I *would* like to *lead* a life of complete leisure." and "7. People *should seek* as much leisure as possible in their lives." As a validation concern, even though the items unintentionally belong to three components, factors can emerge, reliabilities can be demonstrated, and inter-factor correlations can result, without regard to the concept's content. The problem is a validity issue, not a statistical evidence of factor structure or reliabilities.

Second, concerning what was raised above about the empirical difficulty in testing concurrent validity, Ragheb and Beard included Crandall and Slivken's scale in their development of another attitude scale. Based on their analysis, they found that the reliability of Crandall and Slivken's scale could be improved by the deletion of the negatively stated item about guilt feelings. Moreover, in their pilot study, Ragheb and Beard realized that ALL negatively stated items of leisure attitude obtained low point-biserial correlations between the item and the total subscale score. Empirically, this suggests — based on current evidence — not using negatively stated items for the development of future leisure attitude measures. This is simply because they may not tap something of value to respondents' leisure attitude or they may create confusion in respondents' responses.

It is important to note that all of the above-mentioned scales are assessing leisure in its totality. In comparison, this strategy is the opposite of how leisure involvement is handled, concentrating almost exclusively on assessing involvement in specific leisure activities such as tennis, camping, or family vacations. (For more details, see Chapter 20 in this book on measuring leisure involvement.)

One of the exceptions to assessment of total attitudes — mainly pertinent to physical education — is the development of activity-specific scales of attitudes toward fitness, exercising, physical activities, and play. Examples of such scales are Attitudes Toward Physical Activity (Kenyon, 1968); Attitudes Toward Exercise and Physical Activity (McPherson and Yuhasz, 1968); Attitudes Toward Jogging Questionnaire (Riddle, 1980); Attitudes Toward Exercise Questionnaire (Anshel, 1991); and Children's Attitude toward Physical Activity Inventory (Schutz et al., 1985). Attention to attitudes toward exercising and physical recreation seems to be equivalent in focus to involvement in specific leisure activities.

Attitude Change

For the benefits of constituents, there are times when leisure professionals need to help users change their leisure attitudes to a more positive outlook. To change an attitude, you may follow a theory such as the one by Festinger (1957), with the attempt to create dissonance. This theory postulates that dissonance, in feelings or views toward objects, is emotionally unpleasant and uncomfortable. Therefore, dissonance sufferers attempt to create consistency among the three components of their attitude.

Consistency is searched for in three steps. First, among what they know (e.g., fatty food, cholesterol, heart attacks). Second, how they feel (e.g., "I like to be healthy"; "I enjoy a healthy and positive outlook.") Last, what they intend to do about it (e.g., "Given the time, I would do more leisure or more exercise.") In the attempt to create consistency, a balance among the three components will be achieved. Festinger's basic theorization is that, if one component is changed, modified, or collapsed, the sufferer will attempt to bring the other two components in line with the new one. Assuming that it is painful and uncomfortable to be inconsistent, searching for harmony between one's ideas or views, feelings, and intensions is something that people will do.

Applications of dissonance theory in leisure are highly needed. These applications will be useful in relation to some newly emerging phenomena: increasing weight problems resulting in obesity, the widespread reliance on fast foods and their negative effects, the lack of movement and its impacts, computer obsessions, and deteriorating health for an increasing number of people. More desirable ways for encouraging people to exercise, to live a healthy and active leisure lifestyle, to seek and achieve

vitality are in dire need of techniques for attitude change.

The following scenario can illustrate the application of the dissonance theory to change an attitude, using one of the following three strategies. If a person scored low on a leisure attitude scale (which was composed of the three components), dissonance can be created based on one of the components:

First, the simplest approach is to present the person with facts, information, or knowledge about the benefits and impacts of leisure, as well as the harm of being inactive. (Propaganda and brainwashing use this approach!) This can create awareness, ideas, and orientations that can reshape beliefs about leisure (e.g., relaxation, tension relief, enjoyment, stress reduction, healthier feelings, improving wellness, and living longer). To use an analogy, an attitude is like a three-legged table: breaking one leg makes it fall or *change* its position. So that imbalance prevents keeping objects upon the table. Therefore, to continue employing Festinger's dissonance theory, changing the affective or the behavioral components would discomfort the individual suffering from ambivalent feelings until s/he balances the other two, creating harmony.

Secondly, dissonance for the affective component could be brought about by using all of the accumulated leisure research findings on how to create "peak experience," "flow," "intrinsic motivation," "aesthetic experience or environment," "control and self-determination" of what is done, "intensity," and "absorption" in the leisure experiences to which the person is exposed. Attempts need to be made to provide personally designed choices with the above qualities, exposing individuals to experiences of their choices that generate pleasure, contentment, and liking (e.g., camping, musical events, or club invitations). If the affective component is improved through exposure to quality leisure encounters and their atmosphere, the other two will be more likely to follow and be consistent with the newly changed component.

Lastly, dissonance for the behavioral component is usually achieved by changing norms (group beliefs), habits, legislation, operating time (scheduling), providing people with more free time opportunities, developing skills, and providing workshops. Actual exposure (behavior) to new activities, experiences, extra time, and skills can help individuals to form ideas and gain knowledge (cognition) and/or experience positive feedback (affectance). These can be fulfilled through feeling good about themselves, experiencing success, and testing how far or high they can go. All are characteristics of the newly growing science of positive psychology.

In an applied sense, for example, some pre-retired persons were identified as having negative leisure attitudes. How can we change these negative attitudes? Employing a hypothetical strategy, we can have a caring policy, planning for pre-retirees to be exposed to leisure environments, activities, and skills at the expense of the corporation. This will help such persons reshape their cognitive orientations in order to develop a taste for, liking for, and positive evaluations of leisure. In turn, the probability of a person changing feelings and behavioral intentions will be greater, unless moderating aspects or constraints are much more dominant than expected. It is important to note that the easiest component to change is the cognitive component.

In some cases, no matter what you do, say, or present, attitudes will not change. A reaction that can illustrate this point is this: "I know that smoking is bad for my health. It will also take four years of my life, but I am not going to quit." Ethically, at least, concerned professionals and systems have done their share. In the case of smoking, changing beliefs might not reshape attitude, but changing health conditions (e.g., a stroke, as an outcome of smoking) can alter feelings and intentions.

Considerations in Studying Measurements of Leisure Attitudes

Are we locked into the traditional social-psychological orientation of the 1960s and 1970s, believing that attitudes are either an affective feeling or a combination of cognitive, affective, and behavioral components? Contemporarily, accumulated evidence suggests some more innovative and creative ideas to consider in assessing attitude components. For instance, based on a mathematical theory of attitude, Stamm and Dube (1994) explored and found evidence of the existence of four attitudinal components: Direction, Intensity, Closure, and Involvement.

Furthermore, in a psychometric study constructing a scale entitled The Computer Attitude Measure, Kay's (1993) analysis revealed four factors: Cognitive, Affective, Behavioral, and Perceived Control. Therefore, new ways, conceptualizations, and orientations need to be identified, explored, and implemented. In this we recognize further attitudes toward leisure, parks, recreation, exercise, play, and facilities, all for the benefit of beneficiaries using their free time and leisure.

Existing Measurements Assessing Leisure Attitudes

The following assessments measure general leisure attitude.

1. Leisure Orientation Scale (LOS) (Burdge, 1961)
2. Measurement of Leisure Attitude (MLA) (Neulinger and Breit, 1971)
3. Leisure Ethic Scale (LES) (Bryan and Alsikafi, 1975)
4. Leisure Ethic Subscale (LES) (Buchholz, 1978)
5. Leisure Attitude Scale (LAS) (Crandall and Slivken, 1980)
6. Leisure Attitude Measurement (LAM) (Ragheb and Beard, 1982)
7. Leisure Coping Belief Scale (LCBS) (Iwasaki and Mannell, 2000)

The following measure attitudes about specific-leisure activities (mostly exercising and fitness).

1. Attitudes Toward Jogging Questionnaire (ATJQ) (Riddle, 1980)
2. Children's Attitude toward Physical Activity Inventory (CATPAI) (Schutz, Smoll, Carre, and Mosher, 1985)
3. Attitudinal Beliefs Regarding Exercise Questionnaire (ABREQ) (Godin, Shephard, and Colantonio 1986)
4. Attitudes Toward Exercise Questionnaire (ATEQ) (Anshel, 1991)

Summary and Conclusions

A careful review of the accumulated body of literature on attitude reveals its implementations in all applied areas. The reason behind this wide attention is that knowing what our constituents know, feel, and intend to do can be utilized as one basis for providing quality services. We can maintain participants' involvement, treat their negative impressions, and maximize rewards and outcomes for their benefit. An attitude toward an object is a very functional chain, connecting a person's core values to her/his expressed views (opinions).

So far, leisure attitude can be represented by a maximum of three components: cognitive, affective, and behavioral. But contemporary findings suggest the possibility of attitudes being based on a structure of more than three components. In many cases, moderating factors intervene altering the nature of relationships among attitudes and a large host of pertinent aspects. Therefore, it is recommended that moderating domains be identified and controlled.

Concerning the availability of leisure attitude scales, unfortunately, despite the importance of the notion of attitude and its application in leisure, only six general leisure attitude scales were identified covering a span of time from 1961 to 2001. Fortunately, however, many more leisure-specific attitude scales were constructed to assess attitudes toward fitness, exercise, and physical movement (see Ostrow, 1996). Professional needs probably are geared more to the uses of leisure-specific attitude scales. Five of these specific scales were reported for their relevance to physical recreation, recreational sports, and exercising as free time choices.

Skills in handling assessment are needed to maximize benefits gained from understanding the nature of leisure attitudes. Moreover, competencies are required in using assessment tools, interpreting results, and applying assessment findings for users' benefits. All this is to be achieved not only for purposes such as attitude change and leisure education, but also for leisure counseling and for leading participants to enjoyment of optimal leisure engagement. One of the values of assessment of leisure attitude is to utilize findings to enable a person to change her/his attitude for more positive functioning. There are some specific approaches founded on theories of attitude: dissonance and consistency.

In conclusion, studies of leisure attitudes are viable and functional in their contributions. Understanding leisure attitudes can serve practice: leisure education, leisure counseling, and programming. It can also serve research, investigating relations of leisure attitude to other life domains to gain knowledge to be incorporated in models and theorizations, explaining contemporary phenomena, and to enhance professional preparation and field services. Furthermore, general and specific leisure attitude scales are needed in the 21st century to respond to changes in lifestyles, gender equality, and the return to the outdoors.

Questions and Exercises

1. Discuss the conceptualization of leisure attitude.
2. How would values, attitudes, and opinions interrelate?
3. Explain the background perspectives of attitude assessment.
4. Why is it important to study attitude? How would attitudes help understanding behavior?
5. Explain the issue of attitude-behavior relationships. Why was the study of attitude "in" then "out" then "in" again?
6. Debate the possible components of attitudes.
7. How would attitude components fluctuate logically in their existence and importance based on changing settings?
8. What is the influence of moderating factors on attitude-behavior relationships?
9. Explain the issues of assessing leisure attitude.
10. How can you change a person's attitude? Explain the process.

Chapter 24

Free Time Boredom: From Concepts to Measurements

Focus of Chapter

To comprehend the impact of free time boredom (FTB) and to be able to plan strategies when we encounter it, two questions need to be answered: What is the nature of boredom? Why do we need to study free time boredom? Strategically, boredom can move into many areas, potentially reaching almost all of our life domains, such as work, family, and friendship. The purpose of this chapter is to demonstrate the interrelationships between boredom and a large number of maladaptive behaviors. Such behaviors can operate as inappropriate self-medication, including gambling and drugs, evolving into pathologies or epidemics. Answering the above questions will prepare us for the next chapter, which looks at the kinds of boredom currently existing in our society. Ultimately, by the virtue of this preparation, a leisure practitioner can diagnose boredom when s/he sees it, utilize preventive measures skillfully, and be able to treat it, when it is prevalent. The practitioner needs to competently employ the appropriate tools or strategies by being equipped with sufficient knowledge on boredom's pathological nature and complexity so that clients' functioning and quality of existence will be enhanced.

Key Terms

- alcoholism
- crime
- depression
- drug abuse
- *ennui*
- gambling
- individual functioning
- lack of interest
- lack of stimulus
- maladaptive behavior
- passivity
- pathology
- placebos

Key Names

- Richard W. Bargdill
- Richard F. Farmer
- Seppo Iso-Ahola
- John R. Kelly
- Susan M. Shaw
- Norman D. Sundberg
- S. J. Vodanovich

Objectives

- Realize why professionals need to understand the nature of free time boredom.
- Recognize characteristics of boredom as pathology.
- Explain how boredom can creep into an individual's life.
- Compare characteristics of boredom to their counterparts in stimulus seeking.
- Describe boredom in a holistic way, incorporating family, work, and free time.

- Identify behavioral disorders associated with boredom, such as gambling, alcoholism, drug abuse, crime, depression, and suicide attempts.

Free time boredom, defined as a state of monotony and inactivity in informal times, is interwoven with boredom in two other critical domains: the family and work. If a person suffers from boredom during free time, family, and/or work, behavioral disorders, such as alcoholism and depression, may manifest themselves. These conditions can negatively impact health, vitality, functioning, and happiness. Therefore, coordination among professionals in work, family, and free time is badly needed to control boredom. (See Kelly and Kelly, 1994, on meaning in three domains: work, family, and leisure.) Boredom escalates to attack the totality of life.

The concept of boredom will be related to free time, leisure, and recreation: The intention is to demonstrate reasons to search for desirable, exciting, and needed wholesome activities. When failing to attain this healthy level of functioning, individuals usually report uncomfortable feelings, consistently referred to as boredom, sometimes (in deteriorating cases) as *ennui*. This state can occur when a person is unable to convert his/her free time into a rewarding leisure experience or positive activity.

The purpose here is to present knowledge about boredom, illustrating uses of this understanding as a means towards achieving desirable leisure and recreation ends. Some of the aims of the leisure delivery systems are to increase participants' active involvement, healthy lifestyles, maximizing gains, rewards, and improvement of quality of existence. O'Connell's (1984) suggestion to recreational therapists (RTs) is relevant to this discussion and is an important idea for all professionals providing leisure and non-leisure activities: The RT should not only provide patients with ways of expressing their difficulties (such as boredom, depression, disorientation, or isolation), says O'Connell, but also should provide patients with active means of reducing and controlling these problems.

Reasons to Understand the Nature of Boredom

Why is it necessary to explore the nature of boredom in free time? By using a comparison with health care practices, the question can be answered appropriately. Medicine's ultimate goal is to maintain health and treat illnesses through knowledge of diseases (origination, cycle, and treatment through pharmaceutics and/or practice), developing the science of pathology.

Similarly, leisure service professionals offer recreation programs and activities, fitness, tourism, arts, play, and different facilities. All are provided for individuals' enjoyment through involvement, excitement, interest, and challenge. But sometimes individuals are dysfunctional in their leisure pursuits, unable to use their free time appropriately to maximize their leisure gains. (Societies throughout the world are suffering from many problems caused by inactivity and the misuse of the free time that technology is yielding.) Speculatively, there are three main reasons for leisure professionals to understand the nature of boredom and its pathological manifestations:

1. To purposely prevent boredom through the maintenance of certain actions in leisure experiences, programs, services, and environments. (As an example of one of the applications, see Hickerson and Beggs, 2007 where findings related to students' leisure time boredom are related to the development and maintenance of campus recreational programs.)
2. To be able to treat boredom when it occurs.
3. To be able to maximize leisure rewards, by minimizing the prevalence of boredom.

Admittedly, certain behavioral and social ills can constrain participants, disallowing positive outcomes and enjoyment. Diseases or pathologies may manifest themselves in the presence of boredom (see Heron, 1957). Therefore, leisure professionals are not only required to help maintain active participation, providing a varied menu of activities, but also to function as therapists. That is, whether they recognize it or not, they are treating (or at best avoiding) social and behavioral ills by offsetting apathy and lethargy that can result in a state of boredom. Such an understanding can help in the development of an "anatomy" of boredom, learning how it manifests itself and spreads. Within this context, practitioners develop skills to control and divert boredom as a pathology that may limit the fulfillment of leisure.

Prevention is less expensive and more efficient than treatment, which can be very expensive and sometimes unattainable. This is the very reason for paying attention to the study and control of free time boredom. The goal is to prevent boredom from constraining a healthy, rewarding, and quality leisure lifestyle. Preventive actions are attained through being aware of boredom's nature and providing exciting outlets.

Over 50 years ago, Heron (1957) recognized this problem and attempted to investigate the pathology of boredom. He used an experiment that prolonged exposure to monotonous environments. Results showed that this exposure caused thinking impairment, childish emotional responses, visual perception disturbance, actual hallucinations, and altered brain wave patterns. Therefore, attempts to reveal the nature of boredom can be employed to prevent, offset, and treat it as a social pathology. Techniques include awareness, leisure education, attitude change, and provision and acquisition of skills.

Relying on common sense, almost all individuals attempt to maximize their leisure and recreational gains but, due to genetics, environment, or a certain situation, boredom may seem difficult to prevent. In a very interesting investigation, which can help to prevent and treat boredom, Mageau et al., (2000) obtained documentation for a possible necessary vent. They found that when all participants had the opportunity to *express* their boredom at the end of the experiment, the level of boredom was significantly higher for the participants that previously *suppressed* their boredom than for the participants of the control group.

Being able to express and act on boredom and the like can be our front line of defense. A very close analogy is that awareness of nutritional foods and their contribution to health can help individuals to act on making the right diet choices. This last finding by Mageau et al. has implications for leisure services, counseling programs, and environments to prevent boredom from starting and stop it from becoming epidemic. (Further elaboration on suppressing the expression of boredom will appear in a later section.)

The Nature of Boredom

Like stress and depression, boredom has unique common features. These attributes are shared among certain settings, environments, and personalities. Knowing and interpreting those features can help to control and avoid boredom's negative impacts. One interpretation of boredom is that most of these features result from the lack of an optimally exciting involvement. In a conceptual effort, Conrad (1999) observed that repetition, lack of interaction, and minimal variation contribute to boredom.

Another interpretation came about as a result of investigating the influence of activities on the length of time. Loehlin (1959) found distinctive, bipolar features such as interest vs. boredom, filled vs. empty, and activity vs. passivity that contribute to the perception of the length of time. So, it seems that emptiness and passivity cluster with boredom to give a perception of time dragging or stagnating.

A third interpretation is that individuals experience boredom when an activity or circumstance lacks social meaning (Barbalet, 1999). In this study, boredom was emotionally characterized as being restless, irritable, and with a need for something interesting.

A fourth interpretation was observed long ago in attempting to describe *ennui* (Dugas, 1929) — that might be more perversely apparent in contemporary times. He viewed *ennui* as the painful experience of being unable to be interested in current happenings.

Finally, in a fifth interpretation, boredom was found to associate with five health symptoms: obsessive-compulsive disorder, somatization, anxiety, interpersonal sensitivity, and depression (Sommers and Vodanovich, 2000). Analogously, perhaps boredom has been used as a "social hanger" — an easy expression of or rationalization for commonly inactive lifestyles, disinterest in current affairs, emptiness of choices, and non-stimulating happenings, all of which make individuals uncomfortable.

In sum, as far as the above five interpretations are concerned, boredom can be characterized as lack of excitement, slow speed of time, lack of social meaning, inability to be significantly involved, and suffering from health symptoms (e.g., depression or anxiety). In other words, it seems that the common theme among all these manifestations is the lack, deficit, or deprivation of flow of interesting physical, mental, and social pursuits. (For further information on the notion of flow or lack thereof, see Csikszentmihalyi, 1990.)

The Nature of Boredom Allegorically, What if it was a Person?!

The Untold Story about the Presence of "The Dot and Nothingness"

What type of personality can boredom resemble? By the virtue of the accumulated knowledge about its nature, features, and behavior, boredom would be like an uninvited and unwanted guest. This Mr. Boredom E. (BE) acts in the most disrespectful way. (The middle initial of Mr. Boredom ought to be E, for *Ennui*. The full-grown version, more severe, circular, and chronic, will be introduced later.) One of the characteristics of Mr. BE's personality is coming and going with his face down, no eye contact, withdrawn. He revolves gently and softly for a long duration as the host chooses. Seemingly, Mr. BE is without a goal or purpose, but he is actually hiding a nasty, long-range, and concealed agenda.

In the early encounters, the host (that can be you or I) may naively ask Mr. BE: "What can I do for you or with you?" The answer is, simply but not as simply, NOTHING. Actually *nothing* is what Mr. BE is there to introduce to the host. The pursuit of nothingness — if it can be called a pursuit — is the beginning of the string to follow. *Technically, from the point of view of existentialists, nothingness is regarded as a ground for anxiety.*

(Italicized statements, in the story, are possible interpretations)

In a host's life, BE starts very humbly, very small, as trivial as the size of a dot or a microscopic particle. Gradually, as the host accepts Mr. BE's presence, he starts to grow on the host, as long as there is consent, no objection, no resistance, and no reversal. The more Mr. BE grows, the more the host diminishes (figuratively) in size. Actually, the host will be losing control of the situation and becoming uninvolved. Ultimately, after BE takes over, the host will be reduced to a dot, exchanging positions with Mr. BE. The host reaches annihilation by host's choice, voluntarily.

BE started unnoticeable, content with nothing, seemingly benign, so to speak. But after a period of time — which Mr. BE does not care to watch — the real agenda evolves undetected and becomes malignant. Mr. BE's intention is to be bigger than what the host was prepared for or aware of, leading the host to self-chosen annihilation (or suicide), with both Mr. BE and the host vanishing.

Characteristically, Mr. BE loves (instinctively or genetically) to die triumphant, preferably young. Mr. BE instinctively knows that for him there is a rebirth, a reincarnation, so to speak; repeating the same

nothingness and annihilator's cycle with another naïve host.

It is most important to note that newly advanced technologies and entertainment devices include in them many unseen potential dots, virus-like. They are newcomers joining the more developed generation of BE in the environment. These advancements might quickly help in changing last names, from being BE to EB (Ennui B. – the more virulent and grownup version of boredom), for its resilience and being chronically existential.

As Mr. BE or EB takes control, slowly or sneakily but deliberately, he will start to invite the host to particular places and actions. Sometimes these involve actions never pursued before. Soon they will be self-initiated, self-destructive, without an idea or a desire to get rid of that veiled guest. *An occupational secret known to EB is that the more the host self-initiates to go to these places and commit these acts, the more EB as a guest will tighten his grip on the host's life, gradually staying longer and longer.*

Progressively and swiftly, Mr. EB will be opening doors widely for the drama to come, facilitating for a broad array of choices, starting softly and ending in violence or death. *From watching television aimlessly, seeking all possible entertainments, spectator behaviors, following fads and fashions, and nude shows. All can serve as preparation for more serious, detrimental acts or maybe dysfunction, such as gambling, smoking, pornography, illegal drugs, alcoholism, and all sorts of delinquency and/or crime.*

All in all, when Mr. EB takes over, disorders can

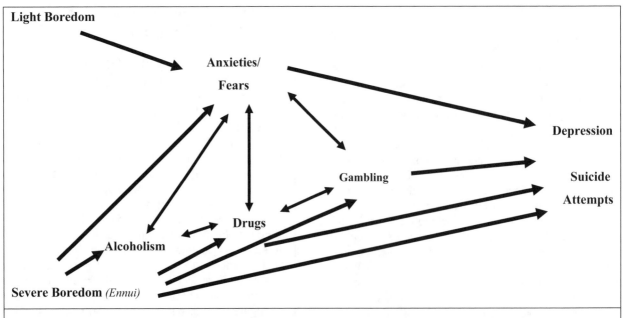

Model 5: Evolution of Mr. Boredom (Ennui)

create a wave or a flow of potentially devastating reactions, taking the host to uncharted waters, more acute sentiments, and negative emotions. These tend to be reoccurring, unending, and more persistent, rushing the host to self-destruction as fast as possible. That is how tricky and paradoxical that guest is, especially when the host fails to realize and oust him by replacing him with something desirable, and at best exciting. *The originally unrealized emotions and sentiments start with anxieties, depression for a duration, especially when combined severely with Mr. EB, ending with greater emptiness and goallessness — resulting in suicidal attempts (see Model 5).*

Potentially Devastating Destruction

How can Mr. EB be defeated? One of the best initial encounters is very simple, as simple as the creeping of the initial, low-key Mr. BE and its nothingness. That step is through AWARENESS: awareness that an unwanted and undesired guest is about to creep in with the intent to take over while the host is not paying attention. *Later, awareness must be followed by full involvement in endeavors that are self-motivated, exciting, and valued (with positive attitude).*

The reverse of the model provides a better outcome. In an early stage of BE's tenure, what will happen when Mr. EB meets or stumbles on Mr. Stimulus Seeker (SS)? This is a different angle to the story, which is the moral lesson here. While Mr. BE is attempting to creep in and slowly getting oriented, Mr. SS, the host — with clear awareness and skills — will be reaching out for exciting choices, unintentionally paying no attention to low-key and genteel but not merciful Mr. BE.

Brilliantly, SS would be leaving what started as a dot, staying as a DOT, or even less. If Mr. SS is involved in activities with intensity and flow, Mr. BE won't even be noticed because there will be no uninteresting activities for him to feed on. Mr. SS will be far away from self-initiated associations with Mr. BE, causing the dot to get smaller and smaller until it is totally annihilated. SS's behavior can function as a desirable preventive medicine, before reaching a stage of pathology or developing friendship with an unwanted guest. (This issue of stimulus seeking will be covered in the next section, as a countermeasure to Mr. BE.)

Moreover, it seems that what can be characterized as "interesting" or "having flow" to offset Mr. BE and EB should exhibit certain qualities known to be optimally arousing and exciting. Comparing Mr. SS to Mr. EB is like comparing day to night, hot to cold; for stimulus seeking and boredom are two opposites, as extrovert versus introvert. Therefore, stimulus-seeking characteristics and phenomena are

useful to comprehend, for what they reveal about the nature of their countermeasure: Mr. E. Boredom.

Stimulus and Arousal Seeking as Counterweights to Boredom

The absence of stimuli, as a theory of motivation, can cause drowsiness, less alertness, and finally boredom. Ellis (1973), in his extensive review and theorization, identified numerous attributes of stimulus seeking and arousal seeking. As demonstrated at length, the counterpart of these attributes results in boredom, as an outcome of the absence of arousal.

The list below was developed to equip leisure practitioners with tools and bases for prescriptions as preventive measures. Evidence, based on Ellis work, is presented below supporting the pertinence of the following list of indicators to achieve or reach a state of stimulus seeking:

- A drive for exploration
- Humor
- Rearranging old ideas
- Dissonance
- Optimal level of excitement
- Ambiguity
- A need for novelty
- Conflict
- Unpredictability
- Mismatch
- Manipulative drive
- Complexity
- Interaction with the environment
- Surprise
- Varied sensory inputs
- Activation
- Generating or containing information
- Uncertainty
- Investigation or testing
- Unfamiliarity

These indicators apply in different ways to each individual, generating optimally arousing encounters and sustaining desirable experiences. There is no specific formula or prescription as to which of these features would be greater contributors to the control of boredom. What works for an individual is a subjective matter. Perhaps mixing and matching through trial and error can show what works for given settings, stages, circumstances, or personal encounters. Besides, the nature of personality will determine what is appropriate to control boredom.

Comprehending antecedents and consequences of stimulus seeking help in dealing with it. The duration of engagement in novel, cognitive, stimulating tasks was found to associate with higher IQ levels (Williams, 1997). Combining the above novelty with Zuckerman et al.'s (1970) finding puts things into perspective: It was found that high sensation seekers preferred more complicated tasks and used more drugs and alcohol.

Investigators suggested a physiological (genetic) predisposition for sensation seeking behavior. Also, Green-Demers' (1991) dissertation revealed that participants in a boring free recall task used five interest-enhancing strategies:

1. Challenge enhancement.
2. Exploitation of stimulation from physical context.
3. Introduction of variety within the task.
4. Provision of self-relevant rationales.
5. Focused intentional involvement on the task.

These five strategies are very strong evidence of the necessity of the above arousal-seeking notion as an anti-boredom mechanism, whether in work, family, or free time.

Moreover, Seib and Vodanovich (1998) found that being attentive or absorbed by the tasks associated negatively with the difficulty in keeping oneself interested and entertained. The Internal Stimulation Subscale of the Boredom Proneness Scale (Farmer and Sundberg, 1986) was utilized to measure boredom. For play being characterized with a multitude of variations, novelty, and complexities, a lack of motivation (amotivation, Deci and Ryan, 1991) to play or recreate can cause inattentiveness, lack of involvement, and disinterest. Based on a discussion of theories of play, Jackson and Angelina (1974) defined play as stimulus-seeking behavior, motivated by a drive for arousal.

In sum, lack of stimulus-seeking opportunities in work, the family, or informal times and activities evolve to result in cognitive inattentiveness, sluggishness, and discomfort that can be called boredom. On a continuum, individuals usually swing between two extremes: from a highly stimulating and interesting point that can be considered "meta-stimulant" to a strong loss of interest in almost everything, as a "meta-unnerved" or "meta-deadened" existence or reaction (see Maslow, 1969, in a similar context).

Scope of Boredom in Daily Encounters and Its Consequences

A human being needs to be looked on as a whole person. Instead of dividing the person into structural parts, roles to play, and reactions toward life domains, a family-work-free-time fit needs to be considered:

Extra focusing on analytic approaches, without a careful balance with holistic and integrative paradigms of the individual tends to provide fragmented explanations and incomplete understandings, distorting resulting outcomes and interpretations.

A human is undividable; all of the life circumstances have to be observed to obtain valid conceptualizations. Therefore, for boredom to be viewed in general, it will be treated in terms of its presence within three major areas of life concerns: family, work or school, and free time. Boredom may be manifested in varying degrees in any of these major areas.

There is evidence in interviews by Bargdill (2000) suggesting that individuals became bored with their lives after they had compromised their life projects for less desired projects. The participants in these interviews adopted passive and avoidant stances toward their lives that allowed their boredom to defuse to more aspects of their existence.

Documenting the notion of boredom spreading from work to other aspects of life (e.g., family or free time) can draw from the generalization theory in leisure and play (see Ellis, 1973) and spillover theory (Kelly and Godbey, 1992). The theories postulate that what individuals do in their work would have a chance to spread, generalize to, or spillover to other pursuits. Realization of any such interrelations is not feasible unless all domains are accounted for simultaneously, as parts of a jigsaw puzzle, to estimate boredom's pervasive ability, speed, and power.

As a result, many disorders associate with boredom that stems from one of these three areas, or a combination thereof. Dysfunctions relating to boredom can range from depression and suicide to drug abuse and obsessive gambling. It is assumed, for a person to fully control boredom, generating interest, and stimulation in one single domain (either family or work or free time) would be a ground to save a person from potential disorders. That single interesting domain can create a limited buffer, resiliency, and defense against full control by boredom.

First, boredom in the above three domains will be introduced, followed by relationships between boredom and disorders, as outlined below:

A. Boredom in Major Life Domains
    1. Boredom in Marriage and the Family
    2. Boredom in Work/School
    3. Boredom in Free Time/Leisure
B. Boredom and Behavioral Disorders
    1. Boredom, Lack of Meaning, and Suicide
    2. Boredom and Depression
    3. Boredom and Alcohol and Drug Abuse

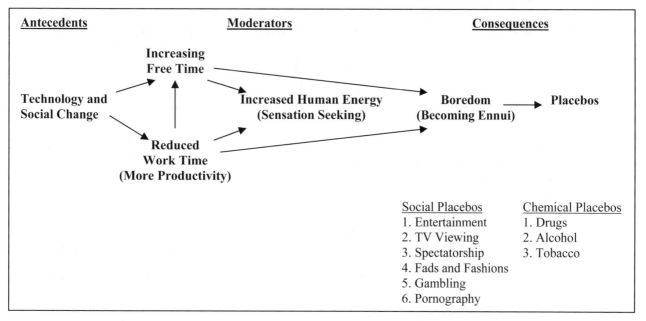

Model 6: Impacts of technology and social change on work, free time, human energy, boredom, and placebos.

4.   Boredom and Gambling
5.   Boredom and Juvenile Delinquency/Crime

It is important to recognize the historical settings of work, family, and free time, as they exist within a larger frame of culture and its conditions. As Model 6 depicts, within a cultural frame of reference, technology and social change have come to influence almost everything: the nature and kinds of work, availability of free time, family relations, and the savings of human energy. As such, contemporary civilizations are experiencing advanced technologies and problems like never before, followed by rapid social changes. Consequently, many cultures are experiencing less strenuous work because of technology. That can lead to boredom, followed by more demands on social and chemical placebos such as entertainment and substance abuse.

As a response to the complexity of life settings and the spread of boredom in almost every life domain, seven measurements have been developed and reported:

1.   The Boredom Proneness Scale (Farmer and Sundberg, 1986)
2.   The Boredom Susceptibility Scale (Zuckerman, 1979)
3.   Sexual Boredom Scale (Watt and Ewing, 1996)
4.   Leisure Boredom Scale (Iso-Ahola and Weissinger, 1987)
5.   Job Boredom Scale (Grubb, 1975)
6.   Lee's Job Boredom Scale (Lee, 1986)
7.   Free Time Boredom Scale (Ragheb and Merydith, 2001)

Complete details about the items of each scale are reported on:
http://uwf.edu/svodanov/boredom/measures.htm
(Retrieved on July 23, 2011).

The above seven scales did not account for boredom in two major life domains; that is school and the family. First, school routine and discipline can result in boredom. Second, there is no doubt that an emotional state can strike the family or seep into it causing damage, such as disloyalty, divorce, and infidelity. To face school boredom, officials need to assess its magnitude and causes; therefore, a scale is needed to serve this purpose. Another scale is needed to assess family boredom; but, due to the sensitivity of the matter, scientists are refraining for approaching this task.

Observations and Exceptions of Model 6

First, what we now call work used to be more aptly described as labor 100-150 years ago, when laborers put in six days a week, 11 hours a day. About 50 years ago, labor turned to work, due to automation. Lately, work turned to push buttons, sometimes touch screens or just talking to a machine to type something or to process a bank transaction. As such, work is much less strenuous than before and it has lessened in its demands. No name can be found for this "lesser demanding work." This type of work can be characterized as "emotional." Less demanding work leaves extra energy and time for other advanced pursuits or it leaves us starving for pursuits. These pursuits can range from the most creative, innovative, fulfilling, and meaningful to the most harmful and destructive to society and self (see Nash, 1953; Maslow, 1954; Frankl, 1962). Starving for pursuits is conducive to boredom.

Second, this model does not apply to a number of groups:

1. Those who do demanding work in terms of time and energy; nothing is left for extra pursuits, or nothing is left for nothingness to be felt.
2. Those who have active and varied leisure lifestyles. They are leisurely aware, occupied, skillful, and educated for their leisure.

This model applies to those who are entrapped in social and chemical placebos in their free time, with choices that can be described as passive, inactive, non-stimulating, and unfulfilling for them. Only those who suffer from repetition, feeling empty, irritable, passive, and restless, experience a sense of boredom.

Boredom in Major Life Domains

To control boredom in life, at least one domain should experience excitement and meaningful involvement. For meta-satisfaction and meta-stimulation, excitement and meaningfulness should be achieved in all three domains. One domain is a minimal protection against boredom's entrapments. Experiencing boredom in the three domains (family and marriage, work or school, and free time) can drive individuals to indulge in certain negative behaviors, called "meta-pathological" by Maslow (1969). Further, these behaviors can turn into disorders. Specifically, boredom in life domains can exist as follows:

1. Boredom in Marriage and the Family

Marriage and the family seem to be an institution that is strongly affected by boredom. Through clinicians' reflections from marital therapy sessions, Nichols (1987) found that boredom was viewed as a symptom of deeper, underlying problems. As demonstrated in another study, as difficulties persist and boredom grows in dominance, the marriage ends. Gigy and Kelly (1992) administered a 27-item checklist of reasons for divorce. "Boredom with the marriage" was observed as the second factor among nine dimensions, with the first being unmet emotional needs/growing apart.

Buffering some underlying problems was the focus of an experiment by Aron et al. (2000), using leisure- and recreation-like involvement. The experiment used a seven-minute shared participation in arousing and novel activities versus a control group. Aron et al. suggested maintaining excitement to control boredom beyond the honeymoon period as

a treatment to boredom. In the context of this chapter, a variety of shared leisure and recreation pursuits in marriage or leisure program settings can buffer potential discomfort and suffering from boredom and/or *ennui*.

In relation to children and Internet addiction, a study explored the effects of parental monitoring, leisure boredom, and leisure activity on teenagers in Taiwan (Lin, et al., 2009). Results showed that leisure boredom, Internet, and social activities increase the probability of Internet addiction; however, family and outdoor activities along with participative and supportive parental monitoring reduce the tendencies. Overall evidence indicates that parental monitoring is an inhibitor of adolescents' Internet addiction. Being bored during leisure time (not having other activities that seemed worthwhile) led to increased time being spent on the Internet.

2. Boredom in Work/School

On the conceptual level of boredom and work, simplification of factory work in the 1960s brought boredom and meaninglessness. The challenge of the work and a sense of commitment (involvement) to work were both removed (Sorcher and Meyer, 1968). In the 1990s, boredom and its underlying lack of personal meaning in work impacted on vitality and creativity in organizations (Gemmill and Oakley, 1992). In a study on young adults, Wiesner, Windle, and Freeman (2005) observed associations between high job boredom, depression, and alcohol use.

Fisher (1993), in an article on "Boredom at work: A neglected concept," accepts traditional explanations of boredom as stemming from outside the person (e.g., repetitive or extremely un-stimulating tasks). Adding a broader view, Fisher suggests that an integration of all aspects is needed to understand boredom in the workplace. This accounts not only for attributes of the task but also the environment, the person, and a person-environmental fit (see Holie, 2000), including boredom in family and free time.

Empirically, Sawin and Scerbo (1995) observed that employees with low proneness to boredom outperformed those with high proneness to boredom. Moreover, in another study, persons who were rated low on proneness to boredom had significantly higher internal work values (Vodanovich et al., 1997). In a study on 292 employees, it was found that individuals scoring high on both state boredom (job) and trait boredom were significantly more dissatisfied with the work itself, pay, promotion, supervision, and co-workers (Kass, Vodanovich, and Callender, 2001).

Schooling is a work-like setting, which is also affected by boredom. Quantitative and qualitative data (see Shaw et al., 1996) yielded evidence of high levels of boredom for a large number of students. This is due to lack of options as well as the imposed adult-structured activities. Therefore, it seems that work/school environments and their tasks are conducive to boredom under certain conditions. Simplification, meaninglessness, lower work values, lack of options, and structure created by others all impact negatively on productivity, vitality, creativity, interest, and satisfaction, yielding a common reaction: boredom.

3. Boredom in Free Time

Free time, as a third identified life domain, seems to provide the highest chance for boredom to seep in. That is due to the nature of free time: less obligating; lacking the type of structure found at work or school (keeping individuals busy, which sometimes prevents boredom); and being potentially inactive, invariant, and passive in nature. For some, free time is more exciting and interesting than work. However, free time is very conducive to behavioral disorders when people are left alone (e.g., depression, alcoholism, and gambling). Therefore, attention needs to be paid to the study of boredom in free time, for preventive and treatment reasons.

The literature provides evidence to prove that the prevalence of free time boredom is increasing. In Germany, Vagt and Kraschinski (1978) observed boredom/lack of activity as the first among seven factors causing problems for adults. Still (1957) reported that the percentage of work time is decreasing and that of leisure (free time) is increasing. As a result, he claims, "a new psychological (*and social*) disease of boredom" has emerged (italics added).

Also, more evidence showed that boredom jeopardized many qualities of the leisure and recreation experience. To that end, Iso-Ahola and Weissinger (1990) demonstrated that higher boredom in leisure decreased leisure satisfaction, health, social competence, intrinsic motivation, and self-esteem. Workers' susceptibility to boredom, shown by restlessness, was manifested frequently in daily habits and leisure time activities (Smith, 1955). Furthermore, in an experiment, Stein et al. (1995) found that subjects in the boredom versus flow treatment did not experience enjoyment, satisfaction, concentration, or control.

For many individuals, free time is increasing (e.g., Robinson, 1990), either by choice or by social force (such as early retirement). (See *Society for the Reduction of Human Labor: Newsletter*, 1992 and 1993.) Meanwhile, to avoid falling into the classical traps of boredom in free time, people need to be consciously aware of what they are up against and get prepared for it. This should be done through education for leisure, acquisition of leisure skills and competencies, improving personal leisure attitudes,

and developing self-understanding to confront free time. Otherwise, ill-manifestations can result. How boredom interacts with disorders and ill-manifestations will be the subject of the following discussion.

Boredom and Behavioral Disorders

Behavioral disorders do not exist accidentally or without a cause. There are distinct determinants for their manifestations, whether we realize them or not. Boredom was observed as a prevalent and influential domain that was associated with many disorders. Relationships among boredom and identified disorders were observed as follows:

1. Boredom, Lack of Meaning, and Suicide

Boredom can impact on health factors, jeopardizing individuals' wellness. The most drastic impact of any disorder on health is for an individual to end his/her life. Conceptually, it seems that severe lack of meaning and purpose in life can lead to suicide (see Frankl, 1962). Possible antecedents include depression, loss of hope, anxiety, and boredom. The road to collapse, then, is an evolving string, which can possibly be predicted. In many instances, the string begins with inactivity and disinterest in most of these domains: work, family life, and free time.

The literature reveals the existence of that string that ends with suicide or its attempts. Blair (2004) identified that the lack of meaning in life may be manifested as boredom or apathy. This can be described, in Frankl's (1988) terms, as "existential frustration" that evolves to an "existential vacuum." Boredom, or apathy, can serve as a stepping-stone toward meaninglessness, or even toward the grave as the moral story of "The Dot and Nothingness" goes. A strong illustration is that of George Sanders (1906-1972), a noted Oscar-winning supporting actor who committed suicide, "leaving a note that stated he was too bored to go on" (Chaneles and Wolsky, 1974: 432). This type of incident has been reported repeatedly, in many cultures, throughout history.

In a case similar to George Sanders, Maltsberger (2000) reported that a 30-year-old man, who twice attempted suicide, said life was boring, a purposeless burden, without meaning; and the only time he felt secure or close to his friends was when he was using marijuana, hashish, mushrooms, or LSD. Comparatively, for children and adolescents, suicide has been on the rise due to a number of reasons (Marfatia, 1975), one of which is adolescent boredom. Heled and Read (2005) reported that problems with alcohol or drugs, boredom, and depression were causes of suicide for New Zealand's high school students. Boredom and lack of meaning at all ages seems to be very costly. Using innovative and preventive strategies and activities — based on accurate assessment and understanding of boredom — can combat the monster of suicide. Through enhancing the search for meaning and controlling potential depression, we may be able to avoid suicide attempts that are preceded by boredom.

2. Boredom and Depression

It seems that the second serious disorder for boredom is depression or sadness. Does being bored cause depression? Or does being depressed about a loss of something significant lead a person to be bored with life? This relationship seems to be circular, with possible reciprocal impact of the two, or they might come together as a package. Assessing the two, or at least observing them in leisure settings, can help professionals to deliver quality therapeutic and humanistic services.

Caruba (2001) observed that depression is a loss of joyful life, a feeling of purposelessness, and difficulty focusing on the most common ways to handle boredom. In Caruba's estimate, there are over ten million Americans suffering from depression, and 10% of them will commit suicide. Possibly, these were among the main reasons Caruba founded the "Boring Institute."

Empirically, there is evidence to prove that boredom and depression associate together (e.g., Bargdill, 2000; Sommers and Vodanovich, 2000; Ejaz et al., 1997; Blaszczynski et al., 1990; Domagalska-Kurdziel et al., 1988; Farmer and Sundberg, 1986). Therefore, it is suggested that leisure professionals reformulate their objectives for this era, to be concerned about the total functioning of humans. These professionals should work toward the enhancement of quality of life and wellness through providing services that offset depression and combat boredom, offering optimally exciting leisure ventures appropriate for each individual, preventively and therapeutically.

3. Boredom, Alcoholism, and Drug Abuse

Somehow, alcoholism, drug abuse, and boredom associate together. Alcohol and drugs are consumed primarily during an individual's free time. Increasing consumption can be attributed to addiction or lack of leisure competencies, awareness, or attitude. In other words, suffering from boredom is operating as a constraint on leisure activities. Reporting on alcoholism, crime, and delinquency in the Soviet society, Field (1955) speculated that boredom, among other factors, might lead to such social problems as drinking, crime, and delinquency.

From Australia, Gordon and Caltabiano (1996) provided evidence that the heaviest substance users were those who scored high on sensation seeking; participation was highest for passive leisure and lowest for active leisure (see also Elia, 1992; Iso-Ahola and Crowley, 1991; Seaburn, 1987; Wilson, 1986). Moreover, in the U.S., Brumbaugh (1998) found that junior high school students who participated in a life skills program were 40% less likely to drink than non-participants.

Conceptually, while Kunz (1997) was serving in an Addiction Research Foundation in Canada, he reviewed research on the interrelationships between leisure and alcohol consumption between 1980 and 1994. Kunz identified four themes that would put the topic into perspective:

1. Alcohol is an integral part of leisure experience,
2. Drinking is an impediment to leisure,
3. Participation in active leisure reduces alcohol use/abuse, and
4. Drinking and leisure have no relation.

In sum, there seem to be consistent reports from one culture to another of the interrelationships between boredom, chemical dependency, drug abuse, and leisure deficiencies as behavioral disorders.

4. Boredom and Gambling

Consistent research evidence has demonstrated the relationship between boredom and gambling (e.g., McNeilly and Burke, 2000; Gunter, Stanley, and St. Clair, 1985). Slot-machine gamblers indicated that they played to alleviate boredom (Carroll and Huxley, 1994). Another study (Blaszczynski et al., 1990) observed that there are three subtypes of pathological gamblers: bored, depressive, and a mixture of the two. (The last subtype of pathology might point to a gradual evolution into entrapment, when nothing seems to work positively and there are no interesting encounters. A person may be bored first, evolving to depression, and then suffering from the two evils.)

More studies provide evidence that problem gamblers score high on sensation seeking or arousal and boredom susceptibility (Kuley and Jacobs, 1988; Dickerson et al., 1987). Gambling, with its many unknown factors and uncertainty of outcome, seems to attract those who have a high desire for sensation but fail to find it. Most likely, this is combined with the absence of challenging, interesting, and novel leisure options. Failing to meet a high desire for sensation is something that many parties can affect, ranging from the person him/herself to the parents and schools and leisure agencies.

5. Boredom, Juvenile Delinquency, and crime

In a study on 418 high school students, evidence indicated that those with higher levels of delinquent behavior reported more negative self-assessment and a higher tendency to experience boredom (Newberry and Duncan, 2001). In another context, Yin et al. (1999) found that less frequent participation in organized leisure and sport activities associated with higher involvement in adolescent delinquency. Organized leisure and sport activities seem to provide anti-boredom ingredients, such as challenge, interest, attention, meaningful involvement, and speed of time, which operate as buffers to prevent boredom.

Tobias (1970) investigated affluent suburban male delinquents in a Midwestern U.S. community. It was observed that boredom was one of the factors contributing to delinquents' antisocial behavior. The same issue was speculated about more than half a century ago (Field, 1955). In some critical stages, if activities and time do not carry certain qualities (such as excitement, intensity, involvement, novelty, and satisfaction), individuals seek other acts. Sometimes those acts are antisocial or criminal, chosen to elevate input and arousal.

Summary

This chapter attempted to demonstrate the prevalence of free time boredom. It demonstrated how leisure professionals need to understand the nature of boredom as a social and behavioral pathology. In all studies of pathology, whether medical, mental, social, or behavioral — to be able to diagnose and treat an illness — experts try to identify relevant features of what practitioners plan to control. This is vital for understanding pathology's causes, characteristics, attributes, behaviors, and how they manifest themselves. Because a state of boredom is undesirable, achieving an optimal level of stimulation is the goal of many providers; including leisure professionals.

In developing sound explanations, free time boredom was put into a larger perspective; incorporating family and work/school domains, achieving a holistic view of the total person and her/his encounters. When boredom strikes one domain, it is possible that it creeps into other domains, too. However, in some cases controlling boredom in one domain can produce resilience and resistance to boredom's entrapments. Boredom in any designated domain or, at worst, all of them may lead to a host of behavioral disorders. A number of disorders operate to elevate the level of arousal and may meet the need for stimulation, but not in a healthy way.

Therefore, a model was presented, theorizing that the root of boredom and uses of unhealthy arousal are imbedded in advanced technologies, modernity, and social change. By the virtue of progress, humans work less and exert less energy to meet life's necessities compared to a century ago, when labor was the theme of life. As a result, more free time is available now, sometimes not used as fully and meaningfully as it may. Add to that the extra human energy saved by performing lighter work, leaving individuals in dire need for sensation seeking. Altogether, with the lack of leisure skills, increasing passivity, and taking an easy way out or suffering from inertia, unhealthy substitutes sneak-in, taking over gently or ferociously, by choice or by imposition.

To counter this tremendous impact of boredom on life's domains, creating behavioral and social epidemics, service providers should be more prepared to encounter it, as presented in the next chapter. They should be able to diagnose free time boredom — within a context of other life domains — treat it, plan, and program societal and community strategies to control it. At least actions should be taken to minimize boredom's destructive impact.

Questions and Exercises

1. What are some of the main reasons to understand boredom?
2. What is the nature of boredom?
3. How would boredom creep in a person's life? Give examples from the story of "The dot and nothingness."
4. Describe the scope of boredom in daily encounters and its consequences.
5. Elaborate on boredom in the three major life domains: work-school, family, and free time.
6. How would boredom contribute to behavioral disorders?
7. Discuss how boredom contributes to each behavioral disorder.

Chapter 25

Applications of Free Time Boredom Concepts in Providing Leisure

Focus of Chapter

After laying some basic groundwork in the previous chapter, actions to benefit constituents and society will be the focus of this chapter. We will look at kinds of boredom that may first impact on free time and then evolve to prevent the enjoyment of a state of leisure. The literature yielded 14 kinds of boredom, speculating on eight contrasting sets of two or three kinds. These kinds of boredom lend themselves to a classification that can be integrated into three major categories. Sorting out the kinds of boredom provides insights into the scope and nature of boredom, showing mainly how boredom manifests itself. Due to the importance of assessment for diagnosis, treatment, and strategizing based on data; measurements of both general (non-leisure) and free time (leisure) boredom were identified. How can an individual overcome the problem of "slowness of time," as a part of one's free time? Using components identified empirically in a methodological study on free time boredom (FTB), a theoretical model will be suggested to solve the problem of the slowness of time as an outcome of boredom. Finally, for professionals and individuals to improve leisure lifestyles, a large number of research findings were accumulated, generating usable implications and suggestions for field applications.

Key Terms

- boredom
- physical involvement
- prevention
- slowness of time
- stages of free time
- treatment

Key Names

- Mihaly Csikszentmihalyi
- Orrin Klapp
- Marvin Zuckerman

Objectives

- Distinguish among identified kinds of boredom.
- Recognize common grounds among kinds of boredom, synthesizing them in fewer, more usable categories.
- Identify possible spreads of FTB categories, to be able to counter them through leisure.
- Assess FTB as a basis for diagnosis, prevention, and treatment.
- Describe stages of measuring boredom in general and in free time since scales originated in the 1920s.
- Identify through a model, the stages of FTB, starting with lack of physical and mental involvement, resulting in slowness of time.
- Describe implications — helping field actions — based on research findings.

While treatment is rather expensive, prevention is less costly. Taming boredom can be as simple as the following common sense statement, which is based on accumulated data and a suggested theoretical model reported below. In essence, for field applications and individual guidance a sound preventive and therapeutic strategy to control boredom can be summarized as follows:

Find or create activities that interest you, do a variety of them, maximize uses of your human machine, involve both body and mind, as much as you are able to, and use your hands and legs, as much as possible.

In application, the distance between common sense and actual adaptation can be great, requiring clear objectives and strategies. Some basic behavioral requirements can include sound leisure education, motivation, and positive leisure attitudes; all backed with necessary leisure skills.

Kinds of Boredom

For practical reasons, to be able to handle boredom in field settings, to assess it, and to relate it to other domains, kinds of boredom were recognized. The types of boredom presented below apply generally, and equally well, to family, work, and free time situations. Accordingly, eight sets of two or more boredom types were reported in the literature, with slight overlaps among them as follows:

First, *response boredom versus chronic boredom* was recognized by Bernstein (1975): Response boredom is caused by environmental arrangements and conditions (from without) that can be temporary, while chronic boredom emanates from within individuals and tends to last longer and reoccur more frequently.

Second, *existential versus interpersonal boredom* was reported by Orcutt (1984): Existential boredom was defined as a lack of purpose in life and tends to be more frequent. (There is a similarity between chronic and existential boredom.) It correlated positively and strongly with alcohol use among men. On the other hand, interpersonal boredom was defined as "small talk," lacking feelings of "happiness with people." Interpersonal boredom inversely associated with quantity of alcohol used by the two genders.

Third, *transitory versus chronic boredom* was identified by Ashford (1997). Transitory boredom is expressed as a deficit in sensation seeking (see Zuckerman et al., 1978), whereas chronic boredom is expressed existentially as lack of meaning (see Frankl, 1962). "Transitory" can be defined as short-term circumstances that an individual passes through relatively quickly. "Chronic boredom" persists, is cyclical, and is deeper. Chronic boredom can deepen to or be considered *ennui* (see Klapp, 1986).

Fourth, *endogenous versus reactive boredom* was conceptualized by Neu (1998). Endogenous boredom tends to color the whole of life, which seems to be overly prolonged. This is similar to depression, coloring everything gray. Also it can relate to the explanation of the top-down theory of life satisfaction (Krause, 1991), a general state of sentiments at the "top" resonates "down" to lower or specific satisfactions. In contrast, reactive boredom seems to arise as a response to particular objects (settings, conditions, or arrangements) that can be considered situational or temporary.

Fifth, *under-stimulating versus disconnecting boredom* was reported by Conrad (1999). Boredom as under-stimulation is characterized by lack of social interaction, repetition, and low variation, whereas disconnecting is viewed as experiencing irrelevance of the activity, situation, and others. Disconnecting relates to one's expectations, values, and personality. Orcutt's "interpersonal boredom" resembles disconnecting boredom.

Sixth Todman (2003) observed *sustained boredom, induced boredom, and chronic boredom* as kinds of boredom. Sustained boredom occurs when its feeling or the drag is prolonged, induced boredom is aroused or formed, and chronic boredom is circular and seems to be unending.

Seventh, *trait versus situational versus habitual boredom* were identified by Bargdill (1999, 2000). Pertinent explanations are as follows:

- Trait boredom is genetically related and runs in certain families. Trait boredom is the inherent lack of capacity or inner lack of interest that predisposes the individual to be bored, everything else being equal. The Boredom Proneness Scale (Farmer and Sundberg, 1986) is evaluated as a trait assessment tool.

- Situational boredom, on the other hand, is described as a reaction to repetitive and monotonous stimuli when a person experiences decreased arousal. Bargdill suggested that individuals who made active choices (some can be recreational) and experienced early success reported lower levels of boredom.

- Habitual boredom, the third kind, is forcefully customary and usual by addictive behavior. It is characterized also as existential. It can make people aware that they are their own source (or lack) of meaning. Habitual boredom can become chronic and even deeper, with the potential to reach the level of harmful *ennui*.

Eighth, *boredom as a lack of inner resourcefulness versus culturally conditioned boredom*: "Inner resourcefulness" (Neulinger, 1974) is relevant to preferences in using already existing personal capabilities such as creativity, physical dispositions, and mental abilities and talents. Mannell's (1985) concept of self-as-entertainment comes very close to using one's inner resourcefulness. Consequently, lack of inner resourcefulness and absence of self-as-entertainment would lead to boredom.

On the other hand, culturally conditioned boredom is fundamentally not only the impact of technology and modernity, but also the influence of norms, expectations, comfort, fads, fashions, and changeable ways of doing things. A list of cultural and social aspects relevant to modernity can illustrate how conditioning can be manipulated in quality and duration: television programs, computers, modern communication devices, microwaves, spectatorship attitudes, fads and fashions, and the number of stadiums existing nationwide. Entertainment resources, means of transportation, uses of appliances and available tools also impact on modernity by reducing time input and physical/mental energy expenditure. Heavy reliance on modern devices (versus primitive living) combined with inactivity can be the most conducive (inducing boredom, Todman, 2003) to the dominance of culturally conditioned boredom (similar to chronic and existential boredom in terms of effect and duration).

Both of these powerful aspects and variations can impact on boredom, operating as prerequisites to position vulnerable individuals to be disengaged, predictable, and disinterested. Hence, boredom is a natural byproduct or a stage in the evolution of this type of conditioning. Lack of inner resourcefulness and cultural conditioning both produce more acute boredom.

Overall, some severe kinds of boredom can create a state of stagnation, like a crippled car in the mud, stuck without tools or instruments (activities or actions) to rescue it. Paradoxically, sometimes equipment is available but unused for odd reasons. Thus, the above eight comparisons of types of boredom can bear practical implications, enabling leisure practitioners to detect signs of boredom and then make plans to counteract and control them. (See the section on implications at the end of this chapter.) Besides, to benefit from knowing these types of boredom in leisure assessment and non-leisure, developers of measurements should be aware of what is assessed: whether the boredom is trait-based, situational, chronic, transitional, habitual, or under-stimulating.

In sum, there are several varieties of boredom, resembling a chameleon in their ability to change time, color, or length. Sometimes, its manifestation is existential or personal, circumstantial or cyclical, imposed from top-down as a feeling toward some conditions, or springing up in response to general boring states, as well as being inherited or induced by the current situation. Integrating and classifying the 19 kinds of boredom help create a shorter, more informative, meaningful, and organized set of categories.

Simplified Model of Boredom

To simplify the above-mentioned 19 kinds of boredom a new set of categories was developed. Three main categories, environmental, acquired habits, and hereditary seem to encompass almost all of the types of boredom described above:

1. Environmentally Imposed Boredom: This category incorporates the majority of the kinds reported. Environmental situational boredom is a response or a reaction to something in the environment, characterized by being for a duration, transitory, and disconnecting individuals. It may be caused by currently occurring actions, surroundings, social interactions, or a lack of boredom-reducing actions.

2. Personally Acquired Boredom Habits (PABH): PABH is mostly due to lack of purpose, goal, and orientation in a given stage of life. This creates an emotional, mental, or spiritual vacuum characterized by being existential, chronic, and cyclical (habitual). Sometimes this is due to cultural and social norms and habits that condition individuals for instant gratification (one of the best allies of boredom). In turn, personal inputs and involvement are reduced, leading to dependence on excitement from external resources (e.g., others, television, computers, or entertainers).

3. Genetically Inherited Trait Boredom: This category is mostly genetic or hereditary. It is possible that some individuals are born bound to be bored more often than others, being vulnerable to boredom. They may have limited capabilities or a lack of inner resourcefulness for self-entertainment. Conditioning and social class can be moderating factors that increase or reduce trait dominance, by either suppressing or facilitating boredom manifestations.

Prevalence of the Three Categories

How widespread in society are these three categories? How dominant is a given category with different groups (e.g., children, teens, college students, employees, retirees, homeless, prisoners, and homemakers)? For practitioners in leisure delivery systems, education, and counseling, what implications can be drawn as bases for diagnosis, prevention, and treatment?

These three major categories vary with individual differences in their degrees of severity and ability to diagnose, prevent, and treat. It is assumed that environmental boredom is the least severe with better possibilities to observe and overcome. This simply requires situational and environmental changes, inducements, and stimuli.

Acquired boredom is more difficult to handle than environmental boredom. This is because it is deeply rooted; formed by accumulated layers of habits, situations, and offerings, turning repetitive boredom into chronic, cyclical, and existential boredom. Sometimes this is labeled as *ennui*. Acquired boredom ranges in severity from moderate to high and can be treated through finding a goal and purpose in life in either one domain or all of leisure, family, and work. The goal is to engage the body and/or mind and/or emotions in something worthwhile to the person by seeking something of interest, such as public service and volunteering, and increasing relevancy and relatedness of what is pursued.

Trait boredom seems to be the most difficult to treat. It requires more attention to overcome because the genetic and hereditary structure and capabilities are relatively more fixed. This disposition operates as a state of readiness, functioning as a limitation, restricting by personal inclination what is done and pursued. To change the situation, newly adapted characteristics must be instilled, which is certainly possible.

A good guide for finding effective approaches was demonstrated in a different context. Cote and Levine (2000) provided evidence that motivation is more important than IQ level in determining academic success. Comparatively, trait boredom can be high, but an individual's determination (motivation) can be increased to overcome inherited limitations or lack of inner resources, such as self-as-entertainment. Therefore, trait boredom can be controlled if there is an intention to seek and pursue active lifestyle. Genetics are almost impossible to alter, while changing personality dispositions, habits, determinations, initial choices, and the environment are easier to improve to provide better outcomes.

Handling Types of Boredom

For field use and service providers, it is important to note four aspects of relevance to the above-integrated classification of boredom:

1. The three categories are considered initial in their explanations. Other scholars can classify the 19 types of boredom differently, yielding better, more meaningful and insightful classifications. This is an open invitation to integrate types of boredom differently, for the benefit of service recipients. In leisure settings, the above integration is only a tentative start.

2. Chronic/Existential Boredom can be more severe than trait boredom sometimes, depending on personal circumstances and subjective handling. In other words, an individual can genetically lack talents, abilities, and resources, but still be adjusted and functioning well, able to live with self and with what is available. It may be much harder to have desirable genetics but be environmentally and repeatedly constrained, conditioned, and prevented from actualizing oneself. The later can be troubling due to "existential frustration," creating anger, a feeling of misery, and dissatisfaction. In the movie, *Coming to America*, actor Eddie Murphy is a perfect illustration of existential frustration. No category operates independently, for many moderators can interfere or enable positively; therefore, their possible impacts and dominance ought to be accounted for.

3. More severe cases of boredom are experienced when two or more classifications are combined. For example, when minor environmental boredom (short duration and task irrelevancies) keep on getting repeated over time, becoming habitual or chronic, they may lead to Personally Acquired Boredom Habit. Another example (at worst) is when the three (environmental, trait, and habit) are combined. These combinations seem to exhibit the utmost degrees of complexity, producing exceptionally severe chronic or existential boredom, "when nothing makes sense anymore." Accordingly, this combination tends to have potentially severe outcomes and is extremely difficult to handle.

4. As of this era, no comments are made as to which category is more or less prevalent in society at large. Moreover, no serious rank order of their dominance and destruction is suggested. More conceptualizations, assessments, and tests of relationships between boredom and other life aspects are needed before such comments, rankings, applications, and universalities are demonstrated and accepted.

In conclusion, the real challenge is how leisure professionals can use the above 19 kinds of boredom and their integrated three classifications. Actions based on pertinent implications are needed in working with individuals, groups, organizations, and centers, as well as society in general. Then we can have offerings and endeavors that are connecting, relevant, interesting, and stimulating — to be employed preventively, therapeutically, and developmentally.

Implications for Types and Categories of Boredom

Integrating all kinds of boredom can reveal some serious underlying implications for leisure professionals to consider. Historically, boredom seems to be evolving outward. In reality, however, it often lurks within the person, where boredom begins, moving to be perverted and anchored in external bases. This stems not only from tasks, situations, surroundings, and environment, but also from social life and finally from the culture at large, hurting the person's speed of time. In other words, as a point in history, it is gradually evolving from micro (internal) positions, which can be controlled and managed, to macro (wider) external positions, from a single person to whole societies.

In rebounding back to the person, it gains strength and dominance, becoming a problem that appears impossible to defeat or even manage, due to its circularity. So it seems that micro levels were dominant in the 1960s and the 1970s when life was simpler. Macro manifestations started with the 1980s, possibly due to high modernity and extensive uses of technologies, as basis for social change (see Model 7). Perhaps, they have combined forces in the 21st century, if not before, becoming a dominant social and behavioral pathology, leading to a variety of ills.

This worst-case scenario, which might already be starting in advanced communities and possibly becoming more prevalent, seems to be the case when micro and macro positions interact and consolidate their negative impacts. The two aspects feed back on each other and join forces. When boredom from within (genetic and personal) and boredom from without (environmental and cultural) mutually reinforce each other or collaborate together, destruction can be expected to escalate.

This demonstrates how serious contemporary professional roles will be in different types of interventions: education, leisure services, sports, rehabilitation, counseling, criminology, social work, justice, police, and even politics. These dynamic interactions and feedback between macro and micro levels can be drastically conducive to an outburst of severe and persistent boredom. A much more serious occurrence can be born out of this state. This state is what was referred to as *ennui*, with a potential for pathology beyond *ennui*, as a third unknown phenomenon (boredom, *ennui*, then beyond *ennui*).

Professionally, what is the role of leisure systems in combating the newly evolving state of extreme boredom? How can we assess its magnitude on different levels, its growth and existence in the above types, and its prevalence in society? How would leisure education, counseling, and guidance handle these states of boredom and *ennui*? Fundamentally, it is suggested that our role is not only to provide fun and games, pleasure and relaxation as it used to be in the past, but also to realize a contemporary professional and social role and a responsibility based on what is occurring in society.

Among the roles of practitioners is that of combating the pathology of boredom, providing diagnosis, prevention, and treatment. The goal is to satisfy the deepest human leisure needs and longings, not superficially contrived or faked ones. The intention is to maximize opportunities for finding the deepest meaning and purpose in what is pursued, to engage and maintain physical and mental health, to facilitate a state of wellness and vitality, and to improve quality of life and total functioning of participants. This takes more than perpetuating the traditional roles of parks and recreation. Instead, the focus should be on humans and their strivings — on social problems and on functioning through leisure choices.

Assessment for Diagnosis, Prevention, and Treatment

To be able to handle almost all kinds of boredom, a specialist needs competencies in assessment and interpretation. Existing boredom scales that are useful to leisure practitioners belong to two levels: general life and informal endeavors. To treat boredom effectively, you need to appraise it accurately.

Practitioners need to know what boredom is (definition) and how to detect it (observation and assessment) before any actions can be taken successfully. Familiarity with boredom measurements will let them be used as diagnostic tools that can be used preventively and/or therapeutically. Moreover, ratings can be utilized as baselines, generating goals and objectives to be sought (see Henderson and Bialeschki, 2002).

Measuring Boredom in General

Investigators use two varieties of scales to study the boredom phenomenon: stimulus/arousal seeking and boredom proneness. Comparatively, scoring low on stimulus and arousal seeking indicates no boredom. They are opposites. A pioneering investigation by L. A. Thompson (1929) attempted to assess susceptibility to monotony. Thompson assumed that repetition causes error and lowers work productivity. He tested the impact of monotony through manipulation of phases: one uniform and the other varied (or having variations). Accordingly, monotony was recognized for its potential effect on boredom, as introduced to scholars with the scale called Measuring Susceptibility to Monotony, more than 80 years ago.

Progressing, but very slowly, 36 years after Thompson's study, "curiosity" as an indicator of stimulus seeking and the reverse of boredom was conceptualized and assessed by Maw and Maw (1965). The Maws' Curiosity Scale was further adopted and verified in India, yielding five components: Thrill Seeking, Novelty Preference, Forbidden Pleasure, Change Seeking, and Boredom (Padhee and Das, 1987). Immediately after the Maws' study, Penney and Reinehr (1966) constructed another scale, the Stimulus-Variation Seeking Scale. Test-retest reliability was obtained as well as discriminant and convergent validity.

Zuckerman (1971) constructed an elaborate and psychometrically verified assessment tool, relevant to boredom, known as the Sensation Seeking Scale (SSS). This scale measured optimal stimulation level. Factor analysis revealed a four-factor structure: Thrill and Adventure Seeking, Experience Seeking, Disinhibition, and Boredom Susceptibility. The first three factors demonstrated reasonable factor and internal reliability. The SSS has been widely and cross-culturally utilized in research. Attempts to adopt it in Germany (see Beauducel et al., 1999) and in China (see Wang et al., 2000) documented its validity, confirming the above structure of four factors.

A 40-item scale was developed by Mehrabian and Russell (1973), entitled Arousal Seeking Tendency Scale (ASTS), which yielded five factors: Change, Unusual Stimuli, Risk, Sensitivity, and New Environments. Test-retest reliability was reported and two validations were provided (concurrent and construct). More than 20 years after ASTS was developed, Baumgartner and Steenkamp (1994) examined its psychometric properties. They obtained high reliability and criterion-related validity for it.

About 10 years after the original ASTS was constructed, another generation of scales was developed. Hamilton, Haier, and Buchsbaum (1984) constructed the Intrinsic Enjoyment and Boredom Coping (IEBC) scale, designed to represent the disposition to restructure one's perceptions and participation in potentially boring activities. Despite the low use of the IEBC scale in general, it has an excellent potential in leisure and recreation (practice and research), since leisure professionals are concerned with coping, creating choices to increase interest, restructuring, involvement, and concentration.

With an increasing momentum, two years following IEBC, a very widely utilized trait (genetic) scale was developed: The Boredom Proneness Scale (BPS) (Farmer and Sundberg, 1986). Factor structure of the BPS was further examined (Vodanovich and Kass, 1990), providing evidence indicating consistency of five factors: External Stimulation, Internal Stimulation, Affective Response, Perception of Time, and Constraint. In Australia, Gordon et al. (1997) obtained evidence supporting Farmer et al.'s BPS validities: convergent, divergent, and predictive. A more recent scale (Cook et al., 1993) assesses very interesting constructs relevant to leisure lifestyles in the Telic Paratelic Scale (TPS). Their 12-item scale yielded three subscales: Playfulness, Arousal Seeking, and Negativity. The scale demonstrated adequate reliability and validity.

In sum, the following nine measurements assess boredom or boredom-related constructs, as presented above.

1. Measuring Susceptibility to Monotony (MSM), Thompson, 1929.
2. Curiosity Scale (CS), Maw and Maw, 1965.
3. Stimulus-Variation Seeking Scale (SVSS), Penney and Reinehr, 1966.
4. Sensation Seeking Scale (SSS), Zuckerman et al, 1971.
5. Arousal Seeking Tendency Scale (ASTS), Mehrabian and Russell, 1973.
6. Intrinsic Enjoyment and Boredom Coping (IEBC), Hamilton, Haier, and Buchsbaum, 1984.
7. Boredom Proneness Scale (BPS), Farmer and Sundberg, 1986.
8. Adopted Curiosity Scale (ACS), Padhee and Das, 1987.
9. Telic Paratelic Scale (TPS), Cook et al, 1993.

Despite the fact that many developed scales, as reported above, were not constructed to assess boredom in leisure and/or free time (such as SSS, SVSS, ASTS, BPS, and IEBC), they can still be very useful in assessing free time types of boredom during informal times. However, more specific measurements are needed to serve recreation and leisure settings. For example, existing scales would be more useful as adapted to confinements in institutions, such as hospitals, rehabilitation centers, homes, and correctional environments. Moreover, scale verifications are needed on individuals exposed to trauma or life changes, such as reduced mobility, vision impairments, or an illness. The major aim here, underlying all assessment efforts, is to enable individuals to function comfortably, use and maintain their competencies to a level near their expectations.

Measuring Boredom in Informal Times

It can be assumed that boredom during informal times determines quantity and quality of recreation, leisure, and play experiences during individuals' free time. But how can pertinent concepts be measured? Unfortunately, boredom in informal times did not gain the assessment attention it deserved, due to its destructiveness through maladaptive behaviors. Investigating phenomena of boredom and behavioral disorders revealed that boredom caused the most destruction during informal times.

Boredom's potential destruction to work can be mainly in productivity, job satisfaction, job turnover, and health — quitting a job might end boredom momentarily. Its destruction to marriage and the family can be in loyalty and satisfaction — divorce might end boredom within the confines of the current marriage. It is not nearly as clear what can help with informal lifestyle.

During informal times, many traps offer opportunities to be inactive, disinterested, suffering from sameness, and feeling empty. A person may quit activities and change places; but, if boredom persists, there seems to be no alternative. All are conditions that lead to a host of disorders and pathologies that have the potential to threaten the core of existence or survival.

The meager attention to the assessment of boredom in informal times is represented by the availability of just three measurements.

1. Leisure Boredom Scale (LBS), Iso-Ahola and Weissinger, 1990.
2. Free Time Boredom (FTB), Ragheb and Merydith, 1995.
3. Measuring the ABC's of Leisure Experience: Awareness, Boredom, Challenge, and Distress, Barnett, 2005.

The Leisure Boredom Scale (a theory-driven, 16-item measurement) by Iso-Ahola and Weissinger (1990) was developed to assess the mismatch between desired arousal-producing characteristics of leisure experiences, perceptions, and actual availability of such experiences. Factor analysis confirmed the existence of only a single factor underlying leisure boredom. The internal reliabilities for the LBS's three samples were .85, .88, and .86.

The Free Time Boredom scale, another theory-based, 20-item scale by Ragheb and Merydith (1995) was constructed to assess the amount of boredom in a person's free time, which may prevent the achievement of a state of leisure and its enjoyment. Factor analysis revealed four distinct factors: Lack of Physical Involvement, Lack of Mental Involvement, Lack of Meaningful Involvement, and Slowness of Time. Alpha reliability coefficients for the four subscales ranged between .78 and .91, with .92 for the total FTB. (For interrelationships among FTB's four components, see the model below.)

In Barnett's (2005) development of a measure to assess the ABC's of leisure experience, boredom was reported as one of four aspects. College students were employed to verify properties of the measurement. The scale's internal consistency was reported.

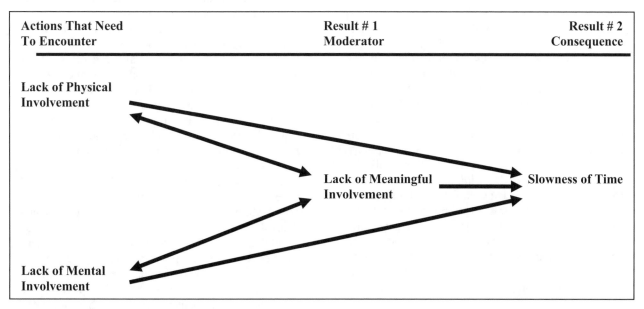

Model 7: Interrelationships among Free Time Boredom's components requiring actions to speed time

Interrelationships among FTB's Four Components

How can the four components found in the Free Time Boredom scale interrelate or impact on each other? In response, a theoretical model was speculated, explaining possible impacts of the four FTB components, as shown in Model 7.

This model implies that lack of physical and mental involvement causes lack of meaningful involvement. Two chapters by Csikszentmihalyi (1990) would echo the root of this interrelation, one is on "The body in flow" and the other is on "The flow of thought." Moreover, lack of physical, mental, and meaningful involvement evolves to cause a feeling of slowness of time. As much as the lack of physical and mental involvement impact *directly* on slowness of time, they also contribute *indirectly* to this reaction via lack of meaning. The validity and applicability of the above theorization can be tested through some statistical procedures such as multiple regression analysis and the use of LISREL.

Implications of Research Findings

Assessment of boredom in different life settings provided interesting and important findings, pointing to potential implications that are valuable to field applications. Professionals serving leisure functions in society can benefit from these research results and conclusions. Based on research outcomes and evidence relevant to boredom, stimulus seeking, and flow, the following implications and recommendations are suggested. (Investigators' findings are in bold, followed by possible implications and applications.)

1. **Conducting a study on the effect of information-seeking strategies on perception, Nidorf (1968) found that a female's cognitive complexity was related to the amount of information sought. The more cognitively complex females sought more information in forming impressions.** Relating these findings to leisure requires some considerations. In particular, due to the dominance of computers, television, and written media, contemporary leisure participants are characterized (especially the younger ages) by extremely high cognitive complexity. The mind might have been formally untaught but was stimulated inwardly by information-seeking needs. These newly occurring phenomena demand accurate leisure assessment to utilize findings as bases for planning uniquely innovative leisure programs, services, and environments that intellectually challenge and match the growing stimulus-seeking needs for information.

2. **Couples participating together in a novel and arousing (versus a more mundane) task experienced greater increases in relationship quality. This was due to the novel, arousing task bearing on boredom in relationships that comes after the honeymoon period (Aron et al., 2000).** It is possible that all leisure programs, services, activities, and actions may have "honeymoon periods" as part of the product's "life cycle." Length of a program's "honeymoon" can be extended and renewed with intimate, novelty-arousing feedback, which are characterized as honeymoon-like impressions. Programs should be characterized as being varied, surprising, rearranged, complex, and providing unpredictable experiences to combat potential boredom. Moreover, leisure users need to be able to choose and change activities, so they can seek novelty, arousal, and variations. This will extend and renew their interests and motivations beyond the initial euphoric stage, after novelty wears-off.

3. **Studying the influence of different activities on the perception of the length of time, Loehlin (1959) employed factor analysis to treat the data. Analysis revealed some pertinent characteristics that contribute to the perception of the length of time: interest versus boredom, filled versus empty (attention to time), repetition of activities versus variety, and activity versus passivity.** Clearly then, to tame boredom leisure services and programs should not only be involving and require a person to be active, but also interesting, filling, fulfilling and meaningful, changeable, and variable. As for leisure endeavors pursued independently, patrons avoid boredom if they are aware and educated in seeking the above features, being active, interested, and creating variations.

4. **A study was conducted on sensation seeking and the use of television for arousal (Perse, 1996). It was observed that sensation seekers (SS) used television to increase complexity and arousal in their environments. Individuals rated high on SS watched television accompanied by distracting activities — changing the channels more often, changing channels out of boredom, or seeking arousal content.** Implications of the above findings are obvious: Leisure programs, choices, and environments should provide for needed complexity (e.g., novelty, variety, challenge, frequent change, feedback). Moreover, high SS persons should be identified. Then, professionals should help them to intentionally develop self-awareness, offering them more novelty. High SS persons could also be grouped with individuals with similar levels of arousal seeking to accommodate for their high-level needs and ensure their satisfaction with the outcomes. Otherwise, as Dumazedier (1974) postulated,

individuals' participation will deteriorate when satisfaction goes down.

5. **While investigating boredom proneness and psychosocial development, Watt and Vodanovich (1999) employed the Student Development Task and Lifestyle Assessment tool to relate it to boredom. They found that low boredom (*or no boredom*) correlated with career planning, lifestyle planning, peer relationships, educational involvement, instrumental (goal-oriented) autonomy, emotional autonomy, independence, academic autonomy, and a salubrious lifestyle.** For leisure professionals to control boredom in their environments, counselors and leisure providers can make use of such findings, They can have participants be a part of the planning process (feedback), help them develop positive relationships with others, offer them chances for goal-oriented initiations, provide autonomy, and promote awareness of wholesome lifestyles.

6. **There is a resemblance between some occupational characteristics and leisure activities or program features, necessitating certain considerations. A study on interests and stimulus seeking by Kish and Donnenwerth (1969) found that sensation seeking is a positive component of occupational interest patterns requiring relatively unstructured activities, which dealt with complex, novel situations and concepts and required flexibility (freedom) of approach. Well-structured and well-defined activities associated negatively with sensation seeking because of attention to details, routine, and order.** Professionals need to assess — formally or informally — participants' levels of sensation seeking before engaging in the arts versus regimented exercises or sports, writing poetry versus practicing musical instruments or ballet. In other words, program offerings or activity choices should match individuals' needs for sensation seeking. Moreover, a prerequisite is required: the need for a classification of activities and programs in terms of their levels of structure. Sometimes, participants prefer very structured activities when competencies and skills are valued. Others might prefer completely unstructured leisure pursuits, depending on persons' needs, stage of development, preferences, personal circumstances, season, age, gender, and peers.

7. **What will happen if boredom is suppressed? Mageau et al. (2000) obtained an interesting answer to the above question that might have multiple implications, not only for leisure and exercise but also for work, marriage, and therapy. Mageau et al. found that when all the participants had the opportunity to express their boredom at the end of the experiment, the level of boredom was significantly higher for the participants who previously suppressed their boredom than for the participants of the control group.** "Facilitation of boredom's expression" in the above-mentioned areas is not quite as easy as it may seem, for what has been long known in social psychology is that "aggression is a learned behavior" (Berkowitz, 1969). Also, "boredom can be a learned behavior" if we unskillfully over-facilitate for its expression. How much is needed and how can professionals allow for individuals to express boredom? It is an issue that needs further study. Over facilitating the expression of boredom might result in participants over-expressing their boredom.

8. **Barbalet (1999), in a conceptual article on boredom and social meaning, emphasized that meaning is necessary in social processes. Absence of meaning in activities leads to boredom, showing up as restlessness, irritability, and a need to change to something more interesting.** Based on these observations, leisure professionals should develop competencies in social facilitation, maximizing meaning from all possible socially oriented leisure endeavors. Moreover, in giving guidance and counseling, participants can develop awareness and insights into the meaningful potential of leisure pursuits that involve others.

9. **In developing a model to transcend boredom, enhancing interest and motivation in individual sports, Green-Demers et al. (1998) observed that self-determined, extrinsic motivation predicted higher levels of intrinsic motivation. Three of the four interest-enhancing strategies they tried were demonstrated to have an effect: creating challenges for oneself, adding variety to the task, and providing oneself with self-relevant rationales for performing the task.** Accordingly, in application, leisure professionals should offer self-challenge, variety, and personal reasons or rationales to engage in activities. Moreover, knowledge accumulated in the field of leisure on self-determination, personal control, and freedom of choice should be put to use to motivate individuals to initiate and continue in their choices.

10. One of the strategies used to avoid boredom is to seek optimum stimulation from a wide array of recognized free time activities. **It was found that fashion, sensuality, and new environments are examples to provide different optimum stimulation to both genders (see Kwon and Workman, 1996).** Professionals should assess participants' optimal stimulation, and then plan to offer a wide variety of services to meet such identified needs.

11. **Based on five experiments, Ratner et al. (1999) investigated consumers' needs for variety seeking responses. Experiments supported the**

assumption that people sometimes choose to switch to less-preferred options (perhaps because of familiarity, monotony, and boredom), even with less expected enjoyment. This has been labeled as "the law of diminishing returns." Leisure professionals should be aware that "the law of diminishing returns" operates also in leisure, recreation, and play. When it happens within informal settings, it indicates a need for activity change, a signal to offer alternatives to help participants make the transition, substitution, or switch smoothly from one choice to another, to further variety, maintaining optimal flow and interest.

12. **For at-risk youth to learn in instructional environments, Dicintio and Gee (1999) found that perceived challenge and perceived control lessened boredom and enhanced motivation for engaging in learning activities.** This implies that, in planning for recreation programs and facilities for youth (or all ages), professionals must involve participants, giving them control over possible details and outcomes, maintaining an optimal level of challenge or difficulty in chosen activities.

13. **From early childhood on, individuals need creative pursuits to actualize their abilities to acquire talents. Mack (1986) argues that schools focus on enhancing intelligence, which has far overshadowed the enhancement of creativity. In turn, neglecting creativity can contribute to boredom and youth crime. The title of Mack's report is "Who Is Enhancing Creativity?"** Implications of this neglect, involve two other powerful institutions: the family and the leisure delivery system. Pioneering agencies and agents in leisure services — mostly through private recreation, initially — fill societal gaps, respond to neglected needs, and work on social problems. Leisure professionals in such settings should realize that enhancing creativity is not completely fulfilled through the educational system. Coordination is badly needed between parents and leisure systems, so that they can work in collaboration, developing creative competencies — not only to control and reduce boredom and crime (which should just be a byproduct), but also to facilitate what we believe in as leisure professionals: personal development, self-actualization, and total functioning.

Summary and Conclusions

With the prevalence of boredom in all life domains, its causes and treatments might be similar in all other domains. For example, the existence of monotony, routine, lack of meaning, and lack of interest seem to share in causing boredom in family, work, and informal times. The attributes are almost the same, while the settings are different. When these characteristics exist in any or all of the three domains, certain consequences will persist in the form of epidemics or pathologies, such as suicide attempts, depression, drug abuse, gambling, and crime. Therefore, results of research about boredom should be integrated to explain and predict boredom in contemporary times. Accordingly, strategies, treatments, interventions, and plans should be devised to suppress, control, and remove boredom in all domains, to control or lessen disorders for most participants.

To achieve these humanistic goals in fighting boredom, professionals should understand the complicated nature of boredom and its relationship to seeking stimuli and arousal. It is assumed here that professionals will never control boredom completely, for it comes under different conditions, in such a variety of types and manifestations. Therefore, orientation to kinds of boredom is important in understanding its very nature. Is it genetic or situational, transitional or chronic? Is the cause a lack of inner resourcefulness or is it culturally conditioned? When all pieces of the puzzle are put together in a predictive model or theory, remedies will be more successful. Boredom seems to encompass all identified types. Usually, this occurs under restrained personal and environmental circumstances, allowing for the observed manifestation, which would lead to the dominance of one kind or the other (chronic or trait, habitual or transitory). Hence, no strategy will be truly effective without coordinating efforts to attack boredom in all domains and in its relationship to all disorders, with the understanding of all the ways it appears.

The state of the art of boredom study shows the magnitude of the demands for its assessment. Practitioners need to be able to measure its severity, recognizing how far it has spread in the body of society (like cancer in a human body), and how is it impacting society. A variety of assessment tools have been constructed, from 1929 until the present, to measure and respond to this very problem. Constructs developed range from susceptibility to monotony to curiosity; from stimulus variation to sensation seeking; from boredom coping to boredom proneness; and from leisure boredom to free time boredom. Professionals, concerned about functioning during informal times, need to adopt and validate instruments that were originally constructed to serve other areas, making them leisure-specific instruments.

Research on boredom has produced results that carry interesting implications for leisure practitioners at all levels of the system. More than a dozen implications were reported, suggesting solutions for newly occurring phenomena. Certain considerations were recommended, such as providing the kinds of activities and programs that match the higher cognitive complexity of younger ages, demanding more stimulation and information to participate in novel and arousing activities. This is intended to sustain interest and control boredom. It was found that expressing boredom after a boring event could help to control it, as compared to those who suppressed that feeling. Implications reported can serve in a variety of settings.

Finally, it seems that boredom is not only here to stay, but also to expand and spread through and with aid of modern advancements, which seems paradoxical (whether we admit it or not). However, the fear now is that what we know as boredom will deteriorate, advancing to a more serious reaction as *ennui*. Not only that, but a third, much more serious reaction can be in the making. What is the name of that third manifestation after boredom and *ennui*? This newborn trouble will demand a name soon. The question, then, is this: What is the role of professionals in human and social services — maintaining mental health — toward these varied manifestations of boredom? Particularly, what is the role of the leisure delivery systems to reduce, control, and tame boredom to facilitate for participants to maximize their leisure rewards?

In conclusion, to entertain a few solutions, it is suggested we conduct a careful study of what used to be done in "the good old days." That is when boredom was in a state of almost non-existence in the time before World War I. Back then there was less technology and limited advancements, which seems to be a blessing. This implies two things: going back to nature and more use of our two hands and legs in life pursuits, mainly leisure activities and experiences. Nature is known to provide unlimited variations, interests, challenges, absorption, infinite encounters, and numerous qualities that are definitely anti-boredom.

Moreover, the use of hands in different leisure, recreation, and play needs to be studied and encouraged. Hands-involvement brings the physical structure of humans and the physical task of nature closer to the mind — a characteristic manifested intensively in the arts, hobbies, outdoors living, and children's physical play. In turn, an individual loses the sense of time or experiences time "flying" when hands and legs are engaged in what is done. That is the very reason why the use of hands in interesting endeavors is definitely another anti-boredom idea.

Modern conveniences are removing our physical and mental involvement, through watching (as in the use of computers, television, and movies), spectatorship, and visual entertainment. It can be proven that the use of hands or eye-hand coordination in personal endeavors, such as the arts (molding and shaping), sports, exercising, outdoor activities, gardening, and writing, can draw the individual to focus on the task at hand. This increases intensity and the possibilities for absorption. There seem to be greater opportunities for actualizing ideas and aspirations. The above two suggestions can have many social and programming implications.

The best prevention and treatment to boredom would sound like common sense; it can be synthesized as follows:

> *Find or create activities that interest you, do a variety of them, maximize uses of your human machine, involve both body and mind as much as your are able to, using your hands and legs as much as possible.*

Questions and Exercises

1. What are the kinds of boredom?
2. Explain the simplified model of boredom that incorporates all the identified kinds.
3. What is the prevalence of the three categories of boredom?
4. How would a leisure practitioner handle the different types of boredom?
5. How would assessment of boredom help diagnosis, prevention, and treatment?
6. Explain the interrelationships among free time boredom components.
7. Elaborate on five implications of research findings relative to boredom.

Chapter 26

Satisfaction in a Context of Life Endeavors: The Place of Leisure

Focus of Chapter

Due to the diversification of the concept of satisfaction, this chapter will outline — as much as possible — its boundaries, mapping its main structure. The approach used here is centered on leisure satisfaction, shedding more light on it within different contexts, concepts, characteristics, and/or theories. Moreover, identified characteristics of life satisfaction (LS) will be reported, ranging from intensity and positive affect to pleasant mood and state of mind. The universality of LS across cultures will be demonstrated comparing Western cultures to Eastern ones. Through a holistic model, LS will be put into the context of its underlying determinants (the other satisfactions that make LS). The satisfactions that an individual values are those that influence the weight of the reported satisfaction. A method to make an estimate of LS based on what is valued will be explained. A set of theories will be presented predicting under which conditions LS occurs. This chapter focuses upon satisfaction elicited from informal domains, namely leisure, recreation, exercise, travel, and play. Another goal of the chapter is to illustrate how the concepts of satisfaction relate to those domains of leisure. The available literature, guided by the psychometric theory presented in the second part of this book, will be used to develop constructs to assess the attributes of satisfaction.

Key Terms

- cross-culture
- happiness
- life satisfaction
- peak experience

- pleasant mood
- positive affect
- state of mind
- well being

Key Names

- Ed Diener
- Viktor Frankl
- George C. Homans

- Abraham Maslow
- Waldyslaw Tatarkiewicz

Objectives

- Differentiate among different concepts of life satisfaction.
- Identify major characteristics of life satisfaction.
- Explain how satisfaction is generalizable and needed in all cultures.
- Recognize major domains or determinants of satisfaction.
- Identify cultural sources and means to shape what is satisfying.
- Report on and differentiate among theories of life satisfaction.

What is the nature of satisfaction? Conceptually, satisfaction is what an individual gets from engaging in an activity. As Homans (1961) views it, "Satisfaction is a matter of reward" (p. 267). He adds that people use the meaning of satisfaction loosely, referring to the activity as satisfying when they actually mean that the "reward" satisfied or benefited them. Homans provided a challenging observation: satisfaction's relationship to other variables is not at all clear. About 40 years after Homans' extensive conceptualization, theories began to be formulated and hypotheses tested to explain and predict the antecedents and consequences of satisfaction (see Sirgy et al., 2000). A set of theories of life satisfaction will be presented later on, helping not only conceptualization and instrument development, but also research studies and practice.

An individual's satisfaction exists in an environmental and situational context. Rojek (1989) has the view that "value free" facts such as "life satisfaction," "pleasure," and "freedom" are inadequately understood. They require examining their contexts. He emphasizes the importance of studying "social values" as a context for facts such as satisfaction. In another conceptual article, Christopher (1999) also argues that culture-free theories or measures of well-being (life satisfaction) are unattainable. He suggests that understanding psychological well-being should be based on moral vision.

In a similar, but broader, empirical endeavor, Oishi et al. (1999) tested life satisfaction in 39 nations. After reporting their interesting findings, they arrived at a synthesis for their findings. The investigation provided support for needs and values as moderators of subjective well-being on a cultural level. They added that people were satisfied with their lives to the extent that their needs and values were satisfied. Different levels of satisfaction are the outcomes of these moderators: what individuals aspire to achieve, what they value and hope for, and how much they still need to accomplish.

Within Maslow's (1954) human motivation theory, many needs, hopes, values, and aspirations can be satisfied to reach a "peak experience" or meta-contentment through many domains, including leisure (love, belonging, esteem, and self-actualization). Moreover, according to Rotter's (1954) self-determination theory, leisure can provide abundant opportunities for exercising control over outcomes and an individual's destiny. Leisure provides the freedom to choose, to decide, and to be responsible for one's own actions.

Furthermore, based on White's (1959) competence-effectance theory, individuals can satisfy numerous needs in leisure and recreation: seeking competence, control, and mastery in choices such as the arts, physical activities, exercising, outdoor pursuits, and social activities. In sum, reinforced positive outcomes, peak satisfaction, self-determined free choices, and competence/mastery of leisure provide rewards and meta-contentment that attract individuals to continue these pursuits to enhance health, well-being, and vitality — achieving and maintaining empowerment.

Characteristics of Life Satisfaction

Scholars identified some interesting characteristics for life satisfaction and happiness, which can be elements of Leisure Satisfaction as well. Diener (2000) suggested that happiness or affective well-being can be equated with the relative amount of time a person experiences positive versus negative affects. In an earlier report, Diener et al. (1985) investigated the impact of intensity and frequency of positive and negative affects on individuals. They concluded that the intensity dimension helps in explaining the relative independence of positive and negative affect. Comparatively, such qualities seem to characterize positive leisure lifestyles at their utmost peak to be considered intrinsically motivated.

How would the duration or frequency of positive affects impact on life satisfaction or subjective well-being? Suh, Diener, and Fujita (1996) found that only life events during the previous three months influenced life satisfaction and positive and negative affect. Moreover, Schimmack and Grob (2000) found that the amount of time that people were in a pleasant mood was negatively correlated with the amount of time that people were in an unpleasant mood. Characteristically — depending on cultural orientations and values — leisure can provide a multitude of positive moods, feelings, emotions, and states of mind for a long duration, which, in turn, impacts significantly on subjective well-being.

The above findings can have very practical implications for diagnosis and treatment and for leisure delivery systems at large. Activities, choices, and services can be utilized instrumentally, even prescribed. They can be utilized not only to treat and correct, but also to heighten leisure experience, improve mood, and create more positive affects or meta-contentment. Like the way vitamins or diets improve health, a good prescribed set of activities can improve the satisfaction of individuals that are assessed to be in need of such treatments. Leisure satisfaction can be increased due to activities and choices made.

Accordingly, ingredients of activities can be used intentionally, by design. In this manner, professionals can deliberately sustain positive dispositions and feelings. Numerous choices can yield such outcomes: travel, exercising, successful events, tournaments, drawing and painting, music, camping, and social gatherings. Experiencing longer duration of intensity can be achieved through facilitating not only for cross-cultural entertainment and amusements, but, more importantly, for focused leisure involvement, intrinsically initiated pursuits, and maintenance of flow, all of which yield positive affects, emotions, and moods. All in all, life satisfaction can be amalgamated from these positive experiences and outcomes.

Generalization of Satisfaction to Different Cultures

How universal is satisfaction? Interestingly, it was found that feelings of life satisfaction vary cross-culturally. Testing Maslow's needs, Oishi et al.'s (1999) study compared life satisfaction in about 40 nations, utilizing two massive sets of samples (54,446, and 6,782 persons). They found that satisfaction with esteem needs (the self and freedom) predicted global life satisfaction more strongly among people in individualistic nations (e.g., the U.S., France) than people in collective nations (e.g., Japan, India, and China).

A possible implication of this finding is related to the nature of free choice for personal development as sources of satisfaction in Western cultures. This can bring leisure and its choices close to the core of the values in the United States, as an individualistic nation. While in Eastern societies such as China, for instance, family norms and interpersonal relations would be emphasized more through leisure. In essence, these findings imply that leisure serves different functions in different cultures, maintaining the fabrics of societies. So it seems that satisfaction is universal across nations, but the sources of satisfaction differ.

What are some of the underlying aspects that make life satisfaction universal? As demonstrated above, the predictors of life satisfaction vary nationally. Those variations can be based on structural aspects such as developmental stages, income levels, social class, career, political orientation, and education. Similarly, means and sources also vary cross-culturally. This is based on cultural ways of life, customs, habits, traditions, values, technology, economics, population density, and governing systems.

Meanwhile, life satisfaction is proven to be universal, without regard to variations in the sources of satisfaction and their magnitude. All humans have needs to survive and to function beyond the survival level. If we consider a need as a container that persons strive to fill, its filling must be satisfied to a given minimum level. As a result, all living organisms, including humans, experience satisfaction of their needs or the lack of fulfillment.

In a line of research similar to Oishi, et al., Suh and associates (1998) tested the basis of life satisfaction judgments, cross-culturally among 61 nations, with N=62,446 persons. In individualistic nations like the U.S., it was found that emotions (such as autonomy, self-sufficiency, identity, and independence) correlated strongly with life satisfaction, while norms (social approval) and emotions were equally strong predictors of life satisfaction in collectivist cultures (such as East Asian societies). Besides norms and emotions, collectivist societies are shaped by and more satisfied on the basis of social roles, public images, and interpersonal relationships. In other words, Eastern and Western containers are going to be filled to a degree, but with different substances or qualities or products.

Briefly, satisfaction is definitely universal, providing positive affects. However, there are distinct variations due to what leads to these moods and emotions (individualistic or collectivist, agricultural, industrial, or post-technological).

Life Satisfaction in a Context of its Determinants

Life satisfaction can be viewed in two mutually inclusive ways: as an end in itself (e.g., to be satisfied with health or family) and/or instrumentally as a means toward a greater end. Happiness can be a composite of valued life domains. For satisfaction to be cultivated or fulfilled as an end in itself, certain antecedents and moderators must act harmoniously and collaboratively with their designated satisfaction. A simple model can illustrate these dynamic operations.

Model 8 presents a diagrammatic evolution of the place of life satisfaction within a context of its specific determinants of satisfaction leading to a greater consequence or pursuit. A domain can operate as an antecedent, moderator, and a consequence, depending on its utility and function within a model.

The easiest parts of the model are the aspects that can be exclusively positioned. These are the extreme left (pure antecedents in the model) and the extreme right (pure consequences). The pure antecedents to life satisfaction are motivations, attitudes, and interests, while the pure consequence is happiness. The middle aspects or moderators are more inclusive and changeable in their weight and existence.

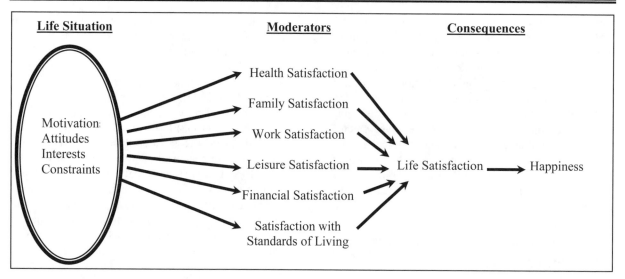

Model 8: Life satisfaction as a function of other types of satisfaction.

Examples of life satisfaction moderators are health satisfaction, family satisfaction, work satisfaction, leisure satisfaction, and financial satisfaction. In one sense, they can be designated as antecedents; while in another, they are regarded as moderators and consequences. Within this model, life satisfaction can be equated with happiness, except that the latter is an abstract, while the former is operational. In other words, life satisfaction is more easily assessed and computed through indexes of the domains of different types of satisfaction.

Examples about financial satisfaction and health satisfaction can illustrate this point clearly. When there are serious health problems, a person's attitudes and motivations to seek health will be heightened to their maximum in an attempt to recuperate, to regain the lost health or mobility, and/or to relearn lost function. Health recovery would supersede almost everything else in life.

In critical illness or accident situations, health satisfaction is sought at almost every possible instant, as an end in itself, or as a prime consequence. An example about sand in the eyes can illustrate this point clearly. While a person is enjoying a hot summer day on the beach, making a million-dollar deal, the wind blows and eyes are filled with sand. Other considerations are lost and maximum attention switches to the recovery of the eyes. After that, fun (or life) resumes as normal. Under these circumstances health satisfaction (functioning) is the source of meta-contentment, momentarily. The same applies when there is an extreme financial difficulty. Financial satisfaction under such circumstances seems to be the person's ultimate goal, at least for the duration of financial difficulty.

Surprisingly, when health and financial needs are taken care of, individuals consistently use those satisfactions instrumentally toward a higher state of affect or fulfillment of meta-contentment — taking health and money for granted. That is, they attempt to find happiness using these types of satisfaction as moderators, aiming at a higher reward.

Satisfaction from leisure activities is similar to health and financial satisfaction. It may be treated as an antecedent, a moderator, or a consequence. Functions and contributions of leisure satisfaction will depend on age, gender, income, work/retirement status, and the time of the week or year. Thus, leisure and satisfaction gained from it will be either an end in itself or a means towards an end.

Overall, it is clear that no relationship between two or more variables will be understood and documented accurately unless fluctuating moderators, which are shifting in their impacts, are accounted for. Conflicting and confusing findings can be attributed sometimes to not accounting for important moderators. Therefore, the dynamic context of the antecedents to life satisfaction and its consequences can be explained, demonstrating first the nature of moderators such as motivation and attitude as follows.

Motivation and Satisfaction

One of the main antecedents to satisfaction and/or happiness is motivation. DuBrin (1972) suggested a logical order for the relationship between the two. His view is that motivation refers to expenditure of effort toward a goal, while satisfaction refers to feelings of contentment resulting from its achievement (see also Mannell, 1989). In exploring this relation further, satisfaction is usually equated with a need or a deficiency. In Latin, the root *satis* mean "enough," as in saturated, satiated, sate, and satiety. These words mean to fill completely, saturate; to satisfy fully or to excess, satiated; to cloy with overabundance, sate; and the quality or state of being fed or gratified to or beyond capacity, satiety (see Homans, 1961).

To illustrate the extent of filling, an interesting study by O'Reilly and Anderson (1980) demonstrated that contributors to satisfaction were the need for information and frequent feedback that individuals were progressing toward their goals. That is the search for "enough," "sufficient" awareness to fill or *satis* the need for knowledge and feedback of individuals' performances. In the pursuit to fill what is needed, a person is pushed, driven, or motivated to seek solutions among available alternatives. That is why "to be filled to a high extent" or meta-content-ment is common to all of the above terms that begin with the root *sat*.

Less than 60 years ago, Morse (1953: 28) postulated that "The greater the amount the individual gets, the greater his satisfaction. At the same time, the more the individual still desires, the less his satisfaction." The first part of Morse's elegant statement is pertinent to the ways that products, services, and life endeavors attempt to please or satisfy individuals, improving the quality of life. The second part is the center of motivation: "The more the individual still desires, the less his satisfaction." Perhaps this is the core of drives and incentives to keep on seeking.

Lack of complete satiation or "enough" seems to make persons aspire for, feel a need for, or keep on working towards something of interest until they gain sufficient filling and fulfilling. In informal times people seek exercising, practicing, performing, repeating, and/or relaxing until a level of saturation is achieved. When people are filled sufficiently, they quit. They start to look for alternatives or other needs that seem to challenge them. This is the root of motivation that determines interest and results in satisfaction, which can determine substitutability of activities (see Iso-Ahola, 1986).

Homans (1961) has an equally interesting view: "The more valuable a reward is to a man, the less likely he is to be satisfied with the amount of that reward he has gotten so far" (p. 269). Examples from leisure can illustrate the above proposition. A youth of 17 years, admiring a sport and its performers or being interested in an artistic hobby, will keep on coming to the recreation center in town until s/he masters the skills, develops competencies, perfects talent, and satisfies her/his intrinsic and extrinsic rewarding mechanisms. Conceptually, motivations (needs) operate as prerequisites or antecedents to any given involvement. Consequently, they also lead to satisfaction.

From the era of Morse and Homans, the concern about the determinants and consequences of satisfaction gained reasonable empirical and conceptual attention. For example, based on reviews of 10 motivation theories, Thierry (1998) concluded that satisfaction is conceived as a construct that usually operates rather independently in empirical research, although it is conceptually closely related to the cycle of motivated behavior. Moreover, findings obtained by Ryan and Deci (2000) led to the postulation of three innate psychological needs — competence, autonomy, and relatedness — which, when satisfied, yield enhanced self-motivation and mental health, while when thwarted lead to diminished motivation and well-being (see also Geller, 2010).

According to the Social Production Function Theory (Ormel et al., 1999), motivation was demon-strated as an antecedent to satisfaction. It was explained that all humans strive (are driven) to optimize physical and social well-being. (For the relationship between altruistic activity as a social orientation and life satisfaction, see Williams et al., 1998.) In sum, lacking motivation to act can block or inhibit all possible rewards and outcomes that can sate, satiate, and saturate.

Attitudes, Involvement, and Satisfaction

An attitude, as defined in a prior chapter, is a mental disposition or a feeling influencing individu-als' responses toward its related object. Attitudes may not associate directly with satisfaction, but rather indirectly through an important moderator — involvement. The conceptual logic or rationale is that a person can have a positive attitude toward an object or a source of satiation, but might not obtain satisfac-tion unless s/he is involved in that object. Direct contact is "the door" to experience satisfaction, most of the time the only door. In almost all cases, immediate contact or interaction "involvement" with objects is a prerequisite to satisfaction. Therefore, relationships between attitudes and involvement will be discussed as intertwined aspects.

Involvement, operating as a mediator between attitudes and satisfaction, gained attention in many fields. Fundamentally, the catastrophe theory of attitude by Latane and Nowak (1994) postulates that attitudes have a joint function, issue involvement and information favorability. This connection between attitudes and involvement found application in marketing (Kokkinaki and Lunt, 1997); advertising (Kokkinaki and Lunt, 1999); management (Askew et al., 2002); persuasion (Maio and Olson, 1995), and in politics (Lavine et al, 2000). Attitudes demonstrated a consistent connection to involvement under condi-tions incorporated in all the above studies (also see,

Hague and White, 2005; Cho and Boster, 2005, Sherif and Sherif, 1967).

Satisfaction in Domains that Compose Satisfaction with Life

Life satisfaction seems to be composed of specific satisfactions. Accumulated empirical evidence in the last 40 or 50 years strongly endorses the idea that life satisfaction of a given developmental stage, group, social class, or culture is made up of *valued benefits* or rewards gained from unique sets of domain satisfactions. As a result, we need to look at the frequently valued domain satisfactions that have been identified and used to form life satisfaction.

Many studies have attempted to answer this question. There is always a search for new ground or further contributors to life satisfaction, based on a person's standing in life. However, no single study could accommodate the diverse domain satisfactions that can be amalgamated together to form life satisfaction for all. Many practical and research reasons contribute to this highly subjective state. Among the reasons are the differences in the nature of populations: their problems, hopes, expectations, aspirations, and constraints. Other reasons can include the level of accumulated knowledge on specific satisfaction, investigators' orientations, the nature and uniqueness of each study, and the complexity and diversification of life satisfaction concepts as demonstrated below.

Nevertheless, in an excellent dissertation entitled "Central Life Interests: An Integrative Review," Kaplan (1997) analyzed and synthesized the results of 139 studies on central life interests. Kaplan identified 15 variables that were tested in relation to DuBrin's (1959) theory. However, Kaplan was disappointed in his conclusion, claiming that little theoretical advancement has been made since 1956, and conceptualizations are not aligned around a unified definition of central life interests. Despite the limitations on the above theoretical advancements, it can be useful to many fields if helping professionals learn about the domains of satisfaction that compose respondents total life satisfaction.

Some studies illustrate differences in the nature of outcomes such as in assessing residents' satisfaction with community-based services (SWC). In this study Sirgy et al. (2001) accounted for satisfactions from work, family, and leisure besides SWC as contributors to LS. In one of the many studies on persons 55 years of age and older, Koivumaa-Honkanen et al. (2000) found that life satisfaction was based on health predictors, social engagement/support, and interest in life.

In another investigation (Glass and Jolly, 1997), variables such as education, religion, positive attitude, volunteerism, and family determined satisfaction in later life among women aged 60 or over. In the same study, good health, income, work life, and leisure were not endorsed as important (were not valued). Yet, in another study the option of voluntary retirement, or lack thereof, impacted upon life satisfaction (Shultz et al., 1998). It was found that those who perceived their retirement to be voluntary had higher life satisfaction scores and rated themselves healthier (physically and mentally) than those who perceived their retirement to be imposed (for further interpretations of Shultz et al.'s findings, see the theories of locus of control by Rotter, 1954, and self-determination, Deci, 1975).

Comprehensively, Pavot et al. (1991) concluded that subjective well-being is a relative global and stable phenomenon, not simply a momentary judgment based on fleeting influences. Bases for life satisfaction that demonstrates stability over time — based on what is valued — are autonomy versus norms, independence versus social roles, and identity versus interpersonal relationships. In turn, stability of what is valued gives consistency to the basis and antecedents of satisfaction in both Western and Eastern cultures, maintaining the fabric and continuation of societies.

Life Satisfaction Leading to Happiness

How would satisfaction relate to happiness? For life satisfaction to function instrumentally as a moderator, happiness (as an end in itself) would be a consequence. Philosophically, "Happiness requires total satisfaction, that is satisfaction with life as a whole," Tatarkiewicz (1976, p. 8) explained, in his book *Analysis of Happiness*, "People who are satisfied partially or relatively do not call themselves happy…. Happiness means lasting satisfaction."

Empirically, Neto (2001) observed that four predictors account for 58% of the variance in happiness, LS is one of them. A prior section by Diener et al. (2000) on the "Identified Characteristics of Life Satisfaction" provides empirical evidence supporting Tatarkiewicz's philosophy.

Furthermore, the "lasting satisfaction" as a basis for happiness was empirically investigated as "Intensity and frequency of positive and negative affects," how the "life events during the previous three months influenced life satisfaction and positive and negative affect," and "the amount of time that people are in a pleasant mood." These intensities and frequencies of positive affects made lasting satisfaction.

Searching for the place of leisure satisfaction, Beard and Ragheb (1980, p. 331) suggested, "Happiness is composed of a number of satisfactions." How would leisure and its satisfaction contribute to this mood? It has been said that Aristotle was known to be not only a philosopher of happiness but also one of leisure. Aristotle's views suggest that happiness is found only in leisure (see de Grazia, 1962; Kraus, 2000). Empirically, in one of the studies on older persons, leisure satisfaction was found to be the highest contributor to LS (Ragheb and Griffith, 1982). Leisure satisfaction alone in this study contributed half of the variance in LS, as compared to satisfactions from other endeavors such as health, family, and standard of living.

However, it is not the search for happiness only that makes people happy. As Frankl (1962) postulates, those who try hardest to be happy are the least likely to experience happiness. There seems to be a paradox about happiness and pleasure. Frankl adds that happiness should not be the ultimate goal of life. He suggests that "the search for meaning" is the ultimate goal. He strongly feels that facing and enduring pain and suffering can enable humans to realize significant meaning and goals for their existence. Logically, the search for happiness and meaning could operate on different levels of affectivity, sometimes simultaneously within an individual's life span. Depending on one's stage of life and other circumstances, happiness and meaning can rotate positions or complement each other, focusing on the latter as a long-range mechanism, and considering that there is happiness in meanings discovered.

Estimating Satisfaction in Contemporary Times

As a sign of this current era, pleasing enough, empirical evidence was established (see Diener and Diener, 1996) that most people in the U.S. are happy (or satisfied with life). Diener and Diener observed a positive level of subjective well-being (SWB): Citizens are satisfied with their marriages, work environments, health, finances, and friendships. Also, they reported that cross-national data suggested a positive level of SWB throughout the globe, with the exception of very poor nations. (Diener and Diener made no mention of leisure, however significant it may be.) Note that, those feelings were in the era around 1996, which was a prosperous time for Western nations. One wonders how the circumstances in the 2010s, concerning the rate of unemployment, housing crises, debt size, and the new economic realities nationally and internationally would impact life satisfaction and happiness.

Based on realized satisfactions, how can we determine a person's total life satisfaction? First, assess and weight satisfactions from different domains (using valid and reliable scales). Second, assess how the person reports what s/he strives for and values. By combining these two scores (weight multiplied by value) we can compose an index based on a simple mathematical formula: A score on a given domain's satisfaction scale (from 1 to 100) is assessed to get the weight, and then multiplied by how valuable this domain is to the individual. (Reported value of domain can range between 1 and 10, where 1 means not valuable at all).

If a person scores 90 of 100 on a given domain's satisfaction scale and rates the value of the domain as 2 out of 10, computed satisfaction from this domain is 90 x 2 = 180 / 1000 = .18 or 18%. Possible scores range from 1 to 1000 as a result of multiplying 100 x 10. (This is actually the case with college students; they take their health for granted, but strive for financial satisfaction.) Although the person is highly satisfied with the domain's rewards (90%), it is only valued at 2 out of 10. Therefore, the impact of this domain on LS is very low (18%). This is seen with someone who is very healthy but does not care or does not give importance to health (usually younger individuals feel this way), or being very rich but does not think of wealth as significant or important; rather valuing the love and romance s/he is deprived of.

It is important to note that the satisfactions that are highly valued are the ones that impact total satisfaction the most. In this regard, it is like depression; when it prevails, it colors everything else gray. In other words, when a highly valued satisfaction is great, all other satisfactions, most likely, will seem okay. A given satisfaction can spill over, causing multiple negatives or positives in other satisfactions.

Adding up satisfaction in all the domains (calculated as above) depicts an individual's level of life satisfaction. To illustrate a more global picture, accounting for scores from six domains, two cases can be computed as follows:
Case 1: LS = 88 + 97 + 85 + 95 + 89 + 90 = 544 divided by 6 domains = 90.66
Case 2: LS = 23 + 19 + 27 + 32 + 16 + 21 = 139 divided by 6 domains = 23.16

The mean scores of 90.66 and 23.16 out of 100 demonstrate the levels of life satisfaction or misery for cases 1 and 2. Scores obtained can have multiple uses, not only for diagnosis, treatment, and referral purposes; but also for program planning, intervention, counseling and guidance, and increasing awareness of what is impacting an individual's life.

Using the assessed value of each satisfaction, a more realistic profile can be reached, demonstrating a person's satisfaction with life.

Assuming that the person in case 1 rated highly the values of the first and the sixth only, what is the final score? Results can be reported as follows:

Satisfaction	value/10	score
88	X 0.9	= 79.2
97	X 0.4	= 38.8
85	X 0.6	= 51.0
95	X 0.5	= 47.5
89	X 0.3	= 26.7
90	X 1.0	= 90.0
544		**333.2**

This adds up to a total from the satisfactions of 333.2 divided by 6 domains for a LS score of 55.53%. Despite the fact that this person is rated high on the first and last satisfactions, total score for life satisfaction is moderate (56%).

For another person rating him/herself high on satisfactions and also high on their values, scores can be like this:

Satisfaction	value/10	score
96	X 0.9	= 86.4
93	X 1.0	= 93.0
97	X 0.8	= 77.6
95	X 0.9	= 85.5
98	X 1.0	= 98.0
94	X 1.0	= 94.0
573		**534.5**

The score for this person is 534.5 / 6 = 89.8%. This is how the value of given satisfactions impact the total LS.

Within a context of individuals' reference groups, scores of satisfaction can be added up and compared, producing a composite for life satisfaction or subjective well-being within a designated culture or subculture. This presents the numerous moderators that make life satisfaction a pivot within a viable frame of reference. Take the example of a person who scored high (80-90) on all life types of satisfactions, but does not value any of them. Such a person will be suffering from emptiness or lack of meaning, as an existential vacuum, which leads to existential frustration.

Specifically, how would leisure satisfaction measure up in comparison to satisfactions gained from other domains? Neither conceptual nor empirical answers are available at this time to answer this question.

Motivations and attitudes operate as antecedents to satisfaction in valued life domains (e.g., health, family, work). If an individual lacks attitudes and motivations, aspiration for their satisfaction will diminish until some necessary changes occur. An individual's synthesis of all satisfactions would form something mysterious — to be imprinted cognitively and affectivity within the person as a stable disposition, most of the time subconsciously. That stable disposition is positively or negatively formed or changed over a relatively long period of time.

Formulating an affective imprint is like Piaget's schemata in children's play, when assimilating and accommodating confronted experiences in play (see Ellis, 1973). Processes of composing domain satisfaction help the individual to place himself/herself on a ladder of life satisfaction, happiness, and meaning. Therefore, Campbell's (1980) view has merit, suggesting that individuals cannot be precise in describing the quality of their lives, although they tend to report valid responses.

Probably, that is due to the gradual, unnoticeable, subconscious development of what is referred to as schemata or integration of synthesized satisfactions within self. Hence, services, treatments, and aspirations consistently attempt to maximize the gains and benefits obtained from their designated domains. These add up to the broader domain, satisfaction, leading to meta-contentment or lack of such. The goal is to maintain or re-synthesize individuals to more positive impressions and outlooks.

What will happen when a person loses access to sources of satisfaction through situations such as empty nest, retiring from work, and health deterioration? As humans get older, they lose sources that matter in providing satisfaction and pleasure, which they usually had, but took for granted. Therefore, two scenarios can evolve in a person's life:

- A passive person can feel helpless and goalless, giving in to shrunken satisfactions arising from work, family, health, and friendships.
- A more active person might take charge of situations, replacing losses with new pursuits: volunteering, acquiring new leisure skills, joining new groups, seeking alternative lifestyles, and planning for travel to new lands.

What can determine these two scenarios? It is possible that personal orientation, readiness, and awareness would determine the course of action or non-action. This would demonstrate whether a person is maximizing rewards or giving in by being actionless, helpless, and hopeless, which usually leads to depression. Clearly, leisure pursuits can play a great role, replacing and empowering lost satisfactions.

Theories of Satisfaction

A variety of theories can provide good bases for understanding the concepts of leisure satisfaction and other satisfactions, as well as their assessment. Examples of theories relevant to leisure satisfaction are

1. Bottom-up and top-down theories.
2. Activity theory of life satisfaction.
3. Theoretical explanations relevant to conditioning to positive rewards and outcomes.
4. Satisfaction of the need for the search for meaning.
5. Discrepancy between actual and past rewards.
6. Social production function.

Some of the basic explanations of these theoretical structures are described below.

Bottom-Up and Top-Down Theories

Two theories by Krause (1991) can contribute to the explanation of leisure satisfaction (the bottom-up theory and top-down theory). The bottom-up theory assumes that the person assesses feelings of satisfaction in domains that are frequently encountered and provide daily gratification. Obtained rewards from specific life domains (e.g., leisure, health, family) make up this satisfaction. The domain-specific views are subsequently synthesized, computed, accommodated, and integrated internally to form an overall sense of satisfaction with life as a whole.

Sirgy et al. (2000), assessing residents' satisfaction with community-based services, obtained evidence supporting the bottom-up spillover explanation. They found that community satisfaction, together with satisfactions from domains such as family, work, and leisure, affect global life satisfaction. Similarly, specifically encountered leisure experiences and rewards from activities such as painting, reading, dancing, and meeting people are synthesized into leisure satisfaction as a total. The many pursuits and experiences at the bottom form a total impression of satisfaction.

The top-down theory, on the other hand, suggests that a person formulates or reaches a certain level of "global satisfaction with life as a whole." In turn, this sense, impression, or idea predisposes her/him to estimate satisfactions with specific domains in ways that are congruent with her/his initially formulated sense of global life satisfaction. Global life satisfaction creates a "Euphoric Mood" that generalizes to all other moods. In other words, if a person is claiming to be highly satisfied with life, then in encountering leisure, health, work, or family, s/he will be prepared to report satisfaction on a similar high level, even if there are difficulties, pains, sorrows, funerals, failures, and minor displeasures that would last for more than a limited duration. The higher-level euphoria cancels out potential negatives or minimizes their impact.

In a leisure context, this also applies to a large extent. For example, if a person has an impression that s/he is highly pleased with leisure, this will tend to predispose him/her to report similar levels of specific rewards, even when there are some leisure constraints, defeats, and frustrations. This was referred to in the top-down theory as the congruence between the whole impression that was previously formulated and the parts that would come after.

How valid is each theory? How much truth is there in each explanation? Which theory is more universal? Also, to tap a person's "true" satisfaction, how representative are both theories? Realistically, it seems that each theory is tapping a unique true dimension of the real satisfaction, valid at times when it is most applicable, and they have similar universalities in individuals' encounters. An integration of both theories can be beneficial and makes satisfaction easier to understand. To fit the two explanations together, satisfaction can be swinging in a pendulum motion.

As individuals experience different domains (e.g., health, family, work), they move up and down between specific experiences and the global experience. These experiences cause the individuals to instantly reformulate their impressions and benefits, from bottom and from top, readjusting both levels in different proportions. No satisfactions exist separately; feedback is always operating between the two. The movement may pause on the top, waiting for changes in the impressions on the bottom or with the specifics. Or it may color impressions on the bottom with the overall satisfaction felt on the top. It swings from up to down and down to up formulating a given level of satisfaction on a given day, moving to formulate a total impression periodically, say every three months.

Sometimes, satisfaction readjustments are made simultaneously on what is encountered momentarily (e.g., specific activities, settings, situations). Nevertheless, general satisfaction from domains (such as financial, leisure, or community) takes longer time and more encounters to improve or deteriorate. It is possible that "improving" satisfaction takes longer than "deterioration," similar to how building a house takes more time than demolishing it. This is besides the acquired resilience and endurance as psychological traits that had been built up. (See resilience and endurance as positive psychological emotions.)

Furthermore, much longer duration and extensive encounters (from the bottom) are required to modify synthesized global life satisfaction (formulated top). In other words, the lower the level of the encounter, the faster the formulation or change of impressions. This is situational. To the contrary, the higher the position of the domain's satisfaction, the slower is its change. On this level, it is a disposition.

There is a constant feedback between the two, never a static situation. Such a process gives satisfaction not only realism and dynamics, but also uniqueness and complexity. In an examination of a controversy between top-down and bottom-up theories, Anderson (2010) devised a correlational method to control possible confounding effects of using the same testing strategies. Investigators found different weights for top-down effects in satisfaction judgments of older persons.

Practically, both theories operate in different degrees and momentum on leisure, recreation, travel and tourism, and exercise lifestyles, requiring further verification. Confirming the predictability of these theories in informal activities can have strong field and scientific implications

Activity Theory of Life Satisfaction

The activity theory of life satisfaction is centered on the concept of engagement and involvement in life pursuits. In essence, the theory postulates, according to Havinghurst et al. (1968), that a satisfied person is an active member in community activities. These activities can be physical, social, artistic, cultural, mental, and/or spiritual, pursuing frequent (optimal) interaction with all sections of society, maintaining a middle-age lifestyle. Knapp (1977) validated the relevance of activity theory of life satisfaction in an English context. Moreover, evidence indicates that to experience subjective well-being, activities must be satisfying, fun, and keep a person busy (Schulz, R. and Kenneth, R., 2006).

Moreover, in comparing contributions of informal, formal, and solitary activities to well-being, Everard (1999) found that informal activities were the only consistent domain to impact on well-being. Griffin and McKenna (1998), in a study on older persons (aged 65-98 years), revealed through multiple regression analysis that less leisure participation associated with poorer health, but leisure satisfaction remained high, due to continued participation in a more limited but still valued number of activities.

This is an issue relevant to the suggested method of making an estimate for total life satisfaction by accounting for a domain's value as a part of the index. Moreover, the comparison between participation and involvement is similar to the above issue: less activities but with high intensity and flow seem

to help in experiencing satisfaction. In another study on midlife females, Parry and Shaw (1999) observed that a physically active leisure lifestyle enhanced health and emotional well-being.

In essence, activity theory of life satisfaction is the closest to leisure and recreation explanations — their satisfaction and their pursuits.

Conditioning to Positive Rewards and Outcomes Theory

This theory is based on one of Thorndike's principles that postulated: repeating a certain choice would emanate from the rewards (satisfaction) obtained (see Kimble, 1961: 10). Rewards function as motives to revisit what once satisfied the person.

In a leisure context, activities and services lose participants if they obtain negative outcomes and impressions (Dumazedier, 1974). Accordingly, leisure, recreation, travel and tourism, and fitness activities can be positively or negatively conditioned, based on the nature of rewards gained or the lack of these rewards (sometimes acting like constraints).

As a further support, Geyer et al. (1987) proposed a model indicating that satisfaction is a function of perceiving more positive than negative emotional and cognitive outcomes. More validation of this theory in leisure and recreation can be beneficial for programming and in knowing about satisfied versus unsatisfied needs.

Satisfaction of the Need for the Search for Meaning

One of the deepest possible and most rooted contributors to leisure satisfaction can be explained by Frankl's (1962) theory: man's search for meaning. Humans seek to discover and realize meaning through performing activities: discovering hidden sides of self, about others, nature, and one's superpower. In achieving that sense of meaning, humans gain hope and reasons for existence. There are many persistent needs for meaning that require satisfaction from work, family, and leisure. Otherwise, emptiness, aimlessness, and purposelessness (see Frankl, 1962) will cause maladaptive behaviors.

In a cross-cultural comparison between Australian and Canadian samples, Prager (1996) investigated 16 sources of meaning employing the Sources of Meaning Profile (SOMP). Subjects in the two cultures agreed that the most important sources of personal meaning are in personal relationships, personal growth, meeting basic needs, participation in leisure activities, and the preservation of values and ideals. (The reader is also referred to a coming satisfaction theory on Social Production Function, to see a possible overlap and need for integrating these two theories.) Many other humanistic psychological theories can provide explanations regarding the satisfying qualities of the leisure experience, such as optimal arousal (Berlyne, 1960), on becoming a person (Rogers, 1956), and the discovery of being (May, 1983).

Discrepancy between Actual and Past Rewards

Discrepancy is viewed as a gap between what an individual has and what s/he hopes to have. According to Helson's (1959) adaptation-level theory, individuals attempt to adapt to what is provided, resulting in an affective state called "satisfaction level." Some of the applications of the theory (mostly applied in commercial, consumer, and marketing settings) can treat leisure satisfaction as a discrepancy between actual (present) and past reward levels.

The adaptation-level theory postulates that a person may expect that the satisfaction derived from a given pursuit is a function, not of the actual level of satisfaction from that pursuit, but rather of the discrepancy between the actual and past levels, as reflected in a person's adaptation level. Since satisfaction is the discrepancy between expectations — based on past encounters — and the actual gain, unmet expectations give rise to dissatisfaction. The opposite is equally true. Discrepancy can be applied in another way, as Stock et al. (1986) viewed it: Discrepancy is the outcome of what a person has (or gains) compared to what s/he aspires to, expects, or deserves.

The concept of adaptation applies to leisure settings where programs, services, and facilities are provided. In turn, the concept can be utilized when services, programs, environments, and resources are offered, as the basis for the assessment of users' satisfaction, comparing what they obtained against what they expected and aspired to receive.

Social Production Function Theory

The social production functions theory, by Ormel et al. (1999) postulates that there are two main goals that humans strive to optimize: physical well-being and social well-being. Apparently, other aspects of well-being such as mental, psychological, emotional, and spiritual seem to serve or to be incorporated within the above-identified ones.

Theorists propose five instrumental goals by which physical and social well-being are satisfied. These are stimulation, comfort, status, behavioral confirmation, and affection. The core aspect of this theory applies perfectly to leisure and recreation satisfaction. Social production function theory proposes that individuals choose and substitute instrumental goals (activities) so as to optimize the production of their well-being, subject to constraints in available means of production.

Comments on the Theories of Life Satisfaction

Satisfaction concepts are broad and adaptable. This is logical and fitting because they need to serve all life stages, almost all personal conditions (gender, age, social class, income, education), and diverse cultures. Daily, any given individual seeks satisfaction, wherever s/he is. Therefore, explanations of satisfaction are naturally broad and complicated. What needs to be satisfied is multifaceted, at many levels, and reoccurring. This seems obvious when a person tries to fit explanations to numerous settings, states of being, stages of life, and personal conditions. These broad varieties give satisfaction concepts uniqueness, importance, and sometimes complexity.

Life satisfaction theories offer elegant explanations that attempt to incorporate the many observed aspects, however specific or limited each interpretation is. In sum, to reconstruct and synthesize available theoretical assumptions of satisfaction, reviewers can assemble the basic assumptions of the theories as follows:

1. Satisfaction is an outcome of many domains (e.g., health, family, and work) and many specific domain encounters. In leisure this might include music, drawing, jogging, and camping. In work we may look at pay, supervision, environment, peers, and responsibilities.
2. Past and present experiences, interwoven within future expectations, formulate, shape, and condition satisfaction.
3. Satisfaction results from a level of involvement or actual doing, not just aspiring to or longing for an engagement in activities or facing an experience.
4. Satisfaction also lends itself to flexible emphasis, such as autonomy or independence in some cultures or subcultures, social roles and norms in other cultures.
5. Satisfaction taps rewards obtained from the lowest levels of needs (e.g., hunger, thirst, and security), to the highest levels, in peak self-actualization, searching for meaning, and meta-contentment, with plenty of benefits in between.
6. Satisfaction optimizes many functions as a result of two major ones: physical and social well-being. Psychological, mental, emotional, and spiritual well-being are theorized to result from

the main two functions or they are the function's by-products.

These explanations can help in fitting and integrating leisure satisfaction into a broader theoretical frame of reference, contributing to field practice and scientific use.

Summary and Conclusion

All people have basic needs that they strive to satisfy. Otherwise, they experience a sense of deprivation and frustration, on some levels misery. Needs are assessed by satisfaction measurements or misery indexes. Need satisfaction seems to determine health, well-being, vitality, quality of life, meta-contentment, and happiness.

There are humanistic, professional, and research reasons to be concerned about satisfactions gained from different domains such as health, work, family, and leisure. The main practical reason for this attention is to improve them. Practically, leisure satisfaction can be met on three unique levels: fun and amusement; discoveries, competencies, and actualizations; and seeking and finding meanings, purposes, and significance in what is pursued. This applies to all humans but in different timings, degrees, and conditions.

The concept of satisfaction can incorporate gains, rewards, and benefits received from actual involvement in activities or their domains. Moreover, there are unique characteristics to satisfaction: a positive affective feeling, a degree of intensity, and a long duration or frequency of positive emotion and mood. Satisfaction is proven to be universal, a part of all humans in all cultures; only their sources vary. While Westerners obtain it from individualistic endeavors, Easterners receive it from collectivity.

Satisfaction is a viable entity that can operate as an ultimate consequence. It can also operate as a moderator or as an antecedent. A model was constructed incorporating many domains of the above. Many aspects can determine it and, in turn, it can impact on other ends or goals, such as happiness or quality of life. Life satisfaction was discussed in detail within a dynamic context relating determinants to it and presenting possible consequences of it. The main purpose for a presented model is to develop a broader context where leisure satisfaction may fit. Moreover, contributions of leisure to specific benefits or satisfaction can include physical, mental, psychological, social, economic, and environmental, as will be explained in the next chapter.

Finally, to explain satisfaction and to construct its assessment tools, some theories are presented. Theories can range from bottom-up/top-down, activity, conditioning, and search for meaning to discrepancy. Explanations of leisure and life satisfaction can be utilized in leisure on a global or holistic level, activity-specific level, or when looking at free time contributions.

Questions and Exercises

1. Explain the nature of satisfaction.
2. What are the characteristics of life satisfaction?
3. Is life satisfaction universal, existing in all cultures? Discuss.
4. What are the possible determinants of life satisfaction?
5. How would motivation, attitudes, and involvement relate to satisfaction?
6. What are the possible domains that compose life satisfaction?
7. Explain the relationship between life satisfaction and happiness.
8. How would you estimate a person's satisfaction based on life encounters? Explain the contribution and value of different satisfactions to make an accurate estimate.
9. Explain the theories of satisfaction.
10. What were the comments made on the theories of life satisfaction? What are your comments?

Chapter 27

Leisure Satisfaction: From Concepts to Measurements

Focus of Chapter

This chapter focuses upon satisfactions elicited from informal domains: leisure, recreation, exercise, travel, and play. Reasons for the attention given to leisure satisfaction are explained. They range from initial human social interaction and consumer satisfaction to service (non-merchandizing) satisfaction. The roots of the application of the concepts of leisure satisfaction are described. To understand the position of leisure satisfaction in life, it was placed in its larger frame of reference, incorporating other satisfactions in a context. Because leisure satisfaction is multifaceted, relevant domains will be explored. Based on available literature, constructs to assess attributes of satisfaction are identified, guided with the uses of the psychometric theory presented in the second part of this book. The few existing Leisure Satisfaction measurements will be presented and discussed. Furthermore, efforts will be made to point to areas where the measurements have shortages and gaps. Hopefully, further efforts will focus on filling the identified gaps.

Key Terms

- benefits
- contentment
- global satisfaction
- life satisfaction

- meta-contentment
- optimal rewards
- specific satisfaction

Key Names

- Donald Campbell

- Allen V. Sapora

Objectives

- Explain the nature of leisure satisfaction.
- Report the main reasons to study leisure satisfaction.
- Identify the roots of the leisure satisfaction concept.
- Outline the larger context of various satisfactions.
- Relate leisure satisfaction to the identified larger context of different satisfactions.
- List benefits gained from leisure satisfaction.
- Differentiate among levels of uses of the leisure satisfaction concept (e.g., levels such as activity, experience, free time, global, and specific).
- Report on existing leisure satisfaction measurements and their quality.

I walked for five miles, which made me thirsty. The deficiency walking created drove me to seek a fluid. As I drank, I sensed pleasure (rewards). Therefore, I kept on drinking until I was satisfied (filled or saturated). Similarly, perhaps another person performed hard work (mentally or physically) during a workweek and felt tired, strained, or stressed, "creating a deficiency for life's fluids," in the form of "relaxation" or "a need for a change." S/he needed to be recharged. That need could drive (motivate) that person to seek non-mental or non-physical outlets, to relax, depending on personal conditions. In other words, outlets are pursued until the person is full and pleased, sometimes saturated or optimally satisfied.

Intake of fluids and ways to recharge energy are both sought for their satisfaction qualities. Satisfaction, the search for contentment, therefore, is the outcome, reward, and gain sought by a person. Individuals seek such pursuits to extract their needed rewards from actions, products, or relationships. It is important to note that the pursuit of satisfaction is sometimes equated in the literature with well being and quality of life (see Campbell, Converse, and Rogers, 1976). The goal is the achievement of meta-contentment or a higher pursuit, including meaning and happiness. All these domains can be viewed and demonstrated instrumentally later in this chapter.

Reasons to Study Leisure Satisfaction

Satisfaction is as old as humanity itself. Through the earliest interactions of humans — most often nonverbal — attempts were made, for example, to please, to reward, to get along, and to complement each other (social satisfaction). Many other satisfactions stemming from different needs were also realized (e.g., work, health, accommodations, and marriage). Accordingly, satisfaction gained from all domains evolved as a major part of the way of life. Lately, as a result of the high volume of industrial productivity, distributors or marketers are very sensitive about the speedy sale of their merchandise or commodities. This is how customer satisfaction became a common practice and a standard way to do business.

Common sense, more than anything else, told us that buyer satisfaction was a key to distribution and eventually a key to success (profit). Therefore, humans got better at the use of satisfaction strategies. In contemporary times, satisfaction has formulated more sophisticated perspectives. For example, a customer is realized to be the lifeblood of the company; a spouse is a cornerstone of the family; and a student is the prime target of academic efforts. Satisfaction of all concerned parties is a prerequisite for success and the ability of providers or marriage "to stay in business."

However, not until the 1950s did services and non-merchandising satisfaction begin to be investigated scientifically (e.g., health, family, and work), accounting and planning for it. Leisure and recreation satisfaction (benefits and rewards) began to be recognized and incorporated into exploratory studies, searching for their possible existence and then their causes. As leisure services started to play an active role in society and its environments such as communities, corporations, military bases, hospitals, and prisons, "user satisfaction" grew as a key for service quality and other successes.

Moreover, "Satisfaction gained from different activities has been of concern to social scientists for several years," observed Ragheb and Beard (1980: 329), "There are humanistic, as well as scientific reasons for that concern. Humanistically, knowledge about satisfaction could enable its attainment by identifying activities, actions, or services that contribute to it. Scientifically, relationships between satisfaction and other relevant variables could be examined to discover how they fit into the total scheme of life." Satisfaction is planned for and expected from every service.

The case of leisure satisfaction is universal among all services such as education, rehabilitation, and mental health. Interestingly, Jackson and Lilley (1990) reiterated that improved life satisfaction (LS) is cited as a fundamental goal for nursing home residents, and an argument is made for the effective achievement of that goal. Besides, they elaborate on the value of activities, mainly leisure and recreation, as an alternative treatment for anxiety and depression, and the cost-effectiveness of activity programs. Also, Pinquart and Schindler (2009) from Germany, they found that the largest group of their sample showed a linear increase in leisure satisfaction during the four years prior to retirement and in the first months of retirement, followed by stability thereafter.

There are growing humanistic trends to incorporate leisure and recreation benefits for the enhancement of the quality of service such as fitness, health, stress reduction, wellness, vitality, and total functioning. Moreover, scientifically explored relationships have been attempting to reveal the concealed impact of leisure satisfaction on human empowerment, adjustment, and the quality of life (Frain, et al., 2009; Iwasaki, Mannell, Smale, and Butcher, 2002). These research efforts and humanistic trends can lead to improving leisure theorizing (see Tinsley and Tinsley, 1986; Dattilo, Kleiber, and Williams, 1998) that can have very beneficial implications and applications by contributing to users' welfare and advancements of leisure delivery systems.

The Roots of Leisure Satisfaction

Satisfaction does not exist randomly or by accident. Fundamentally, satisfaction should be considered an echo or expression of needs and their motivations. In an earlier stage of the evolution of recreation services, Sapora (1966) insightfully emphasized the value of user satisfaction and the importance of its assessment for participants' benefits, as well as for the advancement of the leisure delivery system. Contemporary professionals are striving to achieve what Sapora envisioned more than 40 years ago, satisfying individuals' and society's needs.

Leisure satisfaction is subjective, colored and shaped by needs. To a starving person, for instance, music falls on deaf ears. Definitely, food and shelter are more basic to that starving person's satisfaction, as basic needs that have to be met first before music could be appealing. Hence, satisfaction as a concept is multifaceted in terms of its nature, degree, meaning, and measurement. However, satisfaction in leisure and recreation should be viewed in terms of its unique functions. This is what leisure professionals and scientists attempt to understand and enhance.

Three levels of leisure satisfaction are suggested. On the surface, leisure satisfaction can be obtained by having fun, good times, amusement, entertainment, and relaxation. At a higher level, satisfaction is moving deeper, to mental discoveries and challenges, being useful to others (service), mastering skills, developing competencies, and actualizing self. Then much deeper satisfaction still is accomplished, in seeking and finding meanings and purposes in what is done, usually in significant human relations, in volunteering for causes, and even in enduring life's pains and paradoxes. (These ideas will be further elaborated below.) What are usually observed for a given person are rewards for the senses, while mental and meaningful rewards (or their deficits) are hard to observe, being covert constructs.

Leisure Satisfaction in a Context

For leisure satisfaction to be understood, it must be placed into its frame of reference. In doing so, through available literature, evidence shows that leisure satisfaction is related to life satisfaction (LS) and well-being. In a conceptual development, McPherson (1991) synthesized many findings relevant to LS of the elderly, saying that there is strong evidence that leisure contributes to LS, citing many positive qualities. McPherson goes on by raising a critical issue: Why do we still not understand how or why relationships prevail? More importantly, why are some older adults not involved in leisure pursuits while others, despite being involved, report low levels of LS, well-being, and happiness? A hidden aspect that might have caused inconsistencies of the results is the issue of domain value.

Moreover, at least two problems or methodological difficulties — common to all fields — could have caused McPherson's concerns. First, lack of quality instrumentations and assessment tools usually cause fluctuating and inconsistent results. Moreover, competencies in the use of instruments, data manipulation, and interpretation can make the problems worse. Second, many results that conflict and confuse the issue are because of unrealized moderating aspects that can disrupt the nature of true relationships. Moderating aspects that need to be considered when investigating LS and/or leisure satisfaction may include the state of health, income, human energy, constraints, attitudes, motivation, level of leadership facilitation, skills, awareness, and leisure education.

Among the many findings on leisure satisfaction and LS, Russell (1990) demonstrated that the only significant, direct predictor of quality of life in old age was satisfaction with recreation. Lloyd and Auld (2002) also found that leisure satisfaction was the best predictor of quality of life. Also, Kelly et al. (1987) showed that there was an independent contribution of leisure to LS. Specifically, they found that social activity and travel were associated with higher levels of life satisfaction. One of the potentialities of leisure was suggested empirically as a spillover of work and leisure to LS.

In a conceptual article, MacNeil and Anderson (1999) wrote that personally satisfying leisure is a critical component of mental health and LS. They added an argument that leisure contributes to personal empowerment through self-determination as a quality essential to community adjustment. In another study by Boley (2002), a significant association was found between leisure satisfaction and LS of older persons. Interestingly, a sample of 461 Australians, aged 18 to 91 years, was asked what they considered to be the most and least important sources of meaning in their lives (Prager, 1996). Reported responses were personal relationships, personal growth, meeting basic needs, participation in leisure activities, and preservation of values and ideals. For leisure to be empowering and a source for meaning are considered here indicative of LS and well-being.

Moreover, Iwasaki, Mannell, Smale, and Butcher (2005) found relaxing leisure to be the strongest positive predictor of coping with stress among police and emergency workers. Relaxation is one of the six components of leisure satisfaction as reported by Beard and Ragheb (1980). Also, Tseng, T. A. et al. (2009) observed that leisure behavior and leisure satisfaction had an inverse relationship on two out of three burnout components: Emotional Exhaustion and Depersonalization.

The ways resources are used are critical determinants of leisure satisfaction. Psychological and social benefits of those sources are achieved when individuals have chances to perform, excel, and achieve their goals. In an excellent contribution, Larsen and Stothart (1986) demonstrated three historical developmental stages for the leisure movement by comparing Australia, New Zealand, and Canada in how they resemble the U.S. in their leisure delivery systems. Interestingly, similar historical stages evolved in those three countries, but with a time span difference. The first stage was giving attention to facilities in the 1940s and 1950s, leading to programming in the 1960s, with more attention to human needs and interests from the 1970s on. It was noticed that all stages were centered on meeting identified needs, maximizing citizens' recreation, and leisure satisfaction. Therefore, extensive conceptualization regarding the attributes of leisure satisfaction is needed as a foundation for its understanding, assessment, and contribution to higher-order gains (e.g., life satisfaction, wellness, vitality, meta-contentment, happiness, and the search for meaning).

In sum, leisure and physical recreation seem to have some inherent rewarding characteristics that can consistently contribute to the betterment of participants. "Realization" of the contribution of activities is not enough in itself to gain satisfaction. It is like knowing all about the values of fruits and vegetables (vitamins and minerals), and how they can contribute to the betterment of health, but without eating these products. Similarly, leisure and physical activities are not going to benefit people unless individuals actually engage in them through acting on their attitudes and motivations. Admittedly, there are possible personal or environmental constraints to prevent satisfaction; therefore, every possible effort needs to be made to remove these barriers. At least, effort should be invested, minimizing setting constraints and maximizing leisure benefits.

Possible Impacts of Lack of Leisure Satisfaction

What is the impact of deprivation from leisure satisfaction? Logically, the contributions of leisure and recreation to LS and other positive outcomes are understood for those who, for example, are healthy and have positive attitudes and motivations as a part of their ongoing actions. Meanwhile, how about those who lack the above dispositions? Will they have chances to reap the benefits of leisure and recreation? Meyers (1999) has the concern that leisure, including all of the non-work uses of one's time, potentially

increases during retirement, but adjustment to increased free time is not necessarily positive.

Guidelines, such as the ones suggested by Elejalde-Ruiz (2011), are needed for leisure satisfaction deprivation, making leisure optimally rewarding and satisfying. They suggested incorporating physical movement, thinking, and feelings in both leisure and physical activity for older adults. They also recommended that activity programs should appreciate older persons' anxieties, doubts, and expectations. Therefore, to maximize leisure benefits and rewards, efforts should be made to involve participants in specifying their goals and exercising self-determining means to achieve them.

Despite the above facts — that leisure is characterized by being experiential, attitudinal, and emotional, Sirgy (1998) suggests that overall life satisfaction (quality of life) is partly determined by satisfaction with the person's material situation represented by standards of living. This notion applies most often to recreation resources and leisure environments: parks, clubs, facilities (e.g., tennis courts and swimming pools), fitness areas, and travel and tourism sites. However, material objects and resources can be available, but with little or no contribution to quality of life or to the feelings of deeper satisfaction. Resources are insufficient by themselves for satisfaction to be experienced, as demonstrated above. Actual involvement in resource usage and activities is still a basic requirement.

Contributions of Leisure to Specific Satisfactions

Leisure and recreation have the potential not only to provide multiple physiological and psychological benefits, but also benefits that are emotional, social, economic, and environmental. Specifically, physical gains can be related to the cardiovascular and health. Psychological rewards can include mood improvement, positive feelings, stress control, self-concept, and adjustment as follows:

- Social benefits can be in the form of getting along with others, interpersonal harmony, and gaining others' esteem.
- Economically, leisure spending can increase the volume of trade of leisure goods, allowing individuals to enjoy economic prosperity, mass production, and affordability, with their substantial contributions to leisure satisfaction.
- Environmental benefits can be gained through improving the aesthetics of the surroundings and the layout of communities, neighborhoods, cities, parks, roads, highways, and organizations.

- Finally, there are moral and spiritual gains, which include having hope to achieve and master, aspiration to be or to fulfill. Participants can extract a sense of meaning and purpose from daily endeavors and future encounters.

Two examples of these basic rewards and benefits from leisure and recreation will be elaborated upon below: physical and psychological. (For excellent details on leisure benefits, see Driver et al., 1991 and Froelicher and Froelicher, 1991).

First, due to the obvious importance of physical health, most conceptualizations and studies focused on the body and the health benefits that are obtained from leisure. For instance, there is evidence that physically active leisure enhanced physical and emotional well being (Parry and Shaw, 1999). In another study, Sanchez (2010) found positive relationships between participation in sports and subjective health ratings for persons aged 18 to 65 years. Conceptually, Paffenbarger, Hyde, and Dow (1991) demonstrated that physical recreation contributes to health benefits, as well as cardiovascular functioning. Finally, Griffin and McKenna (1998) reported that less frequent leisure participation is associated with poorer health. In sum, due to its physical and material nature, the impact of leisure and physical recreation is the easiest to observe and test. Other spin-off rewards, such as social, emotional, and spiritual benefits, are more difficult to notice and test.

Second, the psychological rewards of leisure and recreation might be parallel to the physical ones. Two studies demonstrated how certain leisure qualities affect individuals: Guinn (1999) showed that intrinsically motivated leisure from self-determined competence and challenge contributed to positive life satisfaction. Also, Ellis and Witt (1994) provided support for the existence of a perceived freedom factor as a part of leisure satisfaction.

Other psychological benefits of activities and leisure were reviewed and incorporated by Tinsley et al. (1985) as a therapeutic tool in nursing homes, controlling anxiety and depression. Deduced from interrelationships between leisure satisfaction and wellness, Ragheb (1993) suggested that leisure satisfaction can be a major determinant of an individual's vitality and empowerment. Therefore, psychological and other gains from leisure require careful assessment and study to reveal their antecedents and consequences for possible applications and theorizations.

Levels of the Leisure Satisfaction Concept

In application, leisure satisfaction is interwoven in many daily processes that add to its complexity.

Leisure satisfaction can be treated on two levels: in global terms and in specific ones. Furthermore, leisure satisfaction can result from activities or from experiences or from the amount of free time available. In this context, a classification of the above can be explained and sorted in three points. The categories are as follows:

First, leisure satisfaction can be treated in a global or holistic manner, concerned about leisure in general or in its totality (all activities, all experiences, and all free time). Many research studies treated leisure satisfaction in this global manner. Parties concerned about utilizing this approach are not only management that provides recreation and leisure services in communities, corporations, the armed forces, senior homes, campuses, or correctional settings, but also scientists interested in psychology and positive psychology, sociology, and gerontology. In other words, the global and holistic view of leisure satisfaction is highly usable in practice and research.

Second, satisfaction received from specific activities gained most of the attention for program planning functions, such as user satisfaction. Also, there are research reasons to know about satisfaction, for instance, from camping, tennis, the arts, and exercising. Studies reported many benefits and rewards from specific activities, such as Relaxation gained from camping, listening to music, physical activities, and watching television; Achievement obtained from gardening and sewing; Power from physical activities, fitness, travel, and watching television; and Intellection from reading and chess. In sum, it is important to know about the composition of nutritional food: specific substances, elements, and chemicals in specific foods. In the same way it is important to know the leisure benefits of specific activities.

Third, leisure satisfaction is not limited to activities and their experiences, but it is also concerned with satisfaction about the amount of free time. This is a concern of laypersons as well as scientists of industrial and organizational psychology, occupational rehabilitation, and corporate/public management. The intent is to reveal the impact of free time on critical functions. Many of the relations that can be tested are between satisfaction with the length of free time and sick leave, turnover, job satisfaction, productivity, physical and mental health, well-being, and life satisfaction of employees.

Leisure satisfaction exists on many levels, which creates complexity and difficulties in its application. Leisure satisfaction's contributions are varied in nature; therefore, contributions in the outcome of satisfaction are multifaceted. When the issue of leisure satisfaction is encountered in practice and/or research, broad considerations are required. This is because for many groups, settings, and uses, rewards gained can be uniquely personalized.

Measures of Leisure Satisfaction

Despite the growing attention and importance of individual leisure satisfaction and user satisfaction, assessment efforts are still inadequate. Development of measurements of leisure satisfaction is not equivalent to the diversity of uses and growing social concerns. Almost every individual experiences leisure activities, daily or weekly, with the attempt to maximize benefits. Nevertheless, just a few scales exist, without further development. Only four global and two specific leisure satisfaction scales were identified from 1977 to 2004. One of those four global scales, the LSS, was translated to French and validated utilizing factor analysis, showing positive results (see Lysyk et al. 2002). However, more employment of both qualitative and quantitative procedures is needed to further inspect the underlying nature of leisure satisfaction.

In a detailed development, a chapter on leisure satisfaction, Mannell (1989) questioned the use of the global need-satisfying properties of the Leisure Satisfaction Scale (LSS) by Beard and Ragheb (1980). He speculated, "Its adequacy as a measure of leisure-need-satisfaction may be in question" (p. 293). Moreover, Mannell wondered why another scale assessing leisure motivation by the same developers "identified only four major need dimensions" while leisure satisfaction has six domains.

Mannell's questions are answerable. If leisure knowledge is going to advance, instruments and definitions should be refined periodically. This is an issue of validity (see Cohen and Swerdlik, 2002). However, the above-mentioned scales were constructed on meritorious literature and theories available in their era, the early 1980s. Moreover, suggestions are required from instrument evaluators, demonstrating a more valid concept, a newly formulated theoretical structure, or a more advanced methodology. These can be used to develop a psychometrically sounder instrument to replace LSS. Waiting for further verifications, components, indicators, and items ought to be tentatively delineated and presented.

Moreover, Mannell suspected the value of the identified components of the same scale. "Beard and Ragheb's scale has six satisfaction subdomains." He voiced his doubts adding, "However, researchers have typically used only the total scale score in assessing leisure need-satisfaction. Further research is required to determine whether the measurement of these subdimensions provide useful information beyond that provided by the global score" (p.293).

In response to these suspicions, the following can be offered:

1. The six satisfaction components were the outcome of both a careful review of the literature and an empirical support employing factor analysis. Factors obtained were the objective reality of the identified knowledge.
2. More critically, researchers should have used the substantiated six factors, not only their total. Objectively, that is not an inherent problem with the measurement, but rather in the way items and components were handled. Usability and usefulness of the components is up to the users and their skill levels. Components were proven to be very useful in some studies drawing attention to important findings (e.g., Ragheb and Griffith, 1982; Ragheb, 1993; Hsieh, 1999; Munchua, Lesage, Reddon, and Badham, 2003). Scientists' competency in data reduction, usage, analysis, and interpretation determine the value and quality of their findings.

Therefore, Beard and Ragheb's scale can be verified for concurrent validity against a newly developed, theory-guided instrument assessing the same construct. As it is always possible, the LSS might have outlived its lifespan, since it was developed over 30 years ago. Moreover, the six subdimensions need to be exposed to the same treatment and scrutinizing, making changes or replacements, if needed.

Fundamentally, existing scales in general need to be reexamined when needed; hence, revalidated, identifying missing parts or extra parts of the designated concepts based on contemporary theorization. Accordingly, further knowledge of given concepts will be realized, and trustworthy inclusion of constructed scales will be guaranteed.

The limited measures of leisure satisfaction that have been constructed are as follows:

1. Milwaukee Avocational Satisfaction Questionnaire, Overs, Taylor, and Adkins, 1977.
2. Leisure Satisfaction Inventory, Rimmer, 1979.
3. Leisure Satisfaction Measure, Beard and Ragheb, 1980.
4. Racquet Sports Satisfaction Scale, Aguilar and Petrakis, 1989.
5. Physical Activity Enjoyment Scale, Kendzierski and DeCarlo, 1991.
6. Global Leisure Satisfaction Scale, Ellis and Witt, 1994.
7. Leisure Coping Strategy Scale, Iwasaki and Mannell, 2000
8. Leisure Time Satisfaction, Stevens, Coon, Wisniewski, Arguelles, Mendelsohn, Ory, and Haley, 2004.

9. Vitality Through Leisure, Ragheb, 2005.

In conclusion, though the concept of leisure satisfaction is viable and has proved over the years to be critical, qualitative and quantitative assessment procedures have not matched that status. Obviously, more quality scales (reliable and valid) of leisure satisfaction are badly needed. Basically, further application of the psychometric theory is strongly invited to improve the quality of leisure satisfaction instrumentations.

Summary and Conclusion

People have needs that they persist to satisfy; otherwise, they experience a sense of deprivation and frustration. Need satisfaction seems to determine well-being, vitality, empowerment, quality of life, and happiness. There are humanistic and research reasons to be concerned about satisfaction gained from different domains such as health, work, and leisure. The main reason for this attention is to improve them. Leisure satisfaction can be met on three levels: fun and amusement; discoveries, competencies, and actualization; and seeking and finding meanings in what is pursued.

Satisfaction concepts can incorporate gains, rewards, and benefits received from actual involvement in activities or their domains. Moreover, there are unique characteristics to satisfaction: a positive affect; a degree of intensity; and a long duration of frequency of positive emotion and mood.

Questions and Exercises

1. Elaborate on the main reasons for the study of leisure satisfaction.
2. What are the roots of leisure satisfaction?
3. Discuss leisure satisfaction in its context.
4. What are some of the possible impacts of the lack of leisure satisfaction?
5. How does leisure contribute to specific satisfactions?
6. Discuss the levels of leisure satisfaction concepts.
7. What comments can you make on leisure satisfaction measurements?

Leisure Satisfaction Measure

The *Leisure Satisfaction Measure* was developed by Jacob G. Beard and Mounir G. Ragheb and published in the *Journal of Leisure Research*, 1980, Volume 12, Number 1, pp. 20-33. Idyll Arbor, Inc. developed this version with the permission of Beard and Ragheb. Through 2002 the long form of the assessment was used. In 2002 Idyll Arbor, Inc. switched to the short form because there were some concerns about four of the questions on the long form. Scores may be compared between the two versions of the test. Idyll Arbor, Inc. modified the assessment form and wrote a manual for the benefit of the recreational therapists who choose to administer the *Leisure Satisfaction Measure* (*LSM*).

Purpose: The purpose of the *Leisure Satisfaction Measure* is to measure the degree to which a client perceives his/her general "needs" are being met through leisure.

Definitions: Leisure activities are defined as non-work activities in which the individual has a free choice as to whether or not to participate. These activities take place in one's free time and there is no obligation as to what is chosen or to what extent one participates.

Leisure satisfaction is defined as the positive perceptions or feelings that an individual forms, elicits, or gains as a result of engaging in leisure activities and choices. It is the degree to which one is presently content or pleased with his/her general leisure experiences and situations. This positive feeling of contentment results from the satisfaction of felt or unfelt needs of the individual (Beard and Ragheb, 1980).

Areas Measured: Being "satisfied" is a multi-dimensional feeling. An individual may be more satisfied with his/her social life but be unhappy with his/her lack of physical activity. To measure the individual's overall satisfaction on a scale from one to ten without specifying areas of greater or lesser contentment has little meaning for the client and for the therapist. This assessment tool divides satisfaction of one's leisure into six categories:

(The following six description are taken from the *Journal of Leisure Research*, 1980, Volume 12, Number 1, p. 26.)

1. Psychological. Psychological benefits such as: a sense of freedom, enjoyment, involvement, and intellectual challenge.
2. Educational. Intellectual stimulation; helps them to learn about themselves and their surroundings.
3. Social. Rewarding relationships with other people.
4. Relaxation. Relief from the stress and strain of life.
5. Physiological. A means to develop physical fitness, stay healthy, control weight, and otherwise promote well-being.
6. Aesthetic. Aesthetic rewards. Individuals scoring high on this part view the areas in which they engage in their leisure activities as being pleasing, interesting, beautiful, and generally well designed.

Supplies Needed: Idyll Arbor, Inc. form #A146, pen, *LSM* Manual. (No additional copies of the score sheet may be made. The therapist may order more score sheets from Idyll Arbor, Inc., PO Box 720, Ravensdale, WA 98051-9763 360-825-7797.)

Populations: Idyll Arbor, Inc. staff recommend the following guidelines to help determine if a client is cognitively able to comprehend the statements.

- Adapted IQ of 80 or above
- Mental age of 12 years or above
- Rancho Los Amigos level of 7 or above
- Reality orientation level of "Mild to No Orientation Disability"

Time Needed: The recreational therapist should allow between 5 and 20 minutes for the client to answer all 24 statements. Scoring (both sides of the score sheet) should take the therapist under 10 minutes. In most cases the recreational therapist should be able to administer the assessment, score it, and write a brief summary/recommendation statement in 20 minutes or less.

Reliability and Validity: The first step taken by the authors was to conduct a review of the theoretical literature. All the various effects (or gains as a result of engaging in leisure activities) were abstracted and cataloged. Many of the effects seemed to share the same or similar definitions, so they were grouped together. Other effects were difficult to quantify, so these were discarded. After review, the authors arrived at six effects that became the subscales within the assessment tool. A Likert scale was developed for the responses. ("1" Almost Never True, "2" Seldom True, "3" Sometimes True, "4" Often True, and "5" Almost Always True.)

The assessment tool then went through extensive critiques and revisions, as needed, until it was determined to be ready for field testing.

The field test consisted of two separate steps. The tool was first sent out for an expert panel review by

83 individuals. The responses from the expert panel were generally positive with the exception of a general concern over the advanced reading skill required by the tool. The wording of the assessment tool was then modified to make it easier for the general population to read. Overall, the *Leisure Satisfaction Measure* received good face validity.

This modified version of the tool was then administered to 950 individuals (one group of 603, and then later to a group of 347). The data from this sample group was analyzed using conventional item and test analysis techniques. Factor analysis was also used. These analyses were completed on the assessment tool as a whole and on each of the six subscales to test for the degree of intercorrelation between the subscales.

These analyses showed that the psychological, educational, social, and environmental subscales were clearly defined. The other two subscales (relaxation and physiological) were less clearly defined but still within an acceptable range.

The alpha reliability coefficient for the overall *Leisure Satisfaction Measure* is quite high, being .93. This high reliability allows the therapist to administer a short assessment and still have confidence in the results.

When to Administer: The *LSM* ideally should be administered between the 4th and 7th day after admission. If the assessment is administered prior to the 4th day, the results may be undesirably impacted by transitional depression (the normal physiological reaction of people to an unfamiliar environment). If the therapist waits until some time after the 7th day of admission, s/he may run into two problems: the first being the need to start treatment prior to knowing what the client finds satisfying, and the second being that the client may be adapting too well to being in an institution (developing an institution-alized mentality) and the score achieved may reflect that.

In Conjunction with Psychotropic Medications: Psychotropic medications may change a client's feelings about the amount of satisfaction received from leisure. (Whether the change is a positive or negative one may require further assessment and discussion by the treatment team and the client.) On units that frequently use psychotropic medications as one method of treatment, the recreational therapist may want to routinely administer the *LSM* prior to the medication being introduced or changed, and again after the medication has stabilized in the client's system.

Administering the *Leisure Satisfaction Measure*

Verbal Instructions: It is important that the recreational therapist gives each client the same instructions for completing the assessment. The instructions should be the same whether the client is self-administering the assessment or the therapist is reading the assessment to the client.

The therapist should first explain to the client the purpose of the assessment and how the results could benefit the client. This explanation should not take more than four or five brief sentences.

The therapist should also inform the client that there are no "right" or "wrong" answers.

Next, the therapist should read the directions right from the score sheet and then ask the client if s/he understands the instructions. If the therapist is going to be reading the statements for the client, the therapist should place an example of the 1-5 bar graph with the corresponding words (e.g.; "Almost Never True") in front of the client to help cue him/her.

Environment: The therapist should obtain better results if the assessment is administered in a stimu-lus-reduced environment. A comfortable room with adequate light, limited visual and auditory distrac-tions should be the therapist's goal.

Client Self-Administration vs. Therapist Read: Up to 20% of the population of the United States are nonfunctional readers (*World Book Encyclopedia*, 1989). In addition, numerous clients have visual disabilities making it difficult for them to self-administer this assessment. The therapist should always err on the conservative side. If s/he feels that the client's reading level or visual acuity may affect the client's score, the statements should be read out loud.

Instructions for Filling Out the First Page of the *LSM* Form

The purpose of the first page of the *LSM* is to present the 24 statements to the client. The therapist will need to ensure:

1. that the client understands the statements, and
2. that the basic client information is placed across the bottom of the form.

Directions: The *LSM* contains 24 statements. To the left of each statement is a line to indicate how true that statement is. A "1" means that the statement is almost never true, a "2" means that the statement is seldom true, a "3" means that the statement is sometimes true, a "4" means that the statement is often true, and a "5" means that the statement is almost always true. Write down the number that best fits your (the client's) situation.

Instruct the client to select one whole number between 1 and 5 (e.g., "2" not "2.5") for each statement.

The therapist may want to measure the length of time it takes for the client to answer the statements. By collecting this data and comparing it with the times of other clients with similar disabilities and illnesses, the therapist will have a more realistic understanding of the actual time required to administer (and score) the *LSM* within the facility. If this is being done, the therapist needs to let the client know that s/he is being timed. The client should be less threatened if s/he understands that the information is taken to establish the time that needs to be allocated for clients in the future and does not have a bearing on his/her score.

Scoring Instructions

The therapist will need to determine 6 separate subscores. The subscales with the highest total score will indicate the areas that the client finds the most satisfying about his/her leisure. The lowest scores will indicate the areas that the client is the least satisfied with.

Subscore A, Psychological: To determine the client's score in this area use the following equation:
Add the numerical value of the answers given to the first four statements to achieve a total and divide by four.
Scores from: $(1+2+3+4) / 4$ = Satisfaction with the psychological aspect of his/her leisure lifestyle.

Subscore B, Educational: To determine the client's score in this area use the following equation:
Add the numerical value of statements 5-8 to achieve a total and divide by 4.
Scores from: $(5+6+7+8) / 4$ = Satisfaction with the educational aspect of his/her leisure lifestyle.

Subscore C, Social: To determine the client's score in this area use the following equation:
Add the numerical value of the answers given to statements 9-12 to achieve a total and divide by 4.
Scores from: $(9+10+11+12) / 4$ = Satisfaction with the social aspect of his/her leisure lifestyle.

Subscore D, Relaxation: To determine the client's score in this area use the following equation:
Add the numerical value of statements 13-16 to achieve a total and divide by 4.
Scores from: $(13+14+15+16) / 4$ = Satisfaction with the relaxation aspect of his/her leisure lifestyle.

Subscore E, Physiological: To determine the client's score in this area use the following equation:
Add the numerical value of the answers given to statements 17-20 to achieve a total and divide by 4.
Scores from: $(17+18+19+20) / 4$ = Satisfaction with the physiological aspect of his/her leisure lifestyle.

Subscore F, Aesthetic: To determine the client's score in this area use the following equation:
Add the numerical value of the answers given to statements 21-24 to achieve a total and divide by 4.
Scores from: $(21+22+23+24) / 4$ = Satisfaction with the aesthetic aspect of his/her leisure lifestyle.

Scores greater than 4 show a high amount of satisfaction from a particular area. Scores less than 2 show low satisfaction. It is important for the recreational therapist to know the degree to which a client is satisfied with the various components of his/her leisure lifestyle. In addition, the therapist may use the overall score from all 24 statements (total the statements and divide by 24) to determine a general degree of satisfaction.

Interventions

This assessment provides information about the types of leisure activities that the individual finds satisfying. The therapist should be sure that the individual has the opportunity to participate in activities that are satisfying and may need to modify the leisure activities that are available to meet the demonstrated needs of the clients.

Clients will score high in some areas and low in others. The therapist needs to make the decision whether education or opportunities should be provided to increase the satisfaction level in areas where the client has low scores. In making the decision, the therapist should determine if the low score is having a negative impact on the client's ability to make progress on his/her treatment objectives. Low scores in all areas point to a definite need for working with the client to increase his/her satisfaction with leisure.

LEISURE SATISFACTION MEASURE (LSM)

Purpose: The purpose of the Leisure Satisfaction Measure is to determine the degree to which you are currently content with your leisure.

Directions: Listed below are 24 statements. To the left of each statement is a line to indicate how true that statement is. A "1" means that the statement is almost never true, "2" means that it is seldom true, "3" means that it is sometimes true, "4" means that it is often true, and "5" means that it is almost always true. Write down the number that best fits your situation.

Definition: "Leisure Activities" are those things that you do that are not part of your work and are not part of your basic grooming needs.

1	2	3	4	5
ALMOST NEVER TRUE	SELDOM TRUE	SOMEWHAT TRUE	OFTEN TRUE	ALMOST ALWAYS TRUE

____ 1. My leisure activities are very interesting to me.

____ 2. My leisure activities give me self-confidence.

____ 3. My leisure activities give me a sense of accomplishment.

____ 4. I use many different skills and abilities in my leisure activities.

____ 5. My leisure activities increase my knowledge about things around me.

____ 6. My leisure activities provide opportunities to try new things.

____ 7. My leisure activities help me to learn about myself.

____ 8. My leisure activities help me to learn about other people.

____ 9. I have social interaction with others through leisure activities.

____ 10. My leisure activities have helped me to develop close relationships with others.

____ 11. The people I meet in my leisure activities are friendly.

____ 12. I associate with people in my free time who enjoy doing leisure activities a great deal.

____ 13. My leisure activities help me to relax.

____ 14. My leisure activities help relieve stress.

____ 15. My leisure activities contribute to my emotional well being.

____ 16. I engage in leisure activities simply because I like doing them.

____ 17. My leisure activities are physically challenging.

____ 18. I do leisure activities which develop my physical fitness.

____ 19. I do leisure activities which restore me physically.

____ 20. My leisure activities help me to stay healthy.

____ 21. The area or places where I engage in my leisure activities are fresh and clean.

____ 22. The areas or places where I engage in my leisure activities are interesting.

____ 23. The areas or places where I engage in my leisure activities are beautiful.

____ 24. The areas or places where I engage in my leisure activities are well designed.

Chapter 28

Playfulness and Humor: From Concepts to Measurements

Focus of Chapter

This chapter is designed to demonstrate the mutual overlap of humor and playfulness as a main ingredient of children's play and as a part of adults' leisure lifestyles. Therefore, concepts of both humor and playfulness will be presented, followed by their history. Realized functions of humor and playfulness will be presented in a frame of reference from the times of Stanley, McDougall, and Freud. Realized functions are numerous, such as control of depression and pain, coping with problems, arousal, mastery, health, academic achievement, and creativity. In some accounts humor and playfulness are instrumentally utilized to counter low moods with the intention to create positive emotions. A list of scales assessing playfulness and humor are reported.

Key Terms

- laughter
- pain relief
- spontaneous play

Key Names

- Lynn A. Barnett
- Sigmund Freud
- J. N. Lieberman
- William McDougall
- Henry M. Stanley

Objectives

- Define playfulness and humor.
- Identify basic characteristics and concepts of playfulness and humor.
- Explain the history of laughter and humor.
- Describe functions of playfulness and humor.
- Report on how humor and laughter can help offset low moods.
- Differentiate between humor and playfulness.
- Realize the overlap between playfulness and humor and the uniqueness of each.
- Describe how humor and laughter affect positive emotions.
- List measurements of playfulness and humor.

Playfulness and humor share common grounds. Essentially, the former lasts for a longer duration of time, whereas the latter intervenes and intercedes for a shorter period. However, humor's intermittent presence mediates and gives significance and meaning to playfulness. The element of surprise in humor, intermixing it with playfulness, seems to heighten stimuli and therapeutic effects. Moreover, to playfulness, humor is like the soul to the body or if playfulness were the body, humor would be the spirit. Therefore, due to the interplay of humor and playfulness, presenting one of them necessitates also discussing the other.

Concepts of Playfulness and Humor

Playfulness has been defined in a variety of ways — all of which are intertwined with play and humor. For Dodd (1996) it is viewed as a psychological construct involving the disposition of play; for Li (1978) it is the make-believe attitude. As for Guitard, Ferland, and Dutil (2005), playfulness is defined as an internal predisposition characterized by creativity, curiosity, pleasure, sense of humor, and spontaneity. For some others, playfulness is viewed as a state occurring when children modulate their arousal, stimulus seeking, and mastery for fun and enjoyment, with no abstract goals or utilitarian motives in mind (see Chapman, 1978; Fountain, 1995). Finally, for Csikszentmihalyi (1976), play must be redefined as the experiential component of playfulness, not the behavioral concept of playing.

On the other hand, humor is defined as the ability to perceive and express what is funny, joking, amusing, or ludicrous. Humor and playfulness have been interwoven with daily living encounters since the beginning of life. Humans engage spontaneously in these activities, playfully, for their observed rewards, impacts, or consequences.

Common sense alone has conditioned humans to detect a variety of physical and mental effects for humor, joking, and playfulness. Therefore, people repeated those playful behaviors not only for positive emotions, blood circulation, and stimulation, but also for a feeling of well-being, relief from anxiety, control of tension, and protection from harmful physiological changes. These activities of joking, playfulness, and humor can occur in all waking hours, whether the person is working or attending to family responsibilities or during free time. There are no situational boundaries or limits on this behavior in that it can take place in the most serious of situations, such as the times of crises or funerals.

History of the Study of Laughter and Humor

Laughter and humor have been conceptualized and investigated for a long period of time. Hall and Allin (1897) initiated the first empirical study with the title: "The psychology of tickling, laughter, and the comic." This was during the ninth year of the publication of the *American Journal of Psychology*. They reported that hearty laughing is a good thing for children, like occasional crying for babies. It is good for the voice, lungs, diaphragm, and digestion.

A year later, Stanley (1898) introduced concepts about the interwoven nature of laughter and playfulness. He suggested that the pleasurable nature of tickling has been explained by the fact that its reaction comes from playfulness. He also suggested that laughter can be considered a reduplicated and articulated shouting, and the best method for investigating it is through long-term physiological study, and not questionnaire.

McDougall (1923) designated laughter as a biological instinct to control depression and pain. Moreover, Freud (1946) viewed joking as a means to cope with problems. Also, Freud (1957) observed that people laugh to release excess nervous "energy." Empirically, Saunders et al. (1999) and Lieberman (1977) obtained evidence that seems to support Freud's observation. They found a positive relationship between children's levels of playfulness and their coping skills.

Playfulness and laughter seem to be mutually inclusive and interconnected, presenting themselves together. In a development, which has been neglected in the field of recreation and leisure as well as in other areas, Maslow (1969) developed a theory of meta-motivation. He suggested that the reverse of playfulness is humorlessness, with the latter as a part of a table of general meta-pathologies.

Moreover, in an attempt to reveal the therapeutic nature and value of playfulness and humor, Handler (1999) discussed the importance of playfulness as an indicator of psychological health. Also, Parsons (1999) demonstrated the importance of spontaneous play and humor in psychoanalytic therapy. Finally, concerning an underlying structure of playfulness, Smith (1996) identified five components: Physical, Cognitive, Social Spontaneity, Manifest Joy, and Sense of Humor.

Functions Served by Playfulness and Humor

Numerous functions can be served by playfulness and humor. For example, Lichtenberg and Meares (1996) discussed the importance of toddlers' playfulness as experiences essential to the development of a vital sense of self, contributing to the capacity for flexibility and elasticity. Although many scholars have reasons to limit play to childhood and recreation to adults (see Kaplan, 1975; Sapora and Mitchell, 1961; de Grazia, 1962; Kelly, 1996), Solnit (1998) viewed playfulness as common to all life stages. He emphasized the central importance of playfulness throughout life (also, see Guitard, Ferland, and Dutil, 2005). Besides, playfulness was reported as an effective training intervention, impacting on long-term academic achievement (Boyer, 1998).

One of the numerous valuable functions of playfulness is its relationship to creativity. Kocher (1976) reported a relationship between playfulness and creativity measured by creative thinking. Other dispositions, such as self-concept (Hallman, 1976) and mental health (Szurek, 1959) were found to associate with both playfulness and creativity. Moreover, Lieberman (1966) views playfulness as a component in exploratory behavior and variation seeking. Therefore, it seems that playfulness and humor are instrumental in life, enabling individuals to form self-concepts and acquire flexibility. They impact on future academic achievement, mental health, creativity, and exploratory behavior, among other functions.

Humor and Laughter to Counter Low Moods

Humor and laughter seem to be mysterious in their impacts, having secretive qualities, improving individuals' moods. Humor's mystical qualities reside in their surprise and unexpected alteration in an individual's perspective, causing sudden physical, mental, psychological, and emotional reactions. Mystical qualities are part of what humor and laughter present: paradoxes, riddles, contradictions, novelties, and syntheses.

What make humorous reactions are the realities presented, the logic in what is said or done, and the degree of the exact fit to the situation. Filipowicz (2002) breaks humor down into three components that can be pertinent to humor's mystical and mysterious qualities: carrying information, generating affect, and drawing attention. Moreover, Deutsch (2002) observed that humor and laughter were documented to have reinforcing and curative properties: treatments for anxiety, depression, and pain management disorders. Szabo (2003) confirmed a hypothesis that 20 minutes of humor exert greater anxiety-lowering effect than aerobic exercise.

For humor and laughter to achieve their highest impacts on mood, they must be spontaneous, informal, and voluntary. This brings them closer to family life and free time activities. Crandall (2003) tested the potential benefit of approaching stressful situations through the use of humor. It was found that the request to be humorous increased stressfulness instead of demonstrating the expected buffering effect. Furthermore, it was found that participants

who were unaccustomed to using humor, when instructed to do so, did not experience any psychological or physiological benefits. However, another study examined the effect of a brief period of forced laughter on the mood of adults (Foley, Matheis, and Schaefer, 2002). Despite the fact that individuals rated their mood as positive prior to the intervention, after forced laughter they rated positive affect significantly higher. The moderating factor that might have created the difference between forced and spontaneous laughter is the setting, the initiator, and the explained purpose. It is important to note that if this is the impact of forced laughter, what would be the effect of voluntary, spontaneous, and informal laughter on a person's mood?

So it seems that humor can be destroyed or limited when imposed. This is similar to the "state of leisure," which we cannot force someone to feel or benefit from. Self-determination and freedom of choice are core factors that can facilitate for a state of leisure, humor, laughter, and playfulness healing powers. This notion can have serious and beneficial implications and applications for leisure practitioners. The real goal is maximizing spontaneous and voluntary humor and laughter in an informal atmosphere conducive to the improvement of mood.

Impact of Humor and Laughter on Positive Emotions

Humor and laughter have the potential to enhance mood, control illness, and remove depressive feelings. Erdman (1993) presented the notion that while laughter therapy is not a curative treatment, much suffering has been alleviated through its use. Erdman adds that positive emotions provided by hospital humor can improve prescribed medical treatment. Moreover, in a comparison among howling, smiling, and laughter, Neuhoff and Schaefer (2002) found that while howling did not substantially improve mood, both smiling and laughing did, with laughing boosting positive affect more than smiling.

It seems that laughter is a conditioned behavior. A positive emotional response results from another individual's laugh acoustics (Smoski and Bachorowski, 2003). Saper (1988) examined the notion that "laughter is the best medicine" in treating physical and mental disorders. He points out that humor generates positive emotions of joy and laughter that influence physiological components of health and illness.

Laughter and humor are characterized by joy, comfort, ease, informal reactions, use of many muscles, grinning, and relaxing. However, what brings laughter and humor can be the opposite of these characteristics such as bereavement, discomfort, tension, formality, use of limited muscles, and being uptight. In essence, humor and laughter can be intensified; therefore, memorable. Interestingly, Bergen (2002) observed that although many of the humor incidents were very short and many of the manifestations of humor were mild, it was notable that evidences of humor were clearly present in intensity and pleasure (positive emotions).

Laughter, joy, and humor produce positive effects: physiologically (Saper, 1988), neurologically, chemically (Panksepp, 2000), and emotionally (Van der Bolt and Tellegen, 1992). Panksepp elaborates on the brain sources of laughter that contribute to social bonds. These sources are based on a person's neurochemistry that promotes laughter and joy.

Moreover, laughter can result in improved levels of heart rate (Ruch, 1998). In the 1980s, a conference titled "The Role of Love and Laughter in the Healing Process" centered on uses of positive emotions to promote healing (see Warga, 1984). The social domains and encounters in leisure are the best suited for this role, allowing for laughter, humor, and playfulness.

There is no denial that humor and laughter manifest themselves in all other settings, ranging from distressing events, work, times of crises, even during bereavement. To put humor and laughter into a larger perspective, a set of positive emotions should be considered together as pointed out by Cousins (1989) to create desirable outcomes: hope, love, will to live, purpose, and confidence. Careful considerations suggest that there are benefits — as reported above — to reach beyond laughter and attain the above desirable outcomes. Positive emotions are fundamental concepts in positive psychology for their numerous impacts on mood, empowerment, success, and therapy.

Examples of measurements assessing humor and playfulness are as follows:

1. Lieberman's Playfulness Instrument (LPI); Lieberman, 1965, 1966.
2. Coping Humor Scale (CHS); Martin and Leftcourt, 1983.
3. Situational Humor Response Questionnaire (SHRQ); Martin and Leftcourt, 1984.
4. Children's Playfulness Scale (CPS); Barnett, 1991.
5. Adult Playfulness Scale (APS); Glynn and Webster, 1992, 1993.
6. Sense of Humor Scale (SHS); Thorson and Powell, 1993.
7. State-Trait Cheerfulness Inventory (STCI); Ruch, Koehler, and Ban Thriel, 1996.
8. Playfulness Scale (PS); Schaefer and Greenberg, 1997.
9. Test of Playfulness (ToP); Okimoto et al., 2000.
10. Humor Styles Questionnaire (HSQ); Martin, Puhlik-Doris, Larsen, Gray, and Weir, 2003.

Summary and Conclusions

Humor and playfulness, as partners, exist instrumentally to serve functions beyond what they seem to be. Humor and playfulness are not fully comprehended. What we understand so far is that both activities serve the creation of positive feelings, stimulation, and blood circulation, as well as relief from tension and anxiety, and as a guard against harmful physiological changes.

Early psychologists revealed some basic functions of humor and playfulness. Later, it was demonstrated how humor and playfulness can help confront low moods such as depression. Control of illness and health improvements were among the positive emotions realized as outcomes of humor and playfulness. Existing scales assess a variety of dimensions of humor and playfulness.

Questions and Exercises

1. What are the concepts of playfulness and humor?
2. What are the functions served by playfulness and humor?
3. How would humor and laughter counter low mood?
4. How would humor and laughter impact on positive emotions?
5. Comment on the measurements available on assessment of playfulness and humor.

Appendices

Appendix 1

Standards and Ethics Related to Measurement

Ethical Guidelines for Statistical Practice[2]

The following article is the final document of ASA Ethical Guidelines after three years of development and discussion.

Executive Summary

This document contains two parts: I. Preamble and II. Ethical Guidelines. The Preamble addresses **A. Purpose of the Guidelines, B. Statistics and Society**, and **C. Shared Values**. The purpose of the document is to encourage ethical and effective statistical work in morally conducive working environments. It is also intended to assist students in learning to perform statistical work responsibly. Statistics plays a vital role in many aspects of science, the economy, governance, and even entertainment. It is important that all statistical practitioners recognize their potential impact on the broader society and the attendant ethical obligations to perform their work responsibly. Furthermore, practitioners are encouraged to exercise "good professional citizenship" in order to improve the public climate for, understanding of, and respect for the use of statistics throughout its range of applications.

---

[2] Reprinted with permission from the American Statistical Association. Copyright 1999 by the American Statistical Association. All rights reserved. Prepared by the Committee on Professional Ethics Approved by the Board of Directors, August 7, 1999.

The **Ethical Guidelines** address eight general topic areas and specify important ethical considerations under each topic.

A. Professionalism points out the need for competence, judgment, diligence, self-respect, and worthiness of the respect of other people.

B. Responsibilities to Funders, Clients, and Employers discusses the practitioner's responsibility for assuring that statistical work is suitable to the needs and resources of those who are paying for it, that funders understand the capabilities and limitations of statistics in addressing their problem, and that the funder's confidential information is protected.

C. Responsibilities in Publications and Testimony addresses the need to report sufficient information to give readers, including other practitioners, a clear understanding of the intent of the work, how and by whom it was performed, and any limitations on its validity.

D. Responsibilities to Research Subjects describes requirements for protecting the interests of human and animal subjects of research — not only during data collection but also in the analysis, interpretation, and publication of the resulting findings.

E. Responsibilities to Research Team Colleagues addresses the mutual responsibilities of professionals participating in multidisciplinary research teams.

F. Responsibilities to Other Statisticians or Statistical Practitioners notes the interdependence of professionals doing similar work, whether in the same or different organizations. Basically, they must contribute to the strength of their professions overall by sharing nonproprietary data and methods, participating in peer review, and respecting differing professional opinions.

G. Responsibilities Regarding Allegations of Misconduct addresses the sometimes painful process of investigating potential ethical violations and treating those involved with both justice and respect.

H. Responsibilities of Employers, Including Organizations, Individuals, Attorneys, or Other Clients Employing Statistical Practitioners encourages employers and clients to recognize the highly interdependent nature of statistical ethics and statistical validity. Employers and clients must not pressure practitioners to produce a particular "result," regardless of its statistical validity. They must avoid the potential social harm that can result from the dissemination of false or misleading statistical work.

I. PREAMBLE

A. Purpose of the Guidelines

The American Statistical Association's Ethical Guidelines for Statistical Practice are intended to help statistics practitioners make and communicate ethical decisions. Clients, employers, researchers, policy-makers, journalists, and the public should be urged to expect statistical practice to be conducted in accordance with these guidelines and to object when it is not. While learning how to apply statistical theory to problems, students should be encouraged to use these guidelines, regardless of whether their target professional specialty will be "statistician." Employers, attorneys, and other clients of statistics practitioners have a responsibility to provide a moral environment that fosters the use of these ethical guidelines.

Application of these or any other ethical guidelines generally requires good judgment and common sense. The guidelines may be partially conflicting in specific cases. The application of these guidelines in any given case can depend on issues of law and shared values; work-group politics; the status and power of the individuals involved; and the extent to which the ethical lapses pose a threat to the public, to one's profession, or to one's organization. The individuals and institutions responsible for making such ethical decisions can receive valuable assistance by discussion and consultation with others, particularly persons with divergent interests with respect to the ethical issues under consideration.

B. Statistics and Society

The professional performance of statistical analyses is essential to many aspects of society. The use of statistics in medical diagnoses and biomedical research may affect whether individuals live or die, whether their health is protected or jeopardized, and whether medical science advances or gets side-tracked. Life, death, and health, as well as efficiency, may be at stake in statistical analyses of occupational, environmental, or transportation safety. Early detection and control of new or recurrent infectious diseases depend on sound epidemiological statistics. Mental and social health may be at stake in psychological and sociological applications of statistical analysis.

Effective functioning of the economy depends on the availability of reliable, timely, and properly interpreted economic data. The profitability of individual firms depends in part on their quality control and market research, both of which should rely on statistical methods. Agricultural productivity benefits greatly from statistically sound applications to research and output reporting. Governmental policy decisions regarding public health, criminal justice, social equity, education, the environment, the citing of critical facilities, and other matters depend in part on sound statistics.

Scientific and engineering research in all disciplines requires the careful design and analysis of experiments and observations. To the extent that uncertainty and measurement error are involved — as they are in most research — research design, data quality management, analysis, and interpretation are all crucially dependent on statistical concepts and methods. Even in theory, much of science and engineering involves natural variability. Variability, whether great or small, must be carefully examined for both random error and possible researcher bias or wishful thinking.

Statistical tools and methods, as with many other technologies, can be employed either for social good or evil. The professionalism encouraged by these guidelines is predicated on their use in socially responsible pursuits by morally responsible societies, governments, and employers. Where the end purpose of a statistical application is itself morally reprehensible, statistical professionalism ceases to have ethical worth.

C. Shared Values

Because society depends on sound statistical practice, all practitioners of statistics, whatever their training and occupation, have social obligations to perform their work in a professional, competent, and ethical manner. This document is directed to those whose primary occupation is statistics. Still, the principles expressed here should also guide the statistical work of professionals in all other disciplines that use statistical methods. All statistical practitioners are obliged to conduct their professional activities with responsible attention to the following:

1. The social value of their work and the consequences of how well or poorly it is performed. This includes respect for the life, liberty, dignity, and property of other people.
2. The avoidance of any tendency to slant statistical work toward predetermined outcomes. (It is acceptable to advocate a position; it is not acceptable to misapply statistical methods in doing so.)
3. Statistics as a science. (As in any science, understanding evolves. Statisticians have a body of established knowledge, but also many unresolved issues that deserve frank discussion.)
4. The maintenance and upgrading of competence in their work.
5. Adherence to all applicable laws and regulations, as well as applicable international covenants, while also seeking to change any of those that are ethically inappropriate.
6. Preservation of data archives in a manner consistent with responsible protection of the safety and confidentiality of any human being or organization involved.

In addition to ethical obligations, good professional citizenship encourages the following:

7. Collegiality and civility with fellow professionals.
8. Support for improved public understanding of and respect for statistics.
9. Support for sound statistical practice, especially when it is unfairly criticized.
10. Exposure of dishonest or incompetent uses of statistics.
11. Service to one's profession as a statistical editor, reviewer, or association official and service as an active participant in (formal or informal) ethical review panels.

II. ETHICAL GUIDELINES

A. Professionalism

1. Strive for relevance in statistical analyses. Typically, each study should be based on a competent understanding of the subject-matter issues, statistical protocols that are clearly defined for the stage (exploratory, intermediate, or final) of analysis before looking at those data that will be decisive for that stage, and technical criteria to justify both the practical relevance of the study and the amount of data to be used.
2. Guard against the possibility that a predisposition by investigators or data providers might predetermine the analytic result. Employ data selection or sampling methods and analytic approaches that are designed to ensure valid analyses in either frequentist or Bayesian approaches.
3. Remain current in dynamically evolving statistical methodology; yesterday's preferred methods may be barely acceptable today and totally obsolete tomorrow.
4. Ensure that adequate statistical and subject-matter expertise is both applied to any planned study. If this criterion is not met initially, it is important to add the missing expertise before completing the study design.
5. Use only statistical methodologies suitable to the data and to obtaining valid results. For example, address the multiple potentially confounding factors in observational studies and use due caution in drawing causal inferences.
6. Do not join a research project unless you can expect to achieve valid results and you are confident that your name will not be associated with the project or resulting publications without your explicit consent.
7. The fact that a procedure is automated does not ensure its correctness or appropriateness; it is also necessary to understand the theory, data, and methods used in each statistical study. This goal is served best when a competent statistical practitioner is included early in the research design, preferably in the planning stage.
8. Recognize that any frequentist statistical test has a random chance of indicating significance when it is not really present. Running multiple tests on the same data set at the same stage of an analysis increases the chance of obtaining at least one invalid result. Selecting the one "significant" result from a multiplicity of parallel tests poses a grave risk of an incorrect conclusion. Failure to disclose the full extent of tests and their results in such a case would be highly misleading.
9. Respect and acknowledge the contributions and intellectual property of others.
10. Disclose conflicts of interest, financial and otherwise, and resolve them. This may sometimes require divestiture of the conflicting personal interest or withdrawal from the professional activity. Examples where conflict of interest may be problematic include grant reviews, other peer reviews, and tensions between scholarship and personal or family financial interests.
11. Provide only such expert testimony as you would be willing to have peer reviewed.

B. Responsibilities to Funders, Clients, and Employers

1. Where appropriate, present a client or employer with choices among valid alternative statistical approaches that may vary in scope, cost, or precision.
2. Clearly state your statistical qualifications and experience relevant to your work.
3. Clarify the respective roles of different participants in studies to be undertaken.
4. Explain any expected adverse consequences of failure to follow through on an agreed-upon sampling or analytic plan.
5. Apply statistical sampling and analysis procedures scientifically, without predetermining the outcome.
6. Make new statistical knowledge widely available to provide benefits to society at large and beyond your own scope of applications. Statistical methods may be broadly applicable to many classes of problem or application. (Statistical innovators may well be entitled to monetary or other rewards for their writings, software, or research results.)
7. Guard privileged information of the employer, client, or funder.
8. Fulfill all commitments.
9. Accept full responsibility for your professional performance.

C. Responsibilities in Publications and Testimony

1. Maintain personal responsibility for all work bearing your name; avoid undertaking work or coauthoring publications for which you would not want to acknowledge responsibility. Conversely, accept (or insist upon) appropriate authorship or acknowledgment for professional statistical contributions to research and the resulting publications or testimony.
2. Report statistical and substantive assumptions made in the study.
3. In publications or testimony, identify who is responsible for the statistical work if it would not otherwise be apparent.
4. Make clear the basis for authorship order, if determined on grounds other than intellectual contribution. Preferably, authorship order in statistical publications should be by degree of intellectual contribution to the study and material to be published, to the extent that such ordering can feasibly be determined. When some other rule of authorship order is used in a statistical publication, the rule should be disclosed in a footnote or endnote. (Where authorship order by contribution is assumed by those making decisions about hiring, promotion, or tenure, for example, failure to disclose an alternative rule may improperly damage or advance careers.)
5. Account for all data considered in a study and explain the sample(s) actually used.
6. Report the sources and assessed adequacy of the data.
7. Report the data cleaning and screening procedures used, including any imputation.
8. Clearly and fully report the steps taken to guard validity. Address the suitability of the analytic methods and their inherent assumptions relative to the circumstances of the specific study. Identify the computer routines used to implement the analytic methods.
9. Where appropriate, address potential confounding variables not included in the study.
10. In publications or testimony, identify the ultimate financial sponsor of the study, the stated purpose, and the intended use of the study results.
11. When reporting analyses of volunteer data or other data not representative of a defined population, include appropriate disclaimers.
12. Report the limits of statistical inference of the study and possible sources of error. For example, disclose any significant failure to follow through fully on an agreed sampling or analytic plan and explain any resulting adverse consequences.
13. Share data used in published studies to aid peer review and replication, but exercise due caution to protect proprietary and confidential data, including all data that might inappropriately reveal respondent identities.
14. As appropriate, promptly and publicly correct any errors discovered after publication.
15. Write with consideration of the intended audience. (For the general public, convey the scope, relevance, and conclusions of a study without technical distractions. For the professional literature, strive to answer the questions likely to occur to your peers.)

D. Responsibilities to Research Subjects (including census or survey respondents and persons and organizations supplying data from administrative records, as well as subjects of physically or psychologically invasive research)

1. Know about and adhere to appropriate rules for the protection of human subjects, including particularly vulnerable or other special populations

that may be subject to special risks or may not be fully able to protect their own interests. Ensure adequate planning to support the practical value of the research, validity of expected results, ability to provide the protection promised, and consideration of all other ethical issues involved.

2. Avoid the use of excessive or inadequate numbers of research subjects by making informed recommendations for study size. These recommendations may be based on prospective power analysis, the planned precision of the study endpoint(s), or other methods to ensure appropriate scope to either frequentist or Bayesian approaches. Study scope also should take into consideration the feasibility of obtaining research subjects and the value of the data elements to be collected.

3. Avoid excessive risk to research subjects and excessive imposition on their time and privacy.

4. Protect the privacy and confidentiality of research subjects and data concerning them, whether obtained directly from the subjects, other persons, or administrative records. Anticipate secondary and indirect uses of the data when obtaining approvals from research subjects; obtain approvals appropriate for peer review and independent replication of analyses.

5. Be aware of legal limitations on privacy and confidentiality assurances. Do not, for example, imply protection of privacy and confidentiality from legal processes of discovery unless explicitly authorized to do so.

6. Before participating in a study involving human beings or organizations, analyzing data from such a study, or accepting resulting manuscripts for review, consider whether appropriate research subject approvals were obtained. (This safeguard will lower your risk of learning only after the fact that you have collaborated on an unethical study.) Consider also what assurances of privacy and confidentiality were given and abide by those assurances.

7. Avoid or minimize the use of deception. Where it is necessary and provides significant knowledge — as in some psychological, sociological, and other research — ensure prior independent ethical review of the protocol and continued monitoring of the research.

8. Where full disclosure of study parameters to subjects or other investigators is not advisable, as in some randomized clinical trials, generally inform them of the nature of the information withheld and the reason for withholding it. As with deception, ensure independent ethical review of the protocol and continued monitoring of the research.

9. Know about and adhere to appropriate animal welfare guidelines in research involving animals. Ensure that a competent understanding of the subject matter is combined with credible statistical validity.

E. Responsibilities to Research Team Colleagues

1. Inform colleagues from other disciplines about relevant aspects of statistical ethics.

2. Promote effective and efficient use of statistics by the research team.

3. Respect the ethical obligations of members of other disciplines, as well as your own.

4. Ensure professional reporting of the statistical design and analysis.

5. Avoid compromising statistical validity for expediency, but use reasonable approximations as appropriate.

F. Responsibilities to Other Statisticians or Statistics Practitioners

1. Promote sharing of (nonproprietary) data and methods. As appropriate, make suitably documented data available for replicate analyses, metadata studies, and other suitable research by qualified investigators.

2. Be willing to help strengthen the work of others through appropriate peer review. When doing so, complete the review promptly and well.

3. Assess methods, not individuals.

4. Respect differences of opinion.

5. Instill in students an appreciation for the practical value of the concepts and methods they are learning.

6. Use professional qualifications and the contributions of the individual as an important basis for decisions regarding statistical practitioners' hiring, firing, promotion, work assignments, publications and presentations, candidacy for offices and awards, funding or approval of research, and other professional matters. Avoid as best you can harassment of or discrimination against statistical practitioners (or anyone else) on professionally irrelevant bases such as race, color, ethnicity, sex, sexual orientation, national origin, age, religion, nationality, or disability.

G. Responsibilities Regarding Allegations of Misconduct

1. Avoid condoning or appearing to condone careless, incompetent, or unethical practices in

statistical studies conducted in your working environment or elsewhere.

2. Deplore all types of professional misconduct, not just plagiarism and data fabrication or falsification. Misconduct more broadly includes all professional dishonesty, by commission or omission, and, within the realm of professional activities and expression, all harmful disrespect for people, unauthorized use of their intellectual and physical property, and unjustified detraction from their reputations.

3. Recognize that differences of opinion and honest error do not constitute misconduct; they warrant discussion, but not accusation. Questionable scientific practices may or may not constitute misconduct, depending on their nature and the definition of misconduct used.

4. If involved in a misconduct investigation, know and follow prescribed procedures. Maintain confidentiality during an investigation, but disclose the results honestly after the investigation has been completed.

5. Following a misconduct investigation, support the appropriate efforts of the accused, the witnesses, and those reporting the possible scientific error or misconduct to resume their careers in as normal a manner as possible.

6. Do not condone retaliation against or damage to the employability of those who responsibly call attention to possible scientific error or misconduct.

H. Responsibilities of Employers, Including Organizations, Individuals, Attorneys, or Other Clients Employing Statistical Practitioners

1. Recognize that the results of valid statistical studies cannot be guaranteed to conform to the expectations or desires of those commissioning the study or the statistical practitioner(s). Any measures taken to ensure a particular outcome will lessen the validity of the analysis.

2. Valid findings result from competent work in a moral environment. Pressure on a statistical practitioner to deviate from these guidelines is likely to damage both the validity of study results and the professional credibility of the practitioner.

3. Make new statistical knowledge widely available in order to benefit society at large. (Those who have funded the development of statistical innovations are entitled to monetary and other rewards for their resulting products, software, or research results.)

4. Support sound statistical analysis and expose incompetent or corrupt statistical practice. In cases of conflict, statistical practitioners and those employing them are encouraged to resolve issues of ethical practice privately. If private resolution is not possible, recognize that statistical practitioners have an ethical obligation to expose incompetent or corrupt practice before it can cause harm to research subjects or society at large.

5. Recognize that within organizations and within professions using statistical methods generally, statistics practitioners with greater prestige, power, or status have a responsibility to protect the professional freedom and responsibility of more subordinate statistical practitioners who comply with these guidelines.

6. Do not include statistical practitioners in authorship or acknowledge their contributions to projects or publications without their explicit permission.

Key References:

1. U.S. federal regulations regarding human subjects protection are contained in *Title 45* of the Code of Federal Regulations, Chapter 46 (45 CFR 46).

4. *The Belmont Report: Ethical Principles and Guidelines for the Protection of Human Subjects of Research* is available through the Office of Human Research Protections.

5. Title 13, U.S. Code, Chapter 5 — Censuses, Subchapter II — Population, housing, and unemployment, Sec. 141 restricts uses of U.S. population census information. Similar restrictions may apply in other countries.

6. The International Statistical Institute's 1985 *Declaration on Professional Ethics*

7. The United Nations Statistical Commission's 1994 *Fundamental Principles of Official Statistics*

Members of the American Statistical Association Committee on Professional Ethics (1998-99): John Bailar, Paula Diehr, Susan Ellenberg, John Gardenier (chair), Lilliam Kingsbury, David Levy, Lisa McShane, Richard Potthoff, Jerome Sacks, Juliet Shaffer, and Chamont Wang.

Other contributing advisors in the preparation of these guidelines: Martin David, Virginia deWolf, Mark Frankel (American Association for the Advancement of Science), Joseph Kadane, Mary Grace Kovar, Michael O'Fallon, Fritz Scheuren, and William Seltzer.

Helpful reviews of these guidelines were provided by the Council of Sections, Beth Dawson, chair, and by the Council of Chapters, Brenda Cox, chair.

Thanks to many persons who commented on successive drafts or participated in discussions of the guidelines at the 1998 Joint Statistical Meetings in Dallas, Texas. We also thank the various ASA boards and presidents who have supported this effort, especially Lynne Billard, Jon Kettenring, David Moore, and Jonas Ellenberg, as well as ASA Executive Director Ray Waller.

In Defense of a Recreation and Leisure Academic Program

Due to the economic crises facing the US from 2008 and after, education, like many other services, faced cuts and reductions. As a result, Recreation and Leisure Academic programs were included in those cuts. The Florida State University (FSU) made a decision to cancel the Recreation Management Program as of 2011. The new president of FSU, after he was hired in the year 2010, invited the faculty and staff to write to him about their "Big Ideas" that can advance and contribute to the improvement of the university in general.

The conceptual knowledge reported in the last nine chapters of this book, 20 to 28, were based on three structures: the social psychological concepts of leisure and recreation, philosophical views of leisure, and assessment of different functions and operations in recreation, which were utilized as bases for the response to that memo, supporting an action to reinstate the Recreation Management Program at FSU. Furthermore, the content below can be used to identity the goals and intentions of the recreation movement and its role in society. The memo from the author of this book to the president of FSU in response to his request for "Big Ideas" in 2010 was as follows:

It is expected that "Once it is gone, it will be GONE forever." What a loss? What a shame?

Memo to Dr. Eric J. Barron, the President of the Florida State University:

To respond to your initiative, identifying **"Big Ideas"** that can shape the future (as they shaped the past); ideas identified here are not necessarily new, but sometimes they are critical issues that might have been ignored or fallen through the cracks of the system and its budget encounters. These ideas will impact the future.

The "Big Idea" that I am presenting here is a reaction to the *"phasing out"* of a vital academic unit, which was founded in the 1950s, at the Florida State University (FSU). Moreover, that unit is nationally accredited and recognized since the 1980s and it meets many of the state's needs; as mentioned in your initiative, provisions of this unit "**Strengthen**

our life-long connections." This unit is the **Recreation Management Program** of the College of Education.

To start with some fundamental issues, some people may ask: **What are we as a state? What do people identify Florida with? What are some of the basic economic and life activities of the state of Florida? What are the impacts of recreation, leisure, and travel and tourism services on the economy of the state of Florida and its citizens?** The layout of the state, its institutions, corporations, and economic activities are all centered on some long life connections such as travel, tourism, entertainment, warm beaches (663 miles, according to Florida Quick Facts), hotels and restaurants, and retirement communities (baby boomers), which are all in dire need for free time activities.

Mostly the services above belong to commercial, geriatric, and government recreation that attract state, national, and international visitors, who spent $57 billion dollars, which benefit not only state revenues but national employment and economics as well.

(Florida was the top travel destination in the world in 2004, serving 76.8 million visitors; see *Florida Quick Facts*, 2004.) In addition, recreation activities (outdoors, exercise and fitness, and physical recreation) in the state of Florida have been contributing to citizens' welfare: For example, health, wellness, and vitality were found to be outcomes of active lifestyles that impact positively on **longevity**; not only adding years to life, but improving life satisfaction, quality, and happiness. Accounting for a number of satisfactions (health, standard of living, family relations, financial, and leisure), **it was found that leisure satisfaction showed the greatest contribution to life satisfaction of older Floridians**, ages 55 and older (Ragheb and Griffith, 1982).

Furthermore, let us look into some down-to-earth facts and realities. American citizens work to get paid and the unemployed get federal compensation benefits for a period of time, as well as the steady income of retirees. All groups, the employed, the unemployed, and the retirees spend their incomes to meet basic necessities; **what is left from income is mainly spent on recreation and leisure goods and services**. Leisure spending has been proven to be one of the most stimulating aspects to the economy (Americans spent $705 billion in 2005 on recreation and luxury leisure, *Business Publications*). Also, in a Master's thesis conducted at FSU, Bagely (1976) found that leisure satisfaction of the unemployed was higher than the employed. **A society that denies citizens' leisure and recreation needs and services ignores a great domain of their existence.**

Besides, if the school from "K to 12" grades is failing to meet children's and teen's needs for activities such as physical education, extra-curricular skills, and creativity, who will provide for those populations' needs for talent development (in the arts, music, singing, outdoors, sports, and fitness) and free time pursuits? Nature hates a void and this includes human nature; voids are always filled; what will fill that void, if it is not filled with productive enhancements? **Recreational activities and services are "preventive" activities that enhance the quality of life**; otherwise, many costly services for children and teens will increase to fill the void (e.g., police, mental health, jails, hospitals, and rehabilitation). Preventive recreation offers services that confront maladaptive behaviors, such as illegal uses of drugs, alcoholism, crime, juvenile delinquency, at-risk youth, severe boredom and *ennui*, pornography, anxiety, stress, depression, obesity and overweight (57% of adults and 26% of high school students in Florida are overweight or obese as reported by the Florida Obesity Program). **Prevention is cheaper, more efficient, and more effective than treatment.**

As a result, **the state will suffer from the cost of increasing behavioral and social problems**, instead of achieving growth, success, and fulfillment. Services provided by the Recreation Management Program are not only for prevention and treatment, but also for the development and the flourishing of the participant's abilities, skills, and meeting citizens' free time needs for recreation and leisure for self-actualization. In turn that can fulfill the deepest persisting needs, improving the quality of living, life satisfaction, longevity, and happiness. (Floridians' life expectancy is 77.5 years according to NPR; ranked 21 in the US but the first in the southeast.) **Without qualified leaders and managers graduating from Recreation Management and the like, who will meet those critical and persisting needs and fill the *voids* that contribute negatively to domains of life?**

The needs listed above are a few examples of what recreation and leisure management can provide for the multiple domains of life. The diversity of what is offered as recreation is unimaginable sometimes. A simple illustration of the spectrum of settings can clarify the magnitude of services that this program prepares leaders to serve:

- Outdoor recreation — public beaches, forests, lakes, and rivers; mountains in other states
- Park systems — campgrounds, picnic areas, public golf courses, state and city parks
- Public recreation — city, county, state, and national
- Nonprofit recreation — for youth, religious, service clubs, YMCA, YMHA, boys and girls clubs, and scouts
- Private recreation — private clubs, golf courses, hobby groups
- Commercial recreation — travel, tourism, hospitality, resorts, entertainment, special events, and fitness
- Armed forces — MWR (Morale, Welfare, and Recreation)
- Corporate and industrial recreation — for blue- and white-collar personnel and their families
- Geriatric recreation — baby boomers, senior institutions, older citizens' programs and services
- Campus recreation — community colleges, universities, for all sorts of activities
- Therapeutic recreation — serving the disabled and special populations
- Correctional recreation — county, state, and federal correctional institutions

If humans are going to venture in space or on any other planets, recreation and leisure services will be there. **Recreation provisions exist where humans live and exist**; this illustrates the magnitude of this area of services.

Moreover, to stimulate the economy, as employment increases, recreation and leisure opportunities provided by such broad systems, as illustrated above, need to be sustained and offered to increase spending and employment to help rebound the sluggish economic state the country is facing.

The Recreation Management Program at the FSU is known to be the recreation and leisure services' pioneer in Florida and the US. Most of the senior practitioners and executives in our state graduated with a BS and/or a Master's Degree from the recreation and leisure program at FSU. Those **alums are very disappointed and displeased to see their vital and viable program to be phased out** and canceled as of the year 2011.

In my view, it is a truly a "Big Idea" to reevaluate the merit and the impact of the services of the Recreational Management Program, assessing the magnitude, the vitality, and the quality of its services and contributions to our state and the nation, testing its "life-long connections" and contributions that need to be strengthened, not phased out. **Objectively, you can choose a random sample of 10 to 15 executives in the leisure delivery systems of our state and listen to what they suggest.** Moreover, to get deeper in realizing some realities, invite three to five of them to Tallahassee; listen to them and their assessment of the situation and the losses that our university and the state are about to experience. FSU will never regret this reevaluation step; to the contrary, FSU will regret the decision made to phase out the Recreational Management academic program.

I am sure the above will demonstrate that the impact of this program is so great, so spread all over the state (and our alums are so successful and proud to be graduating from FSU) that the program should be re-instated. This is a compelling area of services that FSU should not miss. In all practicality, maintaining this program would go with your statement in

the memo sent to us about an action or **an idea that "has not had a chance to percolate through our leadership."** Knowing the impact of recreation and leisure services in the state of Florida makes me wonder, saying to myself that "**It is a grave mistake to let this program fall through the cracks of the system.**" Florida is not only the "**Fishing Capital in the World**" as the TV ad says, but it has been truly considered the "**Recreation Capital.**" as the playground for visitors and tourists, as well as its natives.

It is a major life difficulty to deprive citizens of the state of Florida and the US of quality leisure and recreation opportunities, it worsens the future and the hard conditions that Floridians are currently facing.

Thank you very much for the opportunity to reflect and focus on some critical realities that will shape and impact the future as they have shaped and impacted the past.

Mounir G. Ragheb, PhD
Professor Emeritus Sport and Recreation
Management
College of Education, Florida State University

*Note: I had the privilege and honor serving in the Recreation Management Program, from 1975 - 2005, under the leadership of **Professor Emeritus Francis C. Cannon**, who is one of the pioneers of the movement of recreation in Florida and the US.*

This semester, I am teaching the class **LEI 4881: Assessment, Research, and Evaluation in Leisure Systems**.

Thanks to **Mr. Tom McMorrow**, a doctoral student in Sport Management at the Florida State University and **Mr. Jim Austin**, one of our alums with a BS and Master's degrees in Recreation and an F15 pilot, US Air Force; for their editing of this memo. Also, I appreciate **current students enrolled in LEI 4881** for reviewing and commenting on the content of this memo.

References

Acosta, O. and Toro, P. A. (2000). Let's ask the homeless people themselves: A needs assessment based on probability sample of adults. *American Journal of Community Psychology, 28*, 343-366.

Additon, H. (1930). And what of leisure? *Journal of Social Hygiene, 16*, 321-334.

Aguilar, T. E. and Petrakis, E. (1989). Development and initial validation of perceived competence and satisfaction measures for racquet sports. *Journal of Leisure Research, 21*, 77-91.

Aiken, L. R. (1989). *Assessment of personality.* Boston, MA: Allyn and Bacon.

Aiken, L. R. (1991). *Psychological testing and assessment.* Boston: Allyn and Bacon.

Allen, L. R. (1982). Murray's personality needs and interests. *Journal of Leisure Research, 14*, 160-170.

Allport, F. H. (1994). *Social Psychology.* Boston, MA: Houghton Mifflin.

Allport, G. (1935). Attitudes. In G. Murchison (Ed.), *Handbook of social psychology* (pp. 798-844). Worcester, PA: Clark University Press.

American Educational Research Association, National Council on Measurement in Education. (1985). *Standards for educational and psychological testing.* Washington, DC: American Psychological Association.

American Psychological Association (1996). *Standards for psychological tests.* Washington DC: Author.

Anastasi, A. (1988). *Psychological testing.* New York, NY: Macmillan Publishing Company.

Anderson, J. (2010). Top-down vs. bottom-up management: What's the best way to set goals? *Management, Oct. 27.*

Anderson, D. F. and Cychosz, C. M. (1994). Development of an exercise identity scale. *Perceptual and Motor Skills, 78*, 747-751.

Anderson, D., Cychosz, C., and Franke, W. (1998). Association of exercise with measures of exercise commitment and psychological indicators of fitness in law enforcement cohort. *J. of Sport Behavior, 21*, 233-241.

Anderson, D., Cychosz, C., and Franke, W. (2000). Association of exercise identity with three measures of exercise commitment in a community sample. *Research Quarterly for Exercise and Sport. 71*, A-24.

Anderson, D., Cychosz, C., and Franke, W. (2001). Preliminary Exercise Identity Scale norms for three adult samples. *J. of Sport Behavior, 24*, 1-9.

Anshel, M. H. (1991). Attitudes toward exercise questionnaire. *Journal of Sport Behavior, 14*, 145-154.

Ap, J., Dimanche, F., and Havitz, M. (1994, October). Involvement and residents' perceptions of tourism impacts. Paper presented at the NRPA Symposium on Leisure Research, Minneapolis, MN.

Aron, A., Norman, C. C., Aron, E. N., McKenna, C., and Heyman, R. E. (2000). Couples' shared participation in novel and arousing activities and experienced relationship quality. *Journal of Personality & Social Psychology, 78*, 273-284.

Arthur, M. W. and Blitz, C. (2000). Bridging the gap between science and practice in drug abuse prevention through needs assessment and strategic community planning. *Journal of Community Psychology, 28*, 241-255.

Asch, S. E. (1987). *Social psychology.* New York, NY: Oxford University Press.

Ashford, M-W. (1997). Boredom as a neglected issue in violence prevention programs in schools. *Dissertation Abstracts International, Section A: Humanities & Social Sciences, 58*, 1507.

Askew, D. A., Clavarino, A. M., Glasziou, P. P. and Del Mar, C. B. (2002). General practice research: Attitude and involvement of Queensland general practitioners. *The Medical Journal of Australia, 177*, 74-77.

Backman, S. L. and Crompton, J. L. (1990). Motivation for joining and reasons for not continuing in leisure. *Leisure Sciences, 10*, 247-259.

Bagely, K. A. (1976). A study of the relationship between leisure satisfaction and the unemployed. Master's Thesis, the Florida State University, Tallahassee, FL.

Baldwin, C. and Caldwell, L. (2003). Development of the Free Time Motivation Scale for adolescents. *Journal of Leisure Research, 35*, 129-151.

Baldwin, K. S. and Tinsley, H. E. (1988). An investigation of the validity of Tinsley and Tinsley's (1986) theory of leisure experience. *Journal of Counseling Psychology, 35*, 263-267.

Bang, H., Ellinger, A. E., Hadjimarcou, J., and Traichal, P. A. (2000). Consumer concern, knowledge, belief, and attitude toward renewable energy: An application of the reasoned action theory. *Psychology of Marketing, 17*, 449-468.

Barbalet, J. M. (1999). Boredom and social meaning. *British Journal of Sociology, 50*, 631-646.

Bargdill, R. W. (1999). Being bored with one's life: An empirical phenomenological study. *Dissertation Abstracts International, Section B: The Sciences & Engineering, 59*, 6482.

Bargdill, R. W. (2000). A phenomenological investigation of being bored with life. *Psychological Reports, 86*, 493-494.

Bargdill, R. W. (2000). The study of life boredom. *Journal of Phenomenological Psychology, 31*, 188-219.

Barkham, M. (1996). *Quantitative research on psychotherapeutic interventions: Methodological issues and substantive findings across three research generations.* London, England: Sage Publishers, Inc.

Barnett, L. (1991). Playfulness: Definition, design, and measurement. *Play & Culture, 3*, 319-336.

Barnett, L. (2005). Measuring the ABC's of leisure experiences: Awareness, boredom, challenge, and distress. *Leisure Sciences, 27*, 131-155.

Barry, M. M., Doherty, A., Hope, A., Sixsmith, J., and Kelleher, C. C. (2000). A community needs assessment for rural mental health promotion. *Health Education Research, 15*, 293-304.

Bar-Tal, Y. (1992). The effect of the experience with attitude object on the relationships among cognitive and affective components of attitude and behavioral intentions. *Psychological Record, 42*, 131-139.

Baudrillard, J. (1970). *La societe de consommation (The consumer society)*. Paris: Gallimard, collection Ideas.

Baumgartner, H. and Steenkamp, J. E. (1994). An investigation into the construct validity of the Arousal Seeking Tendency Scale, Version II. *Educational & Psychological Measurement, 54*, 993-1001.

Beach. (1997). Leisure Deficit Scale.

Beard, J. G. and Ragheb, M. G. (1980). Measuring leisure satisfaction. *Journal of Leisure Research, 12*, 20-33.

Beard, J. G. and Ragheb, M. G. (1983). Measuring leisure motivation. *Journal of Leisure Research, 15*, 219-228.

Beard, J. G. and Ragheb, M. G. (1989). *Leisure Motivation Scale*. Enumclaw, WA: Idyll Arbor.

Beauducel, A., Brocke, B., Strobel, A., and Strobel, A. (1999). Construct validity of sensation seeking: A psychometric investigation. *Zeitschrift fuer Differentielle und Diagnostische Psychologie, 20*, 155-171.

Beck, A. T. (1987). Cognitive therapy. In Zeig, J. K. (Ed.), *The evolution of psychotherapy* (pp. 149-178). New York, NY: Brunner/Mazel.

Becker, H. S. (1960). Notes on the concept of commitment. *American J. of Sociology, 66*, 32-40.

Beggs, B. A. and Elkins, D. J. (2010). The influence of leisure motivation on leisure satisfaction. *The Cyber Journal of Applied leisure and Recreation Research*. Retrieved on August 4, 2011.

Bennett, F. (1995). Qualitative and quantitative methods: In-depth or rapid assessment. *Social Science and Medicine (40)*, 1589-1590.

Bergen, D. (2002). Finding the humor in children's play. *Play and Culture Studies, 4*, 209-220.

Berkowitz, L. (1969). Simple views of aggression: An essay review. *American Scientist, 57*, 372-383.

Berlyne, D. E. (1960). *Conflict, arousal and curiosity*. New York: McGraw Hill.

Bernstein, H. (1975). Boredom and ready-made life. *Social Research, 42*, 512-537.

Bieri, D., Reeve, R., Champion, G., Addicoat, L., and Ziegler, J. (1990). The Faces Pain Scale for the self-assessment of the severity of pain experienced by children: Development, initial validation and preliminary investigation for ratio scale properties. *Pain, 41*: 139-150.

Bishop, D. W. (1970). Stability of the factor structure of leisure behavior. *Journal of Leisure Research, 2*, 160-170.

Blair, R. G. (2004). Helping older adolescents search for meaning in depression. *Journal of Mental Health Counseling, 26,* 333-347.

Blalock, H. M. (1979). Measurement and conceptualization problems: The major obstacles to integrating theory and research. *American Sociological Review, 44*, 881-894.

Blaszczynski, A., McConaghy, N., and Frankova, A. (1990). Boredom proneness in pathological gambling. *Psychological Reports, 67*, 35-42.

Bloch, P. (1993). Involvement with adornments as leisure behavior: An exploratory study. *Journal of Leisure Research, 25*, 245-262.

Bloch, P. and Richins, M. (1983). A theoretical model for the study of product importance perceptions. *Journal of Marketing, 47*, 69-81.

Bodur, H. O., Brinberg, D., and Coupey, E. (2000). Belief, affect, and attitude: Alternative models of the determinants of attitude. *Journal of Consumer Psychology, 9*, 17-28.

Boley, B. (2002). Life satisfaction, leisure satisfaction, and leisure participation among publicly housed older adults. *Dissertation Abstracts International Section A: Humanities and Social Sciences, 62*(8-A), 2881.

Bollen, K. A. (1989). *Structural equations with latent variables*. New York, NY: Wiley.

Bover, W. A. R. (1998). Enhancing playfulness with sensorial stimulation. *Journal of Research in Childhood Education, 12*(1), 78-87.

Bronson, M. K. (2001). Supervision of career counseling. In L. J. Bradley, L. J. and Ladany, C. (Eds.) *Counselor supervision: Principles, process, and practice* (pp. 222-244). Philadelphia, PA: Brunner-Routlege.

Brook, J. and Brook, R. (1989). Exploring the meaning of work and nonwork. *Journal of Organizational Behavior, 10*, 169-178.

Brown, J. S. (1995). Attitudes toward women managers in the corporate structure: Demographic and personality predictors. *Dissertation abstracts international, Section A: Humanities and social sciences, 55*(11-A), 3413.

Brumbaugh, A. (1998*). The cost of untreated chemical dependency*. Santa Monica, CA; The Stillpoint Press.

Bryan, H. (1977). Leisure value systems and recreational specialization: The case of trout fishermen. *Journal of Leisure Research, 9*, 174-187.

Bryan, H. and Alsikafi, M. (1975). *The case of university professors*. Birmingham, AL: University of Alabama, Bureau of Public Administration.

Bryant, W. and Wang, Y. (1990). Time together, time apart: An analysis of wives' solitary time and shared time with spouses. *Lifestyles, 11*, 89-119.

Buchanan, T. (1985). Commitment and leisure behavior: A theoretical perspective. *Leisure Sciences, 7*, 401-420.

Buchholz, R. A. (1978). The work ethic reconsidered. *Industrial and Labor Relations Review, 31*, 450-459.

Burdge, R. (1961). The development of a leisure-orientation scale. Unpublished master's thesis. Columbus, OH: Ohio State University.

burlingame, j. (2001*). Idyll Arbor's therapy dictionary*. Ravensdale, WA: Idyll Arbor.

burlingame, j. and Blaschko, T. (2010). *Assessment tools for recreational therapy and related fields, fourth edition*. Enumclaw, WA: Idyll Arbor.

Burisch, M. (1984). Approaches to personality inventory construction: A comparison of merits. *American Psychologist, 39*, 214-227.

Buros, O. K. (1978, Ed.). *The eighth mental measurement yearbook, 1*. Highland Park, NJ: Gryphon Press.

Business Publications. (2005). Self-actualization drives spending on entertainment and recreation, reports unity marketing; Americans demand luxury of leisure, Business Wire, *Business Publications*, Jan 11, 2005.

Butcher, J. N., Perry, J. N., and Atlis, M. M. (2000). Validity and utility of computer-based test interpretation. *Psychological Assessment, 12*, 6-18.

Butler, G. (1959). *Introduction to community recreation.* New York: McGraw-Hill.

Caldwell, L. L., Smith, E. A., and Weissinger, E. (1992). Development of a leisure experience battery for adolescents: Parsimony, stability, and validity. *Journal of Leisure Research, 24*, 361-376.

Calkins, M. W. (1916). The self in recent psychology. *Psychological Bulletin 13*, 20-27.

Campbell, B.A. (1980) A Theoretical Approach to Peer Influence in Adolescent Socialization. *American Journal of Political Science*, 24(2), 324-344.

Campbell, A., Converse, P. E., and Rogers, W. L. (1976). *The quality of American life: Perceptions, evaluations, and satisfactions.* New York: Russell Sage Foundation.

Carey, G. (1996). *Theory and practice of counseling and psychotherapy.* Pacific Grove, CA: Brooks/Cole Publishing Co.

Carless, S. A. (1999). Career assessment: Holland's vocational interests, personality characteristics, and abilities. *Journal of Career Assessment, 7*(2), 125-144.

Carlson, M., Wilcox, R., Chou, C. P., Chang, M., Yang, F., Blanchard, J., Marterella, A., Kuo, A., and Clark, F. (2001). Psychometric properties of reverse-scored items on the CES-D in a sample of ethnically diverse older adults. *Psychological Assessment, 23*, 558-562.

Carmack, M. A. and Martens, R. (1979). Measuring commitment to running: A survey of runners' attitudes and mental states. *Journal of Sport Psychology, 1*, 25-42.

Carpenter, G. M. and Howe, C. Z. (1985). *Programming leisure experiences.* Englewood Cliffs, NJ: Prentice-Hall.

Carroll, D. and Huxley, J. A. (1994). Cognitive, dispositional, and psychophysiological correlates of dependent slot machine gambling in young people. *Journal of Applied Social Psychology, 24*, 1070-1083.

Carter, H. D. (1940). Resources for the consultant: The development of vocational attitudes. *Journal of Consulting Psychology, 4*, 185.

Carter, M. J., Van Andel, G. E., and Robb, G. M. (1995). *Therapeutic recreation: A practical approach.* Prospect Heights, IL: Waveland Press, Inc.

Caruba, A. (2001). Don't ignore boredom as a cause. *USA Today, 130*, 2675-2677.

Cattell, R. (1966). The Scree test for the number of factors. *Multivariate Behavior Research, 1*, 245-276.

Celsi, R. and Olson, J. (1988). The role of involvement in attention and comprehension processes. *Journal of Consumer Research, 15*, 210-224.

Chaneles, S. and Wolsky, A. (1974). *The movie makers.* English Book illus. Secaucus, NJ: Derbibooks

Chapman, J. A. (1978). Playfulness and the development of divergent thinking abilities. *Child Care, Health, and Development, 4*(6), 371-383.

Chase, S. (1966). Are you alive? In T. D. Berry (Ed.), *Values in American culture.* New York, NY: The Odyssey Press.

Cho, H. and Boster, F. (2005). Development and validation of value-, outcome-, and impression-relevant involvement scales. *Communication Research, 32*, 235-264.

Christopher, J. C. (1999). Situating psychological well-being: Exploring the cultural roots of its theory and research. *Journal of Counseling and Development, 77*, 141-152.

Clark, N. (1986). Central life interests of Australian. *Work and Occupations, 13*, 67-75.

Clary, E. G., Snyder, M., Ridge, R. D., Copeland, J., Stukas, A. A., Haugen, J., and Miene, P. (1998). Understanding and assessing the motivations of volunteers: A functional approach. *Journal of Personality and Social Psychology, 74*, 1516-1530.

Clough, P., Shepherd, J., and Maughan, R. (1990). Motives for participation in recreational running. *Journal of Leisure Research, 21*, 297-309.

Cnaan, R. A. and Goldberg-Glen, R. R. (1991). Measuring motivation to volunteer in human services. *Journal of Applied Behavioral Sciences, 27*, 269-285.

Cohen, R. J. and Swerdlik, M. E. (2002). *Psychological testing and assessment: An introduction to test and measurement*, 5th ed. Boston, MA: McGrawHill Companies, Inc.

Cohen, R. J. and Swerdlik, M. E. (2005). *Psychological testing and assessment: An introduction to test and measurement*, 6th ed.. Boston, MA: McGrawHill Companies, Inc.

Cohen, R. J. and Swerdlik, M. E. (2009). *Psychological testing and assessment: An introduction to test and measurement*, 7th ed. Boston, MA: McGrawHill Companies, Inc.

Cokley, K. O. (2000). Examining the validity of the Academic Motivation Scale by comparing scale construction to self-determination theory. *Psychological Reports, 86*, 560-564.

Coleman, D. and Iso-Ahola, S. (1993). Leisure and health: The role of social support and self-determination. *Journal of Leisure Research, 25*, 111-128.

Comrey, A. L. (1988). Factor-analytic methods of scale development in personality and clinical psychology. *Journal of Consulting and Clinical Psychology, 56*, 754-761.

Conrad, P. (1999). It's boring: Notes on the meanings of boredom in everyday life. In B. Glassner, R. Hertz, et al. (Eds.), *Qualitative sociology as everyday life.* Thousand Oaks, CA: Sage Publications, Inc.

Cook, M. R., Gerkovich, M. M., Potocky, M., and O'Connell, K. A. (1993). Instruments for the assessment of reversal theory states. *Patient Education & Counseling, 22*, 99-106.

Cordes, K. A. and Ibrahim, H. M. (1999). *Applications in recreation and leisure: For today and the future.* Boston, MA: McGraw-Hill.

Corey, G. (2001). *Theory and practice of counseling and psychotherapy.* Pacific Grove, CA: Cole..

Cote, J. E., and Levine, C. G. (2000). Attitude versus aptitude: Is intelligence or motivation more important for positive higher educational outcomes? *Journal of Adolescent Research, 15*, 58-80.

Cousins, N. (1989). *Head first: The biology of hope and healing power of the human spirit.* New York: Penguin Book.

Cowen, E. L. and Kilmer, R. P. (2002). Positive psychology: Some pluses and some open issues. *Journal of Community Psychology, 30,* 449-460.

Crandall, K. (2003). The stress-moderating effect of productive humor. *Dissertation Abstracts International: Section B: The Sciences & Engineering. 64*(3-B). 1485.

Crandall, R. (1979). Social interaction, affect, and leisure. *J. Leisure Research, 11,* 165-181.

Crandall, R. and Slivken, K. (1980). Leisure attitude and their measurement. In S. E. Iso-Ahola (Ed.), *Social psychological perspectives on leisure and recreation* (pp. 261-284). Springfield, IL: C. C. Thomas, Publishers.

Crano, W. D. and Prislin, R. (1995). Components of vested interest and attitude behavior consistency. *Basic and Applied Social Psychology, 17,* 1-21.

Csikszentmihalyi, M. (1975). *Beyond boredom and anxiety.* San Francisco, CA: Jossey-Bass, Inc.

Csikszentmihalyi, M. (1976). What play says about behavior. *Ontario Psychologist, 8*(2), 5-11.

Csikszentmihalyi, M. (1990). *Flow: The psychology of optimal experience.* New York, NY: Harper Perennial.

Culkin, D. F. and Kirsch, S. L. (1986). *Managing human resources in recreation, parks, and leisure services.* New York, NY: Macmillan Publishing Company.

Culkin, D. F. and Kirsch, S. L. (1986). Personnel performance appraisal. *Journal of Park and Recreation Administration, 9,* 59-70.

Dale, E. (1935). Diagnosis in leisure time activities. *Yearbook of the National Society for the Study of Education, 34,* 477-486.

Darley, J. B. and Hagenah, T. (1955). *Vocational interest measurement.* Twin Cities Campus, MN: University of Minnesota Press.

Danner, D. D., Snowdon, D. A., and Friesen, W. V. (2001). Positive emotions in early life and longevity: Findings from the nun study. *Journal of Personality and Social Psychology, 80,* 804-813.

Dattilo, J., Kleiber, D. A., and Williams, R. (1998). Self-determination and enjoyment enhancement: A psychologically-based service delivery model for therapeutic recreation. *Therapeutic Recreation Journal, 32,* 258-271.

de Grazia, S. (1962). *Of time, work, and leisure.* Garden City, NY: Doubleday.

de Wit, R., Victoir, A., and Van den Bergh, O. (1997). "My mind's made up by the way that I feel:" Affect, cognition and intention in the structure of attitudes toward condom use. *Health Education Research, 12,* 15-24.

Deci, E. L. (1975). *Intrinsic motivation.* New York: Plenum Press.

Deci, E. L. and Ryan, R. M. (1985). *Intrinsic motivation and self-determination in human behavior.* New York, NY: Plenum.

Deci, E. L. and Ryan, R. M. (1990). A motivational approach to self: Integration in personality. In R. D. Dienstbier (Ed.). *Nebraska symposium on motivation*: Vol. 38, perspectives on motivation (pp. 237-288). Lincoln: University of Nebraska Press.

Deutsch, D. (2002). Humor as a reinforcer with depressed and nondepressed subjects. *Dissertation Abstracts International: Section B: The Sciences & Engineering University Microfilms International, US, 63*(1-B), 510.

Dimanche, F., Havitz, M., and Howard, D. (1991). Testing the involvement profile scale in the context of selected recreational and touristic activities. *Journal of Leisure Research, 23,* 51-66.

Diamond, E. E. and Zytowski, D. G. (2000). The Kuder Occupational Interest Survey. In C. E. Watkins, Jr., V. L. Campbell, et al. (Eds.). *Testing and assessment in counseling practice* (2nd Ed.). Mahwah, NJ: Lawrence Erlbaum Associates, Inc.

Dicintio, M. J., and Gee, S. (1999). Control is the key: Unlocking the motivation of at-risk students. *Psychology in the Schools, 36,* 231-237.

Dickerson, M., Hinchy, J., and Fabre, J. (1987). Chasing, arousal, and sensation seeking in off-course gamblers. *British Journal of Addiction, 82,* 673-680.

Diener, E. (2000). Subjective well-being: The science of happiness and a proposal for a National Index. *American Psychologist, 55,* 34-43.

Diener, E., and Diener, C. (1996). Most people are happy. *Psychological Science, 7,* 181-185.

Diener, E., Emmons, R. A., Larsen, R. J, and Griffin, S.. (1985). The Satisfaction with Life Scale. *Journal of Personality Assessment, 49,* 71-75.

Dimanche, F., Havitz, M., and Howard, D. (1991). Testing the involvement profile scale in the context of selected recreational and touristic activities. *Journal of Leisure Research, 23,* 51-66.

Dishman, R. K. (1990) Determinants of participation in physical activity. In: C. Bouchard, R. Sheppard, T. Stephens, J. Sutton, and McPherson (Eds.). *Exercise, fitness, and health.* Champaign, IL: Human Kinetics Books.

Dodd, A. T. (1996). The effect of situational context on playful behaviors of young preschool children. *Dissertation Abstracts International, Section A: Humanities & Social Sciences, 57*(2-A), 0571.

Domagalska-Kurdziel, E., Kurzydlo, B., Szary, W., and Ulasinska, R. (1988). Time and space feeling in depressive adolescents. *Dynamische Psychiatrie, 20,* 396-405.

Dreikurs, R. (1953). *Fundamentals of Adlerian psychology.* Chicago, IL: Alfred Adler Institute.

Driver, B. (1976). Quantification of outdoor recreationists' preferences. In B. Van der Smissen (Ed.). *Research, camping, and environmental education* (pp. 165-187). University Park, PA: Pennsylvania State University, HPER Series, 11.

Driver, B. (1977). *Item pool for scales designed to quantify the psychological outcomes desired and expected from recreation opportunities.* Fort Collins, CO: SUDA Forest Services

Driver, B. L., Brown, P. J., and Peterson, G. L. (eds.) (1991). *Benefits of Leisure.* State College, PA, Venture Publishing, Inc.

Dubin, R. (1956). Individual workers worlds: A study of the "central life interests" of industrial workers. *Social Problems, 3,* 131-142.

DuBrin, A. (1972). *The practice of managerial psychology: Concepts and methods for manager and organization development.* New York: Pergamon Press, Inc.

Dugas, L. (1929). The question of ennui. *Psychologie et la Vie, 3,* 162-164.

Dunn-Ross, E. and Iso-Ahola, S. E. (1991). Sightseeing tourists' motivation and satisfaction. *Annals of Tourism Research, 18,* 226-237.

Dumazedier, J. (1967). *Toward a society of leisure.* New York, NY: The Free Press.

Dumazedier, J. (1974*). Sociology of leisure.* New York, NY: Elsevier North-Holland, Inc.

Durrant, L. H. (1986). A multiple approach to prevention of adolescent substance abuse. Doctoral Dissertation, University of Utah. *Dissertation Abstracts International, 47,* 833.

Edginton, C. R., Hanson, C. J., Edginton, S. R., and Hudson, S. D. (1998). *Leisure programming: A service-centered and benefits approach.* Boston, Mass: McGraw-Hill.

Edginton, C. R., Jordan, D. J., DeGraaf, D. G., and Edginton, S. R. (2002). *Leisure and life satisfaction.* Boston, MA: McGraw-Hill.

Edmondson, B. (1991). Burn-out boomers flee to families. *American Demographics, 13,* 17.

Everard, K. M. (1999). The relationship between reasons for activity and older adult well-being. *The Journal of Applied Gerontology, 18,* 325-340.

Einarsdottir, S. and Rounds, J. (2000). Application of three dimensions of vocational interests to the Strong Interest Inventory. *Journal of Vocational Behavior, 56*(3), 363-379.

Ejaz, F. K., Schur, D., and Noelker, L. S. (1997). The effect of activity involvement and social relationships on boredom among nursing home residents. *Activities, Adaptation, & Aging, 21,* 53-66.

Elejalde-Ruiz, A. (2011). How old do you feel inside? *Chicago Tribune,* Oct. 18.

Elia, C. J. (1992). Stimulus reduction and boredom in pathological gamblers. *Dissertation Abstracts International, 53,* 2577.

Elliott, T. and Shewchuk, R. (1995). Social support and leisure activities following severe physical disability: Testing the mediating effects of depression. *Basic and Applied Social Psychology, 16,* 471-487.

Ellis M. J. (1973). *Why people play.* Englewood Cliffs, NJ: Prentice-Hall, Inc.

Ellis, G. D., and Witt, P. A. (1984). The measurement of perceived freedom in leisure. *Journal of Leisure Research, 16,* 110-123.

Ellis, G. D. and Witt., P. A. (1989). Leisure Diagnostic Battery. *Journal of Therapeutic Recreation, 20,* 31-47.

Ellis, G. D., and Witt, P. A. (1994). Perceived freedom in leisure and satisfaction: Exploring the factor structure of the perceived freedom components of the Leisure Diagnostic Battery. *Leisure Sciences, 16,* 259-270.

Erdman, L. (1993). Laughter therapy for patients with cancer. *Journal of Psychosocial Oncology, 11,* 55-67.

Ervin, L., and Stryker, S. (2001). What does self-esteem have to do with it? Theorizing the relationship between self-esteem and identity theory. In: T. Owens, S. Stryker, and N. Goodman (Eds.). *Extending self-esteem theory and research* (pp. 29-55). Cambridge, UK: Cambridge University Press.

Ewert, A. and Hollenhorst, S. (1989). Testing the adventure model: Empirical support for a model of risk participation. *J. Leisure Research, 21,* 124-139.

Farmer, R. and Sundberg, N. D. (1986). Boredom proneness: The development and correlates of a new scale. *Journal of Personality Assessment, 50,* 4-17.

Farrell, J. M., Johnston, M. E., and Twynam, D. (1998). Volunteer motivation, satisfaction, and management at an elite sporting competition. *Journal of Sport Management, 12,* 288-300.

Farrell, P. and Lundegren, H. M. (1993). *The process of recreation programming.* State College, PA: Venture.

Festinger, L. (1957). *A theory of cognitive dissonance.* Stanford, CA: Stanford University Press.

Field, M. G. (1955). Alcoholism, crime, and delinquency in Soviet society. *Social Problems, 3,* 100-109.

Filipowicz, A. (2002). The influence of humor on performance in task-based interactions. *Dissertation Abstracts International: Section A: Humanities & Social Sciences, 63*(4-A), 1437.

Findling, R. L., Schulz, S. C., Kashani, J. H., Harlan, E. (2001). Psychotic disorders in children and adolescents. *Developmental Clinical Psychology Psychiatry, 44.*

Fishbein, M. (1965). A consideration of beliefs, attitudes and their relationship. In I. Steiner and M. Fishbein (Eds.). *Readings in attitude theory and measurement* (pp. 257-266). New York: Rinehart and Winston.

Fisher, C. D. (1993). Boredom at work: A neglected concept. *Human Relations, 46,* 395-417.

Fisher, C. D. (2000). Mood and emotions while working: Missing pieces of job satisfaction? *Journal of Organizational Behavior, 21,* 185-202.

Fisher, R. L. and Price, L. L. (1991). International travel motivations and post vacation cultural attitude change. *J. Leisure Research, 23,* 193-208.

Fiske, D. W. (1971). *Measuring the concepts of personality.* Chicago, IL: Alsine Publishing Company.

Flavell, J. H. (1963). *The developmental psychology of Jean Piaget.* Princeton, NJ: Van Nostrand-Reinhold.

Fleming, T. L., Green, J. L., Martin, J. C., and Wicks, M. N. (2000). Effectiveness of a cardiovascular health promotion education intervention on the attitudes of urban African American school-age children. *Journal of Community Health Nursing, 17,* 49-60.

Fletcher, S. (2000). Competence-based assessment techniques. London: Kogan Page Pub.

Florida Obesity Program. Obesity Discussion Administrator. Retrieved on Oct. 22, 2010.

Florida Quick Facts. State of Florida.com, Retrieved on Oct. 13, 2010.

Foley, E; Matheis, R.; and Schaefe, C. (2002). Effect of forced laughter on mood. *Psychological Reports, 90,* 184.

Forer, B. R. (1948). A diagnostic interest blank. *Rorschach Research Exchange and Journal of Projective Techniques, 12,* 1-11.

Foret, C. (1985). Life satisfaction, leisure satisfaction, and leisure participation among young-old and old-old adults with rural and urban residence. *Dissertation Abstracts*

International 47(02A), 655, AAC 8608486. Texas Woman's University.

Forrester, M. (2000). *Psychology of the image.* New York, NY: Routledge.

Fountain, A. M. (1995). Playful personalities: A study of playfulness, arousal modulation, and cognitive style. *Dissertation Abstracts International, Section B: The Sciences & Engineering, 55*(9-B), 4140.

Frain, M. P., Bishop, M., and Tschopp, M. (2009). Empowerment variables as predictors of outcomes in rehabilitation. *The Journal of Rehabilitation, 33*, 59-65.

Frank, R., Vaitl, D. and Walter, B. (1990). Zur diagnostik korperlichen wohlbefindens. *Diagnostica, 36*, 33-37.

Frankl, V. (1962). *Man's search for meaning: An introduction to logotherapy.* Boston, MA: Beacon Press.

Frankl, V. (1988). *The will to meaning: Foundations and applications of logotherapy* (2nd ed.). New York: Meridian.

Frankl, V. (1992) *Man's search for meaning.* Boston, MA: Bacon Press.

Fredrick, C. and Ryan, R. (1993). Differences in motivation for sport and exercise and their relationship to participation and mental health. *J. of Sport Behavior, 16*, 124-146.

Fredrickson, B. L. (2003). The value of positive emotions. *American Scientist, 91*, 330-335.

Freud, A. (1946). *The psychological treatment of children.* London: Imago.

Freud, S. (1957). Mourning and melancholia. In J. Strachey (Ed.). *The standard edition of the complete psychological works of Sigmund Freud* (Vol. 14, pp. 152-170). London: Hogarth Press. (Original work published 1917).

Frisbie, G. R. (1984). Measurement of leisure interest. *Journal of Career Development, 10*, 101-109.

Froelicher, V. F. and Froelicher, E. S. (1991). Cardiovascular benefits of physical activity, Pp. 59-72. In: B. L. Driver et al., (Ed.) *Benefits of leisure.* State College, Venture Pub., Inc.

Garb, H. N. (2000). Computers will become increasingly important for psychological assessment: Not that there's anything wrong with that. *Psychological Assessment, 12*, 19-30.

Garb, H. N. (2000). Introduction to the special section on the uses of computers for making judgments and decisions. *Psychological Assessment, 12*, 3-5.

Geller, E. S. (2010). Cultivating a self-motivated workforce: The choice, community, and competence of an injury free-culture. *Health and Safety Leaders.* (Retrieved on August 2, 2011).

Gemmill, G. and Oakley, J. (1992). The meaning of boredom in organizational life. *Group & Organization Management, 17*, 358-369.

Getz, D. (1991). *Festivals, special events, and tourism.* New York: Van Nostrand Reinhold.

Geyer, P. D., Brannon, Y. S., and Shearon, R. W. (1987). The prediction of students' satisfaction with community college vocational training. *Journal of Psychology, 121*, 591-597.

Gigy, L., and Kelly, J. B. (1992). Reasons for divorce: Perspectives of divorcing men and women. *Journal of Divorce & Remarriage, 18*, 169-187.

Glass, C. R. and Arnkoff, O. B. (1992). Behavior therapy. In D. K. Freedheim (Ed.), *History of psychotherapy: A century of change* (pp. 587-628). Washington, DC: American Psychological Association.

Glass, J. C. and Jolly, G. R. (1997). Satisfaction in later life among women 60 or over. *Educational Gerontology, 23*, 297-314.

Glasser, W. (1976). *Positive addiction.* New York: HarperCollins.

Glynn, M. and Webster, J. (1992). The Adult Playfulness Scale: An initial assessment scale. *Psychological Reports, 71*, 83-103.

Godin, C., Shephard, R., and Colantonio, R. (1986). The cognitive profile of those who intend to exercise but do not. *Public Health Reports, 101*, 521-526.

Goldstein, M. (1998). An ethnographic study of leisure participation among people with spinal cord injury. *Dissertation Abstracts International, Section A: Humanities & Social Sciences, 58*(12-A), 4807.

Good, D. (1990). Utilizing consumer involvement to market services. *Review of Business, 11*, 3-7.

Goodale, T. L. and Witt, P. A. (1991). *Recreation and leisure: Issues in an era of change.* State College, PA: Venture Publishing, Inc.

Gordon, A., Wilkinson, R., McGown, A., and Jovanoska, S. (1997). The psychometric properties of the Boredom Proneness Scale: An examination of its validity. *Psychological Studies, 42*, 85-97.

Gordon, W. R. and Caltabiano, M. L. (1996). Urban-rural differences in adolescent self-esteem, leisure boredom, and sensation seeking as predictors of leisure-time usage and satisfaction. *Adolescence, 31*, 883-901.

Gorsuch, R. (1983). *Factor analysis.* Hillsdale, NJ: Erlbaum.

Graef, R., Csikszentmihalyi, M., and Gianinno, S. M. (1983). Measuring intrinsic motivation in everyday life. *Leisure Studies, 2*, 155-168.

Gravelle, F., Pare, C., and Laurencelle, L. (1997). Attitude and enduring involvement of older persons in structured programs of physical activity. *Perception of Motor Skills, 85*, 67-71.

Green-Demers, I. (1991). When boredom gives birth to motivation: Interrelations between interest-enhancing strategies, interest, and self-determination. *Dissertation Abstracts International, 59*(7B), 3724.

Green-Demers, I., Pelletier, L. G., Stewart, D. G., and Gushue, N. R. (1998). Coping with the less interesting aspects of training: Toward a model of interest and motivation enhancement in individual sports. *Basic & Applied Social Psychology, 20*, 251-261.

Griffin, J. and McKenna, K. (1998). Influence of leisure and life satisfaction on elderly people. *Physical and Occupational Therapy in Geriatrics, 15*, 1-6.

Gronroos, C. (1982). An applied service marketing theory. *European Journal of Marketing, 16*, 30-41.

Grubb, E. A. (1975). Assembly line boredom and individual differences in recreational participation. *Journal of Leisure Research, 7*, 256-269.

Guinn, B. (1999). Leisure behavior motivation and the life satisfaction of retired persons. *Activities, Adaptation, & Aging, 23*, 13-20.

Guitard, P., Ferland, F., and Dutil, E. (2005) Toward a better understanding of playfulness in adults. *Occupation, Participation & Health, 25*, 9-22.

Gutiérrez, M., Caus, N., Ruiz, L. (2011). The influence of parents on achievement orientation and motivation for sport of adolescent athletes with and without disabilities. *Journal of Leisure Research, 43*(3).

Gunter, B., Stanley, J., St. Clair, R. (1985). *Transitions to leisure*. New York: University Press of America, Inc.

Hall, G. S. and Allin, A. (1897). The psychology of tickling, laughing and the comic. *The American Journal of Psychology, 9*, 1-42.

Hallman, L. K. (1976). The effect of the play experience on playfulness, creativity, and self-concept in adults. *Dissertation Abstracts International, 36*(8-B), 4157-4158.

Hamilton, J. A., Haier, R. J., and Buchsbaum, M. S. (1984). Intrinsic Enjoyment and Boredom Coping scales: Validation with personality, evoked potential, and attention measures. *Personality & Individual Differences, 5*, 183-193.

Handler, L. (1999). Assessment of playfulness: Hermann Rorschach Meets D. W. Winnicott. *Journal of Personality Assessment, 72*(2), 208-217.

Hauge, A. and White, A. (2005). Web-based intervention for changing attitude of obesity among current and future teachers. *Journal of Nutrition Education & Behavior, 37*, 58-66.

Hausenblas, H. A., Hall, C. R., Rogers, W. M., and Munroe, K. J. (1999). Exercise imagery: Its nature and measurement. *Journal of Applied Sport Psychology, 11*, 171-180.

Havinghurst, R. J., et al. (1968). Disengagement and aging. In: Berice L. Neugarten (Ed.) *Middle age and aging*. Chicago: University of Chicago Press.

Havitz, M. and Dimanche, F. (1990). Propositions for testing the involvement construct in recreational and tourism contexts. *Leisure Sciences, 12*, 179-195.

Havitz, M. and Dimanche, F. (1997). Leisure involvement revisited: Conceptual conundrums and measurement advances. *Journal of Leisure Research, 29*, 245-278.

Havitz, M. and Mannell, R. (2005). Enduring involvement, situational involvement, and flow in leisure and non-leisure activities. *Journal of Leisure Research, 37*, 152-177.

Hawkins, B. (1994). Leisure participation and life satisfaction of older adults with mental retardation and Down syndrome. In E. Sutton, A. Factor, B. Hawkins, T. Heller, and G. Seltzer (Eds.). *Older adults with developmental disabilities*. Baltimore, Paul H. Brooks.

Hawkins, B., Ardovino, P., and Hsieh, C. (1998). Validity and reliability of the Leisure Assessment Inventory. *Mental Retardation, 36*, 303-313.

Hawkins, B., Ardovino, P., Rogers, N., Foose, A., and Ohlsen, N. (2002). *Leisure Assessment Inventory* (LAI). Idyll Arbor, Inc., Enumclaw, WA.

Heider, F. (1958). *The psychology of interpersonal relations*. New York, NY: Wiley.

Heled, E. and Read, J. (2005). Young peoples' opinions about the causes of, and solutions to, New Zealand's high youth suicide rate. *Suicide & Life-Threatening Behavior, 35*, 170-180.

Helson, H. (1959). Adaptation-level theory. In S. Koch (Ed.). *Psychology: A study of a science*, 565-621. New York, NY: McGraw-Hill.

Henderson, K. A. (1991). The contribution of feminism to an understanding of leisure constraints. *Journal of Leisure Research, 23*, 263-377.

Henderson, K. A. and Bialeschki, M. D. (2002). *Evaluating leisure services: Making enlightened decisions*. State College, PA: Venture Pub, Inc.

Henry, A. D. (1998). Development of a measure of adolescent leisure interests. *American Journal of Occupational Therapy, 52*, 531-539.

Heron, W. (1957). Disease or pathology and boredom. *Scientific American, 196*, 52-69.

Herzberg, F. (1966). *Work and the nature of man*. Cleveland, OH: Holland.

Hettler, B. (1986). Strategies for wellness and recreation program development. *New Directions for Student Services, 34*, 19-32.

Hickerson, B. D. and Beggs, B. A. (2007). Leisure time boredom: issues concerning college students. *College Student Journal, 41*, 1036-1044.

Hills, P., Argyle, M., and Reeves, R. (2000). Individual differences in leisure satisfactions: An investigation of four theories of leisure motivation. *Personality and Individual Differences, 28*, 763-779.

Holbrook, M. and Hirshman, E. (1982). The experiential aspects of consumption: Consumer fantasies, feelings, and fun. *Journal of Consumer Research, 9*, 132-140.

Holie, P. C. (2000). Improving person-environment fit: Increasing job satisfaction by matching employees' preferred levels of arousal to job complexity within Holland's model of occupational types (John L. Holland). *Dissertation Abstracts International: section B, 61*(5-B), 2804.

Holland, J. L. (1959). A theory of vocational choice. *Journal of Counseling Psychology, 6*, 35-45.

Holland, J. L. (1966). *The psychology of vocational choice: a theory of personality types and model environments*. Waltham, MA: Blaisdell.

Holland, J. L. (1973). *Making vocational choices: A theory of careers*. Englewood Cliffs, NJ: Prentice-Hall.

Holland, J. L. (1978). *Manual for vocational preference inventory*. Palo Alto, CA: Consulting Psychologist Press.

Holland, J. L. (1985). *Making vocational choices: A theory of vocational personalities and work environments*. (2nd ed.) Englewood Cliffs, NJ: Prentice-Hall.

Hollander, P. (1971). *Principles and methods of social psychology*. New York: Oxford University Press.

Homans, G. (1961). *Social behavior: Its elementary forms*. New York: Harcourt, Brace World.

Hood, C. (2003). Women in recovery from alcoholism: The place of leisure. *Leisure Sciences, 25*, 51-79.

Hopkins, W. S. (1966). Research and user preferences. In *Recreation research*, pp. 81-85. New York, NY: National Recreation and Park Association.

House, J. D. (2000). The effect of student involvement on the development of academic self-concept. *Journal of Social Psychology, 140*, 261-263.

Houston, V. M. (1940). A neglected aspect of guidance. *School Executive, 60*, 22-24.

Howard, D. R. (1976). Multivariate relationships between leisure activities and personality. *Research Quarterly, 47*, 226-237.

Howat, G., Absher, J., Crilley, G., and Milne, I. (1996). Measuring customer service quality in sports and leisure centers. *Managing Leisure, 1*, 77-89.

Howe, C. Z. and Rancourt, A. M. (1990). The importance of definition: Selected concepts for leisure inquiry. *Leisure Sciences, 12*, 395-406.

Hsieh, C-M. (1999). Leisure attitudes, motivation, participation, and satisfaction: Test of a model of leisure behavior. *Dissertation Abstracts International, Section A: Humanities & Social Sciences, 59*(9-A), 3644.

Hubert, E. (1969). The development of an inventory of leisure interests. Unpublished doctoral dissertation, University of North Carolina, Chapel Hill.

Huffman, J. C. and Kunik, M. E. (2000). Assessment and understanding of pain in patients with dementia. *Gerontologist, 40*, 574-581.

Hull, R. and Michael, S. (1995). Nature-based recreation, mood change, and stress restoration. *Leisure Sciences, 17*, 1-14.

Hupfer, N. and Gardner, D. (1971). Differential involvement with products and issues: An exploratory study. In D. Gardner. (Ed.). *Proceedings of the Association for Consumer Research* (pp. 262-270),. College Park, MD: Second Conference.

Inglehart, R. (1990). *Culture shift in advance industrial society.* Princeton, NJ: Princeton University Press.

Iso-Ahola, S. (1980). *The social psychology of leisure and recreation.* Dubuque, IA: William C. Brown Company.

Iso-Ahola, S. 1984. Social psychological foundations of leisure and resultant implications for leisure counseling. In E. T. Dowd (Ed.). *Leisure counseling: Concepts and applications* (pp. 97-125). Springfield, IL: Charles C. Thomas,

Iso-Ahola, S. E. (1986). A theory of substitutability of leisure behavior. *Leisure Sciences, 8*, 367-389.

Iso-Ahola, S. E. and Allen, J. R. (1982). The dynamics of leisure motivation: The effects of outcome on leisure needs. *Research Quarterly for Exercise and Sport, 53*, 141-149.

Iso-Ahola, S. E. and Crowley, E. D. (1991). Adolescent substance abuse and leisure boredom. *Journal of Leisure Research, 23*, 260-271.

Iso-Ahola, S. E. and Park, C. J. (1996). Leisure-related social support and self-determination as buffers of stress-illness relationship. *Journal of Leisure Research, 28*, 169-187.

Iso-Ahola, S. E. and Weissinger, E. (1987). Leisure and boredom. *Journal of Social and Clinical Psychology, 5*, 356-364.

Iso-Ahola, S. E. and Weissinger, E. (1990). Perceptions of boredom in leisure: Conceptualization, reliability, and validity of the Leisure Boredom Scale. *Journal of Leisure Research, 22*, 1-17.

Iwasaki, Y. and Mannell, R. C. (1999). Situational and personality influences on intrinsically motivated leisure behavior: Interaction effects and cognitive processes. *Leisure Sciences, 21*, 287-306.

Iwasaki, Y. and Mannell, R. C. (2000). Hierarchical dimensions of leisure stress coping. *Leisure Sciences, 22*, 163-181.

Iwasaki, Y., Mannell, R., Smale, B., and Butcher, J. (2002). A short-term longitudinal analysis of leisure coping used by employees of police and emergency response service workers. *Journal of Leisure Research, 34*, 311-339.

Iwasaki, Y., Mannell, R., Smale, B., and Butcher, J. (2005). Contributions of leisure participation in predicting stress coping and health among police and emergency response services workers. *Journal of Health Psychology, 10*, 79-99.

Jackson, D. W. and Angelino, H. R. (1974). Play as learning. *Theory into Practice, 13*, 317-323.

Jackson, E. L. (1988). Leisure constraints: A survey of past research. *Leisure Services, 10*, 203-215.

Jackson, E. L. (1990). Variations in desire to begin a leisure activity: Evidence of antecedent constraints. *Journal of Leisure Research, 22*, 55-70.

Jackson, L. T. and Lilley, J. (1990). The value of activities: Establishing a foundation for cost-effectiveness — a review of literature. *Activities, Adaptation, and Aging, 14*, 5-20.

Jackson, S. A. and Marsh, H. W. (1996). Development and validation of a scale to measure optimal experience: The Flow State Scale. *Journal of Sport and Exercise Psychology, 18*, 17-35.

Jaeger, R. and Bond, L. (1996). Quantitative research methods and design. In D. Berliner and R. Calfee (Eds.), *Handbook of educational psychology* (pp. 877-898). London, England: Prentice-Hall International.

James, L. R., Demaree, R. G., and Wolf, G. (1984). Estimating within-group interrater reliability with and without response bias. *Journal of Applied Psychology, 69*, 85-98.

Joint Committee on Testing Practices. (1988). *Code of fair testing practices in education.* Washington, DC: American Psychological Association.

Jung, C. G. (1990). *Analytical psychology: its theory and practice.* The Tavistock Lectures, Ark Paperbacks.

Juniu, S., Tedrick, T., and Boyd, R. (1996). Leisure or work? Amateur and professional musicians' perception of rehearsal and performance. *Journal of Leisure Research, 28*(1), 44-56.

Kabanoff, B. and O'Brien, G. (1986). Stress and the leisure needs and activities of different occupations. *Human Relations, 39*, 903-916.

Kao, C-H. (1993). A model of leisure satisfaction. *Dissertation Abstracts International, 54*(4-B), 1922.

Kaplan, M. (1960). *Leisure in America: A social inquiry.* New York: John Wiley and Sons, Inc.

Kaplan, M. (1975). *Leisure: Theory and policy.* New York: John Wiley.

Kaplan, R. S. and Norton, D. P. (1996). Using the balanced scorecard as a strategic management system. *Harvard Business Review*, January-February, 1-13.

Kaplan, S. M. (1997). Central life interests: An integrative review. Dissertation Abstract International: Section B: The Science and Engineering. APA 6th Edition.

Kashima, Y. and Lewis, V. (2000). Where does the behavior come from in attitude-behavior relations? Toward a connectionist model of behavior generation. In

Terry, D. J. and Hogg, M. A. (Eds.) *Attitude, behavior, and social context: The role of norms and group membership.* London: Lawrence Erlbaum Associates.

Kass, S. J., Vodanovich, S. J., and Callender, A. (2001). State-trait boredom: The relationship to absenteeism, tenure, and job satisfaction. *Journal of Business and Psychology, 16*, 317-327.

Kauffman, R. (1984). The relationship between activity specialization and resource related attitudes and expected rewards for canoeists. Unpublished doctoral dissertation. College Park, MD: University of Maryland.

Kay, R. H. (1993). An exploration of theoretical and practical foundations for assessing attitudes toward computers: The Computer Attitude Measure (CAM). *Computers in Human Behavior, 9*, 371-386.

Keller, J. (1983). The relationship between leisure and life satisfaction among older women. Paper presented at the meeting of the NRPA, Kansas City, KS.

Kelly, J. (1972). Work and leisure: A simplified paradigm. *Journal of Leisure Research, 4*, 50-62.

Kelly, J. R. (1974). Socialization toward leisure: A developmental approach. *Journal of Leisure Research, 6*, 181-193.

Kelly, J. R. (1977). Leisure socialization: Replication and extension. *Journal of Leisure Research, 9*, 121-132.

Kelly, J. R. (1996). *Leisure.* Boston, MA: Allyn and Bacon.

Kelly, J. and Godbey, G. (1992). *The sociology of leisure.* State College, PA: Venture Publishing, Inc.

Kelly, J. and Kelly, J. (1994). Multiple dimensions of meaning in the domains of work, family, and leisure. *Journal of Leisure Research, 26*, 250-274.

Kelly, J. R., MacKay, K. J., and Compton, J. L. (1990). Measuring the quality of recreation services. *Journal of Park and Recreation Administration, 8*, 47-56.

Kelly, J. R., Steinkamp, M. W., Kelly, J. R.. (1987). Later life satisfaction: Does leisure contribute? *Leisure Sciences, 10*, 189-200.

Kendzierski, D. and DeCarlo, K. J. (1991). Physical activity enjoyment scale: Two validation studies. *Journal of Sport and Exercise Psychology, 13*, 15-64.

Kenyon, G. S. (1968). Six scales for assessing attitude toward physical activity. *Research Quarterly, 39*, 566-574.

Kerlinger, F. N. and Lee, H. (2000). *Foundations of behavioral research.* New York: Holt, Rinehart, and Winston, Inc.

Kerner, M. S. and Grossman, A. H. (1998). Attitudinal, social, and practical correlates to fitness behavior: A test of the theory of planned behavior. *Perception and Motor Skills, 87*, 1139-1154.

Ketcham, M. and Marion, J. (1982). Wellness: How outdoor recreation helps. *Outdoor Communicator, 12*, 27-30.

Killcross, M. C. and Bates, T. G. (1968). The APU Occupational Interests Guide: A progress report. *Occupational Psychology, 42*, 119-122.

Kimble, G. A. (1961). *Hilgard and Marquis' conditioning and learning.* New York, NY: Appleton-Century Crofts.

Kirkcaldy, B. (1990). Gender and personality determinants of recreational interests. *Studia Psychologica, 1-2*(30), 115-121.

Kirkcaldy, B. D. and Athanasou, J. A. (1995). Leisure interests of German workers: Gender differences and similarities. *Perceptual & Motor Skills, 81*(2), 429-430.

Kish, G. B. and Donnenwerth, G. V. (1969). Interests and stimulus seeking. *Journal of Counseling Psychology, 16*, 551-556.

Klapp, O. E. (1986). *Overload and boredom: Essays on the quality of life in the information society.* Westport, CT: Greenwood Press.

Knapp, M. R. (1977). The activity theory of aging: An examination in the English context. *The Gerontologist, 17*, 553-559.

Kocher, S. A. (1976). A study of the relationships between playfulness and two conceptions of creativity in kindergarten children. *Dissertation Abstracts International, 37*(1-A), 196-197.

Koivumaa-Honkanen, H., Honkanen, R., Viinamäki, H., Heikkilä, K., Kaprio, J. and Koskenvuo, M. (2000). Self-reported life satisfaction and 20-year mortality in healthy Finnish adults. *American Journal of Epidemiology, 152*, 982-991.

Kokkinaki, F. and Lunt, P. (1997). Involvement with the attitude object: Moderators of the attitude-behavior relationship. *The British Journal of Social Psychology, 36*, 497-509.

Kokkinaki, F. and Lunt, P. (1999). The effect of advertising message involvement on brand attitude accessibility. *Journal of Economic Psychology, 20*, 41-51.

Kramer, A. F. and Willis, S. L. (2001). Enhancing vitality of older persons. *Current Direction in Psychological Science, 11*, 173-177.

Kraus, R. (2000). *Leisure in a changing America: Trends and issues for the 21ˢᵗ century.* Boston, MA: Allyn and Bacon.

Kraus, R. and Allen, L. (1987). *Research and evaluation in recreation, parks, and leisure studies.* Columbus, OH: Publishing Horizons, Inc.

Krause, N. (1991). Stressful events and life satisfaction among elderly men and women. *Journal of Gerontology, 46*, 584-592.

Kruger, A. (1995).The adult playfulness scale: A review. *Psychology: A Journal of Human Behavior, 32*, 36-

Kuder, G. F. (1934). *Kuder general interest survey.* Chicago, IL: Science Research Associates.

Kuley, N. B. and Jacobs, D. F. (1988). The relationship between dissociative-like experiences and sensation seeking among social and problem gamblers. *Journal of Gambling Behavior, 4*, 197-207.

Kunz, J. L. (1997). Associating leisure with drinking: Current research and future directions. *Drug & Alcohol Review, 16*, 69-76.

Kwon, Y-H. and Workman, J. E. (1996). Relationship of optimum stimulation level to fashion behavior. *Clothing & Textiles Research Journal, 14*, 249-256.

Lang, C. T. and O'Leary, J. T. (1997). Motivation, participation, and preference: A multi-segmentation approach to the Australian nature travel market. *Journal of Travel and Tourism, 6*, 150-180.

Larsen, J. K. and Stothart, R. A. (1986). The development of recreation education: A comparative study. *World Leisure and Recreation,* February, 14-17.

Larson, R. W. (2000). Toward a psychology of positive youth development. *American Psychologist, 55*, 170-183.

Latane, B. and Nowak, A. (1994). *Attitude as catastrophes: From dimensions to categories with increasing involvement.* In Vallacher, R. R. and Nowak, A. (Eds). Dynamical systems in social psychology, (pp. 219-249). San Diego, CA: Academic Press

Laurent, G. and Kapferer, J. (1985). Measuring consumer involvement profiles. *Journal of Marketing Research, 22*, (1) 41-53.

Lavine, H., Borgida, E., and Sullivan J. L. (2000). On the relationship between attitude involvement and attitude accessibility: Toward a cognitive-motivational model of political information processing. *Political Psychology, 21*, 81-106.

Lavine, H., Thomsen, C. J., Zanna, M. P., and Borgida, E. (1998). On the primacy of affect in the determination of attitudes and behavior: The moderating role of affective-cognitive ambivalence. *Journal of Experimental Social Psychology, 34*, 398-421.

Lawler, R. and Carley, K. (1996). *Case study and computing: Advanced qualitative methods in the study of human behavior.* Norwood, NJ: Ablex Publishing Corporation.

Lawshe C. H. (1975). A quantitative approach to content validity. *Personnel Psychology, 28*, 563-575.

Lazarus, R. S. (2003). Does the positive psychology have legs? *Psychological Inquiry, 14*, 93-102.

Lazer, R. I. and Wikstrom, W. S. (1977). *Appraising managerial performance: Current practices and future directions.* New York, NY: The Conference Board, Inc.

Lee, L. (1990). Leisure involvement and subjective well-being of young adults with mental retardation. *Dissertation Abstracts International, 51*(3-B), 1218.

Lee, T. W. (1986). Toward the development and validation of a measure of job boredom. *Manhattan College Journal of Business, 15*, 22-28.

Martin, R. A. and Lefcourt, H. M. (1983). Sense of humor as a moderator of the relation between stresses and moods. *Journal of Personality and Social Psychology, 45*, 1313-1324.

Martin, R. A. and Lefcourt, H. M. (1984). Situational Humor Response Questionnaire: Quantitative measure of sense of humor. *Journal of Personality and Social Psychology, 47*, 145-155.

Lehman, A. F., Myers, C. P., Corty, E. (2000). Assessment and classification of patients with psychiatric and substance abuse syndrome. *Psychiatric Services, 51*, 1119-1125.

Lehman, H. C. and Witty, P. A. (1927). The play behavior of fifty gifted children. *Journal of Educational Psychology, 18*, 259-265.

Leininger, M. (1994). Evaluation criteria and critique of qualitative research studies. In J. M. Morse, *Critical issues in qualitative research methods.* Thousand Oaks, CA: Sage Publications.

Lester, H. E. and Pattison, H. M. (2000). Development and validation of the attitudes toward the homeless questionnaire. *Medical Education, 34*, 266-268.

Levenson, H. (1973). Multidimensional locus of control in psychiatric patients. *J. of Consulting and Clinical Psychology, 41*, 397-404.

Levin, I., Share, D., and Shatil, E. (1996). A qualitative-quantitative study of preschool writing: Its development and contribution to school literacy. In M. Levy and S. Ransdell (Eds.), *The science of writing: Theories, methods, individual differences, and applications* (pp. 271-293). Hillsdale, NJ: Lawrence Erlbaum Associates.

Lewinsohn, P. M., Munoz, R., Youngren, M., and Zeixx, A. M. (1986). *Control your depression.* New York: Fireside.

Li, A. K. (1978). Effects of play on novel responses in kindergarten children. *Alberta Journal of Educational Research, 24*(1), 31-36.

Li, F. (1999). The exercise motivation scale: Its multifaceted structure and construct validity. *Journal of Applied Sport Psychology, 11*, 97-115.

Lichtenberg, J. D. and Meares, R. (1996). The role of play in things human. *Psychoanalysis & Psychotherapy, 13*(1), 5-18.

Lichtveld, M. (2005). Introduction: Terrorism and human health risk — From assessment to management. *Human and Ecological Risk Assessment, 11*, 483-485.

Lieberman, J. N. (1965). Playfulness and divergent thinking: An investigation of their relationship at the kindergarten level. *J Genet Psychol. 107*(2d Half), 219-224.

Lieberman, J. N. (1966). Playfulness: An attempt to conceptualize a quality of play and of the player. *Psychological Reports, 19*(3), 1278.

Lieberman, J. N. (1977). *Playfulness: Its relationship to imagination and creativity.* New York: Academic Press.

Lin, C., Lin, S., Wu, C. (2009). The effects of parental monitoring and leisure boredom on adolescents' Internet addiction. *Adolescence, 44*, 993-1004.

Lindell, M. K., Brandt, C. J., and Whitney, D. J. (1999). A revised index of interrater agreement for multi-item ratings of a single target. *Applied Psychological Measurement, 23*, 127-135.

Lloyd, K. and Auld, C. (2002). The roles of leisure in determining quality of life: Issues of content and measurement. *Social Indicators Research, 57*, 43-71.

Loehlin, J. C. (1959). The influence of different activities on the apparent length of time. *Psychological Monographs, 73*, p. 27.

Loesch, L. C. and Wheeler, P. T. (1982). *Principles of leisure counseling.* Minneapolis, MN: Educational Media Corporation.

London, M., Crandall, R., and Fitzgibbons, D. (1977). The psychological structure of leisure: Activities, needs, people. *J. Leisure Research, 9*, 252-263.

Lumpe, A. T., Haney, J. J., and Czerniak, C. M. (2000). Assessing teachers' beliefs about their science teaching context. *Journal of Research in Science Teaching, 37*, 275-292.

Lundegren, H. M. and Farrell, P. (1985). *Evaluation for leisure service manages.* Philadelphia, PA: W. B. Saunders Co.

Lysyk, M., Brown G. T., Rodrigues E., McNally J., Loo K. (2002). Translation of the Leisure Satisfaction Scale in

French: a validation study. *Occupational Therapy International, 9,* 76-89.

Mack, R. W. (1986). Who is enhancing creativity? *Journal of Human Behavior & Learning, 3,* 42-45.

MacKay, K. J. and Compton, J. L. (1988). A conceptual model of service quality and its implications for future research. *Leisure Studies, 7,* 41-49.

MacKay, K. J. and Compton, J. L. (1990). Measuring the quality of recreation services. *Journal of Park and Recreation Administration, 8,* 47-56.

MacNeil, R. and Anderson, S. (1999). Leisure and persons with developmental disabilities: Empowering self-determination through inclusion. In P. Retish and S. Reiter (Ed). *Adults with disabilities: International perspectives in the community* (pp. 125-143). Mahwah, NJ: Lawrence Erlbaum Associates, Inc.

Madrigal, R., Havitz, M. E., and Howard, D. R. (1992). Married couples' involvement with family vacation. *Leisure Sciences, 14,* 287-301.

Mageau, G. A., Green-Demers, I., and Pelletier, L. G. (2000). The suppression of our boredom, but at what price? The paradoxical impact of mental control of boredom during a tedious task. *Canadian Journal of Behavioural Science, 32,* 29-39.

Mahoney, J. L. and Stattin, H. (2000). Leisure activities and adolescent antisocial behavior: The role of structure and social content. *Journal of Adolescence, 23,* 113-127.

Maio, G. R., Esses, V. M., and Bell, D. W. (2000). Examining conflict between components of attitudes: Ambivalence and inconsistency are distinct constructs. *Canadian Journal of Behavioural Science, 32,* 71-83.

Maio, G. R. and Olson, J. M. (1995). Involvement and persuasion: Evidence of different types of involvement (outcome-relevant involvement versus value-relevant involvement and attitude). *Canadian Journal of Behavioral Science, 27,* 64-78.

Maltsberger, J. T. (2000). Case consultation: Mansur Zaskar: A man almost bored to death. *Suicide and Life-Threatening Behavior, 30,* 83-90.

Manfredo, M. J. and Driver, B. L. (1996). Measuring leisure motivation: A meta-analysis of the recreation experience preference scales. *Journal of Leisure Research, 28,* 188-213.

Mannell, R. (1980). Social psychological techniques and strategies for studying leisure experiences. In S. Iso-Ahola (Ed.). *Social psychological perspectives on leisure and recreation.* Springfield, IL: C. C. Thomas.

Mannell, R. C. (1984). Personality in leisure theory: The self-as-entertainment. *Society and Leisure, 7,* 229-242.

Mannell, R. C. (1985). Reliability and validity of a leisure-specific personality measure: The self-as-entertainment construct. Abstracts from the 1985 symposium on Leisure Research. Alexandria, VA: National Recreation and Parks Association.

Mannell, R. C. (1989). Leisure satisfaction. In E. L. Jackson and T. L. Burton (Eds.). *Understanding leisure and recreation: Mapping the past, charting the future.* State College, PA: Venture Pub. Inc.

Mannell, R. C. and Kleiber, D. A. (1997). *A Social Psychology of Leisure.* State College, PA: Venture Publishing, Inc.

Mannell, R. C., Zuzanek, J., and Larson, R. (1988). Leisure states and "flow" experiences: Testing perceived freedom and intrinsic motivation hypotheses. *Journal of Leisure Research, 20,* 289-304.

Marcus, B. H., Rakowski, W., and Rossi, J. S. (1992). Assessing motivational readiness and decision making for exercise. *Health Psychology, 11,* 257-261.

Marcus, B. H., Rossi, J. S., Selby, V. C., Niaura, R. S., and Abrams, D. B. (1992). The stages and processes of exercise adoption and maintenance on a work site sample. *Health Psychology, 11,* 386-395.

Marcus, B. H., Selby, V. C., Niaura, R. S., and Rossi, J. S. (1992). Self-efficacy and the stages of exercise behavior change. *Research Quarterly for Exercise and Sport, 63,* 60-66.

Markland, D. and Hardy, L. (1993). The Exercise Motivations Inventory: Preliminary development and validity of a measure of individuals' reasons for participation in regular physical exercise. *Personality & Individual Differences, 15,* 289-296.

Marfatia, J. C. (1975). Suicide in childhood and adolescence. *Child Psychiatry Quarterly, 8,* 13-16.

Marino-Schorn, J. (1985-86). Morale, work, and leisure in retirement. *Physical and Occupational Therapy in Geriatrics, 4,* 49-59.

Markland, D. and Ingledew, D. K. (1997). The measurement of exercise motives: Factorial validity and variance across gender of a revised Exercise Motivations Inventory. *British Journal of Health Psychology, 2,* 361-376.

Martens, R. (1975). *Social psychology and physical activity.* New York, NY: Harper & Row, Publishers.

Martin, R., Puhlik-Doris, P., Larsen, G., Gray, J., and Weir, K. (2003). Individual differences in uses of humor and their relation to psychological well-being: Development of the Humor Styles Questionnaire. *Journal of Research in Personality, 37,* 48-75.

Maslow, A. (1954). *Motivation and personality.* New York, NY: Harper and Row, Pub.

Maslow, A. (1962). *Motivation and personality.* New York, NY: Harper & Row, Publishers.

Maslow, A. H. (1967). A theory of metamotivation: The biological rooting of the value-life. *Journal of Humanistic Psychology 7*(2), 93–127.

Mateer, C. A. (2000). Assessment issues. In *Neuropsychological Management of Mild TBI.* S. A. Raskin and C. A. Mateer (Eds.), pp. 34-72. New York: Oxford University Press.

Maw, W. H. and Maw, E. W. (1977). Nature and assessment of human curiosity. In P. McReynolds (Ed.), *Advances in psychological assessment. Vol. 4.* San Francisco: Jossey-Bass.

May, R. (1983). The discovery of being: Writing in existential psychology. New York: Norton.

McDavid, J. W. and Harari, H. (1968). *Social psychology: Individual, group, and society.* New York, NY: Harper & Row, Publishers.

McDougall, W. (1923). *Outline of psychology.* New York, NY: Scribner's & Sons.

McGrew, K., Johnson, D., and Bruininks, R. (1994). Factor analysis of community adjustments outcome measures for young adults with mild to severe disabilities. *Journal of Psychoeducational Assessment, 12*, 55-66.

McIntyre, N. (1989). The personal meaning of participation: Enduring involvement. *Journal of Leisure Research, 21*, 167-179.

McIntyre, N. (1992). Involvement in risk recreation: A comparison of objective and sub measures of engagement. *Journal of Leisure Research, 24*, 64-71.

McKechnie, G. E. (1974). The psychological structure of leisure: Past behavior. *Journal of Leisure Research, 6*, 27-45.

McKeganey, N. (1995). Quantitative and qualitative research in the addictions: An unhelpful divide. *Addiction* (90), 749-751.

McNeilly, D. P. and Burke, W. J. (2000). Late life gambling: The attitudes and behaviors of older adults. *Journal of Gambling Studies, 16*, 393-415.

McPherson, B. D. (1991). Aging and leisure benefits: A life cycle perspective. Pp. 423-430. In: B. L. Driver et al., (Ed.) *Benefits of leisure*. State College, Venture Pub., Inc.

McPherson, B. M. and Yuhasz, M. S. (1968). Attitudes toward exercise and physical activity. *Research Quarterly, 39*, 218-220.

McQuarrie, E. and Munson, J. (1987). The Zaichkowsky personal inventory: Modification and extension. *Advances in Consumer Research, 14*, 36-40.

Mehrabian, A. and Russell, J. A. (1973). A measure of arousal seeking tendency. *Environment & Behavior, 5*, 315-333.

Meyers, S. (1999). Service learning in alternative education settings. *The Clearing House, 73*(2), 114.

Mirenda, J. (1973). Mirenda leisure interest finder: The computer as a tool in leisure counseling. In A. Epperson (Ed.). *Leisure counseling*. Springfield, IL: C. C. Thomas.

Mitra, Ananda. (2011). *Needs assessment: A systematic approach to data collection*. Urbana, IL: Sagamore Publishing.

Mittal, B. and Lee, M. (1988). Separating brand-choice involvement from product involvement via the consumer involvement profile. *Advances in Consumer Research, 15*, 43-49.

Mittal, B. and Lee, M. (1989). A causal model of consumer involvement. *Journal of Economic Psychology, 10*, 363-390.

Morse, N. (1953). *Satisfaction in the white collar job*. Ann Arbor: University of Michigan Sociological Research.

Mullan, D., Markland, D., and Ingledew, D. K. (1997). A graded conceptualization of self-determination behavior: Development of a measure using confirmatory factor analytic procedures. *Personality and Individual Differences, 23*, 745-752.

Munchua, M., Lesage, D., Reddon, J., and Badham, T. (2003). Motivation, satisfaction, and perceived freedom: A tri-dimensional model of leisure among young offenders. *Journal of Offender Rehabilitation, 38*, 53-64.

Munchua-DeLisle, M. and Reddon, J. (2005). Leisure motivation in relation to psychosocial adjustment. In S. Shohov (Ed.). *Advances in psychology research, 33*, 203-217. Hauppauge, Nova Science Publishers, Inc.

Murphy, J. (2008). *Health and vitality*. Carlsbad, CA: Hay House.

Nash, J. B. (1953). *Philosophy of recreation and leisure*. Dubuque, IA: Wm. C. Brown.

Navar, N. (1980). A rationale for leisure skill assessment with handicapped adults. *Therapeutic Recreation Journal, Vol. 14*, Fourth Quarter.

Navar, N. (1990). State Technical Institute's Leisure Assessment Process (STILAP). Idyll Arbor, Inc., Ravensdale WA.

Navar, N. and Clancy, T. (1979). Leisure skill assessment process in leisure counseling. In D. Szmanski and G. Hitzhusen (Eds.). *Expanding Horizons in Therapeutic Recreation VI*, Colombia, MO: University of Missouri.

Neal, J. D., Sirgy, M. J., and Uysal, M. (1999). The role of satisfaction with leisure travel/tourism services and experience in satisfaction with leisure life and overall life. *Journal of Business Research, 44*, 153-163.

Nelson, J. F. (1934). *Leisure-time interests and activities of business girls: A research study*. New York, NY: The Macmillan Company.

Neto, F. (2001) Personality predictors of happiness. *Psychological Reports, 88*, 817-824.

Neu, J. (1998). Boring from within: Endogenous versus reactive boredom. In W. F. Flack, Jr., J. D. Laird, et al. (Eds.). *Emotions in psychopathology: Theory and research* (pp. 158-170). New York, NY: Oxford University Press, Series in Affective Science.

Neugarten, B. L., Havighurst, R. J., and Tobin, S. S. (1961). The measurement of life satisfaction. *Journal of Gerontology, 16* (2), 134-143.

Neuhoff, C. and Schaefer, C. (2002). Effects of laughing, smiling, and howling on mood. *Psychological Reports, 91*, 1079-1080.

Neulinger, J. (1974). *Psychology of leisure: Research approaches to the study of leisure*. Springfield, IL: Charles C. Thomas, Pub.

Neulinger, J. (1981). *To leisure: An introduction*. Boston: Allyn and Bacon.

Neulinger, J., and Breit, M. (1971). Attitude dimensions of leisure: A replication study. *Journal of Leisure Resources, 3*, 108-115.

Newberry, A. L. and Duncan, R. D. (2001). Roles of boredom and life goals in juvenile delinquency. *Journal of Applied Social Psychology, 31*, 527-541.

Newsletter, *Society for the Reduction of Human Labor* (1996). Our time famine: A critical look at the culture of work and re-evaluation of free time. Iowa City, IA: University of Iowa,.

Nichols, W. C. (1987). Boredom in marital therapy: A clinician's reflections. *Psychotherapy Patient, 3*, 137-146.

Nidorf, L. (1968). Information-seeking strategies in person perception. *Perceptual & Motor Skills, 26*, 355-365.

Niemi, R. G., Hepburn, M. A., and Chapman, C. (2000). Community service by high school students: A cure for civil ills? *Political Behavior, 22*, 45-69.

Nock, S. and Kingston, P. (1989). The division of leisure and work. *Social Science Quarterly, 70*, 24-40.

NPR. Longevity in the United States. Retrieved on Oct. 13, 2010

Nunez, A. F. (2001). Is the focus on recreation provisions or persons' total functioning? Applied to at risk youth and after-school programs. Unpublished personal communication. The Florida State University, Tallahassee, Florida.

Nunnally, J. C. (1978). *Psychometric theory*. New York, NY: McGraw-Hill, Inc.

O'Connell, S. R. (1984). Recreation therapy: Reducing the effects of isolation for the patient in a protected environment. *Children's Health Care, 12*, 118-121.

Oishi, S., Diener, E. F., Lucas, R. E., and Suh, E. M. (1999). Cross-cultural variations in predictors of life satisfaction: Perspectives from needs and values. *Personality & Social Psychology Bulletin, 25*, 980-990.

Okimoto, A., Bundy, A., and Hanzik, J. (2000). Playfulness in children with and without disability: Measurement and intervention. *American Journal of Occupational Therapy, 54*, 73-82.

Orcutt, J. D. (1984). Contrasting effects of two kinds of boredom on alcohol use. *Journal of Drug Issues, 14*, 161-173.

O'Reilly, C. A. and Anderson, J. C. (1980). Trust and communication of performance appraisal information: The effect of feedback on performance and job satisfaction. *Human Communication Research, 6*, 290-298.

Ormel, J., Lindenberg, S., Steverink, N., and Verbrugge, L. M. (1999). Subjective well-being and social production functions. *Social Indicators Research, 46*, 61-90.

Ostrow, A. C. (1996). *Directory of psychological tests in the sport and exercise sciences*. Morgantown, WV: Fitness Information and Technology, Inc., Publishers.

Overs, R. (1977). *Avocational counseling manual*. Menomonee Falls, WI: Signpost Press.

Overs, R., Taylor, S., and Adkins, C. (1977). Milwaukee avocational satisfaction questionnaire. In A. Epperson, P. Witt, G. Hitzhusen. *Leisure counseling: An aspect of leisure education* (pp. 106-136). Springfield, IL: Charles C. Thomas.

Padhee, B. and Das. S. (1987). Reliability of an adapted curiosity scale. *Social Science International, 3*, 27-30.

Paffenbarger, R. S., Hyde, R. T., and Dow, A. (1991). Health benefits of physical activity. In: B. L. Driver et al. (Ed.). *Benefits of leisure*. State College, PA: Venture Pub., Inc.

Panksepp, J. (2000). The riddle of laughter: Neural and psycho-evolutionary underpinnings of joy. *Current Directions in Psychological Science, 9*, 183-186.

Parasuraman, A., Zeithamal, V. A., and Berry, L. (1985). A conceptual model of service quality and its implications for future research. *The Journal of Marketing, 49*, 41-50.

Parry, D. C. and Shaw S. M. (1999). The role of leisure in women's experiences of menopause and mid-life. *Leisure Sciences, 21*, 205-218.

Parsons, M. (1999). The logic of play in psychoanalysis. *International Journal of Psycho-Analysis, 80*(5), 871-884.

Patrick, G. T. (1919). *The psychology of relaxation*. Boston: Houghton-Mifflin.

Patrick, G. T. (1921). The play of a nation. *Scientific Monthly, 13*, 350-362.

Patrick, G. W. (1982). Clinical treatment of boredom. *Therapeutic Recreation J., 16*, 7-12.

Pavot, W., Diener, E., Colvin, C. R., and Sandvik, E. (1991). Further validation of the satisfaction with Life Scale: Evidence for the cross-method convergence of well-being measures. *Journal of Personality Assessment, 57*, 149-161.

Pearson, G. (1995). The quantitative-qualitative dispute: An unhelpful divide, but one to be lived with. *Addiction 90*, 759-776.

Peel, E. A. (1959). The measurement of interests by verbal methods. *British Journal of Statistical Psychology, 12*, 105-118.

Pelletier, L. G., Vallerand, R. J., Green-Demers, I., Blais, M. R., and Brière, N. M. (1996). Construction and validation of the leisure motivation scale. *Leisure and Society, 19*, 529-585.

Pelletier, L. G., Vallern, R. J., Blais, M. R., Brière, N. M. (1991). Leisure motivation scale, *Communication presentee au congres annuel de la SQRP*, Ottawa, ON.

Pelletier, L. G., Fortier, M. S., Vallerand, R. J., Tuson, K. M., Brière, N. M., and Blais, M. R. (1995). Toward a new measure of intrinsic motivation, extrinsic motivation, and amotivation in sports: The Sport Motivation Scale. *Journal of Sport and Exercise Psychology, 17*, 35-53.

Penney, R. K. and Reinehr, R. C. (1966). Development of a stimulus-variation seeking scale for adults. *Psychological Reports, 18*, 631-638.

Perse, E. M. (1996). Sensation seeking and the use of television for arousal. *Communication Reports, 9*, 38-48.

Peter, P. (1979). Reliability: A review of psychometric basics and recent marketing practice. *Journal of Marketing Research, 16*, 6-17.

Peterson, C. and Gunn, S. (1984). *Therapeutic recreation program design: Principles and procedures*. Prentice Hall, Englewood Cliffs, NJ.

Piaget, J. (1948). *The moral judgment of the child*. Glencoe, IL: The Free Press.

Pieper, J. (1963). *Leisure: The basis of culture*. New York: The New American Library.

Pinquart, M. and Schindler, I. (2009). Change of leisure satisfaction in the transition to retirement: a latent-class analysis. *Leisure Sciences, 31*, 311-329.

Posavac, E. and Carey, R. (1997). Program evaluation: Methods in case studies. Upper Saddle River, NY: Prentice-Hall, Inc.

Potter, W. (1996). An analysis of thinking and research about qualitative methods. Mahwah, NJ: Lawrence Erlbaum Associates, Inc.

Prager, E. (1996). Exploring personal meaning in an age differentiated sample: Another look at the Sources of Meaning Profile (SOMP). *Journal of Aging Studies, 10*, 117-136.

Prediger, D. J. (2000). Holland's hexagon is alive and well — though somewhat out of shape: Response to Tinsley. *Journal of Vocational Behavior, 56*, 197-204.

Privette, G. (1983). Peak experience, peak performance, and flow: A comparative analysis of positive human experiences. *Journal of Personality and Social Psychology, 45*, 1362-1368.

Prochaska, J. and DiClemente, C. (1983). Stages and processes of self-change of smoking: Toward an integrative model of change. *J. of Consulting and Clinical Psychology, 51*, 390-395.

Proctor, C. (1962). *Dependence of recreation participation on background characteristics of sample persons in the September 1960 national recreation survey* (Report No. 19). Outdoor Recreation Resources Review Commission Study.

Psychological Assessment Resources, Inc., (1999). *Journal of Career Assessment, 7,* 111+.

Ragheb, M. (1980). Social psychology of leisure behavior: A frame of reference and implications for research. In S. Iso-Ahola (Ed.). *Social psychological perspectives on leisure and recreation.* Springfield, IL: Charles C. Thomas.

Ragheb, M. (1993). Leisure and perceived wellness: A field investigation. *Leisure Sciences, 15,* 13-24.

Ragheb, M. (1996). The search for meaning in leisure pursuits: Review, conceptualization, and a need for a psychometric development. *Leisure Studies, 15,* 245-258.

Ragheb, M. G. (1996). Measuring leisure and recreation involvement. Symposium on Leisure Research, National Recreation, and Park Association. Kansas City, MO.

Ragheb, M. G. (1997). Development and validation of a multidimensional scale: Measuring the search for meaning in leisure and recreation. Symposium on Research, National Recreation and Park Association. Salt Lake City, UT.

Ragheb, M. G. (2001). A psychometric development and validation of a multivariate scale: Measuring recreation and leisure motivation. Sport and Globalization, Scientific International Conference, Helwan University, Giza-Cairo, Egypt, April 4-5.

Ragheb, M. G. (2005). *Vitality Through Leisure.* Enumclaw, WA: Idyll Arbor.

Ragheb, M. G. and Beard, J. G. (1982). Measuring leisure attitude. *Journal of Leisure Research, 14,* 155-167.

Ragheb, M. G. and Beard, J. G. (1992). Measuring leisure interests. *Journal of Park and Recreation Administration, 10,* 1-13.

Ragheb, M. G. and Griffith, C. A. (1982). The contribution of leisure participation and leisure satisfaction to life satisfaction of older persons. *Journal of Leisure Research, 14,* 295 -306.

Ragheb, M. G. and McKinney, J. (1993). Campus recreation and perceived academic stress. *Journal of College Student Development, 34,* 5-10.

Ragheb, M. G. and Merydith, S. P. (1994). Measuring free time boredom. Symposium on Leisure Research, National Recreation, and Park Association. Minneapolis, MN.

Ragheb, M. G. and Merydith, S. P. (1995). *Free time boredom.* Enumclaw, WA: Idyll Arbor.

Ragheb, M. G. and Merydith, S. P. (2000). Development and validation of a multidimensional scale measuring free time boredom. *Leisure Studies, 19,* 1-19.

Ragheb, M. G. and Merydith, S. P. (2001). Development and validation of a multidimensional scale measuring free time boredom. *Leisure Studies, 20,* 41-59.

Ram, S. and Jung, H. (1994). Innovativeness in product usage: A comparison of early adopters and early majority. *Psychology and Marketing, 11,* 57-67.

Ratner, R. K., Kahn, B. E., and Kahneman, D. (1999). Choosing less-preferred experiences for the sake of variety. *Journal of Consumer Research, 26,* 1-15.

Rean, A. (1984). Intensity and attractiveness as parameters of common learning activity. *Voprosy Psikologii, 6,* 102-105.

Reddon, J., Pope, G., Friel, J., and Sinha, B. (1996). Leisure motivation in relation to psychosocial adjustment and personality in young offender and high school samples. *Journal of Clinical Psychology, 52,* 679-685.

Reeves, J. W. and Slater, P. (1947). Age and intelligence in relation to leisure interests. *Occupational Psychology, 21,* 111-124.

Reid, L. M. (1966). Utilizing user preferences in predicting outdoor recreation. . In *Recreation Research* (pp. 86-93). New York, NY: National Recreation and Park Association.

Rennes, P. (1952). Constructing and validating a new interest questionnaire. *Travail Humain, 15,* 41-55.

Richins, M. L., Bloch, P. H., and McQuarrie, E. F. (1992). How enduring and situational involvement combine to create involvement responses. *Journal of Consumer Psychology, 1,* 143-153.

Riddick, C. C. and Russell, R. V. (1999). *Evaluative research in recreation, park, and sport settings: Searching for useful information.* Champaign, IL: Sagamore Publishing.

Riddle, P. K. (1980). Attitudes toward jogging questionnaire. *Research Quarterly for Exercise and Sport, 51,* 663-674.

Rimmer, S. M. (1979). The development of an instrument to assess leisure satisfaction among secondary school students. *Dissertation Abstracts International. 40*(9-A): 4903.

Ritchie, J. R. (1975). On the derivation of leisure activity types: A perception mapping approach. *Journal of Leisure Research, 7,* 128-140.

Robbinson, J. (1990). American's use of time project. In B. Cutler. *Where does the free time go? American Demographics,* 12.

Robinson, J. (1990). The leisure pie (use of leisure time). *American Demographic, 12,* 39.

Roe, A. (1956). *The psychology of occupation.* New York, NY: Wiley.

Roelofs, L. (1992). The meaning of leisure for older persons. *Dissertation Abstracts International.*

Rogers, C. R. (1956). Client-centered theory. *Journal of Counseling Psychology, 3,* 115-120.

Rojek, K. C. (1989). Leisure and recreation theory. Pp. 69-88. In: E. L. Jackson and T. L. Burton. *Understanding leisure and recreation: Mapping the past, charting the future.* State College, PA: Venture Pub. Inc.

Rojek, C. (1995). *Decentering leisure: Rethinking leisure theory.* Thousand Oaks, CA: Sage Pubs.

Rosenheck, R. A. (2000). Cost-effectiveness of services for mentally ill homeless people: The application of research to polity and practice. *American Journal of Psychiatry, 157,* 1563-1570.

Rosenthal, T., Montgomery, L., Shadish, W., and Lichstein, K. (1989). Leisure interest patterns and subjective stress in college students. *Behavioral Research & Therapy, 27,* 321-335.

Rossman, J. R. and Schlatter, B. E. (2000). *Recreation programming: Designing leisure experience.* Champaign, IL: Sagamore Publishing.

Rotter, J. (1954). Social learning and clinical psychology. New York, NY: Prentice-Hall.

Rowland, G. L., Franken, R. E., and Harrison, K. (1986). Sensation seeking and participation in sporting activities. *Journal of Sport Psychology, 8*, 212-220.

Ruch, W. (1998). Sense of humor: A new look at an old concept. Pp. 3-14. In: W. Ruch (Ed). *The sense of humor.* Berlin: Mouton de Gruyter.

Ruch, W., Koehler, G., and Van Thriel, C. (1996). Assessing the "humorous temperament": Construction of the facet and standard trait forms of the State-Trait-Cheerfulness-Inventory — STCI Humor. *International Journal of Humor Research, 9*, 303-339.

Russell, R. (1987). The importance of recreation satisfaction to the life satisfaction of age-segregated retirees. *Journal of Leisure Research, 19*, 273-283.

Russell, R. (1990). Recreation and the quality of life in old age: A causal analysis. *Journal of Applied Gerontology, 32*, 119-128.

Rutledge, A. (1971). *Anatomy of a park: The essentials of recreation are planning and design.* New York: McGraw-Hill.

Ryan, C. and Glendon, I. (1998). Application of Leisure Motivation Scale to tourism. *Annals of Tourism Research, 25*, 169-184.

Ryan, R. M. and Connell, J. P. (1989). Perceived locus of causality and internalization: Examining reasons for acting in two domains. *Journal of Personality and Social Psychology, 57,* 749-761.

Ryan, R. M. and Deci, E. L. (2000). Intrinsic and extrinsic motivation: Classic definitions and new directions. *Contemporary Educational Psychology, 25*, 54-67.

Ryan, R. and Deci, E. (2000). Self-determination theory and facilitation of intrinsic motivation, social development, and well being. *American Psychologist, 55,* 68-78.

Ryan, R. M. and Guardia, J. G. (2000). What is being optimized over development? A self-determined theory on basic psychological needs across the life span. In S. Qualls and N. Abele (Eds.). *Psychology and the aging revolution* (pp. 145-172). Washington, DC: APA Books.

Ryff, C. D. (1989). Happiness is everything, or is it? Exploring on the meaning of psychological wellbeing. *Journal of Personality and Social Psychology, 57,* 1069-1081.

Salvia, J. and Ysseldyke, J. E. (1991). *Assessment.* Boston, MA: Houghton Mifflin Company.

Samdahl, D. M. (1988). A symbolic interactionist model of leisure: Theory and empirical support. *Leisure Science, 10,* 27-39.

Sampson, J. (1998). Using the Internet to enhance test selection, orientation, administration, and scoring. Indianapolis, IN: Annual Meeting of the Association for Assessment in Counseling.

Samra-Grewal, J. and Roesch, R. (2000). The parole attitudes scale (PAS): Development of a 15-item scale to assess attitudes toward conditional release. *Canadian Journal of Criminology, 42,* 157-175.

Sanbonmatsu, D., Prince, K., Vanous, S., and Posavac, S. (2005). The multiple roles of attitudes in decision making. In T. Betsch and S. Haberstroh (Eds). *The routines of decision making* (pp. 101- 116). Mahwah, NJ: Laurence Erbaum Associates, Pub.

Sanchez, M. D. (2010). The influence of physical activity and sport on health and subjective well-being of Spanish people. *Proceedings of European Association of Sociology of Sport Conference 2010, EASS 2010 Porto.* Universidad de Oporto.

Saper, B. (1988). Humor in psychiatric healing. *Psychiatric Quarterly, 59*, 306-319.

Sapora, A. V. (1966). Ascertaining interests for recreation program planning. In *Recreation research*. New York, NY: National Recreation and Park Association.

Sapora, A. V. and Mitchell, E. (1961). *The theory of play and recreation.* New York, NY: Ronald Press.

Saunders, I., Sayer, M., and Goodale, A. (1999). The relationship between playfulness and coping in preschool children: A pilot study. *American Journal of Occupational Therapy, 53*(2), 221-226.

Sawin, D. A. and Scerbo, M. W. (1995). Effects of instruction type and boredom proneness in vigilance: Implications for boredom and workload. *Human Factors, 37*, 752-765.

Schaefer, C. and Greenberg, R. (1997). Measurement of playfulness: A neglected therapist variable. *International Journal of Play Therapy, 6*, 21-31.

Schenk, C. (1993). Use of visual cues to identify leisure interests, motivation, and sensation seeking. In G. Hitzhusen. (Ed.). *Midwest symposium on therapeutic recreation: Executive summary book.* Columbia, MO: University of Missouri.

Schenk, C. (1998). *Leisurescope Plus* and *Teen Leisurescope Plus.* Ravensdale, WA: Idyll Arbor Inc.

Schimmack, U. and Grob, A. (2000). Dimensional models of core affect: A qualitative comparison by means of structural comparison by means of structural equation modeling. *European Journal of Personality, 14*, 325-345.

Schreyer, R. and Beaulieu, J. (1986). Attribute preferences for wildland recreation settings. *Journal of Leisure Research, 18*, 231-247.

Schuett, M. A. (1993). Refining measures of adventure recreation involvement. *Leisure Sciences, 15*, 205-216.

Schultz, D. P. (1977). *Growth psychology: Models of the healthy personality.* New York: Van Nostrand Reinhold.

Shultz, K., Morton, K. R., and Weckerle, J. R. (1998). The influence of push and pull factors on voluntary and involuntary early retiree's retirement decision and adjustment. *Journal of Vocational Behavior, 53*, 45-57.

Schutz, R. W., Smoll, F. L., Carre, F. A., and Mosher, R. E. (1985). Inventories and norms for children's attitudes toward physical activity. *Research Quarterly for Exercise and Sport, 56*, 256-265.

Schutz, R. W., Smoll, F. L., and Wood, T. M. (1981). A psychometric analysis of an inventory for assessing children's attitudes toward physical activity. *J. of Social Psychology, 3*, 321-344.

Schulz, R. and Kenneth, R. (2006). *Activity theory. The encyclopedia of aging* (4th Edition). New York: Springer Pub. Co.

Seaburn, D. B. (1987). Transition boredom. *Psychotherapy Patient, 3-4*, 119-127.

Seassoms, H. D. (1975). Leisure society value systems. Pp. 14-24. In: J. F. Murphy *Concepts of Leisure: Philosophical Implications*. Englewood Cliffs, NJ: Prentice-Hall, Inc.

Sechrest, L. and Sidani, S. (1995). Quantitative and qualitative methods: Is there an alternative? Special Feature: "The Quantitative-Qualitative Debates," *Evaluation and Program Planning (18)*, 77-87.

Seib, H. M. and Vodanovich, S. J. (1998). Cognitive correlates of boredom proneness: The role of private self-consciousness and absorption. *Journal of Psychology, 132*, 642-652.

Seligman, M. E. (1972). Learned helplessness. *Annual Review of Medicine*, 207-412.

Seligman, M. E. (1998). Building human strength: Psychology's forgotten mission. *American Psychological Association Online, Vol. 29*(1), 1.

Selin, S. and Howard, D. (1988). Ego-involvement and leisure behavior: A conceptual specification. *Journal of Leisure Research, 20*, 237-244.

Seward, S. S., Jr. (1930). *The paradox of the ludicrous*. Palo Alto, CA: Stanford University Press.

Shaw, S. (1985). Gender and leisure: Inequality in the distribution of leisure time. *Journal of Leisure Research, 17*, 266-292.

Shaw, S. M., Caldwell, L. L., and Kleiber, D. A. (1996). Boredom, stress, and social control in the daily activities of adolescents. *Journal of Leisure Research, 28*, 274-292.

Sherif, C. and Sherif, M. (1967). *Attitude, ego-involvement, and change*. New York: John Wiley.

Sherif, C., Sherif, M., and Nebergall, R. (1965). *Attitude and attitude de change: the judgment-involvement approach*. Philadelphia, PA: W. B. Saunders.

Sherif, M., and Cantril, H. (1947). *The psychology of ego involvement, social attitudes and identification*. New York, NY: Wiley.

Shields, C., Franks, P., Harp, J., McDaniel, S., and Campbell, T. (1992). Development of the family emotional involvement and criticism scale: A self-report scale to measure expressed emotion. *The Journal of Marital and Family Therapy, 18*, 395-407.

Siegenthaler, K. and Lam, T. (1992). Commitment and ego-involvement in recreational tennis. *Leisure Sciences, 14*, 303-315.

Simon, J. A. and Smoll, F. L. (1974). An instrument for assessing children's attitude toward physical activity. *Research Quarterly for Exercise and Sport, 45*, 407-415.

Sirgy, M. J. (1998). Materialism and quality of life. *Social Indicators Research, 43*, 227-260.

Sirgy, M. J., Efraty, D., Siegel, P. and Lee, D. (2000). A new measure of quality of work life (QWL) based on need satisfaction and spill-over theories. *Social Indicators Research, 55*, 241-302.

Sirgy M. J.; Rahtz D. R.; Cicic M.; Underwood R. (2000). A method for assessing residents' satisfaction with community-based services: A quality-of-life perspective. *Social Indicators Research, 49*, 279-316.

Smissen, B., Moiseichik, M., Hartenburg, V. J., and Twardzik, L. F. (1999). *Management of park and recreation agencies*. Ashburn, VA: The National Recreation and Park Association.

Smith, E. R. and Mackie, D. M. (2000). *Social psychology*. London, Psychology Press Ltd.

Smith, D. S. (1996). Investigating playfulness in family process. *Dissertation Abstracts International, Section A: Humanities & Social Sciences, 57*(2-A), 0880.

Smith, P. C. (1955). The prediction of individual differences in susceptibility to industrial monotony. *Journal of Applied Psychology, 39*, 322-329.

Smith, S. M. and Kampfe, C. M. (2000). Characteristics of diversity and aging: Implications for assessment. *Journal of Applied Rehabilitation Counseling, 31*, 33-39.

Smoski, M. J. and Bachorowski, J. (2003). Antiphonal laughter between friends and strangers. *Cognition and Emotion, 17*, 327-340.

Snyder, C. R. (2006). *Psychology of human motivation*. Oxford University Press, Inc.

Snyder, C. R., Sympson, S. C., Ybasco, F. C., Borders, T. F., Babyak, M. A., Higgins R. L. (1996). Development and validation of the State Hope Scale. *Journal of Personality and Social Psychology, 70*, 321-335.

Snyder, D. K. (2000). Computer-assisted judgment: Defining strengths and liabilities. *Psychological Assessment, 12*, 52-60.

Solnit, A. J. (1998). Beyond play and playfulness. *Psychoanalytic Study of the Child 53*, 102-110.

Sommers, J. and Vodanovich, S. J. (2000). Boredom proneness: Its relationship to psychological- and physical-health symptoms. *Journal of Clinical Psychology, 56*, 149-155.

Sorcher, M. and Meyer, H. H. (1968). Motivation and job performance. *Personnel Administration, 31*, 8-21.

Spence, M. F. (1998). Risk-taking in adolescence: An exploration of basic constructs. *Dissertation Abstracts International, 58*(11-A), 4189.

Stamm, K. and Dube, R. (1994). The relationship of attitudinal components to trust in media. *Communication Research, 21*, 105-123.

Stangl, W. (1991). The leisure interest inventory. *Zeitschrift fuer Differentielle und Diagnostische Psychologie, 12*, 231-244.

Stanley, H. M. (1898). Discussion: Remarks on tickling and laughing. *American Journal of Psychology, 9*(2), 235-240.

Stanton-Rich, H. M. (1996). The interrelationships of leisure attitude, leisure satisfaction, leisure behavior, intrinsic motivation, and burnout among clergy. *Dissertation Abstracts International, Section A: Humanities & Social Sciences, Vol. 57*(3-A), p. 1323.

Stanton-Rich, H. and Iso-Ahola, S. (1998). Burnout and leisure. *Journal of Applied Social Psychology, 28*, 1931-1950.

Stein, G. L., Kimiecik, J. C., Daniels, J., and Jackson, S. A. (1995). Psychological antecedents of flow in recreational sport. *Personality & Social Psychology Bulletin, 21*,

Stephens, T. (1988). Physical activity and mental health in the U.S. and Canada: Evidence from four population surveys. *Preventive Medicine, 17*, 35-47.

Stevens, A., Coon, D., Wisniewski, S., Vance, D., Arguelles, S., Belle, S., Mendelsohn, A., Ory, M., and Haley, W. (2004). Measurement of leisure time satisfaction in family caregivers. *Aging & Mental Health, 8*, 450-459.

Still, J. W. (1957). Boredom: The psychosocial disease of aging. *Geriatrics, 12*, 557-560.

Stock, W. A.; Okun, M. A.; Benin, M. (1986). *Psychology and Aging, 1*(2), 91-102.

Stodolska, M. (2000). Changes in leisure participation patterns after immigration. *Leisure Sciences, 22*, 39-63.

Strong, E. K. (1927). Vocational interests test. *Educational Record, 8*, 107-121.

Stumbo, N. J. and Thompson, S. R. (1986). *Leisure education: A manual of activities and resources.* State College, PA: Venture Publishing. Inc.

Stumbo, N. J. and Peterson, C. A. (1998). The leisure ability model. *Therapeutic Recreation Journal, 32*, 82-96.

Suchman, E. (1976*). Evaluative research: Principles and practice in public service and social actions programs.* New Your, NY: Russell Sage Foundation.

Suh, E., Diener, E., and Fujita, F. (1996). Events and subjective well-being: Only recent events matter. *Journal of Personality and Social Psychology, 70*, 1091-1102.

Suh, E., Diener, e., Oishi, s., and Triandis, H. C. (1998). The shifting basis of life satisfaction judgments across cultures: emotions versus norms. *Journal of Personality and Social Psychology, 74*, 482-493.

Super, D. E. (1949). *Appraising vocational fitness.* New York, NY: Harper.

Super, D. E. (1970). *Manual Work Values Inventory.* Chicago, IL: Riverside Pub.

Super, D. E. (1970). *The psychology of careers.* New York, NY: Harper & Row.

Szabo, A. (2003). The acute effects of humor and exercise on mood and anxiety. *Journal of Leisure Research, 35*, 152-162.

Szurek, S. A. (1959). Playfulness, creativity, and schisis. *American Journal of Orthopsychiatry, 29*, 667-683.

Tarrant, M. A. and Green, G. T. (1999). Outdoor recreation and the predictive validity of environmental attitudes. *Leisure Sciences, 21*, 17-30.

Tatarkiewicz, W. (1976). *Analysis of happiness.* Warzawa, Marinus Nijhoff/The Hague Pwn/Polish Scientific.

Taylor, C. B., Sallis, J. F., and Needle, R. (1985). The relation of physical activity and exercise to mental health. *Public Health Reports, 100*, 195-202.

Tellegen, A. (1982). Brief manual for the multidimensional personality questionnaire. Unpublished manuscript. Minneapolis, MN: University of Minnesota, Department of Psychology.

Terry, D. J., Hogg, M. A., and White, K. M. (2000). Attitude-behavior relations: Social identity and group membership. In D. J. Terry and M. A. Hogg (Eds.), *Attitudes, behavior, and social context: The role of norms and group membership, applied social research.* Mahwah, NJ: Lawrence Erlbaum Associates, Inc.

Theobald, W. (1979). *Evaluation of recreation and park programs.* New York, NY: John Wiley & Sons.

Thierry, H. (1998). Motivation and satisfaction. In P. J. D. Drenth, H. Thierry, C. J. Dewall (Eds.). *Handbook of work and organizational psychology.* Pp. 253-254. Sussex: Psychology Press Ltd.

Thompson, L. A., Jr. (1929). Measuring susceptibility to monotony. *Personnel Journal, 8*, 172-196.

Thornicroft, G. and Bebbington, P. (1996). *Quantitative methods in the evaluation of community mental health services.* New York, NY: Oxford University Press.

Thorson, J. A. and Powell, F. C. (1993). Development and validation of a multi-dimensional sense of humor scale. *Journal of Clinical Psychology, 49*, 13-23.

Thurstone, L. (1946). Comment. *American J. of Sociology, 52*, 39-40.

Tillman, A. (1973). *The program book for recreation professionals.* Palo Alto, CA: National Press Book.

Tinsley, H. E. (2000). The congruence myth: An analysis of the efficacy of the person-environment fit model. *Journal of Vocational Behavior, 56*, 147-179.

Tinsley, H. E., Barrett, T., and Kass, R. (1977). Leisure activities and need satisfaction: A replication and extension. *J. Leisure Research, 11*, 278-291.

Tinsley, H. E. and Eldredge, B. D. (1995). Psychological benefits of leisure participation: A taxonomy of leisure activities based on their need-gratifying properties. *Journal of Counseling Psychology, 42*, 123-132.

Tinsley, H. E. and Kass, R. A. (1980). The construct validity of the leisure activities questionnaire and of the paragraphs about leisure. *Educational & Psychological Measurement, 40*, 219-226.

Tinsley, H. E., Teaff, J. D., Colbs, S. L., and Kaufman, N. (1985). A system of classifying leisure activities in terms of the psychological benefits of participation reported by older persons. *Journal of Gerontology, 40*, 172-178.

Tinsley, H. E. and Tinsley, D. J. (1986). A theory of the attributes, benefits, and causes of leisure experience. *Leisure Sciences, 8*, 1-45.

Tobias, J. J. (1970). The affluent suburban male delinquent. *Crime & Delinquency, 16*, 273-279.

Todman, M. (2003). Boredom and psychotic disorders: Cognitive and motivational issues. *Psychiatry: Interpersonal & Biological Processes, 66*, 146-167.

Toh, K. L. and Yeung, S. Y. (2000). International leisure travel motivations among students in Hong Kong. *International Council for Health, Physical Education, Recreation, Sport, and Dance, 36*, 56-58.

Toogood, R. (1939). A survey of recreational interests and pursuits of college women. *Research Quarterly, 10*, 90-100.

Triandis, H. C. (1971). *Attitude and attitude change.* New York, NY: Wiley.

Trow, W. C. (1927). The leisure activities of students and their instructors. *Pedagogical Seminary, 34*, 406-414.

Tseng, T. A., Chang, D. Y., and Shen, C-C. (2009). The relationships between leisure behaviors and life satisfaction of foreign labors in Taiwan — the case of Thai labors. *Advances in Hospitality and Leisure, 5*, 25-50.

Twynam, G. D. (1993). An analysis of the extent and response forms of complex behavior and those factors which influence consumers to complain with travel contexts. Doctoral dissertation, University of Oregon. *Dissertation Abstracts International, 53*, 2983A.

Tybjee, T. (1979). Response time, conflict, and involvement in brand choice. *Journal of Consumer Research, 6*, 295-304.

Unger, L. and Kernan, J. (1983). On the meaning of leisure: An investigation of some determinants of the subjective experience. *Journal of Consumer Research, 9,* 381-392.

Vagt, G. and Kraschinski, W. (1978). Dimensions and correlates of subjective problems with free time in adults. *Zeitschrift fuer Sozialpsychologie, 9,* 257-264.

Vallerand, R. J. and O'Connor, B. P. (1991). Construction and validation of the scale of motivation for old people. *International Journal of Psychology, 26,* 219-240.

Vallerand, R. J., Pelletier, L. G., Blais, M. R., Brière, N. M., Senecal, C., and Vallieres, E. F. (1992). The Academic Motivation Scale: A measurement of intrinsic, extrinsic, and amotivation in education. *Educational and Psychological Measurement, 52,* 1003-1017.

Van de Ven, P., Bornholt, L., and Bailey, M. (1996). Measuring cognitive, affective, and behavioral components of homophobic reaction. *Archives of Sexual Behavior, 25,* 155-179.

Van der Bolt, L. and Tellegen, S. (1992-3). Involvement while reading: An empirical exploration. *Imagination, Cognition and Personality, 12,* 273-285.

Varca, P. E. and Shaffer, G. S. (1982). Holland's theory: Stability of avocational interests. *Journal of Vocational Behavior, 21,* 288-298.

Verplanken, B., Hofstee, G., and Janssen, H. J. (1998). Accessibility of affective versus cognitive components of attitudes. *European Journal of Social Psychology, 28,* 23-35.

Vodanovich, S. J. and Kass, S. J. (1990). A factor analytic study of the boredom proneness scale. *Journal of Personality Assessment, 55,* 115-123.

Vodanovich, S. J. and Watt, J. D. (1999). The relationship between time structure and boredom proneness: An investigation within two cultures. *Journal of Social Psychology, 139,* 143-152.

Vodanovich, S. J., Watt, J. D, and Piotrowski, C. (1997). Boredom proneness in African-American college students: a factor analytic perspective. *Education, 118,* 229-239.

Vodanovich, S. J., Weddle, C., and Piotrowski. C. (1997). The relationship between boredom proneness and internal and external work values. *Social Behavior & Personality, 25,* 259-264.

Wade, M. (1968). A study of free play patterns of elementary school age children on playground equipment. Unpublished master's thesis: Pennsylvania State University.

Walsh, W. B. and Betz, N. E. (1985). *Tests and assessment.* Englewood Cliffs, NJ: Prentice-Hall, Inc.

Wang, W., Wu, Y., Peng, Z., Lu, S., Yu, L., Wang, G., Fu, X., and Wang, Y (2000). Test of sensation seeking in a Chinese sample. *Personality and Individual Differences, 28,* 169-179.

Warga, C. (1984). The role of love and laughter in the healing process. *Advances, 1,* 38-39.

Watkins, M. (1986). The influence of involvement and information search on consumers' choices of recreation activities. Unpublished doctoral dissertation, University of Oregon, Eugene, OR.

Watson, J. B. (1913). Psychology as the behaviorist views it. *Psychological Review, 20,* 158-177.

Watt, J. D. and Ewing, J. E. (1996). Toward the development and validation of a measure of sexual boredom. *Journal of Sex Research, 33,* 57-66.

Watt, J. D. and Vodanovich, S. J. (1999). Boredom proneness and psychosocial development. *Journal of Psychology, 133,* 303-314.

Webster's Ninth New Collegiate Dictionary. (1986). Springfield, MA: Merriam–Webster.

Weissinger, E. M. (1985). Development and validation of an intrinsic leisure motivation scale. Unpublished doctoral dissertation. University of Maryland, College Park.

Weissinger, E. M. (1986). The development and validation of an intrinsic leisure motivation scale. *Dissertation Abstracts International, 46*(12-A, Pt. 1), 3860.

Weissinger, E. M. (1994). Development, reliability, and validity of a scale to measure intrinsic motivation in leisure. *Society and Leisure, 7,* 217-228.

Weissinger, E., and Bandalos, D. (1995). Development, reliability, and validity of a scale to measure intrinsic motivation in leisure. *J. of Leisure Research, 27,* 379-400.

Wellman, J., Roggenbuck, J., and Smith, A. (1982). Recreation specialization and norms of depreciative behavior among canoeists. *Journal of Leisure Research, 14,* 323-340.

White, R. W. (1959). Motivation reconsidered: The concept of competence. *Psychological Review, 66,* 297-333.

White, W. (1939). *The psychology of making life interesting.* New York, NY: The Macmillan Company.

Whitehead, J. R. and Corbin, C. B. (1988). Multidimensional scales for the measurement of locus of control of reinforcements for physical fitness behavior. *Research Quarterly for Exercise and Sport, 59,* 108-117.

Widmer, M. A. and Ellis, G. D. (1998). The Aristotelian good life model: Integration of values into therapeutic recreation service delivery. *Therapeutic Recreation Journal, 33,* 290-302.

Widmer, M. A., Ellis, G. D., and Munson, W. W. (2003). Development of the Aristotelian ethical behavior in leisure scale short form. *Therapeutic Recreation Journal, 37,* 256-274.

Widmer, M. A., Ellis, G. D., and Trunnell, E. P. (1996). Measurement of ethical behavior in leisure among high- and low-risk adolescents. *Adolescence, 31,* 397-408.

Wiesner, M., Windle, M, and Freeman, A. (2005). Work stress, substance use, and depression among young adult workers: An examination of main and moderator effect model. *Journal of Occupational Health Psychology, 10,* 83-96.

Wild, T. C., Kuiken, D., and Schopflocher, D. (1995). The role of absorption in experimental involvement. *Journal of Personality and School Psychology, 69,* 569-579.

Wiley, C. G., Shaw, S. M., and Havitz, M. E. (2000). Men's and women's involvement in sports: An examination of the gendered aspects of leisure involvement. *Leisure Sciences, 22,* 19-31.

Williams, A. E. and Neal, L. L. (1993). Motivational assessment in organizations: An application of importance-performance analysis. *Journal of Park and Recreation Administration, 11,* 60-71.

Williams, A. V. (1987). Validation of the life interests (leisure/work) inventory for secondary school students. *Dissertation Abstracts International, 47*(11-A), 4049.

Williams, P. S. (1997). The relationship between arousal, affect, and cognition. *Dissertation Abstracts International, Section A: Humanities & Social Sciences, 57*, 3459.

Wilson, G. D. (1986). Eating style, obesity, & health. *Personality & Individual Differences, 7*, 215-224.

Wilson, S. and Nutt, D. (2005). Assessment and management of insomnia. *Clinical Medicine, 5*, 101-104

Witt, P. A. (1971). Factor structure of leisure behavior for high school age youth in three communities. *Journal of Leisure Research, 3*, 213-220.

Witt, P. A. and Ellis, G. D. (1989). *The leisure diagnostic battery users manual*. State College, PA: Venture.

Witzel, M. (2005). Danger of mistaking science of measuring as divine. *CFT Institute: Financial Time, Business Life*, August 2, 2005.

World Book, Inc. *World Book Encyclopedia*. (1989). Chicago, IL: author.

Wright, B. A., Duray, N., and Goodale, T. L. (1992). Assessing perceptions of recreation center service quality: An application of recent advancements in service quality research. *Journal of Park and Recreation Administration, 10*, 33-47.

Wyman, M. (1982). Substitutability of recreation experience. *Leisure Studies, 1*, 277-293.

Yankelovich, D. (1978). The new psychological contracts at work. *Psychology Today, 11*, (May), 46-50.

Yin, Z., Katims, D. S., and Zapata, J. T. (1999). Participation in leisure activities and involvement in delinquency by Mexican American adolescents. *Hispanic Journal of Behavioral Sciences, 21*, 170-185.

Yoesting, D. R. and Burdge, R. J. (1976). Utility of a leisure orientation scale. *Iowa State Journal of Research, 50*, 345-356.

Yusof, A. and Shah, P. M. (2008). Application of leisure scale to sport tourism. *Humanities Conference 08, the Sixth International Conference on New Directions in the Humanities*, Faith University, Istanbul, Turkey, 15-18 July 2008.

Zaichkowsky, J. (1985). Measuring the involvement construct. *Journal of Consumer Research, 12*, 341-352.

Zayas, M. (1990). The relationship between stressful events, locus of control, leisure satisfaction, and state anxiety. *Dissertation Abstracts International, 50*(8-B). New York, NY: Columbia University.

Zuckerman, M. (1971). Dimensions of sensation seeking. *Journal of Consulting & Clinical Psychology, 36*, 45-52.

Zuckerman, M. (1977). Development of a situation-specific trait-state test for the prediction and measurement of affective response. *Journal of Counseling and Clinical Psychology, 45*, 513-523.

Zuckerman, M. (1979). *Sensation Seeking: Beyond the Optimal Level of Arousal*. New York: Lawrence Erlbaum.

Zuckerman, M., Eysenck, S., Eysenck, H. J. (1978). Sensation seeking in England and America: Cross culture age and sex comparisons. *Journal of Consulting and Clinical Psychology, 46*, 139-149.

Zuckerman, M., Neary, R. S., and Brustman, B. A. (1970). Sensation-seeking scale correlates in experience (smoking, drugs, alcohol, "hallucinations," and sex) and preference for complexity (designs). *Proceedings of the Annual Convention of the American Psychological Association, 5*, 317-318.

Index

About the Author

Mounir G. Ragheb, PhD, is a Professor Emeritus at the Florida State University, Tallahassee, Florida; having served in the department of Sport and Recreation Management, College of Education. During his tenure he was involved in the following activities:

- Participated in developing eight standardized measurements that are used in practice and research studies in many different countries.
- Conducted scientific studies on how leisure domains relate to wellness, stress, vitality, boredom or lack of boredom, life satisfaction, and quality of life.
- Presented and published nationally and internationally scholar reports and scientific studies in the USA, Canada, United Kingdom, Spain, Venezuela, Peru, Colombia, Kuwait, Saudi Arabia, and Egypt.
- Served as a graduate coordinator and participated in supervising Master's theses and Doctoral dissertations at the Florida State University.
- Served (1982-1983) as a visiting professor at King Saud University, College of Education, Abha Branch, Kingdom of Saudi Arabia.

Dr. Ragheb taught classes on the following:

- Assessment, Research, and Evaluation in Leisure Systems
- Philosophical, Social, and Behavioral Foundations of Leisure
- Leisure Education
- Leadership in Recreation and Leisure Services
- Social Psychology of Leisure and Recreation (Graduate level)
- Positive Psychology of Leisure and Recreation (Graduate level)
- Scientific Research Methods in Leisure and Recreation (Graduate level)

For ten years, he taught graduate classes to Master's students from all over South America, Central America, and Mexico through the Pan American Institute of Physical Education and Recreation, located in Maracaibo, Venezuela.

In his retirement, he has completed two books in Arabic with the following titles: Olympic Performance: Policies and Institutions (2010), and The Pathway to Sport Excellence (in press).

Dr. Mounir G. Ragheb, PhD
Professor Emeritus
Sports and Recreation Management Department
2211A Stone Building
College of Education
The Florida State University
Tallahassee, FL 32306-4280

Cell: 850-345-9682
Email: mragheb@fsu.edu